The Social
Construction
of Difference
and Inequality

The Social Construction of Difference and Inequality

Race, Class, Gender, and Sexuality

Seventh Edition

Tracy E. Ore
Saint Cloud State University

New York   Oxford
OXFORD UNIVERSITY PRESS

Oxford University Press is a department of the University of Oxford.
It furthers the University's objective of excellence in research, scholarship,
and education by publishing worldwide. Oxford is a registered trade mark of
Oxford University Press in the UK and certain other countries.

Published in the United States of America by Oxford University Press
198 Madison Avenue, New York, NY 10016, United States of America.

For titles covered by Section 112 of the US Higher Education
Opportunity Act, please visit www.oup.com/us/he for the
latest information about pricing and alternate formats.

Library of Congress Cataloging-in-Publication Data

Names: Ore, Tracy E., author.
Title: The social construction of difference and inequality : race, class,
    gender, and sexuality/Tracy E. Ore.
Description: Seventh edition.|New York : Oxford University Press, 2018.|
    Revised edition of the author's The social construction of difference and
    inequality, [2014]
Identifiers: LCCN 2018004267|ISBN 9780190647964 (paperback)
Subjects: LCSH: Cultural pluralism—United States.|Equality—United States.
    |Minorities—United States—Social conditions.|Social classes—United
    States.|Women—United States—Social conditions.|Gays—United
    States—Social conditions.|Discrimination—United States.|United
    States—Social conditions—1980-|United States—Race relations.|United
    States—Ethnic relations.|BISAC: SOCIAL SCIENCE/Sociology/General. |
    SOCIAL SCIENCE / Social Classes.|SOCIAL SCIENCE/Gender Studies.
Classification: LCC HN59.2 .S585 2018|DDC 305.800973—dc23 LC record available at
    https://lccn.loc.gov/2018004267

9 8 7 6 5 4 3 2 1
Printed by LSC Communications Inc., United States of America

This book is dedicated to the memory of my mother,
Virginia Maxine Barton Ore—the smartest woman I have
ever known.
I also dedicate this book to my brother, Brian Curtis Ore,
and to all others lost in the continuing crisis of AIDS.

Tracy E. Ore is a professor of sociology and the Faculty Director of Civic Engagement and Service Learning at St. Cloud State University. She received her PhD in sociology from the University of Michigan, is an active member of the American Sociological Association and the Southern Sociological Society, and is past president of Sociologists for Women in Society. Her teaching areas include social inequality, race and ethnicity, social movements, and the global politics of food. She does research in the areas of food access and sustainable agriculture. She serves as a consultant for multicultural education and curriculum to a variety of organizations and agencies and conducts workshops and trainings related to issues of inequality. In addition to this work, Professor Ore is a long-time activist and community organizer. The connections between her scholarly work and activism are made real in the St. Cloud State University Community Garden, which she established in 2005.

Urban spaces in the United States can serve as landscapes that both reflect and make legible social inequality, particularly along racial and class lines. While news reports indicate that the US economy is in recovery, urban residents remain disproportionately likely to live in areas of concentrated poverty. Efforts to address these disparities fall short due to past and current policies and practices that disproportionately disadvantaged people of color and the poor. For example, government initiated urban renewal policies and projects of the 50s, 60s and 70s intended to address issues of urban decay were supposed to result in more livable cities for all. However, 90 percent of all housing destroyed by urban renewal was not replaced, and two-thirds of those displaced were African American or Latino. While programs labeled "urban renewal" are a thing of the past, their impact remains visible. As we seek to address problems of racial and class inequality, we need to reflect on who is served by our solutions.

CONTENTS

Teaching about issues of inequality in a culture that focuses on individualism can be a daunting task. Having been raised in such a culture, students in my classes often arrive with little knowledge of the systemic nature of inequality in society. While they may be aware of their own experiences of disadvantage (and perhaps privilege), they are generally not aware of how structural arrangements in society result in systems of difference and inequality. This book, which focuses on how race, class, gender, and sexuality are socially constructed as categories of difference and are maintained as systems of inequality, is an effort to help students move toward a more systemic understanding.

WHY ANOTHER RACE, CLASS, GENDER (AND SEXUALITY) READER?

With the plethora of readers on race, class, and gender currently on the market, one may wonder why another is needed. Indeed, some excellent anthologies are available that can be effective in demonstrating the impact of race, class, and gender inequality on the life chances of various individuals and groups in our society. However, few of these texts thoroughly explain how such categories of difference are created, and even fewer demonstrate how social institutions work to maintain systems of inequality. The text here is structured in a way that examines how and why the categories of race, class, gender, and sexuality are socially constructed, maintained, and experienced.

This anthology is divided into four parts. Each part begins with an introductory essay that offers a conceptual framework illustrating concepts and theories (which are designated by boldface type) useful for understanding the issues raised by the readings in that section. These essays are not merely introductions to the readings; rather, they provide material that will enable students to move beyond them. Part I provides a thorough discussion of what it means to think critically, as well as an extensive overview of how and why categories of difference are socially constructed. Part II discusses in greater detail how categories of difference are transformed and maintained as systems of inequality by social institutions. Part III examines how categories of difference and systems of inequality impact the everyday experiences of individuals in our society. Finally, Part IV offers a useful look at perspectives on social change and provides examples of barriers to and opportunities for transforming systems of oppression and privilege into systems of equal access to opportunity.

In each section, the readings and examples were selected to cover a variety of racial and ethnic groups as well as experiences of multiracial identity and immigration. In addition, issues of sexuality are incorporated throughout each part of this book. While a few anthologies have begun to incorporate readings that address inequality on the basis of sexuality, the majority do so on only a superficial level. With the continuing political and social debate regarding civil rights and sexuality, it is important that texts provide sufficient material to address this area of inequality. Overall, the readings represent myriad individuals with various perspectives and life experiences. Such diversity will aid students' ability to understand perspectives and experiences that differ from their own. Finally, the part introductions as well as many of the readings selected demonstrate the intersections of race, class, gender, and sexuality and stress the importance of viewing them as interlocking systems of oppression and privilege. By moving beyond traditional additive models of examining inequality, students will be better able to see how forms of inequality are interconnected.

A NOTE ON LANGUAGE

As discussed in Part II, language serves as a link between all the different forms of culture in a society. Although language enables us to communicate with and understand one another, it also incorporates cultural values. Thus, the words we use to describe ourselves and others with regard to race, class, gender, and sexuality reflect not only our own values but also those of the dominant ideology and popular discourse.

In discussing the experiences of different groups, issues of language can become particularly problematic. For example, as discussed in Part I, categories of race and ethnicity are socially constructed. In addition, the externally created labels for these categories are not always accepted by those viewed as belonging to a particular group. For example, individuals of Latin American descent may not accept the term *Hispanic*. Similarly, those who are indigenous to North America may not accept the term *American Indian*. However, there is rarely agreement among all members of a particular racial or ethnic group regarding the terminology with which they would like to be identified.

Recognizing the problems and limitations of language, I have attempted to be consistent in the terminology I have used in each part introduction. For example, I use the term *Latina/o* to refer to those of Latin American descent, although not all people in this group may identify themselves in this way. I also use the terms *black* and *African American* interchangeably, as I do with *American Indian* and *Native American*. In using such terms it is not my intention to homogenize divergent experiences. Rather, it is done in an effort to allow discussion of common experiences within as well as across groups. The terminology used by the authors of the readings was not altered, however. It is important that readers be mindful of the limitations of my language use as well as that of the other authors within this anthology.

CHANGES TO THIS EDITION

With this seventh edition, I have continued to cover a variety of racial and ethnic groups and to incorporate sexuality throughout. In addition, I have maintained the focus on the intersections of race, class, gender, and sexuality as interlocking systems of oppression. To keep the text current with regard to economic conditions, issues of gender and sexuality, the political and social discourse on race, and recent events in our country and world, I have updated all relevant statistics and changed many readings, adding fifteen new readings. These readings include articles discussing issues of immigration and documentation, updated discussions of the relationship between the growing racial wealth gap and social policy in the United States, and the impact of stereotypes held by case workers regarding poor women's reproductive decisions and relationships that shape policy implementation as explained in the article "Jezebel at the Welfare Office." As with the sixth edition, I have selected readings that are engaging for students and that reflect a variety of experiences. I welcome any feedback that instructors and students may have.

ONLINE RESOURCES

An instructor's manual to accompany this text is located on the Ancillary Resource Center. The instructor's manual contains guidelines for discussion for each reading, short-answer and essay questions, suggestions for classroom activities, and recommendations for films/videos. These items were compiled to help instructors further student comprehension of the issues addressed in this volume.

ACKNOWLEDGMENTS

The inception and completion of this project were made possible through the efforts of many people. Foremost among these, I would like to acknowledge the students at the University of Illinois (1995–98) and their efforts in lobbying for a class on multiculturalism and inequality that would incorporate students doing service in the community. Without their perseverance and commitment, I would likely not have had the opportunity to teach a course that provided such a wonderful foundation for this book. As has been the case throughout my teaching career, my students are my best teachers. Thanks go to all of my students at the colleges and universities where I have taught. I continue to learn from each of them.

I also would like to acknowledge the work of a wonderful team of reviewers: Jodi Burmeister-May, St. Cloud State University; Denise M. Dalaimo, Mt. San Jacinto College; Sharon Elise, California State University at San Marcos; Kristin G. Esterberg, University of Massachusetts at Lowell; Susan A. Farrell, Kingsborough Community College; Lisa M. Frehill, New Mexico State University; Melinda Goldner, Union College; Kelley Hall, DePauw University; Melissa Herbert, Hamline University; Eleanor A. Hubbard, University of Colorado at Boulder; Melissa Latimer, West Virginia University; Betsy Lucal, Indiana University South Bend; Anne Roschelle, State University of New York at New Paltz; Steve Schacht, State University of New York at Plattsburgh; Susan Shaw, Oregon State University; and Brett Stockdill, California State Polytechnic University at Pomona. Their insights, comments, and suggestions served me greatly in clarifying the direction of this project. I value the contribution each of them made to its completion.

For the second edition, I would like to thank the following team of reviewers: Peter Meiksins, Cleveland State University; Jackie Hogan, Bradley University; Philip A. Broyles, Shippensburg University; Heather E. Dillaway, Michigan State University; Elizabeth J. Clifford, Towson University; Tom Gershick, Illinois State University; Susan A. Farrell, Kingsborough Community College; Kristin G. Esterberg, University of Massachusetts–Lowell; and Eleanor A. Hubbard, University of Colorado at Boulder.

For the third edition, I would like to thank the following reviewers: Kristin Esterberg, University of Massachusetts–Lowell; Susan Farrell, Kingsborough Community College;

Eleanor Hubbard, University of Colorado at Boulder; and Peter Meiksins, Cleveland State University. Again, their suggestions and comments enabled me to continue to improve this project.

For the fourth edition, I would like to thank the following team of reviewers: Tiffany Davis, University of Minnesota; Spencer Hope Davis, Elon University; Mary Ferguson, University of Missouri–St. Louis; Christina M. Jimenez, University of Colorado at Colorado Springs; Peter Meiksins, Cleveland State University; Chadwick L. Menning, Ball State University; and Tracy Woodard Meyers, Valdosta State University. Their suggestions and comments were incredibly helpful in continuing to produce a text that will be useful to others.

For the fifth edition, I would like to thank the following team of reviewers: Christina Accomando, Humboldt State University; Rose Brewer, University of Minnesota–Twin Cities; Edith Brotman, Towson University; Julie Rauli, Wilson College; and Mark Rauls, College of Southern Nevada. Their thoughtful reviews helped to guide me in providing a text that will continue to be useful to instructors in the field.

For the sixth edition, I appreciate the work of the following team of reviewers: Debora Barrera Pontillo, Cascadia Community College; Catherine Felton, Central Piedmont Community College; Timothy Pippert, Augsburg College; Yvonne Moody, Chadron State College; Jason Martin, University of Missouri at Kansas City; Ann Wood, University of Missouri at Kansas City; Linda Bynoe, California State University–Monterey Bay; Daniel Egan, University of Massachusetts–Lowell; Lynn Jones, Northern Arizona University; Leslie Richards, University of the District of Columbia; Lissa Yogan, Valparaiso University; Nicole Hendricks, Houston Community College; and Adrianna Bohm, Delaware County Community College. Their input was helpful in assisting me in developing an edition that is timely and relevant.

For the seventh edition, I would like to thank the following team of reviewers: Karen Hossfeld, San Francisco State University; Hortencia Jimenez, Hartnell College; Diane McMahon, La Roche College; Deinya Phenix, St. Francis College; Michael Polgar, Pennsylvania State University; Alfred Prettyman, Ramapo College of New Jersey; Dominick Quinney, Albion College; Rosemary Shinko, American University; Nivedita Vaidya, California State University–Los Angeles; and Christi Young, Southwestern Michigan College. Their invaluable feedback helped me to make the revisions necessary to continue to provide a tool that will be beneficial to educators.

The production of the first edition of this book and its adherence to schedule was due to the work of many people. Specifically, I would like to thank Jan Fisher, Kathryn Mikulic, and Dave Mason at Publication Services for their excellent copyediting and other support. At Mayfield Publishing I would like to thank Mary Johnson, April Wells-Hayes, Marty Granahan, and Jay Bauer. My deepest thanks go to Serina Beauparlant for believing in this project and for supporting me throughout. With her vision and perseverance, I couldn't have asked for a better editor.

The creation of the second edition is due to the work of Jill Gordon, Sally Constable, Amy Shaffer, Ruth Smith, Lori Koetters, Jenny El-Shamy, Nathan Perry, and Dan Loch at McGraw-Hill. I appreciate your patience, creative efforts, and attention to detail.

The creation of the third edition is due to the work of Sherith Pankratz, Trish Starner, Larry Goldberg, Jill Gordon, Kim Menning, Melissa Williams, and Randy Hurst at McGraw–Hill. I appreciate your work, imagination, and thoroughness.

The creation of the fourth edition is due to the work of Gina Boedeker, Amanda Peabody, Leslie Oberhuber, Rich DeVitto, and Margarite Reynolds at McGraw–Hill. I am in great appreciation of your patience and commitment.

The creation of the fifth edition is due to the work of Andrea Edwards and Meghan Campbell at McGraw–Hill. I am grateful for your persistence and excellent work.

The production of the sixth edition was supported by Sara Jaeger at McGraw–Hill. I greatly appreciate all that she did to assist me with the completion of the project.

This most recent edition is the result of the most able assistance of Grace Li at Oxford University Press. I am especially appreciative of her patience as the project was delayed because of unforeseen circumstances. Her professionalism and commitment went beyond all my expectations.

Completing this project was also made possible through the support and caring of a wonderful community of friends. I could always count on them for unconditional support, and I am thankful to them for sharing their knowledge and insight. Thanks also go to my fellow activists who help me to always keep one foot in reality so that I do not lose perspective. Finally, I am incredibly grateful to my partner Kramer, a consistent and stable force in my life. Her love, support, and understanding continue to be all I need to get by.

Tracy E. Ore

PART

Constructing Differences

Introduction

In the United States, the Census Bureau attempts to conduct a complete accounting of all residents every ten years. The data gathered by the Census Bureau are extremely important because they serve to determine the distribution of federal dollars to support housing assistance, highway construction, employment services, schools, hospital services, programs for the elderly, and other funding targets. In the year 2000, persons filling out census forms were given a unique opportunity. For the first time, those with mixed racial heritage were permitted to select more than one racial category. As a result of new governmental policy, the category *multiracial* is now a reality in the United States.

Does this mean that people who are multiracial have never before existed in this country? Of course not. Even a superficial exploration of US history will show that multiracial people have been present throughout. The recent study using DNA tests to confirm that Thomas Jefferson was the father of at least one child by his slave Sally Hemings (Foster et al. 1998) is but one example of how the history of slavery in the United States has contributed to the existence of people of multiracial descent. However, until recently, government policies in the United States have not allowed for the recognition of a multiracial identity. Rather, they have enforced policies such as the rule of **hypodescent**—one drop of black blood makes you black—to maintain distinct racial categories.

The preceding example clearly illustrates that the categories we use to describe ourselves and those around us are the product of social rather than biological factors. Biologically, people who are multiracial certainly exist throughout the United States. Indeed, it is unlikely that anyone is racially pure. Nevertheless, it is the social recognition, definition, and grouping of these factors that make them culturally significant in our daily interactions. Our reliance on such distinct categories is made clear when we ask someone whose race is not immediately discernible to us, what are you?

These culturally defined classifications are also significant in that they are structured as categories that are fundamentally different from one another. Thus, we expect people to be black or white, never in between.[1] It is important to point out, however, that difference is not necessarily a negative quality. On the contrary, the existence of categories of difference adds a great deal of richness to our lives. The presence of different cultural traditions, types of food, forms of music, and styles of dance serves to make society more interesting. It is not the differences that are the causes of inequality in our culture. Rather, it is the meanings and values applied to these differences that make them harmful. For example, it is not that people of color are defined as different from whites in the United States, but that whites are viewed as superior and as the cultural standard against which all others are judged that transforms categories of race *differences* into a system of racial *inequality*.

The readings in this text explore how categories of difference with regard to race/ethnicity, social class, sex/gender, and sexuality are constructed and then transformed into systems of inequality. We will investigate what creates these categories and how they are constructed, and we will consider some explanations about why these categories are created. It is important that we understand how the processes that construct these categories simultaneously create structures of **social stratification**—a system by which society ranks categories of people in a hierarchy—and how social stratification results in systems of inequality. The readings in this text will aid us in understanding the effects that categories of difference have on all members of our society and how this inequality can be addressed. By examining closely the processes that construct categories of difference, we will better understand how they impact our lives. Furthermore, by recognizing how systems of inequality are socially created, we can gain a greater understanding of how to transform such systems into ones of equality.

Critical Thinking

A fundamental component in examining constructions of difference and systems of inequality is **critical thinking** about the social constructs on which systems of inequality rely. This requires us to examine how the social structure has affected our values, attitudes, and behaviors. The object of this text is not to negate your current belief system and provide you with a new one, but rather to provide the tools that will allow you to think critically about the attitudes and opinions you have been given. By thinking critically, we are better able to develop a belief system that we can claim as our own.

Many of us are unsure of what is meant by critical thinking. According to various scholars, critical thinking can involve logical reasoning, reflective judgment, exploring assumptions, creating and testing meanings, identifying contradictions in arguments, and determining the validity of empirical findings and generalized conclusions. For the purposes of this text, to think critically is to ask questions about what is assumed to be real, valued, and significant in our culture. Stephen Brookfield (1987) offers a useful framework for asking these questions. He sees critical thinking as having four primary elements.

First, we must identify and challenge assumptions. We should try to identify the assumptions that are at the foundation of the concepts, values, beliefs, and behaviors that we deem important in our society. Once we have identified these assumptions, we need to explore their accuracy and legitimacy, considering whether what we take for granted does indeed reflect the realities we experience. For example, a common assumption in the United States is that women are inherently more nurturing than men and that men are inherently more aggressive than women. When thinking critically, we ask whether such assumptions reflect reality or if they shape what we observe in the behaviors of women and men. In other words, do we observe women indeed being more nurturing, or do we make note of only their nurturing behavior? In addition, we need to ask whether our expectations of women and men shape the ways in which they act. For example, do men behave in a more aggressive manner because that is what is expected of them? Through identifying and challenging assumptions, we become more aware of how uncritically examined assumptions shape our perceptions and our understanding of our environment.

Second, thinking critically involves awareness of our place and time in our culture. When asking questions about aspects of our culture, we need to be aware of our own **standpoint**—the position from which we are asking these questions. In other words, we need to be aware of our location at a particular intersection of culture and history; how that is influenced by our race/ethnicity, social class, sex/gender, sexuality, ability, age, and other factors; and how these in turn influence the questions we ask and the answers we accept. For example, a millionaire examining the strengths and weaknesses of the US economic system would likely see different problems and solutions to these problems than would a working-class individual. Their respective class standpoints (as well as their race/ethnicity, sex/gender, sexuality, etc.) affect the ways in which they examine the world.

One's standpoint also influences what one sees as normal or ordinary behavior. This relates to the concept of **enculturation**—immersion in our own culture to the point where we assume that our way of life is natural or normal. Because we are so enculturated into our own societal standards and practices, we often assume that they are the only options and, as a result, we are unaware of alternatives. Furthermore, we often view those who have other cultural standards or practices as behaving in a strange or unnatural manner. For example, people raised in a culture with strict religious teachings based on the idea of a supreme being may be so enculturated that they view those with different notions of religion (or none at all) as strange or odd. As a consequence of the depth of our enculturation, we also often possess some level of **ethnocentrism**—the practice of judging another culture using the standards of one's own. Such judging is based on the assumption that one's own group is more important than or superior to other groups (Sumner [1906] 1959). Thus, we may judge those who possess different religious beliefs than ourselves not only as strange but also as wrong. For example, many non-Muslim Americans, fueled by media stereotypes, view the practices of those who follow Islam as inappropriate, if not un-American.

It is important to point out, however, that ethnocentrism is not in and of itself problematic. Every social system to some degree promotes its ideas and standards. Ethnocentrism becomes a problem when such ideas are used as a basis for treating people in an unequal manner. An alternative to ethnocentrism is **cultural relativism**—judging a culture by its own cultural rules and values. By being cultural relativists, we can gain a better understanding of the real meaning of another culture's ideas and standards. In thinking critically it is important that we recognize the depth of our enculturation and how it is manifested in our ethnocentrism, so that we can become aware of our own standpoint and be better able to judge other cultures by their own values and ideas.

Third, when thinking critically we need to search for alternative ways of thinking. This means examining the assumptions that form the basis of our ideas and ways of behaving. For example, the United States is currently a society based on the notion of **civil rights**—a system based on majority rule. When we vote, the will of the majority becomes the will of all. This system is designed to bring the greatest good for the greatest number. In addition, there is a fundamental belief that if one is a good citizen, one earns rights within society, such as liberty. In a civil rights system some people inevitably do not benefit. Implicit in the statement "the greatest good for the greatest number" is the assumption that society cannot provide for everyone. To think critically about a civil rights system, we must imagine an alternative to this reality. For example, what might it be like to live in a society that operates under a **human rights** framework? Such a system recognizes each person as an individual and as valuable. It is based on the belief that everyone has inalienable rights to housing, food, education, and health care and that society must provide these rights to people who are unable to provide for themselves. What structural changes are necessary to bring about such a society? Furthermore, if we were to create such a society, how might our own lives be transformed? Considering alternatives to current ways of thinking can provide us with new insights about widely accepted ideas.

Fourth, to think critically one must develop a reflective analysis. Such an analysis requires that we be skeptical, not in the sense that we do not believe anything we see, but rather that we question rigid belief systems. For example, once we become aware that it is possible to have a society that operates under a human rights framework, we come to question those who claim that a system based on civil rights is the only way to operate. A reflective analysis requires that we challenge dominant ideas and popularly held notions regarding solutions to social problems.

Thinking critically frees us from personal, environmental, and institutional forces that prevent us from seeing new directions (Habermas 1979). Furthermore, once we become critical thinkers, we are no longer passive recipients of knowledge and products of socialization. Rather, through practicing thoughtful scrutiny and continuously asking questions, we become active participants and arrive at our own ideas and commitments. As a result, we ground our ideas on a solid and informed foundation, all the while realizing that we may still be wrong. When we face challenges to our ideas, we are better prepared to provide justification and evidence in their support. The readings in this text provide us with many essential tools for becoming discerning critical thinkers.

Essentialism and Social Construction

As mentioned earlier, in the United States we have a system of stratification that is based on many categories of difference, including race/ethnicity, social class, sex/gender, and sexuality. We tend to view this system as fixed because of our assumptions that these categories are unchangeable. Such assumptions are often based on a belief of **essentialism**—the tenet that human behavior is natural, predetermined by genetic, biological, or physiological mechanisms and thus not subject to change. Human behaviors that show some similarity are assumed to be expressions of an underlying human drive or tendency. In the United States, gender and sexuality are among the last realms to have their natural or biological status called into question. For most of us, essentialism informs the way we think about such things as gender and remains the **hegemonic** or culturally dominant belief in our culture. For example, many of us attribute great importance to what we perceive as biological differences between women and men and see them as central to the organization of human society. Essentialism guides the way we order our social world and determines what we value as well as what we devalue.

This text proceeds from a different perspective, however. As you read the selections in Part I, you will note that they all begin with the premise that categories such as race/ethnicity, social class, sex/gender, and sexuality are socially constructed. Peter Berger and Thomas Luckmann, on whose work this premise is based, state that "social order is not part of the 'nature of things,' and it cannot be derived from the 'laws of nature.' Social order exists *only* as a product of human activity" (1966, 52). **Social construction theory** suggests that what we see as real (in this case, cultural categories of difference and systems of inequality) is the result of human interaction. Through such interaction we create aspects of our culture, objectify them, internalize them, and then take these cultural products for granted. A suitable companion to critical thinking, social construction theory encourages us to ask new questions but does not imply a particular answer. Using a critical thinking framework based on the notion of social construction requires that we be committed to asking questions and challenging assumptions that impair our ability even to imagine these questions.

Adopting a framework based on social construction theory means understanding that we are not born with a sense of what it means to be male, female, or intersexual; with a disability or not; black, Latina/o, Asian, white, or Native American; gay, straight, asexual, or bisexual; or rich, working class, poor, or middle class. We learn about these categories through social interaction, and we are given meanings and values for these categories by our social institutions, peers, and families. What we learn depends on the culture in which we live as well as on our place within that culture. Further, how we are defined by our culture often determines how we experience our social world. As W. I. Thomas noted, if we "define situations as real, they are real in their consequences" ([1931] 1966, 301). For example, when we define one group as inferior to another, this does not make that group inferior, yet it may result in the group being experienced as inferior. To illustrate this, consider the vicious cycle that results from the assignment of substandard resources to people who are poor. For example, low-income housing is generally located in geographic areas that lack quality resources such as good public schools and access to adequate health care. Lacking such quality resources results in further social disadvantage, which can perpetuate the poverty of this group. Thus, although reality is initially *soft* as it is constructed, it can become *hard* in its effects. We will examine these effects throughout this text.

According to Berger and Luckmann (1966), reality is socially constructed in three stages. In the first stage, **externalization**, we create cultural products through social interaction. These cultural products may be material artifacts, social institutions, or values or beliefs concerning a particular group. When these products are created, they become "external" to those who have produced them; they become products outside ourselves. For example, as Judith Lorber describes in Reading 7, "The Social Construction of Gender," the construction of gender identity starts at birth with placement within a sex category (male or female). Through dress and adornment, others become aware of the sex of the child and they treat the child according to the gendered expectations they have for that particular sex. Children then behave and respond differently because of the different treatment they receive. A situation defined as real thus becomes real in its consequences. Girls and boys are taught to act differently from each other and thus *do* act differently. As a result, boys and girls are seen as *being* different from each other.

A second example of externalization can be found in the first reading, "Racial Formations," by Michael Omi and Howard Winant. They note that the concept of race has varied over history and is subject to a great deal of debate. Using the term **racial formation**, they describe "the process by which social, economic, and political forces determine the content and importance of racial categories, and by which they shape racial meanings." The example cited at the beginning of this essay clearly illustrates the social forces involved in determining racial categories. The recognition of a multiracial identity involves more than individuals being identified as multiracial. Rather, interaction that takes place at the social, economic, and political levels serves to construct such categories of race.

The second stage, **objectivation**, occurs when the products created in the first stage appear to take on a reality of their own, becoming independent of those who created them. People lose awareness that they themselves are the authors of their social and cultural environment and of their interpretations of reality. They feel as if the products have an objective existence, and they become another part of reality to be taken for granted. For example, most of us take race categories for granted, employing an essentialist perspective that views race categories as the result of biological or genetic factors. However, as mentioned earlier, a variety of social, economic, and political forces are involved in the construction of race categories. When we forget our part in the social construction of race or fail to recognize the social forces that operate to construct race categories and the meanings associated with them, these categories take on objective realities. The objective realities that many of us attribute to racial categories can be seen in the findings of the 2010 census conducted by the US Census Bureau. Nationwide, just under 3 percent of respondents identified themselves as being of mixed race. The reasons for such a low response rate vary from a lack of knowledge of the options to a strong identification with one race, regardless of one's multiracial heritage. These findings demonstrate that most respondents hold on to what they see as the objective reality of clear and mutually exclusive race categories.

In the final stage, **internalization**, we learn the supposedly objective facts about the cultural products that have been created. This occurs primarily through **socialization**, the process of social interaction in which one learns the ways of the society and one's specific **roles**—the sets of rules and expectations attached to a social position (or **status**) in that society. In this stage we make these facts part of our subjective consciousness. Because of the process of internalization, members of the same culture share an understanding of reality and rarely question the origins of their beliefs or the processes by which the beliefs arose. For example, as Gregory Mantsios discusses in Reading 5, "Media Magic: Making Class Invisible," the mass media serve as a powerful tool for shaping the way we think. A significant part of our culture, mass media operate as an extremely important socialization mechanism. What we see presented in the mass media, as well as how it is presented, delivers important messages about who and what is or is not valued. Specifically, mass media help us to internalize certain constructs about class in our society, perpetuating a variety of myths. Among these myths are that poverty is not a significant problem in this country, that those who are poor have only themselves to blame, that we are a middle-class society, and that blue-collar and union workers are to blame for declining economic security. As mass media present us with these images, we develop a particular view of the class structure in our country. In addition, we internalize beliefs about members of a specific class (e.g., the poor are lazy) as if they were objective facts. The role of the media in maintaining constructions of difference and the resulting systems of inequality will be explored in Part II of this text.

It is important to note here that viewing cultural products as being produced in stages does not imply that the creation of reality occurs in a neat and overt progression. In some cases, the process of externalization in the creation of a social category is clear. However, the construction of reality is not always such a clear process. Thinking in terms of a cultural product as produced in stages, however, provides a general understanding of how the knowledge that guides our behavior is established and how it becomes a part of culture and common sense. In addition, it is important to be aware that while categories of difference are being constructed and subsequently transformed into systems of inequality, such systems of inequality are often being maintained by the same social forces and practices. To clearly understand how categories of difference become systems of inequality, we begin by examining the processes that construct them. The social factors that serve to maintain these constructs and their corresponding systems of inequality will be examined in detail in Part II.

What Constructs Categories of Difference?

The readings in this text explore how the categories of race, class, gender, and sexuality are socially constructed and transformed into systems of inequality. The preceding in-depth explanation of social construction theory was intended to give us an understanding of how these categories are socially constructed. To thoroughly comprehend this process, however, it is important to understand what social factors are at work in creating these categories.

Simply put, categories of difference are the result of human activity guided by the values of our culture. When parents teach their child how to behave like a lady or act like a gentleman, when one child labels another gay as discussed in the reading "'If You Don't Kiss Me, You're Dumped': Boys, Boyfriends and Heterosexualised Masculinities in the Primary School" (Reading 11), or when a girl decides to stop playing rough to avoid being labeled a tomboy, each is engaged in the process of creating categories of difference. We take these everyday actions for granted, but they play a fundamental role in how we view the world. The kinds of categories we create, as well as the meanings we give to them, are guided by our cultural values regarding who or what is important.

The process of creating these categories occurs in a variety of contexts that we encounter every day. Perhaps the most significant of these is the **institutional context**. An **institution** is the set of rules and relationships that govern the social activities in which we participate to meet our basic needs. The major social institutions that we will examine are as follows:

The family: responsible for reproducing and socializing and protecting the young, regulating sexual behavior, and providing emotional comfort and support for each of its members

Education: responsible for teaching members of society the knowledge, skills, and values considered most important for survival of the individual and society

The economy: creates, controls, and distributes the human and material resources of a society

The state: possesses the legal power to regulate the behavior of members of that society, as well as the relationship of that society to others

The media: responsible for supplying members of society with information, for reinforcing the policies of other institutions, and for socializing members of society with regard to appropriate ways of behaving and accepted cultural values

From the policies and practices of each of these institutions, influenced by our cultural values, categories of difference are created. Thus, when parents teach their child how to behave like a lady or act like a gentleman, they create categories of difference within the institutional context of the family.

Another context in which we create categories of difference is the **interpersonal context**—our daily interactions with others. In these interactions we rely on common guidelines for behavior (**norms**) to define situations and create these categories. For example, when an individual, operating on stereotypes based on race and ethnicity, labels another a foreigner, she or he is relying on what are assumed images of what is an American. As a result, she or he creates categories of difference within an interpersonal context.

Finally, we create categories of difference in **internal contexts** by internalizing the values and beliefs established in institutional and interpersonal contexts. When a girl decides to stop playing rough to avoid being labeled a tomboy, she is internalizing the ideas of what it means to be a girl that were taught to her by her family as well as her peers.

Constructing Race and Ethnicity

The institution of the state, which determines how the census should be taken and how individuals should be counted, plays an integral role in defining race categories in an institutional context. **Race** denotes a group of people who perceive themselves and are perceived by others as possessing distinctive hereditary traits. **Ethnicity** denotes a group of people who perceive themselves and are perceived by others as sharing cultural traits such as language, religion, family customs, and food preferences. As Omi and Winant illustrate in "Racial Formations," what is important about the construction of race categories is not necessarily our perception of our own race, but the recognition by social institutions of our membership in that race category. Furthermore, racial and ethnic categories are significant in that they are constructed in a hierarchy from superior to inferior. Additionally, as illustrated by Roberto Gonzales in "Learning to Be Illegal" (Reading 3), a person's position in the racial stratification system may shift as policies define and redefine which groups are granted legal status.

Racial categories are also constructed in interpersonal contexts. As Waters discusses in "Optional Ethnicities" (Reading 2), many of us, particularly whites, will ask someone whose race or ethnicity is not immediately apparent, what are you? We do not, however, generally ask such a question of those whom we perceive to be white. Thus, in our efforts to define others we not only attempt to construct distinct racial categories but also create white as an unmarked category and as a standard against which all others are judged.

Finally, race is constructed in internal contexts, where we reinforce those categories and the meanings associated with them within ourselves. This process is particularly evident when a person of color who is light skinned attempts or desires to "pass" as a white person. Through internalizing the idea that to be other than white is to be less valued, they participate in constructing race categories as well as the meanings associated with them.

Constructing Social Class

The categories of social class are also constructed within institutional contexts. Although we may view social class as a result of how much **income** (wages and salaries from earnings and investments) and **wealth** (the total amount of valuable goods) a person possesses, it is in fact more than this. What class we belong to is determined not only by how much money we have or the material possessions we own, but also by the institutions of our society, including state policies and the structuring of the economy. For example, definitions of poverty created by the government affect the access some members of our society have to certain important resources. The Thrifty Food Plan—the least costly of four nutritionally adequate plans designed by the Department of Agriculture, based on their 1955 Household Food Consumption

Survey—demonstrates how the establishment of the **poverty line**, an annual income level below which a person or family was defined as poor and therefore entitled to certain benefits, creates who is seen as poor. The poverty line is problematic, however, in the way it is determined because it relies on material standards of the 1950s rather than contemporary standards. For example, expenses for items we consider essential today—for things such as transportation, childcare, and technology—were not essential costs for families of the 1950s. As a result, while the government determined in 2017 that the poverty line for a family of four was $28,290, a more accurate calculation, employing contemporary standards, would have been closer to $48,000. The more accurate figure would result in doubling if not tripling the number of individuals defined as poor. Additionally, it is important to note that measures such as the poverty line miss a significant aspect of what it means to be poor. Poverty is more than how much money one has; it is also a process of social exclusion (Neal 2004). According to the United Nations, "poverty is more than a shortage of income. It is the denial of opportunities and choices most basic to human development—to lead a long, healthy, creative life and to enjoy a decent standard of living, freedom, dignity, self-esteem, and respect of others" (Townson 2000). When institutions establish definitions and measures, they determine a person's access to resources (i.e., the ability of people living in poverty to receive aid from the government). In this way, constructions of class provide the foundation for a system of inequitably distributed resources. The impact of such a system will be discussed in greater detail later in this text.

In addition to establishing who is poor, institutions such as the economy and its related public policies also function to create a social class stratification system that is increasingly divided by a "wealth gap," as illustrated by Laura Sullivan, Tatjana Meschede, Lars Dietrich, Thomas M. Shapiro, Amy Traub, Catherine Reutschlin, and Tamara Draut in "The Racial Wealth Gap" (Reading 4). Finally, the values that we place on members of social classes are further influenced by social institutions such as the media, as explained by Gregory Mantsios in "Media Magic: Making Class Invisible" (Reading 5). According to Mantsios, those who control the media (i.e., the upper class) can use this institution to create class divisions and to define our attitudes about members of different social classes. Both these articles clearly illustrate that the rules, practices, and policies of social institutions serve to construct categories of class differences and establish a system of class inequality.

Categories of social class are also constructed in interpersonal contexts. We define who is rich, poor, middle class, and so forth in our interactions with others. In addition, we attach meanings to each of these categories. For example, if we see a well-dressed, clean-cut individual driving an expensive car, we not only may judge the individual as belonging to the upper class but also admire her or him and the class position we assume she or he has achieved. However, if we observe people purchasing groceries with food stamps and then taking the bus, we not only judge them as poor but also are likely to think less of them as a result of their presumed class. In each instance, we rely on **stereotypes**—rigid, oversimplified, often exaggerated beliefs that are applied both to an entire category of people and to each individual in that category. As a result of stereotypes, we treat individuals according to the values we attribute to these classes.

The individuals in the preceding examples likely would be aware of the assumptions made about them on the basis of their social class. Mantsios illustrates that such stereotypes about class dominate our media. As these individuals internalize these messages, their sense of self-worth is impacted. In addition, these individuals aid in creating categories of class and the meanings associated with them.

Constructing Sex and Gender

Categories of sex and gender are also socially constructed in institutional contexts. This claim may, at first glance, seem strange. Whether a person is female or male is generally seen as a biological condition. However, as Judith Lorber in "The Social Construction of Gender" (Reading 7) and Cheryl Chase in "Square Pegs" (Reading 8) discuss, the categories of male and female are not always sufficient to describe the variety of sexes that exist in reality. For example, individuals born **intersex**—the physical manifestation of genital/genetic/endocrinological differentiation that is viewed as different from the norm—may constitute as many as 4 percent of live births. However, these infants are placed in a program of hormonal and surgical management almost immediately after birth so that they can become "normal" males or females in society. Thus, the institutions of science and medicine and advances in physiology and surgical technology aid in constructing a reality in which there are only two sexes.

What is significant about **sex**—the genetic (and sometimes scientific) determination of male and female—is the corresponding expectations that we place on people occupying these categories with regard to **gender**—the socially defined roles expected of males and females. As Lorber and others clearly explain, gender constructs are created and justified by a variety of institutions, including the family, the state, and the economy. Thus, gender constructs are transformed into a **gender system** in which men and masculinity are at the top of the hierarchy and women and femininity are at the bottom. Our ideas about gender therefore influence the way people are sorted into social positions. For example, our expectations of women to be feminine and our corresponding assumptions about their ability to handle certain kinds of strenuous or stressful work contribute to the underrepresentation of women as chief executive officers and heads of governing bodies. Similarly, our expectations that males be masculine and our corresponding assumption that they are less able to be nurturing contribute to their being less likely to pursue careers as nurses or elementary school teachers, for example. Because such a gendered division of labor is established in a society that is based on **patriarchy**—a form of social organization in which males dominate females—what results is not only a gendered division of labor but also an occupational hierarchy in which the work of men is valued over that of women.

Further examples of how we construct categories of sex and gender are found in interpersonal contexts. We construct these categories by acting out the two polar sex categories and fulfilling the corresponding gendered expectations that have been constructed by the social institutions of the family, education, and others. As West and Zimmerman (1987) note, we do gender through our attempts to define others and through our expectations that others display appropriate gender identity. Similar to the ways in which we view race, we are often frustrated with ambiguities of sex and gender. If the sex/gender of another individual does not fit our expectations of opposite sex categories with corresponding gendered behavior, we often seek to define the person, again asking, what are you? In so doing we aid in the process of constructing a sex/gender system that allows for only two sexes and requires gender categories to be distinct and polar opposites.

Finally, gender is also created in internal contexts. As sociologist Michael Kimmel (1994) has illustrated, males often insecure in their manhood will thus act as bullies to prove their manhood, not only to others but also to themselves. Furthermore, feelings of **alienation** (a sense of not belonging to the culture or the community, as is the case with males fearing they will be labeled sissy if they do not act like men) as well as feelings of **self-alienation** (hatred for one's own position and oneself) play a significant role in how we create these categories within ourselves. As a result, we often perpetuate the ways in which these categories are constructed in other contexts.

Constructing Sexuality

Categories of sexuality are also constructed within institutional contexts. Claims that sexuality is constructed may at first appear as strange as claims of sex being a social construct. Just as we generally recognize only two categories of sex, we often recognize sexuality as existing in only two opposing categories: gay and straight. Furthermore, we tend to see these categories as polar opposites, with one fundamentally different from the other. However, current notions of sexuality are but one way of imagining the social relations of the sexes. Like all of the previously discussed categories, sexuality is a complex yet culturally defined construct. **Sexuality** can involve attraction on a physical, emotional, and social level as well as fantasies, sexual behaviors, and self-identity (Klein 1978). However, just as we may be required to distill our variations in racial and ethnic heritage into one of a few categories, we are often required to place all the varying aspects of our sexuality into one of two categories. Thus, a complex part of who we are becomes socially defined within rigid and limiting constructs.

What is significant about categories of sexuality is that they are transformed into systems of inequality, where one form of sexuality is valued and viewed as more appropriate than others. In the United States, the policies and practices of the federal government have historically recognized some forms of sexuality and not others. For example, the Defense of Marriage Act allowed some states to exclude same-sex couples from the right to marry. Despite the existence of such an act, thirty states had constitutional amendments that banned civil unions, marriage equality, and, in a few instances, any and all legal protection for lesbian and gay families. In 2008, the voters of California passed Proposition 8, the California Marriage Protection Act, which designated that only marriage between a man and a woman is valid or recognized in California. Such actions served to grant access to resources to heterosexuals but deny that access to lesbians and gays, thus creating systems of inequality. In 2015, the US Supreme Court ruled that same-sex couples have the right to marry in all fifty states, nullifying these institutional policies.

We also create different sexuality categories in interpersonal contexts. As Emma Renold notes in "'If You Don't Kiss Me, You're Dumped': Boys, Boyfriends and Heterosexualised Masculinities in the Primary School" (Reading 11), in addition to Kate Bornstein's discussion in "Naming All the Parts" (Reading 10), constructions of sexuality are culturally linked to constructions of gender. Each of these readings illustrates not only how constructions of difference in institutional contexts are reflected in interpersonal interactions, but also how the social construction of one category of difference is generally dependent on the social construction of another. The interrelatedness of various constructions of difference will be addressed later.

We also create categories of sexuality in internal contexts. Again, this is generally done in response to the ways sexuality is defined in the larger society. Our descriptions of sexuality divisions and our own membership in them are determined by the sexual landscape of the culture and what are viewed as appropriate or available categories. As we define ourselves, we perpetuate the ways in which these categories are created in other contexts.

In summary, the construction of categories of difference occurs within a variety of contexts. The readings in Part I illustrate this process. In addition, they demonstrate how the meanings we attach to these categories result in structures of inequality.

Why Categories of Difference?

Often the most difficult aspect of understanding the construction of categories of difference is not the how or the what, but the *why*. We have difficulty understanding why such categories are created and transformed into systems of inequality. Many explanations regarding why categories of difference and their corresponding hierarchies are constructed have been offered from several perspectives.

The readings in Part I offer a variety of explanations. For example, Omi and Winant in "Racial Formations" discuss some of the reasons European explorers created separate categories for the people who were indigenous to the lands that they "discovered." They explain that when the European explorers came upon people who looked different from them, their assumptions about the origin of the human species were called into question. As a result, religious debates regarding creation and whether God created a single species of humanity led to questions about whether the natives of the New World could be "saved," as well as about how they should be treated. By deeming the European settlers children of God and indigenous people *other*, the European settlers not only were able to maintain their worldview but also were able to justify systems of mistreatment, including slavery, coercive labor, and extermination.

Social theorists also offer explanations regarding why elements of social structure work to create systems of stratification. For example, Kingsley Davis and Wilbert Moore (1945) assert, in what has come to be known as the **Davis–Moore thesis**, that social stratification is a universal pattern because it has beneficial consequences for the operation of society. This is the case, they reason, because societal inequality has important functions for social organization. They note that society is a complex system of occupational positions, each of which has a particular importance. Some jobs, they argue, are easy to do (with a little instruction) and can be performed by just about anyone. Others are far more challenging and can only be accomplished by certain people who possess certain scarce talents. Functionally speaking, according to Davis and Moore, the latter positions of high day-to-day responsibility are the most important.

Other social theorists argue, however, that such a perspective is too conservative and fails to point out the inequality and exploitation of such systems of stratification. Thus, they argue that social stratification is a system by which some people gain advantages at the expense of others. Karl Marx ([1859] 1959), for example, contended that systems of class stratification involve inequality and exploitation and are created so that capitalists can maximize their profits. He went on to say that the economy has primary importance as the social institution with the greatest influence on the rest of society. Other institutions also create systems of stratification but do so, in general, to support the operation of the economy.

Still other theorists, such as Marilyn Frye (1983), argue that the social construction of difference is initiated with the purpose of discrimination and **oppression**—a relationship in which the dominant group benefits from systematic abuse, exploitation, and injustice directed at a subordinate group. Thus, the construction of difference is not arbitrary but systematically created and transformed into systems of inequality in an effort to advantage some at the expense of others. The roles of domination and subordination in the construction of difference and the maintenance of inequality will be addressed in greater detail in Part II.

Categories of Difference within a Matrix of Domination

Candace West and Sarah Fenstermaker (1995) note that, although gender, race, and class (and sexuality) involve different attributes and effects, they are comparable devices for creating social inequality. To this point in our discussion we have looked distinctly at the construction of each category of difference—race/ethnicity, social class, sex/gender, and sexuality—yet the similarities in the processes of construction serve to provide a foundation for understanding how their subsequent systems of oppression interconnect. To fully understand the process of transforming difference into inequality, it is necessary to recognize the interrelationships between these systems.

What we have discussed as distinct categories of difference and systems of inequality are, according to hooks (1989), systems of oppression that interconnect in an overarching structure of domination. She argues that oppression based on race, class, gender, and sexuality is part of an interlocking politics of domination which is "a belief in domination, and a belief in the notions of superior and inferior, which are components of all of those systems" (175). Patricia Hill Collins (1991) refers to this interlocking system as a **matrix of domination**. This model provides the framework for our efforts in this text in seeking to understand how categories of difference are transformed into systems of inequality and maintained as systems of oppression. Such a framework will allow us to move beyond simply describing the similarities and differences between various systems of oppression and will help us to focus on how they interconnect. We will thereby be better able to see how each system of oppression relies on the others. The ways in which these systems of oppression rely on each other to maintain inequality will be discussed in detail in Part II.

The matrix of domination also provides a framework that permits us to avoid additive analyses of systems of oppression (e.g., a black woman being viewed as doubly oppressed as a white woman). Such analyses are problematic in that they suggest that oppression can be quantified. Attempts to do this would result in our placing ourselves in competition with one another, arguing over who is more oppressed and which form of oppression is the worst. Such debates generally divide us and prevent us from working toward equality. Viewing oppression and inequality in the form of a matrix of domination enables us to see commonalities in the sources of inequality and thus provides a clearer perspective on how these inequalities should be addressed.

Viewing constructions of difference and corresponding systems of inequality as interconnected also helps us to see how all groups experience both privilege and oppression in one socially constructed system. Each of us has had a life experience that is unique, and each of us has likely experienced both oppression and privilege. As Collins (1991) notes, a person may occupy the position of oppressor, oppressed, or both. The matrix of domination permits us to understand how we all experience both oppression and privilege.

Just as categories of difference are constructed in a variety of contexts, so, too, is the matrix of domination. To thoroughly understand the process of social construction, as well as to understand the matrix of domination, it is important to understand what is constructed, what does the constructing, how these constructs are created, and how their corresponding systems of inequality intersect. As you read the selections in Part I, note the explanations provided by each of the authors and be aware of your reactions to them. These readings will provide you with a framework to better understand contemporary constructions of race/ethnicity, social class, sex/gender, and sexuality in the United States. In addition, by understanding the process of social construction we can be more optimistic in working toward positive social change. If we recognize the processes by which systems of inequality are constructed as interlocking systems of oppression, we can gain a greater understanding of how to deconstruct these systems while constructing systems of equality.

A Final Comment

As stated earlier, this text will help us begin the process of understanding contemporary constructions of race/ethnicity, social class, sex/gender, and sexuality in the United States. A fundamental component to examining these constructs is to think critically. In addition, it is important to employ **empathy**—the ability to identify with the thoughts and experiences of another, although you have not shared those thoughts and experiences. Thus, it is important to remain aware of your own standpoint—your location in society and how that is impacted by your race/ethnicity, social class, sex/gender, sexuality, ability, age, and other personal qualities. As you read about experiences that you have not had or are challenged by perspectives offered by the authors, try not to shut yourself off to what they have to say. Rather, use this challenge as an opportunity to better understand your own ideas. As the process of critical thinking indicates, becoming aware of alternative experiences and perspectives can result in a greater understanding of why we think what we do. Finally, you may find that you come away from this text with more questions than you had on entering. If so, see this as a positive outcome, because it is not only a sign of success in learning to think critically, but also an indication that the process of critical thinking will continue beyond this text.

Note

1. This is most notable in public discourse about the racial identity of the former US president Barack Obama. As the child of Ann Dunham, a white woman from Kansas, and Barack Obama Sr., a man of Lou ethnicity from Nyanza Province, Kenya, former President Obama's multiracial identity is a well-known fact. Nevertheless, he is predominantly recognized as an African American, not a person with a multiracial identity.

References

Berger, Peter L., and Thomas Luckmann. 1966. *The Social Construction of Reality: A Treatise in the Sociology of Knowledge.* New York: Doubleday.

Brookfield, Stephen D. 1987. *Developing Critical Thinkers: Challenging Adults to Explore Alternative Ways of Thinking and Acting.* San Francisco: Jossey–Bass.

Collins, Patricia Hill. 1991. *Black Feminist Thought: Knowledge, Consciousness, and the Politics of Empowerment.* New York: Routledge.

Davis, Kingsley, and Wilbert Moore. 1945. "Some Principles of Stratification." *American Sociological Review* 10 (2): 242–49.

Foster, Eugene A., M. A. Jobling, P. G. Taylor, P. Donnelly, P. De Knijff, Rene Mieremet, T. Zerjal, and C. Tyler-Smith. 1998. "Jefferson Fathered Slave's Last Child." *Nature* 396: 27–28.

Frye, Marilyn. 1983. *The Politics of Reality: Essays in Feminist Theory.* Trumansburg, NY: Crossing Press.

Habermas, Jurgen. 1979. *Communication and the Evolution of Society.* Translated by Thomas McCarthy. Boston: Beacon Press.

hooks, bell. 1989. *Talking Back: Thinking Feminist, Thinking Black.* Boston: South End Press.

Kimmel, Michael S. 1994. "Masculinity as Homophobia: Fear, Shame, and Silence in the Construction of Gender Identity." In *Theorizing Masculinities,* edited by Harry Brod. Thousand Oaks, CA: Sage.

Klein, Fritz. 1978. *The Bisexual Option.* New York: Arbor House.

Marx, Karl. (1859) 1959. "A Contribution to the Critique of Political Economy." In Karl Marx and Friedrich Engels, *Marx and Engels: Basic Writings on Politics and Philosophy,* edited by Lewis S. Feurer, 42–46. Garden City, NY: Anchor Books.

Neal, Rusty. 2004. *Voices: Women, Poverty and Homelessness in Canada.* Ottawa: National AntiPoverty Organization.

Sumner, William Graham. (1906) 1959. *Folkways.* New York: Dover.

Thomas, W. I. (1931) 1966. "The Relation of Research to the Social Process." In *W. I. Thomas on Social Organization and Personality,* edited by Morris Janowitz, 289–305. Chicago: University of Chicago Press.

Townson, Monica. 2000. *A Report Card on Women and Poverty.* Ottawa: Canadian Centre for Policy Alternatives.

West, Candace, and Sarah Fenstermaker. 1995. "Doing Difference." *Gender & Society* 9 (1): 8–37.

West, Candace, and Don H. Zimmerman. 1987. "Doing Gender." *Gender & Society* 1 (2): 125–51.

Racial Formations

MICHAEL OMI AND HOWARD WINANT

In the following reading, authors Michael Omi and Howard Winant examine the sociohistorical processes that are involved in constructing what we know as race in the United States. This excerpt from their book Racial Formations in the United States: From the 1960s to the 1980s *(1986) illustrates the process of social construction explained in the introduction to this section. It is important to note that their explanation of the process of racial formation involves the actions of groups and individuals, as well as changes in social structures and institutions, in constructing racial differences while simultaneously establishing racial inequalities.*

In 1982–83, Susie Guillory Phipps unsuccessfully sued the Louisiana Bureau of Vital Records to change her racial classification from black to white. The descendant of an eighteenth-century white planter and a black slave, Phipps was designated "black" in her birth certificate in accordance with a 1970 state law which declared anyone with at least one-thirty-second "Negro blood" to be black. The legal battle raised intriguing questions about the concept of race, its meaning in contemporary society, and its use (and abuse) in public policy. Assistant Attorney General Ron Davis defended the law by pointing out that some type of racial classification was necessary to comply with federal record-keeping requirements and to facilitate programs for the prevention of genetic diseases. Phipps's attorney, Brian Begue, argued that the assignment of racial categories on birth certificates was unconstitutional and that the one-thirty-second designation was inaccurate. He called on a retired Tulane University professor who cited research indicating that most whites have one-twentieth "Negro" ancestry. In the end, Phipps lost. The court upheld a state law which quantified racial identity, and in so doing affirmed the legality of assigning individuals to specific racial groupings.[1]

The Phipps case illustrates the continuing dilemma of defining race and establishing its meaning in institutional life. Today, to assert that variations in human physiognomy are racially based is to enter a constant and intense debate. *Scientific* interpretations of race have not been alone in sparking heated controversy; *religious* perspectives have done so as well.[2] Most centrally, of course, race has been a matter of *political* contention. This has been particularly true in the United States, where the concept of race has varied enormously over time without ever leaving the center stage of US history.

What Is Race?

Race consciousness, and its articulation in theories of race, is largely a modern phenomenon. When European explorers in the New World "discovered" people who looked different than themselves, these "natives" challenged then existing conceptions of the origins of the human species, and raised disturbing questions as to whether *all* could be considered in the same "family of man."[3] Religious debates flared over the attempt to reconcile the Bible with the existence of "racially distinct" people. Arguments took place over creation itself, as theories of polygenesis questioned whether God had made only one species of humanity ("monogenesis"). Europeans wondered if the natives of the New World were indeed human beings with redeemable souls. At stake were not only the prospects for conversion, but the types of treatment to be accorded them. The expropriation of property, the denial of political rights, the introduction of slavery and other forms of coercive labor, as well as outright extermination, all presupposed a worldview which distinguished Europeans—children of God, human beings, etc.—from "others." Such a worldview was needed to explain why some should be "free" and others enslaved, why some had rights to land and property while others did not. Race, and the interpretation of racial differences, was a central factor in that worldview.

In the colonial epoch science was no less a field of controversy than religion in attempts to comprehend the concept of race and its meaning. Spurred on by the classificatory scheme of living organisms devised by Linnaeus in *Systema Naturae*, many scholars in the eighteenth and nineteenth centuries dedicated themselves to the identification and ranking of variations in humankind. Race was thought of as a *biological* concept, yet its precise definition was the subject of debates which, as we have noted, continue to rage today. Despite efforts ranging from Dr. Samuel Morton's studies of cranial capacity[4] to contemporary attempts to base racial classification on shared gene pools,[5] the concept of race has defied biological definition. . . .

Attempts to discern the *scientific meaning* of race continue to the present day. Although most physical anthropologists and biologists have abandoned the quest for a scientific basis to determine racial categories, controversies have recently flared in the area of genetics and educational psychology. For instance, an essay by Arthur Jensen which argued that hereditary factors shape intelligence not only revived the "nature or nurture" controversy, but raised highly volatile questions about racial equality itself.[6] Clearly the attempt to establish a *biological* basis of race has not been swept into the dustbin of history, but is being resurrected in various scientific arenas. All such attempts seek to remove the concept of race from fundamental social, political, or economic determination. They suggest instead that the truth of race lies in the terrain of innate characteristics, of which skin color and other physical attributes provide only the most obvious, and in some respects most superficial, indicators.

Race as a Social Concept

The social sciences have come to reject biologistic notions of race in favor of an approach which regards race as a *social* concept. Beginning in the eighteenth century, this trend has been slow and uneven, but its direction clear. In the nineteenth century Max Weber discounted biological explanations for racial conflict and instead highlighted the social and political factors which engendered such conflict.[7] The work of pioneering cultural anthropologist Franz Boas was crucial in refuting the scientific racism of the early twentieth century by rejecting the connection between race and culture, and the assumption of a continuum of "higher" and "lower" cultural groups. Within the contemporary social science literature, race is assumed to be a variable which is shaped by broader societal forces.

Race is indeed a pre-eminently *sociohistorical* concept. Racial categories and the meaning of race are given concrete expression by the specific social relations and historical context in which they are embedded. Racial meanings have varied tremendously over time and between different societies.

In the United States, the black/white color line has historically been rigidly defined and enforced.

White is seen as a "pure" category. Any racial intermixture makes one "nonwhite." In the movie *Raintree County*, Elizabeth Taylor describes the worst of fates to befall whites as "havin' a little Negra blood in ya'—just one little teeny drop and a person's all Negra."[8] This thinking flows from what Marvin Harris has characterized as the principle of *hypo-descent*:

> By what ingenious computation is the genetic tracery of a million years of evolution unraveled and each man [sic] assigned his proper social box? In the United States, the mechanism employed is the rule of hypo-descent. This descent rule requires Americans to believe that anyone who is known to have had a Negro ancestor is a Negro. We admit nothing in between. . . . "Hypo-descent" means affiliation with the subordinate rather than the superordinate group in order to avoid the ambiguity of intermediate identity. . . . The rule of hypo-descent is, therefore, an invention, which we in the United States have made in order to keep biological facts from intruding into our collective racist fantasies.[9]

The Susie Guillory Phipps case merely represents the contemporary expression of this racial logic.

By contrast, a striking feature of race relations in the lowland areas of Latin America since the abolition of slavery has been the relative absence of sharply defined racial groupings. No such rigid descent rule characterizes racial identity in many Latin American societies. Brazil, for example, has historically had less rigid conceptions of race, and thus a variety of "intermediate" racial categories exist. Indeed, as Harris notes, "One of the most striking consequences of the Brazilian system of racial identification is that parents and children and even brothers and sisters are frequently accepted as representatives of quite opposite racial types."[10] Such a possibility is incomprehensible within the logic of racial categories in the US.

To suggest another example: the notion of "passing" takes on new meaning if we compare various American cultures' means of assigning racial identity. In the United States, individuals who are actually "black" by the logic of hypo-descent have attempted to skirt the discriminatory barriers imposed by law and custom by attempting to "pass" for white.[11] Ironically, these same individuals would not be able to pass for "black" in many Latin American societies.

Consideration of the term "black" illustrates the diversity of racial meanings which can be found among different societies and historically within a given society. In contemporary British politics the term "black" is used to refer to all nonwhites. Interestingly this designation has not arisen through the racist discourse of groups such as the National Front. Rather, in political and cultural movements, Asian as well as Afro-Caribbean youth are adopting the term as an expression of self-identity.[12] The wide-ranging meanings of "black" illustrate the manner in which racial categories are shaped politically.[13]

The meaning of race is defined and contested throughout society, in both collective action and personal practice. In the process, racial categories themselves are formed, transformed, destroyed, and re-formed. We use the term *racial formation* to refer to the process by which social, economic, and political forces determine the content and importance of racial categories, and by which they are in turn shaped by racial meanings. Crucial to this formulation is the treatment of race as a *central axis* of social relations which cannot be subsumed under or reduced to some broader category or conception.

Racial Ideology and Racial Identity

The seemingly obvious "natural" and "common sense" qualities which the existing racial order exhibits themselves testify to the effectiveness of the racial formation process in constructing racial meanings and racial identities.

One of the first things we notice about people when we meet them (along with their sex) is their race. We utilize race to provide clues about *who* a person is. This fact is made painfully obvious when we encounter someone whom we cannot conveniently racially categorize—someone who is, for example, racially "mixed" or of an ethnic/racial group with which we are not familiar. Such an encounter becomes a source of discomfort and momentarily a crisis of racial meaning. Without a racial identity, one is in danger of having no identity.

Our compass for navigating race relations depends on preconceived notions of what each specific racial group looks like. Comments such as, "Funny, you don't look black," betray an underlying image of what black should be. We also become disoriented when people do not act "black," "Latino," or indeed "white." The content of such stereotypes reveals a series of unsubstantiated beliefs about who these groups are and what "they" are like.[14]

In U.S. society, then, a kind of "racial etiquette" exists, a set of interpretative codes and racial meanings which operate in the interactions of daily life. Rules shaped by our perception of race in a comprehensively racial society determine the "presentation of self,"[15] distinctions of status, and appropriate modes of conduct. "Etiquette" is not mere universal adherence to the dominant group's rules, but a more dynamic combination of these rules with the values and beliefs of subordinated groupings. This racial "subjection" is quintessentially ideological. Everybody learns some combination, some version, of the rules of racial classification, and of their own racial identity, often without obvious teaching or conscious inculcation. Race becomes "common sense"—a way of comprehending, explaining, and acting in the world.

Racial beliefs operate as an "amateur biology," a way of explaining the variations in "human nature."[16] Differences in skin color and other obvious physical characteristics supposedly provide visible clues to differences lurking underneath. Temperament, sexuality, intelligence, athletic ability, aesthetic preferences and so on are presumed to be fixed and discernible from the palpable mark of race. Such diverse questions as our confidence and trust in others (for example, clerks or salespeople, media figures, neighbors), our sexual preferences and romantic images, our tastes in music, films, dance, or sports, and our very ways of talking, walking, eating, and dreaming are ineluctably shaped by notions of race. Skin color "differences" are thought to explain perceived differences in intellectual, physical, and artistic temperaments, and to justify distinct treatment of racially identified individuals and groups.

The continuing persistence of racial ideology suggests that these racial myths and stereotypes cannot be exposed as such in the popular imagination. They are, we think, too essential, too integral, to the maintenance of the U.S. social order. Of course, particular meanings, stereotypes, and myths can change, but the presence of a *system* of racial meanings and stereotypes, of racial ideology, seems to be a permanent feature of U.S. culture.

Film and television, for example, have been notorious in disseminating images of racial minorities which establish for audiences what people from these groups look like, how they behave, and "who they are."[17] The power of the media lies not only in their ability to reflect the dominant racial ideology, but in their capacity to shape that ideology in the first place. D. W. Griffith's epic *Birth of a Nation,* a sympathetic treatment of the rise of the Ku Klux Klan during Reconstruction, helped to generate, consolidate, and "nationalize" images of blacks which had been more disparate (more regionally specific, for example) prior to the film's appearance.[18] In U.S. television, the necessity to define characters in the briefest and most condensed manner has led to the perpetuation of racial caricatures, as racial stereotypes serve as shorthand for scriptwriters, directors and actors, in commercials, etc. Television's tendency to address the "lowest common denominator" in order to render programs "familiar" to an enormous and diverse audience leads it regularly to assign and reassign racial characteristics to particular groups, both minority and majority.

These and innumerable other examples show that we tend to view race as something fixed and immutable—something rooted in "nature." Thus we mask the historical construction of racial categories, the shifting meaning of race, and the crucial role of politics and ideology in shaping race relations. Races do not emerge full-blown. They are the results of diverse historical practices and are continually subject to challenge over their definition and meaning.

Racialization: The Historical Development of Race

In the United States, the racial category of "black" evolved with the consolidation of racial slavery. By the end of the seventeenth century, Africans whose specific identity was Ibo, Yoruba, Fulani, etc., were rendered "black" by an ideology of exploitation based on racial logic—the establishment and maintenance of a "color line." This of course did not occur overnight. A period of indentured servitude which was not rooted in racial logic preceded the consolidation of racial slavery. With slavery, however, a racially based understanding of society was set in motion which resulted in the shaping of a specific *racial* identity not only for the slaves but for the European settlers as well. Winthrop Jordan has observed: "From the initially common term *Christian*, at mid-century there was a marked shift toward the terms *English* and *free*. After about 1680, taking the colonies as a whole, a new term of self-identification appeared—*white*."[19]

We employ the term *racialization* to signify the extension of racial meaning to a previously racially unclassified relationship, social practice, or group. Racialization is an ideological process, a historically specific one. Racial ideology is constructed from pre-existing conceptual (or, if one prefers, "discursive") elements and emerges from the struggles of competing political projects and ideas seeking to articulate similar elements differently. An account of racialization processes that avoids the pitfalls of U.S. ethnic history[20] remains to be written.

Particularly during the nineteenth century, the category of "white" was subject to challenges brought about by the influx of diverse groups who were not of the same Anglo-Saxon stock as the founding immigrants. In the nineteenth century, political and ideological struggles emerged over the classification of Southern Europeans, the Irish, and Jews, among other "non-white" categories.[21] Nativism was only effectively curbed by the institutionalization of a racial order that drew the color line *around*, rather than *within*, Europe.

By stopping short of racializing immigrants from Europe after the Civil War, and by subsequently allowing their assimilation, the American racial order was reconsolidated in the wake of the tremendous challenge placed before it by the abolition of racial slavery.[22] With the end of Reconstruction in 1877, an effective program for limiting the emergent class struggles of the later nineteenth century was forged: the definition of the working class *in racial terms*—as "white." This was not accomplished by any legislative decree or capitalist maneuvering to divide the working class, but rather by white workers themselves. Many of them were recent immigrants, who organized on racial lines as much as on traditionally defined class lines.[23] The Irish on the West Coast, for example, engaged in vicious anti-Chinese race-baiting and committed many pogrom-type assaults on Chinese in the course of consolidating the trade union movement in California.

Thus the very political organization of the working class was in important ways a racial project. The legacy of racial conflicts and arrangements shaped the definition of interests and in turn led to the consolidation of institutional patterns (e.g., segregated unions, dual labor markets, exclusionary legislation) which perpetuated the color line *within* the working class. Selig Perlman, whose study of the development of the labor movement is fairly sympathetic to this process, notes that:

The political issue after 1877 was racial, not financial, and the weapon was not merely the ballot, but also "direct action"—violence. The anti-Chinese agitation in California, culminating as it did in the Exclusion Law passed by Congress in 1882, was doubtless the most important single factor in the history of American labor, for without it the entire country might have been overrun by Mongolian [sic] labor and *the labor movement might have become a conflict of races instead of one of classes.*[24]

More recent economic transformations in the U.S. have also altered interpretations of racial identities and meanings. The automation of southern agriculture and the augmented labor demand of the postwar boom transformed blacks from a largely rural, impoverished labor force to a largely urban, working-class group by 1970.[25] When boom became bust and liberal welfare statism moved rightwards, the majority of blacks came to be seen, increasingly, as part of the "underclass," as state "dependents." Thus the particularly deleterious effects on blacks of global and national economic shifts (generally rising unemployment rates, changes in the employment structure away from reliance on labor intensive work, etc.) were explained once again in the late 1970s and 1980s (as they had been in the 1940s and mid-1960s) as the result of defective black cultural norms, of familial disorganization, etc.[26] In this way new racial attributions, new racial myths, are affixed to "blacks."[27] Similar changes in racial identity are presently affecting Asians and Latinos, as such economic forces as increasing Third World impoverishment and indebtedness fuel immigration and high interest rates, Japanese competition spurs resentments, and US jobs seem to fly away to Korea and Singapore.[28] . . .

Once we understand that race overflows the boundaries of skin color, superexploitation, social stratification, discrimination and prejudice, cultural domination and cultural resistance, state policy (or of any other particular social relationship we list), once we recognize the racial dimension present to some degree in every identity, institution, and social practice in the United States—once we have done this, it becomes possible to speak of *racial formation.* This recognition is hard-won; there is a continuous temptation to think of race as an *essence,* as something fixed, concrete and objective, as (for example) one of the categories just enumerated. And there is also an opposite temptation: to see it as a mere illusion, which an ideal social order would eliminate.

In our view it is crucial to break with these habits of thought. The effort must be made to understand race as *an unstable and "decentered" complex of social meanings constantly being transformed by political struggle.* . . .

Notes

1. *San Francisco Chronicle,* 14 September 1982, 19 May 1983. Ironically, the 1970 Louisiana law was enacted to supersede an old Jim Crow statute which relied on the idea of "common report" in determining an infant's race. Following Phipps's unsuccessful attempt to change her classification and have the law declared unconstitutional, a legislative effort arose which culminated in the repeal of the law. See *San Francisco Chronicle,* 23 June 1983.

2. The Mormon church, for example, has been heavily criticized for its doctrine of black inferiority.

3. Thomas F. Gossett notes:

   Race theory . . . had up until fairly modern times no firm hold on European thought. On the other hand, race theory and race prejudice were by no means unknown at the time when the English colonists came to North America. Undoubtedly, the age of exploration led many to speculate on race differences at a period when neither Europeans nor Englishmen were prepared to make allowances for vast cultural diversities. Even though race theories had not then secured wide acceptance or even sophisticated formulation, the first contacts of the Spanish with the Indians in the Americas can now be recognized as the beginning of a struggle between conceptions of the nature of primitive peoples which has not yet been wholly settled. (Thomas F. Gossett, *Race: The History of an Idea in America* [New York: Schocken Books, 1965], p. 16.)

   Winthrop Jordan provides a detailed account of early European colonialists' attitudes about color and race in *White over Black: American Attitudes toward the Negro, 1550–1812* (New York: Norton, 1977 [1968]), pp. 3–43.

4. Pro-slavery physician Samuel George Morton (1799–1851) compiled a collection of 800 crania from all parts of the world which formed the sample for his studies of race. Assuming that the larger the size of the cranium translated into greater intelligence, Morton established a relationship between race and skull capacity. Gossett reports that:

> In 1849, one of his studies included the following results: The English skulls in his collection proved to be the largest, with an average cranial capacity of 96 cubic inches. The Americans and Germans were rather poor seconds, both with cranial capacities of 90 cubic inches. At the bottom of the list were the Negroes with 83 cubic inches, the Chinese with 82, and the Indians with 79. (Ibid., p. 74.)

On Morton's methods, see Stephen J. Gould, "The Finagle Factor," *Human Nature* (July 1978).

5. Definitions of race founded upon a common pool of genes have not held up when confronted by scientific research which suggests that the differences *within* a given human population are greater than those *between* populations. See L. L. Cavalli-Sforza, "The Genetics of Human Populations," *Scientific American* (September 1974), pp. 81–89.

6. Arthur Jensen, "How Much Can We Boost IQ and Scholastic Achievement?" *Harvard Educational Review,* vol. 39 (1969), pp. 1–123.

7. Ernst Moritz Manasse, "Max Weber on Race," *Social Research,* vol. 14 (1947), pp. 191–221.

8. Quoted in Edward D. C. Campbell, Jr., *The Celluloid South: Hollywood and the Southern Myth* (Knoxville: University of Tennessee Press, 1981), pp. 168–70.

9. Marvin Harris, *Patterns of Race in the Americas* (New York: Norton, 1964), p. 56.

10. Ibid., p. 57.

11. After James Meredith had been admitted as the first black student at the University of Mississippi, Harry S. Murphy announced that he, and not Meredith, was the first black student to attend "Ole Miss." Murphy described himself as black but was able to pass for white and spent nine months at the institution without attracting any notice. (Ibid., p. 56.)

12. A. Sivanandan, "From Resistance to Rebellion: Asian and Afro-Caribbean Struggles in Britain," *Race and Class,* vol. 23, nos. 2–3 (Autumn–Winter 1981).

13. Consider the contradictions in racial status which abound in the country with the most rigidly defined racial categories—South Africa. There a race classification agency is employed to adjudicate claims for upgrading of official racial identity. This is particularly necessary for the "coloured" category. The apartheid system considers Chinese as "Asians" while the Japanese are accorded the status of "honorary whites." This logic nearly detaches race from any grounding in skin color and other physical attributes and nakedly exposes race as a juridical category subject to economic, social, and political influences. (We are indebted to Steve Talbot for clarification of some of these points.)

14. Gordon W. Allport, *The Nature of Prejudice* (Garden City, New York: Doubleday, 1958), pp. 184–200.

15. We wish to use this phrase loosely, without committing ourselves to a particular position on such social psychological approaches as symbolic interactionism, which are outside the scope of this study. An interesting study on this subject is S. M. Lyman and W. A. Douglass, "Ethnicity: Strategies of Individual and Collective Impression Management," *Social Research,* vol. 40, no. 2 (1973).

16. Michael Billig, "Patterns of Racism: Interviews with National Front Members," *Race and Class,* vol. 20, no. 2 (Autumn 1978), pp. 161–79.

17. "Miss San Antonio USA Lisa Fernandez and other Hispanics auditioning for a role in a television soap opera did not fit the Hollywood image of real Mexicans and had to darken their faces before filming." Model Aurora Garza said that their faces were bronzed with powder because they looked too white. "I'm a real Mexican [Garza said] and very dark anyway. I'm even darker right now because I have a tan. But they kept wanting me to make my face darker and darker" (*San Francisco Chronicle,* 21 September 1984). A similar dilemma faces Asian American actors who feel that Asian character lead roles inevitably go to white actors who make themselves up to be Asian. Scores of Charlie Chan films, for example, have been made with white leads (the last one was the 1981 *Charlie Chan and the Curse of the Dragon Queen*). Roland Winters, who played in six Chan features, was asked by playwright Frank Chin to explain the logic of casting a white man in the role of Charlie Chan: "The only thing I can think of is,

if you want to cast a homosexual in a show, and you get a homosexual, it'll be awful. It won't be funny . . . and maybe there's something there . . ." (Frank Chin, "Confessions of the Chinatown Cowboy," *Bulletin of Concerned Asian Scholars,* vol. 4, no. 3 [Fall 1972]).

18. Melanie Martindale-Sikes, "Nationalizing 'Nigger' Imagery Through 'Birth of a Nation,'" paper prepared for the 73rd Annual Meeting of the American Sociological Association, 4–8 September 1978 in San Francisco.

19. Winthrop D. Jordan, op. cit., p. 95; emphasis added.

20. Historical focus has been placed either on particular racially defined groups or on immigration and the "incorporation" of ethnic groups. In the former case the characteristic ethnicity theory pitfalls and apologetics such as functionalism and cultural pluralism may be avoided, but only by sacrificing much of the focus on race. In the latter case, race is considered a manifestation of ethnicity.

21. The degree of antipathy for these groups should not be minimized. A northern commentator observed in the 1850s: "An Irish Catholic seldom attempts to rise to a higher condition than that in which he is placed, while the Negro often makes the attempt with success." Quoted in Gossett, op. cit., p. 288.

22. This analysis, as will perhaps be obvious, is essentially DuBoisian. Its main source will be found in the monumental (and still largely unappreciated) *Black Reconstruction in the United States 1860–1880* (New York: Atheneum, 1977 [1035]).

23. Alexander Saxton argues that:

North Americans of European background have experienced three great racial confrontations: with the Indian, with the African, and with the Oriental. Central to each transaction has been a totally one-sided preponderance of power, exerted for the exploitation of nonwhites by the dominant white society. In each case (but especially in the two that began with systems of enforced labor), white workingmen have played a crucial, yet ambivalent role. They have been both exploited and exploiters. On the one hand, thrown into competition with nonwhites as enslaved or "cheap" labor, they suffered economically; on the other hand, being white, they benefited by that very exploitation which was compelling the nonwhites to work for low wages or for nothing. Ideologically they were drawn in opposite directions. *Racial identification cut at right angles to class consciousness.* (Alexander Saxton, *The Indispensable Enemy: Labor and the Anti-Chinese Movement in California* [Berkeley and Los Angeles: University of California Press, 1971], p. 1, emphasis added.)

24. Selig Perlman, *The History of Trade Unionism in the United States* (New York: Augustus Kelley, 1950), p. 52; emphasis added.

25. Whether Southern blacks were "peasants" or rural workers is unimportant in this context. Some time during the 1960s blacks attained a higher degree of urbanization than whites. Before World War II most blacks had been rural dwellers and nearly 80 percent lived in the South.

26. See George Gilder, *Wealth and Poverty* (New York: Basic Books, 1981); Charles Murray, *Losing Ground* (New York: Basic Books, 1984).

27. A brilliant study of the racialization process in Britain, focused on the rise of "mugging" as a popular fear in the 1970s, is Stuart Hall et al., *Policing the Crisis* (London: Macmillan, 1978).

28. The case of Vincent Chin, a Chinese American man beaten to death in 1982 by a laid-off Detroit auto worker and his stepson who mistook him for Japanese and blamed him for the loss of their jobs, has been widely publicized in Asian American communities. On immigration conflicts and pressures, see Michael Omi, "New Wave Dread: Immigration and Intra-Third World Conflict," *Socialist Review,* no. 60 (November–December 1981).

Questions for Critical Thinking

1. Does Omi and Winant's discussion of race as a social rather than biological concept help you to see issues of race in new and different ways? If so, how? If not, why not?

2. How does your membership in a particular race category influence your understanding of or level of agreement with the authors' discussion?

3. Considering the authors' discussion, do you think it is possible or desirable to move beyond racial divisions?

Optional Ethnicities

For Whites Only?

MARY C. WATERS

This second reading, by sociologist Mary C. Waters, illustrates how, like race, ethnicity is a social construct, not a biological one. Drawing on her field research with suburban whites, she explains the concept of **symbolic ethnicity**—*an ethnicity that is individualistic in its origin and without real social cost for the person. However, as she explains, such a choice is not available to all, and understanding ethnicity as an individual choice may make us unaware of the ongoing discrimination experienced by people of color.*

Ethnic Identity for Whites in the 1990s

What does it mean to talk about ethnicity as an option for an individual? To argue that an individual has some degree of choice in their ethnic identity flies in the face of the common sense notion of ethnicity many of us believe in—that one's ethnic identity is a fixed characteristic, reflective of blood ties and given at birth. However, social scientists who study ethnicity have long concluded that while ethnicity is based in a *belief* in a common ancestry, ethnicity is primarily a *social* phenomenon, not a biological one (Alba 1985, 1990; Barth 1969; Weber [1921] 1968, p. 389). The belief that members of an ethnic group have that they share a common ancestry may not be a fact. There is a great deal of change in ethnic identities across generations through intermarriage, changing allegiances, and changing social categories. There is also a much larger amount of change in the identities of individuals over their life than is commonly believed. While most people are aware of the phenomenon known as "passing"—people raised as one race who change at some point and claim a different race as their identity—there are similar life course changes in ethnicity that happen all the time and are not given the same degree of attention as "racial passing."

White Americans of European ancestry can be described as having a great deal of choice in terms of their ethnic identities. The two major types of options White Americans can exercise are (1) the option of whether to claim any specific ancestry, or to just be "White" or American (Lieberson [1985] called these people "unhyphenated Whites"), and (2) the choice of which of their European ancestries to choose to include in their description of their own identities. In both cases, the option of choosing how to present yourself on surveys and in everyday social interactions exists for Whites because of social changes and societal conditions that have created a great deal of social mobility, immigrant assimilation, and political and economic power for Whites in the United States. Specifically, the option of being able to not claim any ethnic identity exists for Whites of European background

in the United States because they are the majority group—in terms of holding political and social
power, as well as being a numerical majority. The
option of choosing among different ethnicities in
their family backgrounds exists because the degree
of discrimination and social distance attached to
specific European backgrounds has diminished
over time.

The Ethnic Miracle

When European immigration to the United States
was sharply curtailed in the late 1920s, a process
was set in motion whereby the European ethnic
groups already in the United States were for all in-
tents and purposes cut off from any new arrivals.
As a result, the composition of the ethnic groups
began to age generationally. The proportion of
each ethnic group made up of immigrants or the
first generation began to gradually decline, and the
proportion made up of the children, grandchildren, and eventually great-grandchildren began to
increase. Consequently, by 1990 most European-
origin ethnic groups in the United States were
composed of a very small number of immigrants,
and a very large proportion of people whose link
to their ethnic origins in Europe was increasingly
remote.

This generational change was accompanied
by unprecedented social and economic changes.
The very success of the assimilation process these
groups experienced makes it difficult to imagine
how much the question of the immigrants' eventual assimilation was an open one at the turn of the
century. At the peak of immigration from southern
and central Europe there was widespread discrimination and hostility against the newcomers by established Americans. Italians, Poles, Greeks, and
Jews were called derogatory names, attacked by nativist mobs, and derided in the press. Intermarriage
across ethnic lines was very uncommon—castelike
in the words of some sociologists (Pagnini and
Morgan 1990). The immigrants and their children
were residentially segregated, occupationally specialized, and generally poor.

After several generations in the United States,
the situation has changed a great deal. The success and social mobility of the grandchildren and
great-grandchildren of that massive wave of immigrants from Europe has been called "The Ethnic
Miracle" (Greeley 1976). These Whites have moved
away from the inner-city ethnic ghettos to White
middle-class suburban homes. They are doctors,
lawyers, entertainers, academics, governors, and
Supreme Court justices. But contrary to what some
social science theorists and some politicians predicted or hoped for, these middle-class Americans
have not completely given up ethnic identity. Instead, they have maintained some connection with
their immigrant ancestors' identities—becoming
Irish American doctors, Italian American Supreme
Court justices, and Greek American presidential
candidates. In the tradition of cultural pluralism, successful middle-class Americans in the late
twentieth century maintain some degree of identity with their ethnic backgrounds. They have remained "hyphenated Americans." So while social
mobility and declining discrimination have created
the option of not identifying with any European
ancestry, most White Americans continue to
report some ethnic background.

With the growth in intermarriage among people
of European ethnic origins, increasingly these
people are of mixed ethnic ancestry. This gives
them the option of which ethnicity to identify with.
The U.S. census has asked a question on ethnic
ancestry in the 1980 and 1990 censuses. In 1980,
52 percent of the American public responded with
a single ethnic ancestry, 31 percent gave multiple
ethnic origins (up to three were coded, but some
individuals wrote in more than three), and only
6 percent said they were American only, while the
remaining 11 percent gave no response. In 1990
about 90 percent of the population gave some response to the ancestry question, with only 5 percent
giving American as a response and only 1.4 percent
reporting an uncodeable response such as "don't
know" (McKenney and Cresce 1992; U.S. Bureau of
the Census 1992).

Several researchers have examined the pattern of responses of people to the census ancestry question. These analyses have shown a pattern of flux and inconsistency in ethnic ancestry reporting. For instance, Lieberson and Waters (1986, 1988, p. 93) have found that parents simplify children's ancestries when reporting them to the census. For instance, among the offspring in situations where one parent reports a specific single White ethnic origin and the other parent reports a different single White origin, about 40 percent of the children are not described as the logical combination of the parents' ancestries. For example, only about 60 percent of the children of English-German marriages are labeled as English-German or German-English. About 15 percent of the children of these parents are simplified to just English, and another 15 percent are reported as just German. The remainder of the children are either not given an ancestry or are described as American (Lieberson and Waters 1986, 1993).

In addition to these intergenerational changes, researchers have found changes in reporting ancestry that occur at the time of marriage or upon leaving home. At the ages of eighteen to twenty-two, when many young Americans leave home for the first time, the number of people reporting a single as opposed to a multiple ancestry goes up. Thus while parents simplify children's ancestries when they leave home, children themselves tend to report less complexity in their ancestries when they leave their parents' homes and begin reporting their ancestries themselves (Lieberson and Waters 1986, 1988; Waters 1990).

These individual changes are reflected in variability over time in the aggregate numbers of groups determined by the census and surveys. Fairly (1991) compared the consistency of the overall counts of different ancestry groups in the 1979 Current Population Survey, the 1980 census, and the 1986 National Content Test (a pretest for the 1990 census). He found much less consistency in the numbers for northern European ancestry groups whose immigration peaks were early

in the nineteenth century—the English, Dutch, Germans, and other northern European groups. In other words each of these different surveys and the census yielded a different estimate of the number of people having this ancestry. The 1990 census also showed a great deal of flux and inconsistency in some ancestry groups. The number of people reporting English as an ancestry went down considerably from 1980, while the number reporting German ancestry went up. The number of Cajuns grew dramatically. This has led officials at the Census Bureau to assume that the examples used in the instructions strongly influence the responses people give. (Cajun was one of the examples of an ancestry given in 1990 but not in 1980, and German was the first example given. English was an example in the 1980 instructions, but not in 1990.)

All of these studies point to the socially variable nature of ethnic identity—and the lack of equivalence between ethnic ancestry and identity. If merely adding a category to the instructions to the question increases the number of people claiming that ancestry, what does that mean about the level of importance of that identity for people answering the census? Clearly identity and ancestry for Whites in the United States, who increasingly are from mixed backgrounds, involve some change and choice.

Symbolic Ethnicities for White Americans

What do these ethnic identities mean to people and why do they cling to them rather than just abandoning the tie and calling themselves American? My own field research with suburban Whites in California and Pennsylvania found that later-generation descendants of European origin maintain what are called "symbolic ethnicities." Symbolic ethnicity is a term coined by Herbert Gans (1979) to refer to ethnicity that is individualistic in nature and without real social cost for the individual. These symbolic identifications are essentially leisure time activities, rooted in nuclear family traditions and reinforced by the voluntary enjoyable aspects of being ethnic (Waters 1990).

Richard Alba (1990) also found later-generation Whites in Albany, New York, who chose to keep a tie with an ethnic identity because of the enjoyable and voluntary aspects to those identities, along with the feelings of specialness they entailed. An example of symbolic ethnicity is individuals who identify as Irish, for example, on occasions such as Saint Patrick's Day, on family holidays, or for vacations. They do not usually belong to Irish American organizations, live in Irish neighborhoods, work in Irish jobs, or marry other Irish people. The symbolic meaning of being Irish American can be constructed by individuals from mass media images, family traditions, or other intermittent social activities. In other words, for later-generation White ethnics, ethnicity is not something that influences their lives unless they want it to. In the world of work and school and neighborhood, individuals do not have to admit to being ethnic unless they choose to. And for an increasing number of European-origin individuals whose parents and grandparents have intermarried, the ethnicity they claim is largely a matter of personal choice as they sort through all of the possible combinations of groups in their genealogies.

Individuals can choose those aspects of being Italian, for instance, that appeal to them, and discard those that do not. Or a person whose father is Italian, and mother part Polish and part French, might choose among the three ethnicities and present herself as a Polish American. With just a little probing, many people will describe a variety of ancestries in their family background, but do not consider these ancestries to be a salient part of their own identities. Thus the 1990 census ancestry question, which estimated that 30 percent of the population is of mixed ancestry, most surely underestimates the degree of mixing among the population. My research, and the research of Richard Alba (1990), shows that many people have already sorted through what they know of their ethnic ancestries and simplified their responses before they ever answer a census or survey question (Waters 1990).

But note that this freedom to include or exclude ancestries in your identification to yourself and others would not be the same for those defined racially in our society. They are constrained to identify with the part of their ancestry that has been socially defined as the "essential" part. African Americans, for example, have been highly socially constrained to identify as Blacks, without other options available to them, even when they know that their forebears included many people of American Indian or European background. Up until the mid-twentieth century, many state governments had specific laws defining one as Black if as little as one-thirty-second of one's ancestors were defined as Black (Davis 1991; Dominguez 1986; Spickard 1989). Even now when the one-drop rule has been dropped from our legal codes, there are still strong societal pressures on African Americans to identify in a particular way. Certain ancestries take precedence over others in the societal rules on descent and ancestry reckoning. If one believes one is part English and part German and identifies in a survey as German, one is not in danger of being accused of trying to "pass" as non-English and of being "redefined" English by the interviewer. But if one were part African and part German, one's self-identification as German would be highly suspect and probably not accepted if one "looked" Black according to the prevailing social norms.

This is reflected in the ways the census collects race and ethnic identity. While the ethnic ancestry question used in 1980 and 1990 is given to all Americans in the sample regardless of race and allows multiple responses that combine races, the primary source of information on people defined racially in the United States is the census race question or the Hispanic question. Both of these questions require a person to make a choice about an identity. Individuals are not allowed to respond that they are both Black and White, or Japanese and Asian Indian on the race question even if they know that is their background. In fact, people who disobey the instructions to the census race question and check off two races are assigned to the first checked race in the list by the Census Bureau.

In responding to the ancestry question, the comparative latitude that White respondents have does not mean that Whites pick and choose ethnicities out of thin air. For the most part people choose an identity that corresponds with some element of their family tree. However, there are many anecdotal instances of people adopting ethnicities when they marry or move to a strongly identified neighborhood or community. For instance Micaela di Leonardo (1984) reported instances of non-Italian women who married into Italian American families and "became Italian." Karen Leonard (1992) describes a community of Mexican American women who married Punjabi immigrants in California. Some of the Punjabi immigrants and their descendants were said to have "become Mexican" when they joined their wives' kin group and social worlds. Alternatively she describes the community acknowledging that Mexican women made the best curry, as they adapted to life with Indian-origin men.

But what do these identities mean to individuals? Surely an identity that is optional in a number of ways—not legally defined on a passport or birth certificate, not socially consequential in terms of societal discrimination in terms of housing or job access, and not economically limiting in terms of blocking opportunities for social mobility—cannot be the same as an identity that results from and is nurtured by societal exclusion and rejection. The choice to have a symbolic ethnicity is an attractive and widespread one despite its lack of demonstrable content, because having a symbolic ethnicity combines individuality with feelings of community. People reported to me that they liked having an ethnic identity because it gave them a uniqueness and a feeling of being special. They often contrasted their own specialness by virtue of their ethnic identities with "bland" Americanness. Being ethnic makes people feel unique and special and not just "vanilla," as one of my respondents put it.

Because "American" is largely understood by Americans to be a political identity and allegiance and not an ethnic one, the idea of being "American" does not give people the same sense of belonging that their hyphenated American identity does. When I asked people about their dual identities—American and Irish or Italian or whatever—they usually responded in a way that showed how they conceived of the relationship between the two identities. Being an American was their primary identity; but it was so primary that they rarely, if ever, thought about it—most commonly only when they left the country. Being Irish American, on the other hand, was a way they had of differentiating themselves from others whom they interacted with from day to day—in many cases from spouses or in-laws. Certain of their traits—being emotional, having a sense of humor, talking with their hands—were understood as stemming from their ethnicity. Yet when asked about their identity as Americans, that identity was both removed from their day-to-day consciousness and understood in terms of loyalty and patriotism. Although they may not think they behave or think in a certain way because they are American, being American is something they are both proud of and committed to.

Symbolic ethnicity is the best of all worlds for these respondents. These White ethnics can claim to be unique and special, while simultaneously finding the community and conformity with others that they also crave. But that "community" is of a type that will not interfere with a person's individuality. It is not as if these people belong to ethnic voluntary organizations or gather as a group in churches or neighborhoods or union halls. They work and reside within the mainstream of American middle-class life, yet they retain the interesting benefits—the "specialness"—of ethnic allegiance, without any of its drawbacks.

It has been suggested by several researchers that this positive value attached to ethnic ancestry, which became popular in the ethnic revival of the 1970s, is the result of assimilation having proceeded to an advanced stage for descendants of

White Europeans (Alba 1985; Crispino 1980; Steinberg 1981). Ironically, people celebrate and embrace their ethnic backgrounds precisely because assimilation has proceeded to the point where such identification does not have that much influence on their day-to-day life. Rather than choosing the "least ethnic" and most bland ethnicities, Whites desire the "most ethnic" ones, like the once-stigmatized "Italian," because it is perceived as bringing the most psychic benefits. For instance, when an Italian father is married to an English or a Scottish or a German mother, the likelihood is that the child will be reported to the census with the father's Italian ancestry, rather than the northern European ancestries, which would have been predicted to have a higher social status. Italian is a good ancestry to have, people told me, because they have good food and a warm family life. This change in the social meaning of being Italian American is quite dramatic, given that Italians were subject to discrimination, exclusion, and extreme negative stereotyping in the early part of the twentieth century.

Race Relations and Symbolic Ethnicity

However much symbolic ethnicity is without cost for the individual, there is a cost associated with symbolic ethnicity for the society. That is because symbolic ethnicities of the type described here are confined to White Americans of European origin. Black Americans, Hispanic Americans, Asian Americans, and American Indians do not have the option of a symbolic ethnicity at present in the United States. For all of the ways in which ethnicity does not matter for White Americans, it does matter for non-Whites. Who your ancestors are does affect your choice of spouse, where you live, what job you have, who your friends are, and what your chances are for success in American society, if those ancestors happen not to be from Europe. The reality is that White ethnics have a lot more choice and room to maneuver than they themselves think they do. The situation is very different for members of racial minorities, whose lives are strongly

influenced by their race or national origin regardless of how much they may choose not to identify themselves in terms of their ancestries.

When White Americans learn the stories of how their grandparents and great-grandparents triumphed in the United States over adversity, they are usually told in terms of their individual efforts and triumphs. The important role of labor unions and other organized political and economic actors in their social and economic successes is left out of the story in favor of a generational story of individual Americans rising up against communitarian, Old World intolerance, and New World resistance. As a result, the "individualized" voluntary, cultural view of ethnicity for Whites is what is remembered.

One important implication of these identities is that they tend to be very individualistic. There is a tendency to view valuing diversity in a pluralist environment as equating all groups. The symbolic ethnic tends to think that all groups are equal; everyone has a background that is their right to celebrate and pass on to their children. This leads to the conclusion that all identities are equal and all identities in some sense are interchangeable—"I'm Italian American, you're Polish American. I'm Irish American, you're African American." The important thing is to treat people as individuals and all equally. However, this assumption ignores the very big difference between an individualistic symbolic ethnic identity and a socially enforced and imposed racial identity. When White Americans equate their own symbolic ethnicities with the socially enforced identities of non-White Americans, they obscure the fact that the experiences of Whites and non-Whites have been qualitatively different in the United States and that the current identities of individuals partly reflect that unequal history.

In the next section I describe how relations between Black and White students on college campuses reflect some of these asymmetries in the understanding of what a racial or ethnic identity means. While I focus on Black and White students in the following discussion, you should be aware that the myriad other groups in the United

States—Mexican Americans, American Indians, Japanese Americans—all have some degree of social and individual influences on their identities, which reflect the group's social and economic history and present circumstance.

Relations on College Campuses

Both Black and White students face the task of developing their race and ethnic identities. Sociologists and psychologists note that at the time people leave home and begin to live independently from their parents, often ages eighteen to twenty-two, they report a heightened sense of racial and ethnic identity as they sort through how much of their beliefs and behaviors are idiosyncratic to their families and how much are shared with other people. It is not until one comes in close contact with many people who are different from oneself that individuals realize the ways in which their backgrounds may influence their individual personality. This involves coming into contact with people who are different in terms of their ethnicity, class, religion, region, and race. For White students, the ethnicity they claim is more often than not a symbolic one—with all of the voluntary, enjoyable, and intermittent characteristics I have described above.

Black students at the university are also developing identities through interactions with others who are different from them. Their identity development is more complicated than that of Whites because of the added element of racial discrimination and racism, along with the "ethnic" developments of finding others who share their background. Thus Black students have the positive attraction of being around other Black students who share some cultural elements, as well as the need to band together with other students in a reactive and oppositional way in the face of racist incidents on campus.

Colleges and universities across the country have been increasing diversity among their student bodies in the last few decades. This had led in many cases to strained relations among students from different racial and ethnic backgrounds. The 1980s and 1990s produced a great number of racial incidents and high racial tensions on campuses. While there were a number of racial incidents that were due to bigotry, unlawful behavior, and violent or vicious attacks, much of what happens among students on campuses involves a low level of tension and awkwardness in social interactions.

Many Black students experience racism personally for the first time on campus. The upper-middle-class students from White suburbs were often isolated enough that their presence was not threatening to racists in their high schools. Also, their class background was known by their residence and this may have prevented attacks being directed at them. Often Black students at the university who begin talking with other students and recognizing racial slights will remember incidents that happened to them earlier that they might not have thought were related to race.

Black college students across the country experience a sizeable number of incidents that are clearly the result of racism. Many of the most blatant ones that occur between students are the result of drinking. Sometimes late at night, drunken groups of White students coming home from parties will yell slurs at single Black students on the street. The other types of incidents that happen include being singled out for special treatment by employees, such as being followed when shopping at the campus bookstore, or going to the art museum with your class and the guard stops you and asks for your I.D. Others involve impersonal encounters on the street—being called a nigger by a truck driver while crossing the street, or seeing old ladies clutch their pocketbooks and shake in terror as you pass them on the street. For the most part these incidents are not specific to the university environment; they are the types of incidents middle-class Blacks face every day throughout American society, and they have been documented by sociologists (Feagin 1991).

In such a climate, however, with students experiencing these types of incidents and talking with each other about them, Black students do experience a tension and a feeling of being singled out.

It is unfair that this is part of their college experience and not that of White students. Dealing with incidents like this, or the ever-present threat of such incidents, is an ongoing developmental task for Black students that takes energy, attention, and strength of character. It should be clearly understood that this is an asymmetry in the "college experience" for Black and White students. It is one of the unfair aspects of life that results from living in a society with ongoing racial prejudice and discrimination. It is also very understandable that it makes some students angry at the unfairness of it all, even if there is no one to blame specifically. It is also very troubling because, while most Whites do not create these incidents, some do, and it is never clear until you know someone well whether they are the type of person who could do something like this. So one of the reactions of Black students to these incidents is to band together.

In some sense then, as Blauner (1992) has argued, you can see Black students coming together on campus as both an "ethnic" pull of wanting to be together to share common experiences and community, and a "racial" push of banding together defensively because of perceived rejection and tension from Whites. In this way the ethnic identities of Black students are in some sense similar to, say, Korean students wanting to be together to share experiences. And it is an ethnicity that is generally much stronger than, say, Italian Americans. But for Koreans who come together there is generally a definition of themselves as "different from" Whites. For Blacks reacting to exclusion, there is a tendency for the coming together to involve both being "different from" but also "opposed to" Whites.

The anthropologist John Ogbu (1990) has documented the tendency of minorities in a variety of societies around the world, who have experienced severe blocked mobility for long periods of time, to develop such oppositional identities. An important component of having such an identity is to describe others of your group who do not join in the group solidarity as devaluing and denying their very core identity. This is why it is not common for successful

Asians to be accused by others of "acting White" in the United States, but it is quite common for such a term to be used by Blacks and Latinos. The oppositional component of a Black identity also explains how Black people can question whether others are acting "Black enough." On campus, it explains some of the intense pressures felt by Black students who do not make their racial identity central and who choose to hang out primarily with non-Blacks. This pressure from the group, which is partly defining itself by not being White, is exacerbated by the fact that race is a physical marker in American society. No one immediately notices the Jewish students sitting together in the dining hall, or the one Jewish student sitting surrounded by non-Jews, or the Texan sitting with the Californians, but everyone notices the Black student who is or is not at the "Black table" in the cafeteria.

Institutional Responses

Our society asks a lot of young people. We ask young people to do something that no one else does as successfully on such a wide scale—that is to live together with people from very different backgrounds, to respect one another, to appreciate one another, and to enjoy and learn from one another. The successes that occur every day in this endeavor are many, and they are too often overlooked. However, the problems and tensions are also real, and they will not vanish on their own. We tend to see pluralism working in the United States in much the same way some people expect capitalism to work. If you put together people with various interests and abilities and resources, the "invisible hand" of capitalism is supposed to make all the parts work together in an economy for the common good.

There is much to be said for such a model—the invisible hand of the market can solve complicated problems of production and distribution better than any "visible hand" of a state plan. However, we have learned that unequal power relations among the actors in the capitalist marketplace, as well as "externalities" that the market cannot account for, such as long-term pollution, or collusion between corporations, or the exploitation of child labor, means that state regulation is often needed. Pluralism and the relations between groups are very similar. There is a lot to be said for the idea that bringing people who belong to different ethnic or racial groups together in institutions with no interference will have good consequences. Students from different backgrounds will make friends if they share a dorm room or corridor, and there is no need for the institution to do any more than provide the locale. But like capitalism, the invisible hand of pluralism does not do well when power relations and externalities are ignored. When you bring together individuals from groups that are differentially valued in the wider society and provide no guidance, there will be problems. In these cases the "invisible hand" of pluralist relations does not work, and tensions and disagreements can arise without any particular individual or group of individuals being "to blame." On college campuses in the 1990s some of the tensions between students are of this sort. They arise from honest misunderstandings, lack of a common background, and very different experiences of what race and ethnicity mean to the individual.

The implications of symbolic ethnicities for thinking about race relations are subtle but consequential. If your understanding of your own ethnicity and its relationship to society and politics is one of individual choice, it becomes harder to understand the need for programs like affirmative action, which recognize the ongoing need for group struggle and group recognition, in order to bring about social change. It also is hard for a White college student to understand the need that minority students feel to band together against discrimination. It also is easy, on the individual level, to expect everyone else to be able to turn their ethnicity on and off at will, the way you are able to, without understanding that ongoing discrimination and societal attention to minority status makes that impossible for individuals from minority groups to do. The paradox of symbolic ethnicity is that it depends upon the ultimate goal

of a pluralist society, and at the same time makes it more difficult to achieve that ultimate goal. It is dependent upon the concept that all ethnicities mean the same thing, that enjoying the traditions of one's heritage is an option available to a group or an individual, but that such a heritage should not have any social costs associated with it.

There are many societal issues and involuntary ascriptions associated with non-White identities. The developments necessary for this to change are not individual but societal in nature. Social mobility and declining racial and ethnic sensitivity are closely associated. The legacy and the present reality of discrimination on the basis of race or ethnicity must be overcome before the ideal of the pluralist society, where all heritages are treated equally and are equally available for individuals to choose or discard at will, is realized.

References

Alba, Richard D. 1985. *Italian Americans: Into the Twilight of Ethnicity.* Englewood Cliffs, NJ: Prentice-Hall.

Alba, Richard D. 1990. *Ethnic Identity: The Transformation of White America.* New Haven, CT: Yale University Press.

Barth, Frederik. 1969. *Ethnic Groups and Boundaries.* Boston: Little, Brown.

Blauner, Robert. 1992. "Talking Past Each Other: Black and White Languages of Race." *American Prospect* (Summer):55–64.

Crispino, James. 1980. *The Assimilation of Ethnic Groups: The Italian Case.* Staten Island, NY: Center for Migration Studies.

Davis, F. James. 1991. *Who Is Black. One Nation's Definition.* University Park: Pennsylvania State University Press.

di Leonardo, Micaela. 1984. *The Varieties of Ethnic Experience: Kinship, Class and Gender among Italian Americans.* Ithaca, NY: Cornell University Press.

Dominguez, Virginia. 1986. *White by Definition: Social Classification in Creole Louisiana.* New Brunswick, NJ: Rutgers University Press.

Fairly, Reynolds. 1991. "The New Census Questions about Ancestry: What Did It Tell Us?" *Demography* 28:411–29.

Feagin, Joe R. 1991. "The Continuing Significance of Race: Antiblack Discrimination in Public Places." *American Sociological Review* 56:101–117.

Gans, Herbert. 1979. "Symbolic Ethnicity: The Future of Ethnic Groups and Cultures in America." *Ethnic and Racial Studies* 2:1–20.

Greeley, Andrew M. 1976. "The Ethnic Miracle." *Public Interest* 45 (Fall):20–36.

Leonard, Karen. 1992. *Making Ethnic Choices: California's Punjabi Mexican Americans.* Philadelphia: Temple University Press.

Lieberson, Stanley. 1985. "Unhyphenated Whites in the United States." *Ethnic and Racial Studies* 8:159–80.

Lieberson, Stanley, and Mary Waters, 1986. "Ethnic Groups in Flux: The Changing Ethnic Responses of American Whites." *Annals of the American Academy of Political and Social Science* 487:79–91.

———. 1988. *From Many Strands: Ethnic and Racial Groups in Contemporary America.* New York: Russell Sage.

———. 1993. "The Ethnic Responses of Whites: What Causes Their Instability, Simplification, and Inconsistency?" *Social Forces* 72(2):421–50.

McKenney, Nampeo R., and Arthur R. Cresce. 1992. "Measurement of Ethnicity in the United States: Experiences of the U.S. Census Bureau." Paper presented at the Joint Canada–United States Conference on the Measurement of Ethnicity, Ottawa, Canada, April 1–3.

Ogbu, John U. 1990. "Minority Education in Comparative Perspective." *Journal of Negro Education* 59(1): 45–57.

Pagnini, Deanna L. and S. Philip Morgan. 1990. "Intermarriage and Social Distance among U.S. Immigrants at the turn of the Century." *American Journal of Sociology* 96 (2): 405–432.

Spickard, Paul R. 1989. *Mixed Blood.* Madison: University of Wisconsin Press.

Steinberg, Stephen. 1981. *The Ethnic Myth: Race, Ethnicity, and Class in America.* Boston: Beacon Press.

U.S. Bureau of the Census. 1992. *Census of Population and Housing, 1990: Detailed Ancestry Groups for States.* Supplementary Reports CP-S-1-2. Washington, D.C.: U.S. Government Printing Office.

Waters, Mary C. 1990. *Ethnic Options: Choosing Identities in America.* Berkeley and Los Angeles: University of California Press.

Weber, Max. 1921. *Economy and Society: An Outline of Interpretive Sociology,* edited by Guenther Roth and Claus Wittich, translated by Ephraim Fischoff. New York: Bedminster Press.

Questions for Critical Thinking

1. What are some of the reasons whites may choose to identify with a particular ethnicity? What purpose does belonging to a particular ethnicity serve?

2. How does the freedom to include or exclude ancestries differ for whites and people of color?

3. How do "optional ethnicities" differ from ethnicities that result from exclusion and oppression? What are some of the advantages and/or disadvantages of each?

Learning to Be Illegal

Undocumented Youth and Shifting Legal Contexts in the Transition to Adulthood

ROBERTO G. GONZALES

In the reading that follows, Roberto Gonzales discusses how the transition to adulthood among the children of undocumented immigrants in the United States involves moving from a status of legal protection to one of considerable vulnerability. Based on research involving 150 interviews with undocumented 1.5-generation young adult Latinos in Southern California, the author illustrates the profound consequences of access to opportunity and social equality for those who experience this shift from de facto legal to illegal status.

During the past 25 years, the number of undocumented immigrants in the United States has grown substantially, from an estimated 2.5 million in 1987 to 11.1 million today (Passel 2006; Passel and Cohn 2010).[1] Scholars contend that this demographic trend is the unintended consequence of policies designed to curb undocumented migration and tighten the U.S.–Mexico border (Nevins 2010), transforming once-circular migratory flows into permanent settlement (Cornelius and Lewis 2006; Massey, Durand, and Malone 2002). Making multiple migratory trips back and forth became increasingly costly and dangerous throughout the 1990s and the first decade of the twenty-first century, so more unauthorized migrants began

creating permanent homes in the United States. And they brought their children with them. According to recent estimates, there are more than 2.1 million undocumented young people in the United States who have been here since childhood. Of these, more than a million are now adults (Batalova and McHugh 2010). Relatively little is known about this vulnerable population of young people, and their unique circumstances challenge assumptions about the incorporation patterns of the children of immigrants and their transitions to adolescence and adulthood.

Building on prior scholarship about immigrant incorporation and the life course, this article offers an up-close examination of the ways in which public schooling and U.S. immigration laws collide to produce a shift in the experiences and meanings of illegal status for undocumented youth at the onset of their transition to adulthood. I am interested in how these young people become aware of, and come to understand, their status under the law—that is, when they begin to notice their legal difference and its effects, and how they experience this shift as they move through late adolescence and young adulthood. The multiple transformations that undocumented youth experience have important implications for their identity formation, friendship patterns, aspirations and expectations, and social and economic mobility, and they also signal movement of a significant subset of the U.S. immigrant population into a new, disenfranchised underclass. In developing a conceptual and theoretical map of how undocumented youth learn to be illegal, this article identifies important mechanisms that mediate transitions to adulthood for the children of immigrants. Therefore, it helps us understand the consequences of non-legal status for undocumented youth as they move from protected to unprotected status, from inclusion to exclusion, and from de facto legal to illegal, during their final years of secondary schooling.

Undocumented Youth and Shifting Contexts

Assimilation and Public Schooling

As today's children of immigrants come of age, contemporary immigration scholarship challenges the conventional expectation that they will follow a linear generational process of assimilation into mainstream U.S. life (Gans 1992; Portes and Rumbaut 2006; Portes and Zhou 1993). Much current theorizing has moved away from a singular focus on human capital toward nuanced approaches that more fully appreciate the context of reception (Portes 1981; Portes and Bach 1985; Portes and Rumbaut 2006). This approach stresses that multiple factors channel the children of immigrants into different segments of society (Portes and Rumbaut 2001, 2006; Portes and Zhou 1993). Studies suggest that increasing fault lines of inequality along race and ethnicity, poor public schools, and differential access to today's labor market may cause recent immigrants' children to do less well than the children of previous waves (Gans 1992; Portes and Rumbaut 2001, 2006; Portes and Zhou 1993; Rumbaut 1997, 2005, 2008; Zhou 1997).

Given the changes in the U.S. economy and labor market, educational attainment has become critical to the social mobility of all children, and the link between school outcomes and future success is a thread that runs throughout much of the literature (Kasinitz et al. 2008; Portes and Rumbaut 2001, 2006; Suárez-Orozco and Suárez-Orozco 1995; Suárez-Orozco, Suárez-Orozco, and Todorova 2008; Waters 1999; Zhou and Bankston 1998). While some young people with modest levels of education manage to find skilled blue-collar jobs, most need a college degree to qualify for jobs that offer decent wages, benefits, job security, and the possibility of advancement. Children from poor and minority families, however, have historically experienced difficulty attaining significant levels of education (Alba and Nee 2003; Portes and Rumbaut 2001; Telles and Ortiz 2008). Disadvantaged students are particularly harmed by highly differentiated curricula and de facto tracking (Lucas and Berends 2002; Oakes 1985), although scholars have found that supplementary educational programs (Zhou 2008), extrafamily mentors (Portes and Fernandez-Kelly 2008; Smith 2008), and positive support networks (Stanton-Salazar 2001) can help overcome these disadvantages.

For generations, the public school system has been the principal institution that educates and integrates the children of immigrants into the fabric of U.S. society. This is especially true today, as more immigrant children spend more waking hours in school than ever before. Suárez-Orozco and colleagues (2008:2–3) identify public schools' critical role in shaping immigrant youths' understanding of their place in society: "It is in school where, day in and day out, immigrant youth come to know teachers and peers from majority culture as well as newcomers from other parts of the world. It is in schools that immigrant youth develop academic knowledge and, just as important, form perceptions of where they fit in the social reality and cultural imagination of their new nation." Certainly, the role of public schools is increasingly critical, as the returns on education have sharply increased over the past few decades. But public schools' socialization mechanisms are also powerful catalysts for promoting the acculturation processes of the children of immigrants. Schools foster what

Rumbaut (1997:944) calls a "unity of experiences and orientation" among their pupils that aid in the development of a "community of purpose and action" with "primary social contacts." This assimilating experience is profoundly different from what most adult immigrants encounter. While their parents may be absorbed into low-wage labor markets and often work with co-ethnics who speak their language and share their cultural practices, children are integrated into the school system, where they grow up side-by-side with the native-born (Gleeson and Gonzales 2012). Their "unity of experiences" with friends and classmates promotes feelings of togetherness and inclusion (Rumbaut 1997:944), and these feelings, in turn, shape immigrant youths' identification and experience of coming of age.

Today's Children of Immigrants Come of Age

Scholarly consensus on contemporary transitions to adulthood suggests that the process of coming of age is taking much longer today (Furstenberg et al. 2002). In particular, young people are spending more time in postsecondary schooling and are delaying exit from the parental household, entry into full-time work, and decisions about marriage and children (Settersten, Furstenberg, and Rumbaut 2005).

Life-course scholars traditionally define the transition to adulthood in terms of five milestones or markers: completing school, moving out of the parental home, establishing employment, getting married, and becoming a parent. The developmentally dense period of transition entails a large number of shifts out of roles that support and foster childlike dependence and into roles that confer adulthood in a relatively short time (Rindfuss 1991). Drawing from Erikson's (1950) early work, life-course scholarship views the transition to adulthood as composed of adolescence (ages 12 to 17 years) and young adulthood (ages 18 to 35 years). Yet recent decades have brought significant shifts in the roles of social institutions as

well as changes in the opportunities for entry into the labor market. By delaying entry into the workforce in favor of additional education, young adults build human capital that will make them more competitive in the high-skilled labor market. Some parents aid this process by assisting children over a longer period and using financial resources to help pay for college, providing down payments for their children's first homes, or defraying some of the costs associated with having children (Rumbaut and Komaie 2010). Theorists have responded to these changes by conceptually disaggregating young adulthood into shorter periods of time that better define contemporary transitions and permit a better understanding of the relationship between broader contexts and life transitions. Arnett (2000) adds emerging adulthood, a stage between adolescence and young adulthood, roughly between ages 18 and 25 years, and Rumbaut (2005) differentiates between the early transition (18 to 24 years), the middle transition (25 to 29 years), and the late transition (30 to 34 years).

Within the larger national context of coming of age, scholars have uncovered key differences by social class, country of origin, nativity, and immigrant generation (Mollenkopf et al. 2005; Rumbaut and Komaie 2010). Many youngsters from less-advantaged immigrant households put off postsecondary schooling because their parents are not able to provide financial assistance or because they carry considerable financial responsibilities in their households that make it impossible for them to make tuition payments (Fuligni and Pedersen 2002; Suárez-Orozco and Suárez-Orozco 1995). Many of the 1.5 and second generations of certain immigrant groups are in reciprocal financial relationships with their parents, often even supporting them (Rumbaut and Komaie 2010). As a result, they do not enjoy the same degree of freedom from the stresses and responsibilities of adult roles. These differences suggest that we should expect the children of immigrants—documented and undocumented alike—to experience coming of age differently from the native-born.

Conceptualizing the Transition to Illegality for Undocumented Youth

For undocumented youth, the transition into adulthood is accompanied by a transition into illegality that sets them apart from their peers. Undocumented youngsters share a confusing and contradictory status in terms of their legal rights and the opportunities available to them (Abrego 2008; Gonzales 2007). On the one hand, because of the Supreme Court ruling in *Plyler v. Doe* (1982), they have the legal right to a K to 12 education.[2] Furthermore, the Family Educational Rights and Privacy Act prevents schools from releasing any information from students' records to immigration authorities, making school a protected space in which undocumented status has little to no negative effect. On the other hand, undocumented young adults cannot legally work, vote, receive financial aid, or drive in most states, and deportation remains a constant threat. Unauthorized residency status thus has little direct impact on most aspects of childhood but is a defining feature of late adolescence and adulthood and can prevent these youth from following normative pathways to adulthood. Therefore, coupled with family poverty, illegal status places undocumented youth in a developmental limbo. As family need requires them to make significant financial contributions and to assume considerable responsibility for their own care, they become less likely to linger in adolescence. At the same time, legal restrictions keep them from participating in many adult activities, leaving them unable to complete important transitions.

Researchers studying immigrant incorporation and the life course have not systematically considered the effects of the legal context on the children of immigrants, that is, the specific challenges facing undocumented immigrant youth and their complex and contradictory routes to adulthood. Current scholarship is limited to conjecture based on what is known in general about children of immigrants from low-skilled groups. Failure to focus on legal status also limits what we know about the linkages between important mechanisms such as education and social mobility. K to 12 schooling certainly plays an important role in the development and integration of immigrant children, but significant questions remain about how undocumented status shapes educational trajectories and how, in turn, it affects the link between educational attainment and social and economic mobility. The scant existing research on undocumented youth notes that undocumented status depresses aspirations (Abrego 2006) and sensitizes them to the reality that they are barred from integrating legally, educationally, and economically into U.S. society (Abrego 2008).

For conceptual help, I turn to recent advances in the literature that move beyond the binary categories of documented and undocumented to explore the ways in which migrants move between different statuses and the mechanisms that allow them to be regular in one sense and irregular in another. In describing the experiences of Salvadoran migrants caught in the legal limbo of Temporary Protected Status, and their feelings of being legally and socially in-between, Menjívar (2006) introduced the concept of liminal legality. This phrase underscores that documented and undocumented categories do not adequately capture the gray areas experienced by many migrants. Menjívar's analysis builds on Coutin's (2000) exploration of the contradictions that lie between migrants' physical and social presence and their official designation as illegal. Several other scholars have called for a shift from generally studying unauthorized migrants and migrations to a more deliberate investigation of the mechanisms that produce and sustain what they term migrant illegality (Coutin 2000; De Genova 2002; Ngai 2004; Willen 2007). This deliberate shift in focus allows us to pay attention to the effects laws have on migrants' day-to-day lives, revealing the ways in which undocumented persons experience inclusion and exclusion and how these experiences can change over time, in interactions with different persons, and across various spaces. It also points to the two-sided nature of citizenship, which can allow the same person, citizen or not, to experience belonging in one context but not in another.

Portes and Rumbaut (2006) emphasize that it is the combination of positive and negative contexts that determines the distinct modes of immigrants' incorporation. While school contexts foster expectations and aspirations that root undocumented youngsters in the United States (Abrego 2006), they leave these young people grossly unprepared for what awaits them in adulthood. This article focuses on the interactions between such favorable and unfavorable contexts during what I call the transition to illegality. I conceptualize this process as the set of experiences that result from shifting contexts along the life course, providing different meanings to undocumented status and animating the experience of illegality at late adolescence and into adulthood. The transition to illegality brings with it a period of disorientation, whereby undocumented youth confront legal limitations and their implications and engage in a process of retooling and reorienting themselves for new adult lives. But this process is not uniform among undocumented youth. Previous qualitative work on youth populations coming of age has uncovered key mechanisms within the school setting that shape divergent trajectories (MacLeod 1987; Willis 1977). Because comparisons between differently achieving youth may help to more clearly identify mechanisms that mediate undocumented status during the transition to adulthood, I compare the experiences of college-going young adults (i.e., college-goers) with those who exit the education system after high school graduation or earlier (i.e., early-exiters).

Methods

While many recent immigrants have dispersed to new destination states in the South and the Midwest (Marrow 2009; Massey 2008; Singer 2004; Zúñiga and Hernández-León 2005), California remains home to the largest undocumented immigrant population in the country. The numbers of undocumented immigrants from countries outside of Latin America have risen slightly since 2000, but immigrants from Mexico continue to account for the majority. In fact, no other sending country constitutes even a double-digit share of the total (Passel and Cohn 2009). I thus focus on Mexican-origin immigrants in California, drawing on 150 individual semi-structured interviews with 1.5-generation young adults ages 20 to 34 years (who migrated before the age of 12). The interviews focused on respondents' experiences growing up in Southern California without legal status. Such close study of the 1.5 generation permits an examination of the unique ways in which undocumented status is experienced in childhood and adolescence (Rumbaut 2004; Smith 2006).

Until very recently, it has been difficult to study undocumented young adults like those interviewed for this study because their numbers have been prohibitively small. Researching hard-to-reach populations adds layers of difficulty, time, and cost to any study. While previous large-scale efforts have been successful at locating and interviewing undocumented Mexicans on both sides of the U.S.–Mexico border, and have provided useful direction for random sampling,[3] today's anti-immigrant climate and localized immigration enforcement present challenges to finding respondents in the United States. These conditions lead many unauthorized migrants to be more fearful in their everyday lives, thus posing significant challenges to random sampling efforts. Data collection for this study involved nearly four and a half years of field work in the periods 2003 to 2007 and 2008 to 2009, during which I conducted interviews and did additional ethnographic research in the Los Angeles Metropolitan Area.[4] I began conducting interviews after spending lengthy periods of time in the field gaining a rapport with respondents and community stakeholders. I recruited respondents from various settings, including continuation schools, community organizations, college campuses, and churches. After gaining trust, I accompanied respondents throughout their school and work days, volunteered at local schools and organizations, and sat in on numerous community meetings. I built on the initial group of respondents by using snowball sampling to identify subsequent respondents.

All 150 1.5-generation respondents interviewed spent much of their childhood, adolescence, and adulthood with undocumented status. With the exception of eight Central Americans (Guatemalan and Salvadoran), all were born in Mexico. I drew the sample from the five-county Los Angeles Metropolitan Area, and respondents come from all five counties. Most had parents who were undocumented (92 percent) and had fewer than six years of schooling (86 percent). Most respondents were also raised by two parents; one-quarter were raised by single parents and six were raised by other family members.

I designed the sampling process to include relatively equal numbers of males and females (71 males and 79 females) and equal numbers of individuals who dropped out of or completed high school (73) and those who attended some college (77). Of the 77 college respondents, nine had advanced degrees at the time of the interview, 22 had earned bachelor's degrees, 26 were enrolled in four-year universities, and 20 were enrolled in or had attended community college. The majority attended a California public college or university. Of the 73 respondents who exited school at or before high school graduation, 31 had not earned a high school degree at the time of interview, and 42 had high school diplomas.

The life history interviews included questions regarding respondents' pasts and their present lives as well as future expectations and aspirations. Interviews ranged in length from 1 hour and 40 minutes to 3 hours and 20 minutes. To analyze interview transcripts, I used open coding techniques. I placed conceptual labels on responses that described discrete events, experiences, and feelings reported in the interviews. Next, I analyzed each individual interview across all questions to identify meta-themes. Finally, I examined responses for common meta-themes across all interviews.

The Transition to Illegality

To better conceptualize the ways in which legal status affects the transition to illegality, I focus on three transition periods—discovery (ages 16 to 18

years), learning to be illegal (ages 18 to 24 years), and coping (ages 25 to 29 years). While the life-course literature defines the early and middle transitions as ages 18 to 24 and 25 to 29, respectively, I add an earlier period to capture the awakening to newfound legal limitations, which elicits a range of emotional reactions and begins a process of altered life-course pathways and adult transitions. Next, as undocumented youth enter early adulthood, they engage in a parallel process of learning to be illegal. During this period, many find difficulty connecting with previous sources of support to navigate the new restrictions on their lives and to mitigate their newly stigmatized identities. At this stage, undocumented youth are forced to alter earlier plans and reshape their aspirations for the future. Finally, the coping period involves adjusting to lowered aspirations and coming to grips with the possibility that their precarious legal circumstances may never change.

Discovery: Ages 16 to 18

Most life-course scholars focus on age 18 as a time of dramatic change for young people. In the United States, 18 is the age of majority, the legal threshold of adulthood when a child ceases to be considered a minor and assumes control over his actions and decisions. This is traditionally the time when young people exit high school and enter college or full-time work. Yet young people adopt semi-adult roles, such as working and driving, while still in high school. Most respondents in this study began to experience dramatic shifts in their daily lives and future outlooks around age 16.

Because public schooling provided respondents with an experience of inclusion atypical of undocumented adult life in the United States (Bean, Telles, and Lowell 1987; Chavez 1991, 1998), respondents spent their childhood and early adolescence in a state of suspended illegality, a buffer stage wherein they were legally integrated and immigration status rarely limited activities. Through school, respondents developed aspirations rooted in the belief that they were part of the fabric of the nation and would have better opportunities than their parents (Gans 1992). They learned to speak English, developed tastes, joined clubs, dated, and socialized—all alongside their U.S.-born and legal resident peers. During this period, school-based relationships with peers and adults provided key sources of support and identity formation (Portes and Fernandez-Kelly 2008). As Marisol, a college-goer, explained, relationships with teachers and friends provided a comfortable space for many like her to learn and develop: "School was an escape from home. I felt happy, calm. . . . I could be myself. I could be recognized at school. My teachers encouraged me to keep going. And my friends, we believed in education and pushed each other. We helped each other with homework and talked about college."

Such positive relationships, however, were not uniformly experienced by respondents. Many early-exiters (those who left the school system at or before completion of high school) recounted feeling disconnected from school and lacking significant relationships with teachers or counselors. They felt they were left to fall through the cracks and cut off from important services; they also reported having limited visits with counselors. Juan, for example, did not meet with a college counselor until late in his junior year. "I wanted to go to college," he told me, "but the counselors didn't let me know the requirements for four-year colleges. I tried to go to see them, but they didn't have time for me." Nevertheless, even respondents who reported having trouble in school believed they would have more options than their parents. Eric, an early-exiter who grew up in Riverside County, told me he had grown up thinking he was going to have a "better life": "I saw my older [U.S.-born] cousins get good jobs. I mean, they're not lawyers or anything like that, but they're not in restaurants or mowing lawns. I thought, yeah, when I graduate from school, I can make some good money, maybe even go to college."

Respondents uniformly noted a jolting shift at around age 16, when they attempted to move through rites of passage associated with their age. Life-course scholars refer to critical events in one's life as "turning points" that "knife off" past from present and restructure routine activities and life-course pathways (Elder 1987:452). These turning points can enable identity transitions and set into motion processes of cumulative advantage and disadvantage (Rumbaut 2005). For undocumented youth, the process of coming of age is a critical turning point that has consequences for subsequent transitions. Finding a part-time job, applying for college, and obtaining a driver's license—all markers of new roles and responsibilities—require legal status as a basis for participation.

As respondents tried to take these steps into adult life, they were blocked by their lack of a Social Security number. These incidents proved to be life changing and were often accompanied by the realization that they were excluded from a broad range of activities. Rodolfo, an early-exiter who is now 27 years old, spoke of his first experience of exclusion:

> I never actually felt like I wasn't born here. Because when I came I was like 10 and a half. I went to school. I learned the language. I first felt like I was really out of place when I tried to get a job. I didn't have a Social Security number. Well, I didn't even know what it meant. You know Social Security, legal, illegal. I didn't even know what that was.

Until this time, Rodolfo had never needed proof of legal residency. The process of looking for a job made the implications of his lack of legal status real to him for the first time. Like Rodolfo, many early-exiters (a little over 68 percent) made such discoveries while applying for jobs or for driver's licenses.

On the other hand, most college-goers (almost 60 percent) reported finding out they were undocumented in the course of the college application process. Jose, for example, was on the academic decathlon and debate teams. He did well in school and was well-liked by teachers. During his junior year, he attempted to enroll in classes at the community college to earn college credits. But without a Social Security number, he could not move forward.

While most respondents did not know of their unauthorized status until their teenage years, some reported knowing in childhood. This was more true of early-exiters (almost 30 percent, compared with a little over 9 percent among college-goers), many of whom lived in households where older siblings had gone through the process of discovery before them. But even these respondents did not realize the full implications their illegal status would have for their futures until much later. Being undocumented only became salient when matched with experiences of exclusion. Early-exiter Lorena started cleaning houses with her mother and sisters at age 12. Even before she began working, reminders from her mother made her aware that she did not have "papers." But she explained to me that "it really hit home" when she tried to branch out to other work in high school and was asked for her Social Security number.

Discovery of illegal status prompted reactions of confusion, anger, frustration, and despair among respondents, followed by a period of paralyzing shock. Most respondents conveyed that they were not prepared for the dramatic limits of their rights. They struggled to make sense of what had happened to them, many feeling as though they had been lied to. "I always thought I would have a place when I grew up," David, an early-exiter, told me. "Teachers make you believe that. It's all a lie. A big lie." They often blamed teachers and parents for their feelings of anger and frustration. Cory, a college-goer, locked herself in her bedroom for an entire week. When she finally emerged, she moved out of her parents' house, blaming them for "keeping [her] in the dark during childhood." Cory said: "They thought that by the time I graduated I would have my green card. But they didn't stop to think that this is my life. . . . Everything I believed in was a big lie. Santa Claus was not coming down the chimney, and I wasn't going to just become legal. I really resented them."

Respondents reported that soon after these discoveries, they experienced a second shock as they came to realize that the changes they were experiencing would adversely affect their remaining adult lives. As they came to grips with the new meanings of unauthorized status, they began to view and define themselves differently. Miguel, a college-goer who has been caught in the part-time cycle of community college and work for six years, told me: "During most of high school, I thought I had my next 10 years laid out. College and law school were definitely in my plans. But when my mom told me I wasn't legal, everything was turned upside down. I didn't know what to do. I couldn't see my future anymore." Miguel's entire identity was transformed, and the shift placed him, like many other respondents, in a state of limbo. Cory put it this way: "I feel as though I've experienced this weird psychological and legal-stunted growth. I'm stuck at 16, like a clock that has stopped ticking. My life has not changed at all since then. Although I'm 22, I feel like a kid. I can't do anything adults do."

Respondents' illegality was paired with a movement into stigmatized status that reinforced their legal exclusion. While laws limited their access to grown-up activities and responsibilities, fears of being found out curbed their interactions with teachers and peers. Ironically, while many respondents believed they had been lied to in childhood, they adopted lying themselves as a daily survival strategy that separated them from the very peer networks that had provided support and shaped a positive self-image. Many reported they were afraid of what their friends would think or how they would react if they learned of their illegal status. These fears were validated by observations of friends' behavior. Chuy, a college-goer who played sports throughout school, explained that after he saw a teammate on his high school soccer team berate players on an opposing team as "wetbacks" and "illegals," he was reticent to disclose his status even to good friends. "I grew up with this guy," he said. "We had classes together and played on the same team for like four years. But wow, I don't know what he would say if he knew I was one of those wetbacks."

Frustration with the present, uncertainty about the future, and the severing of support systems caused many respondents to withdraw, with detrimental effects on their progress during the last half of high school (see also Abrego 2006; Suárez-Orozco et al. 2008). In my interview with Sandra, an early-exiter, she recalled her struggles during junior year: "I felt the world caving in on me. What was I going to do? I couldn't ask my parents. They didn't know about college or anything. I was kind of quiet in school, so I didn't really know my teachers. Besides, I was scared. What would they do if they knew? I was scared and alone." Throughout high school, Luis, an early-exiter, hoped to attend college. During the latter part of his sophomore year, his grades fell considerably. As a result, he did not meet the requirements to gain entrance into the University of California system. His girlfriend convinced him to apply to the lower-tier California State University, but when he found out he was not eligible for financial aid, he gave up: "It took a while to get accepted. But I ended up not going (because of) financial aid. . . . It just kinda brought down my spirit, I guess." Like Sandra and Luis, many respondents had done moderately well in school before the cumulative disadvantages resulting from the transition to illegality caused them to lose motivation to continue. Lacking trusting relationships with teachers or counselors who could help them, they ended up exiting school much earlier than they had planned (Gonzales 2010).

Nationally, 40 percent of undocumented adults ages 18 to 24 do not complete high school, and only 49 percent of undocumented high school graduates go to college. Youths who arrive in the United States before the age of 14 fare slightly better: 72 percent finish high school, and of those, 61 percent go on to college. But these figures are still much lower than the numbers for U.S.-born residents (Passel and Cohn 2009). The combination of scarce family resources and exclusion from financial aid at the state[5] and federal levels makes the path to higher education very steep for undocumented high school students. Estimates reveal that as few as 5 to 10 percent of all undocumented high school graduates ever reach postsecondary institutions (Passel 2003), and the vast majority attend community colleges (Flores 2010). In several states, laws allowing undocumented students to pay in-state tuition have increased the number of high school graduates matriculating to college over the past decade (Flores 2010). Nonetheless, steep financial barriers prohibit many undocumented youth from enrolling in college.

While depressed motivation contributed to many respondents' early exit from the school system, limited financial resources within their families and a general lack of information about how to move forward also played a part in causing early departures. Karina, an early-exiter, maintained a B average in her general-track high school classes. When she applied to college, she had no guidance. Unaware of a California provision that should have made it possible for her to attend school at in-state tuition rates, Karina opted not to go to college: "I didn't know anything about AB 540.[6] Maybe if I knew the information I could have gotten a scholarship or something. That's why I didn't go. I don't know if my counselors knew, but they never told me anything."

The experiences of successful college-goers, by contrast, unlock a key variable to success missing from the narratives of early-exiters: trusting relationships with teachers or other adults. Portes and Fernandez-Kelly (2008:26) find evidence linking school success to the presence of what they call "really significant others" who "possess the necessary knowledge and experience" and "take a keen interest in [their students], motivate [them] to graduate from high school and to attend college." When Marisol began to exhibit decreasing levels of motivation, for instance, her English teacher was there to intervene. Although Marisol felt embarrassed, she was able to talk frankly with her teacher because they had developed a trusting relationship. As a reward for her trust, Marisol's teacher helped her obtain information about college and also took up a collection among other teachers to pay for her first year of tuition at the community college.

Most college-goers reported they had formed trusting relationships with teachers, counselors, and other mentors in high school. These respondents were concentrated in the advanced curriculum tracks in high school; the smaller and more supportive learning environments gave them access to key school personnel. Compared to early-exiters, they disclosed their problems more easily and were able to draw on relationships of trust to seek out and receive help. At critical times when the students' motivations were low, these relationships meant the difference between their leaving school or going to college. When difficulties arose during the college admissions process for college-goer Jose, for instance, he went straight to his counselor, with positive results. The counselor called the college and found out about the availability of aid through AB 540, which neither he nor Jose had been aware of.

Learning to Be Illegal: Ages 18 to 24

For the children of unauthorized parents, success means improving on the quality of jobs and opportunities. Many youths end up only a small step ahead, however. Lacking legal status and a college degree, early-exiters confront some of the same limited and limiting employment options as their parents. Economic circumstances and family need force them to make choices about working and driving illegally. Nearly all respondents contributed money to their families, averaging nearly $300 per month. After high school, early-exiter Oscar, who at 27 still gives his parents $500 a month, moved through a string of short stints in the workforce, not staying in any one job more than six months at a time. He quit jobs because he was dissatisfied with the meager wages and generally uneasy about the ways in which employers treated him. Each new job proved no better than the previous one. Over time, Oscar realized he had few job choices outside of physical labor: "I wasn't prepared to do that kind of work. . . . It's tough. I come home from work tired every day. I don't have a life. . . . It's not like I can get an office job. I've tried to get something better, but I'm limited by my situation."

The effects of stress and difficult work took their toll on other respondents. Simon, who used to play piano, showed me calluses and cuts on his hands. "Can you believe this? I'm so far away from those days," he said. Janet, who has been employed by various maid services, told me she cried every day after work for the first two months: "I can't believe this is my life. When I was in school I never thought I'd be doing this. I mean, I was never an honors student, but I thought I would have a lot better job. It's really hard, you know. I make beds, I clean toilets. The sad thing is when I get paid. I work this hard, for nothing." Janet and others expressed difficulty coming to terms with the narrow range of bad options their illegal status forced on them.

While financial need forced respondents into the workforce, lack of experience put them at a disadvantage in the low-wage job sector, where they became part of the same job pool as their parents and other family members who have much less education but more work experience. During Josue's final year of high school, his grandparents, who had raised him since childhood, decided to move. Instead of enrolling in a new school, Josue decided to try his luck in the labor market. But he soon realized what a great disadvantage his lack of experience was:

> [At first] I thought, "I'm not gonna bust my ass for someone who can be yelling at me for like $5.75, five bucks an hour." Hell no. If I get a job, I wanna get paid 20 bucks an hour. I speak English. But actually I didn't have any experience. So, it's really hard to get a job. Especially now, because those kinds of jobs . . . they're looking for a more experienced person who knows how to work in the field and ain't gonna complain.

Respondents also recounted difficulty negotiating precarious situations because their undocumented status forced them to confront experiences for which K to 12 schooling did not prepare them. Pedro found himself in legal trouble when, after completing a day job, he tried to cash his check at the local currency exchange. A teller called Pedro's employer to verify its legitimacy, and he denied writing the check and called the police. When the police arrived, they found multiple sets of identification in Pedro's possession and took him to jail for identity fraud. This incident awoke Pedro to the reality that his inexperience with undocumented life could have grave consequences, including arrest and even deportation.

Given the limited employment options available to undocumented youth, moving on to college becomes critical. Making a successful transition to postsecondary schooling requires a number of favorable circumstances, however, including sufficient money to pay for school, family permission to delay or minimize work, reliable transportation, and external guidance and assistance. Respondents who enjoyed such conditions were able to devote their time to school and, equally important, avoid activities and situations that would place them in legal trouble. As a result, they suspended many of the negative consequences of unauthorized status.

When I met Rosalba, she had associate's, bachelor's, and master's degrees. Her parents had prohibited her from working, thus allowing her to concentrate fully on school. Throughout her time in school, she benefited from assistance from a number of caring individuals. "I've made it because I've had a support system," she said:

> At every step of my education, I have had a mentor holding my hand. It's a thousand times harder without someone helping you. Being undocumented, it's not about what you know, it's who you know. You might have all of the will in the world, but if you don't know the right people, then as much as you want to, you're gonna have trouble doing it.

When I interviewed Nimo, he was in his final year of college and considering graduate school. His college years had been enjoyable, lacking many of the stressors of legal limitations. A financial sponsor paid his tuition and fees and provided money for books. Nimo worked only minimally, because his mother did not ask for his financial assistance. He was usually able to secure rides to and from school; on other days, he took the bus. Although the two-hour commute each way was time consuming, the time allowed him to "read and think." Nimo's case is exceptional, but it is also instructive. Without the various barriers of financing college, supporting family, and having to work and drive, he was able to concentrate on school. As a result, he maintained a positive attitude and has high aspirations for his future.

Many other respondents, however, found postsecondary education to be a discontinuous experience, with frequent stalls and detours. Several took leaves of absence, and others enrolled in only one school term per year. Faced with the need to work, few scholarships, debt, and long commutes, these respondents managed to attend college, but completing their schooling was an arduous task that required them to be creative, keep their costs low, and in many cases join early-exiters in the low-wage labor market. Several respondents' dreams of higher education did not materialize because financial burdens became too overwhelming. Margarita, for example, aspired to be a pharmacist, but after two years of community college, her mother started asking her to pay her share of the rent. She left school to clean houses, which she had been doing for almost four years when I met her.

Coping: Ages 25 to 29

The impact of not having legal residency status becomes particularly pronounced for respondents in their mid-20s, when prolonged experiences of illegality force them to begin viewing their legal circumstances as more permanent. By this time, most young adults in the United States have finished school, left the parental home, and are working full-time. They have also started to see the returns on their education in better jobs and have gained increased independence from their parents. Although sharp differences in educational returns persist among legal young adults, I found a high degree of convergence among college-goers and early-exiters as they finished the transition to illegality. By their mid-20s, both sets of respondents held similar occupations. While both groups were also starting to leave the parental home, early-exiters were already settled into work routines. Years on the job had provided them with experience and improved their human capital. Many had let go of hopes for career mobility long ago, opting instead for security and stability. While college-going respondents spent much of their late teens and early 20s in institutions of higher learning, by their mid-20s most were out of school and learning that they had few legal employment options, despite having attained advanced degrees.

In his study of working-class youth in Clarendon Heights, MacLeod (1987) chronicled the experiences of two groups of differently achieving working-class students as they came to realize their limitations in the job market. As their aspirations flattened over time, they put a "lid on hope" (p. 62). For my respondents, day-to-day struggles, stress, and the ever-present ceiling on opportunities similarly forced them to acknowledge the distance between their prior aspirations and present realities. The realization was especially poignant for those who managed to complete degrees but ultimately recognized that the years of schooling did not offer much advantage in low-wage labor markets—the only labor markets to which they had access.

These are young people who grew up believing that because their English mastery and education surpassed those of their parents, they would achieve more. Instead, they came face-to-face with the limits on their opportunities—often a very unsettling experience. Early-exiter Margarita underscored this point:

> I graduated from high school and have taken some college credits. Neither of my parents made it past fourth grade, and they don't speak any English. But I'm right where they are. I mean, I work with my mom. I have the same job. I can't find anything else. It's kinda ridiculous, you know. Why did I even go to school? It should mean something. I mean, that should count, right? You would think. I thought. Well, here I am, cleaning houses.

Others conveyed a tacit acceptance of their circumstances. When I interviewed Pedro, he had been out of school for nine years. He had held a string of jobs and was living with childhood friends in a mobile home. He was slowly making progress toward his high school diploma but was not hopeful that education would improve his opportunities or quality of life. I asked him what he wanted for himself. He replied:

> Right now, I want to take care of my legal status, clean up my record for the stupidity I committed and get a decent job. I'm thinking about five years from now. I don't want to extend it any longer. I wish it could be less, you know, but I don't want to rush it either, because when you rush things they don't go as they should. Maybe 10 years from now. I like where I live, and I wouldn't mind living in a mobile home.

Other respondents had similarly low expectations for the future, the cumulative result of years of severely restricted choices. When I first met Gabriel, he was 23 years old. He was making minimal progress at the community college. He had moved out of his mother's home because he felt like a financial burden, and he left his job after his employer received a letter from the Social Security Administration explaining that the number he was using did not match his name. He was frustrated and scared. When I ran into him four years later, near the end of my study, he seemed to be at ease with his life. He was working in a factory with immigrant co-workers and participating in a community dance group. He told me he was "not as uptight" about his situation as he had once been:

> I just stopped letting it [unauthorized status] define me. Work is only part of my life. I've got a girlfriend now. We have our own place. I'm part of a dance circle, and it's really cool. Obviously, my situation holds me back from doing a lot of things, but I've got to live my life. I just get sick of being controlled by the lack of nine digits.

Undoubtedly, Gabriel would rather be living under more stable circumstances. But he has reconciled himself to his limitations, focusing instead on relationships and activities that are tangible and accessible.

Such acceptance was most elusive for respondents who achieved the highest levels of school success. At the time of their interviews, 22 respondents had graduated from four-year universities, and an additional nine held advanced degrees. None were able to legally pursue their dream careers. Instead, many, like Esperanza, found themselves toiling in low-wage jobs. Esperanza had to let go of her long-held aspiration to become a journalist, in favor of the more immediate need to make ends meet each month. In high school, she was in band and AP classes. Her hopes for success were encouraged by high-achieving peers and teachers. Nothing leading up to graduation prepared her for the reality of her life afterward. Now three years out of college, she can find only restaurant jobs and factory work. While she feels out of place in the sphere of undocumented work, she has little choice:

> The people working at those places, like the cooks and the cashiers, they are really young, and I feel really old. Like what am I doing there if they are all like 16, 17 years old? The others are like senoras who are 35. They dropped out of school, but because they have little kids they are still working at the restaurant. Thinking about that makes me feel so stupid. And like the factories, too, because they ask me, "Que estas haciendo aqui? [What are you doing here?] You can speak English. You graduated from high school. You can work anywhere."

Discussion and Conclusions

The experiences of unauthorized 1.5-generation young adults shed some important light on the powerful role played by immigration policy in shaping incorporation patterns and trajectories into adulthood. Contemporary immigration theory has made great strides in its ability to predict inter-generational progress. In doing so, however, it has paid less attention to the here-and-now experiences and outcomes of today's immigrants and their children. As Portes and Fernandez-Kelly (2008)

point out, focusing exclusively on inter-generational mobility contributes to a failure to uncover key mechanisms that produce delayed, detoured, and derailed trajectories. Indeed, by focusing on individuals they call the "final survivors"—two to three generations out—we neglect the struggles of individuals today who end up disappearing from view. Many respondents in this study possess levels of human capital that surpass those of their parents, who tend to speak little English and have fewer than six years of schooling. We may be tempted to see this outcome as a sign of inter-generational progress. But these young men and women describe moving from an early adolescence in which they had important inclusionary access, to an adulthood in which they are denied daily participation in most institutions of mainstream life. They describe this process as waking up to a nightmare.

While life-course scholars note that most U.S. youngsters today face some difficulty managing adolescent and adult transitions, undocumented youth face added challenges. Their exclusion from important rites of passage in late adolescence, and their movement from protected to unprotected status, leave them in a state of developmental limbo, preventing subsequent and important adult transitions. Their entry into a stigmatized identity has negative and usually unanticipated consequences for their educational and occupational trajectories, as well as for their friendships and social patterns. Unlike documented peers who linger in adolescence due to safety nets at home, many of these youngsters must start contributing to their families and taking care of themselves. These experiences affect adolescent and adult transitions that diverge significantly from those of their documented peers, placing undocumented youth in jeopardy of becoming a disenfranchised underclass.

Positive mediators at the early (discovery) and middle (learning to be illegal) transitions help cushion the blow, and a comparison of early-exiters and college-goers reveals a lot about the power, and the limitations, of these intermediaries. The keys to success for my respondents—extrafamilial mentors, access to information about postsecondary options, financial support for college, and lower levels of family responsibility—are not very different from those required for the success of members of other student populations. For undocumented youth, however, they take on added significance. In adult mentors, they find trusting allies to confide in and from whom to receive guidance and resources. The presence of caring adults who intervene during the discovery period can aid in reducing anxiety and minimizing barriers, allowing undocumented youth to delay entry into legally restricted adult environments and to make successful transitions to postsecondary institutions. Eventually, however, all undocumented youth unable to regularize their immigration status complete the transition to illegality.

My findings move beyond simply affirming that immigrant incorporation is a segmented process. Analyses of this group of undocumented young adults also suggest that successful integration may now depend, more so than ever before in U.S. history, on immigration policy and the role of the state. Historically, assimilation theory has been concerned with the factors that determine incorporation into the mainstream. Scholars argue that human capital is a key determinant for upward mobility (Zhou 1997). However, as I demonstrate here, blocked mobility caused by a lack of legal status renders traditional measures of inter-generational mobility by educational progress irrelevant: the assumed link between educational attainment and material and psychological outcomes after school is broken. College-bound youths' trajectories ultimately converge with those who have minimal levels of schooling. These youngsters, who committed to the belief that hard work and educational achievement would garner rewards, experience a tremendous fall. They find themselves ill-prepared for the mismatch between their levels of education and the limited options that await them in the low-wage, clandestine labor market.

The young men and women interviewed for this study are part of a growing population of undocumented youth who have moved into adulthood.

Today, the United States is home to more than 1.1 million undocumented children who, in the years to come, will be making the same sort of difficult transitions, under arguably more hostile contexts (Massey and Sanchez 2010). These demographic and legal realities ensure that a sizeable population of U.S.-raised adults will continue to be cut off from the futures they have been raised to expect. Efforts aimed at legalizing this particular group of young people have been in the works for more than 10 years without success. Political experts believe there will not be legislative movement at the federal level for at least two more years. In the meantime, proposals aimed at ending birthright citizenship for U.S.-born children of undocumented immigrants and barring their entry to postsecondary education threaten to deny rights to even greater numbers. These young people will very likely remain in the United States. Whether they become a disenfranchised underclass or contributing members to our society, their fate rests largely in the hands of the state. We must ask ourselves if it is good for the health and wealth of this country to keep such a large number of U.S.-raised young adults in the shadows. We must ask what is lost when they learn to be illegal.

Acknowledgments

Joanna Dreby, Cecilia Menjívar, Rubén G. Rumbaut, Celeste Watkins-Hayes, the *ASR* editors and reviewers, and audiences at Brown University, Cornell University, UC–Berkeley, the University of Michigan, the University of Kansas, and the University of Washington provided helpful comments on previous versions of this article.

Funding

This project was supported by the National Poverty Center using funds received from the U.S. Department of Health and Human Services, Office of the Assistant Secretary for Planning and Evaluation, grant number 1 U01 AE000002-01. The opinions and conclusions expressed herein are solely those of the author and should not be construed as representing the opinions or policy of any agency of the Federal government. To protect confidentiality, all names of individuals have been replaced with pseudonyms.

Notes

1. The Immigration Reform and Control Act (IRCA) of 1986 provided the last large-scale legalization program. The 1987 estimate represents the undocumented population after many of the 2.7 million estimated illegal immigrants had moved into legal categories under IRCA.
2. Under *Plyler*, the Supreme Court ruled that undocumented children are entitled to the equal protection under the law afforded by the 14th Amendment of the Constitution and therefore cannot be denied access to public elementary and secondary education on the basis of their legal status (see Olivas 2005).
3. See, in particular, the Mexican Migration Project (MMP), a bi-national research effort co-directed by Jorge Durand (University of Guadalajara) and Douglas S. Massey (Princeton University). Since 1982, the MMP has collected economic and social data from more than 140,000 Mexicans including many migrants; most of the households in the MMP random samples were interviewed in Mexico.
4. Given the respondents' immigration status, I went to great lengths to ensure confidentiality. Having gone through a thorough Human Subjects process, I took several measures to avoid any identifiers that would directly link data to specific respondents. I gave pseudonyms to all respondents at the time of the initial meeting, and I never collected home addresses. Because of these precautions, personal information does not appear anywhere in this research. Respondents provided verbal consent rather than leaving a paper trail with a written consent form. I destroyed all audio tapes immediately after transcription. I conducted all interviews in English, and I gave respondents gift cards for their participation.
5. Only New Mexico (SB 582) and Texas (HB 1403) allow undocumented students to apply for state aid.
6. Assembly Bill 540 (2001) gives undocumented youth in California who have gone to a state high school for three years and graduated the ability to pay tuition at in-state rates. Many undocumented immigrant students have benefited from this provision.

References

Abrego, Leisy J. 2006. "I Can't Go to College Because I Don't Have Papers: Incorporation Patterns of Undocumented Latino Youth." *Latino Studies* 4: 212–31.

Abrego, Leisy J. 2008. "Legitimacy, Social Identity, and the Mobilization of Law: The Effects of Assembly Bill 540 on Undocumented Students in California." *Law & Social Inquiry* 33:709–34.

Alba, Richard and Victor Nee. 2003. *Remaking the American Mainstream: Assimilation and Contemporary Immigration*. Cambridge: Harvard University Press.

Arnett, Jeffrey J. 2000. "Emerging Adulthood: A Theory of Development from Late Teens through the Twenties." *American Psychologist* 55:469–80.

Batalova, Jeanne and Margie McHugh. 2010. "DREAM vs. Reality: An Analysis of Potential DREAM Act Beneficiaries." Washington, DC: Migration Policy Institute (http://www.migrationpolicy.org/pubs/ DREAM-Insight-July2010.pdf).

Bean, Frank D., Edward Telles, and B. Lindsey Lowell. 1987. "Undocumented Migration to the United States: Perceptions and Evidence." *Population and Development Review* 13:671–90.

Chavez, Leo R. 1991. "Outside the Imagined Community: Undocumented Settlers and Experiences of Incorporation." *American Ethnologist* 18:257–78.

Chavez, Leo R. 1998. *Shadowed Lives: Undocumented Immigrants in American Society*. Fort Worth, TX: Harcourt Brace College Publishers.

Cornelius, Wayne A. and Jessa M. Lewis, eds. 2006. *Impacts of Border Enforcement on Mexican Migration: The View from Sending Communities*. Boulder, CO: Lynne Rienner Publishers and Center for Comparative Immigration Studies, UCSD.

Coutin, Susan B. 2000. *Legalizing Moves: Salvadoran Immigrants' Struggle for U.S. Residency*. Ann Arbor: University of Michigan Press.

De Genova, Nicolas. 2002. "Migrant 'Illegality' and Deportability in Everyday Life." *Annual Review of Anthropology* 31:419–47.

Elder, Glen H., Jr. 1987. "War Mobilization and the Life Course: A Cohort of World War II Veterans." *Sociological Forum* 2:449–72.

Erikson, Erik. 1950. *Childhood and Society*. New York: Norton.

Flores, Stella M. 2010. "State Dream Acts: The Effect of In-State Resident Tuition Policies and Undocumented Latino Students." *Review of Higher Education* 33:239–83.

Fuligni, Andrew J. and Sara Pedersen. 2002. "Family Obligation and the Transition to Young Adulthood." *Developmental Psychology* 38:856–68.

Furstenberg, Frank, Thomas Cook, Robert Sampson, and Gail Slap. 2002. "Early Adulthood in Cross National Perspective." *ANNALS of the American Academy of Political and Social Science* 580:6–15.

Gans, Herbert J. 1992. "Second Generation Decline: Scenarios for the Economic and Ethnic Futures of the Post-1965 American Immigrants." *Ethnic and Racial Studies* 15:173–92.

Gleeson, Shannon and Roberto G. Gonzales. 2012. "When Do Papers Matter? An Institutional Analysis of Undocumented Life in the United States." *International Migration* 50 : 1–19.

Gonzales, Roberto G. 2007. "Wasted Talent and Broken Dreams: The Lost Potential of Undocumented Students." *Immigration Policy: In Focus* 5:13. Washington, DC: Immigration Policy Center of the American Immigration Law Foundation.

Gonzales, Roberto G. 2010. "On the Wrong Side of the Tracks: The Consequences of School Stratification Systems for Unauthorized Mexican Students." *Peabody Journal of Education* 85:469.

Kasinitz, Philip, John H. Mollenkopf, Mary C. Waters, and Jennifer Holdaway. 2008. *Inheriting the City: The Children of Immigrants Come of Age*. Cambridge: Harvard University Press.

Lucas, Samuel R. and Mark Berends. 2002. "Sociodemographic Diversity, Correlated Achievement, and De Facto Tracking." *Sociology of Education* 75: 328–48.

MacLeod, Jay. 1987. *Ain't No Makin' It: Aspirations and Attainment in a Low-Income Neighborhood*. Boulder, CO: Westview Press.

Marrow, Helen B. 2009. "Immigrant Bureaucratic Incorporation: The Dual Roles of Professional Missions and Government Policies." *American Sociological Review* 74:756–76.

Massey, Douglas S. 2008. *New Faces in New Places: The New Geography of American Immigration*. New York: Russell Sage Foundation.

Massey, Douglas S., Jorge Durand, and Nolan J. Molone. 2002. *Beyond Smoke and Mirrors: Mexican Immigration in an Era of Economic Integration*. New York: Russell Sage Foundation.

Massey, Douglas and Magaly Sánchez R. 2010. *Brokered Boundaries: Creating Immigrant Identity in Anti-Immigrant Times*. New York: Russell Sage Foundation.

Menjivar, Cecilia. 2006. "Liminal Legality: Salvadoran and Guatemalan Immigrants' Lives in the United States." *American Journal of Sociology* 111:999–1037.

Mollenkopf, John H., Mary Waters, Jennifer Holdaway, and Philip Kasinitz. 2005. "The Ever-Winding Path: Ethnic and Racial Diversity in the Transition to Adulthood." Pp. 454–97 in *On the Frontier of Adulthood: Theory. Research, and Public Policy*, edited by R. Settersten Jr., F. F. Furstenberg Jr., and R. G. Rumbaut. Chicago: University of Chicago Press.

Nevins, Joseph. 2010. *Operation Gatekeeper and Beyond: The War on "Illegals" and the Remaking of the U.S.–Mexico Boundary*. New York: Routledge.

Ngai, Mae. 2004. *Impossible Subjects: Illegal Aliens and the Making of Modern America*. Princeton, NJ: Princeton University Press.

Oakes, Jeannie. 1985. *Keeping Track: How Schools Structure Inequality*. New Haven, CT: Yale University Press.

Olivas, Michael A. 2005. "The Story of *Plyler v. Doe*, the Education of Undocumented Children, and the Polity." Pp. 197–220 in *Immigration Stories*, edited by D. Martin and P. Schuck. New York: Foundation Press.

Passel, Jeffrey S. 2003. *Further Demographic Information Relating to the DREAM Act*. Washington, DC: The Urban Institute.

Passel, Jeffrey S. 2006. "The Size and Characteristics of the Unauthorized Migrant Population in the U.S.: Estimates based on the March 2005 Current Population Survey." Washington, DC: Pew Hispanic Center (http://pewhispanic.org/files/reports/61.pdf).

Passel, Jeffrey and D'Vera Cohn. 2009. "A Portrait of the Unauthorized Migrants in the United States."

Washington, DC: Pew Hispanic Center (http://pewhispanic.org/files/reports/107.pdf).

Passel, Jeffrey and D'Vera Cohn. 2010. "U.S. Unauthorized Immigration Flows Are Down Sharply Since Mid-Decade." Washington, DC: Pew Hispanic Center (http://pewhispanic.org/files/reports/126.pdf).

Portes, Alejandro. 1981. "Modes of Structural Incorporation and Present Theories of Labor Immigration." Pp. 279–97 in *Global Trends in Migration: Theory and Research on International Population Movements*, edited by M. M. Kritz. New York: Center for Migration Studies.

Portes, Alejandro and Robert Bach. 1985. *Latin Journey: Cuban and Mexican Immigrants in the United States*. Berkeley: University of California Press.

Portes, Alejandro and Patricia Fernandez-Kelly. 2008. "No Margin for Error: Educational and Occupational Achievement among Disadvantaged Children of Immigrants." *ANNALS of the American Academy of Political and Social Science* 620:12–36.

Portes, Alejandro and Rubén G. Rumbaut. 2001. *Legacies: The Story of the Immigrant Second Generation*. Berkeley: University of California Press.

Portes, Alejandro and Rubén G. Rumbaut. 2006. *Immigrant America: A Portrait*, 3rd ed. Berkeley: University of California Press.

Portes, Alejandro and Min Zhou. 1993. "The New Second Generation: Segmented Assimilation and its Variants." *ANNALS of the American Academy of Political and Social Science* 530:74–96.

Rindfuss, Ronald R. 1991. "The Young Adult Years: Diversity, Structural Change and Fertility." *Demography* 28:493–512.

Rumbaut, Rubén G. 1997. "Assimilation and its Discontents: Between Rhetoric and Reality." *International Migration Review* 31:923–60.

Rumbaut, Rubén G. 2004. "Ages, Life Stages, and Generational Cohorts: Decomposing the Immigrant First and Second Generations in the United States." *International Migration Review* 38:1160–1205.

Rumbaut, Rubén G. 2005. "Turning Points in the Transition to Adulthood: Determinants of Educational Attainment, Incarceration, and Early Childbearing among Children of Immigrants." *Ethnic and Racial Studies* 28:1041–86.

Rumbaut, Rubén G. 2008. "The Coming of the Second Generation: Immigration and Ethnic Mobility in Southern California." *ANNALS of the American Academy of Political and Social Science* 620:196–236.

Rumbaut, Rubén G. and Golnaz Komaie. 2010. "Immigration and Adult Transitions." *The Future of Children* 20:39–63.

Settersten, Jr., Richard A., Frank F. Furstenberg, and Rubén G. Rumbaut. 2005. *On the Frontier of Adulthood: Theory, Research, and Public Policy*. Chicago: University of Chicago Press.

Singer, Audrey. 2004. "The Rise of New Immigrant Gateways." Washington, DC: The Brookings Institution (http://www.brookings.edu/urban/pubs/20040301_gateways.pdf).

Smith, Robert Courtney. 2006. *Mexican New York: Transnational Lives of New Immigrants*. Berkeley: University of California Press.

Smith, Robert Courtney. 2008. "Horatio Alger Lives in Brooklyn: Extrafamily Support, Intrafamily Dynamics, and Socially Neutral Operating Identities in Exceptional Mobility among Children of Mexican Immigrants." *ANNALS of the American Academy of Political and Social Science* 620:270–90.

Stanton-Salazar, Ricardo. 2001. *Manufacturing Hope and Despair: The School and Kin Support Networks of U.S.-Mexican Youth*. New York: Teachers College Press.

Suárez-Orozco, Carola and Marcelo Suárez-Orozco. 1995. *Transformations: Migration, Family Life, and Achievement Motivation among Latino Adolescents*. Stanford, CA: Stanford University Press.

Suárez-Orozco, Carola, Marcelo M. Suárez-Orozco, and Irina Todorova. 2008. *Learning a New Land: Immigrant Students in American Society*, Cambridge: Harvard University Press.

Telles, Edward E. and Vilma Ortiz. 2008. *Generations of Exclusion: Mexican Americans, Assimilation, and Race*. New York: Russell Sage Foundation.

Waters, Mary C. 1999. *Black Identities: West Indian Immigrant Dreams and American Realities*. New York: Russell Sage Press.

Willen, Sarah S. 2007. "Towards a Critical Phenomenology of 'Illegality': State Power, Criminalization, and Abjectivity among Undocumented Migrant Workers in Tel Aviv, Israel." *International Migration* 45: 7–38.

Willis, Paul. 1977. *Learning to Labour: How Working Class Kids Get Working Class Jobs.* New York: Columbia University Press.

Zhou, Min. 1997. "Segmented Assimilation: Issues, Controversies, and Recent Research on the New Second Generation." *International Migration Review* 4:825–58.

Zhou, Min. 2008. "The Ethnic System of Supplementary Education: Non-profit and For-profit Institutions in Los Angeles' Chinese Immigrant Community." Pp. 229–51 in *Toward Positive Youth Development: Transforming Schools and Community Programs,* edited by B. Shinn and H. Yoshikawa. New York: Oxford University Press.

Zhou, Min and Carl L. Bankston III. 1998. *Growing Up American: How Vietnamese Children Adapt to Life in the United States.* New York: Russell Sage Foundation.

Zúñiga, Victor and Rubén Hernández-León, eds. 2005. *New Destinations: Mexican Immigration in the United States.* New York: Russell Sage Foundation.

Questions for Critical Thinking

1. How does Gonzales's discussion of the transition to adulthood for undocumented Latino young adults impact your understanding of the impact of social policy on one's identity?

2. As the author illustrates, youth today are taking longer to transition to adulthood. How is this transition different for youth based on class immigration status?

3. How does the author's discussion impact your perspective on the need for immigration policy reform?

The Racial Wealth Gap
Why Policy Matters

LAURA SULLIVAN, TATJANA MESCHEDE, LARS DIETRICH, THOMAS M. SHAPIRO, AMY TRAUB, CATHERINE REUTSCHLIN, AND TAMARA DRAUT

As discussed in Part II of this text, the racial wealth gap continues to grow ever wider. In the following essay, authors Laura Sullivan, Tatjana Meschede, Lars Dietrich, Thomas M. Shapiro, Amy Traub, Catherine Reutschlin, and Tamara Draut examine the role of public policies in closing this gap. Using a new tool, the Racial Wealth Audit, they evaluate the impact of housing, education, and labor markets on the wealth gap among black, Latino, and white households and assess how far policies that equalize outcomes in these areas could go toward reducing the gap.

Introduction

America is becoming both a more diverse nation and a more unequal one. Over the past four decades, wealth inequality has skyrocketed, with nearly half of all wealth accumulation since 1986 going to the top 0.1 percent of households. Today the portion of wealth shared by the bottom 90 percent of Americans is shrinking, while the top 1 percent controls 42 percent of the nation's wealth.[1] At the same time, an increasing share of the American population is made up of people of color, and wealth is starkly divided along racial lines: the typical Black household now possesses just 6 percent of the wealth owned by the typical white household and the typical Latino household owns only 8 percent of the wealth held by the typical white household.[2] These wealth disparities are rooted in historic injustices and carried forward by practices and policies that fail to reverse inequitable trends. As a result, racial wealth disparities, like wealth inequality overall, continue to grow.

Political thinkers increasingly recognize that rapidly growing inequality threatens economic stability and growth. But in a country where people of color will be a majority by mid-century, any successful push to reduce inequality must also address the structural racial inequities that hold back so many Americans. To create a more equitable future, we must confront the nation's growing racial wealth gap and the public policies that continue to fuel and exacerbate it.

Stratospheric riches on the scale of the wealthiest Americans will never be accessible to the vast majority. Yet access to some degree of wealth is critical for every family's economic security. Wealth functions as a financial safety net that enables families to deal with unexpected expenses and disruptions of income without accumulating large amounts of debt. At the same time, wealth can improve the prospects of the next generation through inheritances or gifts. Inter-generational transfers of wealth can play a pivotal role in helping to finance higher education, supply a down payment for a first home, or offer start-up capital for launching a new business.[3] Because households of color have less wealth today, Black and Latino

Laura Sullivan, Tatjana Meschede, Lars Dietrich, Thomas M. Shapiro, Amy Traub, Catherine Ruetschlin, and Tamara Draut, "The Racial Wealth Gap: Why Policy Matters" (New York: Demos, 2015).

young adults are far less likely than young white people to receive a large sum—or any money at all—from family members to make these investments in their future.[4] The result is that the racial wealth gap perpetuates from generation to generation, with profound implications for the economic security and mobility of future generations.

The racial wealth gap is reinforced by federal policies that largely operate to increase wealth for those who already possess significant assets. The Corporation for Enterprise Development finds that more than half of the $400 billion provided annually in federal asset-building subsidies—policies intended to promote homeownership, retirement savings, economic investment and access to college—flow to the wealthiest 5 percent of taxpaying households.[5] Meanwhile, the bottom 60 percent of taxpayers receive only 4 percent of these benefits and the bottom 20 percent of taxpayers receive almost nothing. Black and Latino households are disproportionately among those receiving little or no benefit. Unless key policies are restructured, the racial wealth gap—and wealth inequality in general—will continue to grow.

In this report, we assess the major factors contributing to the racial wealth gap, considering how public policies around housing, education, and labor markets impact the distribution of wealth by race and ethnicity. Each factor is evaluated using a new tool: the Racial Wealth Audit developed by the Institute on Assets and Social Policy (IASP) to assess the impact of public policy on the wealth gap between white and Black and Latino households with the aim of guiding policy development. The Racial Wealth Audit draws on a baseline of representative data discussed in this paper to provide an empirical foundation for existing wealth among groups and the major determinants of wealth accumulation.

In this report, we briefly discuss the historic and policy roots of the wealth gap in each area and quantify the extent to which each policy area contributes to the current gap. Next, we look at the extent to which changes in housing, education,

and labor market trends would affect the wealth gap—for example, the wealth impact of increasing the rate of Black and Latino homeownership to match white homeownership rates, and the impact of increasing the wealth returns that households of color receive as a result of homeownership to match white returns. We note policy ideas for reducing the racial wealth gap in each area.[6]

The greatest utility of the Racial Wealth Audit is evident in this policy analysis. From the starting position of existing disparities, the Audit predicts wealth increases or decreases for affected populations according to the components of a proposed policy. The Audit uses the most conservative assumptions possible, avoiding overstating changes in the gap. Finally, the Audit provides insight into the impact of policies on the racial wealth gap within a discrete time period, such as 1 year or 5 years ahead.

The Racial Wealth Audit is designed to fill the void in our understanding of the racial wealth gap and enhance our ability to reduce the gap through policy. It is an essential new measurement framework for assessment to facilitate informed decisions about the role of policy in asset-building, economic stability, and the racial wealth gap. Equally important, it can prevent the unintended side effects of policies that are not explicitly aimed at household wealth or financial disparities, yet contribute to worsening inequality.

Defining the Racial Wealth Gap

In this report, we define the racial wealth gap as the absolute difference in wealth holdings between the median household among populations grouped by race or ethnicity. In the U.S. the racial wealth gap shows that the typical white household holds multiple times the wealth of Black and Latino households. Using the SIPP, we estimate that the median white household had $111,146 in wealth holdings in 2011, compared to $7,113 for the median Black household and $8,348 for the median Latino household.[7]

In relative terms, Black households hold only 6 percent of the wealth owned by white households,

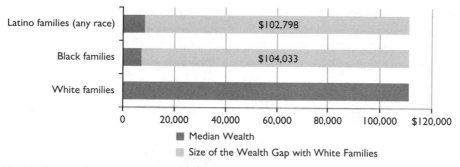

Figure 1 Wealth Accumulation and Size of the Racial Wealth Gap, 2011.
Source: Survey of Income and Program Participation (SIPP), 2008 Panel Wave 10, 2011.

which amounts to a total wealth gap of $104,033, and Latino households hold only 8 percent of the wealth owned by white households, a wealth gap of $102,798 (see Figure 1). In other words, a typical white family owns $15.63 for every $1 owned by a typical Black family, and $13.33 for every $1 owned by a typical Latino family.

How Homeownership Contributes to the Racial Wealth Gap

For most families in the U.S., home equity marks the largest segment in their wealth portfolio; however, home ownership is unequally distributed by racial and ethnic lines. Disparities in homeownership rates (73 percent of whites as compared to 47 percent of Latinos and 45 percent of Blacks [see Figure 2]), typical home equity ($86,800 for white homeowners at the median as compared to $50,000 for Black homeowners and $48,000 for Latino homeowners),[8] and neighborhood values where whites and people of color live substantially contribute to the racial wealth gap. In addition, tracing the same households over 25 years revealed that the number of years a household owned their home explained 27 percent of the growing racial wealth gap.[9] Because white families are more likely to receive inheritances and other family assistance to put a down payment on a home, they are often able to start acquiring home equity many years earlier than Black and Latino families, offering a valuable head start on wealth-building.[10]

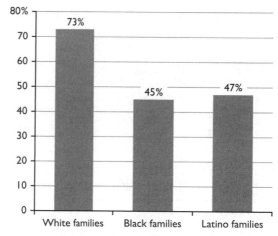

Figure 2 Homeownership Rates.
Source: Survey of Income and Program Participation (SIPP), 2008 Panel Wave 10, 2011.

This section will explore the factors contributing to homeownership disparities in greater depth, and will analyze how equalizing rates of homeownership and returns to homeownership between whites, Blacks, and Latinos would each impact the racial wealth gap. We note that because the disparity in rates and returns to homeownership operate simultaneously to impair wealth building among households of color, policies that only address one aspect will not solve the entire portion of the racial wealth gap driven by homeownership.

Homeownership Policy Shapes the Wealth Gap

Lower homeownership rates among Blacks and Latinos have many roots, ranging from lasting legacies of past policies to disparate access to real estate ownership. The National Housing Act of 1934, for example, redlined entire Black neighborhoods, marking them as bad credit risks and effectively discouraging lending in these areas, even as Black home buyers continued to be excluded from white neighborhoods. While redlining was officially outlawed by the Fair Housing Act of 1968, its impact in the form of residential segregation patterns persists with households of color more likely to live in neighborhoods characterized by higher poverty rates, lower home values, and a declining infrastructure compared to neighborhoods inhabited predominantly by white residents.

Discriminatory lending practices persist to this day. When households of color access mortgages, they are more often underwritten by higher interest rates.[11] Mainstream lending institutions were deeply implicated in discriminatory lending: in 2012 Wells Fargo Bank admitted that they steered thousands of Black and Latino borrowers into subprime mortgages when non-Hispanic white borrowers with similar credit profiles received prime loans.[12] In addition, the proliferation of high-cost credit options such as payday lenders in many neighborhoods of color, combined with the scarcity of banks and credit unions, is another likely contributor to weak credit. The fact that Black and Latino families are more likely to have taken on subprime mortgages in recent years contributed significantly to the devastating impact of the housing collapse that began in 2006.

In addition to these longstanding homeownership and home equity disparities, the foreclosure crisis during the Great Recession of 2007–2008 dipped even further into families of color's housing wealth. While the median white family lost 16 percent of their wealth in the housing crash and Great Recession, Black families lost 53 percent and Latino families lost 66 percent.[13] Foreclosures both directly destroy housing wealth and have a lasting negative impact on

credit, ensuring that mortgages and other loans will be offered on more costly terms in the future.

While homeownership plays a central part in building family wealth in the United States, the nation's public policies have systematically operated to shut Black and Latino families out of numerous opportunities to build housing wealth that benefitted white families. Today, Latinos and Blacks are less likely to own their homes and accrue less wealth, at the median, as a result of homeownership than white families. The next two sections use empirical estimates to explore impacts on the racial wealth gap if these disparities were eliminated.

How Equalizing Homeownership Rates Affects the Wealth Gap

We tested the effects of equalizing homeownership rates among white, Black, and Latino families on the racial wealth gap. Our model looks at wealth accumulation by race and ethnicity if the existing home owning population among Black and Latino households matched the 73 percent rate of white families. In other words, what if Black and Latino homeowners made up 73 percent of each of their respective population subgroups, without changing typical home values for whites or households of color? The model did not control for other characteristics that might distinguish homeowners from non-homeowners.

The results suggest that equalizing homeownership rates has substantial effects on the wealth accumulation of Black and Latino households. Median wealth among Black households rose from $7,113 to $39,226—adding $32,113 to the median Black household's wealth (see Figure 3). Median wealth among Latino households rose from $8,348 to $37,561—adding $29,213 to the median Latino household's wealth. Those numbers represent a 451 percent wealth increase for Black households, and a 350 percent wealth gain for Latino households.

Equalizing Black and Latino homeownership rates with those of whites raises wealth among Black and Latino families, and substantially reduces the racial wealth gap. The wealth gap between white and Black families decreases by $32,113 to $71,920.

Figure 3 Reduction of the Wealth Gap after Equalizing Homeownership Rates.
Source: Survey of Income and Program Participation (SIPP), 2008 Panel Wave 10, 2011.

	Wealth Gap with White Families Before Equalizing Homeownership Rates	Wealth Gap with White Families After Equalizing Homeownership Rates	Change in the Racial Wealth Gap	Percent Change in the Racial Wealth Gap
Black families	$104,033	$71,920	−$32,113	−31%
Latino families (any race)	$102,798	$73,585	−$29,213	−28%

Figure 4 Changes in the Racial Wealth Gap if Rates of Homeownership were Equalized.
Source: Survey of Income and Program Participation (SIPP), 2008 Panel Wave 10, 2011.

This is a 31 percent reduction in the Black–white wealth gap. The wealth gap between white and Latino families decreases by $29,213 to $73,585, or a reduction of 28 percent (see Figure 4).

How Equalizing the Return to Homeownership Affects the Wealth Gap

We tested the effects on the racial wealth gap of changing the wealth return on homeownership to Black and Latino households to equalize the return to homeownership for white households. The first step in this model estimates the wealth returns to homeownership using a multivariate median regression model for the white population. That model estimates that white households benefit from a $96,248 return on with homeownership.

Using a similar model to estimate the wealth effects of homeownership on Black households, we find that the wealth returns to homeownership for Black households amount to $71,715—just 75 percent of the returns that accrue to white households (see Figure 5). This difference of $24,533 means that for every $1 in wealth that a Black family builds as a result of homeownership, white families accrue $1.34.[14] Meanwhile, the wealth returns to homeownership for Latino households amount to $62,647—just 65 percent of the returns that accrue to white households. This difference of $33,601 means that for every $1 in wealth that accrues to Latino families as a result of homeownership, white families accrue $1.54.

In order to construct a model that equalizes the returns to homeownership across groups, we

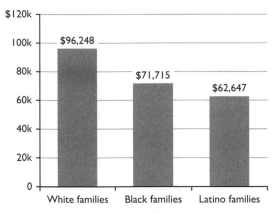

Figure 5 Median Wealth Return to Homeownership.
Source: Survey of Income and Program Participation (SIPP), 2008 Panel Wave 10, 2011.

assigned home equity at the rate accumulating to the median white household—$96,248—to Black and Latino households with home equity values less than that threshold. This assignment raises Black and Latino wealth by the difference between their existing median equity and the white median.

As a result of equalizing the return to Black homeownership to the level of return that accrues to whites, Black families' median wealth grew by $17,113 to $24,226—a 241 percent increase in median Black household wealth (see Figure 6).

As a result of equalizing the return to homeownership among Latinos to the level of return that accrues to whites, Latino families' median wealth grew by $41,652 to $50,000—a 499 percent increase in Latino median wealth.

Equalizing wealth returns to homeownership raised wealth among Black and Latino families while white wealth was held constant, significantly reducing the racial wealth gap. Equalizing the returns to homeownership reduces the wealth gap between white and Black families by $17,133 to $86,920. This is a 16 percent reduction in the Black–white wealth gap (see Figure 7). Meanwhile the wealth gap between white and Latino families decreases by $41,652 to $61,146—a reduction of 41 percent.

Homeownership Policies to Reduce the Wealth Gap

Positing Black and Latino homeownership rates and returns equal to those of white families helps to clarify the contours of the racial wealth gap, but it's quite different from having policy proposals that would actually accomplish these aims—or even approach them. Yet just as past and continuing policies have helped to shape the distribution of wealth in America today, policy change could alter the existing trends for better or worse. A bold, comprehensive approach would be required to

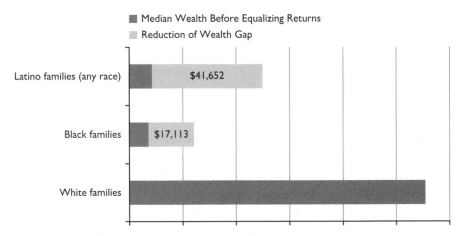

Figure 6 Reduction of the Wealth Gap after Equalizing Homeownership Returns.
Source: Survey of Income and Program Participation (SIPP), 2008 Panel Wave 10, 2011.

	Wealth Gap with White Families Before Equalizing Homeownership Returns	Wealth Gap with White Families After Equalizing Homeownership Returns	Change in the Racial Wealth Gap	Percent Change in the Racial Wealth Gap
Black families	$104,033	$86,920	−$17,113	−16%
Latino families (any race)	$102,798	$61,146	−$41,652	−41%

Figure 7 Changes in the Racial Wealth Gap if Returns on Homeownership were Equalized.
Source: Survey of Income and Program Participation (SIPP), 2008 Panel Wave 10, 2011.

move us towards the level of equality in homeownership modeled in our analyses; however, a number of policy efforts could bring us closer to expanding opportunities to build wealth through homeownership in the U.S. While far from a comprehensive list, here are three sample homeownership policies that could help to build housing wealth for people of color and shrink the racial wealth gap.

- **Stricter enforcement of housing anti-discrimination laws.** As noted above, residential segregation is a key reason that Black and Latino homeowners do not benefit from as great a rate of return on homeownership as their white counterparts. By limiting the residential market, segregation means that homes in predominantly Black and Latino neighborhoods accrue less value. Studies find that Black and Latino homebuyers still face barriers to purchasing homes in predominantly white areas.[15] Stricter enforcement of housing anti-discrimination laws would increase the ability of people of color to buy homes in higher-value neighborhoods, offering significant potential for reducing the racial wealth gap.

- **Authorizing Fannie Mae and Freddie Mac to reduce mortgage principal and make other loan modifications for struggling homeowners.** As we've seen, Black and Latino homeowners are more likely than white homeowners to have obtained subprime mortgages and to have homes at risk of foreclosure. A policy that enables these federally-chartered institutions to reduce mortgage principal and modify mortgage loans in other ways that make them more sustainable would help to protect the home equity wealth of Black and Latino homeowners, potentially reducing the racial wealth gap.

- **Lowering the cap on the mortgage interest tax deduction.** As we have seen, typical Black and Latino homeowners own homes of less value than typical white homeowners. As a result, Black and Latino households benefit less from the tax deduction, which allow homeowners to deduct the cost of interest paid on up to $1 million in mortgage debt. A variety of different caps have been recommended, including an Obama Administration proposal to cap deductions at 28 percent for high-income households, those earning more than $250,000. Such a policy could be helpful in reducing the racial wealth gap, particularly if the additional tax revenues were used to fund foreclosure prevention programs and first-time homebuyers' assistance programs, which are more likely to benefit Black and Latino households.

How Education Contributes to the Racial Wealth Gap

Attaining a college education has never been more important to a household's ability to thrive in the labor market, attain financial stability, and build wealth. Today, more students than ever before are entering 4-year colleges. However, despite rising college attendance rates among Black and Latino households, barriers to completing a degree have actually widened the college attainment gap between whites and people of color over the past decade. In 2011, 34 percent of whites completed a four-year college degree, compared to just 20 percent of Blacks and 13 percent of Latinos (see Figure 8).[16] One key barrier is the rapid growth in college costs, which forces households to take on significant debt in order to attend institutions of higher education—even in cases where students do not ultimately graduate. Gaps in college attainment by race and ethnicity also reflect other inequities in the K–12 education system and in household income.

In addition to attainment gaps, the returns to college education differ across racial and ethnic groups. At the median, a white family sees a return of $55,869 in wealth from completing a four-year college degree, while the median Black and Latino families attain just a small fraction of this return: $4,846 and $4,191 respectively. The returns to Black and Latino families are impacted by, among other things, their greater need to take on debt to pay

for college and their disparate experiences in the labor market after graduation. According to previous research from IASP, differences in college completion rates accounted for about 5 percent of the growth in the racial wealth gap over a 25 year period (1984–2011).

This section looks more closely at the factors contributing to disparities in higher education, and evaluates how equalizing rates of college completion (defined as graduating with a four-year degree) and returns to college completion between whites, Blacks, and Latinos would each impact the racial wealth gap.

Education Policy Shapes the Wealth Gap

Public policy decisions are critical to understanding why Latinos and Blacks are less likely to have completed a four-year college degree than whites, as well as why Latino and Black graduates build less wealth as a result of their degrees. Educational inequities have deep historical roots in policies that prohibited slaves from learning to read and the century of substandard "separate but equal" educational facilities that followed, leaving many students of color poorly prepared for college. These past educational inequities matter today because parents' educational level—as well as family incomes and wealth itself—significantly predict children's educational success across their lifetimes.[17] At the same time, contemporary policy choices, from the retreat from integration in K–12 education to the declining public support for affordable higher education, shape the educational opportunities available to youth of color who are more likely to need financial support for college, thereby contributing to the existing racial wealth gap.

Disparities in education begin early in the lives of children in the U.S. and current education policies often foster inequities.[18] The policy decision not to invest in quality preschool education for all young people sets the stage for racial disparities that persist throughout the educational system from K–12 to higher education. While quality K–12

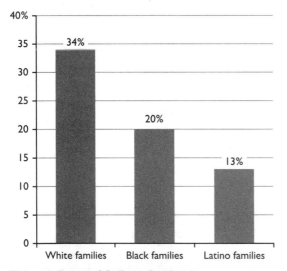

Figure 8 Rates of College Graduation.
Source: Survey of Income and Program Participation (SIPP), 2008 Panel Wave 10, 2011.

education is essential for college readiness, residential segregation leaves many Black and Latino students, particularly those from low-income families, concentrated in low-quality, under-resourced schools. As policy has shifted away from efforts to integrate public education that prevailed after the Brown v. Board of Education Supreme Court decision in 1954, research has documented dramatic increases in segregation, with Black and Latino students increasingly attending the same schools.[19] Predominantly Black and Latino schools spend less per student than predominantly white schools, a disparity that is only partly accounted for by the different property-tax bases of school districts creating a highly unequal educational system across the country.[20]

Once students reach college, racial and ethnic disparities in family economic resources and the soaring costs of attending college mean that students of color often confront unsustainable expenses as they pursue higher education, leading to huge debt burdens and lower graduation rates. At public institutions, increasing tuition and fees are primarily a result of declining state support for higher education shifting a greater share of the costs to students.[21] As a result, Black and Latino students with less family wealth than white students are more likely to struggle with higher costs, seek out less expensive schools, work excessive hours, reduce study time to work, and/or take on more student loan debt.[22]

For young people who come from families without substantial wealth, education has long been seen as the pathway to greater opportunity and economic security. However rather than facilitating economic mobility, according to our analyses, current educational inequalities end up being a small, direct net contributor to the racial wealth gap. In addition, it is also likely influencing a number of other variables that shape unequal asset-building opportunities. The next two sections present our empirical analysis exploring how the racial wealth gap would change if educational disparities were reduced.

How Equalizing College Graduation Rates Affects the Wealth Gap

We tested the effects of equalizing college graduation rates among white, Black, and Latino families on the racial wealth gap. This test did not control for other characteristics that might distinguish those who finish college from those who do not. Instead, it looks at wealth accumulation by race and ethnicity if the proportion of Black and Latino households with a college degree matched the 34 percent college completion rate of whites.

Compared to the effects of changes in homeownership rates on the racial wealth gap, the effects of changing college attainment rates on household wealth for Black and Latino families are modest. Median wealth among Black households rises from $7,113 to $8,426—adding $1,313 to the median Black household's wealth (see Figure 9). Median wealth among Latino households rises from $8,348 to $11,876—adding $3,528 to the median Latino household's wealth. Those gains represent an 18 percent wealth increase for Black households, and a 42 percent wealth increase for Latino households.

The equalization of college graduation rates raised wealth among Black and Latino families while white wealth was held constant, modestly reducing the racial wealth gap. The wealth gap between white and Black families was reduced by $1,313, which amounts to just 1 percent of the racial wealth gap (see Figure 10). The wealth gap between white and Latino families was reduced by $3,528, a reduction of 3 percent.

The fact that the reduction in the racial wealth gap from equalizing college graduation rates is small does not automatically imply that raising educational attainment is an ineffective means of closing the racial wealth gap. Instead, it suggests that matching the *current* levels of college degree attainment of white households—in which the benefits of a four-year college degree reach only about a third of households—is unlikely to substantially reduce the wealth gap.

Figure 9 Reduction of the Wealth Gap after Equalizing College Graduation Rates.
Source: Survey of Income and Program Participation (SIPP), 2008 Panel Wave 10, 2011.

	Wealth Gap with White Families Before Equalizing Graduation Rates	Wealth Gap with White Families After Equalizing Graduation Rates	Change in the Racial Wealth Gap	Percent Change in the Racial Wealth Gap
Black families	$104,033	$102,720	−$1,313	−1%
Latino families (any race)	$102,798	$99,270	−$3,528	−3%

Figure 10 Changes in the Racial Wealth Gap if Rates of College Graduation were Equalized.
Source: Survey of Income and Program Participation (SIPP), 2008 Panel Wave 10, 2011.

How Equalizing the Return to College Graduation Affects the Wealth Gap

Next, we tested the effects on the racial wealth gap of changing the return on completing a four-year college degree for Black and Latino households to equal the return to graduation of white households. As seen above, the first step in this process estimates the wealth returns to a college degree using a multivariate median regression model for the white population. That model estimates that white households benefit from a wealth return of $55,869 associated with college graduation.

In analyzing the experiences of Black households, the wealth returns to a college education for Black households amount to just $4,846—only 9 percent of the returns that accrue to white households (see Figure 11). This difference of $51,023 means that for every $1 in wealth that accrues to Black families

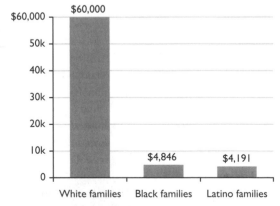

Figure 11 Median Wealth Return to College Graduation.
Source: Survey of Income and Program Participation (SIPP), 2008 Panel Wave 10, 2011.

associated with a college degree at the median, white families accrue $11.49. Meanwhile, the wealth returns to a college education for Latino households amount to $4,191—just 8 percent of what accrues to white households. This difference of $51,678 means that for every $1 in wealth that accrues to Latino families from a college education, white families accrue $13.33.

In order to construct a model equalizing the returns to a college education across groups, we assigned Black and Latino households that had completed college with a value of total wealth equal to the return to college graduation for the median white household: $55,869. Black and Latino college graduates who already had household wealth above this value did not have their wealth adjusted. This change does not alter the differential rates of college graduation and thus affects only a subset of the Black and Latino populations.

As a result of equalizing the return to a college education to the level of return accruing to whites, Black families' median wealth grows by $10,786 to $17,899—a 152 percent increase in Black household wealth (see Figure 12). As a result of equalizing the return to a college education to the level of return accruing to whites, Latino families' median wealth grows by $5,878 to $14,226—a 70 percent increase in Latino wealth.

The equalization of returns to a college education raises the medial level of wealth among Black and Latino families, while white median wealth remains constant, modestly reducing the racial wealth gap. Equalizing the returns to a college education reduces the wealth gap between white and Black families by $10,786 to $93,247. This is a 10 percent reduction in the Black–white wealth gap (see Figure 13). Meanwhile, the wealth gap between

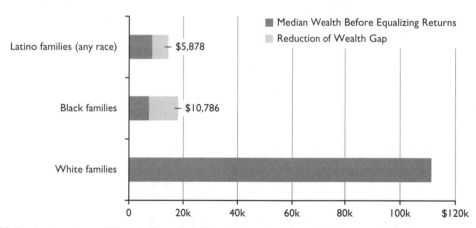

Figure 12 Reduction of the Wealth Gap after Equalizing Returns to College Graduation.
Source: Survey of Income and Program Participation (SIPP), 2008 Panel Wave 10, 2011.

	Wealth Gap with White Families Before Equalizing Graduation Returns	Wealth Gap with White Families After Equalizing Graduation Returns	Change in the Racial Wealth Gap	Percent Change in the Racial Wealth Gap
Black families	$104,033	$93,247	–$10,786	–10%
Latino families (any race)	$102,798	$96,920	–$5,878	–6%

Figure 13 Changes in Racial Wealth Gap if Returns on College Graduation were Equalized.
Source: Survey of Income and Program Participation (SIPP), 2008 Panel Wave 10, 2011.

white and Latino families decreases by $5,878 to $96,920—a reduction of 6 percent.

One reason the reduction in the racial wealth gap is modest when the return to college education is equalized is because the affected households—the 20 percent of Blacks and 13 percent of Latinos that have attained a four-year college degree—is a relatively small proportion of the overall Black and Latino population. Raising college completion rates at the same time that the returns to a college degree increase would be expected to impact a greater number of households and to decrease the racial wealth gap more significantly.

Education Policies to Reduce the Wealth Gap

Disparities in attaining a college education account for only a small portion of the racial wealth gap. Our findings suggest that increasing college completion rates among Black and Latino youth and improving their returns on a college degree would reduce the wealth gap only modestly at the median. Nevertheless, a number of promising education policies do show potential to make a difference in shrinking racial wealth disparities. The following sample policies are not a comprehensive list:

- **Invest in universal, high-quality preschool education.** Black and Latino children see some of the greatest benefits from attending preschool, but many three- and four-year-olds lack access to affordable early childhood education. Establishing universally-available public preschool as a growing number of cities are now doing has the potential to reduce the racial wealth gap by helping students of color to enter school better-prepared to learn.
- **Make K–12 education funding more equitable.** Black and Latino students are more likely to attend under-resourced schools with less experienced teachers and fewer advanced courses, leaving them less well-prepared for college than their white counterparts. Federal, state, and district funding systems could be improved to address disparities. At the federal level, Black and Latino students would benefit from school funding formulas under Title I of the Elementary and Secondary Education Act that better target funding to schools with high concentrations of students in poverty. At the state level, funding systems that draw primarily on local property taxes could be re-envisioned, as they reflect residential segregation patterns along racial lines. Local governments also need to reconsider racialized patterns of funding distribution within school districts.
- **Recommit to racially integrated schools, colleges, and universities.** While recent Supreme Court decisions have made it difficult to promote the racial and ethnic integration of public schools, there is substantial evidence that desegregation worked to reduce racial disparities and produce a sense of common educational fate among students of different racial and ethnic groups. Therefore, policies that promote racially and ethnically integrated schools have the potential to decrease racial and ethnic wealth disparities.
- **Establish an Affordable College Compact.** Greater state investment in public higher education would help to ensure that Black and Latino students can attend college without incurring debt or experiencing financial hardship. Lower college costs would enable more students of color to enroll in and complete college. At the same time, eliminating the need to take on debt would increase the return to a college degree. The federal government could encourage states to reinvest in higher education by offering higher education matching grants to states that commit to maintain minimum per-student funding levels, and could offer a greater match to states that commit to offering debt-free higher education for low- and moderate-income students.

How Labor Markets Contribute to the Racial Wealth Gap

American households derive much of their economic security from the labor market, with earned income, employer-provided health coverage, paid leave, and workplace retirement plans offering greater opportunities to build wealth for the employees who have access. The greater a household's income, for example, the more money household members have to save and invest. Meanwhile if an employer provides an affordable health insurance plan, employees often spend less than if they had to purchase their own coverage or risk incurring substantial medical expenses that can drain wealth. Pensions and 401(k)-type plans with an employer contribution offer a mechanism for employers to contribute directly to household wealth, adding to retirement savings. Yet labor markets are one of the primary drivers of the racial wealth gap, accounting for 20 percent of its growth in the last 25 years.[23] In addition, unemployment, which causes many families to draw on and deplete their assets, explains an additional 9 percent of the growth in the racial wealth gap.

Disparities in labor market outcomes arise from a variety of sources, including employment discrimination, lack of geographic access to jobs, and disparate social capital. Income disparities affect both current consumption and wealth building opportunities. Median Black and Latino families have lower incomes than white families: while the typical white family makes $50,400 a year, the typical Latino family makes just $36,840 and the typical Black family has an annual income of only $32,028 (see Figure 14).

In addition to lower incomes, Black and Latino families also see less of a wealth return on the incomes they earn—in effect, they are less able to translate each additional dollar of income into wealth. For each dollar in income white families earn, they see a return of $19.51, compared to a return of only $4.80 on each dollar for Black families and just $3.63 for Latino families. A number

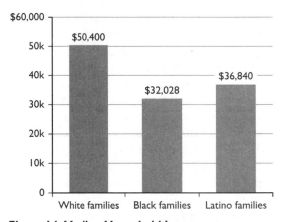

Figure 14 Median Household Income.
Source: Survey of Income and Program Participation (SIPP), 2008 Panel Wave 10, 2011.

of labor market dynamics contribute to these disparities: Blacks and Latinos are less likely to have jobs that include core employer-provided benefits such as health coverage, a retirement plan, or paid time off. As a result, families of color have fewer opportunities to save because they must use their current income to deal with more of life's vicissitudes. Similarly, Black workers have higher rates of unemployment and longer average unemployment spells, which drains wealth and adds to labor market instability.

The following section will more closely consider the factors that contribute to disparities in labor market outcomes and assesses how equalizing family incomes and returns to income (the ability to translate a dollar of income into wealth) between whites, Blacks, and Latinos would impact the racial wealth gap.

Labor Market Policy Shapes the Wealth Gap

Racial and ethnic inequality in American labor markets was codified and maintained by law for much of U.S. history. It was not until the Civil Rights Act of 1964 that federal law prohibited job discrimination on the basis of race, color, religion, sex, and national origin. Yet public policy decisions—from the enduring exclusion of certain job categories to the protections of the Fair Labor Standards Act to immigration laws that inhibit workers from exercising their full rights in the workplace—continue to shape the U.S. labor market in ways that systematically disadvantage Blacks and Latinos, helping to explain why people of color bring in lower incomes and receive lower wealth returns than white families.

For most Americans, the vast majority of income comes from a paycheck. Black and Latino workers are not only paid less, but are also more likely to be employed in jobs that fail to offer key benefits such as health coverage, paid leave, or retirement plans. The disparity in benefits helps to explain why families of color accrue less of a return on each dollar of wealth earned than white families: Blacks and Latinos are more likely to pay for necessities like health care out-of-pocket and therefore, to have less to save and invest for the future. This also means that households of color are more likely to miss out on the tax incentives and wealth-building vehicles provided by employer benefits.

Why don't Black and Latino workers simply move into better-paying jobs? The lower rates of college degree completion discussed previously is one important factor. However, white workers with and without college degrees out-earn their Black and Latino counterparts with similar levels of education. The persistence of job discrimination is a critical part of the explanation for the lower incomes of Black and Latino workers. Here the problem is partly a failure of effective policy enforcement: employment discrimination on the basis of race or national origin has been illegal for decades, yet there is substantial research evidence that it endures, whether through overt bigotry or implicit bias.[24] In addition, since Americans lead largely segregated lives, whites disproportionately benefit from social networking advantages.[25] Because networks reproduce racial wealth inequalities, public policy interventions are required to disrupt this cycle.

For the Latino workforce in particular, immigration policy is a barrier to better jobs and higher incomes. While the nation's worker protection laws officially extend to all employees regardless of immigration status, in practice immigrant workers face barriers to exercising their rights in the workplace, resulting in lower earnings. Limited English, lack of familiarity with the U.S. labor market, and concern about immigration status may also encourage immigrant workers to remain in occupations and industries they are familiar with, even if these jobs pay less and offer fewer benefits.

With the exception of those who are already very wealthy, Americans need good jobs to build assets. Yet, policy choices have contributed to the segregation of labor markets, both reducing the incomes of Black and Latino workers compared to whites and reducing the ability of people of color to turn additional income gains into wealth. As a result, labor market disparities are one of the primary contributors to the racial wealth gap. The next two sections highlight our empirical analysis exploring how the racial wealth gap would change if incomes and returns on income were more equal.

How Equalizing Incomes Affects the Wealth Gap

We tested the effects of eliminating income disparities among white, Black, and Latino families on the racial wealth gap by equalizing the patterns of household income distribution by race and ethnicity. In the current income distribution, white families are disproportionately likely to be at the top while Black and Latino families are overrepresented among lower income households. For our analysis, we estimated the income distribution of the white population alone and identified the thresholds for each income decile (for example, the top ten percent of white households in terms of income, the next ten percent after that, and so on); we then assigned weights to the Black and Latino households that appear in each decile of the white distribution until those households represent 10 percent of the Black and Latino populations. This test did not control for other characteristics that might distinguish those in any particular decile. In other words, we shifted the number of estimated households across the income distribution such that whites, Blacks, and Latinos were represented across the income distribution in equal proportions to their presence in the overall population.

As a result of the redistribution, median wealth among Black households rises from $7,113 to $18,601—adding $11,488 to the median Black household's wealth (see Figure 15). Median wealth among Latino households rises from $8,348 to $17,113—adding $8,765 to the median Latino household's wealth. Those gains represent a 162 percent wealth gain for Black households, and a 105 percent wealth gain for Latino households.

Equalizing Black and Latino incomes to match the white income distribution increases wealth among Black and Latino families who see higher incomes, while white wealth remains constant, modestly reducing the racial wealth gap. The wealth gap between white and Black families was decreased by $11,488, but leaves a remaining gap of $92,545. The change amounts to 11 percent of the racial wealth gap (see Figure 16). The wealth gap between white and Latino families decreases by $8,765, leaving a racial wealth gap of $94,033. The change in the racial wealth gap as a result of equalizing the income distribution is 9 percent.

How Equalizing the Return to Income Affects the Wealth Gap

We also tested the effects of changing the return to an additional $1 of income for Black and Latino households to equal the return for white households. The first step in this model estimates the

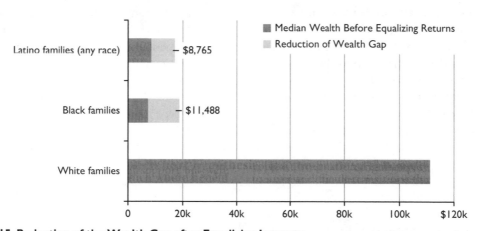

Figure 15 Reduction of the Wealth Gap after Equalizing Incomes.
Source: Survey of Income and Program Participation (SIPP), 2008 Panel Wave 10, 2011.

	Wealth Gap with White Families Before Equalizing Incomes	Wealth Gap with White Families After Equalizing Incomes	Change in the Racial Wealth Gap	Percent Change in the Racial Wealth Gap
Black families	$104,033	$92,545	−$11,488	−11%
Latino families (any race)	$102,798	$94,033	−$8,765	−9%

Figure 16 Changes in the Racial Wealth Gap if Incomes were Equalized.
Source: Survey of Income and Program Participation (SIPP), 2008 Panel Wave 10, 2011.

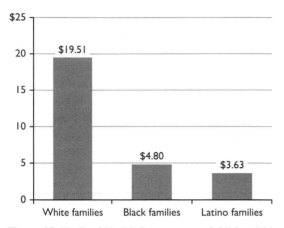

Figure 17 Median Wealth Return to an Additional $1 of Income.
Source: Survey of Income and Program Participation (SIPP), 2008 Panel Wave 10, 2011.

wealth returns to an additional $1 of income using a median regression model for the white population. That model estimates that white households experience a return of $19.51 in wealth on each additional dollar in income.

The wealth returns to an additional dollar of income for Black households amount to $4.80—only 25 percent of the returns that accrue to white households. This means that for every dollar in wealth that accrues to Black families associated with higher incomes, a white family gets $4.06 (see Figure 17). Meanwhile, the wealth returns to an additional dollar of income for Latino households amount to $3.63—19 percent of the return for whites. This means that for every dollar in wealth that accrues to Latino families associated with higher incomes, a white family typically gets $5.37.

Improving Black families' return to an additional dollar of income to equal whites' returns increases Black families' wealth by $44,963 to a total of $52,076—a 632 percent increase in Black household wealth. Meanwhile, equalizing Latino families' returns to an additional dollar of income boosts Latino wealth by $51,552 to a total of $59,900—a 618 percent increase in Latino household wealth.

Equalizing returns to an additional dollar of income raises wealth among Black and Latino families while white wealth remains constant, substantially reducing the racial wealth gap. Equalizing the returns to income reduces the wealth gap between white and Black families by $44,963 to a total of $59,070 (see Figure 18). This is a 43 percent reduction in the Black–white wealth gap. Meanwhile, the

Figure 18 Reduction of the Wealth Gap after Equalizing Returns to Income.
Source: Survey of Income and Program Participation (SIPP), 2008 Panel Wave 10, 2011.

	Wealth Gap with White Families Before Equalizing Returns on Income	Wealth Gap with White Families After Equalizing Graduation Returns	Change in the Racial Wealth Gap	Percent Change in the Racial Wealth Gap
Black families	$104,033	$59,070	–$44,963	43%
Latino families (any race)	$102,798	$51,246	–$51,552	50%

Figure 19 Changes in Racial Wealth Gap if Returns on Income were Equalized.
Source: Survey of Income and Program Participation (SIPP), 2008 Panel Wave 10, 2011.

wealth gap between white and Latino families is reduced by $51,552 to a total of $51,246—a reduction of 50 percent.

Labor Market Policies to Reduce the Wealth Gap

The range of labor market policies that could boost job quality for Black and Latino workers—raising wages, improving benefits, and offering more opportunities for career advancement—is extensive, even before we consider measures to reduce unemployment and increase the ability to turn income into wealth. Below is a sample of three policies with the potential to shrink the racial wealth gap from income and labor market outcomes. The list is far from comprehensive.

- **Establish a direct federal job creation program.** Despite an improving economic outlook, Black unemployment remains high, and unemployment for Black teenagers is particularly widespread. A direct federal hiring program would put people back to work and employ workers to produce useful goods and services for the public's benefit, such as maintaining and upgrading infrastructure, and providing child care, elder care, and cultural enrichment. By targeting communities where joblessness is much higher than the national average, this policy could significantly reduce unemployment among Blacks, while raising incomes and reducing the racial wealth gap in the process.
- **Raise the minimum wage.** Black and Latino workers are disproportionately likely to be employed in positions that pay the minimum wage or just above and would benefit the most from an increase in the federal minimum wage.[26] With new research indicating that minimum wage increases have not reduced employment, a hike in the federal minimum wage from its current low rate of $7.25 would boost the incomes of many of the lowest paid Black and Latino workers and have the potential to decrease the racial wealth gap.
- **Make it easier for workers to form unions.** In earlier decades, white-dominated labor unions often acted to exclude Black and Latino workers from high-quality unionized jobs. Yet, today unionization rates are higher for Black workers than for white workers. Blacks and Latinos see greater wage premiums as a result of union membership than white workers and union membership does more to increase access to key employment benefits like health coverage and retirement plans for people of color than it does for whites.[27] Making it easier for workers to form and join unions could therefore be expected to boost pay and benefits for Black and Latino workers and decrease the racial wealth gap.

Conclusion

When it comes to tackling the racial wealth gap, policies matter tremendously. Simply increasing rates of Black and Latino achievement (whether it is homeownership, college graduation, or income parity) is not sufficient to fully eliminate the gaps in wealth between Black and Latino families and their white counterparts. In almost every case, equalizing the *returns* to any given achievement makes a greater difference for the racial wealth gap than eliminating disparities in home purchases, college graduation rates, or wages. The challenge is that improving the economic returns that households gain requires confronting and changing the deeply entrenched structures discussed throughout this report—from residential segregation to jobs that lack the benefits that enable households to build assets. Policymakers must act both to remove barriers to access and achievement and also challenge the deeply-rooted structures that reproduce disproportionate advantages for white households.

Our results suggest that policies that successfully address disparities in homeownership rates and returns to income are likely to be the most effective in reducing the racial wealth gap. At the same time, policy details matter. As policymakers craft proposals and evaluate legislation, the Racial Wealth Audit will be a valuable tool for understanding how policy impacts one of the most pressing questions of our time—the nation's growing economic divergence along racial and ethnic lines.

Notes

1. Emmanuel Saez, and Gabriel Zucman, "Wealth Inequality in the United States since 1913: Evidence from Capitalized Income Tax Data," NBER Working Paper No. 20625 (2014).
2. Unless otherwise noted, all data derive from our empirical analysis of the SIPP. The words typical and median are used interchangeably throughout this paper.
3. Nathan Grawe, "Wealth and Economic Mobility," Urban Institute (2008).
4. Melvin Oliver and Thomas Shapiro, Black Wealth, White Wealth: A New Perspective on Racial Inequality (Routledge, 1997).
5. Beadsie Woo, Ida Rademacher, and Jillien Meier, "Upside Down: The $400 Billion Federal Asset-Building Budget," CFED and Annie E. Casey Foundation (2010).
6. Throughout this report, we use the term "return" to represent the estimated growth in wealth in relation to variables linked to building wealth. In the case of income, for example, "return" refers to the expected increase in wealth due to an increase in income. However, because our analysis is based on cross-sectional survey data, we cannot determine a causal relationship between these relationships nor can we predict wealth impacts over time.
7. This report analyzes data on white, Black, and Latino households. The terms Black and white are used to refer to the representative respondents of a household who identified as non-Latino Black or white in the Survey of Income and Program Participation (SIPP). Latinos include everyone who identified as Hispanic or Latino and may be of any race. Throughout this report, we use the term "racial wealth gap" to refer to the absolute differences in wealth (assets minus debt) between Black and white households as well as between Latino and white households. All dollar figures are in 2011 dollars.

   The variable used in this analysis from the SIPP is the net worth variable (THHTNW), a summation of all assets owned by a household minus unsecured debt. Assets incorporated into the wealth measure include: home equity, net equity in vehicles, real estate equity, business equity, interest earning assets, equity in stock and mutual funds, and retirement accounts, such as IRA, KEOGH, 401(k) and Thrift savings accounts.
8. Authors' analysis of Survey of Income and Program Participation (SIPP) 2008 Panel, Wave 10.
9. Thomas Shapiro, Tatjana Meschede, and Sam Osoro, "The Roots of the Widening Racial Wealth Gap: Explaining the Black–White Economic Divide," Institute on Assets on Social Policy, Brandeis University (2013).
10. Ibid.
11. Carolina Reid and Elizabeth Laderman, "The Untold Costs of Subprime Lending: Examining the Links among Higher-Priced Lending, Foreclosures and Race in California," Federal Reserve Bank of San Francisco (2009); Wilhelmina A. Leigh and Danielle Huff, "African Americans and Homeownership: The Subprime Lending Experience, 1995 to 2007," Joint Center for Political and

Economic Studies (2007); Paul S. Calem, Jonathan E. Hershaff and Susan M. Wachter, "Neighborhood Patterns of Subprime Lending: Evidence from Disparate Cities," *Housing Policy Debate* 15(3), (2004).

12. "Justice Department Reaches Settlement with Wells Fargo Resulting in More Than $175 Million in Relief for Homeowners to Resolve Fair Lending Claims," United States Department of Justice, Office of Public Affairs (2012). http://www.justice.gov/opa/pr/justice-department-reaches-settlement-wells-fargo-resulting-more-175-million-relief

13. Rakesh Kochhar, Richard Fry and Paul Taylor, "Wealth Gaps Rise to Record Highs Between Whites, Blacks, Hispanics," Pew Research Center (2011).

14. For all analyses that compare the typical wealth gains achieved by median Black, white, and Latino households, we are presenting the typical gains experienced by households at the 50th percentile of the wealth distribution of each race/ethnicity subgroup separately. Due to existing racial wealth disparities, as seen in the report, the median white household holds significantly more wealth than the median Black or Latino household; thus, the analysis compares typical households for each group, rather than households of similar wealth levels. For all analyses that compare the typical wealth gains achieved by median Black, white, and Latino households, we are presenting the typical gains experienced by households at the 50th percentile of the wealth distribution of each race/ethnicity subgroup separately. Due to existing racial wealth disparities, as seen in the report, the median white household holds significantly more wealth than the median Black or Latino household; thus, the analysis compares typical households for each group, rather than households of similar wealth levels.

15. Margery Austin Turner, Rob Santos, and Diane K. Levy et. al. "Housing Discrimination Against Racial and Ethnic Minorities 2012," U.S. Department of Housing and Urban Development (2013).

16. Demographic data measured at the individual level is provided by a reference member of the household to represent the household.

17. Eric F. Dubow, Paul Boxer, and L. Rowell Huesmann, "Long-term Effects of Parents' Education on Children's Educational and Occupational Success: Mediation by Family Interactions, Child Aggression, and Teenage Aspirations," Merrill-Palmer quarterly (Wayne State University. Press) 55.3 (2009); Sean F. Reardon, "The widening academic achievement gap between the rich and the poor: New evidence and possible explanations," in *Whither Opportunity? Rising Inequality and the Uncertain Life Chances of Low-Income Children*, ed., R. Murnane & G. Duncan (New York: Russell Sage Foundation Press, 2011).

18. Farah Z. Ahmad and Katie Hamm, "The School-Readiness Gap and Preschool Benefits for Children of Color," Center for American Progress (2013).

19. Gary Orfield, Erica Frankenberg, Jongyeon Ee and John Kuscera, "Brown at 60: Great Progress, a Long Retreat and an Uncertain Future," Civil Rights Project/Proyecto Derechos Civiles, University of California (2014).

20. Ary Spatig-Amerikaner, "Unequal Education," Center for American Progress (August 2012).

21. John Quinterno and Viany Orozco, "The Great Cost Shift: How Higher Education Cuts Undermine The Future Middle Class," Demos (2012).

22. Alisa F. Cunningham and Deborah Santiago, "Student Aversion to Borrowing: Who Borrows and Who Doesn't," Institute for Higher Education Policy and Excelencia in Education (2008).

23. Shapiro, Meschede, and Osoro Op. Cit.

24. Devah Pager, Bruce Western and Bart Bonikowski, "Race at Work: A Field Experiment of Discrimination in Low-Wage Labor Markets," paper presented at Princeton University workshop (2008); Marianne Bertrand and Sendhil Mullainathan, "Are Emily and Brendan more employable than Latoya and Tyrone? Evidence on racial discrimination in the labor market from a large randomized experiment," *American Economic Review* 94, no. 4 (2004): 991–1013.

25. Nancy DiTomaso, *The American Non-Dilemma: Racial Inequality Without Racism* (Russell Sage Foundation, 2012).

26. Sylvia A. Allegretto and Steven C. Pitts, "To Work With Dignity: The Unfinished March Toward a Decent Minimum Wage," Economic Policy Institute (2013).

27. Lawrence Mishel, "Unions, Inequality, and Faltering Middle-Class Wages," Economic Policy Institute (2012).

Questions for Critical Thinking

1. How does the authors' discussion of the wealth gap help you to understand the importance of addressing economic inequality in the United States?

2. How does your personal experience with regard to class influence your understanding of or level of disagreement with the authors' discussion?

3. The idea of the American Dream (if a person works hard, he or she will get ahead) is still common in the United States. How does this idea perpetuate misconceptions of those who are poor? Of those who are wealthy?

Media Magic

Making Class Invisible

GREGORY MANTSIOS

The mass media serve as a powerful tool for shaping the way we think. A significant part of our culture, mass media operate as an extremely important social-ization mechanism. In the following article, Gregory Mantsios explains how the media influence the values that we learn to place on members of social classes. According to Mantsios, those who control the media (i.e., the upper class) can use this institution to create class divisions and to define our attitudes about mem-bers of different social classes.

Of the various social and cultural forces in our society, the mass media is arguably the most influential in molding public consciousness. Americans spend an average twenty-eight hours per week watching television. They also spend an undetermined number of hours reading periodi-cals, listening to the radio, and going to the movies. Unlike other cultural and socializing institutions, ownership and control of the mass media is highly concentrated. Twenty-three corporations own more than one-half of all the daily newspapers, magazines, movie studios, and radio and televi-sion outlets in the United States.[1] The number of media companies is shrinking and their control of the industry is expanding. And a relatively small number of media outlets is producing and pack-aging the majority of news and entertainment programs. For the most part, our media is national in nature and single-minded (profit-oriented) in purpose. This media plays a key role in defining our cultural tastes, helping us locate ourselves in history, establishing our national identity, and as-certaining the range of national and social possi-bilities. In this essay, we will examine the way the mass media shapes how people think about each other and about the nature of our society.

The United States is the most highly stratified society in the industrialized world. Class distinc-tions operate in virtually every aspect of our lives, determining the nature of our work, the quality of our schooling, and the health and safety of our loved ones. Yet remarkably, we, as a nation, retain illusions about living in an egalitarian society. We maintain these illusions, in large part, because the media hides gross inequities from public view. In those instances when inequities are revealed, we are provided with messages that obscure the nature of class realities and blame the victims of class-dominated society for their own plight. Let's briefly examine what the news media, in particular, tells us about class.

About the Poor

The news media provides meager coverage of poor people and poverty. The coverage it does provide is often distorted and misleading.

The Poor Do Not Exist

For the most part, the news media ignores the poor. Unnoticed are forty million poor people in the nation—a number that equals the entire population of Maine, Vermont, New Hampshire, Connecticut, Rhode Island, New Jersey, and New York combined. Perhaps even more alarming is that the rate of poverty is increasing twice as fast as the population growth in the United States. Ordinarily, even a calamity of much smaller proportion (e.g., flooding in the Midwest) would garner a great deal of coverage and hype from a media usually eager to declare a crisis, yet less than one in five hundred articles in the *New York Times* and one in one thousand articles listed in the *Readers Guide to Periodic Literature* are on poverty. With remarkably little attention to them, the poor and their problems are hidden from most Americans.

When the media does turn its attention to the poor, it offers a series of contradictory messages and portrayals.

The Poor Are Faceless

Each year the Census Bureau releases a new report on poverty in our society and its results are duly reported in the media. At best, however, this coverage emphasizes annual fluctuations (showing how the numbers differ from previous years) and ongoing debates over the validity of the numbers (some argue the number should be lower, most that the number should be higher). Coverage like this desensitizes us to the poor by reducing poverty to a number. It ignores the human tragedy of poverty—the suffering, indignities, and misery endured by millions of children and adults. Instead, the poor become statistics rather than people.

The Poor Are Undeserving

When the media does put a face on the poor, it is not likely to be a pretty one. The media will provide us with sensational stories about welfare cheats, drug addicts, and greedy panhandlers (almost always urban and Black). Compare these images and the emotions evoked by them with the media's treatment of middle-class (usually white) "tax evaders," celebrities who have a "chemical dependency," or wealthy businesspeople who use unscrupulous means to "make a profit." While the behavior of the more affluent offenders is considered an "impropriety" and a deviation from the norm, the behavior of the poor is considered repugnant, indicative of the poor in general, and worthy of our indignation and resentment.

The Poor Are an Eyesore

When the media does cover the poor, they are often presented through the eyes of the middle class. For example, sometimes the media includes a story about community resistance to a homeless shelter or storekeeper annoyance with panhandlers. Rather than focusing on the plight of the poor, these stories are about middle-class opposition to the poor. Such stories tell us that the poor are an inconvenience and an irritation.

The Poor Have Only Themselves to Blame

In another example of media coverage, we are told that the poor live in a personal and cultural cycle of poverty that hopelessly imprisons them. They routinely center on the Black urban population and focus on perceived personality or cultural traits that doom the poor. While the women in these stories typically exhibit an "attitude" that leads to trouble or a promiscuity that leads to single motherhood, the men possess a need for immediate gratification that leads to drug abuse or an unquenchable greed that leads to the pursuit of fast money. The images that are seared into our mind are sexist, racist, and classist. Census figures reveal that most of the poor are white, not Black or Hispanic, that they live in rural or suburban areas, not urban centers, and hold jobs at least part of the year.[2] Yet, in a fashion that is often framed in an understanding and sympathetic tone, we are told that the poor have inflicted poverty on themselves.

The Poor Are Down on Their Luck

During the Christmas season, the news media sometimes provides us with accounts of poor individuals or families (usually white) who are down on their luck. These stories are often linked to stories about soup kitchens or other charitable activities and sometimes call for charitable contributions. These "Yule time" stories are as much about the affluent as they are about the poor: they tell us that the affluent in our society are a kind, understanding, giving people—which we are not.* The series of unfortunate circumstances that have led to impoverishment are presumed to be a temporary condition that will improve with time and a change in luck.

Despite appearances, the messages provided by the media are not entirely disparate. With each variation, the media informs us what poverty is not (i.e., systemic and indicative of American society) by informing us what it is. The media tells us that poverty is either an aberration of the American way of life (it doesn't exist, it's just another number, it's unfortunate but temporary) or an end product of the poor themselves (they are a nuisance, do not deserve better, and have brought their predicament upon themselves).

By suggesting that the poor have brought poverty upon themselves, the media is engaging in what William Ryan has called "blaming the victim."[3] The media identifies in what ways the poor are different as a consequence of deprivation, then defines those differences as the cause of poverty itself. Whether blatantly hostile or cloaked in sympathy, the message is that there is something fundamentally wrong with the victims—their hormones, psychological makeup, family environment, community, race, or some combination of these—that accounts for their plight and their failure to lift themselves out of poverty.

But poverty in the United States is systemic. It is a direct result of economic and political policies that deprive people of jobs, adequate wages, or legitimate support. It is neither natural nor inevitable: there is enough wealth in our nation to eliminate poverty if we chose to redistribute existing wealth or income. The plight of the poor is reason enough to make the elimination of poverty the nation's first priority. But poverty also impacts dramatically on the nonpoor. It has a dampening effect on wages in general (by maintaining a reserve army of unemployed and underemployed anxious for any job at any wage) and breeds crime and violence (by maintaining conditions that invite private gain by illegal means and rebellion-like behavior, not entirely unlike the urban riots of the 1960s). Given the extent of poverty in the nation and the impact it has on us all, the media must spin considerable magic to keep the poor and the issue of poverty and its root causes out of the public consciousness.

About Everyone Else

Both the broadcast and the print news media strive to develop a strong sense of "we-ness" in their audience. They seek to speak to and for an audience that is both affluent and like-minded. The media's solidarity with affluence, that is, with the middle and upper class, varies little from one medium to another. Benjamin DeMott points out, for example, that the *New York Times* understands

---

* American households with incomes of less than $10,000 give an average of 5.5 percent of their earning to charity or to a religious organization, while those making more than $100,000 a year give only 2.9 percent. After changes in the 1986 tax code reduced the benefits of charitable giving, taxpayers earning $500,000 or more slashed their average donation by nearly one-third. Furthermore, many of these acts of benevolence do not help the needy. Rather than provide funding to social service agencies that aid the poor, the voluntary contributions of the wealthy go to places and institutions that entertain, inspire, cure, or educate wealthy Americans—*art museums, opera houses*, theaters, orchestras, ballet companies, private hospitals, and elite universities. (Robert Reich, *"Secession of the Successful,"* *New York Times Magazine*, February 17, 1991, p. 43.)

affluence to be intelligence, taste, public spirit, responsibility, and a readiness to rule and "conceives itself as spokesperson for a readership awash in these qualities."[4] Of course, the flip side to creating a sense of "we," or "us," is establishing a perception of the "other." The other relates back to the faceless, amoral, undeserving, and inferior "underclass." Thus, the world according to the news media is divided between the "underclass" and everyone else. Again the messages are often contradictory.

The Wealthy Are Us

Much of the information provided to us by the news media focuses attention on the concerns of a very wealthy and privileged class of people. Although the concerns of a small fraction of the populace, they are presented as though they were the concerns of everyone. For example, while relatively few people actually own stock, the news media devotes an inordinate amount of broadcast time and print space to business news and stock market quotations. Not only do business reports cater to a particular narrow clientele, so do the fashion pages (with $2,000 dresses), wedding announcements, and the obituaries. Even weather and sports news often have a class bias. An all news radio station in New York City, for example, provides regular national ski reports. International news, trade agreements, and domestic policies issues are also reported in terms of their impact on business climate and the business community. Besides being of practical value to the wealthy, such coverage has considerable ideological value. Its message: the concerns of the wealthy are the concerns of us all.

The Wealthy (as a Class) Do Not Exist

While preoccupied with the concerns of the wealthy, the media fails to notice the way in which the rich as a class of people create and shape domestic and foreign policy. Presented as an aggregate of individuals, the wealthy appear without special interests, interconnections, or unity in purpose. Out of public view are the class interests of the wealthy, the interlocking business links, the concerted actions to preserve their class privileges and business interests (by running for public office, supporting political candidates, lobbying, etc.). Corporate lobbying is ignored, taken for granted, or assumed to be in the public interest. (Compare this with the media's portrayal of the "strong arm of labor" in attempting to defeat trade legislation that is harmful to the interests of working people.) It is estimated that two-thirds of the U.S. Senate is composed of millionaires.[5] Having such a preponderance of millionaires in the Senate, however, is perceived to be neither unusual nor anti-democratic; these millionaire senators are assumed to be serving "our" collective interests in governing.

The Wealthy Are Fascinating and Benevolent

The broadcast and print media regularly provide hype for individuals who have achieved "super" success. These stories are usually about celebrities and superstars from the sports and entertainment world. Society pages and gossip columns serve to keep the social elite informed of each others' doings, allow the rest of us to gawk at their excesses, and help to keep the American dream alive. The print media is also fond of feature stories on corporate empire builders. These stories provide an occasional "insider's" view of the private and corporate life of industrialists by suggesting a rags to riches account of corporate success. These stories tell us that corporate success is a series of smart moves, shrewd acquisitions, timely mergers, and well thought out executive suite shuffles. By painting the upper class in a positive light, innocent of any wrongdoing (labor leaders and union organizations usually get the opposite treatment), the media assures us that wealth and power are benevolent. One person's capital accumulation is presumed to be good for all. The elite, then, are portrayed as investment wizards, people of special talent and skill, whom even their victims (workers and consumers) can admire.

The Wealthy Include a Few Bad Apples

On rare occasions, the media will mock selected individuals for their personality flaws. Real estate investor Donald Trump and New York Yankees owner George Steinbrenner, for example, are admonished by the media for deliberately seeking publicity (a very un–upper class thing to do); hotel owner Leona Helmsley was caricatured for her personal cruelties; and junk bond broker Michael Milken was condemned because he had the audacity to rob the rich. Michael Parenti points out that by treating business wrongdoings as isolated deviations from the socially beneficial system of "responsible capitalism," the media overlooks the features of the system that produce such abuses and the regularity with which they occur. Rather than portraying them as predictable and frequent outcomes of corporate power and the business system, the media treats abuses as if they were isolated and atypical. Presented as an occasional aberration, these incidents serve not to challenge, but to legitimate, the system.[6]

The Middle Class Is Us

By ignoring the poor and blurring the lines between the working people and the upper class, the news media creates a universal middle class. From this perspective, the size of one's income becomes largely irrelevant: what matters is that most of "us" share an intellectual and moral superiority over the disadvantaged. As *Time* magazine once concluded, "Middle America is a state of mind."[7] "We are all middle class," we are told, "and we all share the same concerns": job security, inflation, tax burdens, world peace, the cost of food and housing, health care, clean air and water, and the safety of our streets. While the concerns of the wealthy are quite distinct from those of the middle class

(e.g., the wealthy worry about investments, not jobs), the media convinces us that "we [the affluent] are all in this together."

The Middle Class Is a Victim

For the media, "we" the affluent not only stand apart from the "other"—the poor, the working class, the minorities, and their problems—"we" are also victimized by the poor (who drive up the costs of maintaining the welfare rolls), minorities (who commit crimes against us), and by workers (who are greedy and drive companies out and prices up). Ignored are the subsidies to the rich, the crimes of corporate America, and the policies that wreak havoc on the economic well-being of middle America. Media magic convinces us to fear, more than anything else, being victimized by those less affluent than ourselves.

The Middle Class Is Not a Working Class

The news media clearly distinguishes the middle class (employees) from the working class (i.e., blue collar workers) who are portrayed, at best, as irrelevant, outmoded, and a dying breed. Furthermore, the media will tell us that the hardships faced by blue-collar workers are inevitable (due to progress), a result of bad luck (chance circumstances in a particular industry), or a product of their own doing (they priced themselves out of a job). Given the media's presentation of reality, it is hard to believe that manual, supervised, unskilled, and semiskilled workers actually represent more than 50 percent of the adult working population.[8] The working class, instead, is relegated by the media to "the other."

In short, the news media either lionizes the wealthy or treats their interests and those of the middle class as one in the same. But the upper class and the middle class do not share the same interests or worries. Members of the upper class worry about stock dividends (not employment), they profit from inflation and global militarism, their children attend exclusive private schools, they eat and live in a royal fashion, they call on (or are called upon by) personal physicians, they have few consumer problems, they can escape whenever they want from environmental pollution, and they live on streets and travel to other areas under the protection of private police forces.*⁹

The wealthy are not only a class with distinct life-styles and interests, they are a ruling class. They receive a disproportionate share of the country's yearly income, own a disproportionate amount of the country's wealth, and contribute a disproportionate number of their members to governmental bodies and decision-making groups—all traits that William Domhoff, in his classic work *Who Rules America,* defined as characteristic of a governing class.¹⁰

This governing class maintains and manages our political and economic structures in such a way that these structures continue to yield an amazing proportion of our wealth to a minuscule upper class. While the media is not above referring to ruling classes in other countries (we hear, for example, references to Japan's ruling elite),¹¹ its treatment of the news proceeds as though there were no such ruling class in the United States.

Furthermore, the news media inverts reality so that those who are working class and middle class learn to fear, resent, and blame those below, rather than those above them in the class structure. We learn to resent welfare, which accounts for only two cents out of every dollar in the federal budget (approximately $10 billion) and provides financial relief for the needy,† but learn little about the $11 billion the federal government spends on individuals with incomes in excess of $1,000,000 (not needy),¹² or the $17 billion in farm subsidies, or the $214 billion (twenty times the cost of welfare) in interest payments to financial institutions.

Middle-class whites learn to fear African Americans and Latinos, but most violent crime occurs within poor and minority communities and is neither interracial‡ nor interclass. As horrid as such crime is, it should not mask the destruction and violence perpetrated by corporate America. In spite of the fact that 14,000 innocent people are killed on the job each year, 100,000 die prematurely, 400,000 become seriously ill, and 6 million are injured from work-related accidents and diseases, most Americans fear government regulation more than they do unsafe working conditions.

Through the media, middle-class—and even working class—Americans learn to blame blue-collar workers and their unions for declining purchasing power and economic security. But while workers who managed to keep their jobs and their unions struggled to keep up with inflation, the top 1 percent of American families saw their average incomes soar 80 percent in the last decade.¹³ Much of the wealth at the top was accumulated as stockholders and corporate executives moved their companies abroad to employ cheaper labor (56 cents per hour in El Salvador) and avoid paying taxes in the United States. Corporate America is a world made up of ruthless bosses, massive layoffs, favoritism and nepotism, health and safety violations, pension plan losses, union busting, tax evasions, unfair competition, and price gouging, as well as

---

* The number of private security guards in the United States now exceeds the number of public police officers. (Robert Reich, *"Secession of the Successful,"* New York Times Magazine, February 17, 1991, p. 42.)

† A total of $20 billion is spent on welfare when you include all state funding. But the average state funding also comes to only two cents per state dollar.

‡ In 92 percent of the murders nationwide the assailant and the victim are of the same race (46 percent are white/white, 46 percent are black/black), 5.6 percent are black on white, and 2.4 percent are white on black. (FBI and Bureau of Justice Statistics, 1985–1986, quoted in Raymond S. Franklin, *Shadows of Race and Class*, University of Minnesota Press, Minneapolis, 1991, p. 108.)

fast buck deals, financial speculation, and corporate wheeling and dealing that serve the interests of the corporate elite, but are generally wasteful and destructive to workers and the economy in general.

It is no wonder Americans cannot think straight about class. The mass media is neither objective, balanced, independent, nor neutral. Those who own and direct the mass media are themselves part of the upper class, and neither they nor the ruling class in general have to conspire to manipulate public opinion. Their interest is in preserving the status quo, and their view of society as fair and equitable comes naturally to them. But their ideology dominates our society and justifies what is in reality a perverse social order—one that perpetuates unprecedented elite privilege and power on the one hand and widespread deprivation on the other. A mass media that did not have its own class interests in preserving the status quo would acknowledge that inordinate wealth and power undermines democracy and that a "free market" economy can ravage a people and their communities.

Notes

1. Martin Lee and Norman Solomon, *Unreliable Sources,* Lyle Stuart (New York, 1990), p. 71. See also Ben Bagdikian, *The Media Monopoly,* Beacon Press (Boston, 1990).
2. Department of Commerce, Bureau of the Census, "Poverty in the United States: 1992," *Current Population Reports, Consumer Income,* Series P60–185, pp. xi, xv, 1.
3. William Ryan, *Blaming the Victim,* Vintage (New York, 1971).
4. Benjamin Demott, *The Imperial Middle,* William Morrow (New York, 1990), p. 123.
5. Fred Barnes, "The Zillionaires Club," *The New Republic,* January 29, 1990, p. 24.
6. Michael Parenti, *Inventing Reality,* St. Martin's Press (New York, 1986), p. 109.
7. *Time,* January 5, 1979, p. 10.
8. Vincent Navarro, "The Middle Class—A Useful Myth," *The Nation,* March 23, 1992, p. 1.
9. Charles Anderson, *The Political Economy of Social Class,* Prentice Hall (Englewood Cliffs, N.J., 1974), p. 137.
10. William Domhoff, *Who Rules America?,* Prentice Hall (Englewood Cliffs, N.J., 1967), p. 5.
11. Lee and Solomon, *Unreliable Sources,* p. 179.
12. *Newsweek,* August 10, 1992, p. 57.
13. *Business Week,* June 8, 1992, p. 86.

Questions for Critical Thinking

1. What assumptions do you have about members of different socioeconomic classes? Does Mantsios's discussion help you to understand the sources of these assumptions?
2. How do media representations influence our understandings of the sources of economic inequality? According to these representations, who is to blame for such inequality?
3. How do media representations of class influence policies that are created to respond to economic inequality? In your opinion, do these policies effectively address the source of the problem? Why or why not?

What Trump Can and Can't Do to Immigrants

DAVID BACON

At the time of this writing, there is a heightened sense of fear in immigrant communities in the United States regarding how a new administration may impact their ability to do what many have come to this country for—to achieve the "American Dream." In the following article, author David Bacon illustrates that, while presidential administrations change, the economic system at the foundation of government policy does not. As a result, most policy responds to the interest of industry rather than that of voters, and economic inequality remains. To address the concerns of immigrant rights and economic inequality, the author argues, we will need to work for a deeper understanding and greater unity between recent immigrants and those born in the United States.

> *People make their own history, but they do not make it as they please; they do not make it under self-selected circumstances, but under circumstances existing already, given and transmitted from the past.*
> —Karl Marx, "The Eighteenth Brumaire of Louis Bonaparte," 1852

While the government officials developing and enforcing U.S. immigration policy will change on January 20, 2017, the economic system in which they make that policy will not. As fear sweeps through immigrant communities in the United States, understanding that system helps us anticipate what a Trump administration can and can't do in regard to immigrants, and what immigrants themselves can do about it.

Over the terms of the last three presidents, the most visible and threatening aspect of immigration policy has been the drastic increase in enforcement. President Bill Clinton presented anti-immigrant bills as compromises, and presided over the first big increase in border enforcement. George W. Bush used soft rhetoric, but sent immigration agents in military-style uniforms, carrying AK-47s, into workplaces to arrest workers, while threatening to fire millions for not having papers. Under President Barack Obama, a new requirement mandated filling 34,000 beds in detention centers every night. The detention system mushroomed, and over 2 million people were deported.

Enforcement, however, doesn't exist for its own sake. It plays a role in a larger system that serves capitalist economic interests by supplying a labor force employers require. High levels of enforcement also ensure the profits of companies that manage detention and enforcement, who lobby for deportations as hard as Boeing lobbies for the military budget.

Immigrant labor is more vital to many industries than it's ever been before. Immigrants have always made up most of the country's farm workers in the West and Southwest. Today, according to the U.S. Department of Labor, about 57% of the country's entire agricultural workforce is undocumented. But the list of other industries dependent on immigrant labor is long—meatpacking, some construction trades, building services, healthcare, restaurant and retail service, and more.

During the election campaign, candidate Donald Trump pledged in his "100-day action plan to Make America Great Again" to "begin removing the more than two million criminal illegal immigrants from the country" on his first day in office. In speeches, he further promised to eventually force all undocumented people (estimated at 11 million) to leave.

In a society with one of the world's highest rates of incarceration, crimes are often defined very broadly. In the past, for instance, under President George W. Bush federal prosecutors charged workers with felonies for giving a false Social Security number to an employer when being hired. He further proposed the complete enforcement of employer sanctions—the provision of the 1986 Immigration Reform and Control Act that forbids employers from hiring workers without papers. Bush's order would have had the Immigration and Customs Enforcement agency (ICE) check the immigration status of all workers, and required employers to fire those without legal immigration status, before being blocked by a suit filed by unions and civil rights organizations.

Under President Obama, workplace enforcement was further systematized. In just one year, 2012, ICE audited 1600 employers. Tens of thousands of workers were fired during Obama's eight years in office. Given Trump's choice of Alabama Senator Jeff Sessions as Attorney General, greater workplace enforcement is extremely likely. Sessions has been one of the strongest advocates in Congress for greater immigration enforcement, and has criticized President Obama for not deporting enough people. Last year he proposed a five-year prison sentence for any undocumented immigrant caught in the country after having been previously deported.

Industry Needs Immigrants

Both deportations and workplace firings face a basic obstacle—the immigrant workforce is a source of immense profit to employers. The Pew Hispanic Center estimates that, of the presumed 11 million people in the country without documents, about 8 million are employed (comprising over 5% of all workers). Most earn close to the minimum wage (some far less), and are clustered in low-wage industries. In the Indigenous Farm Worker Survey, for instance, made in 2009, demographer Rick Mines found that a third of California's 165,000 indigenous agricultural laborers (workers from communities in Mexico speaking languages that pre-date European colonization) made less than minimum wage.

The federal minimum wage is still stuck at $7.50/hour, and even California's minimum of $10/hour only gives full-time workers an annual income of $20,000. Meanwhile, Social Security says the national average wage index for 2015 is just over $48,000. In other words, if employers were paying the undocumented workforce the average U.S. wage it would cost them well over $200 billion annually. That wage differential subsidizes whole industries like agriculture and food processing. If that workforce were withdrawn, as Trump threatens, through deportations or mass firings, employers wouldn't be able to replace it without raising wages drastically.

As president, Donald Trump will have to ensure that the labor needs of employers are met, at a price they want to pay. The corporate appointees in his administration reveal that any populist rhetoric about going against big business was just that—rhetoric. But Hillary Clinton would have faced the same necessity. And in fact, the immigration reform proposals in Congress from both Republicans and Democrats over the past decade shared this understanding—that U.S. immigration policy must satisfy corporate labor demands.

During the Congressional debates over immigration reform, the Council on Foreign Relations (CFR) proposed two goals for U.S. immigration policy. In a report from the CFR-sponsored Independent Task Force on U.S. Immigration Policy, Senior Fellow Edward Alden stated, "We should reform the legal immigration system so that it operates more efficiently, responds more accurately to labor market needs, and enhances U.S. competitiveness." He went on to add, "We should restore the integrity of immigration laws, through an enforcement regime that strongly discourages employers and employees from operating outside that legal system." The CFR, therefore, coupled an enforcement regime—with deportations and firings—to a labor-supply scheme.

This framework assumes the flow of migrating people will continue, and seeks to manage it. This is a safe assumption, because the basic causes of that flow have not changed. Communities in Mexico continue to be displaced by 1) economic reforms that allowed U.S. corporations to flood the country with cheap corn and meat (often selling below the cost of production—known as "dumping"—thanks to U.S. agricultural subsidies and trade agreements like NAFTA), 2) the rapacious development of mining and other extractive concessions in the countryside, and 3) the growing impoverishment of Mexican workers. Violence plays its part, linked to the consequences of displacement, economic desperation, and mass deportations. Continuing U.S. military intervention in Central America and other developing countries will produce further waves of refugees.

While candidate Trump railed against NAFTA in order to get votes (as did Barack Obama), he cannot—and, given his ties to business, has no will to—change the basic relationship between the United States and Mexico and Central America, or other developing countries that are the sources of migration. Changing the relationship (with its impact on displacement and migration) is possible in a government committed to radical reform. Bernie Sanders might have done this. Other voices in Congress have advocated it. But Trump will do what the system wants him to do, and certainly will not implement a program of radical reform.

H-2A Guest Workers

The structures for managing the flow of migrants are already in place, and don't require Congress to pass big immigration reform bills. In Washington State alone, for instance, according to Alex Galarza of the Northwest Justice Project, the Washington Farm Labor Association brought in about 2,000 workers under the H-2A guest worker program in 2006. In 2013, the number rose to 4,000. By 2015, it grew to 11,000. In 2016, it reached 16,000. That kind of growth is taking place in all states with a sizeable agricultural workforce.

The H-2A program allows growers to recruit workers outside the country for periods of less than a year, after which they must return to their country of origin. Guest workers who lose their jobs for whatever reason—whether by offending their employer, or not working fast enough, for example—have to leave the country, so joining a union or protesting conditions is extremely risky. Growers can only use the program if they can show they can't find local workers, but the requirement is often unenforced.

The program for foreign contract labor in agriculture is only one of several like it for other industries. One study, "Visas, Inc.," by Global Workers Justice, found that over 900,000 workers were brought to the United States to work every year under similar conditions. The number is growing.

In the context of the growth of these programs, immigration enforcement fulfills an important function. It heralds a return to the *bracero* era, named for the U.S. "guest worker" program that brought millions of Mexican farmworkers to the United States between 1942 and 1964. The program was notorious for its abuse of the *braceros*, and for pitting them against workers already in the United States in labor competition and labor conflict. In 1954 alone, the United States deported over a million people—while importing 450,000 contract workers. Historically, immigration enforcement has been tied to the growth of contract labor, or "guest worker" programs.

Arresting people at the border, firing them from their jobs for not having papers, and sending people to detention centers for deportation, all push the flow of migrants into labor schemes managed to benefit corporations. The more a Trump administration pushes for deportations and internal enforcement, the more it will rely on expanding guest worker programs.

The areas where programs like H-2A are already growing were heavy Trump supporters. In eastern Washington, a heavily Trump area, immigration agents forced the huge Gebbers apple ranch to fire hundreds of undocumented workers in 2009, and then helped the employer apply for H-2A workers. While the undocumented workers of eastern Washington had good reason to fear Trump's threats, employers knew they didn't have to fear the loss of a low-wage workforce.

Deportations and workplace enforcement will have a big impact on unions and organizing rights. Immigrant workers have been the backbone of some of the most successful labor organizing of the last two decades, from Los Angeles janitors to Las Vegas hotel workers to Republic Windows and Doors in Chicago. At the same time, the use of the E-Verify database under President Obama often targeted workers active in labor campaigns like Fight for $15, as did earlier Bush and Clinton enforcement efforts.

Unions and immigrant communities have developed sophisticated tactics for resisting these attacks, and will have to use them effectively under Trump. Janitors in Minneapolis fought the firing of undocumented fast-food workers in Chipotle restaurants. The International Longshore and Warehouse Union (ILWU) teamed up with faith-based activists, immigrant-rights groups, and environmentalists to stop firings of undocumented workers in Bay Area recycling facilities, winning union representation and higher wages as a result. The same unions and community organizations that have fought enforcement in the workplace have also fought detentions and deportations.

These efforts will have to depend on more than a legal defense. The Supreme Court has already held that undocumented workers fired for organizing at work can't be rehired, and their employers don't have to pay them back pay.

Border Enforcement

Trump's threatened enforcement wave extends far beyond the workplace. He promised increased enforcement on the U.S.–Mexico border, expanding the border wall, and increasing the number of Border Patrol agents beyond the current 25,000. Immigration enforcement already costs the government more than all other federal law enforcement programs put together.

Trump proposed an End Illegal Immigration Act, imposing a two-year prison sentence on anyone who re-enters the U.S. after having been deported, and five years for anyone deported more than once. Under President Obama, the United States deported more than two million people. Hundreds of thousands, with children and families in the United States, have tried to return to them. Under this proposed law, they would fill the prisons.

One of Trump's "first day" commitments is to "cancel every unconstitutional executive action, memorandum and order issued by President Obama." This promise includes Obama's executive order giving limited, temporary legal status to undocumented youth brought to the United States by their parents (Deferred Action for Childhood Arrivals, or DACA). DACA has been attacked by the right-wing ideologues advising Trump's transition team since Obama issued his order.

The 750,000 young people who gained status under DACA—the "Dreamers"—have been one of the most active sections of the U.S. immigrant-rights movement. But they had to give the government their address and contact information in order to obtain a deferment, making them vulnerable to deportation sweeps. Defending them will likely be one of the first battles of the Trump era.

Trump further announced that on his first day in office he will "cancel all federal funding to Sanctuary Cities." More than 300 cities in the United States have adopted policies saying that they will not arrest and prosecute people solely for being undocumented.

Many cities, and even some states, have withdrawn from federal schemes, notably the infamous "287(g) program," requiring police to arrest and detain people because of their immigration status. Trump's proposed order would cancel federal funding for housing, medical care, and other social services to cities that won't cooperate. As attorney general, Sessions can be expected to try to enforce this demand. After the election, many city governments and elected officials were quick to announce that they would not be intimidated.

The Dreamers especially see direct action in the streets as an important part of defending communities. In the push for DACA, youth demonstrations around the country sought to stop deportations by sitting in front of buses carrying prisoners to detention centers. Dreamers defended young people detained for deportation, and even occupied Obama's Chicago office during his 2012 re-election campaign.

In detention centers themselves, detainees have organized hunger strikes with the support of activists camping in front of the gates. Maru Mora Villapando, one of the organizers of the hunger strikes and protests at the detention center in Tacoma, Wash., says organizers cannot just wait for Trump to begin his attacks, but have to start building up defense efforts immediately. She advocates pressuring the Obama administration to undo as much of the detention and deportation machinery as possible before leaving office. "We don't want him just to hand over the keys to this machine as it is right now," she warns.

The success of efforts to defend immigrants, especially undocumented people, depends not just on their own determination to take direct action, but on support from the broader community. In Philadelphia, less than a week after the election, Javier Flores García was given sanctuary by the congregation of the Arch Street United Methodist Church after being threatened by federal immigration agents. "Solidarity is our protection," urged the Reverend Deborah Lee of the Interfaith Movement for Human Integrity in California. "Our best defense is an organized community committed to each other and bound together with all those at risk.... We ask faith communities to consider declaring themselves 'sanctuary congregations' or 'immigrant welcoming congregations.'"

But while many workers may have supported Trump because of anger over unemployment and the fallout from trade agreements like NAFTA, they also bought his anti-immigrant political arguments. Those arguments, especially about immigrants in the workplace, even affect people on the left who opposed Trump himself. Some of those arguments have been made by Democrats, and used to justify enforcement measures like E-Verify included in "comprehensive immigration reform" bills. One union activist, Buzz Malone, wrote a piece for *In These Times* arguing for increased enforcement of employer sanctions, although he envisioned them more as harsher penalties for employers who hire the undocumented. "Imprison the employers . . . and all of it would end," he predicted. "The border crossings would fizzle out and many of the people would leave on their own."

What Is to Be Done?

To defeat the Trump enforcement wave, immigrant activists in unions and communities will have to fight for deeper understanding and greater unity between immigrants and U.S.-born people. Workers in general need to see that people in Mexico got hit by NAFTA even harder than people in the U.S. Midwest—and their displacement and migration isn't likely to end soon. In a diverse workforce, the unity needed to defend a union or simply win better conditions depends on fighting for a country and workplace where everyone has equal rights. For immigrant workers, the most basic right is simply the right to stay. Defending that right means not looking the other way when a coworker, a neighbor or a friend is threatened with firing, deportation, or worse.

The rise of a Trump enforcement wave spells the death of the liberal centrism that proposed trading increased enforcement and labor supply programs for a limited legalization of undocumented people. Under Trump, the illusion that there is some kind of "fair" enforcement of employer sanctions and "smart border enforcement" will be stripped away. Sessions will have no interest in "humane detention," with codes of conduct for the private corporations running detention centers. The idea of guest worker programs that don't exploit immigrants or set them against workers already in the United States will face the reality of an administration bent on giving employers what they want.

So in one way the Trump administration presents an opportunity as well—to fight for the goals immigrant rights advocates have historically proposed, to counter inequality, economic exploitation, and the denial of rights. As Sergio Sosa, director of the Heartland Workers Center in Omaha, Nebr., puts it, "we have to go back to the social teachings our movement is based on—to the idea of justice."

References

"Donald Trump's Contract with the American Voter" (donaldjtrump.com); Chico Harlan, "The private prison industry was crashing—until Donald Trump's victory," Wonkblog, *Washington Post*, Nov. 10, 2016 (washingtonpost.com); U.S. Immigration and Customs Enforcement, "Delegation of Immigration Authority Section 287(g) Immigration and Nationality Act" (ice.gov); Interfaith Movement for Human Integrity (im4humanintegrity.org); Community Initiatives for Visiting Immigrants in Confinement, "End the Quota" (endisolation.org); Jens Manuel Krogstad, Jeffrey S. Passel, and D'Vera Cohn, "Five facts about illegal immigration in the U.S.," Pew Research Center, Nov. 3, 2016 (pewresearch.org); Bureau of Labor Statistics, "Foreign-Born Workers: Labor Force Characteristics, 2016," May 19, 2016 (bls.gov); Jie Zong and Jeanne Batalova, "Frequently Requested Statistics on Immigrants and Immigration in the United States," Migration Information Service, April 14, 2016 (migrationpolicy.org); "Selected Statistics on Farmworkers," Farmworker Justice, 2014 (farmworkerjustice.org); "Indigenous Mexicans in California Agriculture," Indigenous Farmworker Study (indigenousfarmworkers.org); "U.S. Immigration Policy Task Force Report," Council on Foreign Relations, August 2009 (cfr.org); "Visas, Inc.: Corporate Control and Policy Incoherence in the U.S. Temporary Foreign Labor System," Global Workers Justice Alliance, May 31, 2012 (globalworkers.org); "H-2A Temporary Agricultural Workers," U.S. Citizenship and Immigration Services (uscis.gov); Buzz Malone, "Stop Blaming Immigrants and Start Punishing the Employers Who Exploit Them," Working *In These Times*, Nov. 15, 2016 (inthesetimes.com); David Bacon, *Illegal People* (Beacon Press, 2008); David Bacon, *The Right to Stay Home* (Beacon Press, 2013); David Bacon, author interviews with Alex Galarza, Maru Mora Villapando, Deborah Lee, and Sergio Sosa (2016); Mae M. Ngai, *Impossible Subjects: Illegal Aliens and the Making of Modern America* (Princeton University Press, 2004); Ronald L. Mize and Alicia C. Swords, *Consuming Mexican Labor: From the Bracero Program to NAFTA* (University of Toronto Press, 2010).

Questions for Critical Thinking

1. How does Bacon's discussion of immigration policy and its enforcement impact your understanding of this issue?
2. As the author discusses, strict enforcement of immigration law would have a profound effect on our economy. What would be the impact on consumers if there were suddenly fewer immigrant workers?
3. What changes are necessary to immigrant policy in the United States that would counter the inequality and economic exploitation often faced by immigrant workers?

The Social Construction of Gender

JUDITH LORBER

In the following essay, sociologist and gender scholar Judith Lorber describes how the process of gender identity construction begins at birth with placement within a sex category (male or female). As Lorber clearly explains, gender constructs are created and justified by a variety of institutions, including the family, the state, and the economy, thereby transforming them into a gender system in which men and masculinity are at the top of the hierarchy and women and femininity are at the bottom.

Talking about gender for most people is the equivalent of fish talking about water. Gender is so much the routine ground of everyday activities that questioning its taken-for-granted assumptions and presuppositions is like thinking about whether the sun will come up.[1] Gender is so pervasive that in our society we assume it is bred into our genes. Most people find it hard to believe that gender is constantly created and re-created out of human interaction, out of social life, and is the texture and order of that social life. Yet gender, like culture, is a human production that depends on everyone constantly "doing gender" (West and Zimmerman 1987).

And everyone "does gender" without thinking about it. Today, on the subway, I saw a well-dressed man with a year-old child in a stroller. Yesterday, on a bus, I saw a man with a tiny baby in a carrier on his chest. Seeing men taking care of small children in public is increasingly common—at least in New York City. But both men were quite obviously stared at—and smiled at, approvingly. Everyone was doing gender—the men who were changing the role of fathers and the other passengers, who were applauding them silently. But there was more gendering going on that probably fewer people noticed. The baby was wearing a white crocheted cap and white clothes. You couldn't tell if it was a boy or a girl. The child in the stroller was wearing a dark blue T-shirt and dark print pants. As they started to leave the train, the father put a Yankee baseball cap on the child's head. Ah, a boy, I thought. Then I noticed the gleam of tiny earrings in the child's ears, and as they got off, I saw the little flowered sneakers and lace-trimmed socks. Not a boy after all. Gender done.

Gender is such a familiar part of daily life that it usually takes a deliberate disruption of our expectations of how women and men are supposed to act to pay attention to how it is produced. Gender signs and signals are so ubiquitous that we usually fail to note them—unless they are missing or ambiguous. Then we are uncomfortable until we have successfully placed the other person in a gender status; otherwise, we feel socially dislocated. In our society, in addition to man and woman, the status can be *transvestite* (a person who dresses in

Excerpted from Paradoxes of Gender, by Judith Lorber, pp. 13–15, 32–36. Reprinted with permission of Yale University Press. © 1994.

opposite-gender clothes) and *transsexual* (a person who has had sex-change surgery). Transvestites and transsexuals construct their gender status by dressing, speaking, walking, gesturing in the ways prescribed for women or men—whichever they want to be taken for—and so does any "normal" person.

For the individual, gender construction starts with assignment to a sex category on the basis of what the genitalia look like at birth.[2] Then babies are dressed or adorned in a way that displays the category because parents don't want to be constantly asked whether their baby is a girl or a boy. A sex category becomes a gender status through naming, dress, and the use of other gender markers. Once a child's gender is evident, others treat those in one gender differently from those in the other, and the children respond to the different treatment by feeling different and behaving differently. As soon as they can talk, they start to refer to themselves as members of their gender. Sex doesn't come into play again until puberty, but by that time, sexual feelings and desires and practices have been shaped by gendered norms and expectations. Adolescent boys and girls approach and avoid each other in an elaborately scripted and gendered mating dance. Parenting is gendered, with different expectations for mothers and for fathers, and people of different genders work at different kinds of jobs. The work adults do as mothers and fathers and as low-level workers and high-level bosses, shapes women's and men's life experiences, and these experiences produce different feelings, consciousness, relationships, skills—ways of being that we call feminine or masculine.[3] All of these processes constitute the social construction of gender.

Gendered roles change—today fathers are taking care of little children, girls and boys are wearing unisex clothing and getting the same education, women and men are working at the same jobs. Although many traditional social groups are quite strict about maintaining gender differences, in other social groups they seem to be blurring. Then why the one-year-old's earrings? Why is it still so important to mark a child as a girl or a

boy, to make sure she is not taken for a boy or he for a girl? What would happen if they were? They would, quite literally, have changed places in their social world.

To explain why gendering is done from birth, constantly and by everyone, we have to look not only at the way individuals experience gender but at gender as a social institution. As a social institution, gender is one of the major ways that human beings organize their lives. Human society depends on a predictable division of labor, a designated allocation of scarce goods, assigned responsibility for children and others who cannot care for themselves, common values and their systematic transmission to new members, legitimate leadership, music, art, stories, games, and other symbolic productions. One way of choosing people for the different tasks of society is on the basis of their talents, motivations, and competence—their demonstrated achievements. The other way is on the basis of gender, race, ethnicity—ascribed membership in a category of people. Although societies vary in the extent to which they use one or the other of these ways of allocating people to work and to carry out other responsibilities, every society uses gender and age grades. Every society classifies people as "girl and boy children," "girls and boys ready to be married," and "fully adult women and men," constructs similarities among them and differences between them, and assigns them to different roles and responsibilities. Personality characteristics, feelings, motivations, and ambitions flow from these different life experiences so that the members of these different groups become different kinds of people. The process of gendering and its outcome are legitimated by religion, law, science, and the society's entire set of values.

Gender as Process, Stratification, and Structure

As a social institution, gender is a process of creating distinguishable social statuses for the assignment of rights and responsibilities. As part of a stratification system that ranks these statuses unequally, gender is a major building block in the social structures built on these unequal statuses.

As a *process,* gender creates the social differences that define "woman" and "man." In social interaction throughout their lives, individuals learn what is expected, see what is expected, act and react in expected ways, and thus simultaneously construct and maintain the gender order: "The very injunction to be given gender takes place through discursive routes: to be a good mother, to be a heterosexually desirable object, to be a fit worker, in sum, to signify a multiplicity of guarantees in response to a variety of different demands all at once" (J. Butler 1990, 145). Members of a social group neither make up gender as they go along nor exactly replicate in rote fashion what was done before. In almost every encounter, human beings produce gender, behaving in the ways they learned were appropriate for their gender status, or resisting or rebelling against these norms. Resistance and rebellion have altered gender norms, but so far they have rarely eroded the statuses.

Gendered patterns of interaction acquire additional layers of gendered sexuality, parenting, and work behaviors in childhood, adolescence, and adulthood. Gendered norms and expectations are enforced through informal sanctions of gender-inappropriate behavior by peers and by formal punishment or threat of punishment by those in authority should behavior deviate too far from socially imposed standards for women and men.

Everyday gendered interactions build gender into the family, the work process, and other organizations and institutions, which in turn reinforce gender expectations for individuals.[4] Because gender is a process, there is room not only for modification and variation by individuals and small groups but also for institutionalized change (J. W. Scott 1988, 7).

As part of a *stratification* system, gender ranks men above women of the same race and class. Women and men could be different but equal. In practice, the process of creating difference depends to a great extent on differential evaluation.

As Nancy Jay (1981) says: "That which is defined, separated out, isolated from all else is A and pure. Not-A is necessarily impure, a random catchall, to which nothing is external except A and the principle of order that separates it from Not-A" (45). From the individual's point of view, whichever gender is A, the other is Not-A; gender boundaries tell the individual who is like him or her, and all the rest are unlike. From society's point of view, however, one gender is usually the touchstone, the normal, the dominant, and the other is different, deviant, and subordinate. In Western society, "man" is A, "woman" is Not-A. (Consider what a society would be like where woman was A and man Not-A.)

The further dichotomization by race and class constructs the gradations of a heterogeneous society's stratification scheme. Thus, in the United States, white is A, African American is Not-A; middle class is A, working class is Not-A, and "African-American women occupy a position whereby the inferior half of a series of these dichotomies converge" (P. H. Collins 1990). The dominant categories are the hegemonic ideals, taken so for granted as the way things should be that white is not ordinarily thought of as a race, middle class as a class, or men as a gender. The characteristics of these categories define the Other as that which lacks the valuable qualities the dominants exhibit.

In a gender-stratified society, what men do is usually valued more highly than what women do because men do it, even when their activities are very similar or the same. In different regions of southern India, for example, harvesting rice is men's work, shared work, or women's work: "Wherever a task is done by women it is considered easy, and where it is done by [men] it is considered difficult" (Mencher 1988, 104). A gathering and hunting society's survival usually depends on the nuts, grubs, and small animals brought in by the women's foraging trips, but when the men's hunt is successful, it is the occasion for a celebration. Conversely, because they are the superior group, white men do not have to do the "dirty work," such as housework; the most inferior group does it, usually poor women of color (Palmer 1989).

Freudian psychoanalytic theory claims that boys must reject their mothers and deny the feminine in themselves in order to become men: "For boys the major goal is the achievement of personal masculine identification with their father and sense of secure masculine self, achieved through superego formation and disparagement of women" (Chodorow 1978, 165). Masculinity may be the outcome of boys' intrapsychic struggles to separate their identity from that of their mothers, but the proofs of masculinity are culturally shaped and usually ritualistic and symbolic (Gilmore 1990).

The Marxist feminist explanation for gender inequality is that by demeaning women's abilities and keeping them from learning valuable technological skills, bosses preserve them as a cheap and exploitable reserve army of labor. Unionized men who could easily be replaced by women collude in this process because it allows them to monopolize the better-paid, more interesting, and more autonomous jobs: "Two factors emerge as helping men maintain their separation from women and their control of technological occupations. One is the active gendering of jobs and people. The second is the continual creation of sub-divisions in the work processes, and levels in work hierarchies, into which men can move in order to keep their distance from women" (Cockburn 1985, 13).

Societies vary in the extent of the inequality in social status of their women and men members, but where there is inequality, the status "woman" (and its attendant behavior and role allocations) is usually held in lesser esteem than the status "man." Since gender is also intertwined with a society's other constructed statuses of differential evaluation—race, religion, occupation, class, country of origin, and so on—men and women members of the favored groups command more power, more prestige, and more property than the members of the disfavored groups. Within many social groups, however, men are advantaged over women. The more economic resources, such as education

and job opportunities, are available to a group, the more they tend to be monopolized by men. In poorer groups that have few resources (such as working-class African Americans in the United States), women and men are more nearly equal, and the women may even outstrip the men in education and occupational status (Almquist 1987).

As a *structure*, gender divides work in the home and in economic production, legitimates those in authority, and organizes sexuality and emotional life (Connell 1987, 91–142). As primary parents, women significantly influence children's psychological development and emotional attachments, in the process reproducing gender. Emergent sexuality is shaped by heterosexual, homosexual, bisexual, and sadomasochistic patterns that are gendered—different for girls and boys, and for women and men—so that sexual statuses reflect gender statuses.

When gender is a major component of structured inequality, the devalued genders have less power, prestige, and economic rewards than the valued genders. In countries that discourage gender discrimination, many major roles are still gendered; women still do most of the domestic labor and child rearing, even while doing full-time paid work; women and men are segregated on the job and each does work considered "appropriate"; women's work is usually paid less than men's work. Men dominate the positions of authority and leadership in government, the military, and the law; cultural productions, religions, and sports reflect men's interests.

In societies that create the greatest gender difference, such as Saudi Arabia, women are kept out of sight behind walls or veils, have no civil rights, and often create a cultural and emotional world of their own (Bernard 1981). But even in societies with less rigid gender boundaries, women and men spend much of their time with people of their own gender because of the way work and family are organized. This spatial separation of women and men reinforces gendered differences, identity, and ways of thinking and behaving (Coser 1986).

Gender inequality—the devaluation of "women" and the social domination of "men"—has social functions and social history. It is not the result of sex, procreation, physiology, anatomy, hormones, or genetic predispositions. It is produced and maintained by identifiable social processes and built into the general social structure and individual identities deliberately and purposefully. The social order as we know it in Western societies is organized around racial, ethnic, class, and gender inequality. I contend, therefore, that the continuing purpose of gender as a modern social institution is to construct women as a group to be the subordinates of men as a group.

The Paradox of Human Nature

To say that sex, sexuality, and gender are all socially constructed is not to minimize their social power. These categorical imperatives govern our lives in the most profound and pervasive ways, through the social experiences and social practices of what Dorothy Smith calls the "everday/evernight world" (1990). The paradox of human nature is that it is *always* a manifestation of cultural meanings, social relationships, and power politics; "not biology, but culture, becomes destiny" (J. Butler 1990, 8). Gendered people emerge not from physiology or sexual orientations but from the exigencies of the social order, mostly from the need for a reliable division of the work of food production and the social (not physical) reproduction of new members. The moral imperatives of religion and cultural representations guard the boundary lines among genders and ensure that what is demanded, what is permitted, and what is tabooed for the people in each gender is well known and followed by most (C. Davies 1982). Political power, control of scarce resources, and, if necessary, violence uphold the gendered social order in the face of resistance and rebellion. Most people, however, voluntarily go along with their society's prescriptions for those of their gender status, because the norms and expectations get built into their sense of worth and identity as [the way we] think, the way we see and hear and speak, the way we fantasy, and the way we feel.

There is no core or bedrock in human nature below these endlessly looping processes of the social production of sex and gender, self and other, identity and psyche, each of which is a "complex cultural construction" (J. Butler 1990, 36). *For humans, the social is the natural.* Therefore, "in its feminist senses, gender cannot mean simply the cultural appropriation of biological sexual difference. Sexual difference is itself a fundamental—and scientifically contested—construction. Both 'sex' and 'gender' are woven of multiple, asymmetrical strands of difference, charged with multifaceted dramatic narratives of domination and struggle" (Haraway 1990, 140).

Notes

1. Gender is, in Erving Goffman's words, an aspect of *Felicity's Condition:* "any arrangement which leads us to judge an individual's . . . acts not to be a manifestation of strangeness. Behind Felicity's Condition is our sense of what it is to be sane" (1983:27). Also see Bem 1993; Frye 1983, 17–40; Goffman 1977.
2. In cases of ambiguity in countries with modern medicine, surgery is usually performed to make the genitalia more clearly male or female.
3. See J. Butler 1990 for an analysis of how doing gender is gender identity.
4. On the "logic of practice," or how the experience of gender is embedded in the norms of everyday interaction and the structure of formal organizations, see Acker 1990; Bourdieu [1980] 1990; Connell 1987; Smith 1987.

References

Acker, Joan. 1990. "Hierarchies, jobs, and bodies: A theory of gendered organizations," *Gender & Society* 4: 139–58.

Almquist, Elizabeth M. 1987. "Labor market gendered inequality in minority groups," *Gender & Society* 1: 400–14.

Bem, Sandara Lipsitz. 1993. *The Lenses of Gender: Transforming the Debate on Sexual Inequality.* New Haven: Yale University Press.

Bernard, Jessie. 1981. *The Female World*. New York: Free Press.

Bourdieu, Pierre. [1980] 1990. *The Logic of Practice*. Stanford, Calif.: Stanford University Press.

Butler, Judith. 1990. *Gender Trouble: Feminism and the Subversion of Identity*. New York and London: Routledge.

Chodorow, Nancy. 1978. *The Reproduction of Mothering*. Berkeley: University of California Press.

Cockburn, Cynthia. 1985. *Machinery of Dominance: Women, Men and Technical Know-how*. London: Pluto Press.

Collins, Patricia Hill. 1990. "The social construction of black feminist thought," *Signs* 14: 745–73.

Connell, R. [Robert] W. 1987. *Gender and Power: Society, the Person, and Sexual Politics*. Stanford, Calif.: Stanford University Press.

Coser, Rose Laub. 1986. "Cognitive structure and the use of social space," *Sociological Forum* 1: 1–26.

Davies, Christie. 1982. "Sexual taboos and social boundaries," *American Journal of Sociology* 87: 1032–63.

Dwyer, Daisy, and Judith Bruce (eds.). 1988. *A Home Divided: Women and Income in the Third World*. Palo Alto, Calif.: Stanford University Press.

Frye, Marilyn. 1983. *The Politics of Reality: Essays in Feminist Theory*. Trumansburg, N.Y.: Crossing Press.

Gilmore, David D. 1990. *Manhood in the Making: Cultural Concepts of Masculinity*. New Haven: Yale University Press.

Goffman, Erving. 1977. "The arrangement between the sexes," *Theory and Society* 4: 301–33.

Haraway, Donna. 1990. "Investment strategies for the evolving portfolio of primate females," in Jacobus, Keller, and Shuttleworth.

Jacobus, Mary, Evelyn Fox Keller, and Sally Shuttleworth (eds.). (1990). *Body/politics: Women and the Discourse of Science*. New York and London: Routledge.

Jay, Nancy. 1981. "Gender and dichotomy," *Feminist Studies* 7: 38–56.

Mencher, Joan. 1988. "Women's work and poverty: Women's contribution to household maintenance in South India," in Dwyer and Bruce.

Palmer, Phyllis. 1989. *Domesticity and Dirt: Housewives and Domestic Servants in the United States, 1920–1945*. Philadelphia: Temple University Press.

Scott, Joan Wallach. 1988. *Gender and the Politics of History*. New York: Columbia University Press.

Smith, Dorothy. 1987. *The Everyday World as Problematic: A Feminist Sociology*. Toronto: University of Toronto Press.

———. 1990. *The Conceptual Practices of Power: A Feminist Sociology of Knowledge*. Toronto: University of Toronto Press.

West, Candace, and Don Zimmerman. 1987. "Doing gender." *Gender & Society* 1: 125–51.

Questions for Critical Thinking

1. In what ways do you see yourself "doing gender"?

2. Lorber argues that gender is a social rather than a biological construct, yet the dominant notion in our society is that gender is linked to biological factors. What do you see as the reasoning behind assertions that gender is biological? What would be the implications of accepting the notion that gender is socially constructed and therefore mutable?

3. Lorber discusses many reasons why a culture maintains constructions of gender differences. What are your own ideas regarding why we maintain such constructs?

Square Pegs

Affronting Reason

CHERYL CHASE

The next essay in this section recounts the experiences of Cheryl Chase, who learned as an adult that she was born intersexual. Her story illustrates the personal impact of the institutions of science and medicine in constructing a reality in which there is only room for two sexes.

"It seems that your parents weren't sure for a time whether you were a girl or a boy," Dr. Christen explained, as she handed me three, fuzzy, photostatted pages. I was twenty-one years old and had asked her to help me obtain records of a hospitalization that had occurred when I was a year and a half old, too young for me to recall. I was desperate to obtain the complete records, to determine who had surgically removed my clitoris, and why. I wanted to know against whom my rage should be directed. "Diagnosis: true hermaphrodite. Operation: clitorectomy." The hospital record showed Charlie admitted, age eighteen months. His typewritten name had been crudely crossed out and "Cheryl" scribbled over it.

Though I recall clearly the scene of Dr. Christen handing me the records and dismissing me from her office, I can recall nothing of my emotional reaction. How is it possible that I could be a *hermaphrodite?* The hermaphrodite is a mythological creature. I am a woman, a lesbian woman, though I lack a clitoris and inner labia. What did my genitals look like before the surgery? Was I born with a penis?

Fifteen years of emotional numbness passed before I was able to seek the answers to these and many other questions. Then, four years ago, extreme emotional turmoil and suicidal despair arrived suddenly, threatening to crush me. "It's not possible," I thought. "This cannot be anyone's story, much less mine. I don't want it." Yet it *is* mine. I mark that time as the beginning of my coming out as a political intersexual, an "avowed intersexual," to borrow the epithet that until recently adhered to homosexuals who refused to stay invisible.

The story of my childhood is a lie. I know now that after the clitorectomy my parents followed the physicians' advice and discarded every scrap of evidence that Charlie had ever existed. They replaced all of the blue baby clothing with pink and discarded photos and birthday cards. When I look at grandparents, aunts, uncles, I am aware that they must know that one day Charlie ceased to exist in my family, and Cheryl was there in his place.

The medical establishment uses the terms *hermaphrodite* and *intersexual* to refer to us. The word hermaphrodite, with its strong mythological associations, reinforces the notion that hermaphroditism is a fantasy, not your neighbor, your friend, your teacher, or—especially—your baby. And, because it falsely implies that one individual possesses two sets of genitals, it allows my clitoris to be labeled as a penis and the clitorectomy performed on me to be justified as "reconstructive surgery." For these reasons, I prefer the term intersexual. Kira Triea, one of many who has joined me in speaking openly about her intersexuality, also feels strongly about this point. "It irks me so when I am trying to explain to someone who I am, what my experience has been, and they begin to quote Ovid to me." For Triea—an intersexual assigned male at birth, raised as a boy, who began to menstruate through her penis at puberty, and who now lives as a lesbian-identified woman—hermaphroditism is a real presence in her life every day; she need not look to poetry penned in Latin two millennia ago.

At the beginning of my process of coming out as intersexual, I chose to examine again the three pages of medical records that I had set aside for fifteen years. The word "hermaphrodite" was horribly wounding; it drove me to the brink of suicide. I thought back to my earlier process of coming out as lesbian. The way out of this pain was to reclaim the stigmatized label, to manufacture a positive acceptance of it. This second coming out was far more painful and difficult. As a teenager recognizing my attraction to women, I visited the library, stealthily examined Del Martin and Phyllis Lyon's *Lesbian/ Woman* (1991) and Radclyffe Hall's *The Well of Loneliness* (1990). I learned that other lesbians existed, that they somehow managed to live and to love women. Somehow I would find them; there was a community where my lesbianism would be understood and welcome. No such help was available to reclaim my intersexuality. The only images I found were absolutely pathologized case histories in medical texts and journals, closeups of genitals being poked, prodded, measured, sliced, and sutured, full body shots with the eyes blacked out.

For many months, I struggled to reclaim the label "hermaphrodite." I knew that I had been horribly mutilated by the clitorectomy, deprived of the experience of sexuality that most people, male

or female, take for granted. What would my life be had I been allowed to keep my genitals intact? "No," I thought. "I don't wish to have a penis between my legs, for my body to look like a man's body. I could never relate sexually to a woman as if I were a man." The physicians who removed my clitoris considered instead performing a long series of surgeries to make my genitals look more male, to support the male sex assignment rather than changing it to female. Though I can offer little evidence to support the idea, I am convinced that, had I been kept male, I would now be a gay man.

"Never mind, just don't think about it," was the advice of the few people to whom I spoke, including two female therapists: "You look like a woman." There is a powerful resistance to thinking about intersex. Because they look at me and make a female attribution, most people find it impossible to imagine that my experience and my history are not female. The resistance to thinking about what my sexual experience might be is even more profound. Most people, including the two therapists mentioned above, are paralyzed by the general prohibition on explicit sex talk. But sex radicals and activists are little better. They assume that I am having "vaginal orgasms" or even "full-body orgasms." If I persist in asserting my sexual dysfunction, many patronize me. "I am completely confident that you will learn how to orgasm," one man told me, then continued his explanation of how male circumcision was just as damaging as clitorectomy, my experience to the contrary.

What is most infuriating is to read, nearly every day in popular media, denunciations of African female genital mutilation as barbaric abuses of human rights, which fail to mention that intersexed children's clitorises are removed every day in the United States. Such writers occasionally note that clitorectomy has been practiced in the United States but always hurry to assure the reader that the practice ended by the 1930s. Letters to these authors receive no reply. Letters to editors pointing out the inaccuracy are not published. In 1996, Congress passed H.R. 3610 (Department of

Defense Appropriations Act), prohibiting "the removal or infibulation (or both) of the whole or part of the clitoris, the labia minor, or the labia major" (p. H11829). However, the next paragraph specifically excludes from prohibition these operations if they are performed by a licensed medical practitioner who deems them necessary. As early as 1993, Brown University Professor of Medical Science Anne Fausto-Sterling had joined intersexuals to ask Congresswoman Pat Schroeder, in drafting the prohibition, not to neglect genital surgery performed on intersexed infants. Ms. Schroeder's office made no reply. Newspaper accounts in 1996 lauded the bill's passage as an end to clitorectomy in the United States.

It took months for me to obtain the rest of my medical records. I learned that I had been born, not with a penis, but with intersexed genitals: a typical vagina and outer labia, female urethra, and a very large clitoris. Mind you, "large" and "small," as applied to intersexed genitals, are judgments that exist only in the mind of the beholder. From my birth until the surgery, while I was Charlie, my parents and doctors considered my penis to be monstrously small, and with the urethra in the "wrong" position. My parents were so ashamed and traumatized by the appearance of my genitals that they allowed no one to see them—no baby-sitters, no possibility of tired parents being spelled for diaper-changing by a helpful grandmother or aunt. Then, in the moment that intersex specialist physicians pronounced that my "true sex" was female, my clitoris was suddenly monstrously large. All this occurred without any change in the objective size or appearance of the appendage between my legs.

Intersex is a humanly possible but (in our culture) socially unthinkable phenomenon. In modern industrial cultures, when a child is born, the experts present, whether midwives or physicians, assign a sex based on the appearance of the infant's genitals. They are required—both legally and by social custom—to assign the child as either male or female. Were parents to tell inquiring friends and relatives that their newborn's sex was "hermaphrodite," they

would be greeted with sheer disbelief. Should the parents persist in labeling their child "hermaphrodite" rather than "male or female with a congenital deformity requiring surgical repair," their very sanity would be called into question.

Thus, intersexed children are always assigned to either male or female sex. In making these problematic sex assignments, specialist physicians are generally consulted; the assignment may not be made for several days, and it is sometimes changed, as was done with me. In fact, there are documented cases in which the sex assignment has been changed without soliciting the opinion of or even *informing* the child, as many as three times.[1] Most people take for granted, even assume as "scientific fact," that there are two, and only two, sexes. In reality, however, about one in two thousand infants is born with an anatomy that refuses to conform to our preconceptions of "male" and "female." Few outside the medical profession are even aware of our existence. I now know that hundreds of thousands of people in the United States alone share my experience, and we are organizing ourselves through the Intersex Society of North America.[2] My ability to embrace the term hermaphrodite, at first halting and uncertain, has grown in depth, conviction, and pride, as I have met other intersexuals; we have shared our stories, our lives, and our anger.

Struggling to understand why society so utterly denies the phenomenon of intersexuality, I read widely in such diverse fields as philosophy, history, psychology, and ethnography. I was excited to discover that in recent years a number of scholars in these fields have begun to examine the ways in which sex and gender are socially constructed (Butler, 1990; Foucault, 1980b; Kessler and McKenna, 1978; Laqueur, 1990; Vance, 1991). These and related works constitute a recognition that the paradigms of previous investigators have caused them to overlook information about nonreproductive sexual conduct, practices, and categories. Data that were at odds with their culturally determined, heterosexist, dimorphic point of view were ignored because they could not be accounted for.

In many other cultures, however, the phenomenon of intersexuality is well known, and an intersexed child may be recognized and assigned as such at birth. Unfortunately, interpretations by ethnographers have been straightjacketed by the absolute sexual dualism that has dominated Western thinking since Darwin. Recently though, ethnographers have given us examples of cultures in which intersexual assignment confers high status, low status, or even condemns an infant to death by exposure, as an evil omen (Edgerton, 1964; Furth, 1993; Herdt, 1994; Nanda, 1994; Roscoe, 1991). The Jewish Talmud discusses hermaphrodites in many locations and lays out regulations governing matrimony, priesthood, inheritance, and other matters for intersexuals (Berlin and Zevin, 1974). The Talmudic sages held variously that the hermaphrodite was: of uncertain sex, but in some essential way actually either male or female; part male and part female; definitely male, but only in respect to certain laws. And, in an eerie echo of modern medical practice, one Talmudic writer even differentiates the hermaphrodite, whose sex can never be resolved, from the *Tumtum,* whose sex is ascertainable through surgery.

Americans, though, are apt to express disbelief when confronted with evidence of intersexuality. Modern Western culture is the first to rely upon technology to *enforce* gender dichotomy: since the 1950s or so, surgical and hormonal means have been used to erase the evidence from intersexed infants' bodies. Medical literature speaks with one voice on the necessity of this practice, even when it concedes that surgical intervention may damage sexual function (Conte and Grumbach, 1989; Emans and Goldstein, 1990; Hendricks, 1993). Silence has been considered evidence of patient satisfaction.

For over forty years, some form of clitorectomy or clitoroplasty has been used to treat little girls with adrenogenital syndrome (one of dozens of reasons why an infant may be born intersexed). The only indication for performing this surgery has been to improve the body image of these children so that they feel "more normal" . . .*Not one has complained of loss of sensation even when the entire clitoris was removed. . . . The clitoris is clearly not necessary for orgasm* (Edgerton, 1993, p. 956).[3]

What are genitals for? It is my position that *my* genitals are for *my* pleasure. In a sex-repressive culture with a heavy investment in the fiction of sexual dichotomy, infant genitals are for discriminating male from female infants. It is very difficult to get parents, or even physicians, to consider the infant as a future adult and sexual being. Medical intersex specialists, however, pride themselves on being able to do just that.

For intersex specialists, male genitals are for active penetration and pleasure, while female genitals are for passive penetration and reproduction: men have sex; women have babies. Asked by a journalist why standard practice assigns 90 percent of intersexed infants as females (and surgically enforces the assignment by trimming or removing the clitoris), one prominent surgical specialist reasoned, "you can make a hole, but you can't build a pole" (Hendricks, 1993, p. 15). Notice how John Gearhart, a noted specialist in genital surgery for intersex children, evades questioning about orgasmic function following the presentation of his paper on additional surgeries for repair of vaginas surgically constructed in intersexed infants. (Dr. Frank, in attendance at the presentation, shares a professional interest in such surgery; the discussion was published in the *Journal of Urology* along with the paper.)

> DR. FRANK: How do you define successful intercourse? How many of these girls actually have an orgasm, for example? How many of these had a clitorectomy, how many a clitoroplasty, and did it make any difference to orgasm?
>
> DR. GEARHART: Interviews with the families were performed by a female pediatric surgeon who is kind and caring, and who I think got the maximum information from these patients. Adequate intercourse was defined as successful vaginal penetration. . . . (Bailez et al., 1992, p. 684)

Gearhart has since condemned outspoken intersexed adults as "zealots" (Angier, 1996, p. E14), and minimized reports by former patients of damaged sexual function after clitoral surgery because "some women who have never had surgery are anorgasmic" (Chase, 1996, p. 1140).

Intersex specialists often stress the importance of a heterosexual outcome for the intersexed children consigned to their care. For instance, Slijper and colleagues state, "parents will feel reassured when they know that their daughter can develop heterosexually just like other children" (Slijper et al., 1994, p. 15). Dr. Y, a prominent surgeon in the field of intersexuality, agreed to be interviewed by Ellen Lee only under condition of anonymity. He asserts that the ultimate measure of success for sex assignment of intersexed children is the "effectiveness of intercourse" they achieve as adults (Lee, 1994, p. 60). Intersexuals assigned female who choose women as sexual partners, and those assigned male who choose men as sexual partners, must then represent failures of treatment in the eyes of our parents and of intersex specialists. Indeed, my mother's reaction upon learning that I was sexual with women was to reveal to my siblings, but not to me, my hermaphroditism and history of sex change and to regret that she had allowed physicians to assign me female, rather than male.

My mother and father took me into their room one day to share a secret with me. I was ten years old, still utterly ignorant about sexual matters. "When you were a baby, you were sick," they explained. "Your clitoris was too big; it was *enlarged.*" The way they spoke the word *enlarged,* it was clear that it was being given some special, out of the ordinary, meaning. "You had to go into the hospital, and it was removed." "What is a 'clitoris'?" I asked. "A clitoris is a part of a girl that would have been a penis if she had been a boy. Yours was *enlarged,* so it had to be removed. Now everything is fine. But don't ever tell this to anyone else."

Who am I? I look at my body. It *looks* female. Yet I have always harbored a secret doubt. I remember myself as a withdrawn, depressed adolescent,

trying to steal a glance of a woman's genitals. Do hers look like mine? I had never seen a naked woman up close. I had no idea that my genitals were missing parts. In fact, one cannot discern the difference between my genitals and those of any other woman without parting the outer labia. I do recall learning, from a book, about the phenomenon of masturbation. Try as I might, I could not locate a focus of pleasurable sensation in my genitals, couldn't accomplish the trick that I had read about. I wasn't able to associate this failure with the secret about the *enlarged* clitoris that had been removed. I simply couldn't take in that such an irreversible harm had been done to me and by adults who were responsible for my well-being. I often woke from a nightmare in which my life was in danger, my gender in question, and my genitals were somehow horribly deformed, spilling out of me like visceral organs. It wasn't until I became a young adult that I was able to make the connection between the removal of my clitoris and my feeble sexual response and inability to experience orgasm.

Who am I? I now assert both my femininity and my intersexuality, my "not female"-ness. This is not a paradox; the fact that my gender has been problematized is the source of my intersexual identity. Most people have never struggled with their gender, are at a loss to answer the question, "How do you know you are a woman (a man)?"

I have been unable to experience myself as totally female. Although my body passes for female, women's clothing does not fit me. The shoulders are too narrow, the sleeves too short. Most women's gloves won't go on my hands, nor women's shoes on my feet. For most women, that wouldn't be more than an inconvenience. But when the clothing doesn't fit, I am reminded of my history. Of course, men's clothing doesn't fit either. The straight lines leave no room for my large breasts or broad hips. Still, I experience something about the way that I work and move in the world as relatively masculine. And when a man expresses an intimate attraction to me, I often suspect that he may be wrestling with a conflicted homosexual orientation—attracted to a masculine part of me, but my feminine appearance renders his attraction safely heterosexual.

As woman, I am less than whole—I have a secret past; I lack important parts of my genitals and sexual response. When a lover puts her hand to my genitals for the first time, the lack is immediately obvious to her. Finally, I simply do not feel myself a woman (even less a man). But the hermaphrodite identity was too monstrous, too other, too freakish, for me to easily embrace—a medical anomaly, patched up as best the surgeons could manage. I had an article from a medical journal that stated that only twelve "true hermaphrodites" (the label applied to me by my medical records) had *ever* been recorded (Morris, 1957, p. 540).

For whose benefit does this mechanism of medical erasure and social silencing operate? Certainly, it does not benefit intersexed children. I have been brutally mutilated, left to wonder and to search for the truth in utter silence and isolation. When at age thirty-six, I finally confronted my mother, I asked her how she could possibly have kept her silence for all those years, left me to learn my history as Charlie and the label of hermaphroditism from medical records. Her response? "Well, you could have *asked* me." (I wonder what other improbable questions I should be certain to ask while she is alive. . .)

At first, I was horribly vexed by this issue of identity. My earlier experience of coming out as a lesbian helped me to see the solution to my predicament. The terms homosexual and lesbian, as with the term intersex, were inventions of medical discourse used to pathologize disapproved sexualities. I must proudly assert my identity and insist that the medical construction of intersexuality as disease is oppression, not science. I must find others who share my experience—others who will speak out with me. A community can provide emotional and logistical support for its members and mount a much more powerful resistance than individuals acting alone.

It wasn't easy to overcome my feelings of intense shame. I remember furtively using the printer,

copier, and fax machine at the office, heart pounding with the fear that someone would see the documents that I was working with—medical records, articles from medical journals, a journal of my emotional progress. I still believed that intersexuality was so rare that I might never find another whose experience was similar to mine. Instead, I first sought out and spoke with transsexuals. Alice Walker had just published *Possessing the Secret of Joy,* a novel which focused Western attention on the African cultural rite euphemistically referred to as female circumcision. I thrilled to read the elderly midwife, whose long life had been spent performing clitorectomies, castigate her former victim for suggesting clitorectomy might be justified for hermaphrodites, if not for females. "It's all normal, as far as that goes, says M'lissa. You didn't make it, so who are you to judge?" (Walker, 1992, p. 257). I located and spoke with African women mutilated in this way, who are now organizing in the United States against the practices of their homelands. The examples of all these brave people helped me to deal with my shame.

I began to speak, at first indiscriminately, with friends and acquaintances about what had been done to me. Within a year, I had turned up half a dozen other intersexuals; most of them were also genitally mutilated; two were living with their atypical genitals intact. A woman clitorectomized during her teens, though she knew from masturbation that her clitoris was the focus of sexual pleasure, she was unable to express this or otherwise resist the pressure of parents and doctors; a child who had been clitorectomized just two years previous (in 1990); a woman who was grateful that her mother had resisted years of medical pressure to remove her daughter's large clitoris; a man who had been raised as a girl, switched to living as a man (with intact intersexed genitals) after he developed a masculine body at puberty; a man whose penis had been severely damaged by repeated surgeries to "correct" the position of his urethral meatus;[4] a man who had discovered that the childhood surgery which no one would explain to him had actually removed his uterus and single ovary. None of these people had ever spoken with another intersexual.

Surgeons assert that the reason why they fail to provide us with counseling is that they cannot locate mental health professionals with experience in dealing with intersexuality (Lee, 1994). Yet, surgeons perpetuate this situation by mutilating, traumatizing, stigmatizing, and silencing us, their intersexed patients. We grow up with so much shame that as adults we are not able to discuss our experience openly, and the phenomenon of intersexuality remains invisible. Indeed, as recently as 1996, one entrant in a medical ethics contest won a cash prize for her essay encouraging physicians to lie to their intersexed patients in order to prevent them from knowing their diagnoses (Natarajan, 1996). In adulthood, many who were treated as children by medical intersex specialists feel so betrayed that they shun all medical care.

What do I see when I look in the mirror? I see a female body, though scarred and missing some important genital parts. When I interact in daily life with others, though, I experience a strange sort of bodily dissociation—my perception of myself is as a disembodied entity, without sex or gender. I view healing this split as an important element of personal growth that will allow me to reclaim my sexuality and to be more effective as an intersex advocate. My body is not female; it is intersexed. Nonconsensual surgery cannot erase intersexuality and produce whole males and females; it produces emotionally abused and sexually dysfunctional intersexuals. If I label my postsurgical anatomy female, I ascribe to surgeons the power to create a *woman by removing* body parts; I accede to their agenda of "woman as lack"; I collaborate in the prohibition of my intersexual identity. Kessler quotes an endocrinologist who specializes in treating intersexed infants: "In the absence of maleness, you have femaleness... It's really the basic design" (Kessler, 1990, p. 15).

Must things be this way? In all cultures, at all times? Anthropologist Clifford Geertz contrasted the conceptualization of intersexuals by the Navajo and the Kenyan Pokot—"a product, if a somewhat unusual product, of the normal course of things"— with the American attitude. "Americans . . . regard femaleness and maleness as exhausting the natural categories in which persons can conceivably come: what falls between is a darkness, an offense against reason" (Geertz, 1984 p. 85). The time has come for intersexuals to denounce our treatment as abuse, to embrace and openly assert our identities as intersexuals, and to intentionally affront that sort of reason which requires that we be mutilated and silenced.

Even before intersexuals began to speak out, there were a few stirrings of awareness that something fishy was going on at the boundaries of the sexes. In 1980, Ruth Hubbard and Patricia Farnes pointed out that the practice of clitorectomy was not limited to the Third World but also occurs "right here in the United States, where it is used as part of a procedure to 'repair' by 'plastic surgery' so-called genital ambiguities" (Farnes and Hubbard, 1980, p. 9). Reacting to intersex specialist John Money's explanation to a three-year-old girl that clitorectomy "will make her look like all other girls," Anne Fausto-Sterling wryly noted, "If the surgery results in genitalia that look like those shown in [Money's] book, then [he is] in need of an anatomy lesson!" (Fausto-Sterling, 1985, p. 138). Five years later Suzanne Kessler, whose work has been influential in motivating the current discourse on gender as a social construction, interviewed physicians who specialize in managing intersexed children. She concluded that genital ambiguity is treated with surgery "not because it is threatening to the infant, but because it is threatening to the infant's culture" (Kessler, 1990, p. 25). Finally, Fausto-Sterling suggested that genital surgery should not be imposed on intersexed infants (Fausto-Sterling, 1993).

A letter to the editor in which I responded to Fausto-Sterling's article, announcing the formation of the Intersex Society of North America (ISNA), brought emotional responses from other intersexuals (Chase, 1993). One, Morgan Holmes, has completed an extended analysis of the reasons why medical technology has been used to erase intersexuality in general, and from her own body in particular (Holmes, 1994). Until she contacted me, Holmes shared her experience of intersexuality with no living being. The only other intersexual in her universe was Herculine Barbin, the nineteenth-century French hermaphrodite whose journals were edited and published by Foucault (Foucault, 1980a). Barbin's life ended in suicide. By 1996, ISNA had grown to include more than 150 intersexuals throughout the United States and Canada, and several in Europe, Australia, and New Zealand.

In Britain, as well, intersexuals have begun to speak out against the extreme secrecy, shame, and freakishness surrounding their condition. The British movement was given a boost when the respected *British Medical Journal* carried an exchange that led to publication of an address for a support group.

> Mine was a dark secret kept from all outside the medical profession (family included), but this is not an option because it both increases the feelings of freakishness and reinforces the isolation. (Anonymous, 1994b)

> It's not that my gynecologist told me the truth that angers me (I'd used medical libraries to reach a diagnosis anyway), but that neither I nor my parents were offered any psychological support but were left to flounder in our separate feelings of shame and taboo. (Anonymous, 1994a)

Both writers have androgen insensitivity syndrome (AIS). During gestation, their XY sex chromosomes caused them to have testes, and their testes produced testosterone. But because their cells were incapable of responding to testosterone, they were born with genitals of typical female appearance but having a short vagina, without cervix or uterus. Raised as girls, with bodies that develop many adult female characteristics at puberty, women with AIS are often traumatized to read in medical records or texts that they are "genetic males" and "male pseudohermaphrodites." The publication of these letters led to a swell of visibility

and participation in Britain's AIS Support Group, which by 1996 had chapters in the United States, Canada, the Netherlands, Germany, and Australia.

In Germany, intersexuals have formed the Workgroup on Violence in Pediatrics and Gynecology for mutual support and in opposition of medical abuse. In Japan, intersexuals have formed Hijra Nippon, with a similar agenda. In the United States, HELP and the Ambiguous Genitalia Support Network were separately founded by mothers who opposed the drastic surgical interventions and secrecy that medical specialists recommended for their intersexed children.[5] One of these women has a suit pending against physicians who removed her son's testes against her stated wishes.

Some intersexuals whose bodies resemble mine have an XX, some an XY karyotype; others have a mosaic karyotype, which differs from cell to cell. There is no possible way to discern my karyotype without sending a tissue sample to a laboratory. If the result were "XX," should this information bolster my identity as a female? As a lesbian? If "XY," should I reconceptualize myself as a heterosexual man? It is ludicrous that knowledge of the result of a laboratory test in which cell nuclei are stained and photographed under a microscope should determine the perception of anyone's sex or gender.

The International Olympic Committee has learned this the hard way. Since the IOC began to karyotype women in 1968, one in 500 female athletes tested have been rejected because of their unusual chromosomes; in some cases, the decision was made only after the event, and the woman was stripped of title and barred from future competition. To this writer's knowledge, only one person treated in this way has thus far been willing to speak openly about her experience. When meet officials presented Maria Patino with the news that she was "genetically male," they advised her to fake an injury and leave quietly (Pool, 1994).

When I first began to seek out other intersexuals, I expected, I wanted, to find people whose experience exactly matched mine. What I have discovered is that in one sense we are very different—the range of personalities, politics, and anatomies in our nascent intersexual movement is broad. Some of us live as women, some as men, some as open intersexuals. Many of us are homosexual, if that term is narrowly understood in terms of the social gender roles of the partners. Some of us have never been sexual. But, in another sense, our experiences are surprisingly coherent: those of us who have been subjected to medical intervention and societal invisibility share our experience of it as abuse.

I claim lesbian identity because women who feel desire for me experience that desire as lesbian, because I feel most female when being sexual, and because I feel desire for women as I do not for men. Many intersexuals share my sense of queer identity, even those who do not share this homosexual identity. One, assigned female at birth and lucky enough to escape genital surgery through a fluke, has said that she has enjoyed sex with both women and men but never with another intersexual. "I'm a heterosexual in the truest sense of the word" (Angier, 1996, p. E14).

Healing is a process without end. The feeling of being utterly alone may be the most damaging part of what has been done to us. My work as an activist—listening to, counseling, and connecting other intersexuals, and working to save children born every day from having to repeat our suffering—has been an important part of my own healing and of feeling less overwhelmed by grief and rage.

Notes

1. Money describes a child who was assigned male at birth, female a few days later, male at age three weeks, and female at age four and a half. She was clitorectomized in conjunction with the final sex change. Her history of sex reassignments was kept secret from her, tabooed from family discussion, although she recalled it in dreams (Money, 1991, p. 239).

2. Intersex Society of North America, P.O. Box 31791, San Francisco, CA 94131. E-mail info@isna.org. http://www.isna.org.

3. Although this statement was written in connection with an article about "clitoroplasty without loss of sensitivity," the authors provide no evidence that this standard procedure, which removes nearly the entire clitoris and relocates the remainder, leaves sexual sensation intact. On the other hand, Morgan Holmes, who was subjected to it as a child, characterizes it as a "partial clitorectomy" (Holmes, 1994). Another woman, who had the procedure performed as an adult and is able to contrast her sexual experience before and after the surgery, calls it "incredibly desensitizing" (Chase, 1994, p. 3).

4. Approximately one in three or four hundred infants is born with a condition called hypospadias, in which the portion of the urethra that traverses the penis is partially or completely open. This condition is rarely harmful; it looks unusual, and the boy or man may have to sit to urinate. Hypospadias "correction" surgery is probably the second most common form of cosmetic genital surgery performed in the United States, following "routine" male circumcision.

5. AIS Support Group US, 4203 Genessee #103–436, San Diego, CA 92117–4950. E-mail <aissg@aol.com>. AG Gewalt in der Padiatrie and Gynecologie, Brandtstrasse 30, Bremen 28 215, Germany. E-mail <aggpg@t-online.de>. Hijra Nippon, Suita Yubinkyoku Todome, Honami cho 4–1 Suita shi, Osaka T564, Japan. HELP, PO Box 26292, Jacksonville, FL 32226. E-mail <help@jaxnet.com>. Ambiguous Genitalia Support Network, P.O. Box 313, Clements, CA 95227.

References

Angier, Natalie. 1996. Intersexual healing: An anomaly finds a group. *The New York Times* (February 4): 14.

Anonymous. 1994a. Be open and honest with sufferers. *British Medical Journal* 308 (April 16): 1041–1042.

Anonymous. 1994b. Once a dark secret. *British Medical Journal* 308 (February 19): 542.

Bailez, M. M., John P. Gearhart, Claude Migeon, and John Rock, 1992. Vaginal reconstruction after initial construction of the external genitalia in girls with salt-wasting adrenal hyperplasia. *Journal of Urology* 148: 680–684.

Berlin, Meyer, and Shlomo Josef Zevin. 1974. *Encyclopedia Talmudica.* Jerusalem: Phillip Feldheim, pp. 386–399.

Butler, Judith. 1990. *Gender Trouble: Feminism and the Subversion of Identity*. New York: Routledge.

Chase, Cheryl. 1993. Letters from readers. *The Sciences* (July/August): 3.

Chase, Cheryl. 1994. Winged labia: Deformity or gift? *Hermaphrodites with Attitude* (Winter): 3.

Chase, Cheryl. 1996. Re: Measurement of evoked potentials during feminizing genitoplasty: Techniques and applications (letter). *Journal of Urology* 156 (3): 1139–1140.

Conte, Felix A., and Melvin M. Grumbach. 1989. Pathogenesis, classification, diagnosis, and treatment of anomalies of sex. In *Endocrinology*, edited by L. J. De Groot. Philadelphia: Saunders, pp. 1810–1847.

Department of Defense Appropriations Act of 1996, 104th Congress, second session, H.R. 3610 Sec 645, Congressional Record: September 28, 1996 (House), p. HI 1829.

Edgerton, Milton T. 1993. Discussion: Clitoroplasty for clitoromegaly due to adrenogenital syndrome without loss of sensitivity (by Nobuyuki Sagehashi). *Plastic and Reconstructive Surgery* 91 (5): 956.

Edgerton, Robert B. 1964. Pokot intersexuality: An East African example of the resolution of sexual incongruity. *American Anthropologist* 66 (6): 1288–1299.

Emans, S. Jean Herriot, and Donald Peter Goldstein. 1990. *Pediatric and Adolescent Gynecology*, third edition. Boston: Little, Brown, and Co.

Farnes, Patricia, and Ruth Hubbard. 1980. Letter to editor. *Ms Magazine* (April): 9–10.

Fausto-Sterling, Anne. 1985. *Myths of Gender: Biological Theories about Women and Men*, second edition. New York: Basic Books.

Fausto-Sterling, Anne. 1993. The five sexes: Why male and female are not enough. *The Sciences* (March/April): 20–25.

Foucault, Michel. 1980a. *Herculine Barbin, Being the Recently Discovered Memoirs of a Nineteenth-Century Hermaphrodite*. Translated by Richard McDougall. New York: Colophon.

Foucault, Michel. 1980b. *The History of Sexuality, Volume I: An Introduction*. Translated by Robert Hurley. New York: Viking.

Furth, Charlotte. 1993. Androgynous males and deficient females: Biology and gender boundaries in sixteenth- and seventeenth-century China. In *The Lesbian and Gay Studies Reader*, edited by Henry Abelove, Michellé Aina Barale, and David Helperin. New York: Routledge, pp. 479–497.

Geertz, Clifford. 1984. *Local Knowledge*. New York: Basic Books.

Hall, Radclyffe. 1990. *The Well of Loneliness*. New York: Anchor.

Hendricks, Melissa. 1993. Is it a boy or a girl? *Johns Hopkins Magazine* (November): 10–16.

Herdt, Gilbert. 1994. Mistaken sex: Culture, biology, and the third sex in New Guinea. In *Third Sex, Third Gender: Beyond Sexual Dimorphism in Culture and History*, edited by G. Herdt. New York: Zone Books, pp. 419–446.

Holmes, Morgan. 1994. Medical Politics and Cultural Imperatives: Intersexuality Beyond Pathology and Erasure. Master's Thesis, Interdisciplinary Studies, York University, Toronto.

Kessler, Suzanne. 1990. The medical construction of gender: Case management of intersexual infants. *Signs: Journal of Women in Culture and Society* 16 (1): 3–26.

Kessler, Suzanne J., and Wendy McKenna. 1978. *Gender: An Ethnomethodological Approach*. Chicago: The University of Chicago Press.

Laqueur, Thomas. 1990. *Making Sex: Body and Gender from the Greeks to Freud*. Cambridge: Harvard University Press.

Lee, Ellen Hyun-Ju. 1994. Producing Sex: An Interdisciplinary Perspective on Sex Assignment Decisions for Intersexuals. Senior Thesis, Human Biology: Race and Gender, Brown University, Providence.

Martin, Del, and Phyllis Lyon. 1991. *Lesbian/Woman*. Volcano, CA: Volcano Press.

Money, John. 1991. Biographies of gender and hermaphroditism in paired comparisons. In *The Handbook of Sexology*, edited by J. Money and H. Musaph. New York: Elsevier.

Morris, John McL. 1957. Intersexuality. *Journal of the American Medical Association* 163 (7): 538–542.

Nanda, Sarena. 1994. Hijras: An Alternative Sex and Gender Role in India. In *Third Sex, Third Gender: Beyond Sexual Dimorphism in Culture and History*, edited by G. Herdt. New York: Zone Books, pp. 373–418.

Natarajan, Anita. 1996. Medical ethics and truth-telling in the case of androgen insensitivity syndrome. *Canadian Medical Association Journal* 154: 568–570.

Pool, Robert E. 1994. *Eve's Rib: The Biological Roots of Sex Differences.* New York: Crown Publishers.

Roscoe, Will. 1991. *The Zuni Man-Woman.* Albuquerque: University of New Mexico Press.

Slijper, F. M. E., S. L. S. Drop, J. C. Molenaar, and R. J. Scholtmeijer. 1994. Neonates with abnormal genital development assigned the female sex: Parent counseling. *Journal of Sex Education and Therapy* 20 (1): 9–17.

Vance, Carol S. 1991. Anthropology rediscovers sexuality: A theoretical comment. *Social Science and Medicine* 33: 875–884.

Walker, Alice. 1992. *Possessing the Secret of Joy.* New York: Simon and Schuster.

Questions for Critical Thinking

1. Chase discusses the impact of maintaining the false notion of the existence of only two sexes on her life as well as the lives of other intersex individuals. Given the devastation she and others experience, what do you see as the responsibility of medical professionals to alter their practices with regard to sex assignment of intersex children at birth?

2. Chase's experiences challenge the notion that being male or female is a biological fact. How do you answer her question, how do you know you are a woman or a man?

3. Currently, the medical profession has more power than parents in determining the sex of intersex children. Why do you think this is? What do you see as the likelihood of this practice changing?

"Ain't I a Woman?"

Transgender and Intersex Student Athletes in Women's Collegiate Sports

PAT GRIFFIN

Athletics is an aspect of U.S. society that is significantly involved in maintaining the idea that males and females are distinct groups. In this essay, Pat Griffin, the founding director of Changing the Game (a project of the Gay, Lesbian, and Straight Education Network), addresses the barriers transgender athletes face that keep them from full participation in sports and offers solutions that would work toward equality for all.

The title of this chapter is borrowed from Sojourner Truth's powerful demand that white feminist abolitionists in the nineteenth century expand their awareness to include the needs of black women in their fight for race and sex equality. Her question, "Ain't I a Woman," seems fitting for the twenty-first century also with regard to the inclusion in women's sports of transgender women and men and women who have intersex conditions. Increasing numbers of athletes who are transgender or have intersex conditions are challenging gender boundaries in sports as they insist on their right to participate according to their self-affirmed genders. Recent controversies surrounding the eligibility of South African runner Caster Semenya to compete in women's events and the participation of transgender athletes, such as George Washington University basketball player, Kye Allums and professional golfer Lana Lawson, challenge the traditional boundaries of sex and gender in sport.

This chapter explores how the gender and sex binary assumptions upon which the organization of sports competition is based can create problems when people whose gender identities or variations in sexual development do not conform to these assumptions assert their right to participate. I discuss how transgender and intersex athletes challenge assumptions about the essential nature of the category "woman." At the same time, I show how sexist and heterosexist stereotypes converge to affect the gender performance of all women in sports, with a particularly limiting effect on people whose gender identity, gender expression, biological sex, and/or sexual orientation do not conform to cultural norms.

After a description of relevant language related to this topic, I review selected historical events describing concerns about women athletes' sex, femininity, and heterosexuality. I then explore how these concerns and the gender-binary assumptions undergirding them affect policies governing the eligibility of transgender and intersex athletes to participate in women's collegiate athletic events. I conclude the chapter with a discussion of current efforts to provide transgender and intersex athletes with opportunities to participate in school-based women's athletic competitions.

A Word about Words

The language of sex and gender can be confusing and complicated. Many of the concepts feminist scholars and gender activists use challenge conventional notions about gender and sex. Moreover, the language is evolving, and many feminist scholars and gender activists disagree about how the language should be used. For example, the terms "sex" and "gender" are used interchangeably by some writers, while others find it useful to provide specific and separate definitions for each of these terms. I find it helpful, at least on a conceptual level, to define these two key terms separately.

According to Gender Spectrum, an education and advocacy organization for gender-variant children and teens, "sex" is biological and includes physical attributes, such as sex chromosomes, gonads, sex hormones, internal reproductive structures, and external genitalia. At birth, individuals are typically categorized as male or female based on the appearance of their external genitalia. This binary categorization ignores the spectrum of biological sex characteristics that confound attempts to fit everyone neatly into either male or female categories. The term "gender" is similarly complicated. According to Genderspectrum.org, "Along with one's physical traits, it is the complex interrelationship between those traits and one's internal sense of self as male, female, both or neither as well as one's outward presentations and behaviors related to that perception." I find it helpful to make this differentiation, especially when discussing these terms in relationship to sports, where physical attributes are integral aspects of the discussion.

Gender is not inherently related to sex. A person who identifies as transgender has a gender identity (an internal sense of gender: being male or female, trans, or other gender sensibility) that does not match the sex (or gender) they were assigned at birth based on an inspection of their physical characteristics. A transgender woman or girl may be born with a body identified as male and, on the basis of that body, assigned to the gender category "boy," even though she identifies

as a girl. The reverse is true for a transgender man or boy. Transgender people choose to express their genders in many ways: changing their names and self-referencing pronouns to better match their gender identities; choosing clothes, hairstyles, or other aspects of self-presentation that reflect their gender identities; and generally living and presenting themselves to others consistently with their gender identities. Some, but not all, transgender people take hormones or undergo surgical procedures to change their bodies to better reflect their gender identities. Transgender encompasses a vast range of identities and practices; however, for the purposes of this essay, I use the term "transgender" more specifically to refer to women who have transitioned from their assigned male gender at birth to their affirmed gender as women and to men who have transitioned from their assigned female gender at birth to their affirmed gender as men.

People with intersex conditions may be born with chromosomes, hormones, genitalia, or other sex characteristics that do not match the patterns that typify biological maleness or femaleness. Many intersex people are not aware of their intersex status unless it is revealed as part of a medical examination or treatment. People with intersex conditions are assigned a gender at birth; many live and identify with that assigned gender throughout their lives, although many do not. In this essay, I use "intersex women" to refer to women with intersex conditions who have always identified as women (for more information about intersex conditions, go to www.accordalliance.org).

The participation of transgender and intersex women poses related but different challenges to gendered divisions in sports. Transgender women and intersex women are viewed by many sports leaders, women competitors, and the general public as men or as "not normal" women whose participation in women's sports threatens the notion of a "level playing field." In the context of sex-segregated women's sports, these athletes' bodies are viewed as male, and they are often perceived to have an unfair competitive advantage over non-intersex or non-transgender women athletes. But trans and intersex visibility and participation belies the myth of the level playing field and the myth of binary gender on which it rests.

Sports and the Gender Binary

Although some school athletic teams, such as sailing, are composed of men and women who compete without regard to the sex or gender of participants, mixed-sex competition is the exception at all levels of sports. In most sports that women and men play, schools sponsor separate men's and women's teams—basketball, volleyball, swimming, track, and field, lacrosse, or soccer, for example. This sex division is based on the assumption that sex-separate competitive opportunities are the best route to equal opportunity and fair competition for all. Title IX, the 1972 landmark federal legislation prohibiting sex discrimination in education, includes guidelines for providing comparable school-based athletic opportunities for girls and women and boys and men on sex-separate teams to provide equal participation opportunities (Brake 2010; Hogshead-Makar and Zimbalist 2007).

Dividing participants into sex-separate teams is based on two assumptions: (1) Sex and gender are binary and immutable characteristics, and (2) salient physical differences between males and females substantially affect athletic performance to the advantage of males in most sports.

Rather than a binary of athletic performance based on sex, it would be more accurate to describe sex differences as a spectrum, with females and males occupying overlapping positions. Although it is fair to say that most adult male athletes are bigger, taller, and stronger than most adult female athletes, some female athletes outperform their male counterparts in sport. So, even among athletes who are not transgender or intersex, sex-separated teams do not always adequately accommodate the diversity of skill, motivation, and physical characteristics among female and male athletes. Some boys or men might find a better competitive match competing on a girls' team, and some girls' athletic performances are more comparable to those on a boys' team.

Some girls and boys have been allowed to participate on teams designated for the other sex, particularly if a school only sponsors a team in that sport for one sex. For example, girls sometimes compete on boy's wrestling or football teams, and boys sometimes compete on girls' field hockey or volleyball teams. However, cross-sex participation on sports teams is always an exception and is often greeted with skepticism by other competitors, parents, and fans. Even among prepubescent girls and boys where size and strength are similar or where girls are often taller, stronger, and faster than boys, sports are typically divided by sex. Such is the entrenched nature of the belief in a static and immutable gender and sex binary in sports.

For most athletes whose gender identity is congruent with their gender assigned at birth or whose physical sex anatomy is congruent with their sex assigned at birth, the answer to the question of which team to play for is simple. However, for athletes whose gender identity does not match the gender they were assigned at birth or for athletes with differences of sexual development, the separation of sports into participation categories based on binary sex has often resulted in humiliation and discrimination. Transgender and intersex athletes challenge the gender binary in sports and force sports leaders to reflect on how and where to draw gender boundaries for the purposes of identifying on which teams an athlete is allowed to compete.

Because women athletes have always challenged the hegemonic notion of athleticism as a masculine trait and because sports participation has historically been a male privilege to which girls and women were not entitled, the fight for equal sports opportunities for women is ongoing. Gendered expectations for girls and women have not comfortably included such characteristics as "competitive," "athletic," or "muscular"; as a result, women athletes have always had to prove their "normalcy" based on socially constructed assumptions about femininity, heterosexuality, and an unquestioned acceptance of a gender binary. Women who excel in sports *and* whose appearance, behavior, and/or identity does not conform to traditional notions of who is a woman, how a woman should look and act, and who a woman should be sexually attracted to are viewed with suspicion and as illegitimate participants in women's sports competitions (Cahn 1994; Festle 1996; Griffin 1998).

History of Gender Anxiety in Women's Sport

During the early twentieth century, women participating in athletic competitions were subjected to white middle-class criticism from medical doctors, media commentators, psychologists, and others who warned of a range of catastrophic effects of athletic competition they believed would cause physiological and psychological damage. Based on the belief that white women were physically and psychically frail, sports participation was viewed as dangerous to their health and well-being. The prevailing medical and social perspective was that women who did compete in sports were subjected to a number of "masculinizing" effects on their appearance, behavior, and sexual interests that would prevent them from living as "normal" women whose proper roles were wives and mothers. Thus, the early seeds of gender suspicion about women athletes were planted. Advocates for women's sports participation and women athletes themselves often responded defensively to these criticisms by highlighting their femininity (according to racially white heteronormative standards) and heterosexual interests, and by portraying their sports interest as a complement to their focus on motherhood and marriage (Cahn 1994).

These fears are best illustrated in public reaction to Babe Didrikson, a multisport athlete who won Olympic medals in track and field and played baseball, basketball, and tennis before later focusing on professional golf. Didrikson was a well-known cultural icon whose brash manner, quick sense of humor, and competitive fire always made for a good story. Unfortunately, Didrikson was treated

as a gender freak and ridiculed for her lack of femininity, her "masculine" appearance, and her athletic prowess. Called a "muscle moll" and worse, it is no wonder that by midcentury, Didrikson initiated an international public-relations campaign to reassure the American public that she was a "normal" woman after all, despite her athletic achievements. (Cayleff 1995). She began wearing dresses and talking about her love of cooking, and, to seal the deal, she married wrestling champion George Zaharias. These efforts succeeded in quieting the concerns of male sports reporters and the general public about Didrikson's femininity and heterosexuality.

As women's competition in Olympic sports and professional golf and tennis became more visible in the 1940s through the 1970s, another wave of suspicion about the gender and sexuality of women athletes prompted some women's sports advocates and athletes themselves to take an apologetic stance by focusing on disproving sexist assumptions about the "masculine" lesbian women who lived in the sports world. These efforts included the institution of feminine dress codes, instructions about makeup application and hair styling, and direction of media attention to the "pretty ones," who served as goodwill ambassadors who contradicted the unsavory image of "masculine" women athletes (Gerber, Felshin, and Wyrick 1974).

These fears, coupled with the belief that women are inherently athletically inferior to their male counterparts, caused increased gender suspicions about outstanding athletic performances by female athletes. These questions were raised in the 1964 Olympics by Russian hammer-throwers and shot-putters Tamara and Irina Press, whose muscular appearances and medal-winning performances provoked suspicion that they were actually men posing as women.

In 1976, Renée Richards, a transgender woman, was denied entry in the Women's U.S. Open by the U.S. Tennis Association (USTA) on the basis that she was not a "born woman." The New York Supreme Court ruled against the USTA and enabled Richards to compete in the women's event.

Despite this court ruling, the Ladies Professional Golf Association (LPGA) maintained a "born woman" requirement for membership until 2010; when faced with a lawsuit by transgender woman golfer Lana Lawson, the LPGA dropped its prohibition against transgender participants. Transgender women, such as Richards and Lawson, are viewed by some suspicious tennis players and golfers as illegitimate women who have male bodies that confer an unfair competitive advantage when competing against so-called "natural" women.

In 1966, in response to fears of male cheaters competing as women, the International Olympic Committee (IOC) instituted mandatory "gender" verification testing of all female competitors. (The tests were called "sex tests," and their purpose was to confirm that competitors were female-bodied and, later, that their chromosomal makeup was female.) The first such tests required all Olympic competitors entered in women's events to appear naked before a panel of "experts," who, by visual inspection, determined whether the prospective competitors were eligible to compete as female.

Not surprisingly, athletes and other sports observers criticized this humiliating process. Medical experts also criticized the process, because, in addition to the invasive and voyeuristic nature of the "gender test," it was also a crude and ineffective means of determining whether a competitor was female.

Eventually, more "scientific" procedures were developed in which women athletes were subjected to buccal smear tests in which mouth swabs yielded cellular samples from which the chromosomal makeup could be identified. Athletes whose chromosomal makeup was other than XX were determined to be ineligible to compete as women. Women who "passed" the test were given "certificates of femininity" and allowed to compete.

These supposedly more-scientific tests also failed to achieve their intended goal. Rather than identifying male imposters, the only competitors who were ever disqualified were women with atypical chromosomal makeup who had lived their entire lives as women and were not attempting to gain an unfair competitive advantage. The resulting traumatic and public shaming that followed their identifications as "not women" not only terminated their athletic careers but damaged their personal lives as well.

Current Policy Governing the Participation of Transgender and Intersex Athletes

These "gender" tests revealed the folly of identifying a simple and fair, not to mention respectful, means of determining who is a woman. Nonetheless, although mandatory "gender verification" testing was discontinued prior to the 2000 Olympic Games, individual women athletes who trigger suspicions about their sex are now tested on a case-by-case basis. Unfortunately, these sex challenges are typically triggered by such ambiguous and culturally biased gender criteria as short hair, small breasts, preferences for "masculine" clothes, deep voices, muscular physiques, and excellence of athletic performance. Thus, the challenge of identifying who is and is not a woman for the purpose of determining eligibility to compete in women's sports events continues to be controversial.

During the 2009 Track and Field World Championships, South African runner Caster Semenya astounded the international track establishment with her gold-medal performance in the women's eight-hundred-meter run, leaving her competition far back on the track. Semenya was identified as a female at birth, has always identified as a woman, and is accepted as a woman by her family and friends. However, unconfirmed speculations are that she has an intersex condition. Immediately following her victory, some of her competitors and race officials from other countries filed challenges to the International Association of Athletics Federation (IAAF) under the IAAF's case-by-case "gender-verification" policy. (Mirroring the IOC, the IAAF policy had replaced mandatory "gender" verification testing of women athletes in favor of a case-by-case process.)

After months of subjecting Semenya to medical examinations, public speculation about whether she is a woman, public humiliation, and egregious breaches of confidentiality by the IAAF, she was allowed to keep her gold medal. Eleven months later, after secretive IAAF deliberations, she was cleared for competition in women's events. The IAAF released this decision without an explanation of its process, criteria, or reasoning. When Semenya won her first two races after returning to competition and finished third in another, some of her competitors again began complaining that they were unfairly forced to compete against a man or, at the very least, a "woman on the fringe of normalcy," as one competitor described Semenya.

Whether being intersex confers any performance advantage is open to speculation. No scientific data are available to indicate that it does or does not. However, Semenya's competitors assume that she is a man or not a "normal" woman and that she has an unfair competitive advantage that should disqualify her from competing in women's events. These objections to Semenya's eligibility to compete as a woman are based on her margin of victory over the other women in the 2009 World Championships and on her "masculine" physical appearance, clothing, and deep voice. All these characteristics challenge the gender binary upon which sports competition is based as well as binary assumptions about who is a woman and therefore eligible to compete in women's events.

In 2004, in a surprisingly proactive decision by a typically conservative organization, the IOC adopted a policy outlining criteria enabling transgender athletes to compete in IOC-sponsored events:

- The athlete's gender must be legally recognized on official identity documents.
- The athlete must have completed genital reconstructive surgery and had his or her testes or ovaries removed.
- The athlete must complete a minimum two-year postoperative hormone treatment before she or he is allowed to compete.

The IOC policy is the first attempt by a mainstream sports organization to identify specific criteria governing the participation of transgender athletes. However, transgender-rights advocates criticize the policy, noting the class and sex bias built into the policy as well as problems related to privacy and medical confidentiality. Moreover, some transgender medical experts have provided some data indicating that a one-year waiting period is adequate for the athletes' hormonal levels to be within the range of non-transgender women and men. To date, no transgender athlete has competed in the Olympic Games under this policy.

Despite its considerable flaws, USA Track and Field, the U.S. Golf Association, and a few state high school athletic governing organizations have adopted the IOC policy (for example, those in Colorado, Connecticut, and Rhode Island). The participation criteria identified in the IOC policy would make it virtually impossible for transgender student athletes to compete in high school sports. The requirements of genital reconstructive surgery, mandatory sterilization, and changing the sex indicated on official identity documents impose financial and legal burdens that even many adult transgender athletes cannot or choose not to pursue. The two-year waiting period is not supported by medical data and is not practical in school sports, where a student athlete's eligibility is already limited to four or five years.

As of 2011, no national governing organization for high school sports has adopted a policy concerning the participation of intersex athletes in school-based sports events. However, in 2008, the Washington State Interscholastic Activity Association (WIAA) adopted the most progressive policy to date governing the participation of transgender student athletes on high school sports teams. This policy requires neither surgery nor change of identity documents. Transgender students can participate in their affirmed genders after appealing to the state interscholastic activities association and providing written documentation of the student's gender from the student and parent/guardian and/or a health-care provider. To date, the policy has been used successfully to enable transgender students to participate on sex-separate teams.

At the collegiate level, the National Collegiate Athletic Association (NCAA) released a statement in 2004 clarifying that the organization does not prohibit transgender student athletes from competing in NCAA-sanctioned events but that student athletes must compete in the sex identified on their official identity documents. NCAA legal advisers believed that this provision was a simple solution to addressing the question of transgender participation in NCAA athletic programs. Because of significant differences among state requirements for changing the sex indicated on official identity documents, however, this requirement is discriminatory and creates complications when athletes from different states compete against each other. More recently, the NCAA has recognized the need for a more nuanced and inclusive policy. In 2011, it adopted the first-ever national policy regarding transgender athletes in collegiate athletics; the policy allows transgender athletes to compete in sex-segregated sports if, and only if, their hormonal treatment is consistent with current medical standards—standards that themselves suggest different treatment requirements for trans men and trans women (Lawrence 2011).

As of 2010, only two collegiate openly transgender student athletes had competed in NCAA-sponsored events. Keelin Godsey competed on the women's track and field team at Bates College and in the Olympic trials in the women's hammer throw. Allums currently is a member of the George Washington University women's basketball team. Godsey and Allums are female-bodied transgender men who are not taking testosterone so they can continue to compete in women's events. Because they are not taking testosterone, an NCAA-banned substance, and are competing in the sex identified on their official identity documents as specified by the NCAA and IOC, Godsey and Allums are eligible to compete on women's teams.

Whether the perceived threats to women's sports are identified as male imposters, transgender women, transgender men not taking testosterone, intersex women, butch-looking straight women, or lesbians, protecting the boundaries of women's sports from these gender transgressors by upholding the gender binary has become increasingly difficult as the myth of the gender binary and the myth of the level playing field have been exposed.

The Myth of the Level Playing Field

Just as some people view lesbians as threats to women's sports because they fear association with the stereotypes of lesbians as unsavory, so, too, do many athletes and the general public view transgender and intersex women athletes with particular suspicion. Although lesbians may be viewed as women who look or act like men, some people view transgender and intersex women as actually *being* men, in most places making them ineligible to compete in women's sports. The most-often-cited concern about the participation of transgender or intersex women in women's sports is that they threaten a "level playing field." Many competitors, coaches, and parents assume that transgender and intersex women, because of their male bodies, have an unfair competitive advantage over women who are not perceived to be trans or intersex.

Even without the participation of transgender or intersex women in women's sports, the playing field is hardly level. The entire focus of sports competition is to gain a competitive advantage, as long as that advantage is defined as being within the rules. Training hard to gain a competitive advantage is fair. Taking performance-enhancing drugs is not fair. Competitive advantages in women's sports come in many different forms; social, economic, environmental, psychological, and physiological, to name a few. Some women grow up in cultures where girls' sports participation is supported by social norms. These girls have a competitive advantage over other girls whose cultures restrict female athleticism. Girls whose families have the financial resources that enable them to train with the best coaches, to use the best equipment, to have access to good nutrition and health care, and to compete with the best athletes have a competitive advantage. Girls who live in places with clean air and water and safe streets have a competitive advantage. Girls who have inner resources of mental toughness and competitive drive have a competitive edge over physically talented but less mentally tough opponents. Some women have competitive advantages over opponents in their sports because of their genetics. Even some genetic conditions, such as Marfan syndrome, which results in unusual height, can be a competitive advantage in some sports where being tall is an advantage. All these competitive advantages are viewed in sports as fair and part of the game. All these advantages expose the myth of the level playing field even among women who are not transgender or intersex.

Why then is it that all these competitive advantages are accepted as fair variations among women athletes that can account for athletic-performance differences, but the competitive advantages that may or may not be enjoyed by some transgender or intersex women are viewed as unfair and threats to a level playing field warranting banishment from women's competition?

Competitive advantages assumed to be conferred by perceived maleness or masculinity are viewed as unfair competitive advantages. Transgender women, intersex women, or any women who do not conform to social expectations of femininity and heterosexuality are threats to the image of athletic women as gender conformists. As long as women athletes can be cast as feminine, heterosexual women, they do not pose a threat to the dominance of men in sports and male privilege in sports. This is the price of acceptance that women in sports have had to pay since the early twentieth century, when they began participating in sports in large numbers.

Gender Binary Meets Transgender and Intersex Athletes: What Is the Way Forward?

Women who by their inability or refusal to conform to binary gender norms in sports also challenge the mythical gender binary altogether. Given

that athletics as an institution has been built on sexist assumptions about the natural superiority of men's sports performance over that of women and that the gender binary forms the basis for how sports are structured into sex-separate participation categories, how should women's sports address the question of including transgender and intersex athletes?

Policy development designed to address this question can take several forms: (1) Protect the gender binary by using sex-verification testing to exclude "non-women," (2) address challenges to the gender binary on a case-by-case basis, (3) eliminate gender as a sport-participation category, and (4) expand gender categories to include participants whose bodies and/or gender identities do not conform to the gender binary.

Protect the gender binary with mandatory sex-verification testing of all female participants. This policy has been discredited as impractical, discriminatory, invasive, and ineffective. The IOC abandoned this policy in 1999, and nothing suggests that any improvement of testing procedures will bring it back as a mandatory process.

Use sex-verification testing on a case-by-case basis as challenges to individual female participants arise. This is the IOC/IAAF policy now in effect. The controversy surrounding the challenge to Semenya's eligibility to compete in women's events illustrates many of the problems with this policy. The criteria for challenging an individual athlete's gender are based on a combination of sexist assumptions about female athletic performance and bodies, socially constructed-gendered expectations for appearance and behavior, and a selective belief in the level playing field in sports in which some competitive advantages, particularly those based on genetic differences, are viewed as fair while others are not. Testing on a case-by-case basis eliminates the impracticality of testing all competitors entered in women's events and avoids the mass anxiety inherent in the process. However, the sex testing of individual competitors on a case-by-case basis is based on myths about gender and a level playing field that subject the athletes who are targeted to an invasive and humiliating, and often public, process. The effects of these tests are questionable given the arbitrary nature of determining when a woman's physiological makeup crosses a socially constructed line to become "too" male to qualify to compete against other women.

The IOC policy for determining the eligibility of transgender women athletes on a case-by-case process includes criteria that require surgical intervention and legal documentation of transition that create insurmountable obstacles for most transgender people. The policy also requires an excessive waiting period once hormone treatment has begun that is not supported by current medical research.

Eliminate sex and gender as sports-participation categories.
Some LGBT legal advocates believe that eliminating men's and women's sports in favor of other criteria for determining sports participation is the only way to address the complexities and challenges of including transgender and intersex athletes. These advocates argue that dividing sports participation on the basis of a sex and gender binary is inherently unfair. Some feminist legal critics of Title IX believe that the law, by assuming that sex-separate teams are the best route to equality for women in sport, has enshrined sex inequality and relegated women's sports to a permanent second-class status. Their assumption is that Title IX establishes a "separate but equal" goal even though this legal concept has been discredited in lawsuits challenging racial and disability discrimination (McDonagh and Pappano 2008).

The logic and goals of such legalistic arguments for the elimination of sex-separate sports as a way to address the myth of the gender and sex binary, inequality in women's sports, and the inclusion of transgender and intersex women athletes are appealing in some ways. Dividing sports by such performance-related physical criteria as height, jumping ability, or weight might be a reasonable

strategy to eliminate discrimination based on sex and gender identity. Using actual performance in sports, such as running or swimming speed, agility, balance, points scored, or batting averages, also provides alternatives for dividing competitors into teams to level the playing field.

Although is it true that the gender binary creates a questionable division between the athletic interests, talent, and performance of men and women, it is also accurate to say that, for adults, most male athletes are bigger and stronger than most women athletes. As a result, dividing school teams by such "non-gendered" criteria as physical characteristics and athletic performance at this point in the history of women's sports would likely result in most athletic teams consisting of men and a few select women (including trans and intersex athletes). Second teams, if schools chose to field them, would probably consist of men and women in more equal numbers (including trans and intersex women). Third teams, in the unlikely event that schools chose to expand their support for more than two teams per sport, would probably consist of mostly women (including men and some trans and intersex athletes) and some men.

It is also questionable whether these performance-based criteria are really non-gendered. Many of the physiological differences between male and female bodies do give men a competitive advantage over women, depending on the sport. However, gendered social and cultural expectations still encourage and reward male athletes more than they do female athletes. Sexism in sports still limits women athletes' access to sports and the resources that support athletic teams. Much like the rationale behind affirmative action as a way of correcting past race and sex discrimination, sex-separate sports enable women to overcome past sex discrimination in sports. Studies documenting the impressive increases in girls' and women's participation in sports and the increasing quality and quantity of women's sports experiences since the passage of Title IX demonstrate the law's undeniable positive effects (Carpenter and Acosta 2004). At the same time, despite these successes, resistance to Title IX compliance and persistent sexism are still obstacles to full women's equality in sports.

I worry that eliminating women's sports in favor of "non-gendered" sports opportunities will, at this point in the development of women's sports, relegate the majority of women athletes either to the junior varsity or to the sidelines. Sport is gendered by social and cultural expectations. Even criteria meant to be "gender-free" are still embedded in historical and contemporary societal structures of sex inequality that disadvantage female athletes while advantaging male athletes. I keep imagining an incredibly talented athlete, such as the University of Connecticut women's basketball player Maya Moore, sitting on the bench for a varsity college team made up of mostly taller, stronger men or starting on a junior varsity team that receives less attention and fewer resources than the varsity team. Moreover, Moore is an exceptional athlete. How does the elimination of women's teams benefit the majority of college women athletes (including trans women and intersex women) who are not as talented as she is?

Expand gender categories to include participants whose bodies and/or gender identities do not conform to the gender binary. I believe that, despite compelling criticisms of the problems posed by dividing sports participation into sex-separate participation categories, this structure is the best way, at this point in women's sports history, to achieve sex equality in sports. Sex-separate sports teams provide the most participation opportunities for the most girls and women. Title IX, although not perfect, has demonstrated that, when opportunities are available, girls and women come to play in increasingly larger numbers with every successive generation. I do not believe that this would be so if girls and women were competing not only against each other but also against boys and men for these opportunities.

If sex-separate sports are indeed the best route to sex equality, the question is how can we expand our criteria to include competitors in women's sports who challenge the rigidity of the gender binary? Can we respect the self-affirmed gender identities of transgender athletes and the differences of sex development in intersex women by including them in our definitions of "woman" so their right to participate on women's teams is also protected?

Current Efforts to Create Inclusive Collegiate Athletic Policy Governing the Participation of Transgender and Intersex Athletes

In October 2009, the National Center for Lesbian Rights and the Women's Sports Foundation co-sponsored a national think tank titled "Equal Opportunities for Transgender Student-Athletes." The attendees were legal, medical, athletic, and advocacy leaders with expertise in transgender issues. The think tank's goal was to develop recommended policies for high school and collegiate athletic programs. The report from this think tank, *On the Team: Equal Opportunities for Transgender Student-Athletes,* includes a comprehensive discussion of issues, policy recommendations for high school and college athletics, and a list of best practices for sport administrators, coaches, student athletes, and parents (Griffin and Carroll 2010).

The following guiding principles served as a foundation for the think tank's discussions and the policy recommendations included in the report:

1. Participation in interscholastic and intercollegiate athletics is a valuable part of the education experience for all students.
2. Transgender student athletes should have equal opportunity to participate in sports.
3. The integrity of women's sports should be preserved.
4. Policies governing sports should be based on sound medical knowledge and scientific validity.
5. Policies governing sports should be objective, workable, and practicable; they should also be written, available, and equitably enforced.

6. Policies governing the participation of transgender students in sports should be fair in light of the tremendous variation among individuals in strength, size, musculature, and ability.
7. The legitimate privacy interests of all student athletes should be protected.
8. The medical privacy of transgender students should be preserved.
9. Athletic administrators, staff, parents of athletes, and student athletes should have access to sound and effective educational resources and training related to the participation of transgender and gender-variant students in athletics.
10. Policies governing the participation of transgender students in athletics should comply with state and federal laws protecting students from discrimination based on sex, disability, and gender identity and expression.

To maintain the integrity of women's sports while including transgender and intersex women athletes on women's sports teams requires that sports-governing organizations at all levels develop policies enabling women who challenge the gender binary to play. These policies must be focused on providing equal opportunities to a broad spectrum of women and be based on current medical and legal information rather than on unchallenged acceptance of the gender binary, female athletic inferiority, and a selective view of what constitutes a level playing field. This endeavor will require confronting our anxieties about blurring gender and sexuality boundaries and recognizing the arbitrary manner in which we define who is a woman to maintain a comfortable but oppressive understanding of gender and sexuality. We must recognize that the enforcement of exclusionary definitions of who qualifies as a woman denies some students the opportunity to play on school sports teams. We must understand that enabling transgender and intersex students to participate on women's sports teams is an important step toward greater equality for all women and strengthens women's sports in the same way that addressing the needs of lesbians, women

with disabilities, and women of color strengthens the broader social movement for women's equality.

Most colleges and universities include as part of their education missions commitments to equality and fairness. As reflected in nondiscrimination statements and educational programming focused on social justice and diversity, schools endeavor to invite students and staff to think more critically about privilege and disadvantage based on social and cultural identities. Policy development in collegiate athletics should reflect the broader goals and values of the schools they are part of and not allow competitive goals or financial gain to shape policies (Buzuvis 2011). Policies governing the inclusion of transgender and intersex student athletes must be based on a commitment to providing all students with equal opportunities to participate on school sports teams, while at the same time protecting the integrity of women's sports as the best strategy for achieving sex equality in sports.

References

Brake, Deborah. 2010. *Getting in the Game: Title IX and the Women's Sports Revolution*. New York: New York University Press.

Buzuvis, Erin E. 2011. *The Feminist Case for the NCAA's Recognition of Competitive Cheer as an Emerging Sport for Women*, 52 B.C. L. REV. 439.

Cahn, Susan. 1994. *Coming on Strong: Gender and Sexuality in Twentieth-Century Women's Sport*. New York: Free Press.

Carpenter, Linda Jean, and R. Vivian Acosta. 2004. *Title IX*. Champaign, IL: Human Kinetics.

Cayleff, Susan E. 1995. *Babe: The Life and Legend of Babe Didrikson Zaharias*. Urbana, IL: University of Illinois Press.

Festle, Mary Jo. 1996. *Playing Nice: Politics and Apologies in Women's Sports*. New York: Columbia University Press.

Gerber, Ellen W., Jan Felshin, and Waneen Wyrick. 1974. *The American Woman in Sport*. Reading, MA: Addison–Wesley.

Griffin, Pat. 1998. *Strong Women, Deep Closets: Lesbians and Homophobia in Sport*. Champaign, IL: Human Kinetics.

Griffin, Pat, and Helen J. Carroll. 2010. On the Team: Equal Opportunities for Transgender Student-Athletes. National Center for Lesbian Rights and Women's Sports Foundation. Available at: http://www.nclrights.org/site/DocServer/TransgenderStudentAthleteReport.pdf?docID=7901.

Hogshead-Makar, Nancy, and Andrew Zimbalist, eds. 2007. *Equal Play: Title IX and Social Change.* Philadelphia, PA: Temple University Press.

Lawrence, Marta. 2011. *Transgender Policy Approved.* September 13, NCAA.org. Available at http://www.ncaa.org/wps/wcm/connect/public/NCAA/Resources/Latest+News/2011/September/Transgender+policy+approved.

McDonagh, Eileen, and Laura Pappano. 2008. *Playing with the Boys.* New York: Oxford University Press.

Questions for Critical Thinking

1. How does the notion of transgender challenge the ways that you view gender? Does it encourage you to see issues of gender in new and different ways? Why or why not?

2. How does your gender identity influence your understanding of or level of agreement with the author's discussion?

3. Considering Griffin's discussion, do you think it is possible or desirable to expand or eliminate socially defined gender roles, particularly in the field of athletics?

Naming All the Parts

KATE BORNSTEIN

The first reading of this section by playwright and gender scholar Kate Bornstein links constructions of gender to those of sexuality. She notes that, although gender is a social construct, we typically assume that it is biological. As a result, we marginalize other ways of conceptualizing and experiencing gender. Additionally, she discusses the problems that result from conflating concepts of gender and sex with those of sexuality. By doing so, we construct ideas of what is normal sexuality and what is not, and we limit the dynamic aspects of our sexual identities.

For the first thirty-or-so years of my life, I didn't listen, I didn't ask questions, I didn't talk, I didn't deal with gender—I avoided the dilemma as best I could. I lived frantically on the edge of my white male privilege, and it wasn't 'til I got into therapy around the issue of my transsexualism that I began to take apart gender and really examine it from several sides. As I looked at each facet of gender, I needed to fix it with a definition, just long enough for me to realize that each definition I came up with was entirely inadequate and needed to be abandoned in search of deeper meaning.

Definitions have their uses in much the same way that road signs make it easy to travel: they point out the directions. But you don't get where you're going when you just stand underneath some sign, waiting for it to tell you what to do.

I took the first steps of my journey by trying to define the phenomenon I was daily becoming.

There's a real simple way to look at gender: Once upon a time, someone drew a line in the sands of a culture and proclaimed with great self-importance, "On this side, you are a man; on the other side, you are a woman." It's time for the winds of change to blow that line away. Simple.

Gender means *class.* By calling gender a system of classification, we can dismantle the system and examine its components. Suzanne Kessler and Wendy McKenna in their landmark 1978 book, *Gender: An Ethnomethodological Approach,* open the door to viewing gender as a social construct. They pinpoint various phenomena of gender, as follows:

Gender Assignment

Gender assignment happens when the culture says, "This is what you are." In most cultures, we're assigned a gender at birth. In our culture, once you've been assigned a gender, that's what you are; and for the most part, it's doctors who dole out the gender assignments, which shows you how emphatically gender has been medicalized. These doctors look down at a newly-born infant and say, "It has a penis; it's a boy." Or they say, "It doesn't have a penis; it's a girl." It has little or nothing to do with vaginas. It's all penises or no penises: gender assignment is both phallocentric and genital. Other cultures are not or have not been so rigid.

In the early nineteenth century, Kodiak Islanders would occasionally assign a female gender to a child with a penis: this resulted in a woman who would bring great good luck to her husband, and a larger dowry to her parents. The European umbrella term for this and any other type of Native American transgendered person is *berdache*. Walter Williams in *The Spirit and the Flesh* chronicles nearly as many types of *berdache* as there were nations.

> *Even as early as 1702, a French explorer who lived for four years among the Illinois Indians noted that berdaches were known "from their childhood, when they are seen frequently picking up the spade, the spindle, the ax [women's tools], but making no use of the bow and arrow as all the other small boys do."*
>
> —Pierre Liette, *Memoir of Pierre Liette on the Illinois Country*

When the gender of a child was in question in some Navajo tribes, they reached a decision by putting a child inside a *tipi* with a loom and a bow and arrow—female and male implements, respectively. They set fire to the *tipi,* and whatever the child grabbed as he/she ran out determined the child's gender. It was perfectly natural to these Navajo that the child had some say in determining its own gender. Compare this method with the following modern example:

> *[The Montana Educational Telecommunications Network, a computer bulletin board,] enabled students in tiny rural schools to communicate with students around the world. Cynthia Denton, until last year a teacher at the only public school in Hobson, Montana (population 200), describes the benefit of such links. "When we got our first messages from Japan, a wonderful little fifth-grade girl named Michelle was asked if she was a boy or a girl. She was extraordinarily indignant at that, and said, 'I'm Michelle—I'm a girl of course.' Then I pointed out*

> *the name of the person who had asked the question and said, 'Do you know if this is a boy or a girl?' She said, 'No, how am I supposed to know that?' I said, 'Oh, the rest of the world is supposed to know that Michelle is a girl, but you have no social responsibility to know if this is a boy or a girl?' She stopped and said, 'Oh.' And then she rephrased her reply considerably."*
>
> —Jacques Leslie, *The Cursor Cowboy*, 1993

Is the determination of one another's gender a "social responsibility"?

Do we have the legal or moral right to decide and assign our own genders?

Or does that right belong to the state, the church, and the medical profession?

If gender is classification, can we afford to throw away the very basic right to classify ourselves?

Gender Identity

Gender identity answers the question, "Who am I?" Am I a man or a woman or a what? It's a decision made by nearly every individual, and it's subject to any influence: peer pressure, advertising, drugs, cultural definitions of gender, whatever.

Gender identity is assumed by many to be "natural"; that is someone can feel "like a man," or "like a woman." When I first started giving talks about gender, this was the one question that would keep coming up: "Do you feel like a woman now?" "Did you ever feel like a man?" "How did you know what a woman would feel like?"

I've no idea what "a woman" feels like. I never did feel like a girl or a woman; rather, it was my unshakable conviction that I was not a boy or a man. It was the absence of a feeling, rather than its presence, that convinced me to change my gender.

What **does** a man feel like?

What does a woman feel like?

Do **you** feel "like a man?"

Do you feel "like a woman?"

I'd really like to know that from people.

Gender identity answers another question: "To which gender (class) do I want to belong?" Being and belonging are closely related concepts when it comes to gender. I felt I was a woman (being), and more importantly I felt I belonged with the other women (belonging). In this culture, the only two sanctioned gender clubs are "men" and "women." If you don't belong to one or the other, you're told in no uncertain terms to sign up fast. . . .

. . . I remember a dream I had when I was no more than seven or eight years old—I might have been younger. In this dream, two lines of battle were drawn up facing one another on a devastated plain: I remember the earth was dry and cracked. An army of men on one side faced an army of women on the other. The soldiers on both sides were exhausted. They were all wearing skins—I remember smelling the untanned leather in my dream. I was a young boy, on the side of the men, and I was being tied down to a roughly-hewn cart. I wasn't struggling. When I was completely secured the men attached a long rope to the cart, and tossed the other end of the rope over to the women. The soldiers of the women's army slowly pulled me across the empty ground between the two armies, as the sun began to rise. I could see only the sun and the sky. When I'd been pulled over to the side of the women, they untied me, turned their backs to the men, and we all walked away. I looked back, and saw the men walking away from us. We were all silent.

I wonder about reincarnation. I wonder how a child could have had a dream like that in such detail. I told this dream to the psychiatrist at the Army induction center in Boston in 1969—they'd asked if I'd ever had any strange dreams, so I told them this one. They gave me a 1-Y, deferred duty due to psychiatric instability.

Gender Roles

Gender roles are collections of factors which answer the question, "How do I need to function so that society perceives me as belonging or not belonging to a specific gender?" Some people

would include appearance, sexual orientation, and methods of communication under the term, but I think it makes more sense to think in terms of things like jobs, economic roles, chores, hobbies; in other words, positions and actions specific to a given gender as defined by a culture. Gender roles, when followed, send signals of membership in a given gender.

Gender Attribution

Then there's gender attribution, whereby we look at somebody and say, "that's a man," or "that's a woman." And this is important because the way we perceive another's gender affects the way we relate to that person. Gender attribution is the sneaky one. It's the one we do all the time without thinking about it; kinda like driving a sixteen-wheeler down a crowded highway . . . without thinking about it.

In this culture, gender attribution, like gender assignment, is phallocentric. That is, one is male until perceived otherwise. According to a study done by Kessler and McKenna, one can extrapolate that it would take the presence of roughly four female cues to outweigh the presence of one male cue: one is assumed male until proven otherwise. That's one reason why many women today get "sirred" whereas very few men get called "ma'am."

Gender attribution depends on cues given by the attributee, and perceived by the attributer. The categories of cues as I have looked at them apply to a man/woman bi-polar gender system, although they could be relevant to a more fluidly-gendered system. I found these cues to be useful in training actors in cross-gender role-playing.

Physical cues include body, hair, clothes, voice, skin, and movement.

I'm nearly six feet tall, and I'm large-boned. Like most people born "male," my hands, feet, and forearms are proportionally larger to my body as a whole than those of people born "female." My hair pattern included coarse facial hair. My voice is naturally deep—I sang bass in a high school choir and quartet. I've had to study ways and means of either changing these physical cues, or drawing attention away from them if I want to achieve a female attribution from people.

Susan Brownmiller's book, *Femininity,* is an excellent analysis of the social impact of physical factors as gender cues.

Behavioral cues include manners, decorum, protocol, and deportment. Like physical cues, behavioral cues change with time and culture. *Dear Abby* and other advice columnists often freely dispense gender-specific manners. Most of the behavioral cues I can think of boil down to how we occupy space, both alone and with others.

Some points of manners are not taught in books of etiquette. They are, instead, signals we learn from one another, mostly signals acknowledging membership to an upper (male) or lower (female) class. But to commit some of *these* manners in writing in terms of gender-specific behavior would be an acknowledgment that gender exists as a class system.

Here's one: As part of learning to pass as a woman, I was taught to avoid eye contact when walking down the street; that looking someone in the eye was a male cue. Nowadays, sometimes I'll look away, and sometimes I'll look someone in the eye—it's a behavior pattern that's more fun to play with than to follow rigidly. A femme cue (not "woman," but "femme") is to meet someone's eyes (usually a butch), glance quickly away, then slowly look back into the butch's eyes and hold that gaze: great hot fun, that one!

In many transsexual and transvestite meetings I attended, when the subject of the discussion was "passing," a lot of emphasis was given to manners: who stands up to shake hands? who exits an elevator first? who opens doors? who lights cigarettes? These are all cues I had to learn in order to pass as a woman in this culture. It wasn't 'til I began to read feminist literature that I began to question these cues or to see them as oppressive.

Textual cues include histories, documents, names, associates, relationships—true or false—which support a desired gender attribution. Someone trying to be taken for male in this culture might

take the name Bernard, which would probably get a better male attribution than the name Brenda.

Changing my name from Al to Kate was no big deal in Pennsylvania. It was a simple matter of filing a form with the court and publishing the name change in some unobtrusive "notices" column of a court-approved newspaper. Bingo—done. The problems came with changing all my documents. The driver's license was particularly interesting. Prior to my full gender change, I'd been pulled over once already dressed as a woman, yet holding my male driver's license—it wasn't something I cared to repeat.

Any changes in licenses had to be done in person at the Department of Motor Vehicles. I was working in corporate America: Ford Aerospace. On my lunch break, I went down to the DMV and waited in line with the other folks who had changes to make to their licenses. The male officer at the desk was flirting with me, and I didn't know what to do with that, so I kept looking away. When I finally got to the desk, he asked "Well, young lady, what can we do for you?"

"I've got to make a name change on my license," I mumbled.

"Just get married?" he asked jovially.

"Uh, no," I replied.

"Oh! Divorced!" he proclaimed with just a bit of hope in his voice, "Let's see your license." I handed him my old driver's license with my male name on it. He glanced down at the card, apparently not registering what he saw. "You just go on over there, honey, and take your test. We'll have you fixed up soon. Oh," he added with a wink, "if you need anything special, you just come back here and ask old Fred."

I left old Fred and joined the line for my test. I handed the next officer both my license and my court order authorizing my name change. This time, the officer didn't give my license a cursory glance. He kept looking at me, then down at the paper, then me, then the paper. His face grim, he pointed over to the direction of the testing booths. On my way over to the booths, old Fred called out,

"Honey, they treating you all right?" Before I could reply, the second officer snarled at old Fred to "get his butt over" to look at all my paperwork.

I reached the testing booths and looked back just in time to see a quite crestfallen old Fred looking at me, then the paper, then me, then the paper. **Mythic cues** include cultural and sub-cultural myths which support membership in a given gender. This culture's myths include archetypes like: weaker sex, dumb blonde, strong silent type, and better half. Various waves of the women's movement have had to deal with a multitude of myths of male superiority.

Power dynamics as cue include modes of communication, communication techniques, and degrees of aggressiveness, assertiveness, persistence, and ambition.

Sexual orientation as cue highlights, in the dominant culture, the heterosexual imperative (or in the lesbian and gay culture, the homosexual imperative). For this reason, many male heterosexual transvestites who wish to pass as female will go out on a "date" with another man (who is dressed as a man)—the two seem to be a heterosexual couple. In glancing at the "woman" of the two, an inner dialogue might go, "It's wearing a dress, and it's hanging on the arm of a man, so it must be a woman." For the same man to pass as a female in a lesbian bar, he'd need to be with a woman, dressed as a woman, as a "date."

> I remember one Fourth of July evening in Philadelphia, about a year after my surgery. I was walking home arm in arm with Lisa, my lover at the time, after the fireworks display. We were leaning in to one another, walking like lovers walk. Coming towards us was a family of five: mom, dad, and three teenage boys. "Look, it's a coupla faggots," said one of the boys. "Nah, it's two girls," said another. "That's enough outa you," bellowed the father, "one of 'em's got to be a man. This is America!"

So sex (the act) and gender (the classification) are different, and depending on the qualifier one is using for gender differentiation, they may or may not be dependent on one another. There are probably as many types of gender (gender systems) as could be imagined. Gender by clothing, gender by divine right, gender by lottery—these all make as much sense as any other criteria, but in our Western civilization, we bow down to the great god Science. No other type of gender holds as much sway as:

Biological gender, which classifies a person through any combination of body type, chromosomes, hormones, genitals, reproductive organs, or some other corporal or chemical essence. Belief in biological gender is in fact a belief in the supremacy of the body in the determination of identity. It's biological gender that most folks refer to when they say *sex*. By calling something "sex," we grant it seniority over all the other types of gender—by some right of biology.

So, there are all these *types* of gender which in and of themselves are *not* gender, but criteria for systemic classification. And there's sex, which somehow winds up on top of the heap. Add to this room full of seeds the words *male, female, masculine, feminine, man, woman, boy, girl*. These words are not descriptive of any sexual act, so all these words fall under the category of gender and are highly subjective, depending on which system of gender one is following.

But none of this explains why there is such a widespread insistence upon the conflation of *sex* and *gender*. I think a larger question is why Eurocentric culture needs to see *so much* in terms of sex.

> It's not like gender is the *only* thing we confuse with sex. As a culture, we're encouraged to equate sex (the act) with money, success, and security; and with the products we're told will help us attain money, success and security. We live in a culture that succeeds in selling products (the apex of accomplishment in capitalism) by aligning those products with the attainment of one's sexual fantasies.

> Switching my gender knocked me for a time curiously out of the loop of ads designed for men or women, gays or straights. I got to look at sex without the hype, and ads without the allure. None of them, after all, spoke to me, although all of them beckoned.

Kinds of Sex

It's important to keep *gender* and *sex* separated as, respectively, *system* and *function*. Since function is easier to pin down than system, sex is a simpler starting place than gender.

Sex does have a primary factor to it which is germane to a discussion of gender: *sexual orientation,* which is what people call it, if they believe you're born with it, or *sexual preference,* which is what people call it if they believe you have more of a choice and more of a say in the matter.

> [W]e do not need a sophisticated methodology or technology to confirm that the gender component of identity is the most important one articulated during sex. Nearly everyone (except for bisexuals, perhaps) regards it as the prime criterion for choosing a sex partner.
> —Murray S. Davis, *Smut: Erotic Reality/Obscene Ideology,* 1983

The Basic Mix-Up
A gay man who lived in Khartoum
Took a lesbian up to his room.
They argued all night
Over who had the right
To do what, and with what, to whom.
> —Anonymous limerick

Here's the tangle that I found: sexual orientation/preference is based in this culture solely on the gender of one's partner of choice. Not only do we confuse the two words, we make them dependent on one another. The only choices we're given to determine the focus of our sexual desire are these:

- *Heterosexual model:* in which a culturally-defined male is in a relationship with a culturally-defined female.
- *Gay male model:* two culturally-defined men involved with each other.
- *Lesbian model:* two culturally-defined women involved with each other.
- *Bisexual model:* culturally-defined men and women who could be involved with either culturally-defined men or women.

Variants to these gender-based relationship dynamics would include heterosexual female with gay male, gay male with lesbian woman, lesbian woman with heterosexual woman, gay male with bisexual male, and so forth. People involved in these variants know that each dynamic is different from the other. A lesbian involved with another lesbian, for example, is a very different relationship than that of a lesbian involved with a bisexual woman, and *that's* distinct from being a lesbian woman involved with a heterosexual woman. What these variants have in common is that each of these combinations forms its own clearly-recognizable dynamic, and none of these are acknowledged by the dominant cultural binary of sexual orientation: heterosexuality/homosexuality.

Despite the non-recognition of these dynamics by the broader culture, *all these models depend on the gender of the partner.* This results in minimizing, if not completely dismissing, other dynamic models of a relationship which could be more important than gender and are often more telling about the real nature of someone's desire. There are so many factors on which we *could* base sexual orientation. The point is there's more to sex (the act) than gender (one classification of identity).

> Try making a list of ways in which sexual preference or orientation could be measured, and then add to that list (or subtract from it) every day for a month, or a year (or for the rest of your life). Could be fun!

Sex without Gender

There are plenty of instances in which sexual attraction can have absolutely nothing to do with the gender of one's partner.

> When Batman and Catwoman try to get it on sexually, it only works when they are both in their caped crusader outfits. Naked heterosexuality is a miserable failure between them. . . . When they encounter each other in costume however something much sexier happens and the only thing missing is a really good scene where we get to hear the delicious sound of Catwoman's latex rubbing on Batman's black

rubber/leather skin. To me their flirtation in capes looked queer precisely because it was not heterosexual, they were not man and woman, they were bat and cat, or latex and rubber, or feminist and vigilante: gender became irrelevant and sexuality was dependent on many other factors. . . .

You could also read their sexual encounters as the kind of sex play between gay men and lesbians that we are hearing so much about recently: in other words, the sexual encounter is queer because both partners are queer and the genders of the participants are less relevant. Just because Batman is male and Catwoman is female does not make their interactions heterosexual—think about it, there is nothing straight about two people getting it on in rubber and latex costumes, wearing eyemasks and carrying whips and other accoutrements.

—Judith Halberstam, "Queer Creatures," On Our Backs, Nov./Dec., 1992

Sexual preference *could* be based on genital preference. (This is not the same as saying preference for a specific gender, unless you're basing your definition of gender on the presence or absence of some combination of genitals.) Preference could also be based on the kind of sex *acts* one prefers. But despite the many variations possible, sexual orientation/preference remains culturally linked to our gender system (and by extension to gender identity) through the fact that it's most usually based on the gender of one's partner. This link probably accounts for much of the tangle between sex and gender.

The confusion between sex and gender affects more than individuals and relationships. The conflation of sex and gender contributes to the linking together of the very different subcultures of gays, lesbians, bisexuals, leather sexers, sex-workers, and the transgendered.

A common misconception is that male cross-dressers are both gay and prostitutes, whereas the truth of the matter is that most cross-dressers that I've met hold down more mainstream jobs, careers, or professions, are married, and are practicing heterosexuals.

A dominant culture tends to combine its subcultures into manageable units. As a result, those who practice non-traditional sex are seen by members of the dominant culture (as well as by members of sex and gender subcultures) as a whole with those who don non-traditional gender roles and identities. Any work to deconstruct the gender system needs to take into account the artificial amalgam of subcultures, which might itself collapse if the confusion of terms holding it together were to be settled.

In any case, if we buy into categories of sexual orientation based solely on gender—heterosexual, homosexual, or bisexual—we're cheating ourselves of a searching examination of our real sexual preferences. In the same fashion, by subscribing to the categories of gender based solely on the male/female binary, we cheat ourselves of a searching examination of our real gender identity. And now we can park sex off to the side for a while, and bring this essay back around to gender.

Desire

I was not an unattractive man. People's reactions to my gender change often included the remonstrative, "But you're such a good-looking guy!" Nowadays, as I navigate the waters between male and female, there are still people attracted to me. At first, my reaction was fear: "What kind of pervert," I thought, "would be attracted to a freak like me?" As I got over that internalized phobia of my transgender status, I began to get curious about the nature of desire, sex, and identity. When, for example, I talk about the need to do away with gender, I always get looks of horror from the audience: "What about desire and attraction!" they want to know, "How can you have desire with no gender?" They've got a good point: the concepts of sex and gender seem to overlap around the phenomenon of desire. So I began to explore my transgendered relationship to desire.

About five months into living full-time as a woman, I woke up one morning and felt really good about the day. I got dressed for work, and checking the mirror before I left, I liked what I saw—at last! I opened the door to leave the building, only to find two workmen standing on the porch, the hand of one poised to knock on the door. This workman's face lit up when he saw me. "Well!" he said, "Don't you look beautiful today." At that moment, I realized I didn't know how to respond to that. I felt like a deer caught in the headlights of an oncoming truck. I really wasn't prepared for people to be attracted to me. To this day, I don't know how to respond to a man who's attracted to me—I never learned the rituals.

To me, desire is a wish to experience someone or something that I've never experienced, or that I'm not currently experiencing. Usually, I need an identity appropriate (or appropriately inappropriate) to the context in which I want to experience that person or thing. This context could be anything: a romantic involvement, a tennis match, or a boat trip up a canal. On a boat trip up the canal, I could appropriately be a passenger or a crew member. In a tennis match, I could be a player, an audience member, a concessionaire, a referee, a member of the grounds staff. In the context of a romantic involvement, it gets less obvious about what I need to be in order to have an appropriate identity, but I would need to have *some* identity. Given that most romantic or sexual involvements in this culture are defined by the genders of the partners, the *most* appropriate identity to have in a romantic relationship would be a gender identity, or something that passes for gender identity, like a gender role. A gender role might be butch, femme, top, and bottom—these are all methods of acting. So, even without a gender identity per se, some workable identity can be called up and put into motion within a relationship, and when we play with our identities, we play with desire. Some identities stimulate desire; others diminish desire. To make ourselves attractive to someone, we modify our identity, or at least the appearance of an identity—and this includes gender identity.

I love the idea of being without an identity; it gives me a lot of room to play around; but it makes me dizzy, having nowhere to hang my hat. When I get too tired of not having an identity, I take one on: it doesn't really matter what identity I take on, as long as it's recognizable. I can be a writer, a lover, a confidante, a femme, a top, or a woman. I retreat into definition as a way of demarcating my space, a way of saying "Step back, I'm getting crowded here." By saying "I am the (fill in the blank)," I also say, "You are *not,* and so you are not in my space." Thus, I achieve privacy. Gender identity is a form of self-definition: something into which we can withdraw, from which we can glean a degree of privacy from time to time, and with which we can, to a limited degree, manipulate desire.

Our culture is obsessed with desire: it drives our economy. We come right out and say we're going to stimulate desire for goods and services, and so we're bombarded daily with ads and commercial announcements geared to make us desire things. No wonder the emphasis on desire spills over into the rest of our lives. No wonder I get panicked reactions from audiences when I suggest we eliminate gender as a system; gender defines our desire, and we don't know what to do if we don't have desire. Perhaps the more importance a culture places on desire, the more conflated become the concepts of sex and gender.

As an exercise, can you recall the last time you saw someone whose gender was ambiguous? Was this person attractive to you? And if you knew they called themselves neither a man nor a woman, what would it make you if you're attracted to that person? And if you were to kiss? Make love? What would you be?

Questions for Critical Thinking

1. Bornstein discusses how constructs of sex and gender are connected to sexuality. Do her ideas challenge the way in which you view gender and sexuality? Why or why not?
2. How does your own gender and sexual identity influence your understanding of or level of agreement with the author's discussion?
3. To many of us, it is important that we are able to identify the sex of another individual. When there is ambiguity, we often have a sense of frustration. Why do you think this is? If we were to have a greater tolerance for such ambiguity, how might that impact our level of tolerance for ambiguity with regard to sexuality?

"If You Don't Kiss Me, You're Dumped"

Boys, Boyfriends and Heterosexualised Masculinities in the Primary School

EMMA RENOLD

In the essay that follows, author Emma Renold, professor of childhood studies, explores how the primary or elementary school serves as a site for constructing heterosexual identities. Drawing from her ethnographic research with ten- and eleven-year-old boys, she illustrates how these constructions of sexuality are often linked with normative assumptions of gender and sexism as well as homophobia.

Introduction

The sanctioning and institutionalisation of heterosexuality within school arenas has been empirically explored in a now growing volume of US, UK and Australian research (Mahony & Jones, 1989; Thorne, 1993; Mac an Ghaill, 1994, 1996; Laskey & Beavis, 1996; Epstein, 1997a, b; Kehily & Nayak, 1997; Epstein & Johnson, 1998; Letts & Sears, 1999; Epstein *et al.*, 2001). Schools and schooling processes are now recognised as key social sites in the production and reproduction of male heterosexualities and boys' sexual cultures (Kehily, 2000). Researchers have extended their understanding of "heterosexual" practices, from sexual activity, to a wide range of discourses and performances, through which boys (and girls) define, negotiate and essentially construct their gendered selves. For example, Mac an Ghaill (1994) and Connell (1995) have shown how hegemonic masculine performances are inextricably tied to dominant notions of heterosexuality. They and others have argued that by problematising and interrogating the "heterosexual presumption," within educational organisations, its "normalisation" and subsequent "dominance" is made visible (Epstein & Johnson, 1994). This has led to a number of school-based investigations into the processes by which heterosexual identities are produced and desired and how that dominance is secured and maintained.

Overwhelmingly, these investigations have focused upon the production of older male heterosexualities (Mac an Ghaill, 1994, 1996; Epstein & Johnson, 1994; Kehily & Nayak, 1996, 1997, 2000; Nayak & Kehily, 1997; Haywood, 1996; Redman 2000, 2001; Frosh *et al.*, 2002). Little research attention has been paid to (hetero)sexualised pupil cultures within the primary school (although see Wallis & VanEvery, 2000; Redman, 1996) and in particular the diversity and ambiguities surrounding boys' heterosexual cultures within primary/elementary school research (see Skelton 2001, pp. 149–154). This paper hopes to offer some insight into the different ways in which Year 6 boys (aged 10/11) engage with, practice and occupy "heterosexualities" and how integral, yet complex and contradictory heterosexual performances are to the production of "proper" boys. It foregrounds children's own accounts and constructions of dominant notions of heterosexualised masculinities which were, for some boys, produced through the precarious and fragile subject position of "boyfriend" but also through heterosexual fantasies/sex-play, homophobic, anti-gay and misogynistic talk and behaviour and the sexualised harassment of female classmates.

The Study: Researching and Theorising Children's Gender and Sexual Relations

The data and analyses presented in this paper derive from doctoral research in the form of a year-long ethnography exploring the construction of children's gender and sexual identities in their final year (Year 6) of primary school (Renold, 1999). The fieldwork was conducted during the academic year 1995/1996 in two primary schools, Tipton Primary and Hirstwood (both pseudonyms) situated in a small semi-rural town in the east of England [1]. Fifty-nine children from two Year Six classes participated in the research [2]. Alongside observation, unstructured exploratory friendship group interviews was the main method used to explore children's gender and sexual relations because it maximised children's ability to create spaces (physical and discursive) from which they could freely discuss what they felt to be important and significant to them. As discussed elsewhere (Renold 2000, 2002a) I did not set out to study children's sexual cultures. However, as in many qualitative studies, the reflexivity and flexibility of the ethnographic process, combined with the longitudinal element of the research, led to a progressive focusing of ideas. From examining gender relations, I found myself increasingly witnessing a complex, interactive and daily network of heterosexual performances by both boys and girls as they negotiated their gendered selves. And from the first few weeks in the field, the inter-connectedness of sexuality and gender was becoming increasingly visible and I began exploring how dominant notions of heterosexuality underscore much of children's identity work and peer relationships as they "live out" the categories "girl" and "boy."

I also began to disrupt the myth of the primary school as an "asexual" environment and explore how young children are each subject to the pressures of "compulsory heterosexuality" (Rich, 1980) and "the heterosexual matrix" (Butler, 1990)—where to be a "normal" boy and girl involves the projection of a coherent and abiding heterosexual self:

> I use the term *heterosexual matrix* . . . to designate that grid of cultural intelligibility through which bodies, genders, and desires are naturalised . . . a hegemonic discursive/epistemological model of gender intelligibility that assumes that for bodies to cohere and make sense there must be a stable sex expressed through a stable gender (masculine expresses male, feminine expresses female) that is oppositionally and hierarchically defined through the compulsory practice of heterosexuality. (Butler, 1990, p. 151)

This paper seeks to examine the acting out of Butler's (1990) "heterosexual matrix" in which the "real" expression of masculinity and femininity is embedded within a presupposed heterosexuality. It explores how boys, multiply positioned through generational ("child") and gendered discourses ("boy"), make sense of the oppositionality of sex/gender through the often hierarchical heterosexualised economies of classroom and playground relations.

The Social World of Boyfriends and Girlfriends: A Case of Mixed Messages

A number of studies have explored the salience of (hetero)sexualities and the discursive practices of dating, dumping and two-timing within a boyfriend/girlfriend network that permeates and structures most upper primary school children's social relations [3] (Thorne, 1993; Hatcher, 1995; Redman, 1996). This study was no exception (see Renold, 2000). For example, simple mixed-sex interactions like borrowing a pencil or helping with a class-task could be (hetero)sexualised (usually by teasing the boy/girl involved that they "fancy" each other). What became apparent, however, was that having a girlfriend and being a boyfriend seemed to be an increasingly *overt* "compulsory" signifier for the public affirmation of a boy's heterosexuality, and a further performative signifier of their hegemonic masculinity [4]. The following group interview extract goes some way to highlight the pressures, pleasures and fears of the heterosexual matrix at work via a ritualised, yet diverse language of "fancying," "going-out," "love" and "embarrassment":

ER: OK, you can talk about what you like . . . .

MARTIN: Erm erm erm erm cool . . . erm Jenna fancies Michael, Michael fancies Jenna

MICHAEL: No I don't

MARTIN: Only joking

ER: How do you /feel about Jenna fancying you Michael?

MARTIN: I was only joking

MICHAEL: Not very good

ER: Why not?

MARTIN: She's a fat cow

COLIN: She put, she put on his dictionary, erm, "good luck, I love you"

ER: Really? . . . (he nods) Have you spoke to her at all?

MICHAEL: (shakes his head to signify "no")

MARTIN: He's shy . . . he's getting embarrassed

COLIN: I'll speak for him, "no"

MARTIN: She's a cow

Despite the ubiquitous presence, and often highly desirable status of boyfriend, actually "going out" [5] with a girl created conformative pressures for boys and girls. Indeed as the latter extract illustrates "coming out" as heterosexual in this way, was often a complex and contradictory process. Despite the connection, heterosexual performances, or "having a girlfriend," did not automatically signify hegemonic masculinity. It was usually only the boys who were good at sport (usually football), and who were deemed "hard," "tough," "cool" or "good-looking" by their peers, who were reported to be the most romantically desirable. While more gentle and non-sporting boys invested and participated in the heterosexual network of boyfriends and girlfriends, they were more often positioned as "heterosexual failures" and subject to much teasing and ridicule, usually for pursuing or being pursued by "non-desirable" girls (see Renold, 2002b). For the majority of girls in this study, the most sought after boys constituted the "A" team (football). Heterosexual hierarchies were thus produced and the cycle of heterosexuality, sport and hegemonic masculinity reinforced.

I have discussed elsewhere how competing discourses surrounding the sexually innocent child and the sexual adolescent created contradictions and conflicts for many girls in ways that were not reported or observed in boys' sexual cultures (Renold, 2000). Rather, boys' contradictions lay in their ambivalent attitude towards proximity to girls. This could give rise to teasing behaviours associated with fear of the "feminine" (often via a language of pollution, disease and contamination) or could publicly represent and confirm a boy's heterosexual masculinity. In sum, physical or emotional closeness to girls could be both masculinity confirming and masculinity denying. Indeed, teasing and ridicule, as illustrated in the extract above, predominantly occurred when boys, like Martin, rarely located themselves in heterosexual/romantic discourses and when there was a lack of boys in the group who were "going out" or who previously had a "girlfriend." Furthermore, attempts to re-secure "masculinity," often led boys to draw on alternative hegemonic discourses such as misogynist comments which usually involved the objectification of girls ("she's a cow"). The fine line between romance and sexual harassment (Skelton, 2001) is discussed in more detail later in the paper.

"It's Always the Girls That Use You": Heterosexual/Romantic Delusions

With a few exceptions, most of the boys who were observed to fleetingly engage in the subject position "boyfriend" and the heterosexualised practices of "fancying" and "going out" rarely felt at ease or reported any sustained pleasure. Many boys described their experiences in a less than positive light:

MARTIN: If you have a girlfriend you have everyone saying "oh can you come and kiss me/, can you come and kiss meee" (singsong)

COLIN: Yeah it's all that/and the next day

MARTIN: Will you kiss me, will you kiss me, will you kiss me?

ER: And you don't want to?

COLIN: NO and Harriet/is like

MARTIN: Jane and Hayley, they'll be going, if you don't kiss me you're dumped

While some boys were teased for not having a girlfriend, those that did, like Martin and Colin, were often overwhelmed by girls' expectations of boys to express their commitment in a physical way ("will you kiss me," "if you don't kiss me, you're dumped"). Indeed, Martin's concern over kissing further emphasises the ambiguity surrounding the desire for yet resistance of sexual maturity and "older child identities" (Redman, 1996). Alternatively, other boys (below) experienced what they considered to be more than their fair share of "dumping" (i.e. when a "relationship" is terminated). Indeed, it seemed that a great deal of power could be exercised and experienced by being able to "dump" relationships and girls were more ready to and more frequently changed their boyfriends than boys [6]:

PETE: I used to be going out with Fiona but I didn't like having a relationship with her because she always used to dump me

DARREN: Yeah that's what Victoria used to do—what she used to do when I was in a stress was she used to get in a bigger stress and then dump me . . . and then about five minutes later she always comes back to me and thinks it's all right again, "do you still love me" and she expects everything to be all right again

ER: And what does that make you feel like?

DARREN: They just use you . . . it's not fair

Indeed, the feelings of powerlessness embedded in Darren and Pete's frustration at being "always dumped" and "used" and the pressures of engaging in "older" sexual activities suggest that neither one of these boys experienced the dominant subject position and power relations associated perhaps with the more traditional heterosexual discourses of patriarchy. At best, most boys experienced heterosexual relationships as fragile, ambiguous and with a mixture of unease and tension. Given these experiences, it seems difficult to understand why many boys continued to pursue girls for "girlfriends" or subject themselves to the precarious role of "boyfriend." A possible explanation could be that the pressures of "compulsory heterosexuality" (i.e. their investment at all costs to perform as heterosexual subjects), the status attached to "older (sexually mature) identities" and the wider media/cultural discourses that bind heterosexuality with hegemonic masculinity (from TV to magazines) leave boys little discursive space for any systematic resistance without throwing into doubt their "masculinity."

"I'm Waiting until the Comp": Delayed (Hetero)Sexualities and Re(a)lationships

Some boys, however, did actively resist "being a boyfriend" and avoid engaging in the heterosexualised discourses and practices of "going-out." As the extracts below illustrate, they either expressed a desire for a "proper" relationship proceeding primary school, which involved intimate sexual activities. Or, they stressed that they were "too young" or "not ready" to have a girlfriend:

DAVID: We don't really care about the girls in our school

RYAN: Yeah

ER: At other schools?

DAVID: In Year Seven, but they're too old for us

* * *

ER: Why's that?

SEAN: Coz we don't want to

JAKE: I'm waiting until the comp

ER: You're waiting until the comp are you?

RYAN: Yeah, and I'm waiting till my brother brings one home then I'll know what to do

* * *

[responding to a discussion on the lack of sexual activity amongst boyfriends and girlfriends in their class]

RYAN: They don't do anything, they just hold hands

DAVID: Yeah, real boyfriends and girlfriends kiss properly and stuff and go around each other's houses

Drawing upon developmental discourses of childhood innocence (i.e. sexual immaturity), and exposing and positioning their peers' "relationships" as phoney (not "real"), Ryan, David, Jake and Sean provide a legitimate rejection to be part of the heterosexualised culture of their peers, whilst simultaneously confirming their imagined, and perhaps superior ("proper"), albeit delayed heterosexualised trajectories as older "comprehensive" boys. It also allowed them to position boys who "just sit and talk" with their girlfriends as subordinate and (hetero)sexually inferior [7]. However, it was not an easy position to maintain. Their "heterosexuality" could be called into question if they failed to successfully demonstrate hegemonic forms of masculinity in other ways (usually through "fighting" or "football"). As I have reported in earlier papers (Renold, 1997, 2000) and as others have noted (Connolly, 1994) the two routes through which boys defined their hegemonic masculinity were usually girlfriends and sport. For example, Ryan's positioning, as successful "sportsman," immediately follows his negative response to having a girlfriend:

ER: So what about you three, any girlfriends, David? (shakes his head), Ryan? (shakes his head), Jake? (shakes his head) . . . so no girlfriends/

RYAN: I got up to novice two in [go]carting.

However, the need for boys to outwardly perform their heterosexualised masculinity to others could not solely be achieved by demonstrating their sporting skills. Indeed, in the pursuit of a hegemonic heterosexual masculinity, which seemed to be increasingly undermined by the refusal of girls to occupy passive sexual subject positions in "real" boyfriend/girlfriend relationships (Renold, 2000), heterosexual identifications were displayed in ways that were not directly undermined or challenged.

"God, I Wish I Could Have Sex": Heterosexual Fantasies, "Sex Talk," Misogyny and Sexualised Harassment

Boys who did not regularly "go-out" or form heterosexual relationships with girls and even some of those who did, would define and construct their "heterosexuality" through publicly projecting their heterosexual fantasies and desires. They located themselves firmly as (hetero)sexual subjects both within and outside classroom spaces in a variety of ways from public and private declarations for greater sexual knowledge to the sexual objectification of girls and women.

Public Desire for Sexual Knowledge
(comments follow from a sex education lesson)

PETE: We want to know more about the girls

ER: OK, so what did you want to know more about the girls? . . . (few seconds silence and embarrassed looks)

PETE: We are interested because when you get older you've got to sometime er er . . . coz when I'm older I won't be able to do it will I, I won't be able to/

COLIN: Yeah sometime or other you'll have to do something beginning with "s" and ending in "x"/

ER: Sex

COLIN AND DARREN: Yeah

TIMOTHY: You wouldn't know how to would you/

* * *

PETE: What's the point of having sex education if you, if it's not really showing it and it's just showing your genitals and all that stuff

* * *

PETE: Yeah it hasn't got enough detail, it hasn't got enough details/
ER: So you want more detail
PETE AND TIMOTHY: Yeah
PETE: We want to know we want to have a man and a lady, real, having it off/

* * *

TIMOTHY: Today when that bloke was shaving naked they had him on for about three minutes and had the girl on/
DARREN: For three seconds bathing this other girl
PETE: All it shows was their boobies
ER: So you wanted to see more?
DARREN: More breast stroke (they all laugh)

Sexualising Lyric

The bell rings, signalling the end of break-time. Adrian walks across the playground singing out loud his version of Michael Jackson's *Earth Song* which has a number of lines beginning "what about . . .". He changes the end of the line with "what about erections?," "what about sex?," "what about masturbation?"

Sexualising Classroom Talk

Mrs Fryer tries to quieten the class down. She asks them to put their lips together. Adrian shouts out "oo err, I'm not kissing everyone in this class." Many of the boys and girls start laughing. Mrs Fryer looks at me, smiles, rolls her eyes and gives Adrian a long look (of disapproval?).

Sexual Objectification of Girls and Women

David and Sean prepare the tables for group artwork by covering them in old newspapers. As they spread the newspapers around David comes across a picture of three topless women posed in an intimate embrace. "Cor—look at this—I wouldn't mind a bit of that" and he shows up the picture to Sean and a number of boys crowd round. The boys start giggling and Mrs Fryer walks over, saying "what's the fuss, they're just naked, haven't you seen naked ladies before?" She takes the paper from them and goes back to her marking.

Sexualisation of Body Parts

TIMOTHY: Stuart gets erections
COLIN: Yeah (they all laugh) he was talking when the video was on and goes "I've got a stiffy" (more laughter)

Positioning themselves as dominant sexual subjects was achieved in a number of ways. David's public declaration of his sexual desires for supermodels (in this case, topless models) and Darren's sexualisation of the girl in the sex education video through his call for more "breast stroke" illustrates how some boys overtly located themselves as heterosexual using dominant discourses in which "women are represented as passive objects of male sexual urges, needs and desires" (Mac an Ghaill, 1994, p. 92). Other (hetero)sexualised performances were maintained through more light-hearted engagements, such as altering song lyrics to sexualise the content or introducing sexual innuendo to everyday pedagogic relations. Moreover, the first extract highlights how some boys' thirst for hetero/sexual knowledge far exceeded official sex education programmes. Like Mac an Ghaill's (1994, p. 92) findings amongst older teenage boys, the boys' "sex-talk" seemed "publicly to validate their masculinity to their male friends." All the extracts to some extent reveal boys' experimentation with sex and sexuality as a means of regulating their hetero/sexualities, transcending "official" (school) sexual discourses and releasing sexual tension through humour (last extract). Pete's fear of being caught-out, not knowing what to do (when the time comes) in future sexual relationships, however, does suggest that some boys could communicate their private insecurities.

Positioning themselves as dominant sexual subjects was also achieved, however, through overt and covert forms of sexualised harassment to their female classmates and peers.

Symbolic Sexual Gestures

The class have been told they can go out—it is now break-time. Neil gets up and as he is walking out, he stops at Carrie's table. Carrie is still sitting down. Neil bends over in front of her so that his face is parallel with hers and wags his tongue up and down directly in front of her face, then walks off. Carrie looks confused and unsettled for a moment and then continues to chat with her friends.

Sexual Swear Words

ER: So what about you Darren?

PETE: Well he's been out with Mandy, I mean, not Mandy, I mean er er Victoria about three times in the past three months init? or something like that and once he went out with her for about a month didn't ya?

DARREN: Mmm

ER: What happened, why aren't you seeing her anymore?

PETE: Because she, because he called her a fucking bitch

Physical Sexual Harassment

ER: Do boys pick on you like they do to their friends?

TRUDY: They punch you in the boobs

ANABEL: Yeah they punch you in the boobs sometimes and pull your bra and that really kills/

TRUDY: Yeah, they go like that (shows me)

ER: Who does that?

ALL: Stu

ANABEL: And Ryan and that

ER: So what do you do to that/

ANABEL: Nothing, we just walk away going like this (hugging chest), "don't touch me"

Heterosexualised harassment usually took the form of denigrating girls through sexually abusive and aggressive language, gestures or behaviours and in most cases were not reported to teaching (or non-teaching) staff (see Renold, 2002b, for a fuller discussion of sexualised bullying and harassment). On two occasions, a group of boys also took to positioning their class teacher as sexually subordinate (see Walkerdine, 1981) by calling her a "slag" and a "bitch" (in an interview): first, when football was banned on the playground and second, when they felt they were receiving unnecessary disciplinary treatment in the classroom. These forms of sexualised harassment/offensive sexualised behaviours were often engaged in by boys who were located lower down the heterosexual hierarchies (Darren for example was continuously "dumped" in a string of relationships).

What I hope these extracts go some way to illustrate are the overt ways in which boys "perform" their heterosexuality in a need to confirm their hegemonic heterosexual masculinity and how such performances, particularly the sexual objectification of women and the sexualised harassment (verbal and physical) of their female classmates, re-instated boys' heterosexual dominance, often undermined and denied through conventional and "real" boyfriend/girlfriend relationships, as Mac an Ghaill explains:

> Externally and internally males attempt to reproduce themselves as powerful within social circumstances which remain out of their control. (1996, p. 200)

With many boys coupling heterosexual activity with maturity and "older boys," these sexualised performances could also be interpreted as a direct challenge to the perceived "asexuality" of the primary school environment and discourses of "childhood innocence." They could also be one of the ways in which boys "collectively explore(d) the newly available forms of authority and autonomy conferred by their position at the 'top of the school'" (Redman, 1996, p. 178). Indeed, their entry into heterosexuality and heterosexual discourses/practices could have thus been further reinforced by their chronological positioning within the school.

Anti-gay Talk and "Homophobic" [8] Narratives

As many secondary school-based studies have illustrated, "homophobic" discourses and anti-gay/lesbian talk and behaviours saturate boys' peer-group cultures, social relations and masculinity-making activities. However, as some primary school-based research (Letts & Sears, 1999) is beginning to uncover, younger children are *also* drawing upon the term "gay" either as a general form of abuse, where the intention is to unsettle or upset their (usually male) peers, or to target particular boys who fail or choose not to access hegemonic masculine discourses or practices. I would argue, from my own research, that towards the end of children's primary school years, boys outwardly demonstrate a fear and loathing of homosexualities and are highly aware of how anti-gay talk/behaviours (labelling and teasing other boys as "gay") can police and produce acceptable heterosexual masculinities. I stress "also" because some authors (Redman, 1996) suggest that "homosexual anxieties" are not employed as a means of defining and constituting "normal" heterosexualities until boys are at least 12 to 13 years of age. The following extracts provide a rare discussion of how "homosexuality" was perceived negatively, with a mixture of fear and disgust:

> RYAN: There was a programme on the other day [it is AIDS week] I turned it off after a while, it was disgusting/
> ER: Why?
> RYAN: Because it showed these er two men who dressed up as women and they were er they were having sex and it was really horrible
> ER: And you didn't like it, so you turned it off?
> RYAN: Yeah
> ER: OK . . . why do you think you didn't like it?
> RYAN: Well like if you see a women and a man doing it I don't really care and er/
> DAVID: Coz everyone does it, every night
> RYAN: You see you see people doing it that way then you don't really mind coz that's what most people do and then you see like two men doing it and you know that's horrible, disgusting

* * *

> ER: When you say gay Jake what do you mean by that?
> JAKE: You know, like/really sad
> SEAN: A bender (Sean, Ryan and Jake laugh)/
> RYAN: And you can sound gay can't you/
> DAVID: Simon/he sounds gay
> RYAN: Our next door neighbour/

* * *

> JAKE: You know that "supermarket sweep" (game show)?
> ER: Yeah
> JAKE: Well there was this man on there/
> DAVID: And he (host of show) goes, "you're really pretty aren't you"
> JAKE: Yeah and he won it right, about 2000 pounds and he goes up to him and he can't stop kissing him (laughing) he kisses him about 2000 times/
> RYAN: Yeah that's like Michael Barrymore/
> JAKE: Yeah and/he smacked Michael Barrymore in the other day/Sean and Ryan: Yeah (they all cheer and clap)/
> DAVID: Who did?
> ER: Why is that good?
> SEAN: Coz he's gay

Anti-gay talk and homophobic performances were expressed more often by boys who did not engage in overt heterosexual boyfriend/girlfriend relationships and more frequently than boys who *did* "have girlfriends" and who *were* "going out." Indeed, the powerlessness experienced by many boys participating in the boyfriend/girlfriend cultures (i.e. being dumped or being used), the precarious position of "boyfriend" and indeed the ambiguity of initiating physical or emotional intimacies with girls at all, produced some very confusing messages and some rather contradictory heterosexual identities.

Processes of differentiation (from "homosexualities") and subordination (of alternative masculinities) were all ways in which these boys asserted and attempted to make coherent their heterosexual identities, which Mac an Ghaill and others (Kehily & Nayak, 1997; Redman, 2000) suggest involve external (social) and internal (psychic) processes:

> Heterosexual male students were involved in a double relationship of traducing the Other, including women and gays (external relations), at the same time as expelling femininity and homosexuality from within themselves (internal relations). (Mac an Ghaill, 1994, p. 90)

However, the differences in attitudes and homophobic behaviours in my study, seemed not to be based not on "class" (as in Mac an Ghaill's research) but on their success at being "tough," "sporty" and "cool," and in particular their sustained participation in heterosexual relationships. Unfortunately, what this study does lack, is a detailed discussion of boys' views towards homosexuality. Because of the sensitivity of discussing non-heterosexualities with primary school children, only the boys' perspectives who instigated discussions on homosexuality were recorded. This is surely an area which would benefit from further investigation.

Conclusions

> Young children, according to commensense understandings, are innocent. They neither do, nor should they, know anything about sexuality. The fear is that contemporary children "grow up too soon" or are "not yet ready" for sexual knowledge. (Epstein *et al.*, 2001, p. 134)

This paper is situated within a growing recognition that primary schools are far from asexual environments and primary school children cannot be presumed (sexually) innocent (Thorne & Luria, 1986; Davies, 1993; Thorne, 1993; Redman, 1996;

Connolly, 1998; Hatcher, 1995; Wallis & VanEvery, 2000; Skelton, 2001). Rather, as Wallis and VanEvery argue, "sexuality (especially heterosexuality) is not only present but crucial to the organisation of primary schools, both explicitly and implicitly" (2000, p. 411) and thus in ways similar to secondary and further education sectors, a key social and cultural site for the production of children's sexual relations and identities. Primarily, the purpose of this paper has been to make visible and thus break the silence around young children's (hetero)sexual cultures and shed some analytic light on a specific aspect of the organisational heteronormativity of the primary school—boys' sexual cultures and in particular how hegemonic masculinities involve the "heterosexual presumption." That is, how being a "proper boy" involves establishing or at least investing in and projecting a recognisable (and hegemonic) heterosexual identity.

Throughout the paper I have highlighted how all boys are to some extent subject to the pressures of "compulsory heterosexuality" (most evident in the boyfriend/girlfriend cultures of the school, which even if they were not directly engaged in, were forever positioned in relation to it). I have also shown how boys can feel confused, anxious, and powerless because of the contradictions involved in constructing heterosexualised masculinities through boyfriend/girlfriend discourses (i.e. that intimacy with girls could be simultaneously contaminating *and* masculinity confirming). In an attempt to make coherent ultimately fragile masculinities I argue that the majority of boys come to define and produce their heterosexualities through various public projections of (hetero) sexual fantasies, imagined (hetero)sexual futures, misogynistic objectifications of girls and women and homophobic/anti-gay performances towards boys and sexualised forms of harassment towards girls. Furthermore, all of these "performances" permeated and thus ultimately affected everyday classroom and playground interactions and as such became a significant site of learning as Kehily

(2002) highlights in her discussion of gender, sexuality and pedagogy in the secondary school:

> Students develop an understanding of the meanings and implications of sex–gender categories and also create their own meanings in a range of informal encounters. (2002, p. 125)

Indeed, some boys drew upon discourses of "childhood innocence" and "older sexualities" to legitimate delaying their active role in boyfriend/girlfriend networks, where others (see Renold, 2002) readily took up the subject position "boyfriend" to maintain close friendships with female classmates.

Most disturbing, however, was how the regulation of hegemonic heterosexualities through the policing and shaming of gender (Butler, 1993) which usually occurred when investment in overt heterosexual practices (girlfriends) did not automatically signify hegemonic masculinity. In these cases, such performances have real social and emotional consequences which are damaging for both boys and girls. For example, homophobic/anti-gay performances not only had the effect of subordinating alternative masculinities and non-hegemonic sexualities, but implicitly subordinates femininities and all things "feminine" (i.e. majority of girls/"girl's activities"). However, in a moral and political climate where children's sexuality and moreover sex/uality education is a contested and contentious space (see the numerous and competing struggles in the UK over the repeal of Section 28 [9]), schools are "legitimately anxious about the reactions of some parents and worse, the popular press if they stray into territory considered to be too risky" (Epstein et al., 2001, p. 136). Headteachers and teachers are thus placed in a difficult position to openly discuss children's emerging gender and sexual identities and knowledges in ways that can challenge the more prevailing heteronormativity of boys' (and girls') peer group cultures and indeed draw upon the services or formulate the policies needed to support children's more painful and oppressive practices of gender-based and sexualised forms of harassment.

On a more positive note, primary headteachers and teachers committed to creating an anti-oppressive environment that strives for gender equity and celebrates and supports diversity within gender/sexual relations can be encouraged in a number of ways:

- First, there has been a shift in UK education policy under the Local Government Act 2000 (Section 104) stating that teachers must take steps to "prevent any form of bullying," including "homophobic bullying" (Social Inclusion: Pupil Support Circular 10/99). This circular also includes a specific reference to peer bullying as a result of "or related to sexual orientation" (1.32) and includes strategies to address sexual and racial harassment (4.47). Furthermore, the government's anti-bullying pack for schools (DfEE, 2000) also offers detailed advice and guidance to prevent bullying because of perceived or actual sexual orientation. The phrasing, "related to their sexual orientation" is an important one in relation to the findings of this study insofar as much of the homophobic/anti-gay insults directed at boys are more often related to their gender deviance (from recognisable "masculine" traits) than their perceived or actual sexual orientation [10]. For those primary headteachers and governers wary of incorporating the term "sexuality" into their bullying policies, conceptualising and including gender-based harassment as a form of "bullying" will go some way to raising awareness and challenge the heteronormative status quo (because of the ways in which gender is mediated by and embedded within sexuality).

- While governing bodies have no legal obligation to provide sex education for primary school pupils, the vagueness of primary sex education guidelines creates gaps which any school can harness to tackle the more oppressive forms of gendered and sexualised harassment and bullying and develop a broader understanding of sex/uality education (Redman, 1994). For example, Brown (1997) suggests that the National Curriculum Council's (NCC) recommendations on primary sex education which stress *positivity, self-image, bodies, sexuality and relationships* and most importantly, in relation to children, *agency* and *responsibility* can be effectively deployed to construct a more comprehensive and inclusive sex/uality education policy.

- Third, as this research and other studies illustrate, many boys (and girls) are aware of the contradictions and difficulties of securing a hegemonic heterosexual masculinity and respond to "gentle challenges about the effects of narrowly constructed masculinities" (see Frosh et al., 2002, p. 262). Indeed, group discussions provide a forum for some boys to openly, and sometimes critically, discuss the constraining nature of hegemonic masculinities and can thus be deployed by teachers as one way to explore the "knock-on effect" of "doing boy" in hegemonic ways (see MacNaughton, 2000). Group-based activities, if sensitively handled, can also be useful "starting points" (see Kenway et al., 1997) for those teachers creating policies that are grounded in children's own experiences. This is especially important given the increasing recognition that pupils be more involved and active in the policy making process (Alderson, 2000). As Skelton (2001) notes, however, any specific strategy (whether it be to tackle homophobic bullying or sexualised harassment more widely) must be integrated within a whole-school approach to gender equity and one that focuses on gender relations—girls *and* boys, masculinities *and* femininities and the power relations at play in their often oppositional construction.

While there are obviously no quick-fix solutions there are opportunities and developments (and gaps) in both policy and practice for committed teachers to support pupil's emerging gender and sexual identities and combat the damaging consequences of negotiating a heteronormative world.

Notes

1. Tipton Primary's catchment area served white "working" and "middle" class families, while Hirstwood served predominantly white "middle" class families.

2. Each child participated in a series of group interviews/discussions (six times in total) over the period of a year. Indeed, I visited each school for 2/3 days every fortnight during that year.

3. Other studies have highlighted how even 4- and 5-year-olds "practice heterosexuality" through dating games and kiss chase (Epstein, 1997a; Connolly, 1998; Skelton, 2001).

4. The subject positions of "boyfriend" and "girlfriend" were discursively reproduced and maintained daily via "messengers" (usually female) who mediated and relayed love letters, dumping letters and requests to be X's boyfriend or girlfriend.

5. Despite the active connotation of the phrase "going out," couples rarely went anywhere. "Going out" was a particular discourse which signified and made available the subject position "boyfriend" or "girlfriend" and could range from a "couple" spending time together in their lunch break (holding hands, chatting, kissing) to simply *saying* you were "going out" with someone.

6. I have argued elsewhere how some girls reported experiencing a great deal of power from being able to terminate relationships. For some, it seemed the only domain in which they could "get one over the boys."

7. Indeed, I argue in another paper how some boys draw upon the discourses and engage in the practices of the boyfriend/girlfriend culture to maintain close friendships with girls and avoid the macho-making activities associated with fighting and football free (almost) from ridicule and speculation over their gender/sexual identities (Renold, 2002).

8. I am using the term "homophobic" to define those behaviours and practices which signify a fear of "homosexuality" and the term "anti-gay" to define talk and behaviour that signifies any

negative sentiment regarding same-sex identities, practices or relationships. While there is obviously some overlap, differentiating "homophobia" from "anti-gay" sentiment offers a way of situating the realm of the unconscious within wider social and cultural relations (see Redman, 2000, for a fuller discussion of the usefulness of the term "homophobia" as an analytic tool).

9. Section 28 of the 1988 Local Government Act prohibits local education authorities from "promoting" the teaching of "homosexuality as a pretended family relationship." While Section 28 has been repealed in Scotland it has undergone two defeated repeals in England and Wales (see Redman, 1994; Epstein, 2000, and Moran, 2001, for a wider discussion of Section 28).

10. However, advice and guidance to date have centred on older children and teenagers.

References

Alderson, P. 2000. Children as Researchers. In *Research with Children,* Christensen P, James, A (eds). Falmer Press: London: pp. 241–257.

Brown, T. (1997) Sex Education, in: M. Cole, D. Hill & S. Shan (Eds) *Promoting Equality in Primary Schools* (London, Routledge).

Butler, J. (1990) *Gender Trouble: Feminism and the Subversion of Identity* (London, Routledge).

———. (1993) *Bodies That Matter: On the Discursive Limits of Sex* (London, Routledge).

Connell, R. W. (1995) *Masculinities: Knowledge, Power and Social Change* (Cambridge, Polity Press).

Connolly, P. (1994) Boys will be boys? Racism, sexuality and the construction of masculine identities amongst infant boys, in: J. Holland & M. Blair (Eds) *Debates and Issues in Feminist Research and Pedagogy* (Clevedon, Multilingual Matters).

———. (1998) *Racisms, Gendered Identities and Young Children: Social Relations in a Multi-ethnic, Inner-city Primary School* (London, Routledge).

Davies, B. (1993) *Shards of Glass: Children Reading and Writing Beyond Gendered Identities* (New Jersey, Hampton Press).

Epstein, D. (1997a) Cultures of schooling/cultures of sexuality, *International Journal of Inclusive Education,* 1, pp. 37–53.

———. (1997b) Boyz' own stories: masculinities and sexualities in schools, *Gender and Education,* 9, pp. 105–117.

———. (2000) "Promoting homophobia: Section 28, schools and young people," *ChildRight,* 164, pp. 14–15.

Epstein, D. & Johnson, R. (1994) On the straight and narrow: the heterosexual presumption, homophobias and schools, in: D. Epstein (Ed.) *Challenging Lesbian and Gay Inequalities in Education* (Buckingham, Open University Press).

Epstein, D. & Johnson, R. (1998) *Schooling Sexualities* (Buckingham, Open University Press).

Epstein, D., O'Flynn, S. & Telford, D. (2001) "Othering" education: sexualities, silences and schooling, *Review of Research in Education,* 25, pp. 127–179.

Frosh, S., Phoenix, A. & Pattman, R. (2002) *Young Masculinities* (Hampshire, Palgrave).

Hatcher, R. (1995) Boyfriends, girlfriends: gender and "race" in children's cultures, *International Play Journal,* 3, pp. 187–197.

Haywood, C. (1996) Out of the curriculum: sex talking, talking sex, *Curriculum Studies,* 4, pp. 229–251.

Kehily, M.J. (2000) Understanding heterosexualities: masculinities, embodiment and schooling, in G. Walford & C. Hudson (eds.) *Genders and Sexualities in Educational Ethnography,* New York: Elsevier.

———. (2002) Issues of gender and sexuality in schools, in: B. Francis & C. Skelton (Eds) *Investigating Gender: Contemporary Perspectives in Education* (Buckingham, Open University Press).

Kehily, M. J. & Nayak, A. (1996) Playing it straight: masculinities, homophobias and schooling, *Journal of Gender Studies,* 5, pp. 211–229.

———. (1997) Lads and laughter: humour and the production of heterosexual hierarchies, *Gender and Education,* 9, pp. 69–87.

———. (2000) Schoolgirl Frictions: young women sex education and social experiences, in G Walford & C. Hudson (eds.) Genders and Sexualities in Educational Ethnography, New York: Elsevier.

Kenway, J. & Willis, S. with Blackmore, J. & Rennie, L. (1997) Are boys victims of feminism in schools?: Some answers from Australia, *International Journal of Inclusive Education,* 1, pp. 19–35.

Laskey, L. & Beavis, C. (1996) *Schooling and Sexualities: Teaching for a Positive Sexuality* (Geelong, Victoria, Deakin University Centre for Change).

Letts IV, W. & Sears, J. T. (Eds) (1999) *Queering Elementary Education: Advancing the Dialogue About Sexualities and Schooling* (New York, Rowman and Littlefield).

Mac an Ghaill, M. (1994) *The Making of Men: Masculinities, Sexualities and Schooling* (Open University Press, Buckingham).

———. (1996) Deconstructing heterosexualities within school arenas, *Curriculum Studies,* 4, pp. 191–207.

MacNaughton, G. (2000) *Rethinking Gender in Early Childhood Education* (London, Paul Chapman).

Mahony, P. & Jones, C. (Eds) (1989) *Learning Our Lines: Sexuality and Social Control in Education* (London, Women's Press).

Moran, S. (2001) Childhood sexuality and education: the case of Section 28, *Sexualities,* 4, pp. 73–89.

Nayak, A. & Kehily, M. J. (1997) Masculinities and schooling: why are young men so homophobic?, in: D.L. Steinberg, D. Epstein & R. Johnson (Eds) *Border Patrols: Policing the Boundaries of Heterosexuality* (Cassel, London).

Redman, P. (1994) Shifting ground: rethinking sexuality education, in: D. Epstein (Ed.) *Challenging Lesbian and Gay Inequalities in Education* (Buckingham, Open University Press).

———. (1996) Curtis loves Ranjit: heterosexual masculinities, schooling, and pupils' sexual cultures, *Educational Review,* 48, pp. 175–182.

———. (2000) Tarred with the same brush: homophobia and the unconscious in school-based cultures of masculinity, *Sexualities,* 3, pp. 483–499.

———. (2001) The discipline of love: negotiation and regulation in boys' performance of a romance-based heterosexual masculinity, *Men and Masculinities,* 4, pp. 186–200.

Renold, E. (1997) All they've got on their brains is football: sport, masculinity and the gendered practices of playground relations, *Sport, Education and Society,* 2, pp. 5–23.

———. 1999. Presumed innocence: an ethnographic investigation into the construction of children's gender and sexual identities in the primary school. Unpublished Doctoral Dissertation.

———. 2000. "Coming out": gender (hetero)sexuality and the primary school. *Gender and Education,* 12: 309–327.

———. (2002a) *Primary school studs: (de)constructing heterosexual masculinities in the primary school,* paper presented at British Association Annual Conference, 25–27 March 2002, University of Leicester.

———. (2002b) "Presumed innocence": (hetero) sexual, homophobic and heterosexist harassment amongst children in the primary school, *Childhood,* 9, pp. 415–433.

Rich, A. (1980) "Compulsory Heterosexuality and Lesbian Existence," *Journal of Women's History*, 15, Autumn 2003, pp. 11–48.

Skelton, C. (2001) *Schooling the Boys: Masculinities and Primary Education* (Buckingham, Open University Press).

Thorne, B. (1993) *Gender Play: Boys and Girls in School* (Buckingham, Open University Press).

Thorne, B. & Luria, Z. (1986) Sexuality and gender in children's daily worlds, *Social Problems,* 33, pp. 176–190.

Walkerdine, V. (1981) "Sex, power and pedagogy," *Screen Education*, 38: 14–24.

Wallis, A. & VanEvery, J. (2000) Sexuality in the primary school, *Sexualities,* 3, pp. 409–423.

Questions for Critical Thinking

1. Renold discusses the ways in which children in primary schools construct heterosexual identities, even at very early ages. What are some of the ways that you have witnessed the gendered behaviors of girls and boys that later influence the construction of their sexuality as women and men?

2. The experiences of the children in this article indicate that heterosexual behavior does not necessarily come naturally to girls and boys but is constructed. In your opinion, how does this challenge everyday representations of heterosexuality as the norm?

3. Do you think it is possible that we can deconstruct sexuality? What would be the implications for society if we were to be successful in doing so?

What's so Cultural about Hookup Culture?

LISA WADE

The following essay by sociologist Lisa Wade explores the norms and practices that make up college students' experience of hookup culture. Connected with her research for her book American Hookup: The New Culture of Sex on Campus, *Wade illustrates that sex on college campuses is more than just what people do and that hookup culture is a phenomenon that impacts all students, whether they participate or not.*

Arman was 7,000 miles from his family, one of the roughly million international students who were enrolled in U.S. colleges last year. Dropped into the raucous first week of freshman year, he discovered a way of life that seemed intensely foreign, frightening, and enticing. "It's been a major shock," he wrote.

The behavior of some of his fellow students unnerved him. He watched them drink to excess, tell explicit sexual stories, flirt on the quad and grind on the dance floor. He received assertive sexual signals from women. It was, Arman wrote, "beyond anything I have experienced back home."

By his second semester, Arman's religious beliefs had been shaken. He was deeply torn as to whether to participate in this new social scene. "Stuck," he wrote, "between a sexually conservative background and a relatively sexually open world." Should he "embrace, accept, and join in?" Or, he wondered, using the past tense like a Freudian slip, "remember who I was and deprive myself of the things I actually and truly want deep down inside?"

He struggled. "Always having to internally fight the desire to do sexual things with girls is not easy," he wrote. One night, he succumbed to temptation. He went to a party, drank, and kissed a girl on the dance floor. When the alcohol wore off, he was appalled at his behavior. "How much shame I have brought onto myself," he recalled with anguish.

A few months later, he would lose his virginity to a girl he barely knew. His feelings about it were deeply ambivalent. "I felt more free and unbounded," he confessed, "but at the same time, guilt beyond imagination."

For my book, *American Hookup: The New Culture of Sex on Campus*, I followed 101 college students through a semester of their first year. They submitted weekly journal entries, writing about sex and dating on campus however they wished. In total, the students wrote over 1,500 single-spaced pages and a million words. I dovetailed their stories with 21 follow-up interviews, quantitative data from the Online College Social Life Survey, academic literature, hundreds of essays written by students for college newspapers, and 24 visits to campuses around the country.

Arman was an outlier. Very few students are strongly motivated to abstain from sex altogether, but it's typical for students to report mixed feelings about the opportunity to have casual sex. Thirty-six of the 101 students I studied reported being simultaneously attracted to and repelled by hookup culture upon arrival at college, compared to thirty-four who opted out entirely, twenty-three who opted in with enthusiasm, and eight who sustained monogamous relationships.

For students like Arman, who are unsure of whether they want to participate, hookup culture has a way of tipping the scales. Its logic makes both abstaining from sex and a preference for sex in committed relationships difficult to justify, and its integration into the workings of higher education makes hooking up hard to avoid.

The Logic of Hookup Culture

Hooking up is immanently defensible in hookup culture. Students believe, or believe that their peers believe, that virginity is passé and monogamy prudish; that college is a time to go wild and have fun; that separating sex from emotions is sexually liberating; and that they're too young and career-focused for commitment. All of these ideas are widely circulated on campus—and all make reasonable sense—validating the choice to engage in casual sex while invalidating both monogamous relationships and the choice to have no sex at all.

For the students in my study who were enthusiastic about casual sex, this worked out well, but students who found casual sex unappealing often had difficulty explaining why, both to themselves or others. Many simply concluded that they were overly sensitive or insufficiently brave. "I honestly admire them," wrote one Latina student about her friends who enjoyed casual sex, "because I just cannot do that." A White middle-class student implored herself to not be so "uptight." "Sometimes I wish I could just loosen up," she wrote. A sexually sophisticated pansexual student wondered aloud if she was a "prude." "I'm so embarrassed by that," she confessed. "I feel as if by not voluntarily taking part in it, I am weird and abnormal."

If culture is a "toolkit" offering culturally competent actors a set of ideas and practices with which

to explain their choices, to use Ann Swider's metaphor from her article "Culture in Action," then hookup culture offers students many tools useful for embracing casual sex, but few for articulating why they may prefer other kinds of sexual engagement, or none at all. Faced with these options, many students who are ambivalent decide to give it a try.

The New Culture of College

In the colonial era, colleges were downright stodgy. Student activities were rigidly controlled, curricula were dry, and harsh punishments were meted out for misbehavior. The fraternity boys of the early 1800s can be credited with introducing the idea that college should be fun. Their lifestyle was then glamorized by the media of the 1920s and democratized by the alcohol industry in the 1980s after *Animal House*. Today, the reputation of higher education as a place for an outlandish good time is second only to its reputation as a place of learning.

Not just any good time, though. A particular kind of party dominates the social scene: drunken, wild, and visually titillating, throbbing with sexual potential. Such parties are built into the rhythm and architecture of higher education. They occur at designated times, such that they don't interfere with (most) classes, and are usually held at large, off-campus houses (often but not always fraternities) or on nearby streets populated by bars and clubs. This gives the institutions plausible deniability, but keeps the partying close enough to be part of colleges' appeal.

Almost all of the students in *American Hookup* were living in residence halls. On weekend nights, dorms buzzed with pre-partying, primping, and planning. Students who stayed in were keenly aware of what they weren't doing. Eventually residence halls would empty out, leaving eerie quiet; revelers returned drunker, louder. Students were sometimes kicked out of their own rooms to facilitate a roommate's hookup. A few had exhibitionistic roommates who didn't bother to kick them out at all.

The morning after, there would be a ritual retelling of the night before. And the morning after that, anticipation for the next weekend of partying began. Being immersed in hookup culture meant being surrounded by anticipation, innuendo, and braggadocio. As one of the African-American men in my study wrote: "Hookup culture is all over the place."

For students who went to parties, hookups felt, as several put it, "inevitable." Sooner or later, a student had one too many drinks, met someone especially cute, or felt like doing something a little wild. For young people still learning how to manage sexual desire, college parties combining sex with sensory overload and mind-altering substances can be overwhelming. Accordingly, anyone who regularly participates in the routine partying built into the rhythm of higher education will likely find themselves opting in to hooking up.

Sex on college campuses is something people do, but it's also a cultural phenomenon: a conversation of a particular kind and a set of routines built into the institution of higher education. When students arrive on campus, they don't just encounter the opportunity to hook up, they are also immersed in a culture that endorses and facilitates hookups. Ceding to or resisting that culture then becomes part of their everyday lives.

"Even if you aren't hooking up," said an African-American woman about her first year on campus, "there is no escaping hookup culture." Residential colleges are what sociologist Erving Goffman called "total institutions," planned entities that collect large numbers of like individuals, cut them off from the wider society, and provide for all their needs. And because hookup culture is totally institutionalized, when students move into a dorm room on a college campus, they become a part of it—whether they like it or not.

Students wish they had more options. Some pine for the going-steady lifestyle of the 1950s. Many mourn the utopia that the sexual revolution promised but never fully delivered. Quite a few would like things to be a lot more queer and gender fluid. Some want a hookup culture that is kinder—warm as well as hot. And there are still a handful who would prefer stodgy to sexy. Satisfying these diverse desires will require a shift to a more complex and rich cultural life on campus, not just a different one.

Questions for Critical Thinking

1. How does Wade's discussion of the prevalence of hookup culture on college campuses reflect your own experiences? How do you think this culture impacts your interactions with others?

2. Wade argues that everyone is impacted by hookup culture, whether they participate in it or not. What evidence have you seen to support or refute this argument?

3. Do you think it is possible or even necessary to eliminate hookup culture on college campuses? If so, how so? If not, why not?

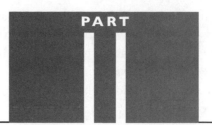

Maintaining Inequalities: Systems of Oppression and Privilege

Introduction

On April 6, 2016, Khairuldeen Makhzoomi, an Iraqi asylee and student at the University of California, Berkeley, was removed from a Southwest Airlines flight and questioned by the FBI. He had recently attended a speech by United Nations secretary general Ban Ki-moon and was excited to call his uncle to tell him about the event. While on the phone, he told his uncle about the chicken dinner they were served and the moment when he got to stand up and ask the secretary general a question about the Islamic State. A nearby passenger overheard the conversation and reported him to the crew for making "potentially threatening comments." Makhzoomi had ended his call with his uncle with a common phrase in Arabic, *inshallah*, meaning "god willing."

On March 4, 2011, Masudur Rahman and Mohamed Zaghloul, two Muslim Imams—recognized religious leaders and teachers of Islam—were on their way to a conference on prejudice against Muslims. Having been cleared by security agents, they boarded an Atlantic Southeast Airlines flight to Charlotte, North Carolina. Shortly after the aircraft left the gate, the pilot announced that the plane needed to return. When it did, the Imams were asked to go back to the boarding gate, where they were told the pilot was refusing to accept them because other passengers could be uncomfortable. The event came amid a flurry of similar incidents since the death of Osama bin Laden, according to the Council on American–Islamic Relations.

On January 1, 2009, Atif Irfan, his brother, their wives, a sister, and three children were headed to Orlando to meet with family and attend a religious conference. As they boarded the AirTran Airways plane, Irfan wondered aloud with his sister-in-law, Inayet Sahin, where the safest place to sit on the plane was. Some time later, while the plane was still at the gate, an FBI agent boarded the plane and asked Irfan and his wife to leave the plane. The rest of the family was removed shortly thereafter, along with a family friend, Abdul Aziz, a Library of Congress attorney and family friend. Although the FBI subsequently cleared the passengers and called the incident a misunderstanding, AirTran refused to seat them on another flight, forcing them to purchase last-minute tickets on another airline that had been secured with the FBI's assistance. Although the men had traditional beards and the women wore headscarves, AirTran denied that their actions were based on the passengers' appearance. A spokesman for AirTran initially defended the airline's actions and said they would not reimburse the passengers for the cost of the rebooked tickets. The following day, after the incident received widespread media coverage, AirTran reversed its position and issued a public apology, adding that it would, in fact, reimburse the passengers.

On November 20, 2006, six Muslim Imams were removed from US Airways flight 300 from Minneapolis to Phoenix. They were returning to Phoenix after attending a conference of the North American Imams Federation in Minneapolis. Their removal was instigated by what passengers and crew identified as suspicious behavior. The group drew attention initially because they were praying in the departure lounge prior to boarding.

On August 12, 2006, Raed Jarrar, an architect of Iraqi descent, was forced to remove a T-shirt bearing the slogan "We will not be silent" in English and Arabic before boarding a flight in New York. Passengers expressed concern over the meaning of the Arabic words, requesting that Jarrar remove his shirt. The slogan had been adopted by opponents to the Iraq War and other Middle Eastern conflicts and had derived from a group resistant to Nazi rule in Germany.

On September 21, 2004, Yusuf Islam, formerly known as the popular music star Cat Stevens, was refused entry into the United States. His flight from London to Washington, DC, was rerouted to Bangor, Maine, where he was questioned by officials and then taken to Boston to catch a connecting flight in Washington for London. The justification for his barred entry was the charitable donations that he had made to humanitarian causes. His donations have helped to support children affected by the wars in Bosnia and Iraq, as well as victims of the September 11, 2001, attacks against America.

On September 17, 2001, Ashraf Khan, bearing a first-class ticket, boarded Delta Airlines flight 1469 to Dallas. This was to be the first part of a two-day trip to Pakistan to attend his brother's wedding. Khan, an eleven-year US resident, was approached by the pilot, who asked to speak with him in the gate area. There, the pilot informed Mr. Khan that he and the crew did not feel safe flying with him on board. Further, the pilot questioned Khan about how he had obtained a first-class ticket.

On September 20, 2001, Kareem Alasady, a US citizen, and his two companions were denied seats on a Northwest Airlines flight from Minneapolis to Salt Lake City. A spokesperson for the airline stated that the crew took the appropriate action because the majority of the passengers felt uncomfortable flying with them.

In Tampa, Florida, Mohamed el-Sayed, a US citizen of Egyptian origin, was denied boarding on a United Airlines flight to Washington on September 21, 2001. An airport manager told him apologetically that the pilot refused to fly with him on board, explaining, "We've reviewed your profile; your name is Mohamed."

Since the events of September 11, 2001, passengers who are perceived to be Arab or followers of Islam—which has included people who are South Asian, Latino, Indian, and Mexican—have been removed from airplanes because of the refusal by crew members and passengers to fly with them. Calling it "flying while Arab," Michel Shehadeh, former West Coast regional director of the American-Arab Anti-Discrimination Committee, asserts that any Arab (or person perceived to be Arab) is thought to be a terrorist. Indeed, the legal department of the committee has addressed over sixty occurrences of discrimination against men of Middle Eastern or South Asian origins by airline crew members across the country (Shora 2002). This form of racial profiling is certainly nothing new.[1] Rather, it is based on a long history of US government anti-Arab programs and policies. However, racial profiling of people perceived to be Arab or Muslim has increased greatly as the result of a September 12, 2001, directive from the Federal Aviation Administration to the nation's airlines instructing security to immediately conduct "random identification checks," stating,

> Extremist groups, with a history of targeting civil action, are actively targeting U.S. interests, particularly in the Middle East. They retain a capability to conduct airline bombings, hijackings, suicide attacks, and possess surface-to-air missiles.

Such a directive is reinforced by other federal policies, such as the National Security Entry Exit Registration System, which was established in 2002 and required the special registration of all male nationals over the age of fifteen from twenty-five countries (with the exception of North Korea, all countries were Arab and Muslim). This registration obligated these males to report to the government to register and be fingerprinted, photographed, and questioned. Those failing to register were subject to detention and/or immediate deportation (American Civil Liberties Union 2004). Because of the ineffectiveness of this policy, the US Department of Homeland Security delisted the countries under the system in April 2011, although the regulatory structure stayed largely intact until December 2016.

Such profiling is similar to that experienced by blacks and Latinos for some time. For example, in May 1992 the Maryland State Police stopped a car in the early morning hours just outside of Cumberland, Maryland. The occupants—Washington, DC, attorney Robert Wilkins and members of his family—were questioned, ticketed, and made to stand in the rain while a dog sniffed for drugs in their car. Mr. Wilkins sued, and the resulting litigation uncovered a memorandum instructing police to watch for "predominantly black" drug couriers.

In Illinois, a defense attorney hired a Latino private investigator to drive across certain counties to test the validity of assertions that the state police stopped Latinos and African Americans in disproportionate numbers. Peso Chavez, a twenty-year veteran investigator and a former elected official from Santa Fe, New Mexico, was followed by an assistant to verify the legality of his driving. Although the assistant saw no violation, state police officers stopped Chavez for a traffic offense. They asked him for permission to search his car and, when he asked whether he had to allow the search, a drug-sniffing dog was brought to the scene. Despite Chavez's unmistakable objection and his request that he be permitted to leave, the police used the dog on his car. The officers then told Chavez that the dog had alerted them to the presence of drugs. Chavez was put into the back of a patrol car and probed with questions as he watched the police search every part of his vehicle, open his luggage, and go through all of his personal possessions.

These are examples of a practice known as **pretext stops**—the use of traffic stops as an excuse to stop African Americans, Latinos, and other people of color to search their cars and question the occupants about possession of drugs. There is considerable evidence of the pervasiveness of this practice. For example, in Volusia County, Florida, a review of 1,100 videotaped traffic stops made during a drug interdiction effort revealed that approximately 70 percent of the drivers stopped were black. Black drivers were more likely to have their cars searched after being stopped than were whites, and their stops usually lasted twice as long (Harris 1998). An investigation of drivers stopped by Maryland state troopers from January 1995 to December 1997 showed that 70 percent of drivers stopped on Interstate 95 were black. According to a survey by the American Civil Liberties Union, only 17.5 percent of the drivers (and likely traffic violators) on that road were black (Cole 1999).

A follow-up investigation in 2008 found similar disparities, despite a 2003 consent decree where the Maryland State Police agreed to thoroughly investigate all complaints of racial profiling. More recently, a 2012 Department of Justice report found that the Alamance County Sheriff's Office in North Carolina engages in a pattern or practice of misconduct that violates the Constitution and federal law. Some of the key findings of the report were that Alamance County deputies were between four and ten times more likely to stop Latino drivers than non-Latinos. Additionally, they routinely located checkpoints just outside Latino neighborhoods, requiring residents to endure police checks when entering or leaving their communities (Department of Justice 2012). Subsequent analyses of records of traffic stops in the state from 2009 through 2014 found evidence of widespread discrimination against black and Hispanic drivers (Pierson et al. 2017). As an additional example, we can look to a statewide investigation in Minnesota of **racial profiling**—the practice of police and other officials targeting people of color for traffic stops because they believe that people of color are more likely to be engaged in criminal activity. This study revealed that police stopped African American, Latino, and American Indian drivers at a greater rate than white drivers. Such a pattern was particularly pronounced in suburban areas, with African Americans being stopped in some areas over 300 percent more often than expected. Once they were stopped, African Americans were subject to discretionary searches over twice as often as expected, although only 11 percent were found in possession of illegal substances as compared to 18 percent of whites who were searched (Institute on Race and Poverty, Research, Education and Advocacy 2003). Pretext stops are so common that members of black and Latino communities refer to them as DWB: driving while black or driving while brown (Fletcher 1996).

These examples illustrate the way in which institutions maintain inequality based on categories of difference. Police officers and airline crew members, acting not on the basis of their own attitudes but on institutional policies (e.g., memorandums instructing to watch for predominantly black drug couriers, directives to conduct random checks mentioning "extremist groups . . . particularly in the Middle East"), help to maintain racial inequality.

As the 2009 *Climate of Fear* report from the Southern Poverty Law Center illustrates (Reading 32), practices of racial profiling can exacerbate anti-immigrant sentiments. In Suffolk County, New York, a largely white suburban area of Long Island, Latinos make up roughly 14 percent of the population. Yet they comprise nearly half of the defendants appearing in court for traffic violations. New laws, such as Arizona's SB 1070, further support these racial profiling practices. This law requires officials and agencies at the state and local levels to make "a reasonable attempt to determine the immigration status of a person" if they come into contact with someone they have reasonable suspicion to believe is undocumented. Such a perpetuation of a stereotype of Latino immigrants as criminals is often used as a justification for violence that is directed toward members of the Latino community.

Individuals are stopped because of their **status,** the socially defined position that they occupy in society. Note that only one status is important here. Although Mr. Wilkins occupied different statuses (lawyer, spouse, father, etc.), as did Mr. Chavez (investigator, former elected official, etc.), what mattered to the police was their presumed membership in a racial or ethnic group. Thus, their **master status**—the most important status they occupied—was their race or ethnicity.

Each of us occupies a variety of statuses at any given moment in terms of our race, class, gender, sexuality, age, religion, (dis)ability, height, weight, and so on. While we may feel that one status is more important to ourselves than another, we do not always get to pick which is most important to others. Just as Mr. Wilkins and Mr. Chavez were singled out for their race, each of us has likely been singled out by other individuals for some aspect of ourselves. In this section we will investigate how institutions—family, education, economy, the state, and media—support this practice and thus maintain inequality based on categories of difference.

Categories of Difference Maintained as a System of Oppression and Privilege

The value of the statuses that we occupy is determined by how they have been defined. When our statuses are defined as having value within the social structure, we experience **privilege**—a set of (not necessarily) earned rights or assets belonging to a certain status. If our statuses are devalued, the result is **oppression**, defined in Part I as a relationship of domination and subordination in which the dominant group benefits from the *systematic* abuse, exploitation, and injustice directed at a subordinate group. Oppression occurs in three forms: **institutionalized oppression**, that which is built into, supported by, and perpetuated by social institutions; **interpersonal oppression**, that which is manifested between individuals; and **internalized oppression**, that which is directed at oneself.

The Role of Ideology

Maintaining systems of inequality relies on a foundation constructed of several components. Central to this foundation is the presence of an **ideology**—a set of cultural values, beliefs, and attitudes that provide the basis for inequality and thus, in part, endorse and justify the interests of the dominant group. Systems of racial inequality in the United States rely on ideologies that include judgments about racial differences to maintain white privilege. Similarly, systems of class inequality rely on ideologies that include valuing the rich over the poor to uphold class privilege. Furthermore, ideologies based in **androcentrism**—the notion that males are superior to females—preserve systems of sex and gender inequality. Finally, an ideology that includes moral or religious judgments about what is and is not an appropriate sexual orientation is used to justify a system of inequality on the basis of sexuality.

The readings in this section demonstrate that the ideologies that maintain systems of inequality are built into the rules, policies, and practices of our social institutions. In addition, these ideologies often depend on one another, further illustrating the matrix of domination discussed in Part I. For example, as several of the readings in this section illustrate, the foundation of class inequality in the United States is an ideology based in capitalism. More than just the private ownership of goods, capitalism, according to some social theorists, involves exploitation because those who control the ownership of goods use the labor of workers to make a profit. Profit making, they argue, is based on paying workers less than the full value of what they produce. To justify paying one group less than another, we establish ideologies in which one group is viewed as less valuable than others. Thus, ideologies justifying inequality in terms of race/ethnicity, sex/gender, and sexuality perpetuate class inequality.

These interdependent ideologies and the resulting interlocking systems of inequality illustrate that oppression is *systematic*. According to Marilyn Frye, **oppression** involves

> a system of interrelated barriers and forces which reduce, immobilize and mold people who belong to a certain group, and effect their subordination to another group. (1983, 33)

Thus, our circumstances are shaped not by accidental or avoidable events but by systematically related forces. To illustrate how pervasive and institutionalized oppression is, Frye offers the following analogy:

> Consider a birdcage. If you look very closely at just one wire in the cage, you cannot see the other wires. If your conception of what is before you is determined by this myopic focus, you could look at that one wire, up and down the length of it and be unable to see why a bird would not just fly around the wire any time it wanted to go somewhere. . . . There is no physical property of any one wire, *nothing* that the closest scrutiny could discover, that will reveal how a bird could be inhibited or harmed by it except in the most accidental way. It is only when you step back, stop looking at the wires one by one, microscopically, and take a macroscopic view of the whole cage, that you see why the bird doesn't go anywhere; and then you will see it in a moment. . . . It is perfectly *obvious* that

the bird is surrounded by a network of systematically related barriers, no one of which could be the least hindrance to its flight, but which, by their relations to each other, are as confining as the walls of a dungeon. (Frye 1983, 35)

As this analogy illustrates, comprehensive systems of oppression maintain the inequality that many experience in our culture. To fully comprehend this system, we must employ a macro- rather than microscopic perspective, using a systemic frame of analysis to understand how each form of oppression is interrelated and maintained by our social institutions.

Defining Forms of Oppression

Employing a systemic frame of analysis requires that we redefine the ways we categorize issues of discrimination. To label unjust ideas and actions, many of us usually think in terms of **prejudice**, a negative attitude toward members of a group or social category, and **discrimination**, the unequal treatment of people determined by their membership in a group. However, these concepts do not acknowledge the ways in which inequality is institutionalized. The definitions of forms of oppression that follow incorporate a more systematic perspective.

To understand issues of racial oppression within the United States, we must examine **institutional racism.** This refers to the systematic and institutionalized policy or practice by which people of color are exploited or controlled because of their perceived physical characteristics. Racism is part of our institutional structure, not simply the product of individual actions. In the previous examples, racism does not simply consist of the actions of the individual officers. Rather, it is the fact that these actions are supported by police *policy* that defines them as racist behaviors.

Furthermore, to fully understand racism we need to see how white people in the United States benefit from institutionalized racism regardless of their own individual actions. For example, as Dave Zirin discusses in "The Florida State Seminoles: The Champions of Racist Mascots" (Reading 31), some institutions of higher education make use of Native American images and symbols in creating mascots for their sports teams. Despite the protest of a substantial number of American Indian individuals and organizations, places such as the University of Illinois, the home of the Fighting Illini, institutionalize racist notions of American Indians by continuing to use these images.[2] White students at that university benefited from this practice, regardless of their participation in it, by not having their race objectified and dehumanized at each sporting event and on numerous university souvenirs.

Similar to racism, oppression based on social class also relies on the rules, policies, and practices of social institutions. As discussed in Part I, social class is a great deal more than individual characteristics. Rather, it is determined by a variety of factors in our social structure. Social institutions, including the state and the economy, that rely on a capitalist system create class structures that benefit some at the expense of others. The result is a heavily skewed distribution of income and wealth. According to the US Census Bureau's Current Population Survey, the median household income in 2016 was $59,039. The 20 percent of households with the highest earnings (with mean earnings of about $213,941) received 51.5 percent of all income, while the bottom 20 percent (with mean earnings of $12,943) received only about 3.1 percent. The distribution of income is illustrated in Figure 1. The distribution of wealth is even more concentrated than the distribution of income. According to economist Edward Wolff (2016), in 2013 the top 20 percent of the population of the United States owned 88.9 percent of the financial wealth—total net worth minus the value of one's home. As Figure 2 illustrates, 1 percent of the United States owned 36.7 percent of the financial wealth (with their average net worth over $10 million), while the bottom 80 percent possessed just 11.1 percent of the nation's financial wealth. What makes this unequal distribution even more significant is the difference in kind of wealth at various places in the social class system. For example, the majority of the net worth of the bottom 90 percent consists of assets tied up in the family home and trusts, while the distribution of stocks, financial securities, and business equity is concentrated in the richest 10 percent of the population (see Fig. 3). Government policies that disproportionately tax workers while granting tax breaks to the wealthy perpetuate a skewed distribution of income and

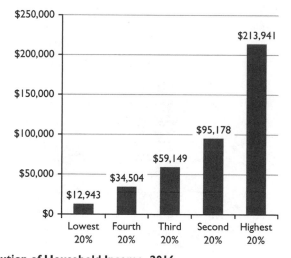

Figure 1 Distribution of Household Income, 2016.
Source: U.S. Census Bureau Current Population Reports, P60-259, Income and Poverty in the United States: 2016.

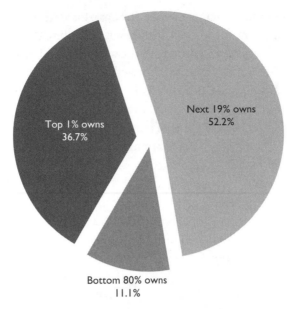

Figure 2 Distribution of Wealth, 2013: Share of Total Financial Wealth.
Source: E. N. Wolff, *Deconstructing Household Wealth Trends in the United States, 1983–2013*, National Bureau of Economic Research Working Paper No. 22704 (Cambridge, MA: National Bureau of Economic Research, 2016).

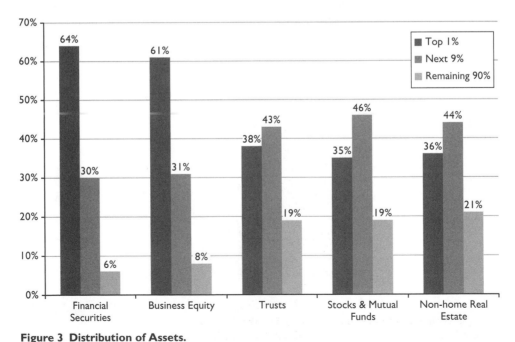

Figure 3 Distribution of Assets.
Source: E.N. Wolff. 2012. *The Asset Price Meltdown and the Wealth of the Middle Class.* New York: New York University).

wealth. As can be seen in Figure 4, the wealthy have historically received an inordinate amount of tax breaks from the federal government, with the wealthiest 1 percent of the country receiving 53 percent. Although these tax cuts were set to expire in 2013, they remained for all taxpayers earning less than $400,000 until recently. As can be seen in Figure 5, proposed tax cuts under the Trump administration continue a similar pattern of disproportionately benefitting the wealthy.

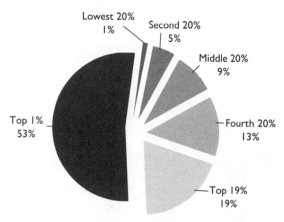

Figure 4 Distribution of Bush-era Tax Cuts in 2010.
Source: From Bob McIntyre, "President Bush Has Made Tax Day Easier for the Rich—at the Expense of Everyone Else" (Citizens for Tax Justice, April 14, 2008), http://www.ctj.org/pdf/taxday2008.pdf. Used by permission.

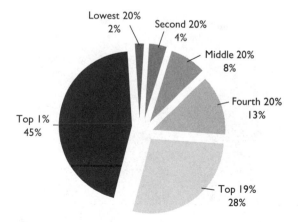

Figure 5 Distribution of Proposed Trump Era Tax Cuts in 2016.
Source: Citizens for Tax Justice, "Impact of Donald Trump's Revised Tax Plan" (Citizens for Tax Justice, September 26, 2016), http://www.ctj.org/the-distributional-and-revenue-impact-of-donald-trumps-revised-tax-plan.

Meanwhile, payroll taxes have significantly increased since 1980, disproportionately affecting workers. The overall impact of such a shift can be seen in the sources of federal revenues, with individual taxes accounting for 83 percent in 2017, while they only accounted for 77 percent in 1962 (see Fig. 6). According to Collins et al. (2004), such a shift of the tax burden from investment to wage income means that a wealthy person relying on earnings from dividends paid a marginal tax rate of approximately 15 percent in 2003, while a person such as a schoolteacher earning $28,400 paid a payroll tax of 15.3 percent as well as a marginal tax rate of 25 percent, for a total tax rate of over 40 percent.

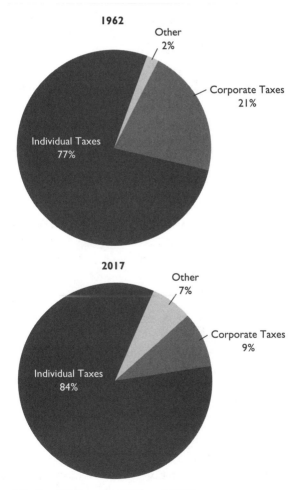

Figure 6 Sources of Federal Revenues, 1962 and 2017.
Source: Congressional Budget Office, "Taxes," September 2017. "Individual taxes" includes income, social insurance (payroll), excise, and estate taxes. "Other" includes customs duties and miscellaneous receipts. https://www.cbo.gov/topics/taxes.

Such systematic class inequality is defined as **classism**—a system of beliefs rooted in the institutions of society where the wealthy are privileged with a higher status at the expense of the oppression of the poor. The ways in which this system is maintained, as well as how issues of class intersect with race/ethnicity and sex/gender, will be discussed later.

Using a systemic analysis to understand issues of sex/gender oppression and privilege requires that we incorporate the role of institutions in definitions of sexism. Thus, for the purposes of this discussion, **sexism** is a systematic and institutionalized policy or practice in which women are exploited or controlled because of perceptions that their sex or gender characteristics are inferior. Again, in recognizing that sexism is systematic, we acknowledge that it is a product of our institutional structure, not necessarily individual actions. As a result, men do not need to individually behave in a sexist manner to benefit from a sexist system. For example, many physical requirements for occupations (such as height) advantage men while they disadvantage women, although they may have little to do with the actual requirements for the job. Additional ways in which sex and gender inequality is reinforced by social institutions will be discussed later.

Finally, inequality with regard to sexuality is also institutionalized. Thus, privilege experienced by heterosexuals and the oppression experienced by those who are or are perceived to be lesbian, gay, bisexual, or transgender is perpetuated through the practices and policies of social institutions. For example, the failure to pass the **Employment Non-Discrimination Act**—a bill to prohibit employment discrimination on the basis of sexual orientation—perpetuates the advantage experienced by heterosexuals and the stigma experienced by lesbian, gay, bisexual, and transgender individuals. Additionally, as mentioned in Part I, the passage of state constitutional amendments—and the campaign by President George W. Bush for a nationwide constitutional amendment—that banned civil unions, marriage equality, and legal protections for lesbian and gay families for decades denied access to resources for lesbian, gay, bisexual, and transgender families.[3] **Heterosexism,** as defined by Cherríe Moraga, applies directly to this example:

> The view that heterosexuality is the "norm" for all social/sexual relationships and as such the heterosexist imposes the model on all individuals through homophobia (fear of homosexuality). S/he supports and/or advocates this continued institutionalization of heterosexuality in all aspects of society—including legal and social discrimination against homosexuals and the denial of homosexual rights as a political concern. (1983, 105)

Moraga indicates here that a person who is heterosexist is an active participant in oppressing those who are or are perceived to be lesbian, gay, bisexual, or transgender.

However, as with all other forms of oppression, it is not necessary to actively partici-pate in discrimination against others to benefit from their systematic exploitation. For example, mainstream media continue to perpetuate stereotypes of lesbians, gay men, bisexuals, and transgendered people. According to the Gay and Lesbian Alliance against Defamation), representation of lesbian, gay, bisexual, and transgender indi-viduals account for just under 5 percent of all scripted-series regular characters in the 2016–2017 broadcast television schedule. This figure is up from just under 3 percent in 2011 and 1.1 percent in 2007. While such characters may be more present on stream-ing services and cable programs, as well as on more widely accessible network pro-grams (although these numbers have declined in recent years), lesbian, gay, bisexual, and transgender people and families are nearly invisible (Macias 2004). Additional-ly, efforts to present messages inclusive and accepting of lesbian, gay, bisexual, and transgender persons are often excluded by broadcast networks. For example, a 2004 advertisement by the United Church of Christ portrayed a gay couple (along with other members of marginalized groups) being kept out of a church by two bouncers. The message was "Jesus didn't turn people away, neither do we." Major broadcasting networks, including CBS and NBC, rejected this advertisement. A heterosexual seek-ing to find images in the media of someone who represents her or his own sexuality is likely to find numerous examples. This ability to find representations of self is a benefit that not only is often overlooked by those who are privileged but also does not require any direct discrimination on the part of the individual who benefits.

As each of these examples illustrates, oppression on the basis of race, class, gender, and sexuality does not require the overt discrimination of bigots that we often think of when examining issues of inequality. Acts of oppression in interper-sonal contexts maintain systems of inequality by engaging in oppressive practices that are a reflection of oppressive social institutions.

In summary, our experiences of oppression and privilege occur within a com-prehensive system of interconnected social institutions. Thus, issues of prejudice and discrimination are transformed into experiences of institutionalized *oppres-sion*. The remainder of this section will explore the ways in which the social insti-tutions of family, education, work and the economy, the state, and media, along with the social forces of language and social control, maintain systems of inequal-ity. As you consider the following, remember to keep in mind how the ideologies depend on one another, forming interlocking systems of oppression.

Social Institutions: Maintaining Systems of Oppression and Privilege

As an intangible aspect of the social structure, the role of social institutions in maintaining inequality often goes largely unnoticed. Rather, we tend to view insti-tutionalized oppression or privilege as the way things are. For example, when we hear of racist acts on the part of individuals, such as in the brutal killing of James Byrd in Jasper, Texas,[4] we are often rightfully outraged and horrified. At the same time, however, few of us are likely to notice the residential segregation that systematically excludes blacks from certain neighborhoods. Although the federal government eliminated overtly racially biased housing, tax, and transportation policies in the 1960s, as a new analysis of data from the US Department of Education documented, a high level of racial segregation nevertheless continues to exist (Orfield, Kucsera, and Siegel-Hawley 2012). Feagin and Sikes (1994) note that practices such as redlining (the systematic refusal on the part of some lenders to make loans in certain areas because of racial composition), racial steering, animosity on the part of whites, and discriminatory practices by mortgage lenders help maintain this segregation. The impact of such segregation influences not only wealth, but also access to important resources, such as education, employment, and good health. In this section we will examine the practices and policies of institutions to understand the ways in which they maintain systems of oppression.

As discussed in Part I, social institutions play a significant role in creating inequality. They define race, class, gender, and sexuality not only in terms of what does and does not exist, but also in terms of the values that we associate with each category. Thus, they confer privilege on some while oppressing others. This is done through the establishment and enforcement of policies constructed by these institutions.

The readings in this section illustrate how social institutions maintain systems of oppression and privilege and how they, in turn, impact access to resources. Ranging from money and property to medical care and education, **resources** are anything that is valued in society. Resources are generally considered scarce because of their unequal distribution among different groups. For example, the unequal distribution of income and wealth, as illustrated earlier, results in the perception that resources such as money and property are scarce.

The ways in which resources are distributed greatly impact an individual's **life chances**—the material advantages or disadvantages that a particular member of a social category can expect to receive based on his or her status (Weber 1946; Dahrendorf 1979). One of the most significant life chances is the distribution of health care and the resulting impact on one's quality of life. For example, according to an article in the *New York Times* by Erica Goode (1999), social class is one of the most powerful predictors of health—more powerful than genetics and even more than smoking. As a result of an unequal distribution of resources, the lower one's rung on the socioeconomic ladder, as illustrated in "Stressing Out the Poor" (Reading 22), the greater the likelihood of negative health effects that have long-ranging consequences. Furthermore, experiences of being marginalized, residing in racially segregated areas, and other forms of institutionalized racism were also found to magnify the impact of social class on health.

This example illustrates that social institutions, with their unequal distribution of valuable resources, perpetuate a cycle of disparate life chances. If someone experiences poor health as a result of occupying a lower social class or living in a racially segregated neighborhood, she or he is going to be less able to fully participate in the social system and less able to develop skills and achieve career goals than is someone who belongs to a higher social class with correspondingly better health.

Family

As a primary social institution, the family is central to maintaining systems of oppression and privilege based on race, class, gender, and sexuality. In addition, because it is so closely connected with other social institutions, such as the state and the economy, the structure of the family significantly influences and is influenced by the structure and actions of these institutions. While many of the ways systems of inequality are maintained are interconnected, perhaps the strongest connection is the relationship of family to the social structure.

For example, Lillian Rubin in "Families on the Fault Line" (Reading 14) illustrates how changes in our economic system resulted in a crisis in the family. Out of economic necessity, many women in white working-class families are now participating more fully in the paid workforce. When both parents attempt to work full-time, they need to find ways to pay for their childcare. However, these families lack the economic resources that middle- and upper-class families have to seek quality childcare. Rubin illustrates that social institutions such as the economy and the state have not responded in ways that support working-class families. As a result, they maintain systems of class inequality.

Notions of citizenship also maintain systems of oppression in a variety of ways. As Leisy Abrego explains in "Illegality as a Source of Solidarity and Tension in Latino Families" (Reading 15), the status of illegal impacts all members of a family, even when only one person or a few people are categorized as undocumented or only temporarily protected. This results in tensions for people whose disadvantages are heightened by structural inequality because of immigration laws.

Education

The institution of education also maintains systems of oppression and privilege. This institution reproduces the existing race, class, and gender structure through a variety of mechanisms, including the distribution of cultural capital and the existence of a hidden curriculum. In "The Racial Achievement Gap, Segregated Schools, and Segregated Neighborhoods" (Reading 17), Richard Rothstein clearly illustrates how the institution of education, over fifty years after *Brown v. Board of*

Education, perpetuates race and class inequalities through the way it is structured. As his article notes, whether a student attends a resource-rich or a resource-poor educational system will impact his or her access to **cultural capital**—social assets that include beliefs, values, attitudes, and competencies in language and culture. A concept proposed by Bordieu and Paseron (1977), cultural capital consists of ideas and knowledge people draw on as they participate in social life, including proper attitudes toward education; socially approved dress and manners; and knowledge about books, music, and other forms of high and popular culture. Because cultural capital is essential for succeeding, children with less cultural capital often have fewer opportunities. In addition, the dominance of white, patriarchal, affluent class notions of what counts as cultural capital generally excludes the ideas and beliefs of the poor and people of color. Schools with fewer economic resources, which are often disproportionately attended by African American, Latina/o, or Native American students, are less able to provide students with what is viewed by the dominant culture as important cultural capital, thus affecting their opportunities in the future. As a result, the educational system, with its unequal distribution of cultural capital, perpetuates a system of stratification based not only on race but also on class.

The institution of education also maintains race and class inequality through the existence of a **hidden curriculum**—the transmission of cultural values and attitudes, such as conformity and obedience to authority, through implied demands found in rules, routines, and regulations of schools. Because of the existence of a hidden curriculum, the values and attitudes that are reinforced in one school are not necessarily those that are promoted at another. For example, curriculum directed toward working-class students often focuses on rote memorization without much decision making, choice, or explanation of why something is done. Curriculum directed at middle-class students, however, emphasizes figuring and decision making in getting the right answer. The curriculum directed at affluent students often stresses the expression of ideas and creative activities, while that directed at elite students stresses critical thinking skills and developing analytical powers to apply abstract principles to problem solving. As the readings in this section illustrate, our education system is largely segregated on the basis of class. In addition, there is also significant evidence of de facto racial segregation. As a result, the hidden curriculum maintains class as well as racial inequality.

Mary Crow Dog and Richard Erdoes further illustrate in "Civilize Them with a Stick" (Reading 18) the ways policies in the institution of education perpetuate racial inequality. As a result of these policies, in combination with policies of the state, Native American children were forced to leave their reservations and attend boarding or day schools. These efforts to assimilate members of this group are but one example of how the institution of education maintains racial inequality.

The institution of education also constructs and perpetuates categories of difference on the basis of sex and gender. Various studies have shown that teachers pay more attention to boys in the classroom than to girls, and the ramifications of this differential treatment are numerous. For example, in "Missing in Interaction" (Reading 19), Myra and David Sadker examine a variety of ways the elementary classroom setting maintains sex and gender inequality. For example, teachers often force boys to work out problems that they do not understand but tell girls what to do, go easier on girls when disciplining their students, and reward girls for non-academic achievements such as neat penmanship or getting along with others. These and other behaviors on the part of teachers and students maintain clear sex and gender divisions that contribute to differential ways of viewing and valuing males and females in our culture as well as the inequalities that females experience in our society.

Finally, the policies and practices of the institution of education can also maintain a system of stratification in which students who are perceived to be heterosexual are deemed more important and are thus more embraced by the institution than those who are perceived to be lesbian, gay, bisexual, or transgender. Examples of heterosexism can even be found in what may be viewed as harmless school traditions (e.g., proms and other social events), but it can also be seen in more overt and meaningful ways. For example, in recent years the US Congress has voted on proposals to eliminate federal aid to schools that "promote" homosexuality. In addition, a policy enacted by the Merrimack, New Hampshire, School Board stated,

> The Merrimack School District shall neither implement nor carry out any program or activity that has either the purpose or effect of encouraging or supporting homosexuality as a positive lifestyle alternative. A program or activity, for purposes of this item, includes the distribution of instructional materials, instruction, counseling, or other services on school grounds, or referral of a pupil to an organization that affirms a homosexual lifestyle.

Although this policy was later repealed, similar policies have been passed in other school districts. Some of the policies are phrased more bluntly than the one above and simply forbid any discussion of homosexuality at all—be it positive or negative. Regardless, the ramifications of official policies such as these, as well as implicit practices based on heterosexism, are severe.

Such overt and covert ways of valuing heterosexuality result in **heteronormativity**—the ways in which the practices of social institutions prescribe heterosexuality as the norm. This can have a profound effect on those who do not fit into such a norm. As a result of heterosexist school traditions and policies like those described above, lesbian, gay, bisexual, transgender, or questioning students are likely to experience feelings of alienation and self-alienation. For example, according to the Centers for Disease Control, gay youth are four to five times more likely to have attempted or seriously considered suicide than their heterosexual peers. Lesbian, gay, and bisexual youth, as well as students who are questioning their sexuality, often need counseling that is only available in schools. Official and unofficial policies and practices based on heterosexism ignore these concerns and maintain inequality based on sexuality.

Work and the Economy

The institution of work and the economy is perhaps the most fundamental in maintaining systems of inequality. As already noted, changes in the structure of the economy significantly impact other institutions. At times, these changes offer new opportunities and privilege to some, and at other times, these changes foster continued oppression. In "Black Men and the Struggle for Work: Social and Economic Barriers Persist" (Reading 20), James Quane and others illustrate that continued structural barriers to opportunity disproportionately prevent economic self-sufficiency for poor black men and, as a result, poor black families. Indeed, increases in the jobless rate disproportionately affect those who are on the low end of the economic spectrum because they are less likely to have other sources of support (e.g., savings or social networks leading to new jobs).

Additionally, through selective recruitment and biased hiring strategies, employers favor white applicants at the expense of others. As Figure 7 indicates, there is a significant wage gap with regard to race in the United States. Policies impacting employee recruitment, hiring, promotion, and termination maintain this gap. Finally, policies of the social institution of work and the economy also perpetuate inequality with regard to sex and gender. As research of men's underrepresentation in predominantly female professions has illustrated, sex segregation continues to exist within the US labor force (Williams 1992). This research also reveals policies and practices with regard to hiring and supervising. These policies maintain a gap in the incomes of women and men, as illustrated in Table 1, and as a result, they maintain a system of inequality.

The State and Public Policy

The state and public policy is another social institution that contributes to inequality. Often confused with the government, the state acts as a blueprint for how various procedures of the government should be carried out. In maintaining inequality,

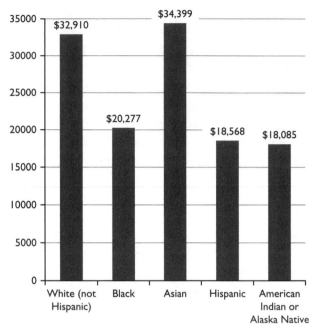

Figure 7 2015 Median Per-Capita Income
Source: U.S. Census Bureau *American Community Survey.* United States Census Bureau. 2015. https://factfinder.census.gov. September 2017

the state acts in the interest of the dominant group or groups in society, reinforcing policies that work in their favor.

Currently, social policies regarding welfare reform have been the subject of much debate. As a result of the myths and stereotypes regarding people who receive aid within the welfare system, US policies regarding Aid to Families with

Table 1 Median Weekly Earnings of Full-Time Workers by Sex and Age, 2017

Age	Males	Females	Female income as percentage of male income (%)
All workers, 16 years and older	$ 934	$780	83.5
16–24	$ 524	$496	94.7
25–34	$ 828	$727	87.8
35–44	$1,065	$877	82.3
45–54	$1,094	$851	77.8
55–64	$1,058	$869	82.1
65 years and older	$1,005	$800	79.6

Source: US Department of Labor, US Bureau of Labor Statistics, *Economic News Release,* July 19, 2017, https://www.bls.gov/news.release/wkyeng.t03.htm.

Dependent Children and similar entitlement programs have undergone considerable change in recent years. State policies often ignore how issues of race and class intersect. As Figure 8 illustrates, poverty is unequally distributed according to race, with people of color disproportionately representing those who are poor. Issues of poverty are exacerbated by stratification on the basis of sex, with women being more likely to be poor than men (14 percent compared to 11.3 percent according to 2016 census data). In addition, female-headed households with children are also disproportionately poor, with 36.5 percent living in poverty compared to 22.1 percent for male-headed families with children. Recent changes in welfare reform only maintain these economic inequalities.

The criminal justice system, also ruled by state policies, reinforces inequality, particularly with regard to race and class, especially as it depends on unequal racial and class patterns in prosecution and incarceration. The evidence of such continuing institutionalized racism can serve as justification of the need for corrective programs such as affirmative action. While such programs have often been accused of discriminating against those in the majority, such policies rarely do this. Rather, they tend to enhance productivity and encourage improved employment practices.

Finally, as stated earlier, public policies established by the state maintain the interest of the majority. For example, state policies prohibiting concepts of

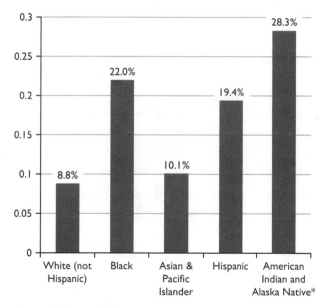

Figure 8 Poverty Rates by Race, 2016.
Source: U.S. Census Bureau *Income and Poverty in the United States: 2016*. https://www.census.gov/content/dam/Census/library/publications/2017/demo/P60-259.pdf. *Data for American Indian and Alaska Native are for 2014, the most recent year available. *Source:* U.S. Census Bureau, https://www.census.gov/newsroom/facts-for-features/2015/cb15-ff22.html.

multiraciality were established during the colonial period to sustain the distinction between master and slave. These and other public policies were created to maintain the control of whites over others. This motivation is reflected in contemporary policies as well, and whites continue to benefit from such a system in the United States.

Media

Like other social institutions, the media convey dominant ideologies about systems of inequality. Often the images reflected in the media represent the policies, practices, and prevailing attitudes of other social institutions. We can see policies of inclusion and exclusion regarding lesbian, gay, bisexual, and transgender individuals reflected in our television media. For example, when the Employment Non-Discrimination Act failed, denying lesbian, gay, bisexual, and transgender individuals the right to be free from employment discrimination on the basis of sexual orientation, *Ellen,* the first prime-time series to feature an out lesbian as the main character, was canceled. As mentioned earlier, television has failed to accurately reflect the diversity of sexuality in the United States.

Television is perhaps the most influential form of media today—viewers in the United States watch approximately thirty-four hours a week. As a result, this form of media possesses the power not only to influence but also to maintain our perceptions of reality, as the distorted images perpetuate not only our stereotypes of these groups but also their continued oppression. Further, the media engage in practices of **media framing**—the process by which information and entertainment are put together by the media to convey a particular message to an audience. Thus, we are less able to distinguish between the realities of class in the United States and the ways in which it is portrayed in the mass media.

The institution of the media also maintains systems of oppression on the basis of sex and gender. For example, images in music, movies, television, and advertising degrade women. One of the ways this is accomplished is through the process of **objectification,** which Catharine MacKinnon defines as

> the primary process of subjugation of women. It unites act with word, construction with expression, perception with enforcement, myth with reality (1982, 541).

Through such a process, the media support the privileges of men and the oppression of women.

As the preceding discussion illustrates, social institutions, often acting in tandem, play a significant role in maintaining inequality. As you read the selections in this section, keep in mind the earlier discussions of the matrix of domination and look closely to see the ways in which these social institutions work together to maintain interlocking systems of oppression and privilege.

Language and Maintaining Inequality

One significant, yet often unexplored mechanism for maintaining inequality is language. Functioning in a manner similar to a social institution, the ways in which we use language can maintain the values, roles, norms, and ideologies of the dominant culture. The readings on language in this section demonstrate that it is a powerful tool of culture, determining how members of a society interpret their environment. According to social construction theory, our social world has no inherent meaning. Rather, the meaning of the social world is constructed, in part, through language. Language serves as the link between all of the different elements of culture and maintains a system of inequality.

There are those who feel that examining the role of language in the maintenance of inequality is trivial or misplaced. However, as illustrated in "How the Right Made Racism Sound Fair" (Reading 29), issues of language are particularly significant, especially in framing how we think of groups that are different from ourselves. In addition, one of the significant functions of language is to serve the purpose of **cultural transmission**—the passing of culture (values, beliefs, symbols, behaviors) from one generation to the next. Through language, children learn about their cultural heritage and develop a sense of personal identity in relation to their group. In addition, language also helps them learn about socially constructed categories of difference and the meanings associated with them.

Language consists of words that are symbols with meaning and serves as a tool for interpreting our environment. The power of words lies in the fact that the members of a culture share their meanings and valuations. It is our common language that allows us to communicate and understand one another, and this makes for order in society. Philosopher Ernst Cassirer (1978) identified several different functions of the ability of humans to use symbols, explaining that they help to define, organize, and evaluate experiences of people. Julia Wood (1997) uses the assertions of Cassirer to illustrate the ways in which we use language to indicate cultural values and views of women and men, thereby maintaining inequality.

First, Wood argues that language *defines sex and gender*. It serves to define women and men as well as what can and cannot exist. For example, generic language (e.g., using the pronoun *he* to refer to both women and men or using words like *fireman, mankind, man-hour,* etc.) excludes women and dismisses their importance. As a result, men and their experiences are presented as the norm while women and their experiences are seen as deviant. In addition to establishing *who* exists, Wood argues that language defines *what* exists. For example, since we use the masculine word as the base to make compounds in the English language, it might appear that women's ability to rule or own may seem impossible in that we can have a kingdom but not a queendom. Does this mean that only men can have land over which they rule? Certainly not. Rather, it illustrates that we attend to what we name and tend not to recognize that which we do not name. For example, words like *sexual harassment* or *date rape* are recent creations. That does not mean that these are new phenomena; rather, they are phenomena that we have only recently attended to and been willing to acknowledge.

Additional ways that language is used to define our perceptions of women and men can be seen in how women are defined by their relationships. Consider, for example, the commonly used titles of respect for men and women in our society. Men are addressed as Mr., which reveals nothing about their relationship to women. But how are women typically addressed? The titles Miss and Mrs. define women in terms of their relationship to men. Even when a woman has earned a higher-status title, such as Dr., she is still likely to be addressed as Miss or Mrs. On an interesting note, many states in the United States have required women to take their husband's name on marrying. It was only in 1975 that a Hawaiian statute requiring women to give up their birth names on marriage was ruled unconstitutional.

The second way that language illustrates our perceptions of women and men, according to Wood, is that it *organizes our perceptions of sex and gender*. The ability of language to organize our experiences and perceptions enables us to express cultural views of sex and gender by stereotyping men and women. In addition, the ways in which we talk about women and men in the English language encourage dualistic notions of sex and gender. For example, when we stereotype women as emotional and men as rational, we limit our abilities to recognize rationality in women and men's abilities to express emotion. Furthermore, because of the heavy emphasis that the English language places on polarity (good–bad, wrong–right, male–female), it is often difficult for us to think of things such as gender as existing along a continuum. In reality, few of us fit on the polar ends of what a male or female is supposed to be. Rather, most of us are somewhere in the middle. Yet we are all expected to conform to the two polar ends or suffer the consequences for not being seen as gender appropriate.

Third, Wood argues that language *evaluates our perceptions of women and men*. Language is ideological, reflecting the values that are important in our culture. In the case of our use of the English language, we can find a great deal of evidence of linguistic sexism—the ways in which a language devalues members of one sex, almost invariably women. To illustrate this concept, consider the following word pairs: *brothers* and *sisters, husband* and *wife, men* and *women, hostess* and *host, madam* and *sir, Eve* and *Adam*. As you read these word pairs, it is likely that those in which the female term preceded the male term sounded awkward or incorrect. This is not coincidental; rather, it is a practice based on a long tradition. As Baron (1986) notes, eighteenth-century grammarians established the rule precisely to assert that "the supreme Being . . . is in all languages Masculine, in as much as the masculine sex is the superior and more excellent" (3). According to these grammarians, to place women before men was to violate the natural order.

In addition, the English language often trivializes or diminishes women and things defined as feminine. There has often been a debate in college athletic associations regarding whether the names generally applied to female sports teams trivialize or diminish the role of women in sport. While male teams are generally set as the standard, being assigned team names with little or no gender meaning (e.g., the Polar Cats, the Volunteers), female teams generally receive feminized team names (e.g., the Polar Kittens, the Lady Volunteers). Many argue that such a practice devalues the role of women in sport and thus in society.

An additional example of how language trivializes things that are feminine is in the use of diminutive suffixes for occupations held by women (e.g., actress, waitress, stewardess) and through the use of terms like *girls* for adult females. Furthermore, when we consider word pairs like *governor* and *governess, master* and *mistress,* or *bachelor* and *spinster,* it becomes clear that the words associated with men have different implied meanings than those associated with women, with the latter consistently negative or demeaning. The male words suggest power or positively valued status, whereas the female words have negative connotations. Although many of these words originally had neutral connotations, over time these words declined in value, a process known as **semantic derogation.** Smith notes that "once a word or term becomes associated with women, it often acquires semantic characteristics that are congruent with social stereotypes and evaluations of women as a group" (1985, 48). Because such values about women are reflected in our language, our perception that women have less value than men is perpetuated. According to the **Sapir–Whorf hypothesis,** "people perceive the world through the cultural lens of language" (Sapir 1949, 162). Thus, language shapes our reality.

As the preceding discussion illustrates, language plays a significant role in maintaining inequality. The readings in this section expand on this illustration. For example, Irving Kenneth Zola argues in "Self, Identity, and the Naming Question" (Reading 30) that those who occupy marginalized groups are not often given the opportunity to name themselves. Rather, names are generally imposed on them by those with social power, maintaining a system in which the marginalized group is oppressed. In addition, Dave Zirin discusses in "The Florida State Seminoles: The Champions of Racist Mascots" (Reading 31) the use of American Indian names and images in sports. Their discussion explains that such a practice maintains a system of stratification in which Native Americans are not only seen as less valuable than whites but also often objectified and seen as less than human. Each of the readings demonstrates that language is a pervasive tool of culture. In maintaining cultural values, roles, norms, and ideologies, language maintains inequality.

Violence and Social Control

Increasing violence in the United States—particularly evident in the school shootings most recently in Roseburg, Oregon; Newtown, Connecticut; Red Lake, Minnesota; Atlanta, Georgia; Cold Spring, Minnesota; Fort Gibson, Oklahoma; Deming, New Mexico; Conyers, Georgia; Littleton, Colorado; Pearl, Mississippi; West Paducah, Kentucky; Jonesboro, Arkansas; and Springfield, Oregon—has resulted in considerable discussion regarding the causes of and solutions to this problem. While some have been quick to blame the media or lax gun-control laws, focusing on violence as an act of individuals, it is important that we understand violence as a pervasive form of **social control**—the regulation of human behavior in any social group. As the findings of a May 1999 Gallup Poll linking antigay and racist attitudes with student-on-student violence illustrates, violence used as a mechanism for social control maintains inequality.

Several of the readings in this section illustrate how violence is used as a means of social control. For example, the Southern Poverty Law Center's report *Climate of Fear* (Reading 32) exposes the practice of *beaner hopping*, where youth in suburban areas go out looking for a Hispanic to beat up. This practice has resulted in most Latino immigrant families living in fear. The role of violence in controlling women is further demonstrated in the article "Ruling Out Rape" (Reading 33). In their discussion, Lisa Wade, Brian Sweeney, Amelia Seraphia Derr, Michael A. Messner, and Carol Burke illustrate the factors that contribute to the existence of a **rape culture**—a set of values and beliefs that create an environment conducive to rape—in perpetuating violence against women. Each of these examples illustrates that violence is used as a mechanism of social control to reinforce interlocking systems of oppression. All forms of violence have a severe impact on an individual's ability to participate fully in society. As a result, violence perpetuates inequality.

Examining violence and social control further illustrates the interconnectedness of race, class, gender, and sexuality oppression. In working to understand the escalating violence within the United States and the world, it is important also to understand how systems of oppression interconnect. In so doing, we will gain a better understanding of how violence is used to maintain interlocking systems of inequality.

Conclusion

As discussed in this section, constructions of difference regarding race, class, gender, and sexuality are transformed into interlocking systems of oppression and privilege. As a result, it is important that we understand how one system relies on another. The readings in this section examine the ways in which the social institutions of family, education, the economy, the state, and the media work together with language and violence and social control to maintain inequality. Once we are aware of this process, we will have a greater understanding of how to transform systems of inequality.

Note

1. The phrase "flying while Arab" or "flying while Muslim" was likely coined at the June 1999 meeting of the American Muslim Political Coordination Council.
2. Because of pressure from the National Collegiate Athletic Association, officials at the University of Illinois decided to end the Chief Illiniwek tradition. The chief made his last performance on February 21, 2007.
3. On July 8, 2010, this denial of resources was recognized through the finding of a federal judge in Massachusetts who ruled that the Defense of Marriage Act, a law that barred the federal government from recognizing same-sex marriage, was unconstitutional, ruling that gay and lesbian couples deserved the same federal benefits as heterosexual couples. Additionally, the US Supreme Court struck down the Defense of Marriage Act as unconstitutional on June 26, 2013, and dismissed California's Proposition 8 appeal. In 2015, the US Supreme Court ruled that same-sex couples have the right to marry in all fifty states, nullifying these institutional policies.
4. James Byrd, forty-nine, was beaten unconscious and then dragged by a chain to his death from the back of a pickup truck after accepting a ride from three white men in Jasper, Texas, in June 1998. One of the men, John William King, was found guilty and given the death penalty for his role in the killing. Another man, Lawrence Brewer, was also found guilty and sentenced to death. The third suspect, Shawn Berry, was sentenced to life in prison. Byrd's body was dismembered in the assault, and many of his body parts were found about a mile from his torso. When he was found, his body was so badly disfigured that Byrd had to be identified by his fingerprints.

References

American Civil Liberties Union. 2004. *Sanctioned Bias: Racial Profiling since 9/11.* New York: American Civil Liberties Union.

Baron, Dennis E. 1986. *Grammar and Gender.* New Haven, CT: Yale University Press.

Bordieu, Pierre, and Jean-Claude Paseron. 1977. *Society, Culture, and Education.* Beverly Hills, CA: Sage.

Cassirer, Ernst. 1978. *An Essay on Man.* New Haven, CT: Yale University Press.

Cole, David. 1999. *No Equal Justice: Race and Class in the American Criminal Justice System.* New York: New Press.

Collins, Chuck, Chris Hartman, Karen Kraut, and Gloribell Mota. 2004. *Shifty Tax Cuts: How They Move the Tax Burden off the Rich and onto Everyone Else.* Boston, MA: United for a Fair Economy.

Dahrendorf, Ralf. 1979. *Life Chances.* London: Weidenfeld & Nicolson.

Department of Justice. 2012. "Justice Department Releases Investigative Findings on the Alamance County, N.C., Sheriff's Office." September 18. http://www.justice.gov/opa/pr/2012/September/12-crt-1125.html.

Feagin, Joe R., and Melvin P. Sikes. 1994. *Living with Racism: The Black Middle-Class Experience.* Boston: Beacon Press.

Fletcher, Michael A. 1996. "Driven to Extremes: Black Men Take Steps to Avoid Police Stops." *Washington Post,* March 29, A1.

Frye, Marilyn. 1983. *The Politics of Reality: Essays in Feminist Theory.* Trumansburg, NY: Crossing Press.

Goode, Erica. 1999. "For Good Health, It Helps to Be Rich and Important." *New York Times,* June 1, D-1, D-9.

Harris, David A. 1998. "The Use of Traffic Stops against African Americans: What Can Be Done?" American Civil Liberties Freedom Network. http://www.aclu.org/issues/policepractices/harris_statement.html.

Institute on Race and Poverty, Research, Education and Advocacy. 2003. *Minnesota Statewide Racial Profiling Report.* Saint Paul, MN: Institute on Race and Poverty, Research, Education and Advocacy.

Macias, Stephen. 2004. *Reality Check: GLAAD Examines the 2004–2005 Primetime Television Season.* New York: Gay and Lesbian Alliance Against Defamation.

MacKinnon, Catharine A. 1982. "Feminism, Marxism, Method, and the State: An Agenda for Theory." *Signs* 7 (3): 515–44.

Moraga, Cherríe. 1983. *Loving in the War Years.* Boston: South End Press.

Orfield, Gary, John Kucsera, and Genevieve Siegel-Hawley. 2012. *E Pluribus . . . Separation: Deepening Double Segregation for More Students.* Los Angeles: Civil Rights Project.

Pierson, Emma, Camelia Simoiu, Jan Overgoor, Sam Corbett-Davies, Vignesh Ramachandran, Cheryl Phillips, and Sharad Goel. 2017 "A Large-scale Analysis of Racial Disparities in Police Stops Across the United States." Working paper.

Sapir, Edward. 1949. *Selected Writings of Edward Sapir in Language, Culture, and Personality,* edited by David G. Mandelbaum. Berkeley: University of California Press.

Shora, Kareem. 2002. "Guilty of Flying While Brown." *Air and Space Lawyer* 17.

Smith, Philip M. 1985. *Language, the Sexes, and Society.* New York: Blackwell.

Weber, Max. 1946. From *Max Weber: Essays in Sociology,* edited and translated by Hans Gerth and C. Wright Mills. New York: Oxford University Press.

Williams, Christine L. 1992. "The Glass Escalator: Hidden Advantages for Men in the 'Female' Professions." *Social Problems* 39 (3): 253–67.

Wolff, Edward N. 2012. *The Asset Price Meltdown and the Wealth of the Middle Class.* New York: New York University.

Wolff, Edward N. 2016. "Household Wealth Trends in the United States, 1962 to 2013: What Happened over the Great Recession?" *Russell Sage Foundation Journal of the Social Sciences* 2 (6): 24–43.

Wood, Julia T. 1997. *Gendered Lives: Communication, Gender, and Culture.* 2nd ed. Belmont, CA: Wadsworth.

Why Won't African Americans Get (and Stay) Married? Why Should They?

SHIRLEY A. HILL

In this essay by sociologist Shirley Hill, the author examines the impact of historical and class, racial, and gender inequalities on marriages among African Americans. Despite the additional burdens placed on these marriages, there continues to be strong ideological support for marriage in the African American community. To increase the rate of successful marriages among African American families, Hill argues that it is essential to address the racial, class, and gender inequality experienced by African Americans.

The extent to which African American families conform to mainstream family ideologies was the focus of much scholarly debate throughout the twentieth century, with the prevalence of single-mother families being at the center of that debate. Early research explained single-mother families as a legacy of slavery and offered a class analysis of black families that characterized them as matriarchal, dysfunctional, and a barrier to socioeconomic mobility. This work, however, was thoroughly challenged during the civil-rights era of the 1960s as revisionist scholars studied the family lives of enslaved black people (Blassingame 1972; Gutman 1976) and drew parallels between the family systems of precolonial Africans, slaves, and contemporary African American families (Nobles 1974).

Social historians studying enslaved families argued that two-parent families were and had always been the statistical norm among African Americans, even during slavery, and that persistent racism was more responsible for single-mother families than slavery (Gutman 1976). This broader scholarship led those who were studying contemporary African American families to shift their focus from their deficiencies to their cultural strengths, often highlighting the adaptive strategies (e.g., extended families) that had enabled them to survive slavery, economic exclusion, and institutional racism (Allen 1978; Billingsley 1968; 1972; Stack 1974).

This cultural-strengths framework still informs much research on African American families, but it is not without critics. More recent researchers, for example, have contested the notion that two-parent families were the norm among enslaved African Americans, asserting that this assumes a universality in their family experiences that simply did not exist. Instead, social-structural factors produced a diversity of family forms among slaves (Dunaway 2003; Franklin 1997). The decline in the quality of life for low-income African American families during the 1980s, as seen in weaker extended family ties, a decrease in marriage, and the rise in nonmarital childbearing and welfare dependency, also seemed to assert the primacy of social-structural forces, namely the rise of the postindustrial economy (Wilson 1978), in shaping families. Cultural theorists were at a loss to explain why the cultural traditions that had enabled black families to survive centuries of slavery and racial oppression were so weakened by economic restructuring. Moreover, the historic focus on the strengths of *families* had never offered much analysis of African American *marriages,* yet by the 1990s black women were the *least* likely to marry and the *most* likely to become single mothers.

Between 1930 and 1944, black men married at an earlier age than white men (23.3 compared to 24.3) (Koball 1998). Heather Koball notes that during this era black men, mostly as tenant-farmers, were more likely to be employed full-time than white men and benefited from the labor of their wives and children. But even more important, she argues, was the fact that their life options were constrained by their low levels of education and concentration in the poor, rural South. Despite this high rate of marriage, very little is known about the quality and resilience of African American marriages during this era, but it is likely that both cultural traditions (e.g., female-centered families) and structural forces (e.g., racism, economic hardship, northward migration) converged to heighten their risk of marital separation and divorce (Frazier 1957; Marks 1989).

By 1945 a racial crossover in marriage had occurred, with blacks marrying later and less often than whites (Koball 1998). By the 1950s, 88 percent of African American and 95 percent of white American women entered marriage (Cherlin 2008). The marriage decline continued at an accelerated rate for African Americans in the ensuing decades. During the 1970s, the rate of marriage among women under the age of twenty fell for all racial groups, but much more dramatically for African American women (Fitch and Ruggles 2000). Moreover, the rate of nonmarriage among African American women more than doubled between 1970 and the 1990s, rising from 17 to 40

percent. By the late 1990s, only about 15 percent of black women between the ages of twenty and twenty-four had married, compared to one-third of white women; by the age of forty, 93 percent of white women had married, compared to only 65 percent of black women (Cherlin 2008; Huston and Melz 2004). Thus, marriage rates among African American women reached a historic low during the latter decades of the twentieth century, sparking concern over the welfare of children and the impact of social-welfare policies on families.

In this chapter, I begin with a historical overview of African American marriages that shows how centuries of slavery compromised African marriage traditions, yet precluded African Americans from embracing American traditions. As noted, the extent to which enslaved black families formed two-parent families has now become a matter of some debate; however, it seems clear that most sought to legalize their marital unions after slavery was abolished. Their ability to reap the benefits of marriage, however, was curtailed by racist policies and dominant gender ideologies, thus undermining the viability of their marriages and perpetuating a strong tradition of single-mother and extended families. Next, I show how social scientists have characterized African American families, arguing that theorists have often ignored marriage and the demands of the traditional marriage contract, which were inconsistent with the cultural traditions and economic resources of African Americans. I explore how the intersection of race, gender, and class inequalities continue to affect African American families and relationships adversely, and I conclude with a look at the future of marriage for African Americans.

Marriage among African Americans: A Historical Perspective

Although marriage and families are universal institutions that are often seen as the bases for societal stability, the rules and norms that govern these institutions are a product of differing cultural ideologies and economic forces. In West African societies, marriage was often arranged and polygamous and, given the importance placed on fertility, was sometimes preceded by the birth of children (Cherlin 2008). Both American and African marriages embraced patriarchal traditions, but the implications of male authority were muted in African societies by the economic roles of women, the primacy of the mother–child relationship, female-centered kin relationships, and the fact that blood relationships were often seen as more important than marital relationships (Caldwell 1996; Young 1970). Thus, Africans brought to the United States their own marital and family traditions, some of which were destroyed by the demands of slavery (e.g., polygamy), while others were reinforced by slavery (e.g., female work roles, extended families). Enslaved blacks undoubtedly merged West African and American family traditions in ways that enabled them to survive, but faced formidable obstacles to conforming fully to either family system. For example, the marriages of enslaved blacks had no legal sanction and were often unstable, and slavery coerced and controlled their labor and lives in ways that undermined family life. Black families were often defined as mothers and their children. Equally arduous labor was required for men and women, and men, even when present in families, were neither the primary providers nor heads of their families. These factors made it impossible for marriage to become thoroughly institutionalized among African Americans, but also freed them from rigid gender norms and the notion that love, sexuality, and family had to be centered in a legally sanctioned marriage contract (Hill 2005).

Emancipation had a destabilizing effect on African American families, often resulting in starvation, migration, marital separation, and the desertion of spouses and children. During the Civil War, armies invaded and disrupted plantation life, setting thousands of black people adrift and leading many to abandon their spouses and children (Frazier 1957). Resisting the loss of cheap labor, white southerners sometimes refused to allow black soldiers returning

from war to claim their wives and children (Landry 2000), and some states passed laws allowing whites to "indenture" (or re-enslave) the children of black couples who were unmarried or unemployed (Scott 1985). As racism intensified, African American men lost many of the skilled jobs they had held during slavery. Frequently charged with crimes like vagrancy and rape, they increasingly faced the prospects of being lynched, incarcerated, or forced into labor contracts (Booker 2000). As Booker has explained, many southerners argued that slavery had a civilizing influence on black people, but without it they were regressing to their primitive state, such as giving in to their natural tendency toward sexual immorality.

Amid myths of dangerous, unbridled sexuality among African Americans, a campaign was waged to legalize their marital unions, with marriage described as elevating "freedpeople to a new level of civilization" (Giddings 1984; Higginbothan 1993; Schwalm 1997). Former slaves were sometimes forced to legalize fairly casual sexual relationships; Frankel, for example, found an 1870 Mississippi law declaring all African American couples "who have not married, but are now living together, cohabiting as man and wife, shall be taken and held, for all purposes in the law, as married" (Frankel 1999). The legalization of marriage was also urged for economic reasons—the need to reorganize the labor of black people for the sharecropping system.

Evidence suggests that the majority of African Americans married after slavery ended; however, a significant minority remained single and/or formed single-mother families. There was, for example, much regional variation in marriage rates. Dabel found that two-thirds of free black women living in New York City between 1850 and 1870 did not marry (Dabel 2002); perhaps they were live-in domestics or had fewer potential marriage partners, since most blacks lived in the South. Indeed, in earlier research (Hill 2005, 2006), I have argued that while most African Americans married after slavery ended, there was also a nonmarriage ethos among a significant minority of black women, since the costs of being married outweighed the benefits. For example, many had developed a tradition of self-reliance during slavery, could perform labor that was still in demand, and were participants in female-centered kin networks that were not easily abandoned in favor of marriage. But even those who married did not necessarily adhere to mainstream family ideologies or abandon black cultural traditions such as relying on extended families and fostering children to other families. The latter may account for the fact that Steven Ruggles found that in 1850 nearly half of all free black children lived with one or neither of their parents, and by the 1880s (a few years after slavery was abolished) parental absence was five times more common among blacks than whites (Ruggles 1994).

Northward migration further diminished marital stability among African Americans, as many migrants failed to gain the economic foothold they had expected. The tradition of working wives was simply transferred from rural to urban areas (Landry 2000), where the tendency of white families to insist on live-in maids threatened the ability of African American women to prioritize caring for their own families (Marks 1989). Efforts to create married couple families were also countered by growing rates of unemployment among African American men during the 1950s (Billingsley 1992), the same decade that marriage rates began to decline. In fact, the birthrate among single African American women tripled between 1940 and 1957 (Franklin 1997), which suggests that nonmarital parenting, although neither normative nor the ideal, was not strongly stigmatized among blacks. Still, the growing concentration of single-mother families in urban areas and on welfare rolls made them more visible and controversial, thus setting the stage for twentieth-century debates about African American families.

Theorizing African American Families

The early sociological study of families was guided by the theoretical premises of structural functionalism, which saw the breadwinner–homemaker family model as ideal for social mobility in the rapidly industrializing economy. Centuries of slavery and racism had made it difficult for most African Americans to form such families; yet racist thinking often led scholars to explain the "deficiencies" in black families using theories of biological inferiority. Even those at the Chicago School of Sociology, which was known for its focus on the primacy of social and environmental forces, sometimes fell sway to the belief that different human populations were "endowed with different *biologically transmitted* cultural capacities" (Hall 2002). Among those opposing such reasoning was E. Franklin Frazier, an influential black scholar who argued that African American families had been shaped by social structural forces. Like other liberal scholars of the era, Frazier essentially offered a class analysis of African American families.

The Class (or Social Deficit) Perspective

Early twentieth-century sociologists focused heavily on processes of assimilation among racial–ethnic minorities who were moving into urban areas, and most sought to refute biological theories of racial inequality by emphasizing the impact of social structural forces on families. Thus, they often highlighted the similarities between middle-class black and white families that had assimilated into mainstream society, but provided dire portrayals of poor black families that had been unable to do so, especially those headed by single mothers (Davis and Havighurst 1946; Kardiner and Ovesey 1951). Frazier also emphasized class diversity among African American families (Frazier 1957), and he thought slavery had destroyed their African culture and was responsible for fostering single-mother families. He argued that single-mother (or matriarchal) families among African Americans had often worked well in the South, but they impeded socioeconomic mobility in a rapidly modernizing society. Never doubting the premises of the dominant theory of his era, structural-functionalism, or the merits of assimilating into the dominant culture, Frazier saw single-mother families as a legacy of slavery and two-parent, patriarchal families as ideal. This theme resonated with most African American activists and leaders throughout the 1950s; however, when reiterated in the Moynihan Report, it became the catalyst for a new genre of research on black families (Moynihan 1965).

The Cultural (or Family Strength) Perspective

The revolutionary era of the 1960s and 1970s produced research that was more critical of hegemonic family, marital, and gender ideologies, and of the social deficit perspective on African American families. The Moynihan Report, although it emphasized that there was significant class diversity among African Americans, was seen during the civil-rights era as attributing the blame for black economic disadvantage to single-mother families rather than racism. The report was widely criticized among activists and scholars, including feminists who bristled at the notion of patriarchal families as inherently superior to those headed by women. In their efforts to refute depictions of African American families as pathological and matriarchal, it became common to valorize the strength and family support networks of single mothers (Stack 1974) and argue that black married couples had created egalitarian relationships (Scanzoni 1977).

Two important themes emerged in the field of African American families studies among these revisionist scholars. First, social historians—in work that ultimately tended to "humanize" slave owners and "masculinize" the study of black families—argued that strong, stable, two-parent families were the norm among enslaved African Americans (Gutman 1976). According to revisionist researchers, enslaved black men exercised considerable authority over their families; indeed, "slaves created impressive norms of family life, including as much of a nuclear family norm as the conditions allowed," and slave owners "rarely if ever denied the moral content of the [marriage] relationship" between slaves (Genovese 1974). More recent scholars

have challenged this work by emphasizing the diversity of experiences among enslaved African Americans, even describing revisionist accounts of family life under slavery as being nothing more than "Disney scripts" (Dunaway 2003).

Second, revisionist scholars rejected the idea that African cultural traditions had been destroyed by slavery. Walter Allen, for example, argued that African American families are best described as "culturally variant" rather than "culturally deviant" (Allen 1978), and Robert Hill described their cultural traditions as including religiosity, extended kin networks, the primacy of blood over marital relationships, multiple parentage, and flexible or egalitarian gender roles (Hill 1972). The premise that African American families were simply culturally different from white families and that most were supported by extended family networks deflected some of the criticism of single-mother families and sparked a virtual cottage industry of studies on the nature, extent, and consequences of their extended family networks.

But the cultural perspective also inadvertently fostered a monolithic depiction of *the* black family as governed by an immutable set of cultural traditions, and failed to offer many insights into African American marriages. In addition, it was at a loss to explain the decline of poor families and their traditions during the post–civil rights era, when, arguably, opportunities for African Americans had expanded. Meanwhile, the political discourse on culture among low-income African Americans had begun to focus on the urban underclass and their lack of family values, with some arguing that escalating rates of nonmarriage and single-mother families were the direct result of generous welfare policies (Murray 1984).

Criticism of the "urban underclass" helped reignite the class perspective on African American families, with William J. Wilson arguing that the rise of the postindustrial economy had severely diminished the employment prospects of young men and produced significant class polarization among African Americans (Wilson 1978). Wilson theorized that class had become more important than race in predicting the life chances of African Americans, and linked the decline in marriage to growing joblessness among men. His narrow focus on the employment–marriage connection, however, failed to place the marriage dilemma of African Americans in historical context or acknowledge the impact of multiple forms of social inequality on marriage.

African American Marriages: A Contemporary Perspective

Scholarly inquiry into the demise of marriage has produced a host of studies showing that attitudinal support for marriage among African Americans has remained strong; indeed, blacks often express greater support for traditional ideals about sexuality, marriage, and family than do white Americans. Despite living lives that contradict their expressed ideals, African Americans are as likely as white Americans to idealize marriage (Edin 2000; Harknett and McLanahan 2004) and are less accepting of nonmarital sex, cohabitation, and divorce than whites (Huston and Melz 2004). How, then, does one explain the discrepancy between their support for marriage and their lived experiences? I argue that marriage has traditionally been based on social norms and ideologies that were at odds with the cultural traditions and economic resources of African Americans, and thus has never been as firmly institutionalized among black people. I use an intersectionality framework to show that class, race, and gender inequalities have made and continue to make it difficult for many African Americans to conform to mainstream marital expectations, and that these structural inequalities have fostered their participation in cultural patterns (such as nonmarriage and single motherhood) that contradict their professed ideals. Neither cultural nor structural theorists have adequately dealt with the intersection of these inequalities, and thus have offered at best partial explanations of the marriage decline.

The traditional marriage contract is rooted in notions of patriarchy, female subordination, distinct roles for men and women, the protection of property, and the production of legitimate children—all of which were negated for African Americans for centuries by the dictates of slavery. Slavery, as noted earlier, demanded diversity and flexibility in the family arrangements of black people, depending on factors such as the type of economy, region, size of the plantation, and solvency of the slave owner (Dunaway 2003; Franklin 1997). At best, slavery nearly always undermined the economic basis for male authority in families, fostered female independence, prevented blacks from owning much property, and defined families primarily as mothers and their children. Most evidence suggests that a majority of African Americans married and formed two-parent families after slavery ended. Clearly, however, a significant minority either remained single (Hill 2005, 2006) or lived in informal or cohabiting relationships (Frankel 1999), at least partly because it was difficult for them to reap the benefits and privileges of married life. For example, most former slaves entered the sharecropping system that demanded the labor of men and women, and that criticized black women who tried to exempt themselves from such work as "aspiring to a model of womanhood that was considered inappropriate for them" (Dill 1988). This labor system made it difficult for black men to claim head-of-household status based on economic provisioning or for wives to prioritize caring for their children and homes. Marriage neither exempted women from productive labor nor substantially improved their standards of living, yet those who married sometimes found their husbands eager to assert patriarchal power in their families—a factor blamed for high rates of domestic violence and marital separation among the newly freed slaves (Franklin 1997). Indeed, mainstream gender expectations, economic marginalization, and racism continued to make it difficult for African Americans to create stable marriages.

The Intersection of Class, Gender, and Racial Inequality

Intersectionality refers to understanding the "interconnectedness of ideas and the social structures in which they occur, and the intersecting hierarchies of gender, race, economic class, sexuality, and ethnicity" (Collins 1999). In applying this concept to the study of marriage, I focus on how structural factors shape cultural ideas and how multiple forms of inequality affect the challenges of marrying and staying married. For example, class matters a great deal as a factor in whether people will get and stay married: researchers have consistently found that higher income and educational attainment predict marriage and marital stability (Cherlin 2008). The rate of poverty among African Americans remains twice as high as that of white Americans, and much of that poverty is related to joblessness among black men (Wilson 1978). Low-income women, although struggling alone to make ends meet, are unwilling to marry men who cannot contribute much to their economic support (Edin 2000). Moreover, joblessness and poverty help push young African American men from mainstream society, and in their pursuit for manhood and respect many embrace behaviors (e.g., violence, hypersexuality) (Anderson 1999) that do not bode well for marriage and often lead to criminal behavior. Indeed, Western and Beckett (1999) have argued the racially motivated sentencing has made the penal system a major strategy in regulating the labor market, with more than 1.6 million people (disproportionately male and black) incarcerated by the late 1990s.

Economic restructuring has lessened the demand for unskilled labor, but racism in the labor market also undercuts the economic position of African Americans. Data from the Bureau of Labor Statistics reveal that among men twenty-five years of age or older in 2005, black men (7.6 percent) were more than twice as likely as white men (3.5 percent) to be unemployed. Moreover, African American men are discriminated against by employers for numerous reasons (Wilson 1987), including the notion that they simply lack the "soft skills" that are now in demand, such as "skills, abilities and traits that pertain to personality, attitude and behavior rather than formal or technical knowledge" (Moss and Tilly 1996). As Moss and Tilly have noted, employers often describe black men as being unmotivated, defensive, and hostile. Similar stereotypes undermine the ability of black women to find work. They are twice as likely as white women to be unemployed, and employers often stereotype them as unreliable single mothers (Browne and Kennelly 1995).

Neither the end of legalized racial segregation nor the gains made since the civil-rights era have eliminated racism or racial inequality; white Americans still endorse a spate of racist assumptions about African Americans and their families (Bobo, Kluegel, and Smith 1997). Racism and racial exclusion adversely affect the feelings of African Americans about their place in society and their quality of life. Hughes and Thomas, for example, found racial disparities in life quality between black and white Americans, and they argued that racism produces identity problems and a sense of rage and resentment among African Americans. Even when age and social class were considered, "African Americans were less satisfied, less happy, more mistrustful, more anomic, had less happy marriages, and rated their physical health worse than whites" (Hughes and Thomas 1998). This sense of being disrespected and disvalued in the larger society can adversely affect the quality of intimate relationships and the likelihood of marriage.

Persistent class and race inequalities intersect with and shape gender ideologies, making it difficult for African Americans to conform to traditional gender expectations or embrace the evolving ideal of gender-egalitarian marriages. For example, their long tradition of work and socioeconomic gains makes it difficult for many African American women to "marry up," or even marry men whose educational and economic position is comparable to their own. Although African American men earn more than black women, mostly because they hold male-typed jobs and more high-paying professional positions, the gains since the 1950s have been greater for black women. African American women, for example, are more likely than men to hold managerial and professional jobs (albeit in areas such as social work and teaching), more likely to have bachelor and especially graduate degrees, and more likely to feel integrated into the values of the dominant culture. This has created an important status gap between black women and men—and numerous books and movies that suggest the problem could be solved if middle-class black women would accept and marry working- or lower-class black men (Hill 2005). But class matters in forming viable marriages and marrying men of a lower class or status may help explain why black women feel less benefited by marriage than white women (Goodwin 2003). Indeed, the ideology of "marrying up" also affects low-income women, who are concerned about the loss of respectability associated with marrying poor and often jobless men (Edin 2000).

These structural inequalities foster cultural practices and behaviors that militate against marriage and marital success. Economic exclusion and persistent racial inequality, for example, ultimately creates an "oppositional culture that devalues work, schooling, and marriage" (Massey and Denton 1993). The courtship practices of young African American men who lack decent jobs or respect in mainstream society are often characterized by deceit, violence, and a general disrespect for women (Anderson 1990). The skewed gender ratio of men to women favors men and shapes their attitudes toward marriage and women; for example, Harknett and McLanahan found that "when men are in short supply, partner quality and relationship quality tend to be worse, and parents place less emphasis on the two-parent, male breadwinner norm" (Harknett and McLanahan 2004). African American men who marry tend to bring to their relationships more conservative gender beliefs than white

men (Blee and Tickamyer 1995) and, despite being more accepting of employed wives, their marriages are characterized by more work–family conflicts, especially when the wife has a career (Bridges and Orza 1996). Gender traditions also persist in the division of domestic work: African American men spend only about half as much time doing housework as their partners (John and Shelton 1997). Overall, black couples are less satisfied in their marriages than white couples; they report sharing fewer activities and experiencing more conflict and distrust (Harknett and McLanahan 2004).

The Marriage Decline: Can (Should) It Be Reversed?

The strongest arguments for marriage are that married couples have higher levels of health and well-being than singles, that marriage reduces poverty, and that children fare better in two-parent families. For these reasons, the 1996 Personal Responsibility and Work Opportunity Act (PRWOA) declared that marriage "is the foundation of a successful society" and "is an essential institution that promotes the interests of children" (Jayakody and Cabrera 2002). Proponents of marriage contend that married people are happier, healthier, and wealthier than single people (Waite and Gallagher 2000). Still, the extent to which this applies to African American couples is debatable. As indicated earlier, there is a racial gap in marital satisfaction, with married African American couples experiencing more conflict and distrust in their relationships than white couples. Although their lower level of marital satisfaction cannot be explained away by noting class differences between blacks and whites, it is undoubtedly exacerbated by the fact that African Americans are more likely to be in the working and lower classes, where divorce and domestic violence are more common. Staying in unhappy marriages correlates with adverse health outcomes, such as elevated levels of psychological distress and poor health (Hawkins and Booth 2005). There is also evidence that marital unhappiness takes a greater toll on the health of wives than of husbands, with unhappy wives having high levels of depression and substance abuse (Coontz 2005).

From an economic standpoint, black married couple families fare better than single-mother families, although their 2001 median household income ($55,618) was much less than that of white married couple families ($71,155) (Conrad and King 2005). Linda Waite has found that several factors reduce the economic benefits of marriage for African Americans, such as lower wage gap between black men and women, the lower returns black women receive for investing in their husband's earnings, and the expense of raising children, who are more likely to be present in the homes of black couples (Waite 1995). For lower-income couples, where the prospects of unemployment, divorce, and domestic violence are high, the economic benefits of marriage may prove even more meager. D. T. Lichter and colleagues report that poverty rates would still be more than twice as high among African American women if they had the same family background and rates of marriage and unwed childbirth as white women (Lichter, Graefe, and Brown 2003). They also found that among economically disadvantaged black women, marriage is associated with downward educational mobility, and those who marry and divorce have higher rates of poverty than those who never married.

Although the growth in single-mother families has leveled off in recent years, nearly 41 percent of American children live in such families, with African American children (53 percent) more likely to do so than white children (22 percent) (Sigle-Rushton and McLanahan 2004). Children benefit from having the emotional and financial support of their fathers; indeed, many studies have shown that children living with single mothers, regardless of their race or social class, are more likely than those living with two biological parents to experience academic failure, behavioral and psychological problems, delinquency, and illegal drug use (Ellwood and Jencks 2004; Sigle-Rushton and McLanahan 2004). Still, single-mother families

and extended family relationships are more institutionalized among African Americans and may have fewer adverse consequences for black children. A study comparing male adolescents living in white and black single-mother families found that lack of involvement with fathers elevated the risk of problematic behaviors only for white sons— at least partially because they were more likely to live in *divorced* single-mother families and were more likely to have lost a father with whom they had a relationship (Thomas, Farrell, and Barnes 1996). For African Americans, the risks of single-mother families may be more the result of the demise of extended family relationships and higher rates of poverty and extreme poverty; for example, in 2001 the median household income for black single mothers was less than $21,000, compared to $29,650 for white single mothers (Conrad and King 2005).

So, should African Americans get married? There are clearly benefits to be gained from marriage, although most evidence suggests that those benefits are not as great for blacks as for whites. But given the diminishing support single mothers are receiving from the state and their extended families, marriage may become more appealing. Moreover, there is strong ideological support for marriage among African Americans; the majority would like to get married, and they equate marriage with respectability, endorsing more traditional marital, gender, and sexual norms than white Americans. Still, a gap has always existed for African Americans between their endorsement of mainstream family values and their lived experiences. As I have argued, many African Americans have historically lacked the economic and cultural resources to conform to the traditional marriage contract, which was based on male-domination, gendered roles, and property. Today, these institutional aspects of marriage have now given way to marriage as a personal relationship based on gender equality and emotional satisfaction (Amato 2004). Such marital expectations should, at least arguably, make it easier for African Americans to achieve marital success, since the emphasis on economics has declined. Still, these new marital expectations are more likely to be embraced by middle-class couples, and African Americans have primarily been in the working and lower classes, where traditional values are more apparent. For example, as Landry has pointed out, employed wives have always been acceptable among African Americans, but "[it] remained for the upper-middle-class black wives to elevate the *acceptable* to the *desirable* in the early decades of the twentieth century" (Landry 2000).

Conclusion

In this chapter, I have argued that multiple forms of social inequality, both historically and currently, have created an important gap between the marital ideals of African Americans and the resources needed to live those ideals. This has made marriage seem less attainable, and thus has fostered cultural alternatives to marriage, such as high rates of single-mother families and nonmarital cohabitation. Mainstream marital traditions, for example, have supported patriarchal marriages headed by men earning the family wage, but exempted African American men from such jobs. These marital traditions have also been based on the primacy of marriage-centered families, but African Americans have often had to rely on extended family networks in order to survive. It has also been traditionally based on a gender division of labor that makes women economic dependents by placing them in the home, yet since slavery African American women have always combined productive and domestic work. Thus, despite high levels of attitudinal support for marriage among black Americans, dominant marital traditions have been at odds with their experiences. In this sense, marriage has never been fully institutionalized among African Americans.

Multiple social inequalities are responsible for the erosion of marriage among African Americans during the twentieth century, and addressing those inequalities is the key to restoring marriage as a vital institution. For example, workshops have sprung up to teach African American men the value of being involved in their children's lives, but less has been done to bring them into the economic mainstream or enhance their employment skills or educational achievement—both of which are important if they are to participate consistently in family life. Similarly, both politicians and religionists who trumpet the value of marriage and two-parent families have not always acknowledged the gender inequities in those arrangements, which women increasingly refuse to tolerate. Welfare-related marriage-promotion programs have more leverage over poor, young mothers than they do the fathers, and some research suggests that such programs place the responsibility on mothers to "swallow their rage and grievances against men" and bring them into the cultural mainstream of marriage (Huston and Melz 2004). Failing to resolve basic gender issues, though, will not lead to successful marriages. Finally, marriages have changed for all Americans over the past few decades, with more employed wives, more dual-income families, more economic independence, and more couples unwilling to stay in marriages that are emotionally unsatisfying. These changes in marriage have made issues such as gender equity in the home, adequate childcare, and family-friendly practices by employers key factors in the maintenance of families.

References

Allen, W. R. 1978. The search for applicable theories of black family life. *Journal of Marriage and the Family 40,* no. 1:117–129.

Amato, P. R. 2004. Tension between institutional and individual views of marriage. *Journal of Marriage and Family 66* (November); 959–965.

Anderson, E. 1990. *Streetwise: Race, class, and change in an urban community.* Chicago: University of Chicago Press.

———. 1999. *Code of the street: Decency, violence, and the moral life of the inner city.* New York: Norton.

Billingsley, A. 1968. *Black families in white America.* Englewood Cliffs, N. J.: Prentice-Hall.

Billingsley, A. and J. M. Giovannoni. 1972 *Children of the Storm: Black Children and American Child Welfare.* New York: Harcourt Brace Jovanovich.

———. 1992. *Climbing Jacob's ladder: The enduring legacy of African-American families.* New York: Simon & Schuster.

Blassingame, J. W. 1972. *The slave community: Plantation life in the antebellum south.* New York: Oxford University Press.

Blee, K. M., and A. R. Tickamyer. 1995. Racial differences in men's attitudes about women's gender roles. *Journal of Marriage and the Family* 57, no. 1: 21–30.

Bobo, L., J. R. Kluegel, and R. A. Smith. 1997. Laissez-faire racism; The crystallization of a kinder, gentler, antiblack ideology. In S. A. Tuch and J. K. Martin, eds., *Racial attitudes in the 1990s: Continuity and change,* 15–42. Westport, Conn.; Praeger.

Booker, C. B. 2000. *"I will wear no chain!" A social history of African American males.* Westport, Conn.; Praeger.

Bridges, J. S., and A. M. Orza. 1996. Black and white employed mothers' role experience. *Sex Roles* 35, nos. 5–6: 337–385.

Browne, I., and I. Kennelly. 1995. Stereotypes and realities: Images of black women in the labor market. In I. Brown, ed., *Latinas and African American women at work: Race, gender, and economic inequality,* 302–326. New York: Russell Sage.

Caldwell, J. C. 1996. The demographic implications of West African family systems. *Journal of Comparative Family Studies* 27:331–352.

Cherlin, A. J. 2008. *Public and private families: An introduction.* New York: McGraw Hill.

Collins, P. H. 1999. Moving beyond gender: Intersectionality and scientific knowledge. In M. M. Ferree, J. Lorber, and B. B. Hess, eds., *Revisioning gender,* 261–284. Thousand Oaks, Calif.: Sage.

Conrad, C. A., and M. C. King. 2005. Single-mother families in the black community: Economic context and policies. In C. A. Conrad, J. Whitehead, P. Mason, and J. Stewart, eds., *African Americans in the U.S. Economy,* 163–174. Lanham, Md.: Rowman & Littlefield.

Coontz, S. 2005. *Marriage, a history: From obedience to intimacy, or how love conquered marriage.* New York: Viking Penguin.

Dabel, J. E. 2002. African American women and household composition in New York City, 1827–1877. In J. L. Conyers Jr., ed., *Black cultures and race relations,* 60–72. Chicago: Burnham.

Davis, A., and R. J. Havighurst. 1946. Social class and color differences in child-rearing. *American Sociological Review* 2:698–710.

Dill, B. T. 1988. Our mothers' grief: Racial ethnic women and the maintenance of families. *Journal of Family History* 13, no. 4: 415–431.

Dunaway, W. A. 2003. *The African American family in slavery and emancipation.* New York: Cambridge University Press.

Edin, K. 2000. What do low-income single mothers say about marriage? *Social Problems* 47, no. 1: 112–113.

Ellwood, D. T., and C. Jencks. 2004. The spread of single-parent families in the United States since 1960. In D. P. Moynihan, T. M. Smeeding, and L. Rainwater, eds., *Future of the family,* 25–65. New York: Russell Sage Foundation.

Fitch, C. A., and S. Ruggles. 2000. Historical trends in marriage formation: The United States 1850–1990. In L. J. Waite, Bachrach, M. Hindin, E. Thomson, and A. Thornton, eds., *The ties that bind: Perspectives on marriage and cohabitation.* New York: Aldine de Gruyter.

Frankel, N. 1999. *Freedom's women: Black women and families in Civil War–era Mississippi.* Bloomington: Indiana University Press.

Franklin, D. L. 1997. *Ensuring inequality: The structural transformation of the African-American family.* New York: Oxford University Press.

Frazier, E. F. 1957. *The Negro in the United States.* New York: Macmillan.

Genovese, E. D. 1974. *Roll, Jordan, roll: The world the slaves made.* New York: Pantheon.

Giddings, P. 1984. *When and where I enter: The impact of black women on race and sex in America.* New York: Bantam.

Goodwin, P. Y. 2003. African American and European American women's marital well-being. *Journal of Marriage and the Family* 65 (August): 550–560.

Gutman, H. G. 1976. *The black family in slavery and freedom, 1750–1925.* New York: Pantheon.

Hall, R. L. 2002. E. Franklin Frazier and the Chicago school of sociology. In J. E. Teele, ed., *E. Franklin Frazier and the black bourgeoisie,* 47–67. Columbia: University of Missouri Press.

Harknett, K., and S. S. McLanahan. 2004. Racial and ethnic differences in marriage after the birth of a child. *American Sociological Review* 69 (December): 790–811.

Hawkins, D., and A. Booth. 2005. Unhappily ever after: Effects of long-term, low-quality marriages on well-being. *Social Forces* 84, no. 1: 451–471.

Higginbothan, E. B. 1993. *Righteous discontent: The women's movement in the black Baptist church, 1880–1920.* Cambridge, Mass.: Harvard University Press.

Hill, R. B. 1972. *The strengths of black families.* New York: Emerson Hall.

Hill, S. A. 2005. *Black intimacies: A gender perspective on families and relationships.* Walnut Creek, Calif.: AltaMira.

———. 2006. Marriage among African Americans: A gender perspective. *Journal of Comparative Family Studies* 37, no. 3: 421–440.

Hughes, M., and M. E. Thomas. 1998. The continuing significance of race revisited: A study of race, class and quality of life in America, 1972 to 1996. *American Sociological Review* 63 (December): 785–795.

Huston, T. L., and H. Melz. 2004. The case for (promoting) marriage: The devil is in the details. *Journal of Marriage and Family* 66 (November): 943–958.

Jayakody, R., and N. Cabrera. 2002. What are the choices for low-income families? Cohabitation, marriage, and remaining single. In A. Booth and A. C. Crounter, eds., *Just living together: Implications of cohabitation on families, children, and social policy,* 85–95. Mahwah, N. J.: Erlbaum.

John, D., and B. A. Shelton. 1997. The production of gender among black and white women and men: The case of household labor. *Sex Roles* 36, nos. 3–4: 171–193.

Kardiner, A., and L. Ovesey. 1951. *The mark of oppression: Explorations in the personality of the American Negro.* New York: Meridian.

Koball, H. 1998. Have African American men become less committed to marriage? Explaining the twentieth century racial cross-over in men's marriage timing. *Demography* 35, no. 2: 251–258.

Landry, B. 2000. *Black working wives: Pioneers of the American family revolution.* Berkeley: University of California Press.

Lichter, D. T., D. R. Graefe, and J. B. Brown. 2003. Is marriage a panacea? Union formation among economically disadvantaged unwed mothers. *Social Problems* 50, no. 1: 60–86.

Marks, C. 1989. *Farewell—we're good and gone: The great black migration.* Bloomington: Indiana University Press.

Massey, D. S., and N. A. Denton. 1993. *American apartheid: Segregation and the making of the underclass.* Cambridge, Mass.: Harvard University Press.

Moss, P., and C. Tilly. 1996. "Soft" skills and race: An investigation of black men's employment problems. *Work and Occupations* 23, no. 3: 252–276.

Moynihan, D. P. 1965. *The Negro family: The case for national action.* Washington, D.C.: Office of Policy Planning and Research.

Murray, C. 1984. *Losing ground: American social policy, 1950–1980.* New York: Basic Books.

Nobles, W. W. 1974. Africanity: Its role in black families. *Black Scholar* 5, no. 9: 10–17.

Ruggles, S. 1994. The origins of African-American family structure. *American Sociological Review* 59 (February): 136–151.

Scanzoni, J. 1977. *The black family in modern society: Patterns of stability and security.* Chicago: University of Chicago Press.

Schwalm, L. A. 1997. *A hard fight for we: Women's transition from slavery to freedom in South Carolina.* Urbana: University of Illinois Press.

Scott, R. J. 1985. The battle over the child: Child apprenticeship and the freedmen's bureau in North Carolina. In N. R. Hiner and J. M. Hawes, eds., *Growing up in America: Children in historical perspective,* 193–207. Chicago: University of Chicago Press.

Sigle-Rushton, W., and S. McLanahan. 2004. Father absence and child well-being: A critical review. In D. P. Moynihan, T. M. Smeeding, and L. Rainwater, eds., *Future of the family,* 116–155. New York: Russell Sage Foundation.

Stack, C. 1974. *All our kin: Strategies for survival in a black community.* New York: Harper & Row.

Thomas, G., M. P. Farrell, and G. M. Barnes. 1996. The effects of single-mother families and nonresident fathers on delinquency and substance abuse in black and white adolescents. *Journal of Marriage and the Family* 58 (November): 884–894.

U.S. Department of Labor, Bureau of Labor Statistics. Household data and annual averages. Retrieved January 25, 2008, from www.bls.gov/cps/cpsaat24.pdf.

Waite, L. 1995. Does marriage matter? *Demography* 32, no. 4: 483–507.

Waite, L., and M. Gallagher. 2000. *The case for marriage: Why married people are happier, healthier, and better off financially.* New York: Doubleday.

Western, B., and K. Beckett. 1999. How unregulated is the U.S. labor market? The penal system as a labor market institution. *American Journal of Sociology* 104, no. 4: 1030–1060.

Wilson, W. J. 1978. *The declining significance of race: Blacks and changing American institutions.* Chicago: University of Chicago Press.

_____. 1987. *The truly disadvantaged.* Chicago: University of Chicago Press.

Young, V. H. 1970. Family and childhood in a southern Negro community. *American Anthropologist* 72, no. 2: 269–288.

Questions for Critical Thinking

1. Hill's discussion of the history of African American families demonstrates the importance of examining race, social class, and gender simultaneously when we examine the institution of family. Do you think that this is important? Why or why not?

2. How do the policies of other institutions (e.g., economy, education, the state) result in additional strains on the family for African Americans that white families do not experience? What policies can you think of that might alleviate some of these strains?

3. How is your own definition of family inclusive or exclusive of a diversity of race, class, or gender experiences?

Families on the Fault Line
America's Working Class Speaks about the Family, the Economy, Race, and Ethnicity

LILLIAN B. RUBIN

The following essay is by sociologist Lillian Rubin, author of the classic book Worlds of Pain *that provided an in-depth examination of working-class family dynamics. In the work that follows, Rubin again explores the working class, drawing on data from nearly four hundred interviews with a diverse array of people. Her analysis illustrates the many ways that continued economic decline disproportionately places stress on families of the working class and how this stress is intensified when we take into consideration inequality based on race and gender.*

Not surprisingly, there are generational differences in what fuels the conflict around the division of labor in families. For the older couples—those who grew up in a different time, whose marriages started with another set of ground rules—the struggle is not simply around how much men do or about whether they take responsibility for the daily tasks of living without being pushed, prodded, and reminded. That's the overt manifestation of the discord, the trigger that starts the fight. But the noise of the explosion when it comes serves to conceal the more fundamental issue underlying the dissension: legitimacy. What does she have a *right* to expect? "What do I know about doing stuff around the house?" asks Frank Moreno, a forty-eight-year-old foreman in a warehouse. "I wasn't brought up

like that. My pop, he never did one damn thing, and my mother never complained. It was her job; she did it and kept quiet. Besides, I work my ass off every day. Isn't that enough?"

For younger couples, those under forty, the problem is somewhat different. The men may complain about the expectation that they'll participate more fully in the care and feeding of the family, but talk to them about it quietly and they'll usually admit that it's not really unfair, given that their wives also work outside the home. In these homes, the issue between husband and wife isn't only who does what. That's there and it's a source of more or less conflict, depending upon what the men actually do and how forceful their wives are in their demands. But in most of these families there's at least a verbal consensus that men *ought* to participate in the tasks of daily life. Which raises the next and perhaps more difficult issue in contest between them: Who feels responsible for getting the tasks done? Who regards them as a duty, and for whom are they an option? On this, tradition rules.

Even in families where husbands now share many of the tasks, their wives still bear full responsibility for the organization of family life. A man may help cook the meal these days, but a woman is most likely to be the one who has planned it. He may take the children to child care, but she

---

virtually always has had to arrange it. It's she also who is accountable for the emotional life of the family, for monitoring the emotional temperature of its members and making the necessary corrections. It's this need to be responsible for it all that often feels as burdensome as the tasks themselves. "It's not just doing all the stuff that needs doing," explains Maria Jankowicz, a white twenty-eight-year-old assembler in an electronics factory. "It's worrying all the time about everything and always having to arrange everything, you know what I mean. It's like I run the whole show. If I don't stay on top of it all, things fall apart because nobody else is going to do it. The kids can't and Nick, well, forget it," she concludes angrily.

If, regardless of age, life stage, or verbal consensus, women usually still carry the greatest share of the household burdens, why is it important to notice that younger men grant legitimacy to their wives' demands and older men generally do not? Because men who believe their wives have a right to expect their participation tend to suffer guilt and discomfort when they don't live up to those expectations. And no one lives comfortably with guilt.

It's possible, of course, that the men who speak of guilt and rights are only trying to impress me by mouthing the politically correct words. But even if true, they display a sensitivity to the issue that's missing from the men who don't speak those words. For words are more than just words. They embody ideas; they are the symbols that give meaning to our thoughts; they shape our consciousness. New ideas come to us on the wings of words. It's words that bring those ideas to life, that allow us to see possibilities unrecognized before we gave them words. Indeed, without words, there is no conscious thought, no possibility for the kind of self-reflection that lights the path of change.[1]

True, there's often a long way between word and deed. But the man who feels guilty when he disappoints his wife's expectations has a different consciousness than the one who doesn't—a difference that usually makes for at least some small change in his behavior. Although the emergence of

this changing male consciousness is visible in all the racial groups in this study, there also are differences among them that are worthy of comment.

Virtually all the men do some work inside the family—tending the children, washing dishes, running the vacuum, going to the market. And they generally also remain responsible for those tasks that have always been traditionally male—mowing the lawn, shoveling the snow, fixing the car, cleaning the garage, doing repairs around the house. Among the white families in this study, 16 percent of the men share the family work relatively equally, almost always those who live in families where they and their wives work different shifts or where the men are unemployed. "What choice do I have?" asks Don Bartlett, a thirty-year-old white handyman who works days while his wife is on the swing shift. "I'm the only one here, so I do what's got to be done."

Asian and Latino men of all ages, however, tend to operate more often on the old male model, even when they work different shifts or are unemployed, a finding that puzzled me at first. Why, I wondered, did I find only two Asian men and one Latino who are real partners in the work of the family? Aren't these men subject to the same social and personal pressures others experience?

The answer is both yes and no. The pressures are there but, depending upon where they live, there's more or less support for resisting them. The Latino and Asian men who live in ethnic neighborhoods—settings where they are embedded in an intergenerational community and where the language and culture of the home country are kept alive by a steady stream of new immigrants—find strong support for clinging to the old ways. Therefore, change comes much more slowly in those families. The men who live outside the ethnic quarter are freer from the mandates and constraints of these often tight-knit communities, therefore are more responsive to the winds of change in the larger society.

These distinctions notwithstanding, it's clear that Asian and Latino men generally participate least in the work of the household and are the least likely to believe they have much responsibility there beyond bringing home a paycheck. "Taking care of the house and kids is my wife's job, that's all," says Joe Gomez flatly.

"A Chinese man mopping a floor? I've never seen it yet," says Amy Lee angrily. Her husband, Dennis, trying to make a joke of the conflict with his wife, says with a smile, "In Chinese families men don't do floors and windows. I help with the dishes sometimes if she needs me to or," he laughs, "if she screams loud enough. The rest, well, it's pretty much her job."

The commonly held stereotype about black men abandoning women and children, however, doesn't square with the families in this study. In fact, black men are the most likely to be real participants in the daily life of the family and are more intimately involved in raising their children than any of the others. True, the men's family workload doesn't always match their wives', and the women are articulate in their complaints about this. Nevertheless, compared to their white, Asian, or Latino counterparts, the black families look like models of egalitarianism.

Nearly three-quarters of the men in the African-American families in this study do a substantial amount of the cooking, cleaning, and child care, sometimes even more than their wives. All explain it by saying one version or another of: "I just figure it's my job, too." Which simply says what is, without explaining how it came to be that way.

To understand that, we have to look at family histories that tell the story of generations of African-American women who could find work and men who could not, and to the family culture that grew from this difficult and painful reality. "My mother worked six days a week cleaning other people's houses, and my father was an ordinary laborer, when he could find work, which wasn't very often," explains thirty-two-year-old Troy Payne, a black waiter and father of two children. "So he was home a lot more than she was, and he'd do what he had to around the house. The kids all had to do their share, too. It seemed only fair, I guess."

Difficult as the conflict around the division of labor is, it's only one of the many issues that have become flash points in family life since mother went to work. Most important, perhaps, is the question: Who will care for the children? For the lack of decent, affordable facilities for the care of the children creates unbearable problems and tensions for these working-class families.

It's hardly news that child care is an enormous headache and expense for all two-job families. In many professional middle-class families, where the child-care bill can be $1,500–2,000 a month, it competes with the mortgage payment as the biggest single monthly expenditure. Problematic as this may be, however, these families are the lucky ones when compared to working-class families, many of whom don't earn much more than the cost of child care in these upper middle-class families. Even the families in this study at the highest end of the earnings scale, those who earn $42,000 a year, can't dream of such costly arrangements.

For most working-class families, therefore, child care often is patched together in ways that leave parents anxious and children in jeopardy. "Care for the little ones, that's a real big problem," says Beverly Waldov, a thirty-year-old white mother of three children, the youngest two, products of a second marriage, under three years old. "My oldest girl is nine, so she's not such a problem. I hate the idea of her being a latchkey kid, but what can I do? We don't even have the money to put the little ones in one of those good day-care places, so I don't have any choice with her. She's just *got* to be able to take care of herself after school," she says, her words a contest between anxiety and hope.

"We have a kind of complicated arrangement for the little kids. Two days a week, my mom takes care of them. We pay her, but at least I don't have to worry when they're with her; I know it's fine. But she works the rest of the time, so the other days we take them to this woman's house. It's the best we can afford, but it's not great because she keeps too many kids, and I know they don't get good attention. Especially the little one; she's just a baby, you know." She pauses and looks away, anguished. "She's so clingy when I bring her home; she can't let go of me, like nobody's paid her any mind all day. But it's not like I have a choice. We barely make it now; if I stop working, we'd be in real trouble."

Even such makeshift solutions don't work for many families. Some speak of being unable to afford day care at all. "We couldn't pay our bills if we had to pay for somebody to take care of the kids."

Some say they're unwilling to leave the children in the care of strangers. "I just don't believe someone else should be raising our kids, that's all."

Some have tried a variety of child-care arrangements, only to have them fail in a moment of need. "We tried a whole bunch of things, and maybe they work for a little while," says Faye Ensey, a black twenty-eight-year-old office worker. "But what happens when your kid gets sick? Or when the baby sitter's kids get sick? I lost two jobs in a row because my kids kept getting sick and I couldn't go to work. Or else I couldn't take my little one to the baby sitter because her kids were sick. They finally fired me for absenteeism. I didn't really blame them, but it felt terrible anyway. It's such a hassle, I sometimes think I'd be glad to just stay home. But we can't afford for me not to work, so we had to figure out something else."

For such families, that "something else" is the decision to take jobs on different shifts—a decision made by one-fifth of the families in this study. With one working days and the other on swing or graveyard, one parent is home with the children at all times. "We were getting along okay before Daryl junior was born, because Shona, my daughter, was getting on. You know, she didn't need somebody with her all the time, so we could both work days," explains Daryl Adams, a black thirty-year-old postal clerk with a ten-year-old daughter and a nine-month-old son. "I used to work the early shift—seven to three—so I'd get home a little bit after she got here. It worked out okay. But then this here big surprise came along." He stops, smiles down fondly at his young son and runs his hand over his nearly bald head.

"Now between the two of us working, we don't make enough money to pay for child care and have anything left over, so this is the only way we can manage. Besides, both of us, Alesha and me, we think it's better for one of us to be here, not just for the baby, for my daughter, too. She's growing up and, you know, I think maybe they need even more watching than when they were younger. She's coming to the time when she could get into all kinds of trouble if we're not here to put the brakes on."

But the cost such arrangements exact on marriage can be very high. When I asked these husbands and wives when they have time to talk, more often than not I got a look of annoyance at a question that, on its face, seemed stupid to them. "Talk? How can we talk when we hardly see each other?" "Talk? What's that?" "Talk? Ha, that's a joke."

Mostly, conversation is limited to the logistics that take place at shift-changing time when children and chores are handed off from one to the other. With children dancing around underfoot, the incoming parent gets a quick summary of the day's or night's events, a list of reminders about things to be done, perhaps about what's cooking in the pot on the stove. "Sometimes when I'm coming home and it's been a hard day, I think: Wouldn't it be wonderful if I could just sit down with Leon for half an hour and we could have a quiet beer together?" thirty-one-year-old Emma Guerrero, a Latina baker, says wistfully.

But it's not to be. If the arriving spouse gets home early enough, there may be an hour when both are there together. But with the pressures of the workday fresh for one and awaiting the other, and with children clamoring for parental attention, this isn't a promising moment for any serious conversation.

Some of the luckier couples work different shifts on the same days, so they're home together on weekends. But even in these families there's so little time for normal family life that there's hardly any room for anyone or anything outside.

For those whose days off don't match, the problems of sustaining both the couple relationship and family life are magnified enormously. "The last two years have been hell for us," says thirty-five-year-old Tina Mulvaney, a white mother of two teenagers. "My son got into bad company and had some trouble, so Mike and I decided one of us had to be home. But we can't make it without my check, so I can't quit.

"Mike drives a cab and I work in a hospital, so we figured one of us could transfer to nights. We talked it over and decided it would be best if I was here during the day and he was here at night. He controls the kids, especially my son, better than I do. When he lays down the law, they listen." She interrupts her narrative to reflect on the difficulty of raising children. "You know, when they were little, I used to think about how much easier it would be when they got older. But now I see it's not true; that's when you really have to begin to worry about them. This is when they need someone to be here all the time to make sure they stay out of trouble."

She stops again, this time fighting tears, then takes up where she left off. "So now Mike works days and I work graveyard. I hate it, but it's the only answer; at least this way somebody's here all the time. I get home about 8:30 in the morning. The kids and Mike are gone. It's the best time of the day because it's the only time I have a little quiet here. I clean up the house a little, do the shopping and the laundry and whatever, then I go to sleep for a couple of hours until the kids come home from school.

"Mike gets home at five; we eat; then he takes over for the night, and I go back to sleep for another couple of hours. I try to get up by 9 so we can all have a little time together, but I'm so tired that I don't make it a lot of times. And by 10, he's sleeping because he has to be up by 6 in the morning. So if I don't get up, we hardly see each other at all. Mike's here on weekends, but I'm not. Right now I have Tuesday and Wednesday off. I keep hoping for a Monday–Friday shift, but it's what everybody wants, and I don't have the seniority yet. It's hard, very hard; there's no time to live or anything," she concludes with a listless sigh.

Even in families where wife and husband work the same shift, there's less time for leisure pursuits and social activities than ever before, not just because both parents work full-time but also because people work longer hours now than they did twenty years ago.[2] Two decades ago, weekends saw occasional family outings, Friday evening bowling, a Saturday trip to the shopping mall, a Sunday with extended family, once in a while an evening out without the children. In summer, when the children weren't in school, a week night might find the family paying a short visit to a friend, a relative, or a neighbor. Now almost everyone I speak with complains that it's hard to find time for even these occasional outings. Instead, most off-work hours are spent trying to catch up with the dozens of family and household tasks that were left undone during the regular work week. When they aren't doing chores, parents guiltily try to do in two days a week what usually takes seven—that is, to establish a sense of family life for themselves and their children.

"Leisure," snorts Peter Pittman, a twenty-eight-year-old African-American father of two, married six years. "With both of us working like we do, there's no time for anything. We got two little kids; I commute better than an hour each way to my job. Then we live here for half rent because I take care of the place for the landlord. So if somebody's got a complaint, I've got to take care of it, you know, fix it myself or get the landlord to get somebody out to do it if I can't. Most things I can do myself, but it takes time. I sometimes wonder what this life's all about, because this sure ain't what I call living. We don't go anyplace; we don't do anything; Christ, we hardly have time to go to the toilet. There's always some damn thing that's waiting that you've got to do."

Clearly, such complaints aren't unique to the working class. The pressures of time, the impoverishment of social life, the anxieties about child care, the fear that children will live in a world of increasing scarcity, the threat of divorce—all these are part of family life today, regardless of class.

Nevertheless, there are important differences between those in the higher reaches of the class structure and the families of the working class. The simple fact that middle-class families have more discretionary income is enough to make a big difference in the quality of their social life. For they generally have enough money to pay for a babysitter once in a while so that parents can have some time to themselves; enough, too, for a family vacation, for tickets to a concert, a play, or a movie. At $7.50 a ticket in a New York or San Francisco movie house, a working-class couple will settle for a $3.00 rental that the whole family can watch together.

Finding time and energy for sex is also a problem, one that's obviously an issue for two-job families of any class. But it's harder to resolve in working-class families because they have so few resources with which to buy some time and privacy for themselves. Ask about their sex lives and you'll be met with an angry, "What's that?" or a wistful, "I wish." When it happens, it is, as one woman put it, "on the run"—a situation that's particularly unsatisfactory for most women. For them, the pleasure of sex is related to the whole of the interaction— to a sense of intimacy and connection, to at least a few relaxed, loving moments. When they can't have these, they're likely to avoid sex altogether—a situation the men find equally unsatisfactory.

"Sex?" asks Lisa Scranton, a white twenty-nine-year-old mother of three who feigns a puzzled frown, as if she doesn't quite know the meaning of the word. "Oh yeah, that; I remember now," she says, her lips smiling, her eyes sad. "At the beginning, when we first got together, it was WOW, real hot, great. But after a while it cools down, doesn't it? Right now, it's down the toilet. I wonder, does it happen to everybody like that?" she asks dejectedly.

"I guess the worst is when you work different shifts like we do and you get to see each other maybe six minutes a day. There's no time for sex. Sometimes we try to steal a few minutes for ourselves but, I don't know, I can't get into it that way. He can. You know how men are; they can do it any time. Give them two minutes, and they can get off.

But it takes me time; I mean, I like to feel close, and you can't do that in three minutes. And there's the kids; they're right here all the time. I don't want to do it if it means being interrupted. Then he gets mad, so sometimes I do. But it's a problem, a real problem."

The men aren't content with these quick sexual exchanges either. But for them it's generally better than no sex at all, while for the women it's often the other way around. "You want to talk about sex, huh?" asks Lisa's husband, Chuck, his voice crackling with anger. "Yeah, I don't mind; it's fine, only I got nothing to talk about. Far as I'm concerned, that's one of the things I found out about marriage. You get married, you give up sex. We hardly ever do it anymore, and when we do, it's like she's doing me a favor."

"Christ, I know the way we've got to do things now isn't great," he protests, running a hand through his hair agitatedly. "We don't see each other but a few minutes a day, but I don't see why we can't take five and have a little fun in the sack. Sure, I like it better when we've got more time, too. But for her, if it can't be perfect, she gets all wound and uptight and it's like . . ." He stops, groping for words, then explodes, "It's like screwing a cold fish."

She isn't just a "cold fish," however. The problems they face are deeper than that. For once such conflicts arise, spontaneity takes flight and sex becomes a problem that needs attention rather than a time out for pleasure and renewal. Between times, therefore, he's busy calculating how much time has passed: "It's been over two weeks"; nursing his wounds: "I don't want to have to beg her"; feeling deprived and angry: "I don't know why I got married." When they finally do come together, he's disappointed. How could it be otherwise, given the mix of feelings he brings to the bed with him— the frustration and anger, the humiliation of feeling he has to beg her, the wounded sense of manhood.

Meanwhile, she, too, is preoccupied with sex, not with thoughts of pleasure but with figuring out how much time she has before, as she puts it, "he walks around with his mouth stuck out. I know I'm in real big trouble if we don't do it once a week. So I make sure we do, even if I don't want to." She doesn't say those words to him, of course. But he knows. And it's precisely this, the knowledge that she's servicing him rather than desiring him that's so hard for him to take.

The sexual arena is one of the most common places to find a "his and her" marriage—one marriage, two different sex lives.[3] Each partner has a different story to tell; each is convinced that his or her version is the real one. A husband says mournfully, "I'm lucky if we get to make love once a week." His wife reports with irritation, "It's two, sometimes three times a week." It's impossible to know whose account is closest to the reality. And it's irrelevant. If that's what they were after, they could keep tabs and get it straight. But facts and feelings are often at war in family life. And nowhere does right or wrong, true or false count for less than in their sexual interactions. It isn't that people arbitrarily distort the truth. They simply report their experience, and it's feeling, not fact, that dominates that experience; feeling, not fact, that is their truth.

But it's also true that, especially for women, the difference in frequency of sexual desire can be a response—sometimes conscious, sometimes not—to other conflicts in the marriage. It isn't that men never withhold sex as a weapon in the family wars, only that they're much more likely than women to be able to split sex from emotion, to feel their anger and still experience sexual desire. For a man, too, a sexual connection with his wife can relieve the pressures and tensions of the day, can make him feel whole again, even if they've barely spoken a word to each other.

For a woman it's different. What happens—or, more likely, what doesn't happen—in the kitchen, the living room, and the laundry room profoundly affects what's possible in the bedroom. When she feels distant, unconnected, angry; when her pressured life leaves her feeling fragmented; when she hasn't had a real conversation with her husband for a couple of days, sex is very far from either her mind or her loins. "I run around busy all the time, and he just sits there, so by the time we go to bed, I'm too tired," explains Linda Bloodworth, a white thirty-one-year-old telephone operator.

"Do you think your lack of sexual response has something to do with your anger at your husband's refusal to participate more fully in the household?" I ask.

Her eyes smoldering, her voice tight, she snaps, "No, I'm just tired, that's all." Then noticing something in my response, she adds, "I know what you're thinking; I saw that look. But really, I don't think it's *because* I'm angry; I really am tired. I have to admit, though, that I tell him if he helped more, maybe I wouldn't be so tired all the time. And," she adds defiantly, "maybe I wouldn't be."

Some couples, of course, manage their sexual relationship with greater ease. Often that's because they have less conflict in other areas of living. But whether they accommodate well or poorly, for all two-job families, sex requires a level of attention and concern that leaves most people wanting much of the time. "It's a problem, and I tell you, it has to be well planned," explains thirty-four-year-old Dan Stolman, a black construction worker. "But we manage okay; we make dates or try to slip it in when the baby's asleep and my daughter's out with a friend or something. I don't mean things are great in that department. I'm not always satisfied and neither is Lorraine. But what can you do? We try to do the best we can. Sex isn't all there is to a marriage, you know. We get along really well, so that makes up for a lot.

"What I really miss is that we don't ever make love anymore. I mean, we have sex like I said, but we don't have the kind of time you need to make love. We talk about getting away for an overnight by ourselves once in a while. Lorraine's mother would come watch the kids if we asked her; the problem is we don't have any extra cash to spare right now."

Time and money—precious commodities in short supply. These are the twin plagues of family life, the missing ingredients that combine to create families that are both frantic and fragile. Yet there's no mystery about what would alleviate the crisis that now threatens to engulf them: A job that pays a living wage, quality child-care facilities at rates people can pay, health care for all, parental leave, flexible work schedules, decent and affordable housing, a shorter work week so that parents and children have time to spend together, tax breaks for those in need rather than for those in greed, to mention just a few. These are the policies we need to put in place if we're to have any hope of making our families stable and healthy.

What we have, instead, are families in which mother goes to work to relieve financial distress, only to find that time takes its place next to money as a source of strain, tension, and conflict. Time for the children, time for the couple's relationship, time for self, time for social life—none of it easily available for anyone in two-job families, not even for the children, who are hurried along at every step of the way.[4] And money! Never enough, not for the clothes children need, not for the doctor's bill, not for a vacation, not even for the kind of child care that would allow parents to go to work in peace. But large as these problems loom in the lives of working-class families, difficult as they are to manage, they pale beside those they face when unemployment strikes, especially if it's father who loses his job.

Notes

1. See Daniel Stern, *The Interpersonal World of the Infant* (New York: Basic Books, 1985), who argues that a child's capacity for self-reflection coincides with the development of language.
2. For an excellent analysis of the increasing amount of time Americans spend at work and the consequences to family and social life, see Juliet B. Schor, *The Overworked American* (New York: Basic Books, 1992). See also Carmen Sirianni and Andrea Walsh, "Through the Prism of Time: Temporal Structures in Postindustrial America," in Alan Wolfe, ed., *America at Century's End* (Berkeley: University of California Press, 1991), for their discussion of the "time famine."
3. For the origin of the term "his and her marriage," see Jessie Bernard, *The Future of Marriage* (New York: Bantam Books, 1973).
4. David Elkind, *The Hurried Child* (New York: Addison–Wesley, 1981).

Questions for Critical Thinking

1. How do economic inequalities in our society place additional burdens on working-class and poor families?
2. How do some of the solutions developed by working-class and poor families to deal with economic difficulties reinforce traditional gender roles? How do they help to challenge these roles?
3. What policy changes in the institutions of the economy or education would aid working-class and poor families? Are such changes necessary? Why or why not?

Illegality as a Source of Solidarity and Tension in Latino Families

LEISY J. ABREGO

The following article is based on extensive interviews with documented and undocumented Latino immigrants from El Salvador, Guatemala, and Mexico in Los Angeles over a ten-year period. In her analysis of these interviews, Leisy Abrego, a professor of Chicana and Chicano studies, illustrates that the status of illegal *impacts all members of a family, even when only one person or a few people are categorized as undocumented or only temporarily protected. As the author notes, this can create tensions for people whose disadvantages are heightened by structural inequality as a result of immigration laws. Alternatively, the presence of a supportive social network can aid families in transforming* illegal *to a source of solidarity and strength.*

I had known 19-year-old Mayra to be a confident, articulate young woman; she was thoughtful and warm in her demeanor, particularly during one-on-one conversations when her shyness usually dissipated.[1] It was surprising, therefore, to witness her sudden fidgeting and eye contact avoidance when we discussed her mother during the interview. Although Mayra was born in the United States and is, as a result, a U.S. citizen, the issue of immigrant legal status (as conferred upon individual migrants through U.S. immigration laws) made her nervous; her mother is an undocumented immigrant from Guatemala. As she explained:

Talking about my mom is hard. It's like there's this whole cloud of, like, a whole heaviness [motions as though she is carrying weight on her shoulders and above her head], I don't know, of things that I was never allowed to say out loud. If she was ever late, if she wasn't back from church or from work right on time, we all worried. . . . Nobody said anything, but we were all thinking it: what if she got caught? . . . That weight, it's just fear, I guess . . . it really sucks to grow up like that.

The deeply divisive and largely misinformed U.S. national debate about undocumented immigrants and immigration laws often masks the great complexity and diversity of legal statuses and their repercussions for Latino immigrants and their families. The discourse suggests that the exclusion and deportability associated with undocumented status affects only the 11.2 million undocumented immigrants in the country (Passel & Cohn, 2011). As the record-breaking number of deportations continues to make news, break families apart, and keep immigrants and their loved ones in fear, it becomes ever more clear that harshly restrictive immigration policies are causing violence against individuals and their entire families (Menjívar & Abrego, 2012). Experiences like Mayra's are proof of the uncontained anguish resulting from the current implementation of U.S. immigration policies.

Previously published in JOLLAS (Journal of Latino/Latin American Studies) 8.1 (2016): 5–21.

Even though she was born a U.S. citizen, Mayra experienced fear of detention and deportation—some of the gravest repercussions associated with undocumented status—in ways that powerfully affected several aspects of her life.

Despite being a U.S. citizen, Mayra grew up carrying the heavy weight of fear because the law's implementation would have had a direct impact on her, even though, from a legal perspective, she is not the target of these laws. Drawing on Mayra's and others' experiences and narratives, this article sheds light on some of the complexities of "illegality" as they play out within different configurations of Latino families. Having to negotiate these repercussions, families learn to live with tension or to develop strategies for mutual support. These experiences, moreover, have long-term consequences for family communication and well-being.

Illegality and Contemporary Latino Families in the United States

Illegality—the historically specific, socially, politically, and legally produced condition of immigrants' legal status and deportability (De Genova, 2002)—intimately and deeply impacts all immigrants. There is nothing inherent in the common understanding or practices associated with someone's undocumented status. Rather, there are historically specific conditions and cues that establish the term's meaning and its consequences in the lives of those categorized in a tenuous legal status at any given time. For example, there have been moments in this country's history when, in practical terms, undocumented status had little meaning (Ngai, 2004). Even immigrants who arrived in the 1970s in Los Angeles were able to obtain a driver's license and work without the intense fear of deportation that now permeates immigrant communities in the city (Abrego, 2014). Increasingly, over the last few decades and especially since the attacks of September 11, 2001, undocumented status, and illegality more broadly, have gained significance in the public eye (Golash-Boza, 2012; Hernández, 2008). Immigrants categorized as undocumented

or temporarily protected have become the target of progressively more harsh laws and ever more hateful speech, all of which work together to criminalize and dehumanize them and their families (Menjívar & Abrego, 2012), even when immigrants' behavior has not changed.

Arguably, Latinos are disproportionately affected. After 9/11, legal moves to criminalize undocumented immigrants were magnified and accelerated (Hernández, 2007, 2008). Programs such as 287(g) and Secure Communities were implemented to allow more communication between local authorities, the FBI, and Immigration and Customs Enforcement (ICE) agencies.[2] In practice, this has meant increased numbers of detentions and deportations, in part through sweeping workplace raids, but also because even routine traffic stops can quickly lead to ICE involvement and, ultimately, to the tearing apart of hundreds of thousands of families. In fact, in recent years the Department of Homeland Security reports that they have deported over 300,000 and closer to 400,000 immigrants annually.[3] The figures of those who are detained and deported are now, therefore, more likely to include the parents of U.S. citizen children. When parents are deported, children are often then placed in foster care with little regard for principles of family unity that presumably guide both immigration and child welfare policies (Wessler, 2011). These record numbers of deportations, moreover, are taking place alongside a wave of hateful speech and growing animosity against Latino immigrants (Chavez, 2008; Menjívar & Abrego, 2012), all of which inevitably affect families' well-being.

Mainstream media's visual representations and powerful public discourses work to dehumanize Latino immigrants—whether documented or undocumented (Chavez, 2001, 2008; McConnell, 2011). While making immigrants' contributions as workers and community members invisible, these images and discourses also make immigrants' very presence in the country hypervisible—but only through the lens of illegality. Although undocumented status has been and largely continues to be a matter of civil law. mainstream media images tend to portray undocumented immigrants as criminals. For example, one common visual used to discuss undocumented immigrants is the image of them being apprehended, handcuffed, and publicly treated in ways that presume they are dangerous criminals (Santa Ana, 2012). In a battle against official statistics that confirm the majority of deported immigrants do not have criminal records (see, for example, National Community Advisory, 2011), these repeated images are unfortunately more convincing to a broad audience. Such persistently negative representations shape the general public's view, but also affect how immigrants and their families understand and experience illegality.

In this article, I heed the call of feminist social scientists to move beyond notions of familism associated with Latino families and instead underscore the role of social structures that delimit the experiences of diverse U.S. Latino groups (Alcalde, 2010; Landale & Oropesa, 2007; Zinn & Wells, 2003). In this tradition, I examine the repercussions for Latino families as they deal with issues associated with illegality during a historical moment that criminalizes and dehumanizes them merely for seeking survival. I am guided by the following questions: In such a harsh legal and political climate, how do Latino immigrant families experience illegality in their day-to-day lives? Moreover, how do individuals negotiate illegality when trying to fulfill their family roles? I explore some of the various ways that immigration laws affect Latino family dynamics, particularly as experienced in transnational, undocumented, and mixed-status families.

Latino Families: Transnational, Undocumented, and Mixed Status

Like other members of the working poor, Latino families dealing with various facets of illegality face notable barriers. Geographically, given undocumented workers' job prospects and legal limitations, most families relying on one or two undocumented parents end up in areas of dense poverty (Chavez, 1998). These communities are typically beset with low-performing schools, high rates of crime, and few opportunities for their residents. These realities, in turn, block families and their next generation from integrating positively and thriving in this country. How do various forms of illegality further mediate these experiences?

One experience of illegality among Latino immigrants is long-term separation as members of transnational families, in which core family members live across borders. Unable to survive in their countries—largely as a result of U.S.-funded wars and neoliberal policies, including free-trade agreements—parents opt to migrate to the United States in search of work to support their children from afar (Abrego, 2014; Dreby, 2010). The vast wage inequalities in the region make this a likely strategy. Once they arrive in the United States, however, immigration laws restrict their chances for family reunification, making for prolonged family separations—often at least a decade (Abrego, 2009). It is difficult to enumerate how many people live in these types of arrangements, but it is a notable proportion for groups from various countries throughout Latin America (Abrego, 2009; Dreby, 2010; Hondagneu-Sotelo & Avila, 1997; Pribilsky, 2004; Schmalzbauer, 2005). In El Salvador, for example, it is estimated that anywhere between 16 and 40 percent of children in various regions of the country are growing up without one or both parents due to migration (García, 2012; Martínez, 2006). For these families, illegality is likely to play out differently than for families forced apart through deportation or who live together in fear.

For Latino undocumented families, in which all or most members are undocumented, they are likely more conscious about illegality's role in their everyday life. It is estimated that there are about 500,000 undocumented children in the United States growing up in families with at least one undocumented parent (Taylor, Lopez, Passel, & Motel, 2011). An additional 4.5 million U.S. citizen children are growing up in mixed-status families in which at least one of their parents is undocumented. Significantly, this figure more than doubled between 2000 and 2011 (Taylor et al., 2011). Illegality is likely to play out in different ways for these families as well. As made clear in the introductory case of this article, U.S.-born citizens are not entirely protected from the consequences of anti-immigrant laws—particularly when their loved ones are undocumented. For mixed-status families who experience the deportation of one or more family members, illegality can mean forced separation, in very painful and difficult ways (Dreby, 2012; Human Rights Watch, 2007; Wessler, 2011). Importantly, even when they are not forced into separation through the deportation of one of their members, mixed-status and undocumented families are also likely to deal with and experience illegality in different ways (Menjívar & Abrego, 2012).

In this article, I examine the ways that illegality permeates family life for Latinos whose relatives include at least one undocumented immigrant. My point is to underscore that illegality affects not only those immigrants who are undocumented. Their families must also grapple with the impact of changing laws, their implementation, and perceptions of undocumented immigrants. The consequences of illegality can lead to various types of experiences for Latino families. Here I focus on the potential for tensions and solidarity as responses to illegality at the family level.

Methods

I draw on various research projects for this article. Between June 2004 and September 2006, I conducted 130 in-depth interviews with Salvadoran parents, children, and caregivers who are members of transnational families that have been separated continuously for 3 to 27 years. In the United States, I interviewed 47 parents (25 mothers and 22 fathers) who had been separated from their children for an average of 11 years. The single-session interviews lasted between one and three hours. I recruited participants in various locations and through different entry points mostly in the greater

Los Angeles region. As part of the same project, I also conducted interviews with 83 relatives of migrants, mostly adolescent and young adult children, whom I recruited in public and private high schools and colleges in El Salvador. The single-session interviews lasted between 45 and 90 minutes. The average age of participants was 17 years old, with a range from 14–29. The average length of separation from their parents was nine years.

I also draw from a separate longitudinal study conducted between 2001–2006 that focused on access to higher education for Guatemalan, Mexican, and Salvadoran undocumented high school and college students in Los Angeles. This project consisted of 43 interviews with 27 informants, some of whom I interviewed a total of three times.[4] In the first round, from July to November 2001, I conducted 12 interviews with undocumented youth. I located all of the respondents at community-based organizations. About half participated in an immigrant rights' youth organization while the rest were enrolled in an art class for school credit. In the second round, from November 2002–January 2003, I re-interviewed eight of the original respondents, all of whom were still undocumented. The third round of interviews took place between December 2005 and June 2006. In this last round, I also conducted interviews with 15 more undocumented students who were attending various colleges and universities throughout California.[5]

The interview data for all phases of each project were heavily supplemented with participant observation conducted on a regular basis over the course of several years at community organizations and in numerous meetings and events. From 2001–2010, I gained access to strikingly similar stories of many more students, parents, and community members in these interactions. Based on the interviewees' narratives and participant observation notes from my ongoing work with immigrant rights' organizations, the article draws on Latina and Latino immigrants' and their children's voices to highlight some patterns that demonstrate the effects of illegality in their lives, whether or not they are undocumented.

Latino Families Negotiating Illegality

My main argument is that all members of Latino families with one or multiple immigrants who are undocumented or only temporarily protected must negotiate the extensive effects of illegality in their lives. How they experience and cope with illegality, however, will vary depending on their resources and local context. Whether neighborhoods and communities are supportive or hostile toward immigrants mediates families' ability to negotiate illegality and its vast consequences. Even though some families include U.S. citizens and legal permanent residents, the narratives of multiple family members reveal the deep pressures and long-term consequences of illegality in all their members' lives.

Transnational Families

Transnational families may be constituted in a number of different ways. Here I focus on families in which parents migrated to support their children who remain in the home country. In these cases female relatives—mothers, grandmothers, aunts, or older sisters—typically care for children (Dreby, 2010; Schmalzbauer, 2005). Parents work in the United States to send remittances to families who often rely solely on these monies to survive. Each member of the family, then, experiences illegality differently.

Unauthorized migrant parents feel the brunt of the criminalization and exclusion associated with illegality beginning from the moment they leave home. The journey north can be a brutal experience that communicates to the migrants they are not welcome and not valued as human beings (Amnesty International, 2010; Martínez 2010). If they reach the United States, they hope never to go through that process again, nor to put their children through such horrors. Instead, the safest option is to stay separated across borders indefinitely (Abrego, 2014).

Once in the United States, life continues to be difficult if immigrant parents are undocumented or only temporarily protected (Abrego, 2011; Abrego & Menjívar, 2011). Limited work opportunities and widespread forms of exploitation in labor sectors that hire undocumented immigrants result in prolonged separations also because parents rarely earn enough money to help their families thrive back in the home countries (Dreby, 2010). Unable to reach their financial goals, even when they work multiple jobs and overtime, immigrant parents experience illegality as frustration and fear of deportation.

Meanwhile, in the home countries, caregivers and children suffer the migrants' illegality from afar. Spouses, mothers, and siblings of migrants are pained in watching the news and knowing of the great likelihood of violence against their loved ones while en route. As one elderly mother of a migrant told me:

> No, look, I really suffered. She's my daughter and I didn't want her to ever suffer any pain. And it's that thing of wanting to watch the news because she wouldn't call, but then you see so many ugly things on television that sometimes I would say, maybe it's better not to watch anything. No, that whole time was just anguish. I wouldn't even sleep those 15 days. That was really terrible.

The inability to do anything, even to remain informed about their loved ones' whereabouts and well-being, is very challenging for relatives. In this example, the journey took two weeks, while in others, it may take one or several months. As the numbers of kidnappings and abuse of migrants continue to escalate (Amnesty International, 2010; Martínez 2010), this part of the experience for transnational families is also increasingly stressful.

When migrants make it to the United States and remain apart from their families for years, their relatives continue to grapple with the consequences of illegality—even if they do not always locate the source of their struggles within immigration laws and their implementation. Much of the tension for transnational families relying on undocumented or only temporarily protected migrants comes from the limited and rare sums of money remitted. Undocumented immigrants are especially likely to be employed in sectors that are dangerous and exploitative (Holmes, 2007; Milkman, González, & Narro, 2010; Walter, Bourgois, & Loinaz, 2004). For transnational families, this results in limited remittances and little improvement in their lives. Undocumented fathers may be prone to injuries that prevent them from fulfilling their financial goals. I met Mauricio, an undocumented immigrant father, at a day labor site. After suffering an injury at his previous job, he was having trouble finding a job. He had not remitted to his children in a few months and preferred not to call them because he was embarrassed that he was not living up to his promise of sending them money regularly:

You see that without papers it is very difficult to be hired just anywhere. So my brother-in-law found me a job [at a warehouse]. That is hard work because they don't care if one is tired, if one needs to rest, or if [the weather is] too hot or too cold. And so, since they didn't even let us rest, I messed up my back and when I told them, they pretended not to hear me, they didn't do anything. I kept complaining and in the end they told me that if I couldn't do the work anymore, I should look for another job because they needed someone who could stay on schedule. And after that I still had to fight with them to get my last paycheck because they were saying that I worked too slowly. Up until now I still can't carry anything too heavy, so I haven't been able to find a steady job.

Because of his undocumented status, Mauricio was afraid to apply for worker's compensation or to denounce the employer who fired him when he complained of back pain. Since losing that job, he spent most of his time at a day labor site, trying to get temporary, short-term jobs. Day labor, however, is unstable employment that does not generate sufficient wages to support his family in El Salvador (cf. Valenzuela Jr., 2002). To further exacerbate the situation, rather than blaming the exploitation made possible by strict immigration laws, parents accept responsibility and feel ashamed. As a result, relatives experience illegality's consequences through continued poverty and increased tension when mothers and fathers cannot meet their parental expectations.

Constantly bombarded by negative images of people like themselves and overcome with uncertainty and lack of solidarity in so many facets of their lives, undocumented immigrant parents can internalize illegality as a sense of worthlessness and helplessness. Mauricio describes how he has internalized illegality:

One comes here thinking that life will be better . . . but without papers, one's life is not worth much. Look at me; I have always been a hard worker . . . but I messed up my back working, carrying heavy things without any protection. . . . What doctor is going to help me if I can't pay? . . . Who's going to hire me now? How will I support my family?

For Mauricio, whose fear of deportation prevents him from applying for workers' compensation, illegality means that he is excluded from basic rights and dignity. Unable to fulfill his role as a father and provider for his family in El Salvador, Mauricio experiences illegality as a personal devaluation when he proclaims that his life is "not worth much." Despite his initially positive migration goals, the sense of being less than a person now pervades him. Moreover, similar situations for undocumented parents in transnational families are especially difficult because the distance across borders further hampers communication between them and their loved ones.

Undocumented immigrants are limited with respect to the kinds of jobs and working conditions they can access. Their unprotected status makes them vulnerable to unscrupulous employers who pay them low wages and withhold health benefits and other basic, legally mandated provisions, such as bathroom breaks, safety training, and protective gear when necessary for the job. Lacking legal recourse, undocumented immigrants can easily fall prey to such dishonest employers and are therefore greatly disadvantaged.

Understanding only that the separation was supposed to lead to financial stability, when this expectation is unmet, children in transnational families can become hurt, confused, and resentful (Abrego, 2009; Menjívar & Abrego, 2009). Sixteen-year-old Lucía in El Salvador, for example, shared her account of how much she had suffered through her mother's absence. Lucía's mother is undocumented, lives in Los Angeles, and, after eight years, has been remitting only about $50 per month due to her limited wages as a nanny. When I asked Lucía what had been the most difficult aspect of being a member of a transnational family, she paused, cried, and shared this thoughtful response:

> You're going to think I'm crazy, but when I was little, I would hear people say that McDonald's was American food so whenever we went downtown by that McDonald's, I would try to peer inside, just look inside the window for as long as I could to see if I could see my mother there.... [Crying] Yes, my life has been pure suffering without her. One never really understands why a mother would abandon you, why she would leave you if nothing changes. Nothing is better. Everything is worse.

The severity of Lucía's suffering is based on the sense of abandonment she feels because she has little to show for the family sacrifice of separation. Her undocumented mother, who like other undocumented immigrants is probably hard-pressed to find better employment, remits consistently but insufficiently. Being undocumented, moreover, prevents Lucía's mother from visiting her daughter because doing so would require a dangerous journey to re-enter the United States. As a result, eight years have gone by for Lucía and her mother without personal interactions, further adding tension to their family dynamics.

Importantly, illegality also intersects with gendered parental expectations to further shape the experiences of transnational families. Fathers, who are expected to be economic providers, can minimize tensions when they send sufficient remittances. Mothers, on the other hand, are held to higher expectations of caring, even from afar, and even if they manage to send sufficient remittances

(Abrego, 2009; Abrego & Menjívar, 2011). For transnational families relying on undocumented mothers, illegality can have extensively painful and difficult consequences. Unable to fulfill the gendered expectations that require them to care for their children intensively and on a daily basis, transnational mothers live with great sadness, guilt, and deprivation (Miranda, Siddique, Der-Martirosian, & Belin, 2005; Parreñas, 2001, 2005; Pratt, 2012). Such was the case for Esperanza. When I interviewed her, she recalled the hardships she underwent to ensure her family's economic well-being in El Salvador:

> I've always sent $300 [monthly] to my mother and I would get paid $100 weekly [working as a live-in nanny]. I would end up with $90 because I also had to pay the fee to wire the money.... It was horrible.... Each week I would buy a dozen ramen noodle soups that I don't even want to see anymore, really, ... so my food was the ramen noodle soup. But I was the happiest woman in the world because my daughter had something to eat!

Like Esperanza, several undocumented mothers in transnational families shared that they had greatly sacrificed themselves and sometimes increased their vulnerability just to be able to remit more money to their children. In the face of great disadvantages as undocumented immigrants, these mothers put themselves on the line to try to attain greater stability for their children. Illegality for them, therefore, meant greater personal risk and deprivation.

For transnational families, more broadly, the consequences of illegality are mostly present through increased tension. Parents suffer the brunt of physical risk and exploitation, but their children and other relatives in the home country experience illegality as stress, poverty, and abandonment. Nonmigrant relatives, moreover, often do not see the source of their suffering in the consequences of illegality. Instead, they blame parents who have not fulfilled their promises and who have been away for too many years.

Undocumented Families

Undocumented families, with all members living together in the United States, are not in the midst of family separation, though many likely spent some time apart, migrating in stages (Suárez-Orozco, Todorova, & Louie, 2002). Illegality, however, plays out differently and in complicated ways for undocumented families. As with transnational families, illegality intersects with gender and other categories to shape individuals' and families' experiences. I now focus on intergenerational relations between members of undocumented families.

Illegality's consequences can create tension and add burdens for undocumented families whose members are already structurally vulnerable. Beyond the usual challenges of communicating and working together across generations, undocumented parents and children may first have to reestablish a family relationship in the likely case they were separated and reunited after years apart (Suárez-Orozco, Bang, & Kim, 2010). Indeed, several undocumented youth mentioned difficult transitions with parents after joining them in the United States. Mario, who came from Guatemala at age six, was 16 when I met him. He still dealt with painful unresolved issues with his father who had migrated when Mario was only a few months old:

> It's not a good feeling. I mean, I knew I had a father, but it was just, he wasn't there. . . . It's still not easy getting along with my dad. We disagree a lot. . . . I was just thinking too highly of my dad, because I never knew him, you know. Things are just not how I figured. . . . I've never been really attached to my dad because of that reason. . . . I guess he expected me to, you know, be like, "Wow, my dad" [in dreamy tone]. But it was just like, how could I show that if he wasn't there? You know?

As Mario explains, being apart from parents over several years can lead to the development of idealized and unrealistic expectations. It is difficult to establish loving bonds and smooth communication when both parents and children expect too much from each other following a painful separation. These experiences of step-migration are especially common among families who travel and live in the United States without authorization (Suárez-Orozco et al., 2010).

Even short separations can be difficult for young children. Luis, whose parents migrated from Mexico to the United States during his early childhood spent only a few months with his grandmother before his own migration at the age of four. He was separated from his father for years, but was apart from his mother for only a few months. Still, in his late teens Luis recalls that through much of his childhood, he felt uneasy about his relationship with his mother:

> Those three months made a huge difference. I didn't remember her. It felt like she wasn't my mom. You know what I mean? It felt like she was someone else. And it was only three months. I remember like when I used to get mad at her, if I was in trouble and she was telling me what to do, in my mind I was like, "What if she's not my mom? What if she's another person?" . . . Yeah, it's just hard. I mean, that's your logic at that age.

Even short separations can confuse children and make them question their parents' authority. As separations are prolonged due to immigrant parents' undocumented status, reunifications are likely to involve difficult transitions that further complicate family dynamics (Suárez-Orozco et al., 2002).

Another challenge for undocumented families is rooted in the vastly different experiences and interpretations of illegality across generations (Abrego, 2011). First-generation immigrants who are usually the parents in these families feel responsible for choosing to migrate, remember clearly the horrific details of the migration journey, and deal with exploitative working conditions on a daily basis. For this generation, illegality is mainly about exclusion from society and great fear of deportation. The 1.5 generation undocumented immigrants, who are usually the children in undocumented families, often remember less about the journey; feel they had little choice in migrating; and enjoy greater levels of membership in U.S. society where they have spent most of their lives (Abrego, 2011). As they learn more details about their status, however, they experience their own forms of exclusion (Abrego, 2008; Gonzales, 2011; Gonzales & Chavez, 2012).

The exclusion associated with illegality can mean different things for various members of undocumented families. For parents, exclusion is most prominent when they are unable to perform the tasks—often gendered—that are expected of them. Mothers often speak of their great worry over their children's well-being if they were to be deported, while fathers feel their lives are worthless if they are unable to access rights, health care, and work to provide for their families. This sense of worthlessness and the fear that pervades undocumented parents are very different from what undocumented children in these families describe as their experience of illegality.

Undocumented immigrants who grow up in the United States and are socialized through schools are more likely to experience illegality as a matter of stigma (Abrego, 2008, 2011). For example, many are embarrassed that they cannot drive a car, go out on dates, go clubbing, or travel abroad like the rest of their peers (see also Gonzales, 2011). Unlike their undocumented parents, moreover, undocumented youth have adapted socially to U.S. social norms and can more easily fit in. This allows them to participate in activities their parents consider too risky, thereby adding tensions to family dynamics when parents disapprove of their children's behavior. This can be frustrating for children because they consider such behavior would, in any other legal context, be perfectly acceptable for someone their age.

Jovani, a 16-year-old undocumented Guatemalan high school student, expressed great resentment toward his parents. His mother, who is also an undocumented immigrant, volunteers at his school and tries to keep an eye on him constantly to keep him out of trouble. Meanwhile, he just wants to get a part-time job and be able to drive like all his friends, but his mother's adamant opposition is challenging for Jovani:

> When I want to get a job, I can't. I want to drive, but I can't. . . . So, most of the time, I just don't think about it, but I mean, there's sometimes when it crosses your mind, you know, you gotta get a job, you want to work, you want to have money. . . . So yeah, it's kind of hard for me. . . . I get mad because my parents brought me. I didn't tell them to bring me, but I get punished for it, for not having the papers.

The consequences of illegality—being excluded from otherwise typical experiences for people his age—deeply frustrate Jovani. But rather than blaming the legal system that prevents him and his family from thriving, he blames his parents. Therefore, despite his mother's best efforts to keep him focused on being a successful student, Jovani rebels. When I met him, he was in danger of failing most of his classes in his second attempt at junior year in high school.

To further complicate intergenerational relations in undocumented families, illegality infused by stigma, as undocumented youth experience it, allows them to develop personal discourses that help them limit the exclusion they feel. For example, undocumented youth try to justify their presence in the country by distancing themselves from negative connotations of illegality. In doing so, they underscore that their liminal status differs from the marginalized and criminalized status of their parents' generation. Most notably, they defend themselves by emphasizing they did not actively choose to come to the United States. Stellar students are especially effective when they can draw on their educational achievements to defend their honor as good people and good citizens of this country. As Isabel states: "The fact that we're students gives us credibility and, in their [anti-immigrant activists] eyes, that's better." This strategy is not available to the more marginalized and publicly targeted undocumented workers and parents in these families and may add greater tension to family dynamics.

Exclusion leads to several other associated experiences of illegality for undocumented immigrants. As Norma, a Mexican first-generation, undocumented immigrant mother, sums it up, "We are here and we know this is not our country. They don't want us here, so you have to be careful. Always be careful." In this experience of illegality, immigrants are made to feel constantly insecure, unaware of who they can trust, and unable to rely even on institutions that should represent safety for all. In such a context, navigating social relationships can be difficult. As Agustín, a first-generation Salvadoran immigrant, shares:

> It just feels like you don't know who you can trust. I tell people that I don't have papers. I feel like I'm not doing anything wrong. I'm not a criminal. But my wife gets mad at me. She tells me to be careful because you never know who could call the migra on you. But I feel like I have nothing to hide.

Most undocumented immigrants feel deeply disconnected from descriptions of themselves as criminals. They migrated in search of work for the sake of their families' survival. But in trying to counter the criminalization of undocumented status, it is difficult to know who they can trust. In this way, illegality and the cloud of distrust around undocumented status cause tension and complicate family dynamics when relatives have different approaches to handling illegality's repercussions in their lives.

Importantly, there are also spaces to build communication and solidarity among members of undocumented families. The following exemplifies this ability to work together to make claims for inclusion in this country. Adela, the undocumented mother of undocumented students who organized a press conference to support the DREAM Act,[6] was one of a few older adults holding signs and standing in support of the event. After 14 years of living in the United States, this was the first time she had participated in such a public and political act and she was nervous, but her children had convinced her to be there. As with undocumented immigrants generally

and for various reasons, parents who arrived in the country as adults are less vocal politically than their children's generation (Abrego, 2011). These different forms of socialization have the potential to create tensions, but can also generate possibilities for communication, as evident in the notes from my conversation with Adela that day.

Adela told me she had never been involved in organizations for immigrant rights. She came from Mexico 14 years ago, but she was dedicated to working and taking care of her kids. The thought of going out to protest or draw attention to herself never crossed her mind. But as her kids got older and the oldest went on to college, she realized how much it hurt them to not have papers. When she came from Mexico, she knew she would have to put up with not having papers and it might mean she could only get hard jobs, but she didn't know it would affect her kids this way—she had no idea—and all she wants is for them to achieve their dreams. It has been painful to watch them struggle just to be able to afford college. Both of her children are great students and are now at a community college. They have been participating in marches and meetings at this organization for a few years now, since high school, and they always invite her to come, but she was always too scared. This year, she finally went to one event and liked what she heard. All she wants to do is support her kids, and now she's committed to being present for them at these rallies and events because she knows how much it means to them.

Her children's persistent requests and her own understanding of how illegality was affecting them gave Adela the courage to become politically engaged. In general, because children of immigrants adapt to U.S. society at a faster pace than their parents, it is often the case that they are socialized politically in school and other spaces and they then socialize their parents (Bloemraad & Trost, 2008). This is becoming increasingly evident even in the immigrant rights' movement—particularly among the most vocal and visible sector at a national level.[7] For these undocumented families then, intergenerational communication may also lead to greater political participation.

Families that include multiple generations of undocumented immigrants experience the consequences of illegality in various ways. Many of these families are likely to have migrated in steps, thereby reuniting after some time apart. In these cases, even the negotiation of a family relationship can be difficult. And when these families overcome the challenges of reunification, the different generational experiences of illegality can also lead to tension when parents, spouses, and children disagree about how to approach their lives and their actions in this country. Finally, the shared experience of illegality, even though it plays out differently in their lives, can also lead to greater solidarity among undocumented members of families.

Mixed-Status Families

Mixed-status families include members with multiple statuses. They share many of the same challenges and experiences of illegality as undocumented families, but also have unique tensions and possibilities as a result of legal internal stratification of their members. Illegality can play out in numerous ways, partly depending on the role of the undocumented persons and their relationships to others. For example, illegality will have different repercussions in a family that includes an undocumented parent and U.S. citizen children versus a family that includes undocumented parents and siblings with various statuses.

Beginning in the late 2000s, journalists and researchers have shed light on the experiences of mixed-status families that include U.S. citizen children and their undocumented parents. One of the most compelling cases is that of Encarnación Bail Romero, a Guatemalan immigrant to the United States (Brané, 2011; Thompson, 2009). In 2007, while working at a poultry plant in Missouri, immigration officials detained Bail Romero in a workplace raid. Her son Carlos, who was then only six months old, spent some time with different caretakers, until a couple approached her about adopting him. She was adamantly against this option, but helpless to

act from a detention center in another state. Her lawyer, who explained the situation to her only in English (a language she did not understand), failed to protect her. Unable to leave detention, she later learned that a judge used her absence in court for a hearing about Carlos's future as evidence of abandonment. The judge terminated her parental rights and Carlos was adopted. Although Ms. Bail spent many years fighting to regain custody of her son, the laws stood against her. As unjust and bizarre as this story may sound, it reflects an increasingly common experience today: the legal system denies undocumented immigrants the same parental rights guaranteed to other parents.

In fact, among the 4.5 million U.S. citizen children growing up in mixed-status families, the chances of undocumented parents being deported have increased considerably over the last decade. With greater communication between local law enforcement and federal immigration agencies, undocumented parents caught during a routine traffic stop, for example, can be detained and deported—for having a broken taillight or driving without a license (Hagan, Eschbach, & Rodríguez, 2008; Hagan, Rodriguez, & Castro, 2011). By 2011, among the record number of deportees, 22 percent were parents of U.S. citizen children (Wessler, 2011). Parents may be detained for simply driving between home and work or dropping off or picking up their kids at school. Such increased targeting adds great stress for families.

Indeed, this sense of insecurity spreads through entire families, whether or not all members are undocumented (Dreby, 2012; Rodriguez & Hagan, 2004; Suárez-Orozco, Yoshikawa, Teranishi, & Suárez-Orozco, 2011; Yoshikawa, 2011). This is evident in the narratives of children of immigrants who grew up with one or two undocumented parents. In Southern California, just over an hour outside of Los Angeles, 20-year-old Nayeli grew up in the outskirts of an affluent city where the majority of inhabitants are white. Throughout her childhood, Nayeli's mother, who is a documented Mexican immigrant, reminded her and her siblings about the need to keep their father's undocumented status a secret. The vocal anti-immigrant groups in the area instilled great fear in Nayeli, and she grew up painfully aware of her family's vulnerability in the face of the consequences of illegality. When asked what the hardest part of the situation had been, she described how she experiences illegality at a personal level: "The silence . . . when it comes to talking about it with people that I trust, it's hard just to even talk about it. It's hard for me to even admit that my father is undocumented. I've kept it a secret for so long, and I feel like it's my secret and I don't want to tell people about it. It's the way I internalize it. We do it to protect my dad."

Nayeli's burden was heavy and constant; her neighbors' hostility exacerbated the potential for harm against her father if her family's secret were revealed. Emotionally, this crushed Nayeli, who cried throughout the interview: "Just my dad, period, is an emotional subject for me. . . . If he took long to get home from work, I feared that he was caught. It's a scary feeling." Her relationship with her father was damaged when the secret prevented them from having open conversations about such an important topic. And to this day, as a young adult, she has difficulty discussing anything related to her father and her childhood generally because the cloud of illegality has been so deeply hurtful.

Not all mixed-status families with undocumented parents have the same experience. In another part of Los Angeles, 20-year-old Aminta, a U.S.-born child with an undocumented Guatemalan father, explains how illegality affected her father and her family:

I think when I was a kid I didn't really understand it. But now as an adult, I feel my dad was frustrated and tired with his job and that he wanted to give us more, but he couldn't. Sometimes my dad seemed very quiet and sad. . . . My mom was the emotional backbone, I think. She always talked about the importance of family, something we had. I'm proud of my parents. They worked hard and that has made me work hard because I know

I have something many people wish they had. And one day, hopefully, I can have the money to get a lawyer that will help my dad get his citizenship status. It just hurts because my dad went almost all his life living through economic challenges.

Aminta's family experienced illegality largely as an economic barrier that limited her father's ability to provide for his family. She suggests that his inability to live up to this gendered expectation weighed heavily on him as he seemed "frustrated," "very quiet and sad," much of the time. This weight can easily extend to the rest of the family. It was her mother's ability to live up to her gendered expectation as the "emotional backbone" of the family that held the family together and allowed them to work around the effects of illegality in their lives.

Aminta's experience in a mixed-status family stands in stark contrast to that of Nayeli. Although both had one undocumented parent and both were U.S. citizens by birth, their different communities mediate how their families experience illegality. While Nayeli grew up in an anti-immigrant community, Aminta's family has lived for decades in the same working class neighborhood where mixed status and undocumented families are common enough to make them seem close to the norm. Aminta, therefore, feels comfortable talking about her experiences and discussing how illegality has shaped her family's participation in the community: "It hasn't been easy, but we feel comfortable in our community. We know we're not the only family who is going through challenges and it feels like we are supportive of each other. My family is very close. We all play an important role. We each do something and the challenges seem less that way."

In Aminta's case, illegality added extra challenges to their lives, but her community's ability to integrate mixed-status families was also helpful. Moreover, illegality and the tenuous status of her father's situation led her family to find ways to increase their solidarity with one another by sharing responsibilities and bringing the family closer together.

Beyond intergenerational challenges, mixed-status families also experience other consequences of illegality when siblings do not share the same legal status. Often there is tension and resentment when U.S. citizen children have access to more resources and opportunities than their undocumented or temporarily protected siblings. Such was the case for Mario, whose younger brother was born in the United States, making him the only member of the family with U.S. citizenship. In the following excerpt, Mario describes resentments resulting from the family's mixed statuses:

Well, basically, I don't have medical insurance. My younger brother, whenever he's sick, they always take him to the hospital, and stuff like that, because the government pays for him. . . . My mom takes him to the dentist yearly, to the doctor, you know, but if I feel really sick, like I have to be dying to go to the hospital. But then, you know, my brother, he feels a stomachache—"let's go to the hospital."

Stratified access to health care means that parents have to provide what seems like preferential treatment for some children owing to their legal status. Despite understanding that his brother had legal access to more resources, Mario harbored resentment toward his brother and his mother for what he experienced as limited concern for his well-being.

Furthermore, because immigration laws change and people move between statuses as they become eligible, families may experience illegality differently at different stages. Andrés, a 21-year-old member of a Mexican mixed-status family, was granted legal residency only a month before high school graduation; he was completing his third year of college when I interviewed him. He reflects on how being undocumented shaped his older brother's experience:

I feel bad for him. He worked even harder than I did in high school, and he should've been graduating from college by now. He even got better grades than me, but just because of his papers he can't go.

LA: What is he doing now?

He works at a warehouse, packing and unpacking things from a truck all day. It makes me feel really bad, guilty because he deserves it as much as I do, but I'm the only one who gets to go [to college].

The way that families experience illegality, therefore, also depends on when statuses shift and how these shifts affect individuals. In this case, Andrés' older brother aged out of a chance to get legal permanent residency, leaving only Andrés to benefit from the change in status. Consequently, illegality played out as guilt for Andrés, who qualified for financial aid and other privileges that continued to be out of reach for his brother.

Among mixed-status families, however, there is sometimes also the opportunity to share rights and protections of one or multiple members with those who have more tenuous legal statuses. For example, Alisa, a 19-year-old Guatemalan undocumented college student, is thankful that her entire family benefits from the privileges of her sisters who are U.S. citizens. As citizens, they are eligible for government assistance, including public housing that is more spacious than what the family (all the rest of whom are undocumented) could otherwise afford:

We moved over here because of the twins. I have two smaller twin sisters, they were born here, but when they were five months old, they got epilepsy, both of them, so it damaged their brain. . . . because of them we moved over here because of the housing. We used to live in a smaller apartment so they gave us a larger apartment for them, because of them, so they could have more room to walk around and stuff.

Although her younger sisters' developmental disabilities have taken a physical and emotional toll on the family, Alisa is grateful that as U.S. citizens, they have access to health care and housing. She is aware of the benefits the entire family receives as a result of the twins' legal status. In this case, the consequences of illegality for a mixed-status family are mediated by the benefits of more spacious housing accorded to the U.S. citizens in the family.

The consequences of illegality in mixed-status families are multiple and varied, depending on the status of each family member and their role in the family. When parents are undocumented, this can lead to limited parental rights and fear of accessing resources for their children, even when children have legal rights to various benefits (Menjívar, 2006; Menjívar & Abrego, 2009; Suárez-Orozco et al., 2011; Yoshikawa, 2011). Illegality, moreover, can weigh heavily on all members of these families, even those who are U.S. citizens by birth or naturalization. Particularly with internal stratification of resources, children can blame each other and develop resentment, but they may also recognize when they benefit from resources given more freely to U.S. citizens in their families. Overall, mixed-status families' experiences of illegality are further mediated by local contexts—whether communities are inclusive or exclusive of immigrants more broadly—and shifts in statuses across time and at different stages in their lives. With these changes, families learn to navigate tensions and solidarity.

Conclusion

Despite the common assumption that immigration laws target only undocumented immigrants, illegality—the historically specific, socially, politically, and legally produced condition of immigrants' legal status and deportability—intimately and deeply impacts a larger proportion of Latinos. Illegality's repercussions are especially present in family dynamics and experiences—forcing parents and children to live across borders over a prolonged period; multiplying families' vulnerability when they are all undocumented and residing together; or complicating family relationships when only one or a few members are in tenuous statuses, but they reside with those who have more rights and protections.

In this article, I examine how illegality encompasses all members of a family, even when only one person is categorized as undocumented. Unsurprisingly, I find that illegality can create tension for people whose disadvantages are heightened by structural limitations related to immigration laws.

On the other hand, illegality can be a source of solidarity and strength when families live in welcoming communities. Based on notions of family and solidarity, some are able to pool resources to help the undocumented member(s) of their families. When they have the right context and resources, this strengthens the family, even in the face of illegality's increased barriers and burdens.

Whether families live apart or together, illegality contextualizes their day-to-day lives and long-term relationships. It limits parents' authority while adding responsibilities for parents and children. Immigrant mothers, for example, experience the violence of illegality when they are unable to care for their children as they would like and as is socially expected of them (Abrego & Menjívar, 2011), while immigrant fathers are likely to be blocked from opportunities to provide for their children. This means that children have to carry part of the burden—sometimes financially, often emotionally—to help the family survive despite the limitations. Illegality, moreover, prevents all parents from accessing social services and other resources to help their children achieve optimal well-being.

When combined, all of illegality's repercussions undermine families' efforts to move out of poverty. Like parents in other working poor families, undocumented parents often work in low-paying, unstable jobs for long periods of time. And like other children who grow up in poverty (documented and undocumented), children of undocumented immigrants also face high levels of danger and few educational opportunities. Furthermore, being undocumented also increases the likelihood that families will lack health insurance (Fortuny, Capps, & Passel, 2007) and lowers their chances of accessing bank accounts and other financial services. Their parents' undocumented status is also detrimental to children in numerous, sometimes indirect ways. For example, due to fear of deportation, such families are less likely to apply for food-stamp benefits, even though their children may be eligible. They may be afraid to go into a government agency to apply for their children's health care benefits.

Children in these families are thus less likely to seek the services they need (Abrego & Menjívar, 2011). In the longer term, undocumented status keeps families in the shadows, avoiding many of the institutions that have traditionally benefited immigrant families (Menjívar, 2006).

Despite these structural and very real challenges, illegality's consequences are also mediated by the demographics and political nature of their local context. People living in communities with a concentration of undocumented immigrants and mixed-status families are more likely to develop networks and access information that can mitigate the fear and insecurity so often associated with illegality. In cases where members of mixed-status communities are able to develop solidarity, they may be able to create safety nets for children and the most vulnerable members among them. However, in communities where few undocumented immigrants are known to reside and where anti-immigration advocates feel emboldened, immigrants and their families are likely to experience illegality as extreme vulnerability that can penetrate even their most intimate relationships.

In many respects, undocumented immigrants and their families are already important members of U.S. society—even if only on the lower rungs of the economic ladder. They contribute to our economy, children are educated in our schools, and all family members envision their futures here. However, these families currently have no available structural paths out of poverty. In a cruel twist, parents' efforts to secure their families' survival by migrating are met with legal obstacles. Current policies restrict their ability to thrive in this country and, for transnational families, to pull children out of poverty in the home countries as well. Without full legal rights, these families are barred from the very mechanisms that have ensured high levels of economic and social mobility to other immigrants throughout U.S. history (Abrego, 2006; Menjívar & Abrego, 2012). Legalization, therefore, is necessary to give Latino families a chance at success in this country.

References

Abrego, L. J. (2006). "I can't go to college because I don't have papers": Incorporation patterns of Latino undocumented youth. *Latino Studies, 4*(3), 212–231. DOI:10.1057/palgrave.1st.8600200

Abrego, L. J. (2008). Legitimacy, social identity, and the mobilization of law: The effects of Assembly Bill 540 on undocumented students in California. *Law & Social Inquiry, 33*(3), 709–734. DOI: 10.1111/j.1747-4469.2008.00119.x

Abrego, L. J. (2009). Economic well-being in Salvadoran transnational families: How gender affects remittance practices. *Journal of Marriage and Family, 71,* 1070–1085. DOI: 10.1111/j.1741-3737.2009.00653.x

Abrego, L. J. (2011). Legal consciousness of undocumented Latinos: Fear and stigma as barriers to claims making for first and 1.5 generation immigrants. *Law & Society Review, 45*(2), 337–370. DOI: 10.1111/j.1540-5893.2011.00435.x

Abrego, L. J. (2014). *Sacrificing families: Navigating laws, labor, and love across borders.* Stanford, CA: Stanford University Press.

Abrego, L. J., & Menjívar, C. (2011). Immigrant Latina mothers as targets of legal violence. *International Journal of Sociology of the Family, 37*(1), 9–26.

Alcalde, M. C. (2010). Violence across borders: Familism, hegemonic masculinity, and self-sacrificing femininity in the lives of Mexican and Peruvian migrants. *Latino Studies, 8*(1), 48–68. DOI:10.1057/1st.2009.44

Amnesty International. (2010). "Invisible victims: Migrants on the move in Mexico." Report published by Amnesty International Publications. London, UK.

Bloemraad, I., & Trost, C. (2008). It's a family affair: Intergenerational mobilization in the Spring 2006 protests. *American Behavioral Scientist, 52*(4), 507–532. DOI: 10.1177/0002764208324604

Brané, M. (2011). Delayed justice for Guatemalan mother Encarnación Bail Romero. Retrieved from http://www.huffingtonpost.com/michelle-bran/delayed-justice-for-guate_b_817191.html

Chavez, L. R. (1998). *Shadowed lives: Undocumented immigrants in American society* (2nd ed.). Fort Worth, TX: Harcourt Brace.

Chavez, L. R. (2001). *Covering immigration: Popular images and the politics of the nation*. Berkeley: University of California Press.

Chavez, L. R. (2008). *The Latino threat: Constructing immigrants, citizens, and the nation*. Palo Alto, CA: Stanford University Press.

De Genova, N. P. (2002). Migrant "illegality" and deportability in everyday life. *Annual Review of Anthropology, 31*, 419–447. DOI: 10.1146/annurev.anthro.31.040402.085432

Dreby, J. (2010). *Divided by borders: Mexican migrants and their children*. Berkeley: University of California Press.

Dreby, J. (2012). The burden of deportation on children in Mexican immigrant families. *Journal of Marriage and Family, 74*, 829–845. DOI: 10.1111/j.1741-3737.2012.00989.x

Fortuny, K., Capps, R., & Passel, J. (2007). The characteristics of unauthorized immigrants in California, Los Angeles County, and the United States. Washington, DC: The Urban Institute.

García, J. J. (2012, January). *20th anniversary of El Salvador's peace accords and implications for transnational development and voting abroad*. Paper presented at the UCLA North American Integration and Development Center, Los Angeles, CA.

Golash-Boza, T. (2012). *Due process denied: Detentions and deportations in the United States*. New York: Routledge.

Gonzales, R. G. (2011). Learning to be illegal: Undocumented youth and shifting legal contexts in the transition to adulthood. *American Sociological Review, 76*(4), 602–619. DOI: 10.1177/0003122411411901

Gonzales, R. G., & Chavez, L. R. (2012). "Awakening to a nightmare": Abjectivity and illegality in the lives of undocumented 1.5 generation Latino immigrants in the United States. *Current Anthropology, 53*(3), 255–281. DOI: 10.1086/665414

Hagan, J., Eschbach, K., & Rodríguez, N. (2008). U.S. deportation policy, family separation, and circular migration. *International Migration Review, 42*(1), 64–88. DOI: 10.1111/j.1747-7379.2007.00114.x

Hagan, J., Rodriguez, N., & Castro, B. (2011). Social effects of mass deportations by the United States government, 2000–10. *Ethnic and Racial Studies, 34*(8), 1374–1391. DOI: 10.1080/01419870.2011.575233

Hernández, D. M. (2007). Undue process: Racial genealogies of immigrant detention. In C. B. Brettell (Ed.), *Constructing borders/Crossing boundaries: Race, ethnicity, and immigration* (pp. 59–86). Lanham, MD: Lexington Books.

Hernández, D. M. (2008). Pursuant to deportation: Latinos and immigrant detention. *Latino Studies, 6*(1–2), 35–63. DOI:10.1057/lst.2008.2

Holmes, S. M. (2007). "Oaxacans like to work bent over": The naturalization of social suffering among berry farm workers. *International Migration, 45*(3), 39–68. DOI: 10.1111/j.1468-2435.2007.00410.x

Hondagneu-Sotelo, P., & Avila, E. (1997). "I'm here, but I'm there": The meanings of Latina transnational motherhood. *Gender & Society, 11*(5), 548–570. DOI: 10.1177/089124397011005003

Human Rights Watch. (2007). Forced apart: Families separated and immigrants harmed by United States deportation policy. New York: Human Rights Watch.

Landale, N., & Oropesa, R. S. (2007). Hispanic families: Stability and change. *Annual Review of Sociology, 33*, 381–405. DOI: 10.1146/annurev.soc.33.040406.131655

Martínez, L. (2006, April 28). El rostro joven de las remesas, *El Diario de Hoy*. Retrieved from http://www.elsalvador.com/noticias/2006/04/28/nacional/nac13.asp

Martínez, O. (2010). *Los migrantes que no importan: En el camino con los centroamericanos indocumentados en México*. Barcelona: Icaria.

McConnell, E. D. (2011). An "incredible number of Latinos and Asians": Media representations of racial and ethnic population change in Atlanta, Georgia. *Latino Studies, 9*(2/3), 177–197. DOI:10.1057/lst.2011.17

Menjívar, C. (2006). Family reorganization in a context of legal uncertainty: Guatemalan and Salvadoran immigrants in the United States. *International Journal of Sociology of the Family, 32*(2), 223–245. Retrieved from http://www.jstor.org/stable/23030196

Menjívar, C., & Abrego, L. (2009). Parents and children across borders: Legal instability and intergenerational relations in Guatemalan and Salvadoran families. In N. Foner (Ed.), *Across generations: Immigrant families in America* (pp. 160–189). New York: New York University Press.

Menjívar, C., & Abrego, L. (2012). Legal violence: Immigration law and the lives of Central American immigrants. *American Journal of Sociology, 117*(5), 1380–1424. DOI: 10.1086/663575

Menjívar, C., & Kanstroom, D. (Eds.). (2013). *Constructing immigrant "illegality": Critiques, experiences, and resistance.* Cambridge: Cambridge University Press.

Milkman, R., González, A. L., & Narro, V. (2010). Wage theft and workplace violations in Los Angeles: The failure of employment and labor law for low-wage workers. Los Angeles: UCLA Institute for Research on Labor and Employment.

Miranda, J., Siddique, J., Der-Martirosian, C., & Belin, T. R. (2005). Depression among Latina immigrant mothers separated from their children. *Psychiatric Services, 56*(6), 717–720. DOI: 10.1176/appi.ps.56.6.717

National Community Advisory. (2011). Restoring community: A National Community Advisory report on ICE's failed "Secure Communities" program. Location: National Community Advisory.

Ngai, M. M. (2004). *Impossible subjects: Illegal aliens and the making of modern America.* Princeton, NJ: Princeton University Press.

Parreñas, R. (2001). Mothering from a distance: Emotions, gender, and intergenerational relationships in Filipino transnational families. *Feminist Studies, 27*(2), 361–390. DOI: 10.2307/3178765

Parreñas, R. (2005). Long distance intimacy: Class, gender and intergenerational relations between mothers and children in Filipino transnational families. *Global Networks, 5*(4), 317–336.

Passel, J., & Cohn. D. (2011). Unauthorized immigrant population: National and state trends, 2010. Washington. DC: Pew Hispanic Center.

Pratt, G. (2012). *Families apart: Migrant mothers and the conflicts of labor and love.* Minneapolis: University of Minnesota Press.

Pribilsky. J. (2004). "Aprendemos a convivir": Conjugal relations, co-parenting, and family life among Ecuadorian transnational migrants in New York City and the Ecuadorian Andes. *Global Networks, 4*(3), 313–334. DOI: 10.1111/j.1471-0374.2004.00096.x

Rodriguez, N., & Hagan, J. M. (2004). Fractured families and communities: Effects of immigration reform in Texas, Mexico, and El Salvador. *Latino Studies, 2*(3), 328–351. DOI: 10.1057/palgrave.lst.8600094

Santa Ana, O. (2012). *Juan in a hundred: The representation of Latinos on network news.* Austin: University of Texas Press.

Schmalzbauer, L. (2005). *Striving and surviving: A daily life analysis of Honduran transnational families.* New York and London: Routledge.

Suárez-Orozco, C., Bang, H. J., & Kim, H. Y. (2010). "I felt like my heart was staying behind": Psychological implications of family separations and reunifications for immigrant youth. *Journal of Adolescent Research, 20*(10), 1–36. DOI: 10.1177/0743558410376830

Suárez-Orozco, C., Todorova, I., & Louie, J. (2002). Making up for lost time: The experience of separation and reunification among immigrant families. *Family Process, 41*(4), 625–643. DOI: 10.1111/j.1545-5300.2002.00625.x

Suárez-Orozco, C., Yoshikawa, H., Teranishi, R. T., & Suárez-Orozco, M. (2011). Growing up in the shadows: The developmental implications of unauthorized status. *Harvard Educational Review, 81*(3), 438–472. Retrieved from http://www.metapress.com/content/G23X203763783M75

Taylor, P., Lopez, M. H., Passel, J., & Motel, S. (2011). Unauthorized immigrants: Length of residency, patterns of parenthood. Washington, DC: Pew Hispanic Center.

Thompson, G. (2009, April 23). After losing freedom, some immigrants face loss of custody of their children *New York Times.* Retrieved from http://www.nytimes.com/2009/04/23/us/23children.html?hpw

Valenzuela Jr., A. (2002). Working on the margins in metropolitan Los Angeles: Immigrants in day-labor work. *Migraciones Internacionales, 1*(2), 6–28.

Walter, N., Bourgois, P., & Loinaz, H. M. (2004). Masculinity and undocumented labor migration: Injured Latino day laborers in San Francisco. *Social Science & Medicine, 59*, 1159–1168. DOI: 10.1016/j.socscimed.2003.12.013

Wessler, S. F. (2011). Shattered families: The perilous intersection of immigration enforcement and the child welfare system. New York: Applied Research Center.

Yoshikawa, H. (2011). *Immigrants raising citizens: Undocumented parents and their young children.* New York: Russell Sage.

Zinn, M. B., & Wells. B. (2003). Diversity within Latino families: New lessons for family social science. In A. S. Skolnick & J. H. Skolnick (Eds.), *Family in transition* (12th ed., pp. 389–415). Boston: Allyn and Bacon.

Notes

1. The names of individual respondents, locations, and organizations have been disguised to preserve anonymity.

2. See Menjívar and Kanstroom 2013 for details on 287(g) and Secure Communities programs.

3. See Table 38 of the Department of Homeland Security's Yearbook of Immigration Statistics: 2010, retrieved from http://www.dhs.gov/files/statistics/publications/YrBk10En.shtm, for a breakdown of the number of deportees with and without histories of criminal offenses.

4. Twelve informants form the basis of the longitudinal part of the study. The remaining 15 participants were recruited only for the interviews that took place in the last two rounds of interviews.

5. For more detailed information about my role as the researcher in these projects, see Abrego, 2009 and Abrego, 2014.

6. The Development, Relief, and Education for Alien Minors (DREAM) Act (S. 2075, H.R. 5131) is a bipartisan piece of legislation that would provide undocumented students who have grown up in the United States with a pathway to legal permanent residency. It has been unsuccessfully introduced multiple times in the U.S. Congress.

7. See, for example, http://immigrantyouthcoalition.org/undocumented-families-come-out-of-the-shadows/

Questions for Critical Thinking

1. The author's research illustrates that the status of illegal impacts all members of a family, even when only one person or a few people are categorized as undocumented or only temporarily protected. How does the author's discussion deepen your understanding of the impact of being an undocumented immigrant?

2. Reflecting on the author's discussion, what are some of the ways that families work to reframe the status of being undocumented as a source of solidarity and strength?

3. Considering the analysis offered in this study, what do you see as solutions to the challenges these families face?

Marriage and Family

LGBT Individuals and Same-Sex Couples

GARY J. GATES

With the recent Supreme Court decision legalizing same-sex marriage, there has been much debate in the public sphere regarding the suitability of same-sex couples to raise children. In the following essay, Gary Gates reviews evidence presented by scholars on both sides of the issue and concludes that same-sex couples are as good at parenting as their different-sex counterparts.

The speed with which the legal and social climate for lesbian, gay, bisexual, and transgender (LGBT) individuals, same-sex couples, and their families is changing in the United States has few historical precedents. Measures of social acceptance related to sexual relationships, parenting, and marriage recognition among same-sex couples all increased substantially in the last two decades. The legal climate followed a similar pattern. In 2005, when the *Future of Children* last produced an issue about marriage and child wellbeing, only one state allowed same-sex couples to legally marry. By June 2015, the Supreme Court had ruled that same-sex couples had a constitutional right to marry throughout the United States.

Analyses of the General Social Survey, a biennial and nationally representative survey of adults in the United States, show that, in the years between 1973 and 1991, the portion who thought that same-sex sexual relationships were "always wrong" varied little, peaking at 77 percent in 1988 and 1991. The two decades since have seen a rapid decline in this figure, from 66 percent in 1993 to 40 percent in 2014.[1] Conversely, the portion of those who say that same-sex sexual relationships are never wrong didn't go much above 15 percent until 1993. From 1993 to 2014, that figure increased from 22 percent to 49 percent. Notably, 2014 marks the first time in the 30 years that the General Social Survey has been asking this question that the portion of Americans who think same-sex sexual relationships are never wrong is substantially higher than the portion who say such relationships are always wrong.

The General Social Survey data demonstrate an even more dramatic shift in support for marriage rights for same-sex couples. In 1988, just 12 percent of U.S. adults agreed that same-sex couples should have a right to marry. By 2014, that figure had risen to 57 percent. Data from Gallup show a similar pattern, with support for marriage rights for same-sex couples increasing from 27 percent in 1996 to 60 percent in 2014.[2] Gallup's analyses document even larger changes in attitudes toward support for adoption by same-sex couples. In 1992, its polling showed that only 29 percent of Americans supported the idea that same-sex couples should have the legal right to adopt children. In a 2014 poll, that figure was 63 percent, even higher than support for marriage among same-sex couples.[3]

Legal Recognition of Same-Sex Relationships

These shifts in public attitudes toward same-sex relationships and families have been accompanied by similarly dramatic shifts in granting legal status to same-sex couple relationships. California was the first state to enact a statewide process to recognize same-sex couples when it created its domestic partnership registry in 1999. Domestic partnership offered California same-sex couples some of the benefits normally associated with marriage, namely, hospital visitation rights and the ability to be considered next of kin when settling the estate of a deceased partner. In 2000, Vermont enacted civil unions, a status designed specifically for same-sex couples to give them a broader set of rights and responsibilities akin to those associated with marriage.

Massachusetts became the first state to legalize marriage for same-sex couples in 2004. In 2013, the U.S. Supreme Court declared unconstitutional the provision of the federal Defense of Marriage Act (passed in 1996) that limited federal recognition of marriages to different-sex couples.[4] That ruling, in *Windsor v. United States*, prompted an unprecedented wave of lawsuits in every state where same-sex couples were not permitted to marry. After numerous rulings in these cases affirming the right of same-sex couples to marry in a series of states, the Supreme Court's June 2015 decision meant that same-sex couples could marry anywhere in the country.[5]

Globally, marriage or some other form of legal recognition through civil or registered partnerships is now widely available to same-sex couples across northern, western, and central Europe, large portions of North and South America, and in South Africa, Australia, and New Zealand.[6] Conversely, homosexuality remains criminalized, in some cases by punishment of death, throughout much of Africa, the Middle East, and Southeast Asia, and in Russia and many Pacific and Caribbean island nations.[7]

Effects on LGBT Relationships and Families

Social norms and legal conditions affect how we live our lives. Psychologists document how social stigma directed toward LGBT people can be quite insidious and damage their health and wellbeing.[8] It can also affect how they form relationships and families. For example, studies from the early 1980s found that same-sex couple relationships were, on average, less stable than different-sex relationships.[9] My own analyses of data from the early 1990s showed that lesbians and gay men were less likely than their heterosexual counterparts to be in a cohabiting relationship.[10] Is this because same-sex couple relationships differ from different-sex relationships in ways that lead to instability? Are lesbians and gay men just not the marrying type? Recent research suggests that the social and legal climate may explain a great deal about why same-sex couples behave differently from different-sex couples in terms of relationship formation and stability. As society has begun to treat same-sex couples more like different-sex couples, the differences between the two groups have narrowed. For example, compared to 20 years ago, proportionately more lesbians and gay men are in cohabiting same-sex relationships, and they break up and divorce at rates similar to those of comparable different-sex couples.[11] As of March 2015, Gallup estimated that nearly 40 percent of same-sex couples were married.[12]

The social and legal climate for LGBT people also affects how they form families and become parents. In a climate of social stigma, LGBT people can feel pressure to hide their identities and have relationships with different-sex partners. Not surprisingly, some of those relationships produce children. Today, most children being raised by same-sex couples were born to different-sex parents, one of whom is now in the same-sex relationship. This pattern is changing, but in ways that may seem counterintuitive. Despite growing support for same-sex parenting, proportionally fewer same-sex couples report raising children today than in 2000. Reduced social stigma means that more LGBT people are coming out earlier in life. They're less likely than their LGBT counterparts from the past to have different-sex relationships and the children such relationships produce.[13]

But that's not the full story. While parenting may be declining overall among same-sex couples, adoption and the use of reproductive technologies like artificial insemination and surrogacy is increasing. Compared to a decade ago, same-sex couples today may be less likely to have children, but those who do are more likely to have children who were born with same-sex parents who are in stable relationships.[14]

Framing the Debate

The legal and political debates about allowing same-sex couples to marry tend to focus on two large themes that can be seen even in the earliest attempts to garner legal recognition of same-sex marriages. These two themes pit arguments about the inherent and traditional relationship between marriage and procreation (including the suitability of same-sex couples as parents) against arguments about the degree to which opposition to legal recognition of same-sex relationships is rooted in irrational animus and discrimination toward same-sex couples or lesbian, gay and bisexual (LGB, used here because these arguments rarely consider the transgender population) individuals more broadly. (Throughout this article, I use LGB rather than LGBT when data or research focuses only on sexual orientation and not on gender identity.)

In the United States, the earliest legal attempt to expand marriage to include same-sex couples began in 1970, when Richard Baker and James McConnell applied for and were denied a marriage license in Hennepin County, Minnesota.[15]

They filed a lawsuit that eventually came before the Minnesota and U.S. supreme courts. The Minnesota court ruling observed that the arguments in favor of allowing the couple to marry were based on the proposition that "the right to marry without regard to the sex of the parties is a fundamental right of all persons and that restricting marriage to only couples of the opposite sex is irrational and invidiously discriminatory." The court wasn't persuaded by these arguments, ruling that "the institution of marriage as a union of a man and woman, uniquely involving the procreation of children, is as old as the book of Genesis."[16] The U.S. Supreme Court dismissed the case on appeal for lack of any substantial federal question.[17]

More than 30 years later, in a ruling from the U.S. Court of Appeals for the Seventh Circuit in *Baskin v. Bogan*, which upheld a lower court's ruling that Indiana's ban on marriage for same-sex couples was unconstitutional, Judge Richard Posner offered a distinctly different perspective from that of the Minnesota court regarding similar arguments made in a case seeking to overturn Indiana's ban on marriage for same-sex couples. He wrote:

At oral argument the state's lawyer was asked whether "Indiana's law is about successfully raising children," and since "you agree same-sex couples can successfully raise children, why shouldn't the ban be lifted as to them?" The lawyer answered that "the assumption is that with opposite-sex couples there is very little thought given during the sexual act, sometimes, to whether babies may be a consequence." In other words, Indiana's government thinks that straight couples tend to be sexually irresponsible, producing unwanted children by the carload, and so must be pressured (in the form of governmental encouragement of marriage through a combination of sticks and carrots) to marry, but that gay couples, unable as they are to produce children wanted or unwanted, are model parents—model citizens really—so have no need for marriage. Heterosexuals get drunk and pregnant, producing unwanted children; their reward is to be allowed to marry. Homosexual couples do not produce unwanted children; their reward is to be denied the right to marry. Go figure.[18]

As in *Baker v. Nelson*, the U.S. Supreme Court opted not to take *Baskin v. Bogan* on appeal. But this time, the court's inaction prompted a rapid expansion in the number of states that allowed same-sex couples to marry.

This article explores the social and legal debates about access to marriage for same-sex couples, how social and legal change is affecting the demographic characteristics of LGBT people and their families, whether parents' gender composition affects children's wellbeing, and how social science research has contributed to those debates and can track the impact of these social changes in the future.

LGBT Families: Demographic Characteristics

Depending on which survey we consider, from 5.2 million to 9.5 million U.S. adults identify as LGBT (roughly 2–4 percent of adults).[19] An analysis of two state-level population-based surveys suggests that approximately 0.3 percent of adults are transgender.[20] More people identify as LGBT today than in the past. Findings from the 2012 Gallup Daily Tracking survey suggest that, among adults aged 18 and older, 3.6 percent of women and 3.3 percent of men identify as LGBT.[21] Nearly 20 years ago, 2.8 percent of men and 1.4 percent of women identified as lesbian, gay, or bisexual in a national survey.[22] These estimates measure the LGBT population by considering who identifies themselves using the terms lesbian, gay, bisexual, or transgender. Self-identity is not necessarily the only way to measure sexual orientation or gender identity. For example, if sexual orientation is measured by the gender of one's sexual partners or sexual attractions, then population estimates increase. Findings from the 2006–08 National Survey of

Family Growth, a national survey of adults aged 18–44 conducted by the National Center for Health Statistics, show that 12.5 percent of women and 5.2 percent of men report at least some same-sex sexual behavior. An estimated 13.6 percent of women and 7.1 percent of men report at least some same-sex sexual attraction.[23]

Estimates for the number of cohabiting same-sex couples in the United States are most commonly derived from U.S. Census Bureau data, either decennial Census enumerations (beginning in 1990) or the annual American Community Survey (ACS). Unfortunately, the accuracy of the Census Bureau figures for same-sex couples has been called into question because of a measurement problem whereby a very small portion of different-sex couples (mostly married) make an error on the survey when recording the gender of one of the partners or spouses, so that the survey appears to identify the couple as same-sex. Findings from various analyses of Census and ACS data suggest that the presence of these false positives among same-sex couples could mean that from one-quarter to one-half of identified same-sex couples may be miscoded different-sex couples.[24]

In 2010, the U.S. Census Bureau released estimates of the number of same-sex couples that were adjusted to minimize the inaccuracies created by the measurement problem. They reported nearly 650,000 same-sex couples in the country, an increase of more than 80 percent over the figure from Census 2000 of 360,000 couples.[25] Same-sex couples represent about 0.5 percent of all U.S. households and about 1 percent of all married and unmarried cohabiting couples. My analyses of the National Health Interview Survey (NHIS), an annual survey of adults conducted by the U.S. Department of Health and Human Services, suggest that there were approximately 690,000 same-sex couples in the United States in 2013, representing 1.1 percent of all couples, a modest increase from the 2010 figures.[26] Gallup estimates from March 2015 suggest that the number of cohabiting same-sex couples may be close to 1 million.[27]

Estimating the number of married same-sex couples in the United States is difficult. Not all states collect administrative marriage data that explicitly identifies same-sex couples. A further complication comes from the measurement issues in Census Bureau data. Estimates of the number of same-sex couples who identify as married are now reported in annual ACS tabulations, but the measurement error that I've discussed likely means that these figures aren't very accurate.[28]

Based on NHIS data, I calculated that there may have been as many as 130,000 married same-sex couples by the end of 2013, approximately 18 percent of all same-sex couples.[29] By contrast, ACS estimates from the same year suggested that there were more than 250,000 married same-sex couples. The NHIS and ACS estimates both were made before the majority of states allowed same-sex couples to marry. Gallup estimates from data collected in March 2015 found 390,000 married same-sex couples.[30] Regardless of the accuracy of these estimates, it's clear that same-sex couples are marrying at a rapid rate. The population of married same-sex couples appears to have doubled or even tripled in just one year.[31]

LGBT and Same-Sex Couple Parents and Families

LGBT individuals and same-sex couples come to be parents in many ways. My own analyses estimate that 37 percent of LGBT individuals have been parents and that as many as 6 million U.S. children and adults may have an LGBT parent.[32] I estimate that while as many as 2 million to 3.7 million children under age 18 may have an LGBT parent, it's likely that only about 200,000 are being raised by a same-sex couple.[33] Many are being raised by single LGBT parents, and many are being raised by different-sex couples where one parent is bisexual. Most surveys find that bisexuals account for roughly half of the LGBT population, and my NHIS analyses suggest that among bisexuals with children, more than six in 10 are either married (51 percent) or partnered (11 percent) with a

different-sex partner.[34] Only 4 percent are living with a same-sex spouse or partner.

Data rarely provide clear information about the birth circumstances of children with LGBT parents or those living with same-sex couples. But, as I've already pointed out, my analyses of ACS data suggest that most children currently living with same-sex couples were likely born in previous different-sex relationships. Two-thirds of children under age 18 living with a same-sex cohabiting couple (married or unmarried) are identified as either the biological child or step-child of one member of the couple. Only about 12 percent of them are identified as adopted or foster children, though that figure has been increasing over time.[35] My research also shows that, among people who have ever had a child, LGB individuals report having had their first child at earlier ages than their non-LGB counterparts.[36] This is consistent with many studies documenting that LGB youth are more likely to experience unintended pregnancy or fatherhood when compared to their non-LGB counterparts.[37] Researchers speculate that social stigma directed toward LGB youth contributes to psychological stress. That stress can sometimes lead them to engage in risky behaviors, including sexual activity that results in unplanned pregnancies.

Analyses of many data sources show that racial and ethnic minorities (particularly African Americans and Latinos) who are LGB or in same-sex couples are more likely to report raising or having had children. The proportion of all same-sex couples raising children tends to be higher in more socially conservative areas of the country, where LGB people may have come out relatively later in life, so were more likely to have children with a different-sex partner earlier in life.[38] These patterns likely also contribute to the broad economic disadvantage observed among same-sex couples and LGB individuals who are raising children. They have lower incomes than their different-sex couple or non-LGB counterparts and have higher levels of poverty.[39] In fact, same-sex couples with children are twice as likely as their married different-sex counterparts to be living in poverty.

The evidence of economic disadvantage among same-sex couples with children is intriguing given the overall high levels of education historically observed among those in same-sex couples. Nearly all research shows that individuals in same-sex couples have higher levels of education than those in different-sex couples.[40] But this pattern differs among couples raising children. While nearly half of those in same-sex couples have a college degree, only a third of those raising children have that much education. Same-sex couple parents also report higher rates of unemployment than their different-sex counterparts. Individuals in same-sex and different-sex couples with children report similar levels of labor force participation (81 percent and 84 percent, respectively), but those in same-sex couples are more likely to be unemployed (8 percent versus 6 percent, respectively). While in the majority of same-sex and different-sex couples with children, both spouses or partners are employed (57 percent and 60 percent, respectively), same-sex couples are more likely to have neither partner employed (8 percent versus 5 percent, respectively).[41]

The percentage of same-sex couples who are raising children began declining in 2006.[42] As I've said, this may actually be a result of social acceptance and LGBT people coming out (being more public about their LGBT identity) earlier in life today than in the past. In a Pew Research Center study, for example, younger respondents reported that they first told someone that they were LGBT at younger ages than did older respondents.[43] It may be that lesbians and gay men are less likely now than in the past to have different-sex sexual relationships while young and, therefore, are less likely to have children with a different-sex partner. Today, about 19 percent of same-sex couples are raising children under age 18, with little variation in that statistic between married and unmarried couples. Among LGB individuals not in a couple, the figure is also 19 percent.[44]

Social Science and Political Debates

To the extent that social scientists have weighed in on the debate about allowing same-sex couples to marry and the consequences that such a change might have on society and families, they have largely focused on parenting. Questions regarding the extent to which LGBT individuals and same-sex couples become parents, how they come to be parents, and whether and how sexual orientation or gender composition of children's parents might affect their health and wellbeing have all been considered within the framework of the debates about legalizing marriage for same-sex couples.

Social Science on Trial

This dynamic may be best observed in the testimony that emerged from a trial in the case of *DeBoer v. Snyder*, a lawsuit filed in the U.S. District Court for the Eastern District of Michigan that challenged the state's ban on marriage for same-sex couples. The case originated when plaintiffs April DeBoer and Jayne Rowse were denied the ability to complete a joint adoption (where both partners are declared a legal parent to the child) because Michigan allowed such adoptions only among married couples. Judge Bernard A. Friedman ordered a trial, the first such trial in a case involving marriage rights for same-sex couples since a challenge to California's Proposition 8 (a 2008 ballot initiative, later overturned by the courts, that made marriage for same-sex couples illegal). Given the origins of the lawsuit, litigants on both sides assembled expert witnesses from the social sciences, including me, to testify regarding what social science tells us about parenting among same-sex couples. . . .

In the end, Judge Friedman, a Reagan appointee to the federal judiciary, issued a strongly worded opinion in favor of the plaintiffs' right to marry.[45] His opinion was later overturned by the U.S. Sixth Circuit Court of Appeals, but upheld by the Supreme Court. In his ruling, Freidman dismissed arguments suggesting that the limitations of social science research with regard to same-sex couple parents were sufficient to cause concern about how allowing same-sex couples to marry would affect children and families. Though Friedman's judicial ruling hardly settles the debates among social scientists about LGBT and same-sex couple parenting, it has affected legal cases that followed. Judge Posner's words that I cited earlier demonstrate that lawyers defending Indiana's ban on marriage for same-sex couples effectively conceded that same-sex couples make entirely suitable parents. Since the Michigan ruling, it has become very rare for those opposed to allowing same-sex couples to marry to base their arguments partly on questions about the suitability of same-sex couples as parents or on possible negative consequences for children's health and wellbeing.

Married Same-Sex Couples

Substantial evidence shows that marriage promotes stability in couples and families.[46] Stability, and the financial and social benefits that come with it, contribute to better outcomes for children raised by married parents. The widespread acceptance of marriage for same-sex couples comes at a time when more of them are pursuing parenting as a couple through adoption and reproductive technologies and fewer are raising children from prior different-sex relationships. Will marriage have the stabilizing effect on same-sex couples and their families that we've seen in different-sex couples? Evidence suggests that it might, since lesbians and gay men have a strong desire to be married and have views about the purpose of marriage that are similar to those of the general population.

Desire for Marriage

In two recent studies, the Pew Research Center has found that 56 percent of unmarried gay men and 58 percent of unmarried lesbians would like to be married someday, compared to 45 percent of unmarried bisexuals and 46 percent of the unmarried general population.[47] The views of bisexuals and the general population may be similar because the

vast majority of coupled bisexual men and women report having different-sex spouses or partners. At the time of the Pew survey, neither marriage nor recognition of a legal relationship through civil union or domestic partnership was yet widely available for same-sex couples in the United States. So it isn't surprising that lesbians and gay men were less likely to be married or in a civil union or registered domestic partnership when compared to bisexuals or the general population. When current marital status was taken into account, approximately 60 percent of LGBT adults in the Pew survey were currently married or said they would like to be married someday, compared to 76 percent of the general population.

Relationship Formation

While desire for marriage may be relatively high among lesbians and gay men, there are differences between the groups, and between LGB individuals and heterosexuals, in patterns of forming relationships. Among LGB men and women, lesbians are the most likely to be in cohabiting relationships, usually at rates very similar to those of non-LGB women. Overall, LGB individuals are less likely than non-LGB individuals to be in a married or unmarried cohabiting relationship. My analyses of the 2013 NHIS show that roughly six in 10 non-LGB adults are living with a partner or spouse, compared to about four in 10 LGB individuals. However, the likelihood of having a cohabiting spouse or partner is markedly higher among lesbians, at 51 percent, than among gay men or bisexual men and women, about one in three of whom are coupled. The difference between lesbians and non-LGB women (58 percent) in the NHIS was not statistically significant.[48] In an older paper, Christopher Carpenter and I also found that cohabiting partnerships were more common among lesbians than among gay men (though the data were from California only) and that lesbians' levels of cohabitation were comparable to those found in heterosexual women.[49]

Findings from a Pew Research Center survey of LGBT adults showed that, consistent with the NHIS analyses, 37 percent of LGBT adults were cohabiting with a spouse or partner. The Pew findings also showed that lesbians were more likely than gay men to have a spouse or partner (40 percent versus 28 percent, respectively). Unlike the NHIS findings, bisexual women were the most likely among LGB men and women to have a spouse or partner at 51 percent, compared to 30 percent of bisexual men. Among the general population, Pew found that 58 percent of adults were cohabiting with a spouse or partner. Regardless of cohabitation, 40 percent of gay men were in a committed relationship, compared to 66 percent of lesbians. Among bisexual men and women, the figures were 40 percent and 68 percent, respectively. In the general population, Pew estimates that about 70 percent were in committed relationships.[50]

As we've seen, lesbians and gay men appear to be partnering at higher rates today than in the past. In analyses of the 1992 National Health and Social Life Survey, a population-based survey of adults focused on sexual attitudes and behaviors, 19 percent of men who identified as gay and 42 percent of women who identified as lesbian reported being in a cohabiting partnership.[51] This suggests that gay men are nearly twice as likely to partner today as they were in the early 1990s. It also confirms that the pattern of higher levels of coupling among lesbians when compared to gay men has persisted over time.

Reasons to Marry

The Pew survey also considered the reasons that people marry. LGBT respondents were no different from the general population in their belief that love, companionship, and making a lifelong commitment were the three most important reasons for a couple to marry. The only substantial difference between LGBT respondents and the general population in this regard was that LGBT people gave more weight to legal rights and benefits as a reason to marry than did the general population.[52] This difference may not be surprising given the substantial media attention focused on the legal rights and benefits that were not available to same-sex couples in places where they could not marry.

The findings also suggested that lesbians and gay men were largely responsible for the fact that rights and benefits were ranked higher among LGBT respondents; lesbians and gay men ranked rights and benefits, as well as financial stability, as much more important than bisexuals did (bisexuals were similar to the general population in this regard, and this portion of the analyses didn't separately consider transgender respondents).[53] Recall that the Pew findings show that most coupled bisexuals are with different-sex partners, while coupled lesbians and gay men are with same-sex partners. Given their more limited access to marriage, rights, benefits, and financial stability might be more important for lesbians and gay men.

Social Impact

When social scientists examine the issue of marriage rights for same-sex couples, they do so largely through the medium of parenting and family studies. Broader public discourse and debate often involves more philosophical (rather than empirical) arguments about marriage as a social and legal institution and the degree to which allowing same-sex couples to marry reflects a fundamental or undesirable change to that institution (a book that pits philosopher John Corvino against political activist Maggie Gallagher, *Debating Same-Sex Marriage*, provides an example of these arguments).[54] However, social scientists certainly have led the way in tracking contemporary changes in patterns of family formation and marriage. Sociologist Andrew Cherlin, for example, has documented many of these changes, including: increases in the age of first marriage; diverging patterns of both marriage and divorce by education, such that those with lower levels of education are less likely to marry and more likely to divorce when compared to those with higher educational attainment; increases in nonmarital births and cohabitation; and increases in the number of children living in families not headed by their married biological mothers and fathers.[55]

Some public debate has emerged regarding the degree to which these social changes are related to allowing same-sex couples to marry. Political commentator Stanley Kurtz argues that marriage for same-sex couples in Europe has contributed to and hastened the institutional decline in marriage, to the detriment of families and children.[56] Journalist Jonathan Rauch disagrees, arguing that allowing same-sex couples to marry will enhance the prestige of the institution and reinvigorate it during a period of decline.[57]

The empirical evidence for a link between the emergence of marriage rights for same-sex couples and broader marriage, divorce, and fertility trends is weak. Economist Lee Badgett has shown that trends in different-sex marriage, divorce, and nonmarital birth rates did not change in European countries after they legalized marriage for same-sex couples.[58] Another study, using data from the United States, found that allowing same-sex couples to marry or enter civil unions produced no significant impact on state-level marriage, divorce, abortion, and out-of-wedlock births.[59] In the Netherlands, where marriage for same-sex couples has been legal for more than a decade, neither the country's domestic partnership law nor the legalization of same-sex marriage appears to have affected different-sex marriage rates. Curiously, however, there appear to be different effects among liberals and conservatives: the introduction of same-sex marriage was associated with higher marriage rates among conservatives and lower rates among liberals.[60]

Conclusions: New Opportunities for Family Research

The demographic and attitudinal data that I've summarized suggest that same-sex and different-sex couples may not look as different in the future as they do today. Already they have similar perspectives on the desire for and purpose of marriage, and increasing numbers of same-sex couples are marrying and having their children as a married couple. Even under the challenging circumstances of social and legal inequality between same-sex and different-sex couples, it's clear that same-sex couples are as good at parenting as their different-sex counterparts, and their children turn out fine. Lesbian and gay parents report outcomes similar to those of their heterosexual counterparts with regard to mental health, stress, and parental competence. Same-sex and different-sex parents show similar levels of parental warmth, emotional involvement, and quality of relationships with their children. So, not surprisingly, few differences have been found between children raised by same-sex and different-sex parents in terms of self-esteem, quality of life, psychological adjustment, or social functioning.[61] As the legal and social playing fields become more equal for same-sex and different-sex couples, we have the opportunity to consider new research questions that can contribute to debates about whether and how parental relationship dynamics affect child wellbeing.

For example, while society has changed in its views about LGBT people and their families, it has also changed in its attitudes about gender and the norms associated with how men and women organize their relationships and families. In 1977, more than half of Americans thought that having a mother who works outside the home could be harmful to children. In 2012, only 28 percent of Americans thought so.[62] Changing social norms concerning gender and parenting likely play a role in explaining the decisions that couples make about how to divide time between work and family. Since those decisions can affect family finances and involvement in parenting, research has considered the effects that family division of labor can have on child wellbeing.[63]

Same-sex couples raising children give us the opportunity to assess how parents divide labor in the absence of gender differences between spouses or partners. However, comparisons between same-sex and different-sex couples are more complicated when same-sex couples don't have access to marriage. Decisions about employment and division of labor among same-sex couples could be directly associated with their inability to marry if, for example, their access to health insurance for each other or their children were contingent on both partners working, because spousal benefits would not be available. But there is also evidence that same-sex couples intentionally favor more egalitarian divisions of labor precisely as a rejection of traditional male/female roles in parenting.[64]

With equal access to marriage among same-sex and different-sex couples and trends toward greater intentional parenting among same-sex couples (as opposed to raising children from prior relationships), the two groups now look more similar in many ways, except, of course, in the couple's gender composition. These are the right conditions for a kind of "treatment" and "control" approach to studying the two groups (or perhaps three, if you think that male and female same-sex couples might behave differently based on gendered behavioral norms) and isolating the influence of gender roles in decisions about how much and which parents work outside the home, how much they interact with their children, and, ultimately, whether any of those decisions affect children's wellbeing. There's already some evidence that children raised by same-sex couples may show fewer gender-stereotyped behaviors and be more willing to consider same-sex sexual relationships (though there is still no evidence that they are more likely than other children to identify as LGB).[65]

The award-winning television program *Transparent* highlights the increasing visibility of parenting among transgender individuals, a relatively understudied subject. In a survey of more than 6,000 transgender individuals in the United States, nearly four in 10 (38 percent) reported having been a parent at some time in their lives.[66] Existing research offers no evidence that children of

transgender parents experience developmental disparities or differ from other children with regard to their gender identity or development of sexual orientation. As with LGB people, several studies have shown that people who transition or "come out" as transgender later in life are more likely to have had children than those who identify as transgender and/or transition at younger ages. This suggests that many transgender parents likely had their children before they identified as transgender or transitioned.[67]

Just like comparing same-sex and different-sex parents, studying transgender parents offers another fascinating opportunity to better understand the relationship between gender and parenting. Transgender parenting research could consider whether the dynamics of parent/child relationships change when a parent transitions from one gender to another. In essence, this would give us another "treatment" and "control" group to explore parent–child relationships when the same parent is perceived as and perhaps conforms behaviors to one gender versus when that parent presents and parents as another gender.

While arguments about what drives trends and changes in marriage and family life may continue, it appears that, with the Supreme Court's ruling that same-sex couples have a constitutional right to marry, heated debates about the subject may be drawing to a close, at least in the United States. Polling data suggest that a substantial majority of Americans now support allowing same-sex couples to marry and raise children. For decades, scholarship regarding LGBT and same-sex couple parenting has occurred in a contentious political and social environment that invited unusual scrutiny. For example, publication of the Regnerus study in 2012 prompted unprecedented responses from scholars who both criticized and supported it.[68] LGBT advocates actually initiated legal action amid charges of academic malfeasance and fraud.[69]

This article highlights how research on LGBT and same-sex couple parenting can not only advance our understanding of the challenges associated with parenting in the face of stigma and discrimination, but also contribute more broadly to family scholarship. While robust political and social debates can be critical in allowing social and political institutions to progress and advance, they can make it hard to advance scholarly goals of objectivity and academic freedom. Let us hope that as the debates about LGBT rights and marriage for same-sex couples cool, scholars can work in a less volatile political and social environment and advance much-needed research that includes and explores parenting and family formation among same-sex couples and the LGBT population.

Notes

1. Figures based on author's analyses of General Social Survey data using the University of California, Berkeley's Survey Documentation and Analysis web-based analysis tool (http://sda.berkeley.edu/index.html).

2. Justin McCarthy, "Record-High 60% of Americans Support Same-Sex Marriage," Gallup, May 20, 2015, http://www.gallup.com/poll/183272/record-high-americans-support-sex-marriage.aspx?utm_source=Social%20Issues&utm_medium=newsfeed&utm_campaign=tiles.

3. Art Swift, "Most Americans Say Same-Sex Couples Entitled to Adopt," Gallup, accessed May 20, 2015, http://www.gallup.com/poll/170801/americans-say-sex-couples-entitled-adopt.aspx.

4. Windsor v. United States 570 US___ (2013).

5. Freedom to Marry, "History and Timeline of the Freedom to Marry in the United States," accessed October 10, 2014, http://www.freedomtomarry.org/pages/history-and-timeline-of-marriage.

6. For a current list of the legal relationship status for same-sex couples around the world, see Freedom to Marry, "The Freedom to Marry Internationally," accessed October 10, 2014, http://www.freedomtomarry.org/landscape/entry/c/international.

7. For a current summary of laws regarding homosexuality and gender identity around the world, see the International Lesbian, Gay, Bisexual, Trans and Intersex Association website, http://ilga.org/.

8. Ilan H. Meyer, "Prejudice, Social Stress, and Mental Health in Lesbian, Gay, and Bisexual Populations: Conceptual Issues and Research Evidence," *Psychological Bulletin* 129 (2003): 674–97, doi: 10.1037/0033-2909.129.5.674.

9. Philip Blumstein and Pepper Schwartz, *American Couples: Money, Work, Sex* (New York: William Morrow & Co., 1983).

10. Dan Black et al., "Demographics of the Gay and Lesbian Population in the United States: Evidence from Available Systematic Data Sources," *Demography* 37 (2000): 139–54.

11. Michael Rosenfeld, "Couple Longevity in the Era of Same-Sex Marriage in the United States," *Journal of Marriage and Family* 76 (2014): 905–18, doi: 10.1111/jomf.12141; M. V. Lee Badgett and Christy Mallory, *Patterns of Relationship Recognition for Same-Sex Couples: Divorce and Terminations* (Los Angeles, CA: Williams Institute, UCLA School of Law, 2014), http://williamsinstitute.law.ucla.edu/wp-content/uploads/Badgett-Mallory-Divorce-Terminations-Dec-2014.pdf.

12. Gary J. Gates and Frank Newport, "An Estimated 780,000 Americans in Same-Sex Marriages," Gallup, accessed May 20, 2015, http://www.gallup.com/poll/182837/estimated-780-000-americans-sex-marriages.aspx.

13. Gary J. Gates, *LGBT Parenting in the United States* (Los Angeles, CA: Williams Institute, UCLA School of Law, 2013), http://williamsinstitute.law.ucla.edu/wp-content/uploads/LGBT-Parenting.pdf.

14. Ibid.

15. William N. Eskridge and Darren R. Spedale, *Gay Marriage: For Better or for Worse? What We've Learned from the Evidence* (New York: Oxford University Press, 2007).

16. Baker v. Nelson. 291 Minn. 310 (1971).

17. Baker v. Nelson. 409 US 810 (1972).

18. Baskin v. Bogan, 7th Cir. No. 14-2386, 2014 WL 4359059 (2014).

19. Gary J. Gates, *LGBT Demographics: Comparisons among Population-Based Surveys* (Los Angeles, CA: Williams Institute, UCLA School of Law, 2014), http://williamsinstitute.law.ucla.edu/wp-content/uploads/lgbt-demogs-sep-2014.pdf.

20. Gary J. Gates, *How Many People Are Lesbian, Gay, Bisexual, and Transgender?* (Los Angeles, CA: Williams Institute, UCLA School of Law, 2011), http://williamsinstitute.law.ucla.edu/wp-content/uploads/Gates-How-Many-People-LGBT-Apr-2011.pdf.

21. Gary J. Gates and Frank Newport, "Special Report: 3.4% of US Adults Identify as LGBT," October 18, 2012, http://www.gallup.com/poll/158066/special-report-adults-identify-lgbt.aspx.

22. Edward O. Laumann et al., *The Social Organization of Sexuality: Sexual Practices in the United States* (Chicago: University of Chicago Press, 1994).

23. Anjani Chandra et al., "Sexual Behavior, Sexual Attraction, and Sexual Identity in the United States: Data from the 2006–2008 National Survey of Family Growth," National Health Statistics Reports no. 36 (Hyattsville, MD: National Center for Health Statistics, 2011).

24. Dan Black et al., "The Measurement of Same-Sex Unmarried Partner Couples in the 2000 US Census," Working Paper 023-07 (Los Angeles, CA: California Center for Population Research, 2007), http://papers.ccpr.ucla.edu/papers/PWP-CCPR-2007-023/PWP-CCPR-2007-023.pdf; Gary J. Gates and Michael D. Steinberger, "Same-Sex Unmarried Partner Couples in the American Community Survey: The Role of Misreporting, Miscoding and Misallocation" paper presented at the Population Association of America Annual Meeting, Detroit, MI, 2009, http://economics-files.pomona.edu/steinberger/research/Gates_Steinberger_ACS_Miscode_May2010.pdf; Martin O'Connell and Sarah Feliz, "Same-Sex Couple Household Statistics from the 2010 Census," Working Paper Number 2011-26 (Washington, DC: Social, Economic and Housing Statistics Division, US Bureau of the Census, 2011), http://www.census.gov/hhes/samesex/files/ss-report.doc.

25. O'Connell and Feliz, "Same-Sex."

26. Gary J. Gates, *LGB Families and Relationships: Analyses of the 2013 National Health Interview Survey* (Los Angeles, CA: Williams Institute, UCLA School of Law, 2014), http://williamsinstitute.law.ucla.edu/wp-content/uploads/lgb-families-nhis-sep-2014.pdf.

27. Gates and Newport, "780,000 Americans."

28. D'Vera Cohn, "Census Confirms More Data Problems in Sorting out the Number of US Gay Marriages," *Fact Tank*, September 22, 2014, http://www.pewresearch.org/fact-tank/2014/09/22/census-confirms-more-data-problems-in-sorting-out-the-number-of-u-s-gay-marriages/.

29. Gates, *LGB Families*.

30. Gates and Newport, "780,000 Americans."

31. Ibid.

32. Gates, *LGBT Parenting*.

33. Ibid.

34. Gates, *LGBT Demographics: Comparisons*.

35. Gates, *LGBT Parenting*; Gary J. Gates, "Family Formation and Raising Children among Same-Sex Couples," *NCFR Report* (Winter 2011), F1–4, http://williamsinstitute.law.ucla.edu/wp-content/uploads/Gates-Badgett-NCFR-LGBT-Families-December-2011.pdf.

36. Gates, "Family Formation."

37. Elizabeth M. Saewyc, "Research on Adolescent Sexual Orientation: Development, Health Disparities, Stigma, and Resilience," *Journal of Research on Adolescence* 21: 256–72 (2011), doi: 10.1111/j.1532-7795.2010.00727.x.

38. Gary J. Gates, *Same-Sex and Different-Sex Couples in the American Community Survey: 2005–2011* (Los Angeles, CA: Williams Institute, UCLA School of Law, 2013), http://williamsinstitute.law.ucla.edu/wp-content/uploads/ACS-2013.pdf.

39. M. V. Lee Badgett et al., *New Patterns of Poverty in the Lesbian, Gay, and Bisexual Community* (Los Angeles, CA: Williams Institute, UCLA School of Law, 2013), http://williamsinstitute.law.ucla.edu/wp-content/uploads/LGB-Poverty-Update-Jun-2013.pdf.

40. Black et al., "Demographics"; Lisa K. Jepsen and Christopher Jepsen, "An Empirical Analysis of the Matching Patterns of Same-Sex and Opposite-Sex Couples," *Demography* 39 (2002): 435–53; Gary J. Gates and Jason Ost, *The Gay and Lesbian Atlas* (Washington, DC: Urban Institute Press, 2004); Gates, *American Community Survey*; Gates, *LGBT Families*.

41. Author's analyses of 2012 American Community Survey Public Use Microdata Sample.

42. Gates, "Family Formation"; Gates, *American Community Survey*.

43. Pew Research Center, *A Survey of LGBT Americans: Attitudes, Experiences and Values in Changing Times* (Washington, DC: Pew Research Center, 2013), http://www.pewsocialtrends.org/files/2013/06/SDT_LGBT-Americans_06-2013.pdf.

44. Gates, *LGB Families*.

45. Bernard A. Friedman, "Findings of Fact and Conclusions of Law," *Deboer v. Snyder*, United States

District Court, Eastern District of Michigan, Southern Division, 12-CV-10285, 2014, https://www.mied.uscourts.gov/PDFFIles/12-10285DeBoerFindings.pdf.

46. Linda Waite and Maggie Gallagher, *The Case for Marriage: Why Married People Are Happier, Healthier, and Better Off Financially* (New York: Broadway Books, 2001).

47. Pew Research Center, *Survey of LGBT Americans*; Pew Research Center, *The Decline of Marriage and Rise of New Families* (Washington, DC: Pew Research Center, 2010), http://www.pewsocialtrends.org/files/2010/11/pew-social-trends-2010-families.pdf.

48. Gates, *LGB Families*.

49. Christopher Carpenter and Gary J. Gates, "Gay and Lesbian Partnership: Evidence from California," *Demography* 45 (2008): 573–90, doi: 10.1353/dem.0.0014.

50. Pew Research Center, *Survey of LGBT Americans*.

51. Black et al., "Demographics."

52. Pew Research Center, *Survey of LGBT Americans*.

53. Ibid.

54. Jon Corvino and Maggie Gallagher, *Debating Same-Sex Marriage* (New York: Oxford University Press, 2012).

55. Andrew J. Cherlin, "Demographic Trends in the United States: A Review of Research in the 2000s," *Journal of Marriage and Family* 72 (2010): 403–19, 10.1111/j.1741-3737.2010.00710.x.

56. Stanley Kurtz, "The End of Marriage in Scandinavia: The 'Conservative Case' for Same-Sex Marriage Collapses," *The Weekly Standard*, February 2, 2004, http://www.weeklystandard.com/Content/Public/Articles/000/000/003/660zypwj.asp.

57. Jonathan Rauch, *Gay Marriage: Why It Is Good for Gays, Good for Straights, and Good for America* (New York: Times Books, 2004).

58. M. V. Lee Badgett, "Will Providing Marriage Rights to Same-Sex Couples Undermine Heterosexual Marriage?" *Sexuality Research and Social Policy* 1 (2004): 1–10, doi: 10.1525/srsp.2004.1.3.1.

59. Laura Langbein and Mark L. Yost, "Same-Sex Marriage and Negative Externalities," *Social Science Quarterly* 90 (2009): 292–308, 10.1111/j.1540-6237.2009.00618.x.

60. Mircea Trandafir, "The Effect of Same-Sex Marriage Laws on Different-Sex Marriage: Evidence From the Netherlands," *Demography* 51 (2013): 317–40, doi: 10.1007/s13524-013-0248-7.

61. Abbie E. Goldberg, Nanette K. Gartrell, and Gary J. Gates, *Research Report on LGB-Parent Families* (Los Angeles, CA: Williams Institute, UCLA School of Law, 2014), http://williamsinstitute.law.ucla.edu/wp-content/uploads/lgb-parent-families-july-2014.pdf.

62. Author's analyses of the General Social Survey. Respondents were asked whether they agreed or disagreed with the statement that having a mother working does not harm children. The figures reported represent the portion who disagreed with that statement.

63. Suzanne M. Bianchi et al., "Housework: Who Did, Does, or Will Do It, and How Much Does It Matter?" *Social Forces* 91 (2012): 55–63, doi: 10.1093/sf/sos120.

64. Abbie E. Goldberg. "'Doing' and 'Undoing' Gender: The Meaning and Division of Housework in Same-Sex Couples," *Journal of Family Theory & Review* 5 (2013): 85–104, doi: 10.1111/jftr.12009.

65. Goldberg, Gartrell, and Gates, *Research Report*.

66. Jaime M. Grant et al., *Injustice at Every Turn: A Report of the National Transgender Discrimination Survey* (Washington, DC: National Center for Transgender Equality and National Gay and Lesbian Task Force, 2011), http://www.thetaskforce.org/static_html/downloads/reports/reports/ntds_full.pdf.

67. Rebecca L. Stotzer, Jody L. Herman, and Amira Hasenbush, *Transgender Parenting: A Review of Existing Research* (Los Angeles, CA: Williams Institute, UCLA School of Law, 2014), http://williamsinstitute.law.ucla.edu/research/parenting/transgender-parenting-oct-2014/.

68. Gary J. Gates et al., "Letter to the Editors and Advisory Editors Social Science Research," *Social Science Research* 41 (2012), doi: 10.1016/j.ssresearch.2012.08.008: 1350–51 ; Byron Johnson et al. "Letter to the Editor," *Social Science Research* 41 (2012): 1352–53, doi:10.1016/j.ssresearch.2012.08.009.

69. Human Rights Campaign, "Judge Overturns Order to Disclose Documents Detailing Publication of Regnerus' Junk Science," news release, April 17, 2014, http://www.hrc.org/press-releases/entry/judge-overturns-order-to-disclose-documents-detailing-publication-of-regner.

Questions for Critical Thinking

1. What do you think constitutes a family? What are its important components? What has led you to define family in the way that you do (e.g., your own family experience, media, friends, other social institutions)?

2. Many things influence the well-being of children. Considering the author's discussion, how might the legalization of same-sex marriage positively impact the children of these relationships?

3. How might same-sex marriages challenge traditional notions of family in the United States? How might recognizing these families lead to greater equality for people of all sexual orientations?

The Racial Achievement Gap, Segregated Schools, and Segregated Neighborhoods

A Constitutional Insult

RICHARD ROTHSTEIN

The following essay is by Richard Rothstein, a research associate of the Economic Policy Institute and a fellow at the Thurgood Marshall Institute of the NAACP Legal Defense Fund and of the Haas Institute at the University of California, Berkeley. As his analysis illustrates, while we no longer have legal segregation in K–12 public schools or legally segregated neighborhoods, segregation continues and, as a result, the racial achievement gap continues to widen. To address this gap, we must understand how education policy is constrained by a history of state-sponsored residential segregation. Without doing so, we will fail to take meaningful steps to remedy this inequality.

We cannot substantially improve the performance of the poorest African American students—the "truly disadvantaged," in William Julius Wilson's phrase—by school reform alone. It must be addressed primarily by improving the social and economic conditions that bring too many children to school unprepared to take advantage of what even the best schools have to offer.

There are two aspects to this conclusion:

- First, social and economic disadvantage—not poverty itself, but a host of associated conditions—depresses student performance, and

- Second, concentrating students with these disadvantages in racially and economically homogenous schools depresses it further.

The individual predictors of low achievement are well documented:

- With less access to routine and preventive health care, disadvantaged children have greater absenteeism (Aysola et al. 2011; Starfield 1997), and they cannot benefit from good schools if they are not present.
- With less literate parents, they are read to less frequently when young and are exposed to less complex language at home (Ayoub et al. 2009; Brooks-Gunn and Markman 2005).
- With less adequate housing, they rarely have quiet places to study and may move more frequently, changing schools and teachers (Mehana and Reynolds 2004; Raudenbush et al. 2011).
- With fewer opportunities for enriching after-school and summer activities, their background knowledge and organizational skills are less developed (Entwisle et al. 2000; Neuman and Celano 2001).
- With fewer family resources, their college ambitions are constrained (Johnson, In Progress).

As these and many other disadvantages accumulate, lower social class children inevitably have lower average achievement than middle-class children, even with the highest quality instruction.

When a school's proportion of students at risk of failure grows, the consequences of disadvantage are exacerbated.

In schools with high proportions of disadvantaged children,

- Remediation becomes the norm, and teachers have little time to challenge those exceptional students who can overcome personal, family, and community hardships that typically interfere with learning.
- In schools with high rates of student mobility, teachers spend more time repeating lessons for newcomers and have fewer opportunities to adapt instruction to students' individual strengths and weaknesses.
- When classrooms fill with students who come to school less ready to learn, teachers must focus more on discipline and less on learning.
- Children in impoverished neighborhoods are surrounded by more crime and violence and suffer from greater stress that interferes with learning (Buka et al. 2001; Burdick-Will et al. 2010; Farah et al. 2006).
- Children with less exposure to mainstream society are less familiar with the standard English that is necessary for their future success (Sampson et al. 2008).
- When few parents have strong educations themselves, schools cannot benefit from parental pressure for higher quality curriculum, children have few college-educated role models to emulate and have few classroom peers whose own families set higher academic standards.

Nationwide, low-income black children's isolation has increased. It is a problem not only of poverty but of race.

- The share of black students attending schools that are more than 90% minority has grown

from 34 to 39% from 1991 to 2011 (Orfield and Frankenberg 2014, Table 8; Orfield and Lee 2006, Table 3). In 1991, black students typically attended schools where 35% of their fellow students were white; by 2011, it had fallen to 28% (Orfield and Frankenberg 2014, Table 4; Orfield et al. 2012, Table 5).
- In 1988, black students typically attended schools in which 43% of their fellow students had low income; by 2006 it had risen to 59% (Orfield 2009).
- In cities with the most struggling students, the isolation is even more extreme. The most recent data show, for example, that in Detroit, the typical black student attends a school where 3% of students are white, and 84% are low income (Detroit Public Schools 2009, Enrollment Demographics as of 11/19/2009).

It is inconceivable that significant gains can be made in the achievement of black children who are so severely isolated.

This school segregation mostly reflects neighborhood segregation. In urban areas, low-income white students are more likely to be integrated into middle-class neighborhoods and less likely to attend school predominantly with other disadvantaged students. Although immigrant low-income Hispanic students are also concentrated in schools, by the third generation their families are more likely to settle in more middle-class neighborhoods. Illustrative is that Latino immigrants who had resided in California for at least 30 years had a 65% homeownership rate prior to the burst of the housing bubble (Myers 2008).[1] It is undoubtedly lower after the bubble burst, but still extraordinary.

The racial segregation of schools has been intensifying because the segregation of neighborhoods has been intensifying. Analyzing Census data, Rutgers University Professor Paul Jargowsky has found that in 2011, 7% of poor whites lived in high-poverty neighborhoods, where more than 40% of the residents are poor, up from 4% in 2000; 15% of poor Hispanics lived in such high-poverty neighborhoods in 2011, up from 14% in 2000; and a breathtaking 23% of poor blacks lived in high-poverty neighborhoods in 2011, up from 19% in 2000 (Jargowsky 2013).

In his 2013 book, *Stuck in Place* (2013), the New York University sociologist Patrick Sharkey defines a poor neighborhood as one where 20% of the residents are poor, not 40% as in Paul Jargowsky's work. A 20-percent-poor neighborhood is still severely disadvantaged. In such a neighborhood, many, if not most other residents are likely to have very low incomes, although not so low as to be below the official poverty line.

Sharkey finds that young African Americans (from 13 to 28 years old) are now ten times as likely to live in poor neighborhoods, defined in this way, as young whites—66% of African Americans, compared to 6% of whites (Sharkey 2013, p. 27, Fig. 2.1). What is more, for black families, mobility out of such neighborhoods is much more limited than for whites. Sharkey shows that 67% of African American families hailing from the poorest quarter of neighborhoods a generation ago continue to live in such neighborhoods today. But only 40% of white families who lived in the poorest quarter of neighborhoods a generation ago still do so (Sharkey 2013, p. 38, Fig. 2.6).

Considering all black families, 48% have lived in poor neighborhoods over at least two generations, compared to 7% of white families (Sharkey 2013, p. 39). If a child grows up in a poor neighborhood, moving up and out to a middle-class area is typical for whites but an aberration for blacks. Black neighborhood poverty is thus more multi-generational, while white neighborhood poverty is more episodic; black children in low-income neighborhoods are more likely than others to have parents who also grew up in such neighborhoods.

The implications for children's chances of success are dramatic: For academic performance, Sharkey uses a scale like the familiar IQ measure, where 100 is the mean and roughly 70% of children score about average, between 85 and 115. Using a survey that traces individuals and their offspring since 1968, Sharkey shows that children who come from middle-class (non-poor) neighborhoods and whose mothers also grew up in middle-class neighborhoods score an average of 104 on problem-solving tests. Children from poor neighborhoods whose mothers also grew up in poor neighborhoods score lower, an average of 96.

Sharkey's truly startling finding, however, is this: Children in poor neighborhoods whose mothers grew up in middle-class neighborhoods score an average of 102, slightly above the mean and only slightly below the average scores of children whose families lived in middle-class neighborhoods for two generations. But children who live in middle-class neighborhoods—yet whose mothers grew up in poor neighborhoods—score an average of only 98 (Sharkey 2013, p. 130, Fig. 5.5).

Sharkey concludes that "the parent's environment during [her own] childhood may be more important than the child's own environment." He calculates that "living in poor neighborhoods over two consecutive generations reduces children's cognitive skills by roughly eight or nine points . . . roughly equivalent to missing two to 4 years of schooling" (Sharkey 2013, pp. 129–131).

Integrating disadvantaged black students into schools where more privileged students predominate can narrow the black–white achievement gap. Evidence is especially impressive for long-term outcomes for adolescents and young adults who have attended integrated schools (e.g., Guryan 2001; Johnson 2011). But the conventional wisdom of contemporary education policy notwithstanding, there is no evidence that segregated schools with poorly performing students can be "turned around" while remaining racially isolated. Claims that some schools, charter schools in particular, "beat the odds" founder upon close examination. Such schools are structurally selective on non-observables, at least, and frequently have high attrition rates (Rothstein 2004, pp. 61–84). In some small districts, or in areas of larger districts where ghetto and middle-class neighborhoods adjoin, school integration can be accomplished by devices such as magnet schools, controlled choice, and attendance zone manipulations. But for African American students living in the ghettos of large cities, far distant from middle-class suburbs, the racial isolation of their schools cannot be remedied without undoing the racial isolation of the neighborhoods in which they are located.

The Myth of de facto Segregation

In 2007, the Supreme Court made integration even more difficult than it already was, when the Court prohibited the Louisville and Seattle school districts from making racial balance a factor in assigning students to schools, in situations where applicant numbers exceeded available seats (Parents Involved in Community Schools v. Seattle School District No. 1 2007).

The plurality opinion by Chief Justice John Roberts decreed that student categorization by race (for purposes of administering a choice program) is unconstitutional unless it is designed to reverse effects of explicit rules that segregated students by race. Desegregation efforts, he stated, are impermissible if students are racially isolated, not as the result of government policy but because of societal discrimination, economic characteristics, or what Justice Clarence Thomas, in his concurring opinion, termed "any number of innocent private decisions, including voluntary housing choices."

In Roberts' terminology, commonly accepted by policymakers from across the political spectrum, constitutionally forbidden segregation established by federal, state or local government action is de jure, while racial isolation independent of state action, as, in Roberts' view, in Louisville and Seattle, is de facto.

It is generally accepted today, even by sophisticated policymakers, that black students' racial isolation is now de facto, with no constitutional remedy—not only in Louisville and Seattle, but in all metropolitan areas, North and South.

Even the liberal dissenters in the Louisville–Seattle case, led by Justice Stephen Breyer, agreed with this characterization. Breyer argued that

school districts should be permitted voluntarily to address de facto racial homogeneity, even if not constitutionally required to do so. But he accepted that for the most part, Louisville and Seattle schools were not segregated by state action and thus not constitutionally required to desegregate.

This is a dubious proposition. Certainly, Northern schools have not been segregated by policies assigning blacks to some schools and whites to others—at least not since the 1940s; they are segregated because their neighborhoods are racially homogenous.

But neighborhoods did not get that way from "innocent private decisions" or, as the late Justice Potter Stewart once put it, from "unknown and perhaps unknowable factors such as in-migration, birth rates, economic changes, or cumulative acts of private racial fears" (Milliken v. Bradley 1974).

In truth, residential segregation's causes are both knowable and known—twentieth century federal, state and local policies explicitly designed to separate the races and whose effects endure today. In any meaningful sense, neighborhoods and in consequence, schools, have been segregated de jure. The notion of de facto segregation is a myth, although widely accepted in a national consensus that wants to avoid confronting our racial history.

De jure Residential Segregation by Federal, State, and Local Government

The federal government led in the establishment and maintenance of residential segregation in metropolitan areas.

From its New Deal inception and especially during and after World War II, federally funded public housing was explicitly racially segregated, both by federal and local governments. Not only in the South, but in the Northeast, Midwest, and West, projects were officially and publicly designated either for whites or for blacks. Some projects were "integrated" with separate buildings designated for whites or for blacks. Later, as white families left the projects for the suburbs, public housing became overwhelmingly black and in most cities was placed only in black neighborhoods, explicitly so. This policy continued one originating in the New Deal, when Harold Ickes, President Roosevelt's first public housing director, established the "neighborhood composition rule" that public housing should not disturb the preexisting racial composition of neighborhoods where it was placed (Hirsch 1998/1983, p. 14; Hirsch 2000, p. 209; e.g., Hills v. Gautreaux 1976; Rothstein 2012). This was de jure segregation.

Once the housing shortage eased and material was freed for post–World War II civilian purposes, the federal government subsidized relocation of whites to suburbs and prohibited similar relocation of blacks. Again, this was not implicit, not mere "disparate impact," but racially explicit policy. The Federal Housing and Veterans Administrations recruited a nationwide cadre of mass-production builders who constructed developments on the East Coast like the Levittowns in Long Island, Pennsylvania, New Jersey, and Delaware; on the West Coast like Lakewood and Panorama City in the Los Angeles area, Westlake (Daly City) in the San Francisco Bay Area, and several Seattle suburbs developed by William and Bertha Boeing; and in numerous other metropolises in between. These builders received federal loan guarantees *on explicit condition* that no sales be made to blacks and that each individual deed include a prohibition on re-sales to blacks, or to what the FHA described as an "incompatible racial element" (FHA 1938; Jackson 1985, pp. 207–209, 238; e.g., Silva 2009). This was de jure segregation.

In addition to guaranteeing construction loans taken out by mass-production suburban developers, the FHA, as a matter of explicit policy, also refused to insure individual mortgages for African Americans in white neighborhoods, or even to whites in neighborhoods that the FHA considered subject to possible integration in the future (Hirsch 2000, pp. 208, 211–212). This was de jure segregation.

Although a 1948 Supreme Court ruling barred courts from enforcing racial deed restrictions, the restrictions themselves were deemed lawful for another 30 years and the FHA knowingly continued, until the Fair Housing Act was passed in 1968, to finance developers who constructed suburban developments that were closed to African Americans (Hirsch 2000, pp. 211–212). This was de jure segregation.

Bank regulators from the Federal Reserve, Comptroller of the Currency, Office of Thrift Supervision, and other agencies knowingly approved "redlining" policies by which banks and savings institutions refused loans to black families in white suburbs and even, in most cases, to black families in black neighborhoods—leading to the deterioration and ghettoization of those neighborhoods (see, e.g., USCCR 1961, pp. 36–37, 42–51). This was de jure segregation.

Although specific zoning rules assigning blacks to some neighborhoods and whites to others were banned by the Supreme Court in 1917, explicit racial zoning in some cities was enforced until the 1960s. The Court's 1917 decision was not based on equal protection but on the property rights of white owners to sell to whomever they pleased. Several large cities interpreted the ruling as inapplicable to their racial zoning laws because they prohibited only residence of blacks in white neighborhoods, not ownership. Some cities, Miami the most conspicuous example, continued to include racial zones in their master plans and issued development permits accordingly, even though neighborhoods themselves were not explicitly zoned for racial groups (Mohl 1987, 2001). This was de jure segregation.

In other cities, following the 1917 Supreme Court decision, mayors and other public officials took the lead in organizing homeowners associations for the purpose of enacting racial deed restrictions. Baltimore is one example where the mayor organized a municipal Committee on Segregation to maintain racial zones without an explicit ordinance that would violate the 1917 decision (Power 1986, 2004). This was de jure segregation.

In the 1980s, the Internal Revenue Service revoked the tax-exemption of Bob Jones University because it prohibited interracial dating. The IRS believed it was constitutionally required to refuse a tax subsidy to a university with racist practices. Yet the IRS never challenged the pervasive use of tax-favoritism by universities, churches, and other non-profit organizations and institutions to enforce racial segregation. The IRS extended tax exemptions not only to churches where such associations were frequently based and whose clergy were their officers, but to the associations themselves, although their racial purposes were explicit and well known. This was de jure segregation.

Churches were not alone in benefitting from unconstitutional tax exemptions. Robert Hutchins, known to educators for reforms elevating the liberal arts in higher education, was president and chancellor of the tax-exempt University of Chicago from 1929 to 1951. He directed the University to sponsor neighborhood associations to enforce racially restrictive deeds in its nearby Hyde Park and Kenwood neighborhoods, and employed the University's legal department to evict black families who moved nearby in defiance of his policy, all while the University was subsidized by the federal government by means of its tax-deductible and tax-exempt status (Hirsch 1998/1983, pp. 144–145; Plotkin 1999, pp. 122–125). This was de jure segregation.

Urban renewal programs of the mid-twentieth century often had similarly undisguised purposes: to force low-income black residents away from universities, hospital complexes, or business districts and into new ghettos. Relocation to stable and integrated neighborhoods was not provided; in most cases, housing quality for those whose homes were razed was diminished by making public housing high-rises or overcrowded ghettos the only relocation option (Hirsch 2000, pp. 217–222; Weaver 1948, p. 324; USCCR 1961, p. 96). This was de jure segregation.

Where integrated or mostly black neighborhoods were too close to white communities or central business districts, interstate highways were routed by federal and local officials to raze those neighborhoods for the explicit purpose of relocating black populations to more distant ghettos or of creating barriers between white and black neighborhoods. Euphemisms were thought less necessary then than today: according to the director of

the American Association of State Highway Officials whose lobbying heavily influenced the interstate program, "some city officials expressed the view in the mid-1950's that the urban Interstates would give them a good opportunity to get rid of the local 'niggertown'" (Schwartz 1976, p. 481–485). This was de jure segregation.

For a sense of how federal policy was infused with segregationist impulses, consider the 1949 Congressional debate over President Harry S. Truman's proposal for a massive public housing program. Conservative Republicans, opposed to federal involvement in the private housing market, devised a "poison pill" guaranteed to defeat the plan. They introduced amendments in the House and Senate requiring that public housing be operated in a non-segregated manner, knowing that if such amendments were adopted, public housing would lose its Southern Democratic support and the entire program would go down to defeat.

The Senate floor leader of the housing program was the body's most liberal member, Paul Douglas, a former economist at the University of Chicago. Supported by other leading liberal legislators (Senator Hubert Humphrey from Minnesota, for example), Senator Douglas appealed on the floor of the Senate to his fellow Democrats and civil rights leaders, beseeching them to defeat the pro-integration amendment: "I should like to point out to my Negro friends what a large amount of housing they will get under this act . . . I am ready to appeal to history and to time that it is in the best interests of the Negro race that we carry through the housing program as planned, rather than put in the bill an amendment which will inevitably defeat it . . ."

The Senate and House each then considered and defeated proposed amendments that would have prohibited segregation and racial discrimination in federally funded public housing programs, and the 1949 Housing Act, with its provisions for federal finance of public housing, was adopted (Davies 1966, p. 108; Julian and Daniel 1989, pp. 668–669). It permitted local authorities in the North as well as the South to design separate public housing projects for blacks and whites, or to segregate blacks and whites within projects. And they did so.

Although there was an enormous national housing shortage at the time, one that denied millions of African Americans a decent place to live, it remains an open question whether it really was in their best interests to be herded into segregated projects, where their poverty was concentrated and isolated from the American mainstream.

It was not, however, federal policy alone that segregated the metropolitan landscape. State policy contributed as well.

Real estate is a highly regulated industry. State governments require brokers to take courses in ethics and exams to keep their licenses. State commissions suspend or even lift licenses for professional and personal infractions—from mishandling escrow accounts to failing to pay personal child support. But although real estate agents openly enforced segregation, state authorities did not punish brokers for racial discrimination, and rarely do so even today when racial steering and discriminatory practices remain (Galster and Godfrey 2005). This misuse of regulatory authority was, and is, de jure segregation.

Local officials also played roles in violation of their constitutional obligations. Public police and prosecutorial power was used nationwide to enforce racial boundaries. Illustrations are legion. In the Chicago area, police forcibly evicted blacks who moved into an apartment in a white neighborhood; in Louisville, the locus of *Parents Involved*, the state prosecuted and convicted (later reversed) a white seller for sedition after he sold his white-neighborhood home to a black family (Braden 1958). Everywhere, North, South, East, and West, police stood by while thousands (not an exaggeration) of mobs set fire to and stoned homes purchased by blacks in white neighborhoods, and prosecutors almost never charged well-known and easily identifiable mob leaders (Rubinowitz and Perry 2002). This officially sanctioned abuse of the police power also constituted de jure segregation.

An example from Culver City, a suburb of Los Angeles, illustrates how purposeful state action to promote racial segregation could be. During World War II, its state's attorney instructed the municipality's air raid wardens, when they went door-to-door advising residents to turn off lights to avoid providing guidance to Japanese bombers, also to solicit homeowners to sign restrictive covenants barring blacks from residence in the community ("Communiques from the housing front" 1943). This was de jure segregation.

Other forms abound of racially explicit state action to segregate the urban landscape, in violation of the Fifth, Thirteenth, and Fourteenth Amendments. Yet the term "de facto segregation," describing a never-existent reality, persists among otherwise well-informed advocates and scholars. The term, and its implied theory of private causation, hobbles our motivation to address de jure segregation as explicitly as Jim Crow was addressed in the South or apartheid was addressed in South Africa.

Private prejudice certainly played a very large role. But even here, unconstitutional government action not only reflected but helped to create and sustain private prejudice. In part, white homeowners' resistance to black neighbors was fed by deteriorating ghetto conditions, sparked by state action. Seeing slum conditions invariably associated with African Americans, white homeowners had a reasonable fear that if African Americans moved into their neighborhoods, these refugees from urban slums would bring the slum conditions with them.

Yet these slum conditions were supported by state action, by overcrowding caused almost entirely by the refusal of the federal government to permit African Americans to expand their housing supply by moving to the suburbs, and by municipalities' discriminatory denial of adequate public services (Colfax 2009; Kerner Commission 1968, pp. 14, 145, 273; Satter 2009). In the ghetto,

- garbage was collected less frequently,
- predominantly African American neighborhoods were re-zoned for mixed (i.e., industrial, or even toxic) use,

- streets remained unpaved,
- even water, power, and sewer services were less often provided.

This was de jure segregation, but white homeowners came to see these conditions as characteristics of black residents themselves, not as the results of racially motivated municipal policy.

The Continuing Effects of State Sponsored Residential Segregation

Even those who understand this dramatic history of de jure segregation may think that because these policies are those of the past, there is no longer a public policy bar that prevents African Americans from moving to white neighborhoods. Thus, they say, although these policies were unfortunate, we no longer have de jure segregation. Rather, they believe, the reason we do not have integration today is not because of government policy but because most African Americans cannot afford to live in middle-class neighborhoods.

This unaffordability was also created by federal, state, and local policy that prevented African Americans in the mid-twentieth century from accumulating the capital needed to invest in home ownership in middle-class neighborhoods, and then from benefiting from the equity appreciation that followed in the ensuing decades.

Federal labor market and income policies were racially discriminatory until only a few decades ago. In consequence, most black families, who in the mid-twentieth century could have joined their white peers in the suburbs, can no longer afford to do so.

The federal civil service was first segregated in the twentieth century, by the administration of President Woodrow Wilson. Under rules then adopted, no black civil servant could be in a position of authority over white civil servants, and in consequence, African Americans were restricted and demoted to the most poorly paid jobs (King 1995).

The federal government recognized separate black and white government employee unions well into the second half of the twentieth century. For example, black letter carriers were not admitted to membership in the white postal service union. Black letter carriers had their own union but the Postal Service would only hear grievances from the white organization ("Same work, different unions" 2011).

At the behest of Southern segregationist Senators and Congressmen, New Deal labor standards laws, like the National Labor Relations Act and the minimum wage law, excluded from coverage, for undisguised racial purposes, occupations in which black workers predominated (Katznelson 2013).

The National Labor Relations Board certified segregated private sector unions, and unions that entirely excluded African Americans from their trades, into the 1970s (Foner 1976; Hill 1977; Independent Metal Workers 1964).

State and local governments maintained separate, and lower, salary schedules for black public employees through the 1960s (e.g., Rothstein and Miles 1995).

In these and other ways, government played an important and direct role in depressing the income levels of African American workers below the income levels of comparable white workers. This, too, contributed to the inability of black workers to accumulate the wealth needed to move to equity-appreciating white suburbs.

Today (2010), median black family income is 61% of the white median, but black median family wealth (net worth or assets minus debts) is an astonishingly low 5% of the white median (Mishel et al. 2012, Tables 2.5 and 6.5). The wealth gap does not only reflect the desperate financial situation of the poorest disadvantaged families. Thomas Shapiro, co-author of *Black Wealth/White Wealth* (1995), has estimated the relative wealth by race for *middle-class* families. Calculating relative wealth for black and white families with annual incomes of $60,000—slightly above the national median—from his most recent data in 2007, he found that black middle-class wealth was only 22% of whites' (T. Shapiro, personal communication, May 3, 2014). This gap has undoubtedly widened since 2007 because the housing collapse harmed blacks—who were targeted disproportionately for exploitative subprime loans and exposed to foreclosure—more than whites.

In short, middle-class African Americans and whites are in different financial straits. Total family wealth (including the ability to borrow from home equity) has more impact than income on high school graduates' ability to afford college. Wealth also influences children's early expectations that they will attend and complete college. White middle-class children are more likely to prepare for, apply to, and graduate from college than black children with similar family incomes. This widely acknowledged difference in educational outcomes is, in considerable part, the enduring effect of de jure segregated housing policies of the twentieth century, policies that prevented African Americans from accumulating, and bequeathing, wealth that they might otherwise have gained from appreciating real estate.

Levittown, described above as a Long Island suburban development built with federal financing and restricted to whites, illustrates these enduring effects. William Levitt sold his houses to whites in 1947 for $7,000, about two and a half times the national median family income (Jackson 1985, pp. 231–245; Williamson 2005). White veterans could get VA or FHA loans with no down payments. Today, these homes typically sell for $400,000, about six times the median income, and FHA loans require 20% down. Although African Americans are now permitted to purchase in Levittown, it has become unaffordable. By 2010 Levittown, in a metropolitan region with a large black population, was still <1% black. White Levittowners can today easily save for college. Blacks denied access to the community are much less likely to be able to do so.

Segregation in many other suburbs is now locked in place by exclusionary zoning laws— requiring large setbacks, prohibiting multi-family construction, or specifying minimum square footage—in suburbs where black families once could have afforded to move in the absence of official segregation, but can afford to do so no longer with property values appreciated.

Mid-twentieth century policies of de jure racial segregation continue to have impact in other ways as well. A history of state-sponsored violence to keep African Americans in their ghettos cannot help but influence the present-day reluctance of many black families to integrate.

Today, when facially race-neutral housing or redevelopment policies have a disparate impact on African Americans, that impact is inextricably intertwined with the state-sponsored system of residential segregation that we established.

Miseducating Our Youth

Reacquainting ourselves with that history is a step towards confronting it. When knowledge of that history becomes commonplace, we will conclude that *Parents Involved* was wrongly decided by the Supreme Court in 2007: Louisville, Seattle and other racially segregated metropolitan areas not only have permission, but a constitutional obligation to integrate.

But this obligation cannot be fulfilled by school districts alone. As noted above, in some small cities, and in some racial border areas, some racial school integration can be accomplished by adjusting attendance zones, establishing magnet schools, or offering more parent–student choice. This is especially true—but only temporarily—where neighborhoods are in transition, either from gradual urban gentrification, or in first-ring suburbs to which urban ghetto populations are being displaced. These school integration policies are worth pursuing, but generally, our most distressed ghettos are too far distant from truly middle-class communities for school integration to occur without racially explicit policies of residential desegregation. Many ghettos are now so geographically isolated from white suburbs that voluntary choice, magnet schools, or fiddling with school attendance zones can no longer enable many low-income black children to attend predominantly middle-class schools (Rothstein and Santow 2012).

Instead, narrowing the achievement gap will also require housing desegregation, which history also shows is not a voluntary matter but a constitutional necessity—involving policies like voiding exclusionary zoning, placing scattered low and moderate income housing in predominantly white suburbs, prohibiting landlord discrimination against housing voucher holders, and ending federal subsidies for communities that fail to reverse policies that led to racial exclusion.

We will never develop the support needed to enact such policies if policymakers and the public are unaware of the history of state-sponsored residential segregation. And we are not doing the job of telling young people this story, so that they will support more integration-friendly policies in the future. Elementary and secondary school curricula typically ignore, or worse, misstate this story. For example,

- In over 1,200 pages of McDougal Littell's widely used high school textbook, *The Americans* (2007, p. 494), a single paragraph is devoted to twentieth century "Discrimination in the North." It devotes one passive-voice sentence to residential segregation, stating that "African Americans found themselves forced into segregated neighborhoods," with no further explanation of how public policy was responsible.
- Another widely used textbook, Prentice Hall's *United States History* (2010, pp. 916–917), also attributes segregation to mysterious forces: "In the North, too, African Americans faced segregation and discrimination. Even where there were no explicit laws, de facto segregation, or segregation by unwritten custom or tradition, was a fact of life. African Americans in the North were denied housing in many neighborhoods."
- *History Alive!* (2008, p. 423), a popular textbook published by the Teachers' Curriculum Institute, teaches that segregation was only a Southern problem: "Even New Deal agencies practiced racial segregation, especially in the South," failing to make any reference to what Ira Katznelson, in his 2013 *Fear Itself*, describes as FDR's embrace of residential segregation nationwide in return for Southern support of his economic policies.

Avoidance of our racial history is pervasive and we are ensuring the persistence of that avoidance for subsequent generations. For the public and policymakers, re-learning our racial history is a necessary step because remembering this history is the foundation for an understanding that aggressive policies to desegregate metropolitan areas are not only desirable, but a constitutional obligation. Without fulfilling this obligation, substantially narrowing the achievement gap, or opening equal educational opportunity to African Americans, will remain a distant and unreachable goal.

Notes

1. Compare to overall national rates in 2007 (in percents): all, 68; whites, 75; blacks, 47; Hispanics (all generations), 50 (U.S. Census Bureau 2014).

References

Alavosus, L. (Ed.). (2008). *History alive!: Pursuing American ideals.* Palo Alto: Teachers' Curriculum Institute.

Ayoub, C., O'Connor, E., Rappolt-Schlictmann, G., Vallotton, C., Raikes, H., & Chazan-Cohen, R. (2009). Cognitive skill performance among young children living in poverty: Risk, change, and the promotive effects of Early Head Start. *Early Childhood Research Quarterly, 24*(3), 289–305. doi:10.1016/j.ecresq.2009.04.001.

Aysola, J., Orav, E. J., & Ayanian, J. Z. (2011). Neighborhood characteristics associated with access to patient-centered medical homes for children. *Health Affairs, 30*(11), 2080–2089. doi:10.1377/hlthaff.2011.0656.

Braden, A. (1958). *The wall between.* New York, NY: Monthly Review Press.

Brooks-Gunn, J., & Markman, L. B. (2005). The contribution of parenting to ethnic and racial gaps in school readiness. *The Future of Children, 15*(1), 139–168.

Buka, S. L., Stichick, T. L., Birdthistle, I., & Earls, F. J. (2001). Youth exposure to violence: Prevalence, risks, and consequences. *American Journal of Orthopsychiatry, 71*(3), 298–310. doi:10.1037/0002-9432.71.3.298.

Burdick-Will, J., Ludwig, J., Raudenbush, S. W., Sampson, R. J., Sonbonmatsu, L., & Sharkey, P. (2010). Converging evidence for neighborhood effects on children's test scores: An experimental, quasi-experimental, and observational comparison. Paper prepared for the Brookings Institution *Project on social inequality and educational disadvantage: New evidence on how families, neighborhoods and labor markets affect educational opportunities for American children.* http://cas.uchicago.edu/workshops/education/files/2010/03/Burdick-Will-Ed-Workshop-20100301.pdf.

Colfax, R. N. (2009, Fall). *Kennedy v. City of Zanesville:* Making the case for water. *Human rights,* 36(4). American bar association. http://www.americanbar.org/publications/human_rights_magazine_home/human_rights_vol36_2009/fall2009/kennedy_v_city_of_zanesville_making_a_case_for_water.html.

Communiques from the housing front: Venice race-hate meet reported on. (1943, November 18). *California eagle,* 64(32), pp. 1–2. http://www.archive.org/details/la_caleagle_reel26.

Danzer, G. A., de Alva, J. J. K., Krieger, L. S., Wilson, L. E., & Woloch, N. (2007). *The Americans.* Evanston, IL: McDougal Littell.

Davies, R. O. (1966). *Housing reform during the Truman administration.* Columbia, MO: University of Missouri Press.

Detroit Public Schools. (2009). *Detroit city school district.* http://detroitk12.org/schools/reports/profiles/district_profile.pdf.

Entwisle, D. R., Alexander, K. L., & Olson, L. S. (2000). Summer learning and home environment. In R. D. Kahlenberg (Ed.), *A notion at risk: Preserving public education as an engine for social mobility* (pp. 9–30). New York, NY: Century Foundation Press.

Farah, M. J., Shera, D. M., Savage, J. H., Betancourt, L., Giannetta, J. M., Brodsky, N. L., et al. (2006). Childhood poverty: Specific associations with neurocognitive development. *Brain Research, 1110*(1), 166–174. doi:10.1016/j.brainres.2006.06.072.

FHA (Federal Housing Administration). (1938). *Underwriting manual: Underwriting and valuation procedure under Title II of the National Housing Act.* Excerpts in J. M. Thomas & M. Ritzdorf (Eds.). (1997). *Urban planning and the African American community: In the shadows* (pp. 282–284). Thousand Oaks, CA: Sage Publications.

Foner, P. S. (1976). *Organized labor and the black worker, 1619–1973.* New York, NY: International Publishers.

Galster, G., & Godfrey, E. (2005). By words and deeds: Racial steering by real estate agents in the U.S. in 2000. *Journal of the American Planning Association, 71*(3), 251–268.

Guryan, J. (2001). *Desegregation and black dropout rates.* Working Paper 8345, Cambridge, MA: National Bureau of Economic Research.

Hill, H. (1977). *Black labor and the American legal system.* Washington, DC: Bureau of National Affairs.

Hills v. Gautreaux. 425 U. S. 284 (1976).

Hirsch, A. R. (1998). *Making the second ghetto: Race and housing in Chicago, 1940–1960. (Original work published 1983).* Chicago, IL: University of Chicago Press.

Hirsch, A. R. (2000). Choosing segregation: Federal housing policy between Shelley and Brown. In J. F. Bauman, R. Biles, & K. M. Szylvian (Eds.), *From tenements to the Taylor Homes: In search of an urban housing policy in twentieth century America* (pp. 206–225). University Park, Pennsylvania: The Pennsylvania State University Press.

Independent Metal Workers, Local 1. 147 N.L.R.B. 1573 (1964).

Jackson, K. T. (1985). *Crabgrass frontier.* New York, NY: Oxford University Press.

Jargowsky, P. A. (2013). *Concentration of poverty in the new millennium: Changes in the prevalence, composition, and location of high-poverty neighborhoods.* The Century Foundation and Rutgers Center for Urban Research and Education. http://www.tcf.org/assets/downloads/Concentration_of_Poverty_in_the_New_Millennium.pdf.

Johnson, R. C. (2011). *Long-run impacts of school desegregation & school quality on adult attainments.* Cambridge, Massachusetts: Working Paper 16664. Cambridge, MA: National Bureau of Economic Research.

Johnson, R. C. (In Progress). *The impact of parental wealth on college enrollment & degree attainment: Evidence from the housing boom & bust.* Working Paper, 2012. University of California Berkeley: Goldman School of Public Policy. http://socrates.berkeley.edu/~ruckerj/RJabstract_ParentalWealth_KidCollege_12-11.pdf.

Julian, E. K., & Daniel, M. M. (1989). Separate and unequal: The root and branch of public housing segregation. *Clearinghouse Review, 23*, 666–676.

Katznelson, I. (2013). *Fear itself: The new deal and the origins of our time.* New York, NY: Liveright Publishing Corporation.

Kerner Commission (National Advisory Commission on Civil Disorders). (1968). *Report of the national advisory commission on civil disorders.* New York, NY: Bantam Books.

King, D. (1995). *Separate and unequal: Black Americans and the U.S. federal government.* Oxford, England: Clarendon Press.

Lapanksy-Werner, E. L., Levy, P. B., Roberts, R., & Taylor, A. (2010). *United States history.* Upper Saddle River, NJ: Pearson.

Mehana, M., & Reynolds, A. J. (2004). School mobility and achievement: A meta-analysis. *Children and Youth Services Review, 26*(1), 93–119. doi:10.1016/j.childyouth.2003.11.004.

Milliken v. Bradley, 418 U.S. 717 (1974).

Mishel, L., Bivens, J., Gould, E., & Shierholz, H. (2012). *The state of working America* (12th Edition). Washington, DC: The Economic Policy Institute. http://www.stateofworkingamerica.org/subjects/overview/?reader.

Mohl, R. A. (1987). Trouble in paradise: Race and housing in Miami during the New Deal era. *Prologue: The Journal of the National Archives, 19*(1), 7–21.

Mohl, R. A. (2001). Whitening Miami: Race, housing, and government policy in twentieth-century Dade County. *The Florida Historical Quarterly, 79*(3), 319–345.

Myers, D. (2008). Immigrants' contributions in an aging America. *Communities and Banking, 19*(3), 3–5. http://www.bostonfed.org/commdev/c&b/2008/summer/myers_immigrants_and_boomers.pdf.

Neuman, S. B., & Celano, D. (2001). Access to print in low-income and middle income communities: An ecological study of four neighborhoods. *Reading Research Quarterly, 36*(1), 8–26. doi: 10.1598/RRQ.36.1.1.

Orfield. G. (2009). *Reviving the goal of an integrated society: A 21st century challenge.* Los Angeles, CA: The Civil Rights Project/Proyecto Derechos Civiles. http://civilrightsproject.ucla.edu/research/k-12-education/ integration-and-diversity/reviving-the-goal-of-an-integrated-society-a-21st-century-challenge/orfield-reviving-the-goal-mlk-2009.pdf.

Orfield, G. & Frankenberg, E. (with Ee, J. & Kuscera, J.). (2014). *Brown at 60: Great progress, a long retreat and an uncertain future.* Los Angeles, CA: The Civil Rights Project/Proyecto Derechos Civiles. http://civilrightsproject.ucla.edu/research/k-12-education/integration-and-diversity/brown-at-60-great-progress-a-long-retreat-and-an-uncertain-future/Brown-at-60-051814.pdf.

Orfield, G., Kucsera, J., & Siegel-Hawley, G. (2012). *E pluribus . . . separation: Deepening double segregation for more students.* Los Angeles, CA: The Civil Rights Project/Proyecto Derechos Civiles. http://civilrightsproject.ucla.edu/research/k-12-education/integration-and-diversity/mlk-national/e-pluribus...separation-deepening-double-segregation-for-more-students/orfield_epluribus_revised_complete_2012.pdf.

Orfield, G. & Lee, C. (2006). *Racial transformation and the changing nature of segregation.* Cambridge, MA: The Civil Rights Project at Harvard University. http://civilrightsproject.ucla.edu/research/k-12-education/integration-and-diversity/racial-transformation-and-the-changing-nature-of-segregation/orfield-racial-transformation-2006.pdf.

Parents Involved in Community Schools v. Seattle School Dist. No. 1, 551 U.S. 701 (2007).

Plotkin, W. (1999). *Deeds of mistrust: Race, housing, and restrictive covenants in Chicago, 1900–1953.* Doctoral Dissertation. Retrieved from Proquest. (9941500).

Power, G. (1986, March). *The development of residential Baltimore, 1900–1930.* Paper presented at the Chancellor's Colloquium, University of Maryland at Baltimore.

Power, G. (2004). Meade v. Dennistone: The NAACP's test case to ". . . sue Jim Crow out of Maryland with the Fourteenth Amendment." *Maryland Law Review, 63*(4), 773–810. http://digitalcommons.law.umaryland.edu/cgi/viewcontent.cgi?article=3230&context=mlr.

Raudenbush, S. W., Jean, M., & Art, E. (2011). Year-by-year and cumulative impacts of attending a high-mobility elementary school on children's mathematics achievement in Chicago, 1995 to

2005. In G. J. Duncan & R. J. Mumane (Eds.), *Whither opportunity: Rising inequality, schools, and children's life chances* (pp. 359–376). New York, NY: Russell Sage Foundation.

Rothstein, R. (2004). *Class and schools: Using social, economic, and educational reform to close the Black–White Achievement Gap.* Washington, D.C. and New York, N.Y.: Economic Policy Institute and Teachers College Press.

Rothstein, R. (2012). Race and public housing: Revisiting the federal role. *Poverty and Race,* 21(6), 1–2; 13–17. http://prrac.org/newsletters/novdec2012.pdf.

Rothstein, R., & Miles, K. H. (1995). *Where's the money gone? Changes in the level and composition of education spending.* Washington, D.C.: The Economic Policy Institute. http://www.epi.org/page/-/old/books/moneygone.pdf.

Rothstein, R., & Santow, M. (2012). *A different kind of choice.* Working Paper. Washington, D.C.: The Economic Policy Institute. http://www.epi.org/files/2012/Different_Kind_Of_Choice.pdf.

Rubinowitz, L. S., & Perry, I. (2002). Crimes without punishment: White neighbors' resistance to black entry. *Journal of Criminal Law and Criminology,* 92(2), 335–428.

Same work, different unions: Carriers content with legacy of segregation. (2011, June). *Postal Record,* 8–13. National Association of letter carriers. http://www.nalc.org/news/precord/ArticlesPDF/june2011/06-2011_segregation.pdf.

Sampson, R. J., Sharkey, P., & Raudenbush, S. W. (2008). Durable effects of concentrated disadvantage on verbal ability among African American children. *Proceedings of the National Academy of Sciences,* 105(3), 845–852. doi:10.1073/pnas.0710189104.

Satter, B. (2009). *Family properties: Race, real estate, and the exploitation of black urban America.* New York, NY: Metropolitan Books.

Schwartz, G. T. (1976). Urban freeways and the interstate system. *Southern California Law Review,* 49(3), 406–513.

Sharkey, P. (2013). *Stuck in place: Urban neighborhoods and the end of progress toward racial equality.* Chicago, IL: University of Chicago Press.

Silva, C. (2009). *Racial restrictive covenants: Enforcing neighborhood segregation in Seattle.* Seattle Civil Rights and Labor History Project, University of Washington. http://depts.washington.edu/civilr/covenants_report.htm.

Starfield, B. (1997). Health indicators for preadolescent school-age children. In R. M. Hauser, B. V. Brown, & W. R. Prosser (Eds.), *Indicators of children's well-being* (pp. 95–111). New York, NY: Russell Sage Foundation.

U.S. Census Bureau (2014). *People and households, housing vacancies and homeownership (CPS/HVS), Historical tables. Table 16: Homeownership rates by race and ethnicity of householder:1994 to present.* Retrieved June 2, 2014 from http://www.census.gov/housing/hvs/data/histtabs.html.

USCCR (United States Commission on Civil Rights). (1961). *Book 4: Housing: 1961 Commission on Civil Rights report.* Washington, D.C.: Government Printing Office. http://www.law.umaryland. edu/marshall/usccr/documents/crl1961bk4.pdf.

Weaver, R. C. (1948). *The negro ghetto.* New York, NY: Russell & Russell.

Williamson, J. (2005). Retrofitting "Levittown." *Places Journal,* 17(2), 46–51. http://escholarship.org/uc/item/0r57v5j3.

Questions for Critical Thinking

1. How does Rothstein's discussion help you to see your own educational experience in new and different ways?

2. In what ways has your class influenced the quality of education that you have received?

3. What do you see as some solutions to the racial achievement gap in education? What do you think is the likelihood of such solutions occurring?

Civilize Them with a Stick

MARY CROW DOG AND RICHARD ERDOES

The following essay is taken from the autobiography of Mary Crow Dog, Lakota Woman, *written with Richard Erdoes, which recounts her experiences growing up Sioux in a white-dominated society. In this excerpt, she reflects on her personal experiences as a student in a boarding school run by the Bureau of Indian Affairs.*

> *. . . Gathered from the cabin, the wickiup, and the tepee,partly by cajolery and partly by threats; partly by bribery and partly by force, they are induced to leave their kindred to enter these schools and take upon themselves the outward appearance of civilized life.*
>
> —*Annual Report of the Department of Interior, 1901*

It is almost impossible to explain to a sympathetic white person what a typical old Indian boarding school was like; how it affected the Indian child suddenly dumped into it like a small creature from another world, helpless, defenseless, bewildered, trying desperately and instinctively to survive and sometimes not surviving at all. I think such children were like the victims of Nazi concentration camps trying to tell average, middle-class Americans what their experience had been like. Even now, when these schools are much improved, when the buildings are new, all gleaming steel and glass, the food tolerable, the teachers well trained and well intentioned, even trained in child psychology—unfortunately the psychology of white children, which is different from ours—the shock to the child upon arrival is still tremendous. Some just seem to shrivel up, don't speak for days on end, and have an empty look in their eyes. I know of an 11-year-old on another reservation who hanged herself, and in our school, while I was there, a girl jumped out of the window, trying to kill herself to escape an unbearable situation. That first shock is always there.

Although the old tiyospaye has been destroyed, in the traditional Sioux families, especially in those where there is no drinking, the child is never left alone. It is always surrounded by relatives, carried around, enveloped in warmth. It is treated with the respect due to any human being, even a small one. It is seldom forced to do anything against its will, seldom screamed at, and never beaten. That much, at least, is left of the old family group among full-bloods. And then suddenly a bus or car arrives, full of strangers, usually white strangers, who yank the child out of the arms of those who love it, taking it screaming to the boarding school. The only word I can think of for what is done to these children is kidnapping.

Even now, in a good school, there is impersonality instead of close human contact; a sterile, cold atmosphere, an unfamiliar routine, language problems, and above all the maza-skan-skan, that damn clock—white man's time as opposed to Indian time, which is natural time. Like eating when you are hungry and sleeping when you are tired, not when that damn clock says you must. But I was not taken to one of the better, modern schools. I was taken to the old-fashioned mission school at St. Francis, run by the nuns and Catholic fathers, built sometime around the turn of the century and not improved a bit when I arrived, not improved as far as the buildings, the food, the teachers, or their methods were concerned.

In the old days, nature was our people's only school and they needed no other. Girls had their toy tipis and dolls, boys their toy bows and arrows. Both rode and swam and played the rough Indian games together. Kids watched their peers and elders and naturally grew from children into adults. Life in the tipi circle was harmonious—until the whiskey peddlers arrived with their wagons and barrels of "Injun whiskey." I often wished I could have grown up in the old, before-whiskey days.

Oddly enough, we owed our unspeakable boarding schools to the do-gooders, the white Indian-lovers. The schools were intended as an alternative to the outright extermination seriously advocated by generals Sherman and Sheridan, as well as by most settlers and prospectors overrunning our land. "You don't have to kill those poor benighted heathen," the do-gooders said, "in order to solve the Indian Problem. Just give us a chance to turn them into useful farmhands, laborers, and chambermaids who will break their backs for you at low wages." In that way the boarding schools were born. The kids were taken away from their villages and pueblos, in their blankets and moccasins, kept completely isolated from their families—sometimes for as long as ten years—suddenly coming back, their short hair slick with pomade, their necks raw from stiff, high collars, their thick jackets always short in the sleeves and pinching under the arms, their tight patent leather shoes giving them corns, the girls in starched white blouses and clumsy, high-buttoned boots—caricatures of white people. When they

found out—and they found out quickly—that they were neither wanted by whites nor by Indians, they got good and drunk, many of them staying drunk for the rest of their lives. I still have a poster I found among my grandfather's stuff, given to him by the missionaries to tack up on his wall. It reads:

1. Let Jesus save you.
2. Come out of your blanket, cut your hair, and dress like a white man.
3. Have a Christian family with one wife for life only.
4. Live in a house like your white brother. Work hard and wash often.
5. Learn the value of a hard-earned dollar. Do not waste your money on giveaways. Be punctual.
6. Believe that property and wealth are signs of divine approval.
7. Keep away from saloons and strong spirits.
8. Speak the language of your white brother. Send your children to school to do likewise.
9. Go to church often and regularly.
10. Do not go to Indian dances or to the medicine men.

The people who were stuck upon "solving the Indian Problem" by making us into whites retreated from this position only step by step in the wake of Indian protests.

The mission school at St. Francis was a curse for our family for generations. My grandmother went there, then my mother, then my sisters and I. At one time or other every one of us tried to run away. Grandma told me once about the bad times she had experienced at St. Francis. In those days they let students go home only for one week every year. Two days were used up for transportation, which meant spending just five days out of 365 with her family. And that was an improvement. Before grandma's time, on many reservations they did not let the students go home at all until they had finished school. Anybody who disobeyed the nuns was severely punished. The building in which my grandmother stayed had three floors, for girls only. Way up in the attic were little cells, about five by five by ten feet. One time she was in church and instead of praying she was playing jacks. As punishment they took her to one of those little cubicles where she stayed in darkness because the windows had been boarded up. They left her there for a whole week with only bread and water for nourishment. After she came out she promptly ran away, together with three other girls. They were found and brought back. The nuns stripped them naked and whipped them. They used a horse buggy whip on my grandmother. Then she was put back into the attic—for two weeks.

My mother had much the same experiences but never wanted to talk about them, and then there I was, in the same place. The school is now run by the BIA—the Bureau of Indian Affairs—but only since about 15 years ago. When I was there, during the 1960s, it was still run by the Church. The Jesuit fathers ran the boys' wing and the Sisters of the Sacred Heart ran us—with the help of the strap. Nothing had changed since my grandmother's days. I have been told recently that even in the '70s they were still beating children at that school. All I got out of school was being taught how to pray. I learned quickly that I would be beaten if I failed in my devotions or, God forbid, prayed the wrong way, especially prayed in Indian to Wakan Tanka, the Indian Creator.

The girls' wing was built like an F and was run like a penal institution. Every morning at five o'clock the sisters would come into our large dormitory to wake us up, and immediately we had to kneel down at the sides of our beds and recite the prayers. At six o'clock we were herded into the church for more of the same. I did not take kindly to the discipline and to marching by the clock, left-right, left-right. I was never one to like being forced to do something. I do something because I feel like doing it. I felt this way always, as far as I can remember, and my sister Barbara felt the same way. An old medicine man once told me: "Us Lakotas are not like dogs who can be trained, who can be beaten and keep on wagging their tails, licking the hand that whipped them. We are like cats, little cats, big cats, wildcats, bobcats, mountain lions. It doesn't matter what kind, but cats who can't be tamed, who scratch if you step on their tails." But I was only a kitten and my claws were still small.

Barbara was still in the school when I arrived and during my first year or two she could still protect me a little bit. When Barb was a seventh grader she ran away together with five other girls, early in the morning before sunrise. They brought them back in the evening. The girls had to wait for two hours in front of the mother superior's office. They were hungry and cold, frozen through. It was wintertime and they had been running the whole day without food, trying to make good their escape. The mother superior asked each girl, "Would you do this again?" She told them that as punishment they would not be allowed to visit home for a month and that she'd keep them busy on work details until the skin on their knees and elbows had worn off. At the end of her speech she told each girl, "Get up from this chair and lean over it." She then lifted the girls' skirts and pulled down their underpants. Not little girls either, but teenagers. She had a leather strap about a foot long and four inches wide fastened to a stick, and beat the girls, one after another, until they cried. Barb did not give her that satisfaction but just clenched her teeth. There was one girl, Barb told me, the nun kept on beating and beating until her arm got tired.

I did not escape my share of the strap. Once, when I was 13 years old, I refused to go to Mass. I did not want to go to church because I did not feel well. A nun grabbed me by the hair, dragged me upstairs, made me stoop over, pulled my dress up (we were not allowed at the time to wear jeans), pulled my panties down, and gave me what they called "swats"—25 swats with a board around which Scotch tape had been wound. She hurt me badly.

My classroom was right next to the principal's office and almost every day I could hear him swatting the boys. Beating was the common punishment for not doing one's homework, or for being late to school. It had such a bad effect upon me that I hated and mistrusted every white person on sight, because I met only one kind. It was not until much later that I met sincere white people I could relate to and be friends with. Racism breeds racism in reverse.

The routine at St. Francis was dreary. Six a.m., kneeling in church for an hour or so; seven o'clock, breakfast; eight o'clock, scrub the floor, peel spuds, make classes. We had to mop the dining room twice every day and scrub the tables. If you were caught taking a rest, doodling on the bench with a fingernail or knife, or just rapping, the nun would come up with a dish towel and just slap it across your face, saying, "You're not supposed to be talking; you're supposed to be working!" Monday mornings we had cornmeal mush, Tuesday oatmeal, Wednesday rice and raisins, Thursday cornflakes, and Friday all the leftovers mixed together or sometimes fish. Frequently the food had bugs or rocks in it. We were eating hot dogs that were weeks old, while the nuns were dining on ham, whipped potatoes, sweet peas, and cranberry sauce. In winter our dorm was icy cold while the nuns' rooms were always warm.

I have seen little girls arrive at the school, first graders, just fresh from home and totally unprepared for what awaited them, little girls with pretty braids, and the first thing the nuns did was chop their hair off and tie up what was left behind their ears. Next they would dump the children into tubs of alcohol, a sort of rubbing alcohol, "to get the germs off." Many of the nuns were German immigrants, some from Bavaria, so that we sometimes speculated whether Bavaria was some sort of Dracula country inhabited by monsters. For the sake of objectivity I ought to mention that two of the German fathers were great linguists and that the only Lakota–English dictionaries and grammars which are worth anything were put together by them.

At night some of the girls would huddle in bed together for comfort and reassurance. Then the nun in charge of the dorm would come in and say, "What are the two of you doing in bed together? I smell evil in this room. You girls are evil incarnate. You are sinning. You are going to hell and burn forever. You can act that way in the devil's frying pan." She would get them out of bed in the middle of the night, making them kneel and pray until morning. We had not the slightest idea what it was all about. At home we slept two and three in a bed for animal warmth and a feeling of security.

The nuns and the girls in the two top grades were constantly battling it out physically with fists, nails, and hair-pulling. I myself was growing from a kitten into an undersized cat. My claws were getting bigger and were itching for action. About 1969 or 1970 a strange young white girl appeared on the reservation. She looked about 18 or 20 years old. She was pretty and had long, blond hair down to her waist, patched jeans, boots, and a backpack. She was different from any other white person we had met before. I think her name was Wise. I do not know how she managed to overcome our reluctance and distrust, getting us into a corner, making us listen to her, asking us how we were treated. She told us that she was from New York. She was the first real hippie or Yippie we had come across. She told us of people called the Black Panthers, Young Lords, and Weathermen. She said, "Black people are getting it on. Indians are getting it on in St. Paul and California. How about you?" She also said, "Why don't you put out an underground paper, mimeograph it. It's easy. Tell it like it is. Let it all hang out." She spoke a strange lingo but we caught on fast.

Charlene Left Hand Bull and Gina One Star were two full-blood girls I used to hang out with. We did everything together. They were willing to join me in a Sioux uprising. We put together a newspaper which we called the *Red Panther*. In it we wrote how bad the school was, what kind of slop we had to eat—slimy, rotten, blackened potatoes for two weeks—the way we were beaten. I think I was the one who wrote the worst article about our principal of the moment, Father Keeler. I put all my anger and venom into it. I called him a goddam wasicun of a bitch. I wrote that he knew nothing about Indians and should go back to where he came from, teaching white children whom he could relate to. I wrote that we knew which priests slept with which nuns and that all they ever could think about was filling their bellies and buying a new car. It was the kind of writing which foamed at the mouth, but which also lifted a great deal of weight from one's soul.

On Saint Patrick's Day, when everybody was at the big powwow, we distributed our newspapers. We put them on windshields and bulletin boards, in desks and pews, in dorms and toilets. But someone saw us and snitched on us. The shit hit the fan. The three of us were taken before a board meeting. Our parents, in my case my mother, had to come. They were told that ours was a most serious matter, the worst thing that had ever happened in the school's long history. One of the nuns told my mother, "Your daughter really needs to be talked to." "What's wrong with my daughter?" my mother asked. She was given one of our *Red Panther* newspapers. The nun pointed out its name to her and then my piece, waiting for mom's reaction. After a while she asked, "Well, what have you got to say to this? What do you think?"

My mother said, "Well, when I went to school here, some years back, I was treated a lot worse than these kids are. I really can't see how they can have any complaints, because we was treated a lot stricter. We could not even wear skirts halfway up our knees. These girls have it made. But you should forgive them because they are young. And it's supposed to be a free country, free speech and all that. I don't believe what they done is wrong." So all I got out of it was scrubbing six flights of stairs on my hands and knees, every day. And no boy-side privileges.

The boys and girls were still pretty much separated. The only time one could meet a member of the opposite sex was during free time, between 4 and 5:30, in the study hall or on benches or the volleyball court outside, and that was strictly supervised. One day Charlene and I went over to the boys' side. We were on the ball team and they had

to let us practice. We played three extra minutes, only three minutes more than we were supposed to. Here was the nuns' opportunity for revenge. We got 25 swats. I told Charlene, "We are getting too old to have our bare asses whipped that way. We are old enough to have babies. Enough of this shit. Next time we fight back." Charlene only said, "Hoka-hay!"

* * *

In a school like this there is always a lot of favoritism. At St. Francis it was strongly tinged with racism. Girls who were near-white, who came from what the nuns called "nice families," got preferential treatment. They waited on the faculty and got to eat ham or eggs and bacon in the morning. They got the easy jobs while the skins, who did not have the right kind of background—myself among them—always wound up in the laundry room sorting out 10-bushel baskets of dirty boys' socks every day. Or we wound up scrubbing the floors and doing all the dishes. The school therefore fostered fights and antagonism between whites and breeds, and between breeds and skins. At one time Charlene and I had to iron all the robes and vestments the priests wore when saying Mass. We had to fold them up and put them into a chest in the back of the church. In a corner, looking over our shoulders, was a statue of the crucified Savior, all bloody and beaten up. Charlene looked up and said, "Look at that poor Indian. The pigs sure worked him over." That was the closest I ever came to seeing Jesus.

I was held up as a bad example and didn't mind. I was old enough to have a boyfriend and promptly got one. At the school we had an hour and a half for ourselves. Between the boys' and the girls' wings were some benches where one could sit. My boyfriend and I used to go there just to hold hands and talk. The nuns were very uptight about any boy–girl stuff. They had an exaggerated fear of anything having even the faintest connection with sex. One day in religion class, an all-girl class, Sister Bernard singled me out for some remarks, pointing me out as a bad example, an example that should be shown. She said that I was too free with my body. That I was holding hands which meant that I was not a good example to follow. She also said that I wore unchaste dresses, skirts which were too short, too suggestive, shorter than regulations permitted, and for that I would be punished. She dressed me down before the whole class, carrying on and on about my unchastity.

* * *

We got a new priest in English. During one of his first classes he asked one of the boys a certain question. The boy was shy. He spoke poor English, but he had the right answer. The priest told him, "You did not say it right. Correct yourself. Say it over again." The boy got flustered and stammered. He could hardly get out a word. But the priest kept after him: "Didn't you hear? I told you to do the whole thing over. Get it right this time." He kept on and on.

I stood up and said, "Father, don't be doing that. If you go into an Indian's home and try to talk Indian, they might laugh at you and say, 'Do it over correctly. Get it right this time!'"

He shouted at me, "Mary, you stay after class. Sit down right now!"

I stayed after class, until after the bell. He told me, "Get over here!" He grabbed me by the arm, pushing me against the blackboard, shouting, "Why are you always mocking us? You have no reason to do this."

I said, "Sure I do. You were making fun of him. You embarrassed him. He needs strengthening, not weakening. You hurt him. I did not hurt you."

He twisted my arm and pushed real hard. I turned around and hit him in the face, giving him a bloody nose. After that I ran out of the room, slamming the door behind me. He and I went to Sister Bernard's office. I told her, "Today I quit school. I'm not taking any more of this, none of this shit anymore. None of this treatment. Better give me my diploma. I can't waste any more time on you people."

Sister Bernard looked at me for a long, long time. She said, "All right, Mary Ellen, go home today. Come back in a few days and get your diploma." And that was that. Oddly enough, that priest turned out okay. He taught a class in grammar, orthography, composition, things like that. I think he wanted more respect in class. He was still young and unsure of himself. But I was in there too long. I didn't feel like hearing it. Later he became a good friend of the Indians, a personal friend of myself and my husband. He stood up for us during Wounded Knee and after. He stood up to his superiors, stuck his neck way out, became a real people's priest. He even learned our language. He died prematurely of cancer. It is not only the good Indians who die young, but the good whites, too. It is the timid ones who know how to take care of themselves who grow old. I am still grateful to that priest for what he did for us later and for the quarrel he picked with me—or did I pick it with him?—because it ended a situation which had become unendurable for me. The day of my fight with him was my last day in school.

Questions for Critical Thinking

1. As discussed by Crow Dog and Erdoes, policies and practices of educational institutions construct Native Americans and Native American culture as deviant. What other cultures are constructed as deviant by our educational institutions?

2. What are some of the ways that we expect marginalized groups to assimilate? How do the policies and practices of the educational institution foster this assimilation process?

3. What would our culture look like if we included the perspectives of Native Americans rather than requiring them to assimilate?

Missing in Interaction

MYRA SADKER AND DAVID SADKER

The following essay, by two authors who gained a national reputation for research and publications promoting equity in education, is from the book Failing at Fairness. *Their essay shows another world of segregation that exists within the K–12 classroom, one that is based on gender. Through their discussion they demonstrate the long-lasting impact on girls and women, boys and men as a result of the differences in treatment in schools.*

"Candid Camera" would have a field day in elementary school. There would be no need to create embarrassing situations. Just set the camera to take a photograph every sixty seconds. Since classroom action moves so swiftly, snapshots slow down the pace and reveal subliminal gender lessons.

Snapshot #1	Tim answers a question.
Snapshot #2	The teacher reprimands Alex.
Snapshot #3	Judy and Alice sit with hands raised while Brad answers a question.
Snapshot #4	Sally answers a question.
Snapshot #5	The teacher praises Marcus for skill in spelling.
Snapshot #6	The teacher helps Sam with a spelling mistake.
Snapshot #7	The teacher compliments Alice on her neat paper.
Snapshot #8	Students are in lines for a spelling bee. Boys are on one side of the room and girls are on the other.

As the snapshots continue, the underlying gender messages become clear. The classroom consists of two worlds: one of boys in action, the other of girls' inaction. Male students control classroom conversation. They ask and answer more questions. They receive more praise for the intellectual quality of their ideas. They get criticized. They get help when they are confused. They are the heart and center of interaction. Watch how boys dominate the discussion in this upper elementary class about presidents.

The fifth-grade class is almost out of control. "Just a minute," the teacher admonishes. "There are too many of us here to all shout out at once. I want you to raise your hands, and then I'll call on you. If you shout out, I'll pick somebody else."

Order is restored. Then Stephen, enthusiastic to make his point, calls out.

STEPHEN: I think Lincoln was the best president. He held the country together during the war.
TEACHER: A lot of historians would agree with you.

MIKE: (seeing that nothing happened to Stephen, calls out): I don't. Lincoln was okay, but my Dad liked Reagan. He always said Reagan was a great president.

DAVID: (calling out): Reagan? Are you kidding?

TEACHER: Who do you think our best president was, Dave?

DAVID: FDR. He saved us from the depression.

MAX: (calling out): I don't think it's right to pick one best president. There were a lot of good ones.

TEACHER: That's interesting.

KIMBERLY: (calling out): I don't think the presidents today are as good as the ones we used to have.

TEACHER: Okay, Kimberly. But you forgot the rule. You're supposed to raise your hand.

The classroom is the only place in society where so many different, young, and restless individuals are crowded into close quarters for an extended period of time day after day. Teachers sense the undertow of raw energy and restlessness that threatens to engulf the classroom. To preserve order, most teachers use established classroom conventions such as raising your hand if you want to talk.

Intellectually, teachers know they should apply this rule consistently, but when the discussion becomes fast-paced and furious, the rule is often swept aside. When this happens and shouting out begins, it is an open invitation for male dominance. Our research shows that boys call out significantly more often than girls. Sometimes what they say has little or nothing to do with the teacher's questions. Whether male comments are insightful or irrelevant, teachers respond to them. However, when girls call out, there is a fascinating occurrence: Suddenly the teacher remembers the rule about raising your hand before you talk. And then the girl, who is usually not as assertive as the male students, is deftly and swiftly put back in her place.

Not being allowed to call out like her male classmates during the brief conversation about presidents will not psychologically scar Kimberly; however, the system of silencing operates covertly

and repeatedly. It occurs several times a day during each school week for twelve years, and even longer if Kimberly goes to college, and, most insidious of all, it happens subliminally. This micro-inequity eventually has a powerful cumulative impact.

On the surface, girls appear to be doing well. They get better grades and receive fewer punishments than boys. Quieter and more conforming, they are the elementary school's ideal students. "If it ain't broke, don't fix it" is the school's operating principle as girls' good behavior frees the teacher to work with the more difficult-to-manage boys. The result is that girls receive less time, less help, and fewer challenges. Reinforced for passivity, their independence and self-esteem suffer. As victims of benign neglect, girls are penalized for doing what they should and lose ground as they go through school. In contrast, boys get reinforced for breaking the rules; they are rewarded for grabbing more than their fair share of the teacher's time and attention.

Even when teachers remember to apply the rules consistently, boys are still the ones who get noticed. When girls raise their hands, it is often at a right angle, arm bent at the elbow, a cautious, tentative, almost insecure gesture. At other times they raise their arms straight and high, but they signal silently. In contrast, when boys raise their hands, they fling them wildly in the air, up and down, up and down, again and again. Sometimes these hand signals are accompanied by strange noises, "Ooh! Ooh! Me! Me! Ooooh!" Occasionally they even stand beside or on top of their seats and wave one or both arms to get attention. "Ooh! Me! Mrs. Smith, call on me." In the social studies class about presidents, we saw boys as a group grabbing attention while girls as a group were left out of the action.

When we videotape classrooms and play back the tapes, most teachers are stunned to see themselves teaching subtle gender lessons along with math and spelling. The teacher in the social studies class about presidents was completely unaware that she gave male students more attention. Only after several viewings of the videotape did she notice how she let boys call out answers but repri-manded girls for similar behavior. Low-achieving boys also get plenty of attention, but more often it's negative. No surprise there. In general, girls receive less attention, but there's another surprise: Unlike the smart boy who flourishes in the class-room, the smart girl is the student who is least likely to be recognized.

When we analyzed the computer printouts for information about gender and race, an intriguing trend emerged. The students most likely to receive teacher attention were white males; the second most likely were minority males; the third, white females; and the least likely, minority females. In elementary school, receiving attention from the teacher is enormously important for a student's achievement and self-esteem. Later in life, in the working world, the salary received is impor-tant, and the salary levels parallel the classroom: white males at the top and minority females at the bottom. In her classroom interaction studies, Jacqueline Jordan Irvine found that black girls were active, assertive, and salient in the primary grades, but as they moved up through elementary school, they became the most invisible members of classrooms.

The "Okay" Classroom Is Not

In our studies of sexism in classroom interaction, we have been particularly fascinated by the ways teachers react to student work and comments because this feedback is crucially important to achievement and self-esteem. We found that teach-ers typically give students four types of responses.

TEACHER *praises:* "Good job." "That was an excel-lent paper." "I like the way you're thinking."
TEACHER *remediates,* encouraging a student to correct a wrong answer or expand and en-hance thinking: "Check your addition." "Think about what you've just said and try again."
TEACHER *criticizes,* giving an explicit statement that something is not correct: "No, you've

missed number four." This category also includes statements that are much harsher: "This is a terrible report."
TEACHER *accepts,* offering a brief acknowledge-ment that an answer is accurate: "Uh-huh." "Okay."

Teachers praise students only 10 percent of the time. Criticism is even rarer—only 5 percent of comments. In many classrooms teachers do not use any praise or criticism at all. About one-third of teacher interactions are comprised of remedia-tion, a dynamic and beneficial form of feedback.

More than half the time, however, teachers slip into the routine of giving the quickest, easi-est, and least helpful feedback—a brief nonverbal nod, a quick "Okay." They rely more on accep-tance than on praise, remediation, and criticism combined. The bland and neutral "Okay" is so pervasive that we doubt the "Okay Classroom" is, in fact, okay.

In our research in more than one hundred class-rooms, we found that while boys received more of all four reactions, the gender gap was greatest in the most precise and valuable feedback. Boys were more likely to be praised, corrected, helped, and criticized—all reactions that foster student achievement. Girls received the more superficial "Okay" reaction, one that packs far less educational punch. In her research, Jacqueline Jordan Irvine found that black females were least likely to receive clear academic feedback.

At first teachers are surprised to see video-tapes where girls are "Okay'd" and boys gain clear feedback. Then it begins to make sense. "I don't like to tell a girl anything is wrong because I don't want to upset her," many say. This vision of females as fragile is held most often by male teachers." What if she cries? I wouldn't know how to handle it."

The "Okay" response is well meaning, but it kills with kindness. If girls don't know when they are wrong, if they don't learn strategies to get it right, then they never will correct their mistakes. And if they rarely receive negative feedback in school, they will be shocked when they are confronted by it in the workplace.

Pretty Is—Handsome Does

Ashley Reiter, National Winner of the 1991 Westinghouse Talent Competition for her sophisticated project on math modeling, remembers winning her first math contest. It happened at the same time that she first wore her contact lenses. Triumphant, Ashley showed up at school the next day without glasses and with a new medal. "Everybody talked about how pretty I looked," Ashley remembers. "Nobody said a word about the math competition."

The one area where girls are recognized more than boys is appearance. Teachers compliment their outfits and hairstyles. We hear it over and over again—not during large academic discussions but in more private moments, in small groups, when a student comes up to the teacher's desk, at recess, in hallways, at lunchtime, when children enter and exit the classroom: "Is that a new dress?" "You look so pretty today." "I love your new haircut. It's so cute." While these comments are most prevalent in the early grades, they continue through professional education: "That's a great outfit." "You look terrific today."

Many teachers do not want to emphasize appearance. "They pull you in," a preschool teacher says. "The little girls come up to you with their frilly dresses and hair ribbons and jewelry. 'Look what I have,' they say and wait for you to respond. What are you supposed to do? Ignore them? Insult them? They look so happy when you tell them they're pretty. It's a way of connecting. I think it's what they're used to hearing, the way they are rewarded at home."

When teachers talk with boys about appearance, the exchanges are brief—quick recognition and then on to something else. Or teachers use appearance incidents to move on to a physical skill or academic topic. In one exchange, a little boy showed the teacher his shiny new belt buckle. Her response: "Cowboys wore buckles like that. They were rough and tough and they rode horses. Did you know that?"

When teachers talk to girls about their appearance, the conversations are usually longer, and the focus stays on how pretty the girl looks. Sometimes the emphasis moves from personal appearance to papers and work. When boys are praised, it is most often for the intellectual quality of their ideas. Girls are twice as likely to be praised for following the rules of form. "I love your margins" is the message.

The Bombing Rate

"How long do you wait for students to answer a question?" When we ask teachers to describe what they do hundreds of times daily in the classroom, their answers are all over the map: One minute. Ten seconds. Five seconds. Twenty-five seconds. Three seconds.

Mary Budd Rowe was the first researcher to frame this question and then try to answer it. Following her lead, many others conducted wait time studies and uncovered an astonishingly hurried classroom. On average, teachers wait only nine-tenths of a second for a student to answer a question. If a student can't answer within that time, teachers call on another student or answer the question themselves.

When questions are hurled at this bombing rate, some students get lost, confused, or rattled, or just drop out of the discussion. "Would you repeat that?" "Say it again." "Give me a minute. I can get it." Requests such as these are really pleas for more time to think. Nobody has enough time in the bombing rate classroom, but boys have more time than girls.

Waiting longer for a student to answer is one of the most powerful and positive things a teacher can do. It is a vote of confidence, a way of saying, "I have high expectations for you, so I will wait a little longer. I know you can get it if I give you a chance." Since boys receive more wait time, they try harder to achieve. As girls struggle to answer under the pressure of time, they may flounder and fail. Watch how it happens:

"Okay, class, get ready for your next problem. Mr. Warren has four cash registers. Each register weighs thirteen kilograms. How many kilograms do the registers weigh altogether? Linda?"

The teacher waits half a second. Linda looks down at her book and twists her hair. She says nothing in the half-second allotted to her.

"Michael?"

The teacher waits two seconds. Michael is looking down at his book. The teacher waits two more seconds. Michael says, "Fifty-two?"

"Good. Exactly right."

Less assertive in class and more likely to think about their answers and how to respond, girls may need *more* time to think. In the real world of the classroom, they receive less. For female achievement and self-esteem, it is a case of very bad timing.

Boy Bastions—Girl Ghettos

Raphaela Best spent four years as an observer in an elementary school in one of Maryland's most affluent counties. She helped the children with school-work, ate lunch with them, and played games with them in class and at recess. As an anthropologist, she also took copious notes. After more than one thousand hours of living with the children, she concluded that elementary school consists of separate and unequal worlds. She watched segregation in action firsthand. Adult women remember it well.

A college student recalled, "When I was in elementary school, boys were able to play basketball and kick ball. They had the side of the playground with the basketball hoops." Another college woman remembers more formal segregation: "I went to a very small grammar school. At recess and gym the boys played football and the girls jumped rope. All except one girl and one boy—they did the opposite. One day they were pulled aside. I'm not exactly sure what they were told, but the next day the schoolyard was divided in two. The boys got the middle and the girls got the edge, and neither sex was allowed on the other's part."

A third grader described it this way: "Usually we separate ourselves, but my teacher begins recess by handing a jump rope to the girls and a ball to the boys." Like the wave of a magic wand, this gesture creates strict gender lines. "The boys always pick the biggest areas for their games," she says. "We have what's left over, what they don't want."

Every morning at recess in schoolyards across the country, boys fan out over the prime territory to play kick ball, football, or basketball. Sometimes girls join them, but more often it's an all-male ball game. In the typical schoolyard, the boys' area is ten times bigger than the girls'. Boys never ask if it is their right to take over the territory, and it is rarely questioned. Girls huddle along the sidelines, on the fringe, as if in a separate female annex. Recess becomes a spectator sport.

Teachers seldom intervene to divide space and equipment more evenly, and seldom attempt to connect the segregated worlds—not even when they are asked directly by the girls.

"The boys won't let us play," a third grader said, tugging at the arm of the teacher on recess duty. "They have an all-boys club and they won't let any girls play."

"Don't you worry, honey," the teacher said, patting the little girl's hair. "When you get bigger, those boys will pay you all the attention you want. Don't you bother about them now."

As we observed that exchange, we couldn't help but wonder how the teacher would have reacted if the recess group had announced "No Catholics" or if white children had blatantly refused to play with Asians.

Barrie Thorne, a participant observer in elementary schools in California and Michigan whose students are mainly from working-class families, captured the tiny incidents that transform integrated classes into gender-divided worlds: Second-grade girls and boys eat lunch together around a long rectangular table. A popular boy walks by and looks the scene over. "Oooh, too many girls," he says, and takes a place at another table. All the boys immediately pick up their trays and abandon the table with girls, which has now become taboo.

Although sex segregation becomes more pervasive as children get older, contact points remain. School life has its own gender rhythm as girls and boys separate, come together, and separate again. But the points of contact, the together games that girls and boys play, often serve to heighten and solidify the walls of their separate worlds.

"You can't get me!" "Slobber Monster!" With these challenges thrown out, the game begins. It may be called "Girls Chase the Boys" or "Boys Chase the Girls" or "Chase and Kiss." It usually starts out one on one, but then the individual boy and girl enlist same-sex peers. "C'mon, let's get that boy." "Help, a girl's gonna get me!"

Pollution rituals are an important part of these chases. Children treat one another as if they were germ carriers. "You've got cooties" is the cry. (Substitute other terms for different cultures or different parts of the country.) Elaborate systems are developed around the concept of cooties. Transfer occurs when one child touches another. Prepared for such attack, some protect themselves by writing C.V. (cooties vaccination) on their arms.

Sometimes boys give cooties to girls, but far more frequently girls are the polluting gender. Boys fling taunts such as "girl stain" or "girl touch" or "cootie girl." The least-liked girls, the ones who are considered fat or ugly or poor, become "cootie queens," the real untouchables of the class, the most contaminating females of all.

Chasing, polluting, and invasions, where one gender attacks the play area of the other, all function as gender intensifiers, heightening perceived differences between female and male to an extreme degree. The world of children and the world of adults is composed of *different*

races, but each gender is socially constructed as so different, so alien that we use the phrase "the *opposite* sex."

It is boys who work hardest at raising the walls of sex segregation and intensifying the difference between genders. They distance themselves, sending the message that girls are not good enough to play with them. Watch which boys sit next to the girls in informally sex-segregated classrooms and lunchrooms; they are the ones most likely to be rejected by male classmates. Sometimes they are even called "girls." A student at The American University remembers his school lunchroom in Brooklyn:

> At lunch our class all sat together at one long table. All the girls sat on one side, and the boys sat on the other. This was our system. Unfortunately, there were two more boys in my class than seats on the boys' side. There was no greater social embarrassment for a boy in the very hierarchical system we had set up in our class than to have to sit on the girls' side at lunch. It happened to me once, before I moved up the class social ladder. Boys climbed the rungs of that ladder by beating on each other during recess. To this day, twenty years later, I remember that lunch. It was horrible.

Other men speak, also with horror, of school situations when they became "one of the girls." The father of a nine-year-old daughter remembered girls in elementary school as "worse than just different. We considered them a subspecies." Many teachers who were victims of sexist schooling themselves understand this system and collaborate with it; they warn noisy boys of a humiliating punishment: "If you don't behave, I'm going to make you sit with the girls."

Most little girls—five, six, seven, or eight—are much too young to truly understand and challenge their assignment as the lower-caste gender. But without challenge over the course of years, this hidden curriculum in second-class citizenship sinks in. Schools and children need help—intervention by adults who can equalize the playing field.

We have found that sex segregation in the lunch-room and schoolyard spills over into the classroom. In our three-year, multi-state study of one hundred classrooms, our raters drew "gender geography" maps of each class they visited. They found that more than half of the classes were segregated by gender. There is more communication across race than across gender in elementary schools.

We have seen how sex segregation occurs when children form self-selected groups. Sometimes the division is even clearer, and so is the impact on instruction.

> The students are seated formally in rows. There are even spaces between the rows, except down the middle of the room where the students have created an aisle large enough for two people standing side by side to walk down. On one side of the aisle, the students are all female; on the other side, all male. Black, white, Hispanic, and Asian students sit all around the room, but no student has broken the gender barrier.
>
> The teacher in the room is conducting a math game, with the right team (boys) against the left team (girls). The problems have been put on the board, and members of each team race to the front of the room to see who can write the answer first. Competition is intense, but eventually the girls fall behind. The teacher keeps score on the board, with two columns headed "Good Girls" and "Brilliant Boys."

The gender segregation was so formal in this class that we asked if the teacher had set it up. "Of course not." She looked offended. "I wouldn't think of doing such a thing. The students do it themselves." It never occurred to the well-meaning teacher to raise the issue or change the seats.

In our research we have found that gender segregation is a major contributor to female invisibility. In sex-segregated classes, teachers are pulled to the more talkative, more disruptive male sections of the classroom or pool. There they stay, teaching boys more actively and directly while the girls fade into the background.

The Character(s) of the Curriculum

At a workshop on sexism in the curriculum, we asked participants, "Have you ever read the book *I'm Glad I'm a Boy! I'm Glad I'm a Girl!*?" Since most of the teachers, principals, and parents had not read it, we showed it to them. *I'm Glad I'm a Boy! I'm Glad I'm a Girl!* is for very young children. One page shows the jobs and activities that boys can do, and the following page shows what is appropriate for girls.

The book announces that boys can be doctors and shows a large male cartoon character with a stethoscope around his neck.

"What do girls do?" we asked the audience.

"They're nurses," the parents and educators chorused as one. They may not have read this book, but they seemed to know the plot line. A little girl nurse pushing a wheelchair is drawn on the page.

"Obviously a case of occupational stereotyping with the girl receiving less of every kind of reward including money, but do you notice anything else?" we asked. Most of the people were puzzled, but a few spotted the subtlety: "Look at how little the girl is." When we showed both pages at once, the boy doctor, a cartoon version of Doogie Howser, towered over the girl pushing the wheelchair.

The next page shows boys as pilots. "What are girls?" we asked.

"Stewardesses," the audience called back. A cartoon girl with a big smile and a short skirt carries a tray of drinks. The audience chuckled as several people remarked, "Look, her underpants are showing." "A little cheesecake for the younger set," someone joked as the next picture emerged, a boy drawn as a policeman.

"What are girls?"

This one had the group confused. "Mommies?" "Criminals?" "Crossing guards?" "Meter maids?" They found it. A tough-looking female figure is shown writing out a ticket for an obviously miserable motorist caught in a parking violation. "She looks as if she's had a steroid treatment," a teacher joked. "She's very big this time." The images continued: boys as those who eat, and girls as the ones who cook; boys as the builders of homes, and girls as the ones who clean them. The picture accompanying the caption about cleaning is that of a smiling cartoon girl pushing a vacuum cleaner. She and the cleaning machine are drawn very large because there is so much work to do. This image upset the audience. "Oh, no," several groaned. Others hissed and booed.

The next caption identified boys as the ones who fix things.

"Girls break things," the audience chorused back. But this time the author had outsmarted them. "Break" was too active. The parents and educators tried other stereotypes: "Girls clean things?" "Play with things?" "Buy things?" "Girls cry over things?"

"These are great responses, but they're all too active."

"Girls watch boys?" an astute parent suggested. She was on to something. Several studies have shown that in basal readers the activity girls are most often engaged in is watching boys in action. They look at boys play baseball, admire them as they perform magic tricks, wave good-bye from behind windows as boys leave for adventure. But in this case even "watch" was too active. The audience was stumped.

"Girls are things!" a young woman burst out. She had actually outdone the author, so we displayed the page: GIRLS NEED THINGS FIXED. The smiling stationary figure is holding the wheel of her doll carriage in her hand. She isn't doing anything with the wheel; she is just standing there beside her tipped-over vehicle, clearly in need of male help. The audience groaned, but the pictures went on with boys shown as inventing while girls are described as using things boys invent. Accompanying this description is an illustration of a girl lying in a hammock and reading, thanks to a lamp invented by a boy. "Who invented the cotton gin?" we asked. Several people from around the room answered, "Eli Whitney." Like Alexander Graham Bell and Thomas Edison, this name is one of the staples of American education. "Has anyone ever

heard of Catherine Littlefield Greene?" The parents and teachers were silent.

We told the story of the woman who, after the death of her husband, Nathaniel, who had been a general in the Revolutionary War, met Eli Whitney. A Yale-educated tutor, Whitney devised a model for the gin while working at Greene's Mulberry Grove Mansion. But his design was flawed; although seeds were pulled from the cotton, they became clogged in the rollers. It was Kitty Greene who came up with the breakthrough idea of using brushes for the seeds. The concept of the machine was so simple that copycat gins sprang up on other plantations. To pay for lawsuits during the fierce battle for patent rights, Kitty Greene sold her estate. It wasn't until seven years later that Eli Whitney won full title to the cotton gin.

"Why wasn't the patent taken out in both names?" a history teacher asked. It was an excellent question, and in the answer is an important lesson for children. At a time when it was unseemly for women to write books (many female authors took male names), it was especially unlikely for a lady to patent an invention. Textbooks tell the story of the names registered in the patent office, but they leave out how sexism and racism denied groups of people access to that registry.

The caricature of gender roles isn't over, and the picture book moves from inventions to politics, showing boys as presidents and girls as their wives.

"Is this some kind of joke?" a teacher asked. "When was it written?"

We threw the question back at the audience.

"The 1920s?" someone called out.

"No, they didn't have stewardesses then. Or meter maids. I think it was the 1950s," another teacher suggested.

Most of the group were stunned to learn that the book was published in 1970 and was in circulation in libraries and schools for years afterward. Few teachers would read a book like this to children today, and if they did, the phone lines would light up in most communities. Twenty-five years ago, books like this were commonplace, and it is a sign of progress that today they are considered outrageous.

"This book is so bad, it's good," a kindergarten teacher said. "I want to show it to my class. A lot of my kids fly on planes and see male flight attendants, and one of my children has a mom who's a doctor."

We agreed that the book with its yesteryear sexism was a good teaching tool. We have shown it to students in every grade level. They had often read it critically and identified the stereotypes, but not always.

Balancing the Books

Few things stir up more controversy than the content of the curriculum. Teachers, parents, students—all seem to be aware intuitively that school-books shape what the next generation knows and how it behaves. In this case research supports intuition. When children read about people in nontraditional gender roles, they are less likely to limit themselves to stereotypes. When children read about women and minorities in history, they are more likely to feel these groups have made important contributions to the country. As one sixth grader told us, "I love to read biographies about women. When I learn about what they've done, I feel like a door is opening. If they can do great things, maybe I can, too."

Double Jeopardy

During the spring of 1992 we visited sixteen fourth-, fifth-, and sixth-grade classes in Maryland, Virginia, and Washington, D.C., and gave students this assignment:

In the next five minutes write down the names of as many famous women and men as you can. They can come from anywhere in the world and they can be alive or dead, but they must be real people. They can't be made up. Also—and this is very important— they can't be entertainers or athletes. See if you can name at least ten men and ten women.

At first the students write furiously, but after about three minutes, most run out of names. On average, students generate eleven male names but only three women's. While the male names are drawn directly from the pages of history books, the female names represent far greater student creativity: Mrs. Fields, Aunt Jemima, Sarah Lee, Princess Di, Fergie, Mrs. Bush, Sally Ride, and children's book authors such as Beverly Cleary and Judy Blume. Few names come from the pages of history. Betsy Ross, Harriet Tubman, Eleanor Roosevelt, Amelia Earhart, Sojourner Truth, Sacajawea, Rosa Parks, Molly Pitcher, and Annie Oakley are sometimes mentioned.

Several students cannot think of a single woman's name. Others have to struggle to come up with a few. In one sixth-grade class, a boy identified as the star history student is stumped by the assignment and obviously frustrated:

"Have you got any girls?" he asks, turning to a classmate.

"Sure. I got lots."

"I have only one."

"Think about the presidents."

"There are no lady presidents."

"Of course not. There's a law against it. But all you gotta do is take the presidents' names and put Mrs. in front of them."

In a fourth-grade class, a girl is drawing a blank. She has no names under her Women column. A female classmate leans over to help.

"What about Francis Scott Key? She's famous." The girl immediately writes the name down. "Thanks," she says. "I forgot about her."

As we are leaving this class, one girl stops us. "I don't think we did very well on that list," she says. "It was too bad you didn't let us put in entertainers. We could've put in a lot of women then. I wrote down Madonna anyway."

Given a time line extending from the earliest days of human history to current events, and given no geographic limits whatsoever, these upper-elementary schoolchildren came up with only a handful of women. The most any single child wrote was nine. In one class the total number of women's names given didn't equal ten. We were stunned!

Something was very wrong—was it with the textbooks? We decided to look at them more closely. During the summer of 1992 we analyzed the content of fifteen math, language arts, and history textbooks used in Maryland, Virginia, and the District of Columbia. When we counted pictures of males and females, we were surprised to find that the 1989 language arts textbooks from Macmillan and D.C. Heath had twice as many boys and men as girls and women. In some readers the ratio was three to one. A 1989 upper-elementary history textbook had four times as many male pictures as females. In the 1992 D.C. Heath *Exploring Our World, Past and Present,* a text for sixth graders, only eleven female names were mentioned, and not a single American adult woman was included. In the entire 631 pages of a textbook covering the history of the world, only seven pages related to women, either as famous individuals or as a general group. Two of the seven pages were about

Samantha Smith, a fifth-grade Maine student who traveled to the Soviet Union on a peace mission. While we felt that Samantha Smith's story brought an interesting message to other students, we wondered why Susan B. Anthony didn't rate a single line. No wonder students knew so little about women. Given the content of their history books, it was a tribute to their creativity that they could list any female names at all.

Every day in America little girls lose independence, achievement, and self-esteem in classes like this. Subtle and insidious, the gender-biased lessons result in quiet catastrophes and silent losses. But the casualties—tomorrow's women—are very real.

Questions for Critical Thinking

1. Reflecting on your own educational experience, in what ways were traditional gender roles reinforced in your schools? In what ways do you think you were given advantage or disadvantage because of being male or female? How do you think this has impacted you today?

2. Do you see evidence of gender bias in your college classes? If so, how do you think this impacts the ways in which women and men participate in the classroom?

3. If gender biases in the educational system were eliminated, how do you think this would impact the roles of women and men in larger society?

Black Men and the Struggle for Work
Social and Economic Barriers Persist

JAMES M. QUANE, WILLIAM JULIUS WILSON, AND JACKELYN HWANG

The following essay explores the continued structural barriers to opportunity that disproportionately prevent economic self-sufficiency for poor black men and, as a result, poor black families. According to the authors, this necessitates an effective, coordinated response of government-funded institutions to support opportunities for economic self-sufficiency for the poor.

Driven by deep dissatisfaction with the economic and social condition of the black family, Daniel Patrick Moynihan hoped, with the release of his 1965 report, to stimulate a national discussion linking economic disadvantage and family instability. Although Moynihan focused on the structural causes of the fragmentation of the black family, critics associated his report with the "culture of poverty" thesis, which implies that poverty is passed from one generation to the next through learned behavior.

A number of those critics emphasized Moynihan's suggestion that the problem "may indeed have begun to feed on itself." From 1948 to 1962, the unemployment rate among black males and the number of Aid to Families with Dependent Children (AFDC) cases were positively correlated, but after 1962, the number of new AFDC cases continued to rise even as black male unemployment declined. "With this one statistical correlation, by far the most highly publicized in the Report," states historian Alice O'Connor, "Moynihan sealed the argument that the 'pathology' had become self-perpetuation."

Still, Moynihan's main concern in the report involved black exclusion from opportunities that fortify economic self-sufficiency. Unlike conservative analysts, he combined economic and cultural explanations for the persistence of poverty. Nevertheless, the controversy that surrounded the report undermined for decades serious research on the complexity of the problem.

A 1987 study by one of this article's authors, William Julius Wilson's *The Truly Disadvantaged*, rekindled the debate with its discussion of institutional and cultural dynamics in the social transformation of the inner city. Research undertaken since that time has reinforced the need for more coordinated, government-directed efforts to dismantle structures that reinforce racial and class-based biases and inequalities. To this end, Moynihan's call for an expansion of such things as youth employment opportunities, improvements in high-quality education programs, greater housing options, and a broadening of income supplements to combat inequality is as pertinent today as it was in 1965.

Concentrated Disadvantage and Socialization in the Inner City

The Truly Disadvantaged chronicles the rise of poor black single women with children, the decline in marriage among the poor, the increase in concentrated urban black poverty, and escalating joblessness among young black males. It links sociodemographic changes in the inner city to shifts in the labor market, the outmigration of higher-income black and white families, and the concomitant decline in services available to poor black families left behind. The analysis suggests that in such neighborhoods, many households lack the resources necessary to sustain stable family life, but it links that fact to structural factors such as persistent exclusion from employment opportunities, social networks, and institutions that are essential for economic mobility.

Both Moynihan and subsequent researchers have acknowledged the critical significance of the family as the primary socializing influence on children and youth. The data show that the percentage of children growing up in single-parent homes has continued to increase. Trends are similar for all races and classes, but the percentages remain highest among families in poor, minority neighborhoods. Indeed, the issue is so acute that law professors June Carbone of the University of Minnesota and Naomi Cahn of George Washington University have recently opined that "marriage has disappeared from the poorest communities" in the U.S.

The numbers by themselves are stark, but when considered in isolation, they do not provide a comprehensive understanding of the major social and economic forces buffeting inner-city black families. In particular, the dramatic mismatch between skill level and employment opportunities among black males has further undermined marriageability in the inner-city black community. In these neighborhoods, poor black children are increasingly likely to grow up in family units whose dire financial circumstances affect every aspect of their physical, emotional, and cognitive development. Their caregivers' abilities to envision and execute a concerted strategy to ensure their children escape poverty is constrained by their own social location, economic circumstances, and restricted access to information.

The Role of Institutions

Many of society's intermediary institutions, whether intended to support social and economic advancement or punish antisocial behavior, have a disproportionate impact on poor black families. Such organizations include public schools, social service agencies, and juvenile and criminal justice systems. Even at the earliest stages in their cognitive development, inner-city black children are less likely to be enrolled in a high-quality child-care arrangement, which puts them at an enormous disadvantage compared to their white and better-off counterparts. Low-income caregivers do not have access to a broad range of choices among high-quality providers of this crucial service. Compared to their higher-income neighbors, caregivers in poorer communities have fewer options when it comes to the provision of regulated child care, and these programs are also disproportionately more likely to experience funding cuts during periods of austerity. Child-care choices among poor inner-city residents are also constrained by issues of trust and safety that often outweigh quality. Inadequate preschool education has important implications for the social and academic domains of child development, and the negative ramifications can last well into adulthood.

When they enter primary school, low-income, inner-city black youth are clustered in failing schools. They are more likely to be suspended or enrolled in special education classes, less likely to graduate from high school on time, and, indeed, more likely to drop out of school altogether.

Consequently, as they enter adulthood, many young blacks, particularly males, are less likely to enter the workforce or postsecondary educational institutions. Young black males have experienced unemployment and been disconnected from schools and vocational institutions at rates ranging from 20 to 32 percent. By 2011, after the end of the last recession, more than one-quarter of young black males were neither employed nor enrolled in school or vocational educational training. The rates for white and Hispanic young people were also very high, around 20 percent, but throughout most of the past few decades rates of disconnection among black youth have been higher than for the other two groups.

Furthermore, many government institutions that have an impact on the lives of poor black families focus more on regulating and controlling behavior than on improving skills and providing opportunity. Poor families who qualify for cash or noncash means-tested benefits are disproportionately exposed to rules that inhibit job seeking and discourage two-parent households.

Moreover, black youth are more likely than their peers to be confined in secure detention and correctional facilities. Admittedly, detention rates since 1977 have been steadily declining for all youth. There are a number of plausible explanations for the decline, including the downward shift in the violent-crime rate among youth in recent years. And the juvenile justice system is now more focused on prevention and rehabilitation as opposed to the harsh sentencing approach of prior decades. That said, black youth, in comparison to white youth, are still disproportionately more likely to be arrested. Furthermore, young black arrestees, compared to their white counterparts, are also more likely to have their case formally adjudicated by the courts, and, following a hearing, they are disproportionately more likely to be placed in an out-of-home detention facility. Black youth were nearly five times as likely to be in detention or correctional facilities in 2011 than white youth.

Contact with school-based disciplinary committees and the juvenile justice system is just a harbinger of a much more ominous trend that is gutting low-income minority communities of their male residents. As a group, black men were six times more likely than white men to be incarcerated in 2010, and blacks constitute nearly half of all people jailed and imprisoned in the U.S. today. The difference between black and white incarceration rates for young men varies greatly by education level. Research conducted by sociologists Bruce Western and Becky Pettit shows a dramatic rise in incarceration rates for young black male high-school dropouts over time. By 2008, approximately 37 percent, or three in eight, were behind bars. The one bit of good news is the noticeable drop—from 11 to 9 percent from 2000 to 2008—in the detention rate of young black males with a high school diploma. Among blacks with some college, the rate falls to around 2 percent, similar to that for young men from other racial and educational backgrounds.

As a result of the escalating incarceration rates among less-educated black males, poor black children are more likely than white or Hispanic children to experience a period when at least one of their parents is incarcerated. Rates for black children with an incarcerated parent more than quadrupled from 1980 to 2008. It should also be noted that close to half of black children with fathers who were high school dropouts had an incarcerated father at some point. The overall implications, therefore, are that poor black children and youth in disadvantaged communities are embedded in family and institutional arrangements that result in socialization experiences that are fundamentally different from those of their peers.

The Role of Neighborhoods

Inner-city neighborhoods are often where all of these dynamics collide, yet youth exposed to these influences are expected to share the aspirations and expectations of their counterparts in better-off communities and to acquire the capacity to make the choices necessary to realize them. Low-income parents are often severely constrained in their ability to help guide their children's engagement with critical facilitators of upward mobility, such as schools, and it is left to youth themselves to formulate and exercise strategic choices that might prove to be avenues out of poverty. These youth are seriously impeded, however, as a result of the gap between the knowledge they accumulate in the restrictive social environment in which they operate and the skills and know-how they need to transcend it.

In high-poverty neighborhoods, the effect on negative youth outcomes increases significantly. Chronically poor neighborhoods, those with poverty rates at or above 40 percent, have higher rates of school dropout, teenage pregnancy, and crime, and lower scores on cognitive and verbal skill tests and health indicators among school-age children. Many poor black and Hispanic children remain disproportionately exposed to conditions in high-poverty neighborhoods with all their deleterious impacts on family well-being.

Between 1990 and 2000—a period of economic growth, tight labor markets, and changes in government welfare policies—the percentage of poor black children living in neighborhoods of concentrated poverty declined from 24 percent to 15 percent. The improvement was short-lived, however, and the concentration of poor black children in high-poverty neighborhoods began to increase again in the next decade. Although not as sharp, the trend line for all black children followed a similar pattern, showing the increased likelihood that black children across all socioeconomic strata reside in disadvantaged neighborhoods compared to poor and nonpoor white children.

The residential distribution of poor (and nonpoor) Hispanic children followed a somewhat different pattern from that of blacks, influenced, in part, by a 29 percent growth in this population since 2000 and their subsequent migration to less blighted regions in the U.S. Like black children, however, Hispanic children of any socioeconomic background are disproportionately more likely to live in high-poverty neighborhoods than white children.

Addressing the Need

Confronting poverty and inequality in the inner city requires that we recognize the complex, interrelated problems facing poor black families. This necessitates an effective, sustained, and coordinated mission of government-funded institutions to support opportunities for economic self-sufficiency among the poor, which has yet to be realized. Recently, the Obama administration funded numerous efforts to revitalize poor, under-resourced neighborhoods by expanding "ladders of opportunity" for youth of color. For example, Choice and Promise Neighborhoods, Promise Zones, and the Strong Cities, Strong Communities initiatives seek to enhance family and community ties and better embed households in networks of institutional supports to improve the in-school and extracurricular experiences of school-age children. Building on neighborhood-empowerment efforts dating from the 1960s, these initiatives seek to create enhanced social contexts that extend choice-making capacity and practical opportunities to act on them. Just as importantly, this emphasis on coalition building has motivated the formation of new alliances among important service providers and community-based organizations that recognize the enormous potential that such collaborations can realize.

Many of these initiatives represent innovative attempts by the federal government to bring the combined resources of inter-agency collaboration to bear on tackling intractable social problems. It is therefore surprising that a more concerted effort is not being made by the administration to tout its significant investments and advances in this regard, and articulate an overarching framework that integrates all of these initiatives and formulates a rationale for how they may complement and inform one another in a cohesive, long-range fashion.

Thus far, the Obama administration's efforts to address the social and physical isolation of disadvantaged and disenfranchised poor families of color lack the size and focus that Moynihan vigorously championed. Many of the administration's place-based strategies can best be considered as multisite demonstration programs, since they only reach a fraction of the beleaguered neighborhoods and disenfranchised children and youth that reside in them. Congress has seriously hampered the replication and expansion of these programs by refusing the administration's repeated requests for additional funds.

Fifty years ago, Moynihan worried that too much responsibility was being placed on community-action programs to address the problems of persistent family poverty. Moynihan implied that these initiatives only go part of the way toward influencing the choice sets available to the poor, as well as the actions such choices energize. Indeed, the combined effects of the multiple forces that we touched upon, ones that disproportionately prevail upon too many poor, urban children of color are not going to be solved by incremental approaches. Under current conditions, many societal institutions exacerbate the disadvantaged status of poor families rather than provide pathways to self-sufficiency and equality of opportunity. Increased efforts must be devoted to rectifying the large-scale fragmentation and lack of uniformity in the mission and practice of schools, social service agencies, and workforce development centers that are intended to support the social and economic mobility of disadvantaged families.

Regrettably, the misinterpretation and intense criticism of the implicit "culture of poverty" observations in Moynihan's report precluded a serious public discussion of the need to tackle these impediments to the progress of the poor. Even more regrettable, the need to acknowledge and address them is all the more urgent 50 years later.

Questions for Critical Thinking

1. How does the authors' discussion impact your own understanding of common notions of unemployment and poverty?
2. How does the authors' discussion of the social and economic barriers that persist broaden your understandings of the disproportionate amounts of poverty in African American communities?
3. The authors offer some strategies for addressing the problems of poverty and unemployment. What do you think of their strategies? What strategies would you offer?

Racializing the Glass Escalator

Reconsidering Men's Experiences with Women's Work

ADIA HARVEY WINGFIELD

Research on the experiences of men in what are usually seen as women's occupations, such as nursing, has long argued that they experience a glass escalator *effect where subtle aspects of the professions push men toward higher statuses. This next essay by sociologist Adia Harvey Wingfield further explores this issue, examining how intersections of gender and race work together to shape experiences for men of color in the traditionally feminine field of nursing. What she finds is that this phenomenon is racialized and not necessarily available to all.*

Sociologists who study work have long noted that jobs are sex segregated and that this segregation creates different occupational experiences for men and women (Charles and Grusky 2004). Jobs predominantly filled by women often require "feminine" traits such as nurturing, caring, and empathy, a fact that means men confront perceptions that they are unsuited for the requirements of these jobs. Rather than having an adverse effect on their occupational experiences, however, these assumptions facilitate men's entry into better paying, higher status positions, creating what Williams (1995) labels a "glass escalator" effect.

The glass escalator model has been an influential paradigm in understanding the experiences of men who do women's work. Researchers have identified this process among men nurses, social workers, paralegals, and librarians and have cited its pervasiveness as evidence of men's consistent advantage in the workplace, such that even in jobs where men are numerical minorities they are likely to enjoy higher wages and faster promotions (Floge and Merrill 1986; Heikes 1991; Pierce 1995; Williams 1989, 1995). Most of these studies implicitly assume a racial homogenization of men workers in women's professions, but this supposition is problematic for several reasons. For one, minority men are not only present but are actually overrepresented in certain areas of reproductive work that have historically been dominated by white women (Duffy 2007). Thus, research that focuses primarily on white men in women's professions ignores a key segment of men who perform this type of labor. Second, and perhaps more important, conclusions based on the experiences of white men tend to overlook the ways that intersections of race and gender create different experiences for different men. While extensive work has documented the fact that white men in women's professions encounter a glass escalator effect that aids their occupational mobility (for an exception, see Snyder and Green 2008), few studies, if any, have considered how this effect is a function not only of gendered advantage but of racial privilege as well.

In this article, I examine the implications of race–gender intersections for minority men employed in a female-dominated, feminized occupation, specifically focusing on Black men in nursing. Their experiences doing "women's work" demonstrate that the glass escalator is a racialized as well as gendered concept.

Theoretical Framework

In her classic study *Men and Women of the Corporation*, Kanter (1977) offers a groundbreaking analysis of group interactions. Focusing on high-ranking women executives who work mostly with men, Kanter argues that those in the extreme numerical minority are tokens who are socially isolated, highly visible, and adversely stereotyped. Tokens have difficulty forming relationships with colleagues and often are excluded from social networks that provide mobility. Because of their low numbers, they are also highly visible as people who are different from the majority, even though they often feel invisible when they are ignored or overlooked in social settings. Tokens are also stereotyped by those in the majority group and frequently face pressure to behave in ways that challenge and undermine these stereotypes. Ultimately, Kanter argues that it is harder for them to blend into the organization and to work effectively and productively, and that they face serious barriers to upward mobility.

Kanter's (1977) arguments have been analyzed and retested in various settings and among many populations. Many studies, particularly of women in male-dominated corporate settings, have supported her findings. Other work has reversed these conclusions, examining the extent to which her conclusions hold when men were the tokens and women the majority group. These studies fundamentally challenged the gender neutrality of the token, finding that men in the minority fare much better than do similarly situated women. In particular, this research suggests that factors such as heightened visibility and polarization do not necessarily disadvantage men who are in the minority.

While women tokens find that their visibility hinders their ability to blend in and work productively, men tokens find that their conspicuousness can lead to greater opportunities for leadership and choice assignments (Floge and Merrill 1986; Heikes 1991). Studies in this vein are important because they emphasize organizations—and occupations—as gendered institutions that subsequently create dissimilar experiences for men and women tokens (see Acker 1990).

In her groundbreaking study of men employed in various women's professions, Williams (1995) further develops this analysis of how power relationships shape the ways men tokens experience work in women's professions. Specifically, she introduces the concept of the glass escalator to explain men's experiences as tokens in these areas. Like Floge and Merrill (1986) and Heikes (1991), Williams finds that men tokens do not experience the isolation, visibility, blocked access to social networks, and stereotypes in the same ways that women tokens do. In contrast, Williams argues that even though they are in the minority, processes are in place that actually facilitate their opportunity and advancement. Even in culturally feminized occupations, then, men's advantage is built into the very structure and everyday interactions of these jobs so that men find themselves actually struggling to remain in place. For these men, "despite their intentions, they face invisible pressures to move up in their professions. Like being on a moving escalator, they have to work to stay in place" (Williams 1995, 87).

The glass escalator term thus refers to the "subtle mechanisms in place that enhance [men's] positions in [women's] professions" (Williams 1995, 108). These mechanisms include certain behaviors, attitudes, and beliefs men bring to these professions as well as the types of interactions that often occur between these men and their colleagues, supervisors, and customers. Consequently, even in occupations composed mostly of women, gendered perceptions about men's roles, abilities, and skills privilege them and facilitate their advancement. The glass escalator serves as a conduit that channels men in women's professions into the uppermost levels of the occupational hierarchy. Ultimately, the glass escalator effect suggests that men retain consistent occupational advantages over women, even when women are numerically in the majority (Budig 2002; Williams 1995).

Though this process has now been fairly well established in the literature, there are reasons to question its generalizability to all men. In an early critique of the supposed general neutrality of the token, Zimmer (1988) notes that much research on race comes to precisely the opposite of Kanter's conclusions, finding that as the numbers of minority group members increase (e.g., as they become less likely to be "tokens"), so too do tensions between the majority and minority groups. For instance, as minorities move into predominantly white neighborhoods, increasing numbers do not create the likelihood of greater acceptance and better treatment. In contrast, whites are likely to relocate when neighborhoods become "too" integrated, citing concerns about property values and racialized ideas about declining neighborhood quality (Shapiro 2004). Reinforcing, while at the same time tempering, the findings of research on men in female-dominated occupations, Zimmer (1988, 71) argues that relationships between tokens and the majority depend on understanding the underlying power relationships between these groups and "the status and power differentials between them." Hence, just as men who are tokens fare better than women, it also follows that the experiences of Blacks and whites as tokens should differ in ways that reflect their positions in hierarchies of status and power.

The concept of the glass escalator provides an important and useful framework for addressing men's experiences in women's occupations, but so far research in this vein has neglected to examine whether the glass escalator is experienced among all men in an identical manner. Are the processes that facilitate a ride on the glass escalator available to minority men? Or does race intersect with gender to affect the extent to which the glass escalator offers men opportunities in women's professions? In the next section, I examine whether and how the mechanisms that facilitate a ride on the glass escalator might be unavailable to Black men in nursing.[1]

Relationships with Colleagues and Supervisors

One key aspect of riding the glass escalator involves the warm, collegial welcome men workers often receive from their women colleagues. Often, this reaction is a response to the fact that professions dominated by women are frequently low in salary and status and that greater numbers of men help improve prestige and pay (Heikes 1991). Though some women workers resent the apparent ease with which men enter and advance in women's professions, the generally warm welcome men receive stands in stark contrast to the cold reception, difficulties with mentorship, and blocked access to social networks that women often encounter when they do men's work (Roth 2006; Williams 1992). In addition, unlike women in men's professions, men who do women's work frequently have supervisors of the same sex. Men workers can thus enjoy a gendered bond with their supervisor in the context of a collegial work environment. These factors often converge, facilitating men's access to higher-status positions and producing the glass escalator effect.

The congenial relationship with colleagues and gendered bonds with supervisors are crucial to riding the glass escalator. Women colleagues often take a primary role in casting these men into leadership or supervisory positions. In their study of men and women tokens in a hospital setting, Floge and Merrill (1986) cite cases where women nurses promoted men colleagues to the position of charge nurse, even when the job had already been assigned to a woman. In addition to these close ties with women colleagues, men are also able to capitalize on gendered bonds with (mostly men) supervisors in ways that engender upward mobility. Many men supervisors informally socialize with men workers in women's jobs and are thus able to trade on their personal friendships for upward mobility. Williams (1995) describes a case where a nurse with mediocre performance reviews received a promotion to a more prestigious specialty area because of his friendship with the (male) doctor in charge. According to the literature, building strong relationships with colleagues and supervisors often happens relatively easily for men in women's professions and pays off in their occupational advancement.

For Black men in nursing, however, gendered racism may limit the extent to which they establish bonds with their colleagues and supervisors. The concept of gendered racism suggests that racial stereotypes, images, and beliefs are grounded in gendered ideals (Collins 1990, 2004; Espiritu 2000; Essed 1991; Harvey Wingfield 2007). Gendered racist stereotypes of Black men in particular emphasize the dangerous, threatening attributes associated with Black men and Black masculinity, framing Black men as threats to white women, prone to criminal behavior, and especially violent. Collins (2004) argues that these stereotypes serve to legitimize Black men's treatment in the criminal justice system through methods such as racial profiling and incarceration, but they may also hinder Black men's attempts to enter and advance in various occupational fields.

For Black men nurses, gendered racist images may have particular consequences for their relationships with women colleagues, who may view Black men nurses through the lens of controlling images and gendered racist stereotypes that emphasize the danger they pose to women. This may take on a heightened significance for white women nurses, given stereotypes that suggest that Black men are especially predisposed to raping white women. Rather than experiencing the congenial bonds with colleagues that white men nurses describe, Black men nurses may find themselves facing a much cooler reception from their women coworkers.

Gendered racism may also play into the encounters Black men nurses have with supervisors. In cases where supervisors are white men, Black men nurses may still find that higher-ups treat them in ways that reflect prevailing stereotypes about threatening Black masculinity. Supervisors may feel uneasy about forming close relationships with Black men or may encourage their separation from white women nurses. In addition, broader, less gender-specific racial stereotypes could also shape the experiences Black men nurses have with white men bosses. Whites often perceive Blacks, regardless of gender, as less intelligent, hardworking, ethical, and moral than other racial groups (Feagin 2006). Black men nurses may find that in addition to being influenced by gendered racist stereotypes, supervisors also view them as less capable and qualified for promotion, thus negating or minimizing the glass escalator effect.

Suitability for Nursing and Higher-Status Work

The perception that men are not really suited to do women's work also contributes to the glass escalator effect. In encounters with patients, doctors, and other staff, men nurses frequently confront others who do not expect to see them doing "a woman's job." Sometimes this perception means that patients mistake men nurses for doctors; ultimately, the sense that men do not really belong in nursing contributes to a push "*out* of the most feminine-identified areas and *up* to those regarded as more legitimate for men" (Williams 1995, 104). The sense that men are better suited for more masculine jobs means that men workers are often assumed to be more able and skilled than their women counterparts. As Williams writes (1995, 106), "Masculinity is often associated with competence and mastery," and this implicit definition stays with men even when they work in feminized fields. Thus, part of the perception that men do not belong in these jobs is rooted in the sense that, as men, they are more capable and accomplished than women and thus belong in jobs that reflect this. Consequently, men nurses are mistaken for doctors and are granted more authority and responsibility than their women counterparts, reflecting the idea that, as men, they are inherently more competent (Heikes 1991; Williams 1995).

Black men nurses, however, may not face the presumptions of expertise or the resulting assumption that they belong in higher-status jobs. Black professionals, both men and women, are often assumed to be less capable and less qualified than their white counterparts. In some cases, these negative stereotypes hold even when Black workers outperform white colleagues (Feagin and Sikes 1994). The belief that Blacks are inherently less competent than whites means that, despite advanced education, training, and skill, Black professionals often confront the lingering perception that they are better suited for lower-level service work (Feagin and Sikes 1994). Black men in fact often fare better than white women in blue-collar jobs such as policing and corrections work (Britton 1995), and this may be, in part, because they are viewed as more appropriately suited for these types of positions.

For Black men nurses, then, the issue of perception may play out in different ways than it does for white men nurses. While white men nurses enjoy the automatic assumption that they are qualified, capable, and suited for "better" work, the experiences of Black professionals suggest that Black men nurses may not encounter these reactions. They may, like their white counterparts, face the perception that they do not belong in nursing. Unlike their white counterparts, Black men nurses may be seen as inherently less capable and therefore better suited for low-wage labor than a professional, feminized occupation such as nursing. This perception of being less qualified means that they also may not be immediately assumed to be better suited for the higher-level, more masculinized jobs within the medical field.

As minority women address issues of both race and gender to negotiate a sense of belonging in masculine settings (Ong 2005), minority men may also face a comparable challenge in feminized fields. They may have to address the unspoken racialization implicit in the assumption that masculinity equals competence. Simultaneously, they may find that the racial stereotype that Blackness equals lower qualifications, standards, and competence clouds the sense that men are inherently more capable and adept in any field, including the feminized ones.

Establishing Distance from Femininity

An additional mechanism of the glass escalator involves establishing distance from women and the femininity associated with their occupations. Because men nurses are employed in a culturally feminized occupation, they develop strategies to disassociate themselves from the femininity associated with their work and retain some of the privilege associated with masculinity. Thus, when men nurses gravitate toward hospital emergency wards rather than obstetrics or pediatrics, or emphasize that they are only in nursing to get into hospital administration, they distance themselves from the femininity of their profession and thereby preserve their status as men despite the fact that they do "women's work." Perhaps more important, these strategies also place men in a prime position to experience the glass escalator effect, as they situate themselves to move upward into higher-status areas in the field.

Creating distance from femininity also helps these men achieve aspects of hegemonic masculinity, which Connell (1989) describes as the predominant and most valued form of masculinity at a given time. Contemporary hegemonic masculine ideals emphasize toughness, strength, aggressiveness, heterosexuality, and, perhaps most important, a clear sense of femininity as different from and subordinate to masculinity (Kimmel 2001; Williams 1995). Thus, when men distance themselves from the feminized aspects of their jobs, they uphold the idea that masculinity and femininity are distinct, separate, and mutually exclusive. When these men seek masculinity by aiming for the better paying or most technological fields, they not only position themselves to move upward into the more acceptable arenas but also reinforce the greater social value placed on masculinity. Establishing distance from femininity therefore allows men to retain the privileges and status of masculinity while simultaneously enabling them to ride the glass escalator.

For Black men, the desire to reject femininity may be compounded by racial inequality. Theorists have argued that as institutional racism blocks access to traditional markers of masculinity such as occupational status and economic stability, Black men may repudiate femininity as a way of accessing the masculinity—and its attendant status—that is denied through other routes (hooks 2004; Neal 2005). Rejecting femininity is a key strategy men use to assert masculinity, and it remains available to Black men even when other means of achieving masculinity are unattainable. Black men nurses may be more likely to distance themselves from their women colleagues and to reject the femininity associated with nursing, particularly if they feel that they experience racial discrimination that renders occupational advancement inaccessible. Yet if they encounter strained relationships with women colleagues and men supervisors because of gendered racism or racialized stereotypes, the efforts to distance themselves from femininity still may not result in the glass escalator effect.

On the other hand, some theorists suggest that minority men may challenge racism by rejecting hegemonic masculine ideals. Chen (1999) argues that Chinese American men may engage in a strategy of repudiation, where they reject hegemonic masculinity because its implicit assumptions of whiteness exclude Asian American men. As these men realize that racial stereotypes and assumptions preclude them from achieving the hegemonic masculine ideal, they reject it and dispute its racialized underpinnings. Similarly, Lamont (2000, 47) notes that working-class Black men in the United States and France develop a "caring self" in which they emphasize values such as "morality, solidarity, and generosity." As a consequence of these men's ongoing experiences with racism, they develop a caring self that highlights work on behalf of others as an important tool in fighting oppression. Although caring is associated with femininity, these men cultivate a caring self because it allows them to challenge racial inequality. The results of these studies suggest that Black men nurses may embrace the femininity associated with nursing if it offers a way to combat racism. In these cases, Black men nurses may turn to pediatrics as a way of demonstrating sensitivity and therefore combating stereotypes of Black masculinity, or they may proudly identify as nurses to challenge perceptions that Black men are unsuited for professional, white-collar positions.

Taken together, all of this research suggests that Black men may not enjoy the advantages experienced by their white men colleagues, who ride a glass escalator to success. In this article, I focus on the experiences of Black men nurses to argue that the glass escalator is a racialized as well as a gendered concept that does not offer Black men the same privileges as their white men counterparts.

Findings

The results of this study indicate that not all men experience the glass escalator in the same ways. For Black men nurses, intersections of race and gender create a different experience with the mechanisms that facilitate white men's advancement in women's professions. Awkward or unfriendly interactions with colleagues, poor relationships with supervisors, perceptions that they are not suited for nursing, and an unwillingness to disassociate from "feminized" aspects of nursing constitute what I term *glass barriers* to riding the glass escalator.

Reception from Colleagues and Supervisors

When women welcome men into "their" professions, they often push men into leadership roles that ease their advancement into upper-level positions. Thus, a positive reaction from colleagues is critical to riding the glass escalator. Unlike white men nurses, however, Black men do not describe encountering a warm reception from women colleagues (Heikes 1991). Instead, the men

I interviewed find that they often have unpleasant interactions with women coworkers who treat them rather coldly and attempt to keep them at bay. Chris is a 51-year-old oncology nurse who describes one white nurse's attempt to isolate him from other white women nurses as he attempted to get his instructions for that day's shift:

> She turned and ushered me to the door, and said for me to wait out here, a nurse will come out and give you your report. I stared at her hand on my arm, and then at her, and said, "Why? Where do you go to get your reports?" She said, "I get them in there." I said, "Right. Unhand me." I went right back in there, sat down, and started writing down my reports.

Kenny, a 47-year-old nurse with 23 years of nursing experience, describes a similarly and particularly painful experience he had in a previous job where he was the only Black person on staff:

> [The staff] had nothing to do with me, and they didn't even want me to sit at the same area where they were charting in to take a break. They wanted me to sit somewhere else. . . . They wouldn't even sit at a table with me! When I came and sat down, everybody got up and left.

These experiences with colleagues are starkly different from those described by white men in professions dominated by women (see Pierce 1995; Williams 1989). Though the men in these studies sometimes chose to segregate themselves, women never systematically excluded them. Though I have no way of knowing why the women nurses in Chris's and Kenny's workplaces physically segregated themselves, the pervasiveness of gendered racist images that emphasize white women's vulnerability to dangerous Black men may play an important role. For these nurses, their masculinity is not a guarantee that they will be welcomed, much less pushed into leadership roles. As Ryan, a 37-year-old intensive care nurse says, "[Black men] have to go further to prove ourselves. This involves proving our capabilities, *proving to colleagues that you*

can lead, be on the forefront" (emphasis added). The warm welcome and subsequent opportunities for leadership cannot be taken for granted. In contrast, these men describe great challenges in forming congenial relationships with coworkers who, they believe, do not truly want them there.

In addition, these men often describe tense, if not blatantly discriminatory, relationships with supervisors. While Williams (1995) suggests that men supervisors can be allies for men in women's professions by facilitating promotions and upward mobility, Black men nurses describe incidents of being overlooked by supervisors when it comes time for promotions. Ryan, who has worked at his current job for 11 years, believes that these barriers block upward mobility within the profession:

> The hardest part is dealing with people who don't understand minority nurses. People with their biases, who don't identify you as ripe for promotion. I know the policy and procedure, I'm familiar with past history. So you can't tell me I can't move forward if others did. [How did you deal with this?] By knowing the chain of command, who my supervisors were. Things were subtle. I just had to be better. I got this mostly from other nurses and supervisors. I was paid to deal with patients, so I could deal with [racism] from them. I'm not paid to deal with this from colleagues.

Kenny offers a similar example. Employed as an orthopedic nurse in a predominantly white environment, he describes great difficulty getting promoted, which he primarily attributes to racial biases:

> It's almost like you have to, um, take your ideas and give them to somebody else and then let them present them for you and you get no credit for it. I've applied for several promotions there and, you know, I didn't get them. . . . When you look around to the, um, percentage of African Americans who are actually in executive leadership is almost zero percent. Because it's less than one percent of the total population of people that are in leadership, and it's almost like they'll go outside of the

system just to try to find a Caucasian to fill a position. Not that I'm not qualified, because I've been master's prepared for 12 years and I'm working on my doctorate.

According to Ryan and Kenny, supervisors' racial biases mean limited opportunities for promotion and upward mobility. This interpretation is consistent with research that suggests that even with stellar performance and solid work histories, Black workers may receive mediocre evaluations from white supervisors that limit their advancement (Feagin 2006; Feagin and Sikes 1994). For Black men nurses, their race may signal to supervisors that they are unworthy of promotion and thus create a different experience with the glass escalator.

Strong relationships with colleagues and supervisors are a key mechanism of the glass escalator effect. For Black men nurses, however, these relationships are experienced differently from those described by their white men colleagues. Black men nurses do not speak of warm and congenial relationships with women nurses or see these relationships as facilitating a move into leadership roles. Nor do they suggest that they share gendered bonds with men supervisors that serve to ease their mobility into higher-status administrative jobs. In contrast, they sense that racial bias makes it difficult to develop ties with coworkers and makes superiors unwilling to promote them. Black men nurses thus experience this aspect of the glass escalator differently from their white men colleagues. They find that relationships with colleagues and supervisors stifle, rather than facilitate, their upward mobility.

Perceptions of Suitability

Like their white counterparts, Black men nurses also experience challenges from clients who are unaccustomed to seeing men in fields typically dominated by women. As with white men nurses, Black men encounter this in surprised or quizzical reactions from patients who seem to expect to be treated by white women nurses. Ray, a 36-year-old oncology nurse with 10 years of experience, states,

> Nursing, historically, has been a white female's job [so] being a Black male it's a weird position to be in. . . . I've, several times, gone into a room and a male patient, a white male patient has, you know, they'll say, "Where's the pretty nurse? Where's the pretty nurse? Where's the blonde nurse?." . . . "You don't have one. I'm the nurse."

Yet while patients rarely expect to be treated by men nurses of any race, white men encounter statements and behaviors that suggest patients expect them to be doctors, supervisors, or other higher-status, more masculine positions (Williams 1989, 1995). In part, this expectation accelerates their ride on the glass escalator, helping to push them into the positions for which they are seen as more appropriately suited.

(White) men, by virtue of their masculinity, are assumed to be more competent and capable and thus better situated in (nonfeminized) jobs that are perceived to require greater skill and proficiency. Black men, in contrast, rarely encounter patients (or colleagues and supervisors) who immediately expect that they are doctors or administrators. Instead, many respondents find that even after displaying their credentials, sharing their nursing experience, and, in one case, dispensing care, they are still mistaken for janitors or service workers. Ray's experience is typical:

> I've even given patients their medicines, explained their care to them, and then they'll say to me, "Well, can you send the nurse in?"

Chris describes a somewhat similar encounter of being misidentified by a white woman patient:

> I come [to work] in my white uniform, that's what I wear—being a Black man, I know they won't look at me the same, so I dress the part—I said good evening, my name's Chris, and I'm going to be your nurse. She says to me, "Are you from housekeeping?" . . . I've had other cases. I've walked in and had a lady look at me and ask if I'm the janitor.

Chris recognizes that this patient is evoking racial stereotypes that Blacks are there to perform menial service work. He attempts to circumvent this very perception through careful self-presentation, wearing the white uniform to indicate his position as a nurse. His efforts, however, are nonetheless met with a racial stereotype that as a Black man he should be there to clean up rather than to provide medical care.

Black men in nursing encounter challenges from customers that reinforce the idea that men are not suited for a "feminized" profession such as nursing. However, these assumptions are racialized as well as gendered. Unlike white men nurses who are assumed to be doctors (see Williams 1992), Black men in nursing are quickly taken for janitors or housekeeping staff. These men do not simply describe a gendered process where perceptions and stereotypes about men serve to aid their mobility into higher-status jobs. More specifically, they describe interactions that are simultaneously raced *and* gendered in ways that reproduce stereotypes of Black men as best suited for certain blue-collar, unskilled labor.

These negative stereotypes can affect Black men nurses' efforts to treat patients as well. The men I interviewed find that masculinity does not automatically endow them with an aura of competency. In fact, they often describe interactions with white women patients that suggest that their race minimizes whatever assumptions of capability might accompany being men. They describe several cases in which white women patients completely refused treatment. Ray says,

> With older white women, it's tricky sometimes because they will come right out and tell you they don't want you to treat them, or can they see someone else.

Ray frames this as an issue specifically with older white women, though other nurses in the sample described similar issues with white women of all ages. Cyril, a 40-year-old nurse with 17 years of

nursing experience, describes a slightly different twist on this story:

> I had a white lady that I had to give a shot, and she was fine with it and I was fine with it, But her husband, when she told him, he said to me, I don't have any problem with you as a Black man, but I don't want you giving her a shot.

While white men nurses report some apprehension about treating women patients, in all likelihood this experience is compounded for Black men (Williams 1989), Historically, interactions between Black men and white women have been fraught with complexity and tension, as Black men have been represented in the cultural imagination as potential rapists and threats to white women's security and safety—and, implicitly, as a threat to white patriarchal stability (Davis 1981; Giddings 1984). In Cyril's case, it may be particularly significant that the Black man is charged with giving a shot and therefore literally penetrating the white wife's body, a fact that may heighten the husband's desire to shield his wife from this interaction. White men nurses may describe hesitation or awkwardness that accompanies treating women patients, but their experiences are not shaped by a pervasive racial imagery that suggests that they are potential threats to their women patients' safety.

This dynamic, described primarily among white women patients and their families, presents a picture of how Black men's interactions with clients are shaped in specifically raced and gendered ways that suggest they are less rather than more capable. These interactions do not send the message that Black men, because they are men, are too competent for nursing and really belong in higher-status jobs. Instead, these men face patients who mistake them for lower-status service workers and encounter white women patients (and their husbands) who simply refuse treatment or are visibly uncomfortable with the prospect. These interactions do not situate Black men nurses in a prime position for upward mobility. Rather, they suggest that the experience of Black men nurses with this particular mechanism of the glass escalator is the manifestation of the expectation that they should be in lower-status positions more appropriate to their race and gender.

Refusal to Reject Femininity

Finally, Black men nurses have a different experience with establishing distance from women and the feminized aspects of their work. Most research shows that as men nurses employ strategies that distance them from femininity (e.g., by emphasizing nursing as a route to higher-status, more masculine jobs), they place themselves in a position for upward mobility and the glass escalator effect (Williams 1992). For Black men nurses, however, this process looks different. Instead of distancing themselves from the femininity associated with nursing, Black men actually embrace some of the more feminized attributes linked to nursing. In particular, they emphasize how much they value and enjoy the way their jobs allow them to be caring and nurturing. Rather than conceptualizing caring as anathema or feminine (and therefore undesirable), Black men nurses speak openly of caring as something positive and enjoyable.

This is consistent with the context of nursing that defines caring as integral to the profession. As nurses, Black men in this line of work experience professional socialization that emphasizes and values caring, and this is reflected in their statements about their work. Significantly, however, rather than repudiating this feminized component of their jobs, they embrace it. Tobias, a 44-year-old oncology nurse with 25 years of experience, asserts,

> The best part about nursing is helping other people, the flexibility of work hours, and the commitment to vulnerable populations, people who are ill.

Simon, a 36-year-old oncology nurse, also talks about the joy he gets from caring for others. He contrasts his experiences to those of white men nurses he knows who prefer specialties that involve less patient care:

> They were going to work with the insurance industries, they were going to work in the ER where it's a touch and go, you're a number literally. I don't get to know your name, I don't get to know that you have four grandkids, I don't get to know that you really want to get out of the hospital by next week because the following week is your birthday, your 80th birthday and it's so important for you. I don't get to know that your cat's name is Sprinkles, and you're concerned about who's feeding the cat now, and if they remembered to turn the TV on during the day so that the cat can watch *The Price is Right*. They don't get into all that kind of stuff. OK, I actually need to remember the name of your cat so that tomorrow morning when I come, I can ask you about Sprinkles and that will make a world of difference. I'll see light coming to your eyes and the medicines will actually work because your perspective is different.

Like Tobias, Simon speaks with a marked lack of self-consciousness about the joys of adding a personal touch and connecting that personal care to a patient's improvement. For him, caring is important, necessary, and valued, even though others might consider it a feminine trait.

For many of these nurses, willingness to embrace caring is also shaped by issues of race and racism. In their position as nurses, concern for others is connected to fighting the effects of racial inequality. Specifically, caring motivates them to use their role as nurses to address racial health disparities, especially those that disproportionately affect Black men. Chris describes his efforts to minimize health issues among Black men:

> With Black male patients, I have their history, and if they're 50 or over I ask about the prostate exam and a colonoscopy. Prostate and colorectal death is so high that that's my personal crusade.

Ryan also speaks to the importance of using his position to address racial imbalances:

> I really take advantage of the opportunities to give back to communities, especially to change the disparities in the African American community. I'm

more than just a nurse. As a faculty member at a major university, I have to do community hours, services. Doing health fairs, in-services on research, this makes an impact in some disparities in the African American community. [People in the community] may not have the opportunity to do this otherwise.

As Lamont (2000) indicates in her discussion of the "caring self," concern for others helps Chris and Ryan to use their knowledge and position as nurses to combat racial inequalities in health. Though caring is generally considered a "feminine" attribute, in this context it is connected to challenging racial health disparities. Unlike their white men colleagues, these nurses accept and even embrace certain aspects of femininity rather than rejecting them. They thus reveal yet another aspect of the glass escalator process that differs for Black men. As Black men nurses embrace this "feminine" trait and the avenues it provides for challenging racial inequalities, they may become more comfortable in nursing and embrace the opportunities it offers.

Conclusions

Existing research on the glass escalator cannot explain these men's experiences. As men who do women's work, they should be channeled into positions as charge nurses or nursing administrators and should find themselves virtually pushed into the upper ranks of the nursing profession. But without exception, this is not the experience these Black men nurses describe. Instead of benefiting from the basic mechanisms of the glass escalator, they face tense relationships with colleagues, supervisors' biases in achieving promotion, patient stereotypes that inhibit caregiving, and a sense of comfort with some of the feminized aspects of their jobs. These "glass barriers" suggest that the glass escalator is a racialized concept as well as a gendered one. The main contribution of this study is the finding that race and gender intersect to determine which men will ride the glass escalator. The proposition that men who do women's work

encounter undue opportunities and advantages appears to be unequivocally true only if the men in question are white.

This raises interesting questions and a number of new directions for future research. Researchers might consider the extent to which the glass escalator is not only raced and gendered but sexualized as well. Williams (1995) notes that straight men are often treated better by supervisors than are gay men and that straight men frequently do masculinity by strongly asserting their heterosexuality to combat the belief that men who do women's work are gay. The men in this study (with the exception of one nurse I interviewed) rarely discussed sexuality except to say that they were straight and were not bothered by "the gay stereotype." This is consistent with Williams's findings. Gay men, however, may also find that they do not experience a glass escalator effect that facilitates their upward mobility. Tim, the only man I interviewed who identified as gay, suggests that gender, race, and sexuality come together to shape the experiences of men in nursing. He notes,

> I've been called awful things—you faggot this, you faggot that. I tell people there are three *F*s in life, and if you're not doing one of them it doesn't matter what you think of me. They say, "Three *F*s?" and I say yes. If you aren't feeding me, financing me, or fucking me, then it's none of your business what my faggot ass is up to.

Tim's experience suggests that gay men—and specifically gay Black men—in nursing may encounter particular difficulties establishing close ties with straight men supervisors or may not automatically be viewed by their women colleagues as natural leaders. While race is, in many cases, more obviously visible than sexuality, the glass escalator effect may be a complicated amalgam of racial, gendered, and sexual expectations and stereotypes.

It is also especially interesting to consider how men describe the role of women in facilitating—or denying—access to the glass escalator. Research on white men nurses includes accounts of ways white women welcome them and facilitate their advancement by pushing them toward leadership positions (Floge and Merrill 1986; Heikes 1991; Williams 1992, 1995). In contrast, Black men nurses in this study discuss white women who do not seem eager to work with them, much less aid their upward mobility. These different responses indicate that shared racial status is important in determining who rides the glass escalator. If that is the case, then future research should consider whether Black men nurses who work in predominantly Black settings are more likely to encounter the glass escalator effect. In these settings, Black men nurses' experiences might more closely resemble those of white men nurses.

Future research should also explore other racial minority men's experiences in women's professions to determine whether and how they encounter the processes that facilitate a ride on the glass escalator. With Black men nurses, specific race or gender stereotypes impede their access to the glass escalator; however, other racial minority men are subjected to different race or gender stereotypes that could create other experiences. For instance, Asian American men may encounter racially specific gender stereotypes of themselves as computer nerds, sexless sidekicks, or model minorities and thus may encounter the processes of the glass escalator differently than do Black or white men (Espiritu 2000). More focus on the diverse experiences of racial minority men is necessary to know for certain.

Finally, it is important to consider how these men's experiences have implications for the ways the glass escalator phenomenon reproduces racial and gendered advantages. Williams (1995) argues that men's desire to differentiate themselves from women and disassociate from the femininity of their work is a key process that facilitates their ride on the glass escalator. She ultimately suggests that if men reconstruct masculinity to include traits such as caring, the distinctions between masculinity and femininity could blur and men "would not have to define masculinity as the negation of femininity" (Williams 1995, 188). This in turn could create a more equitable balance between men and women in women's professions. However, the experiences of Black men in nursing, especially their embrace of caring, suggest that accepting the feminine aspects of work is not enough to dismantle the glass escalator and produce more gender equality in women's professions. The fact that Black men nurses accept and even enjoy caring does not minimize the processes that enable *white* men to ride the glass escalator. This suggests that undoing the glass escalator requires not only blurring the lines between masculinity and femininity but also challenging the processes of racial inequality that marginalize minority men.

Note

1. I could not locate any data that indicate the percentage of Black men in nursing. According to 2006 census data, African Americans compose 11 percent of nurses, and men are 8 percent of nurses (http://www.census.gov/compendia/statab/tables/08s0598.pdf). These data do not show the breakdown of nurses by race and sex.

References

Acker, Joan. 1990. Hierarchies, jobs, bodies: A theory of gendered organizations. *Gender & Society* 4: 139–58.

Britton, Dana. 1995. *At work in the iron cage.* New York: New York University Press.

Budig, Michelle. 2002. Male advantage and the gender composition of jobs: Who rides the glass escalator? *Social Forces* 49 (2): 258–77.

Charles, Maria and David Grusky. 2004. *Occupational ghettos: The worldwide segregation of women and men.* Palo Alto, CA: Stanford University Press.

Chen, Anthony. 1999. Lives at the center of the periphery, lives at the periphery of the center: Chinese American masculinities and bargaining with hegemony. *Gender & Society* 13: 584–607.

Collins, Patricia Hill. 1990. *Black feminist thought.* New York: Routledge.

_____. 2004. *Black sexual politics.* New York: Routledge.

Connell, R. W. 1989. *Gender and power.* Sydney, Australia: Allen and Unwin.

Davis, Angela. 1981. *Women, race, and class.* New York: Vintage.

Duffy, Mignon. 2007. Doing the dirty work; Gender, race, and reproductive labor in historical perspective. *Gender & Society* 21: 313–36.

Espiritu, Yen Le. 2000. *Asian American women and men: Labor, laws, and love.* Walnut Creek, CA: AltaMira.

Essed, Philomena. 1991. *Understanding everyday racism.* New York: Russell Sage.

Feagin, Joe. 2006. *Systemic racism.* New York: Routledge.

Feagin, Joe, and Melvin Sikes. 1994. *Living with racism.* Boston: Beacon Hill Press.

Floge, Liliane and Deborah M. Merrill. 1986. Tokenism reconsidered: Male nurses and female physicians in a hospital setting. *Social Forces* 64: 925–47.

Giddings, Paula. 1984. *When and where I enter; The impact of Black women on race and sex in America.* New York: HarperCollins.

Harvey Wingfield, Adia. 2007. The modern mammy and the angry Black man: African American professionals' experiences with gendered racism in the workplace. *Race, Gender, and Class* 14 (2): 196–212.

Heikes, E. Joel. 1991. When men are the minority: The case of men in nursing. *Sociological Quarterly* 32: 389–401.

hooks, bell. 2004. *We real cool.* New York: Routledge.

Kanter, Rosabeth Moss. 1977. *Men and women of the corporation.* New York: Basic Books.

Kimmel, Michael. 2001. Masculinity as homophobia. In *Men and masculinity,* edited by Theodore F. Cohen. Belmont, CA: Wadsworth.

Lamont, Michelle. 2000. *The dignity of working men.* New York: Russell Sage.

Neal, Mark Anthony. 2005. *New Black man.* New York: Routledge.

Ong, Maria. 2005. Body projects of young women of color in physics: Intersections of race, gender, and science. *Social Problems* 52 (4): 593–617.

Pierce, Jennifer. 1995. *Gender trials: Emotional lives in contemporary law firms.* Berkeley: University of California Press.

Roth, Louise. 2006. *Selling women short: Gender and money on Wall Street.* Princeton, NJ: Princeton University Press.

Shapiro, Thomas. 2004. *Hidden costs of being African American: How wealth perpetuates inequality.* New York: Oxford University Press.

Snyder, Karrie Ann and Adam Isaiah Green. 2008. Revisiting the glass escalator: The case of gender segregation in a female dominated occupation. *Social Problems* 55 (2): 271–99.

Williams, Christine. 1989. *Gender differences at work: Women and men in non-traditional occupations.* Berkeley: University of California Press.

_____. 1992. The glass escalator: Hidden advantages for men in the "female" professions. *Social Problems* 39 (3): 253–67.

_____. 1995. *Still a man's world: Men who do women's work.* Berkeley: University of California Press.

Zimmer, Lynn. 1988. Tokenism and women in the workplace: The limits of gender neutral theory. *Social Problems* 35 (1): 64–77.

Questions for Critical Thinking

1. Williams discusses how sex segregation continues to exist within the US labor force. How do the policies and practices she reveals maintain a gap in the incomes of women and men?

2. What are some ways of correcting gender-biased hiring practices in the workplace? What do you see as the likelihood of such corrective policies being enacted?

3. How does Williams's discussion impact your own expectations for your career?

Stressing Out the Poor

Chronic Physiological Stress and the Income–Achievement Gap

GARY W. EVANS, JEANNE BROOKS-GUNN, AND PAMELA KATO KLEBANOV

The following essay by a team of psychologists explores the link between childhood poverty and the negative effects of prolonged exposure to stressful environments. Their research demonstrates that the chaotic environment that results from childhood poverty generates stress and cognitive dysfunction, which has long-lasting impacts on academic achievement.

It is well known that economic deprivation early in life sets children on a trajectory toward diminished educational and occupational attainment. But why is early childhood poverty so harmful? If we can't answer that question well, our reform efforts are reduced to shots in the dark.

In this article, we offer a new perspective on this question. We suggest that childhood poverty is harmful, in part, because it exposes children to stressful environments. Low-income children face a bewildering array of psychosocial and physical demands that place much pressure on their adaptive capacities and appear to be toxic to the developing brain. Although poor children are disadvantaged in other ways, we focus our analysis here on the new, underappreciated pathway depicted in Figure 1. As shown in this figure, children growing up in poverty demonstrate lower academic achievement because of their exposure to a wide variety of risks. These risks, in turn, build upon one another to elevate levels of chronic (and toxic) stress within the body. And this toxic stress directly hinders poor children's academic performance by compromising their ability to develop the kinds of skills necessary to perform well in school. We will unpack this new Risk-Stress Model in the balance of our article. However, before doing so, it's useful to first go over the evidence regarding the relation between poverty and achievement and then to present some of the well-known pathways through which this relationship is generated. With that background in place, we can then describe the Risk-Stress Model, as represented in Figure 1.

Poverty and Achievement

It is well known that children born into low-income families lag behind their middle- and upper-income counterparts on virtually all indices of achievement. To provide one example, a national study of elementary school children shows that children in the poorest quarter of American households begin kindergarten nearly 10 percent behind their middle-income and affluent classmates in math (Figure 2). Six years later, as they are about to enter middle school, the poorest quarter of American children have fallen even further behind, with the gap between themselves and their most affluent schoolmates nearly doubling.

The splaying pattern revealed here, a general one that holds across various outcomes, may be

Originally appeared in Pathways: A Magazine on Poverty, Inequality, and Social Policy (Winter, 2011). Reprinted with permission of Stanford's Center on Poverty and Inequality.

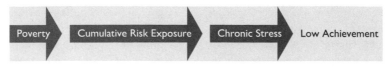

Figure 1 The Risk-Stress Model—A New Pathway to Account for the Income–Achievement Gap.

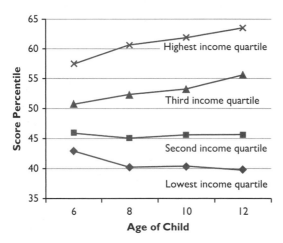

Figure 2 Average Percentile Rank on Peabody Individual Achievement Math.
Source: James J. Heckman (2006). "Skill Formation and the Economics of Investing in Disadvantaged Children." Science, 312(5782):1900–1902

attributed to the tendency for advantage and disadvantage to accumulate over time. This accumulation occurs in various ways; for example, children who score poorly at age six may be tracked into low-achievement school groups, which in turn exposes them to lower expectations, to less rigorous curricula, and to less capable peers, all of which further disadvantage them and generate ever more substantial between-group gaps. The Risk-Stress Model, to which we turn later, suggests that such splaying may also be attributed to the cognitive deficits and poorer health that chronic stress generates. Both cognitive deficits and ill health then repeatedly disadvantage poverty-stricken children in one educational setting after another.

Pathway #1: Parenting Practices

What types of forces have social scientists conventionally understood as explaining the achievement gaps illustrated in Figure 2? One reason poor children lag behind their more affluent peers is that their parents interact with them in ways that aren't conducive to achievement. For example, psychologist Kathryn Grant and her colleagues have documented a strong and consistent relation between socioeconomic disadvantage and harsh, unresponsive parenting. In one national dataset, 85 percent of American parents above the poverty line were shown to be responsive, supportive, and encouraging to their children during infancy and toddlerhood, whereas only 75 percent of low-income parents had the same achievement-inducing parenting style. While most low-income parents (i.e., 75 percent) do provide adequate levels of support and encouragement, these data reveal, then, a nontrivial difference across income levels in the chances that children will experience a problematic parenting style. There is considerable evidence that at least a portion of the cognitive developmental consequences of early childhood poverty is due to this difference.

Pathway #2: Cognitive Stimulation

It's also well known that children from low-income households tend to receive less cognitive stimulation and enrichment. For example, a child from a low-income family who enters first grade has been exposed on average to just 25 hours of one-on-one picture book reading, whereas an entering middle-income child has been exposed on average to more than 1,000 hours of such reading. Likewise, during the first three years of life, a child with professional parents will be exposed to three times as many words as a child with parents on welfare.

And it's not just simple parental effects that account for the achievement deficit. If a child is born into a high-income family, he or she may also benefit from high-quality stimulation and enrichment from extended family, from siblings and friends, and from more formal care providers. All of this redounds to the benefit of higher-income children while further handicapping low-income children.

So much for the well-known pathways by which disadvantage is transmitted. We turn now to another and less-appreciated aspect of low-income environments that may also harm cognitive development. The key concern here: children from impoverished households face a wide array of physical and psychosocial stressors. Their homes, schools, and neighborhoods are much more chaotic than the settings in which middle- and upper-income children grow up. Such conditions can, in turn, produce toxic stress capable of damaging areas of the brain known to underlie cognitive processes—such as attention, memory, and language—that all combine to undergird academic success. In the pages that remain, we document each of the steps in the Risk-Stress Model.

Poverty and Cumulative Risk Exposure

The stressors that poor children face take both a physical and psychosocial form. The physical form is well documented; poor children are exposed to substandard environmental conditions including toxins, hazardous waste, ambient air and water pollution, noise, crowding, poor housing, poorly maintained school buildings, residential turnover, traffic congestion, poor neighborhood sanitation and maintenance, and crime. The psychosocial form is also well documented; poor children experience significantly higher levels of family turmoil, family separation, violence, and significantly lower levels of structure and routine in their daily lives.

An important aspect of early, disadvantaged settings may be exposure to more than one risk factor at a time. A powerful way to capture exposure to such multiple sources of stress and strain is the construct of cumulative risk. Although there

are various ways to quantify cumulative risk, one common approach is to simply count the number of physical or psychosocial risks to which a child has been exposed. In one UK study, the authors counted how often children were exposed to such stresses as: (a) living with a single parent; (b) experiencing family discord; (c) experiencing foster or some other form of institutional care; (d) living in a crowded home; and (e) attending a school with high turnover of both classmates and teachers. It was found in this study that inner-city children experienced far more of these stresses than did the better-off working-class children. The same result holds in the United States (see Figure 3). In rural New England, only 12 percent of middle-income nine-year-olds experienced three or more physical and psychosocial risk factors, whereas nearly 50 percent of low-income children crossed this same threshold (of three risk factors).

In a national U.S. sample of premature and low birth weight infants, Brooks-Gunn and colleagues

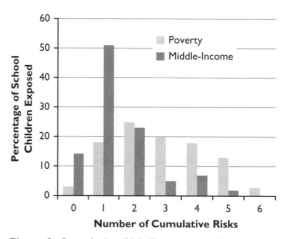

Figure 3 Cumulative Risk Exposure in Relation to Poverty/Not Poverty.

Note: Cumulative risks include family turmoil, violence, child separation from family, noise, crowding, and housing quality.

Source: Gary W. Evans and Kimberly English. 2002. "The Environment of Poverty: Multiple Stressor Exposure, Psychophysiological Stress, and Socioemotional Adjustment." Child Development, 73(4): 1238–48.

similarly found that infants born into low-income families experienced nearly three times more risk factors than their middle-income counterparts by the time they were toddlers. These same low-income toddlers were seven times more likely than their affluent counterparts to experience a very high number of risk factors (>6). The pattern is overwhelmingly clear: being born into early poverty often means exposure to many more physical and psychosocial risk factors.

Cumulative Risk Exposure and Chronic Stress

But does such differential exposure indeed result in higher stress levels among poor children? The simple answer is that it does. In cross-sectional analyses of 9- and 13-year-old children, Evans and colleagues found that the risk exposure described in Figure 3 elevated baseline, resting blood pressure as well as overnight indices of such stress hormones as cortisol. At age 13, when challenged by mental arithmetic problems, children with higher levels of cumulative risk exposure did not show a typical healthy response, instead exhibiting a muted rise in blood pressure. These same children also didn't recover as successfully from the mental challenge posed by these arithmetic problems (as indexed by the longer time it took their blood pressure to return to pre-stressor baseline levels). The evidence thus suggests that children exposed to high levels of cumulative risk are less efficient both in mobilizing and then shutting off physiological activity.

The Risk-Stress Model, as represented in Figure 1, implies that the effect of family poverty on stress is mediated by risk exposure. Although one would ideally like to test that mediation, it's also important to simply document the association between poverty and stress (thereby ignoring the mediating factor). Many investigators have indeed documented that disadvantaged children have higher chronic physiological stress levels, as indicated by elevated resting blood pressure. A smaller number of studies have also uncovered higher levels of chronic stress hormones, such as cortisol, among disadvantaged children. To provide just a few examples, Figures 4 and 5 show elevated resting blood pressure as well as higher overnight urinary stress hormones in a sample of nine-year-old rural children.

The foregoing data, which pertain to nine-year-olds, don't tell us when such stress symptoms emerge. Do poverty-stricken children show evidence of elevated stress early on in their lives?

Or do such symptoms only emerge later? With support from the Stanford Center for the Study of Poverty and Inequality, we sought to answer this question by reanalyzing a national data set of very young at-risk children. The Infant Health and Development Program (IHDP) is a representative sample of low birth weight (<2500 grams) and premature (<37 weeks gestational age) babies born in 1985 at eight medical centers throughout the country. This sample of nearly 1,000 babies is racially and economically diverse (52 percent Black, 37 percent White, 11 percent Hispanic).

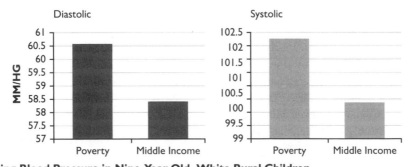

Figure 4 Resting Blood Pressure in Nine-Year-Old, White Rural Children.
Source: Gary W. Evans and Kimberly English. 2002. "The Environment of Poverty: Multiple Stressor Exposure, Psychophysiological Stress, and Socioemotional Adjustment." Child Development, 73(4): 1238–48.

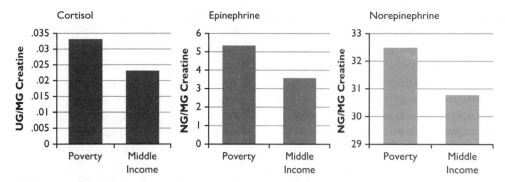

Figure 5 Overnight Stress Hormones in Nine-Year-Old, White Rural Children.
Source: Gary W. Evans and Kimberly English. 2002. "The Environment of Poverty; Multiple Stressor Exposure, Psycho-physiological Stress, and Socioemotional Adjustment." Child Development, 73(4); 1238–48.

We assessed resting blood pressure and child's height and weight at 24, 30, 36, 48, 60, and 78 months of age. The collection of physical health data at such young ages and over time provided us with an unprecedented opportunity to examine the early trajectories of chronic stress among a high-risk sample of babies. Both baseline blood pressure levels and Body Mass Index (BMI) reflect wear and tear on the body and are precursors of lifelong health problems. The former is indicative of cardiovascular health and the latter of metabolic

equilibrium. BMI, which reflects fat deposition, is measured as height divided by weight (kg/m^2).

We sought to assess whether these two measures of stress are elevated in poverty-stricken neighborhoods. Low-income neighborhoods, as defined in our study, have median household incomes below $30,000 (in 1980 dollars), while middle income neighborhoods have median income levels exceeding $30,000 per household. As is evident in Figures 6 and 7, babies growing up in low-income neighborhoods have health trajectories indicative

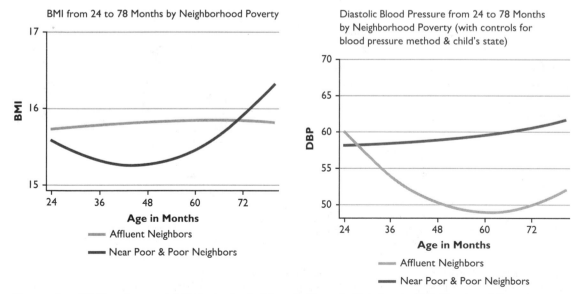

Figures 6 and 7 Developmental Trajectories in Chronic Stress in Relation to Neighborhood Poverty.

of elevated chronic stress. Additional statistical controls for infant birth weight, health, and demographic characteristics did not alter these trajectories. These figures also reveal, even more importantly, that elevated stress emerges very early for children growing up in low-income neighborhoods. BMI, for example, proves to be unusually low among poor children under five years old, but it then takes off as these children grow older. The blood pressure measure, by contrast, registers high among low-income children from almost the very beginning of our measurements (i.e., 24 months). This research confirms, then, that low-income children are more likely than others to develop dangerous stress trajectories very early on in their childhood. As we discuss below, this has profound consequences for their likelihood of success in school and beyond.

Chronic Stress and the Achievement Gap

The next and final step in our chain model pertains to the effects of chronic stress on achievement. Here we turn to an important longitudinal program on poverty and the brain at the University of Pennsylvania conducted by Martha Farah and her colleagues. In a series of studies with multiple samples drawn from lower- and middle-class Black families in Philadelphia, Farah and colleagues show that several areas of the brain appear vulnerable to early childhood deprivation. Using batteries of neurocognitive tests of brain function and brain imaging studies, Farah and other neuroscientists can map the areas of the brain that are recruited by neurocognitive tasks. As shown in Figure 8, among the areas of the brain most sensitive to childhood socioeconomic status (SES) are language, long-term memory, working memory, and executive control. What the graph depicts is the separation, in standard deviation units, between a low- and middle-SES sample of 11-year-old Black children from Philadelphia. For this sample, one standard deviation represents about one-fifth of the total distribution of scores. Samples differing by 3.5 or more standard deviations are virtually

non-overlapping. Given that the samples differ by about 3.5 standard deviations for all four areas of brain functioning, this means that there is virtually no overlap between poor and middle-class Black children when it comes to language, long-term memory, working memory, or executive control. Eleven-year-old Black children from lower SES families reveal dramatic deficits in multiple, basic cognitive functions critical to learning and eventual success in society. These results reveal the starkly cognitive foundation to the poor performance of low-income children.

But is this achievement gap attributable to cumulative risk and chronic stress? With a recent follow-up of the sample depicted in Figures 4 and 5, Evans and colleagues have now provided the first test of the final link in the Risk-Stress Model. The baseline finding from their research is that working memory in early adulthood (i.e., age 17) deteriorated in direct relation to the number of years the children lived in poverty (from birth through age 13). If, in other words, a child lived in poverty continuously, his or her working memory was greatly

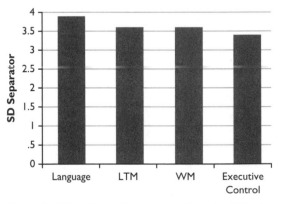

Figure 8 Effect Sizes Measured in Standard Deviations of Separation Between Low-And Middle-Ses 10–12-Year-Old, African American Children.
Source: Martha J. Farah, David M. Shera, Jessica N. Savage, Laura Betancourt, Joan M. Giannetta, Nancy L. Brodsky, Elsa K. Malmud, and Hallam Hurt. 2006. "Childhood Poverty: Specific Associations with Neurocognitive Development." Brain Research, 1110(7): 166–74.

compromised. The main result of interest, however, was that such deterioration occurred only among poverty-stricken children with chronically elevated physiological stress (as measured between ages 9 and 13). That is, chronic early childhood poverty did not lead to working memory deficits among children who somehow avoided experiencing the stress that usually accompanies poverty.

Conclusion

Childhood socioeconomic disadvantage leads to deficits in academic achievement and occupational attainment. It's long been argued that such deficits arise because poor children are exposed to inadequate cognitive stimulation and to parenting styles that don't encourage achievement. We don't dispute the important role of these two variables. But we have outlined here evidence for a new, complementary pathway that links early childhood poverty to high levels of exposure to multiple risks, which in turn elevates chronic toxic stress. This cascade can begin very early in life. Even young babies growing up in low-income neighborhoods already evidence elevated chronic stress. This stress then accounts for a significant portion of the association between

poverty and working memory, a critical cognitive skill involved in language and reading acquisition.

The Risk-Stress Model suggests that the poverty–achievement link can be broken by addressing (a) the tendency of poverty to be associated with physical or psychosocial risks (e.g., environmental toxins, family turmoil), (b) the effects of such risks on stress, and (c) the effects of stress on achievement. If this model bears up under further testing, it would be useful to explore which of these pathways is most amenable to intervention.

Questions for Critical Thinking

1. How does the authors' discussion impact your understanding of the barriers encountered by children of low income?
2. In this article the authors focus on how stress encountered at an early age can have long-lasting impacts on the ability to achieve in education. How does this article broaden your understanding of the continuing achievement gap in the United States?
3. Some argue that policies like universal health care would address some of the problems caused by social inequality. Do you think this would be a sufficient solution? What solutions would you offer?

Jezebel at the Welfare Office
How Racialized Stereotypes of Poor Women's Reproductive Decisions and Relationships Shape Policy Implementation

N. TATIANA MASTERS, TARYN P. LINDHORST, AND MARCIA K. MEYERS

This next essay, by social workers N. Tatiana Masters, Taryn P. Lindhorst, and Marcia K. Meyers, discusses how caseworkers perpetuate negative myths regarding African American women's sexuality and motherhood. Drawing on data from interview transcripts, the authors demonstrate that, regardless of the recipient's individual race, clients were placed into racialized myths through the caseworkers' talk. Their analysis shows that negative ideas about poor women's sexuality persist in welfare policy and are built into its day-to-day implementation.

Welfare workers' conversations with clients about fertility and family formation have the potential to illuminate the discourses on poor women's sexual behavior that are embedded in present-day welfare policy. To understand how poor women's sexuality and fertility are framed during welfare office interviews, this study examined interactions about reproductive decisions and relationships between caseworkers and clients, using transcripts from a multisite study and focusing on caseworkers' language.

A substantial amount of scholarship has grappled with Temporary Assistance to Needy Families (TANF), the program resulting from 1996's welfare reform. Much of this work critically analyzes the policy itself (e.g., A. M. Smith, 2001; Soss & Schram, 2007), assesses the policy's effects (e.g., Burger, 2004; Corcoran, Danziger, Kalil, & Seefeldt, 2000; De Jong, Graefe, & St. Pierre, 2005; Loeb, Fuller, Kagan, & Carrol, 2003), or examines aspects of the policy's implementation (e.g., Hays, 2003; Meyers, 1998; Meyers & Lurie, 2005). Implementation research like ours focuses on interactions between clients and caseworkers to understand how policy mandates are translated within social welfare systems. Research on policy implementation has shown that street-level workers exercise great discretion in their application of formal policy mandates (Lipsky, 1980; Maynard-Moody, Musheno, & Palumbo, 1990; Watkins-Hayes, 2009). Frontline workers are constrained by policy requirements and able to interpret them in such a way as to facilitate or hinder client access to services (Meyers, 1998; Meyers & Lurie, 2005).

An important element of current scholarship on welfare reform implementation studies these efforts at the ground level, using data from interviews or observation and recording in welfare offices. Hays' 2003 book, *Flat Broke with Children*, uses such data to examine the cultural norms, beliefs, and values embedded in welfare reform. She points out that TANF, as written and as implemented, enforces "family values" by discouraging women from raising children alone. Watkins-Hayes' (2009) work focuses on how welfare workers' professional identities and their race and gender locations interact to influence their implementation of policy as they work with clients. Both of these works use day-to-day talk in welfare offices to study implementation, but neither focuses on how workers and clients discuss issues of sexuality and reproduction in the context of the welfare interview.

Welfare office talk matters as a measure of policy implementation and as the kind of language in action that can contribute to perpetuating stigmatizing discourses of poor women's sexuality. Reich's study (2005) of clients' interactions with child protective services sheds light on how everyday practices in government offices draw upon and contribute to racialized and gendered stereotypes of bad parenting; no equivalent work has been done using data from welfare offices. Women on welfare have long been the subjects of derogatory stereotypes, and their sexual behavior and reproductive decisions have been a major element of these negative portrayals (Cassiman, 2006; Collins, 1990, 2004; Lens, 2002; Roberts, 1997, 2002). Such myths, as Dorothy Roberts (1997) puts it, are "more than made-up stories" (p. 8). Myths about people (e.g., poor women, welfare mothers, Black women) affect not only the treatment of specific individuals—unjust in and of itself—but also the treatment of everyone in those people's groups: all women, all mothers, all African Americans. As such, these demeaning myths are of concern in the realms of scholarship and citizenship (Harris-Perry, 2011).

Gilens (1999), in his study of national polling data about welfare policies, found that White Americans responded to racially encoded language: they disapproved of "welfare" (something received, as they saw it, by African Americans), but approved of "assistance for the poor." Likewise, Hancock's (2004) study of references to welfare recipients in newspaper reports and the *Congressional Record* showed how the public identity of welfare recipients was cast as sexually permissive African American women, and Cassiman (2006) delineated the social construction of the "welfare queen"

as "the embodiment of the deviant . . . black, poor, and dependent upon an unearned income" (p. 57). Empirical falsification of such negative myths is often insufficient to diminish their power. For example, the U.S. General Accounting Office (2001) reviewed research on the effect of TANF policies on out-of-wedlock births and concluded that there was no evidence that these policies affected the childbearing choices of women on welfare. In spite of this authoritative statement, the dehumanizing myth of the welfare client having another baby to increase her check persists. Critical analytic descriptions of such myths in action, such as those produced by this study, can potentially contribute to lessening their influence among those who make or implement welfare policy, or who shape it with their public statements or their votes.

The sexual behavior of women and the structure of their families have long been a concern of social policy. The federal Aid to Dependent Children (ADC) program was established in 1935. As the Social Security system was modified in subsequent years, more widowed White women were transferred from ADC to Social Security benefits, and unmarried mothers, particularly African American mothers who were excluded by design from other social assistance programs (Jones, 1995), constituted an increasing percentage of ADC caseloads. ADC became a lightning rod for criticism as this transition occurred, particularly among conservative leaders who believed that providing cash assistance to mother-only families enabled women to avoid the traditional bonds of marriage (Gordon, 1994; Murray, 1984). Poor women were stigmatized by their use of welfare; this stigma was particularly harsh for women of color, as racist attitudes linked the African American women heading these families with irresponsible sexual behavior (Berkowitz, 1991; Collins, 1990; Jones, 1985; Roberts, 1997).

As discriminatory state welfare practices were struck down by the Supreme Court, women previously denied benefits began to receive cash assistance for the care of their children, and welfare rolls grew dramatically (Quadagno, 1994). Cyclically, whenever a system of overtly biased practices was legally overturned, another set of welfare implementation practices seemed to emerge to exclude Black women. Thus as welfare officially became more accessible, state policies also increased scrutiny of poor women's sexual behavior. For example, in 1960, Louisiana discontinued benefits to 95% of its African American clients on the basis of a "suitable home" provision that prohibited welfare benefits for families in which any child had been born out of wedlock (Lindhorst & Leighninger, 2003). Welfare case-workers were also required to conduct raids to find men who were not married to the welfare recipient but were living in the home (Abramovitz, 1996), until legal and administrative challenges by the National Welfare Rights Organization and other groups ended these practices (Neubeck & Cazenave, 2001).

Explanations for welfare use focused increasingly on a "culture of poverty" argument. The culture of poverty thesis, resurrected by Charles Murray (1984), suggests that poverty is caused by the "deviant" values of poor people, particularly poor Black people. One relevant example is his conclusion that poor women, especially African American women, have babies in an entrepreneurial fashion to increase their welfare checks rather than engaging in paid work. Instead of an overtly racist focus on the creation of laws that limit African American women's access to financial assistance, culture of poverty arguments focus on women's transgressive moral and sexual behavior and advocate for conventional gender structures, themes that persist into the current round of welfare reform. Although important refutations of the culture of poverty argument exist (e.g., Katz, 1989; Piven & Cloward, 1971; Quadagno, 1994), it nonetheless continues to exert a powerful influence over U.S. welfare policy.

With welfare reform under the Personal Responsibility and Work Opportunity Reconciliation Act (PRWORA) in 1996, the federal government once again asserted its right to set normative standards for women's sexual behavior, including the prevention of out-of-wedlock pregnancies and the encouragement of marriage. This assertion reinforced welfare's historical devaluing of poor women and women of color as mothers (McCormack, 2005; Roberts 1997, 2002). One example of PRWORA's regulation of reproduction is "family cap" policies that allow states to prohibit increasing a family's financial assistance if the mother has another child while receiving welfare. Twenty-two states have currently implemented family cap provisions (R. J. Smith, 2006). This policy and others sought to eliminate any perceived financial incentive for women receiving welfare to have more children, but empirical evidence of their effectiveness has been mixed (Horvath-Rose, Peters, & Sabia, 2008; Jagannathan & Camasso, 2003).

Welfare rolls dropped dramatically after the passage of PRWORA. Debate continues as to whether these declines were due to discontinuation of recipients who would have been eligible under previous welfare rules, improvements in national economic conditions immediately after PRWORA passed, or increases in the stigma associated with welfare receipt (Danziger, 1999). Under the Bush administration, further efforts were made to encourage marriage through the reallocation of TANF monies to marriage and fatherhood promotion efforts that focused on patriarchal, heterosexual marriage as the primary solution to poverty among women and children (Edin & Kefalas, 2005; Hays, 2003; Weigt, 2010).

The Current Study

Based upon this historical context, we would certainly expect the regulation of women's reproductive decisions and relationships to be a substantial element of frontline workers' implementation of TANF. Our objective with this study was to explore the relationship between welfare workers' conversations with clients and dominant discourses regarding sexual behavior and family structures that are embedded in welfare policy, while also attending to the ways in which gendered and racialized assumptions intertwine in workers' implementation of these policies. Our focus was not on connections between worker rhetoric and welfare case outcomes (e.g., whether a client was granted benefits), but on caseworker language itself. We addressed our research questions by examining conversations related to fertility and family formation in worker–client interactions in welfare offices, using transcripts of these conversations from a multisite study. To date, scholarship on welfare reform has not focused directly on interactions between welfare workers and clients in relation to issues of sexuality and fertility.

Method

Data for this study consisted of transcribed interviews between welfare caseworkers and clients applying for TANF benefits at public welfare agencies in three states. Data were originally collected as part of the Frontline Management and Practice Study conducted by the Rockefeller Institute of Government for the U.S. Department of Health and Human Services (see Lindhorst, Meyers, & Casey, 2008; Meyers, Riccucci, & Lurie, 2001, for further description of the study). The goal of the parent study was to investigate the implementation of welfare reform policies in states with diverse administrative and political structures. This research is a qualitative analysis of a subset of data from this larger study.

The research design for the parent study maximized organizational variation by drawing samples in three stages. The first stage used purposive sampling to select states, based on variation in location, political culture, and TANF agency structures. The states chosen were Georgia, Michigan, and Texas. The second stage used purposive sampling to select nine sites (two to three per state) that represented urban and either rural or suburban locations. Each of these states was below the national median in child well-being indicators (Annie E. Casey Foundation, 2003). The lower child well-being ranking of these states indicates that while they differed from one another somewhat in terms of policy and organizational structures, they were similar in

terms of their levels of poverty and of underlying need for TANF assistance.

Data Collection

Data collection took place in 1999 to 2000. Frontline welfare workers' encounters with clients were captured either through tape recording and transcription or through the taking of detailed notes by a trained observer. Informed consent for observation and recording was obtained from the worker in advance and from the client at the start of the encounter. Research assistants tape recorded and transcribed data in Texas and Michigan. In Georgia, we were unable to obtain permission to tape-record encounters, so research assistants were instructed to record verbatim conversation on 25 topics and activities that were of particular interest, including discussions of reproductive decisions and relationships. Comparison of the Georgia transcripts to the recordings in Texas and Michigan showed no meaningful differences in the length of transcripts or the topics discussed.

Sample

Our aim was to characterize the discourses of fertility and family formation reflected in the routine social and linguistic practices of the welfare encounter. Thus, we focused our preliminary analyses on interviews in which these topics were likely to be discussed. In most welfare systems, clients must participate in an "application interview" that determines their eligibility for benefits; after this, they usually have minimal follow-up contacts with caseworkers. It is during these initial applications (or reapplication interviews for clients renewing their benefits) that conversations about sexuality, fertility and family formation are most likely to occur.

This study's sample has limitations. Data were collected over a decade ago and thus may not reflect current welfare office operations, which may be different in ways to which this study cannot speak. Because locations for data collection were purposefully selected in the context of the parent study (Meyers, 1998), they may not be representative of all U.S. welfare offices. Because we worked with written text, nonverbal worker–client communication that may have provided further insight into these transactions was lost, and the presence of research assistants in offices during welfare interviews may have altered worker behavior in unknowable ways. The data from Georgia may differ from the recordings obtained in Texas and Michigan, potentially affecting its trustworthiness. In spite of these limitations, the available transcripts represent a unique opportunity to examine the spoken discourses with which the welfare system contributes to the construction of poor women's gendered positions through talk about reproductive decisions and relationships.

Our initial data set contained 232 observations of TANF interviews between welfare workers and female clients. The sample of interviews involved 60% female workers and 17% male workers; the remaining workers' genders were not recorded. Forty-four percent of workers were African American, 25% White, 4% Latino/a, 1% Asian American, and 25% of unknown race-ethnicity (percentages do not sum to 100 due to rounding). Seventy-eight percent of clients were African American, 21% White, and 1% Latina; all were women.

To select a subset of interviews and data for in-depth analysis, the first author read and reread all 232 interview transcripts and coded conversations on topics of pregnancy, birth control, family planning, conjugal relationships, and sexual behavior. This topic coding resulted in a subset of 72 interviews that included talk of reproductive decisions and relationships. The second author independently coded a subset of transcripts to validate the topic coding; convergence was excellent overall, and disagreements about topic coding were resolved through discussion. The inclusion criterion for child support conversations deserves special mention. Child support enforcement generally involves workers gathering information about the father's description, location, or social security number for use in finding him and compelling him to pay for the care of his child(ren), and these topics were a part of nearly every welfare interview. We differentiated these routine child support conversations from those that included a pronounced focus on the sexual aspects of the relationship, for example, establishment of children's paternity through questions about the client's sexual relationship with the father. We included child support conversations in the in-depth analysis subset of data only when they had this sexual content in addition to routine, nonsexual discussion of enforcement issues.

Analytical Approach

We drew on a discourse analysis framework to investigate how workers' talk with welfare office clients perpetuated or resisted the negative stereotypes of poor women's reproductive decisions and relationships embedded in welfare policy. Discourse analysis operates from a theoretical perspective that treats social realities such as gender and sexuality as being socially constructed through language and social practices (Cameron & Kulick, 2003). It focuses on what people do with their talk: they "produce versions of events, objects, and people" (Horton-Salway, 2001, p. 153). Focusing on the 72 interviews in which workers discussed reproductive decisions and relationships, we conducted across-case analyses and used techniques of data summarization and display (Miles & Huberman, 1994), categorization (Saldaña, 2009), and comparative analysis (Strauss & Corbin, 1998). We characterized coded statements with brief descriptive labels and grouped related statements together into categories. We refined, split, or merged categories when associations, divisions, or overlap appeared in the data (Hall & Stevens, 1991). The first two authors worked together iteratively to produce the findings and verify their trustworthiness.

Findings

Only about one third of the 232 interviews between caseworkers and clients included conversations that were directly related to clients' sexual behavior. We identified 72 interviews (31%) in which reproductive decisions and relationships were discussed;

these conversations are characterized below. The remaining 160 interviews (69%) involved discussion of other welfare issues such as Food Stamp eligibility, access to child care, work requirement fulfillment, and routine child support enforcement with no discussion of sex or the conjugal relationship. We began these analyses with a focus on how race and gender intertwined in welfare office talk about sex, childbearing, and family organization. Through close reading of the interviews, we identified moments of informal, discretionary talk that focused on moralizing about client behaviors. The more predominant form of talk, however, was a highly bureaucratized exchange of questions and answers. We start with findings related to issues of race and racialized talk within these exchanges, followed by a description of the moralizing and bureaucratic styles of talk.

Race or Racialized Talk?

In the first phase of analysis, we looked at whether race/gender concordance between welfare workers and clients was associated with moralizing or bureaucratic styles of talk. All of the clients and more than one half of the caseworkers in our sample were women. The majority of the clients were African American, as were nearly one half of the caseworkers. The distribution of each of these groups in our sample, as well as our sample size, may have obscured patterns of interaction specific to particular pairings, for example, between a White worker and a Black client, or between two African American women. We did not identify distinct discourses on reproductive decisions and relationships associated with workers' race or gender, clients' race, or the racial or gender makeup of worker–client dyads. Workers were no more likely, for example, to moralize with an African American client, or with a client of a different race or gender than their own. However, the discourse of poor women's reproductive decisions and relationships that emerged from these data on welfare workers' everyday talk with clients was overwhelmingly disrespectful. Regardless of their individual races, clients were subject

to the negative myths that arose out of gendered racism against African American women so powerfully characterized by Roberts (1997) and Collins (1990, 2004).

Although we observed an occasional exception—discussed below—in general, workers' language functioned to create negative subject positions for clients. These positions were remarkably congruent with the stereotypes of African American women's sexuality and reproduction discussed in Collins (1990) and further elaborated by Roberts (1997). Some welfare clients were positioned as the immoral "Jezebel," focused on sexual fulfillment without responsibility; others as the devious "welfare queen" who tricked the state into supporting her and her children; some as "matriarchs" who abandoned marriage in favor of asserting dominance within the family; others as "Mammies" who bore children only to neglect them. In the next section, we present examples of exchanges between workers and clients, highlighting moments when these racialized myths are present in the underlying assumptions expressed in the interview. In quotations from transcripts, we have replaced names with initials, and specific dates with spaces, to protect study participants' confidentiality. When portions of the transcript not relevant to the analysis have been left out, we use this symbol: [. . .].

Styles of Talk

Our analyses identified two overlapping rhetorical styles that supported the stigmatized positioning of welfare clients, with the occasional exception. We labeled the first of these patterns "discretionary moralizing." This style extended the moralistic "suitable home" talk documented among welfare caseworkers of the 1960s (Lindhorst & Leighninger, 2003) into the present. It comprised workers' personal and optional talk regarding the social riskiness of having babies as a poor woman, and the moral deficiencies they ascribed to women who had children and sought state assistance for their support. Discretionary moralizing was layered over the second style, bureaucratic talk, in roughly one third of the interviews analyzed. The bureaucratic style involved statements through which sex-related policy decisions such as the family cap were implemented in the worker–client transaction, reducing reproductive decision making to issues of verification and rule imposition. Unsurprisingly, given that they were official transactions in government offices, all of the 72 welfare interviews involving fertility and family formation included this type of bureaucratic talk.

The bureaucratic examples we discuss below may seem to make less of a contribution to the perpetuation of negative myths regarding welfare clients' sexual and relational behavior than do the examples involving discretionary moralizing. The distinction between these two styles is important to note, however, so that the more subtle action of the bureaucratic imperative is not overlooked. Both strategies—old-fashioned moralizing and neutral-appearing bureaucracy—functioned toward the same end. Through them, welfare clients were positioned as sexually irresponsible supplicants for aid whose fertility and family structures were in need of governmental regulation, rather than as citizens for whom assistance was a right and whose reproductive decisions and relationships were their own.

Discretionary Moralizing

In these cases, in addition to the policy-mandated bureaucratic language present in all the interviews we studied, workers did what we have called "discretionary moralizing"; they spoke in ways that reflected a personal sense of entitlement to judge and regulate clients' reproductive decisions and relationships. These discussions included talk of clients as negligent of their maternal responsibilities, critiques regarding children's paternity and clients' conjugal choices, and talk in which workers took clients to task for their sexual behavior. The moralistic strategy overtly draws on the dominant discourse of irresponsible reproduction and inappropriate family structure in which PRWORA is embedded.

A prominent feature of workers' moralistic talk is statements that position clients as negligent "Mammies" (Collins, 1990; Roberts, 1997), as in this example from Georgia.

WORKER: How many children are in the home?
CLIENT: Five and one on the way.
WORKER: Why would you go ahead and do that? We can talk to y'all until we're blue in the face. You know you won't get any extra money.

Here we see discretionary moralizing layered on top of the bureaucratic imperative as the worker conveys the substance of the family cap regulation in less neutral, more personally judgmental language.

Another instance of morality talk appears in discussions about the fathers of clients' children during workers' attempts to get information for use in child support enforcement. These examples demonstrate workers' personal normative judgments of clients' reproductive relationships.

WORKER: Do you have your current ID? Are you getting child support?
CLIENT: Um, well right now, he's just helping me pay the mortgage so, I guess, yeah.
WORKER: Is he the father of all your children?
CLIENT: The other three, no, he's in prison, the father of the other three.
WORKER: You don't pick them good.

Here the client is talked about as to blame for her own difficulties due to her deficiencies at partner selection and placed in the "Jezebel" role for having children by two different men. The Michigan worker conveys her verdict on the client's partner with the statement, "You don't pick them good." The client is asked to justify the fact that she is not married to the man who fathered her new baby: PRWORA aims to encourage marriage as part of its perspective on appropriate types of family structure, but the worker's discretionary moralizing takes this conversation to a more personally intrusive level.

Discretionary moralizing can also have a sarcastic quality, as when a worker in Georgia said, "You don't have ANY information on their father?"

When the client stated that she and her children's father, "didn't talk," the worker responded "You had to talk sometime, you had three babies." Another worker in Texas expressed disbelief regarding the client's knowledge of her former partner:

WORKER: What's the father's name?
CLIENT: I can only think of his first name, that's _____.
WORKER: How long did you go out with him?
CLIENT: A while. But he's in denial. Only thing I can think of is his first name.
WORKER: If you went out with him a while you should know his last name. [. . .] Oh, I'm getting a message [from the computer]. I never got that before. [. . .] I guess the system couldn't believe someone would only know the first name.

In both examples, the workers take a tone of disbelief that the clients would not have certain information about their childrens' fathers. This language contributes to the workers' positioning of the clients as "Jezebels" who have sex (and children) with men they do not know.

The moralistic rhetorical strategy also occurs in a way that exhorts the client to do better with the kind of tough talk that a coach or parent might use. In Georgia, after discussing tubal ligation with a pregnant client, a worker pointed out that the client's mother worked, saying, "That's probably why she can take care of her children. Like you need to." This quote from a Michigan worker is another minor exception to the overall negativity of caseworkers' positioning of welfare recipients with their moralizing language.

WORKER: You're going to go on and get your GED [Graduate Equivalency Diploma]?
CLIENT: Yes.
WORKER: Because you need that. And you don't need any more children to hinder you. [. . .] You could go to a trade school and learn how to be a nurse. Don't say "don't know"—you just need to do it. And stop having babies. You're too young.

In both of these examples, the worker exhorts the client to pull herself up by her bootstraps. This coaching language is somewhat supportive of the client, positioning her as a potentially strong person who can succeed at school or a career and take care of herself and her children without assistance. It shows some worker resistance to the overwhelmingly negative perspective on poor women's fertility demonstrated in most other examples, and is also congruent with caretaking aspects of TANF policy. However, this paternalistic tone displays no less of an entitlement by the worker to decide what is best for the client regarding reproduction; it simply combines this entitlement with a more parental interpersonal style.

The Bureaucratic Imperative

The dominant discourse of poor women as sexually irresponsible affected talk in the welfare interview through workers' personal and optional talk, but it did so more frequently through its influence on the policy and regulations workers were mandated to implement. The bureaucratic strategy did not involve overtly judgmental language regarding clients' sexual behavior, merely a rote statement of the rules or a seemingly neutral inquiry for information. Much of the content of welfare office encounters was driven by the worker's task of gathering information to complete welfare forms or cover policy-mandated material. Topics of reproductive decisions and relationships (e.g., family cap, child support enforcement) came up in these contexts. Conversations involving the bureaucratic imperative reinforced negative myths regarding poor women's sexual behavior in a low-intensity way without using language that overtly denigrated clients' reproductive decisions or relationships.

We often saw the bureaucratic imperative in encounters where the worker's goal was to get information about the father of the client's children for use in child support enforcement. In this Texas interview the worker's talk had the tone of an interrogation in a police drama on television.

WORKER: All right, this part. Do you know who M's father is?

CLIENT: Nuh-uh.

WORKER: Do you know anything about him? You never see his face or know where he is? OK. You never did find out who he is? (Client shakes her head.) [. . .]

WORKER: Do Z and P have the same father? (Client nods her head.) What's his name?

CLIENT: PM.

WORKER: OK. Um. When was the last time you had contact with him?

CLIENT: About a month ago. [. . .]

WORKER: Did he have any plans to marry you? (Client shakes her head.)

WORKER: OK, do you know his social security number? Date of birth?

CLIENT: September __, 197_.

WORKER: 197_? Is he white? How tall is he?

CLIENT: I don't know.

Here the worker asserts her entitlement as a representative of the welfare system to get information from the client about the father of her children. At the same time, her language positions the client as an immoral "Jezebel" who has been sexually involved with men she cannot remember and as an unwed "matriarch" who is building a family outside marriage (Collins, 1990; Roberts, 1997). The worker demonstrates her skepticism about the client's truthfulness (i.e., "You never see his face?"), but the emphasis of the conversation is discovering information to track down the father rather than moral judgment of the woman.

In addition to across-state policies like child support enforcement, some states had their own reproduction-related policies. One state, Georgia, had a specialized fertility policy, the "family cap," that prevented women who were on welfare from receiving additional financial assistance if they had another child. In the encounter below, the bureaucratic imperative led to a conversation bordering on the absurd.

WORKER: Are you pregnant now?

CLIENT: No.

WORKER: You're not having any more?

CLIENT: No.

WORKER: Are you using any birth control?

CLIENT: I've had my tubes tied.

WORKER: I need you to sign this saying you understand that if you have any more, the baby will not be added to your check.

The dominant discourse of welfare that characterizes clients as at best careless, or at worst, entrepreneurial, about their fertility speaks through the worker so powerfully that even after the client states that she has been sterilized and cannot have more children, the worker continues to talk as if the client is imminently likely to conceive a baby and ask the state to support it. The worker's language enacts within the interview the negative view of welfare clients' reproductive decision-making that permeates welfare policy.

The bureaucratic imperative is also visible in the requirement that pregnancy be medically verified. This documentation requirement in and of itself suggests that welfare clients are likely to fake pregnancy to obtain benefits, even in the absence of a negative tone from the worker:

WORKER: How many months pregnant are you?

CLIENT: 7 months.

WORKER: Have you been to the doctor yet?

CLIENT: Yes.

WORKER: Did they give you a due date or a letter with the due date?

CLIENT: Yes, here it is.

Although this Georgia worker uses neutral language, a negative perspective on poor women's fertility-related behavior nonetheless enters this interview through the documentation requirement. The myth of the devious "welfare queen," who uses her fertility to trick the state into supporting her, informs the policy that workers implement in conversation with clients (Collins, 1990; Roberts, 1997).

There were several instances in which workers discussed reproductive issues with clients using bureaucratic language but resisted participating in the demeaning stereotyping of poor women that imbues welfare policy. These instances arose when workers emphasized assisting clients to comply with TANF's requirements while taking into account women's needs during pregnancy or early motherhood, as in this example from Georgia.

> WORKER: What kind of work—what do you want to do? Do you have a GED?
>
> CLIENT: No. [. . .]
>
> WORKER: You may want to work towards the GED while waiting for the baby. [. . .] We've got a program called New Connections to Work that may be good. Do you know what kind of work you may want?
>
> CLIENT: Nursing. [. . .]
>
> WORKER: We should do the program. Here's some information. [. . .] After you have the child, you go to work—you'll be set. It's a very good program.

Discussion

This research indicates that though sexuality-related topics are not discussed in the majority of welfare interviews, the private sexual decisions and relationships of poor women continue to be a focus of intervention in the day-to-day interactions welfare caseworkers have with their clients. Negative myths regarding poor women's reproductive decisions and relationships (Collins, 1990, 2004; Roberts, 1997) are expressed in welfare offices through their influence on welfare policy and regulations and through the effect these myths have on worker behavior. How workers talk with (and implicitly "frame" clients) is prescribed by bureaucratic mandates whose underlying assumptions reflect racialized myths antagonistic to poor women (Collins, 1990; Hays, 2003; Roberts, 1997). Workers' own informal, discretionary conversations with clients reflected moralizing messages that were also shaped by negative perceptions of poor women's sexuality. Although workers' talk expressing personal judgments of clients may seem more offensive than their bureaucratized language, both styles of speech contribute to the dehumanization of welfare clients. The more subtle action

of the bureaucratic imperative should not be disregarded; both of these strategies reflect the widely accepted false beliefs that poor women on welfare make careless or financially calculating reproductive decisions and that woman-headed families are not legitimate.

Just as the style of mainstream U.S. talk on race has gradually become less overtly and personally racist, more subtle and bureaucratized in its action (Bonilla-Silva, 2006), so analogously has welfare office talk regarding sexuality. By embedding conversations about sexual matters in bureaucratic talk about child support enforcement and the family cap, these conversations are transformed from overtly intrusive discussions of private issues into normalized outcomes of the need to ask for financial help. Women of other class backgrounds would be unlikely to submit to these interrogations, but the United States' current approach to ensuring a social safety net allows this continued focus for poor women (Hays, 2003). This analysis demonstrates that negative ideas about poor women and their fertility and family formation decisions persist in welfare policy and in its day-to-day implementation by caseworkers, but that they are often veiled in bureaucratic language.

Our findings regarding the apparent absence of differences in welfare office talk related to the race or gender of workers or clients are congruent with recent work by welfare implementation scholar Watkins-Hayes (2009), who observes that caseworkers' attitudes and behaviors are not determined by their social group membership alone. Rather, we observed workers' fairly consistent application of an ideology of irresponsible fertility to clients regardless of clients' races or their own. We ascribe this pattern to the racialization of welfare through which the state sanctions discourses (bureaucratic scripts and discretionary utterances) which reinforce underlying negative racial stereotypes, and normalizes the application of these myths to all poor women, regardless of race. Although Black and White women constitute roughly equal proportions of total TANF recipients (35.7%

and 33.4%, respectively), African American women are disproportionately represented among welfare clients (Hays, 2003; U.S. Department of Human Services, 2006). Welfare has been associated with Blackness in the collective mind of the U.S. public ever since African American women gained access to these programs in the 1960s (Gilens, 1999; Quadagno, 1994; Roberts, 1997); in these findings, we see negative myths regarding Black women's sexuality and childbearing extended to include all women on welfare, regardless of their individual races.

Our findings are based on data that are more than 10 years old, and we cannot be certain that the same racialized discourses we identified are employed in welfare offices today. However, scholars of race and policy such as Michelle Alexander (2010) have illuminated a pattern in which new systems of "racial control" in the United States, which tend to be more overtly "colorblind," emerge to replace those that are overturned. In this analysis, which seems likely to extend to welfare office practices, it is probable that these deep negative myths persist and continue to shape caseworker language, though they may look slightly less racially influenced on the surface.

We also noted differences among the three states studied in the amount and the style of conversations on reproductive decisions and relationships. Caseworker–client interactions in Georgia were more likely than those in Texas or Michigan to include sexuality-related topics, however, these conversations were less likely to involve discretionary moralizing by workers than those in other sampled states. In Texas, though interactions were less likely than in Georgia or Michigan to include discussion of clients' sexuality, when such discussions did occur, they were quite likely to involve moralizing discourses in addition to bureaucratic language; such moralizing was also more likely in Michigan than it was in Georgia. One possible explanation for these findings is that negative myths regarding poor women's fertility have a tendency to enter welfare office conversations, and if they do not

do so in bureaucratically mandated ways, they may be more likely to do so through caseworkers' personal moralizing. In states with explicit reproduction-related policies, like Georgia with its "family cap," workers were mandated to discuss sexuality-related topics and thus did so more frequently. Absent such policies in Michigan and Texas, conversations regarding sex and reproduction occurred less often, but because these conversations arose more at workers' discretion, they often included optional, personal moralizing.

In light of these results, it is important to note that individual welfare workers are not solely responsible for talking in ways that position clients negatively (Lindhorst et al., 2008). The actions of these workers reflect a structural reality: Across states and settings, caseworkers are required by law to discuss aspects of the private sexual lives of poor women. Current welfare policy, informed by an ideology that positions poor women as irresponsible in their fertility and illegitimate in their family formation, speaks through these workers.

This study has implications for the theoretical framing of future research on welfare, and for the implementation and creation of welfare policy. Our findings indicate the importance of careful theoretical attention to race and processes of racialization in any study examining welfare. Roberts' (1997) statement that race "fuels the welfare debate even when it is not mentioned" (p. 215) is exemplified by our finding that racialized myths regarding poor women's sexuality enter the welfare interview across multiple dimensions of potential difference. This dehumanizing framing of poor women was expressed through workers' optional moralizing talk about sexuality-related issues and in their bureaucratized language. Regardless of caseworker race, client race, or racial pairing of the worker–client dyad, these stereotypes affected workers' language in welfare interviews. Viewed one way, this finding might be considered null. However, a theoretical attunement to processes of racialization supports a more convincing interpretation:

that the dominant discourse of African American women's irresponsible reproduction and inappropriate family structure in which welfare interviews are embedded acts to "color" all welfare recipients and the language workers use with them.

Regarding policy implications, our analysis suggests that demeaning racialized stereotypes may influence welfare policy's creation and implementation in obvious and subtle ways. Different training and supervision might decrease the amount of discretionary moralizing done by caseworkers. However, such a solution would only address part of the problem. Negative myths regarding poor women's sexuality not only shape workers' optional talk but may also play a role in welfare policy itself. Thus, it is likely that these myths will continue to affect day-to-day talk in welfare offices even if they emerge through the less obviously offensive bureaucratic language mandated by policy. This problem is sustained by tenacious stereotypes that act at many levels.

The pervasiveness of these stereotypes means that attempts to challenge them must focus on depths, not surfaces. To change the discretionary messages welfare workers give their clients, their underlying perceptions of poor women and women of color, and more critically, the perceptions of policy makers, must be changed. This type of deep intervention will not proceed quickly or easily. It will require, at minimum, the kind of open discussion of race and racism that is rare in the United States (Alexander, 2010; Bonilla-Silva, 2006). However, such work has the potential to decrease the influence of negative myths upon those who implement welfare policy as caseworkers as well as reframing these issues for those who make it as elected representatives and those who shape it with participation as citizens.

Current welfare policy emphasizes marriage to "breadwinners" as a way of addressing poor women's need for financial resources for themselves and their children. This policy functions to place women and men into a family structure in which men of severely limited economic means are made financially responsible for women and children, regardless of structural economic factors (e.g., low wages, unemployment) that make meeting this responsibility difficult or impossible (McCall, 2000). It ignores the inconvenient fact that the majority of men who are the would-be husbands of women on welfare, and the fathers of their children, live in poverty as well (McCall, 2000; Roberts, 1997).

Regulating poor women's reproductive decisions and relationships has negative effects on women's freedom and well-being and does not adequately address child poverty (R. J. Smith, 2006; Weigt, 2010). Through regulating sexuality and encouraging marriage, and through other elements of TANF (e.g., work requirements), U.S. welfare policy treats financial provision for children as the almost exclusive responsibility of individual families (Cassiman, 2006). Issues of structural poverty are not considered. Women are made ultimately responsible for ensuring resources for their children by finding husbands who can provide for them financially (Swift, 1995). An alternative policy approach would be for the state to contribute to the support of children regardless of the sexual behavior or gendered positions (i.e. "breadwinner" and "homemaker") of their parents. To take this approach would be to recognize that earners and caregivers are required in families, regardless of whether men or women occupy these roles (Gornick & Meyers, 2009). This perspective could decrease child poverty and the stigmatization of poor women, which in the United States often involves racialized stereotypes that exacerbate existing injustice.

Funding

Data gathering for this work was supported by a grant to Marcia K. Meyers from the Nelson A. Rockefeller Institute of Government, State University of New York. During data analysis and writing, N. Tatiana Masters was partially supported by a fellowship from the National Institute of Mental

Health (F31-MH078732), and Taryn P. Lindhorst was partially supported by a career development award from the National Institute of Mental Health (1K-01-MH72827-01A).

References

Abramovitz, M. (1996). *Regulating the lives of women: Social welfare policy from colonial times to the present.* Boston, MA: South End Press.

Alexander, M. (2010). *The new Jim Crow: Mass incarceration in the age of colorblindness.* New York, NY: New Press.

Annie E. Casey Foundation. (2003). *Kids count databook.* Baltimore, MD: Author.

Berkowitz, E. D. (1991). *America's welfare state: From Roosevelt to Reagan.* Baltimore, MD: Johns Hopkins University Press.

Bonilla-Silva, E. (2006). *Racism without racists: Colorblind racism and the persistence of racial inequality in the United States.* Lanham, MD: Rowman & Littlefield.

Burger, S. (2004). Community health changes under welfare reform. *Journal of Community Health Nursing, 21*(3), 127–140.

Cameron, D., & Kulick, D. (2003). *Language and sexuality.* Cambridge, UK: Cambridge University Press.

Cassiman, S. (2006). Of witches, welfare queens, and the disaster named poverty: The search for a counter-narrative. *Journal of Poverty, 10*(4), 51–66.

Collins, P. H. (1990). *Black feminist thought: Knowledge, consciousness, and the politics of empowerment.* New York, NY: HarperCollins.

Collins, P. H. (2004). *Black sexual politics: African Americans, gender, and the new racism.* New York, NY: Routledge.

Corcoran, M., Danziger, S. K., Kalil, A., & Seefeldt, K. S. (2000). How welfare reform is affecting women's work. *Annual Review of Sociology, 26*, 241–269.

Danziger, S. H. (Ed.). (1999). *Economic conditions and welfare reform.* Kalamazoo, MI: W. E. Upjohn Institute for Employment Research.

De Jong, G. F., Graefe, D. R., & St. Pierre, T. (2005). Welfare reform and interstate migration of poor families. *Demography, 42*(3), 469–496.

Edin, K., & Kefalas, M. (2005). *Promises I can keep: Why poor women put motherhood before marriage.* Berkeley, CA: University of California Press.

Gilens, M. (1999). *Why Americans hate welfare: Race, media, and the politics of anti-poverty policy.* Chicago, IL: University of Chicago Press.

Gordon, L. (1994). *Pitied but not entitled: Single mothers and the history of welfare, 1890–1935.* New York, NY: Free Press.

Gornick, J. C., & Meyers, M. K. (2009). Institutions that support gender equality in parenthood and employment. In J. C. Gornick & M. K. Meyers (Eds.), *Gender equality: Transforming family divisions of labor* (pp. 3–56). New York, NY: Verso.

Hall, J. M., & Stevens, P. E. (1991). Rigor in feminist research. *ANS: Advances in Nursing Science, 13*(3), 16–29.

Hancock, A.-M. (2004). *The politics of disgust: The public identity of the welfare queen.* New York, NY: New York University Press.

Harris-Perry, M. (2011). *Sister citizen: Shame, stereotypes, and Black women in America.* New Haven, CT: Yale University Press.

Hays, S. (2003). *Flat broke with children: Women in the age of welfare reform.* New York, NY: Oxford University Press.

Horton-Salway, M. (2001). The construction of M.E.: The discursive action model. In M. Wetherell, S. Taylor, & S. J. Yates (Eds.), *Discourse as data* (pp. 147–188). London, UK: Sage.

Horvath-Rose, A. E., Peters, H. E., & Sabia, J. J. (2008). Capping kids: The family cap and nonmarital childbearing. *Population Research and Policy Review, 27*, 119–138.

Jagannathan, R., & Camasso, M. J. (2003). Family cap and nonmarital fertility: The racial conditioning of policy effects. *Journal of Marriage and Family, 65*, 52–71.

Jones, J. (1995). *Labor of love, labor of sorrow: Black women, work, and the family, from slavery to the present.* New York, NY: Vintage Books.

Katz, M. B. (1989). *The undeserving poor: From the war on poverty to the war on welfare.* New York, NY: Pantheon Books.

Lens, V. (2002). Welfare reform, personal narratives, and the media: How welfare recipients and journalists frame the welfare debate. *Journal of Poverty, 6*(2), 1–20.

Lindhorst, T., & Leighninger, L. (2003). "Ending welfare as we know it" in 1960: Louisiana's suitable home law. *Social Service Review, 77*(4), 564–584.

Lindhorst, T., Meyers, M., & Casey, E. (2008). Screening for domestic violence in public welfare offices: An analysis of case manager and client interactions. *Violence Against Women, 14*(1), 5–28.

Lipsky, M. (1980). *Street-level bureaucracy: Dilemmas of the individual in public services.* New York, NY: Russell Sage.

Loeb, S., Fuller, B., Kagan, S. L., & Bidemi, C. (2003). How welfare reform affects young children: Experimental findings from Connecticut. *Journal of Policy Analysis and Management, 22*(4), 537–550.

Maynard-Moody, S., Musheno, M. C., & Palumbo, D. (1990). Street-wise social policy: Resolving the dilemma of street-level influence and successful implementation. *Western Political Quarterly, 43*(4), 833–849.

McCall, L. (2000). Increasing inequality in the United States: Trends, problems, and prospects. *Economic and Political Weekly, 35*(21/22), L18–L23.

McCormack, K. (2005). Stratified reproduction and poor women's resistance. *Gender & Society, 19*(5), 660–679.

Meyers, M. K. (1998). *Gaining cooperation at the front lines of service delivery: Issues for the implementation of welfare reform.* Albany, NY: Nelson A. Rockefeller Institute of Government.

Meyers, M. K., & Lurie, I. (2005, June). *The decline in welfare caseloads: An organizational perspective.* Paper presented at the Mixed Methods Research on Economic Conditions, Public Policy, and Family and Child Well-Being conference in Ann Arbor, MI.

Meyers, M. K., Riccucci, N. M., & Lurie, I. (2001). Achieving goal congruence in complex environments: The case of welfare reform. *Journal of Public Administration Research and Theory, 11*(2), 165–201.

Miles, M. B., & Huberman, A. M. (1994). *Qualitative data analysis: An expanded sourcebook* (2nd ed.). Thousand Oaks, CA: Sage.

Murray, C. (1984). *Losing ground: American social policy, 1950–1980.* New York, NY: Basic Books.

Neubeck, K. J., & Cazenave, N. A. (2001). *Welfare racism: Playing the race card against America's poor.* New York, NY: Routledge.

Piven, F. F., & Cloward, R. (1971). *Regulating the poor: The functions of public welfare.* New York, NY: Pantheon Books.

Quadagno, J. S. (1994). *The color of welfare: How racism undermined the war on poverty.* New York, NY: Oxford University Press.

Reich, J. A. (2005). *Fixing families: Parents, power, and the child welfare system.* New York, NY: Routledge.

Roberts, D. E. (1997). *Killing the Black body: Race, reproduction, and the meaning of liberty.* New York, NY: Pantheon.

Roberts, D. E. (2002). *Shattered bonds: The color of child welfare.* New York, NY: Basic.

Saldaña, J. (2009). *The coding manual for qualitative researchers.* Thousand Oaks, CA: Sage.

Smith, A. M. (2001). The sexual regulation dimension of contemporary welfare law: A fifty state overview. *Michigan Journal of Gender and Law, 8,* 121–218.

Smith, R. J. (2006). Family caps in welfare reform: Their coercive and damaging effects. *Harvard Journal of Law and Gender, 29,* 151–200.

Soss, J., & Schram, S. F. (2007). A public transformed? Welfare reform as policy feedback. *American Political Science Review, 101*(1), 111–127.

Strauss, A., & Corbin, J. (1998). *Basics of qualitative research: Techniques and procedures for developing grounded theory.* Thousand Oaks, CA: Sage.

Swift, K. J. (1995). Manufacturing "Bad Mothers": A Critical Perspective on Child Neglect. Toronto: University of Toronto Press.

U.S. General Accounting Office. (2001). *Welfare reform: More research needed on TANF family caps and other policies for reducing out-of-wedlock births* (GAO-01-924). Washington, DC: U.S. General Accounting Office.

Watkins-Hayes, C. (2009). *The new welfare bureaucrats: Entanglements of race, class, and policy reform.* Chicago, IL: University of Chicago.

Weigt, J. (2010). "I feel like it's a heavier burden . . .": The gendered contours of heterosexual partnering after welfare reform. *Gender & Society, 24*(5), 565–590.

Questions for Critical Thinking

1. The authors discuss how caseworkers perpetuate negative myths regarding African American women's sexuality and motherhood. How does their analysis help you to understand how policy, rather than individual or cultural characteristics, perpetuates inequality for recipients of welfare?

2. Reflecting on this reading, what do you believe needs to change with regard to policy and institutional practices to better aid recipients of welfare? What do you see as the likelihood of implementing such changes? What barriers exist that may prevent their implementation?

3. What solutions do you see to poverty in the United States? How are these solutions informed by your own class experience?

Beyond Crime and Punishment

Prisons and Inequality

BRUCE WESTERN AND BECKY PETTIT

The following essay by sociologists Western and Pettit demonstrates how changes in government policy on crime and punishment have resulted in more men of color in prison, at a rate disproportionate to their rate of arrest. Linking race, crime, education, and work, the authors illustrate how the growth of the criminal justice system has masked the extent of economic inequality, which will lead to greater inequality in the future.

Even during the economic boom of the 1990s, more young black men who had dropped out of school were in prison than on the job. Despite rapid growth in employment throughout the economy, released prisoners in the 1990s earned little and were often unemployed. In these two ways—high imprisonment rates among disadvantaged men and poor economic prospects for ex-inmates—the penal system affects inequality in the American society.

Inequality is disguised because data on employment often do not include the mostly poor men who are locked away behind bars. When we count prisoners among the unemployed, we find that racial inequality in employment and earnings is much greater than when we ignore them. Taking prisoners into account substantially alters our understanding of how young black men are faring,

dramatically so when we focus on young black men with little education. In addition, the penal system fuels inequality by reducing the wages and employment prospects of released prisoners. The low-wage, unstable employment they experience when they return to society deepens the divisions of race and class.

For most of the 20th century, imprisonment policies had little effect on social inequality. Prison was reserved for the most violent or incorrigible offenders, and the inmate population was consequently small. This began to change in the early 1970s when stricter law enforcement enlarged the prison population. While incarceration once used to flag dangerousness or persistent deviance, by 2000 it had become a common event for poor minority males.

The Expansion of the Penal System

Between 1920 and 1970, about one-tenth of one percent of Americans were confined in prisons. The prison population increased sixfold in the three decades after 1970. By June 2000, about 1.3 million people were held in state and federal prisons, and 620,000 inmates were in local jails. This translates into a total incarceration rate of seven-tenths of one percent of the U.S. population. The current incarceration rate is five times the historical average of the 1925–70 period and six to eight times the incarceration rates in Western Europe. With the important exception of homicide, however, American levels of crime are similar to those in Western Europe.

These numbers mask the concentration of imprisonment among young black men with little schooling. Although there are no official statistics, we've calculated the proportion of penal inmates among black and white men at different ages and levels of education by combining data from labor force and correctional surveys. Incarceration rates doubled among working-age men between 1980 and 1999 but increased threefold for high school dropouts in their twenties. By 1999, fewer than one percent of working-age white men were behind bars, compared to 7.5 percent of working-age black men (Figure 1). Figures for young black unskilled

men are especially striking: 41 percent of all black male high school dropouts aged 22–30 were in prison or jail at midyear in 1999.

Although 9 out of 10 inmates are male (92 percent), women represent the fastest-growing segment of the inmate population. During the recent penal expansion, the female inmate population has grown more than 60 percent faster than the male inmate population. African-American women have experienced the greatest increase in criminal justice supervision.

Racial disparities in incarceration are even more stark when one counts the men who have ever been incarcerated rather than just those in prison on a given day. In 1989, about 2 percent of white men in their early thirties had ever been to prison compared to 13 percent of black men of the same age (Figure 2).

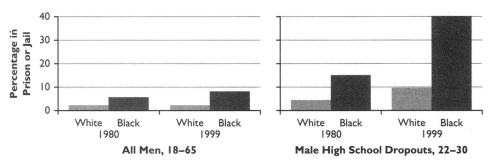

Figure 1 **Percentage of Incarcerated Men, 1980 & 1999, by Race And Education.**

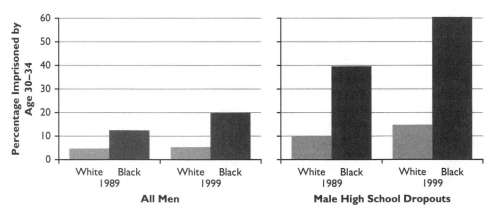

Figure 2 **Percentage of 30 to 34 Year-Old Men Ever Incarcerated, 1989 & 1999, by Race And Education.**

Ten years later, these rates had increased by 50 percent. The risks of going to prison are about three times higher for high school dropouts. At the end of the 1990s, 14 percent of white and 59 percent of black male high school dropouts in their early thirties had prison records.

The high rate of imprisonment among black men is often explained by differences in patterns of arrest and criminal behavior. Blacks are eight times more likely to be incarcerated than whites. With the important exception of drug offenses, blacks are overrepresented among prison inmates due to race differences in crime and arrest statistics. In 1991, for instance, black men accounted for 55 percent of all homicide arrests and 47 percent of homicide offenders in prison. Drug offenses aside, about three-quarters of the racial disparity in imprisonment can be linked to racial differences in arrests and in criminal offending as reported in surveys of crime victims. Although age and educational differences in incarceration have not been studied as closely as race, crime rates are also known to be high among young, poorly educated men. In short, young, black, male high school dropouts are overrepresented in prison mainly because they commit a disproportionate number of crimes (or, at least, street crimes) and are arrested for them. But that is not the whole story.

The explosion of the penal population after 1970 does not reflect increasing crime rates. The prison population has grown steadily every year since 1974, but crime rates have fluctuated up and down with no clear trend. For example 13.4 million crimes were reported to the police in 1980. In that year 182,000 people were admitted to state and federal prisons. In 1998, 12.4 million crimes were reported, and 615,000 people were sent to prison. Crime had gone down (see "Crime Decline in Context," *Contexts,* Spring 2002), but the number of people going to prison had tripled.

To explain the prison boom, we need to look beyond trends in crime. The exceptional pattern of incarceration among drug offenders provides an important clue. Drug offenders account for a rapidly increasing share of the prison population and the surge in drug-related imprisonment coincides with shifts in drug policy. Beginning in the 1970s, state and federal governments increased criminal penalties and intensified law enforcement in an attempt to reduce the supply, distribution and use of illegal narcotics. Drug arrests escalated sharply throughout the 1980s and 1990s, and drug offenders were widely sentenced to mandatory prison terms. While the total state prison population grew at about 8 percent annually between 1980 and 1996, the population of drug offenders in state prisons grew twice as quickly.

The war on drugs was just one part of a broad trend in criminal justice policy that also toughened punishment for violent and repeat offenders. For example, between 1980 and 1996, the average time served in state prison for murder increased from five to more than 10 years. Habitual offender provisions, such as California's three-strikes law, mandated long sentences for second and third felony convictions. Rates of parole revocation have also increased, contributing to more than a third of all prison admissions by the late 1990s.

Why did the punitive turn in criminal justice policy affect young male dropouts so dramatically? Consider two explanations. First, as we have seen, socially marginal men are the most likely to commit crimes and be arrested for them, so simply lowering the threshold for imprisonment—jailing offenders who in an earlier era would have just been reprimanded—will have the biggest impact on this group. Second, some legal scholars claim that policy was redrawn in a way that disproportionately affected young minority males with little schooling. Michael Tonry makes this argument in a prominent indictment of recent anti-drug policy. Street sweeps of drug dealers, mass arrests in inner cities and harsh penalties for crack cocaine were all important elements of the war on drugs. These measures spotlighted drug use among disadvantaged minorities but neglected the trade and consumption of illicit drugs in the suburbs by middle-class whites. From this perspective the drug war did not simply lower the threshold for imprisonment, it also targeted poor minority men.

Although the relative merits of these two explanations have not yet been closely studied, it is clear that going to prison is now extremely common for young black men and pervasive among young black men who have dropped out of school. Imprisonment adds to the baggage carried by poorly educated and minority men, making it harder for them to catch up economically and further widening the economic gap between these men and the rest of society.

Incarceration Conceals Inequality

Regardless of its precise causes, the effects of high incarceration rates on inequality are now substantial. Although the 1990s was a period of economic prosperity, improved job opportunities for many young black men were strongly outweighed by this factor. The stalled economic progress of black youth is invisible in conventional labor force statistics because prison and jail inmates are excluded from standard counts of joblessness.

Employment rates that count the penal population among the jobless paint a bleak picture of trends for unskilled black men in the 1990s. Standard labor force data show that nearly two-thirds of young black male high school dropouts had jobs in 1980 compared to just half in 1999 (Figure 3). When inmates are counted in the population, however, the decline in employment is even more dramatic. In 1980, 55 percent of all young black dropouts had jobs. By the end of the 1990s fewer than 30 percent had jobs, despite historically low unemployment in the labor market as a whole. Incarceration now accounts for most of the joblessness among young black dropouts, and its rapid growth drove down employment rates during the 1990s economic boom.

Because black men are overrepresented in prison and jail, incarceration also affects estimates of racial inequality. A simple measure of inequality is the ratio of white to black employment rates. In 1999, standard labor force data (which do not count convicts) show that young white dropouts were about one and a half times more likely to hold a job than their black counterparts. Once prison and jail inmates are counted among the jobless, the employment rate for young white dropouts is about two and a half times larger than for blacks. If we relied just on the usual labor force surveys, we would underestimate employment inequality for this marginal group by 50 percent.

Isolating many of the disadvantaged in prisons and jails also masks inequality in wages. When low earners go to prison and are no longer counted in the wage statistics, it appears that the average wage of workers has increased. This seeming rise in average wages doesn't represent a real improvement in living standards, however. We estimate that the

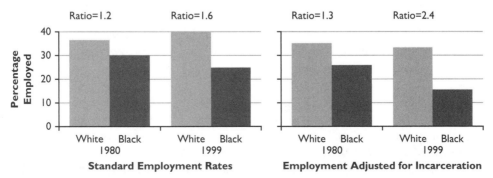

Figure 3 Employment Percentages of Male High School Dropouts, Aged 22 to 30, 1980 & 1999, by Race and Incarceration History.

wage gap between young black and white men would be 20 percent wider if all those not working, including those in prison and jail, were counted.

Incarceration Increases Inequality

The penal system not only conceals inequality, it confers stigma on ex-prisoners and reduces their readiness for the job market. Consequently, ex-convicts often live at the margins of the labor market, precariously employed in low-wage jobs. Ethnographic research paints a vivid picture. For example, in Mercer Sullivan's *Getting Paid,* delinquent youth in New York City cycled through many jobs, each held for just weeks or months at a time. One subject, after entering an ex-offender employment program at age 20, briefly held a factory job, but "he was fired for being absent and then went through three different jobs in the next four months: he tried delivering groceries, being a messenger, and doing maintenance in a nursing home." His experience was typical of Sullivan's subjects.

James Austin and John Irwin's interviews with current and former inmates in *It's About Time* reveal some of the difficulties ex-convicts have finding jobs. Released prisoners may have to disclose their criminal history or risk its discovery in a background check, or jobs may require special licenses or membership unavailable to most ex-convicts. Both may serve as substantial obstacles to employment. For example, a 38-year-old ex-convict living in the San Francisco Bay Area recalls, "I was supposed to get this light industrial job. They kept putting obstacles in front of me and I talked my way over them every time, till she brought up my being on parole and then she went sour on me. If they catch me lying on the application about being in prison or being on parole, they will [report a violation] and give me four months [in prison]." He also was unable to get a job in dry cleaning because he lacked certification: "I had dry-cleaning training a long time ago, but this time I wasn't in long enough to go through the program. It takes several years. You have to have the paper to get a job. I could jump in and clean anything—silks, wools—remove any spot, use all the chemicals, but I don't got any paper. They won't let you start without the paper."

Statistical studies have tried to estimate the toll incarceration takes on earnings after release. Ideally, to measure the effect of prison time, we would compare the pay of groups who were the same in all respects except for their prison records. However, criminal offenders are unusual in ways that are hard to observe. They may be more impulsive or aggressive, and these sorts of characteristics aren't consistently measured by our usual surveys. Thus different studies yield different estimates.

With these caveats in mind, statistical studies suggest that serving time in prison, by itself and with other characteristics of workers accounted for, reduces wages by between 10 and 30 percent. However, this is a simplified picture of how imprisonment affects job opportunities. Research also shows that incarceration affects the growth—and not just the level—of wages. While pay usually increases as men get older, this is not so true for ex-convicts. This suggests that men with prison records find it hard to get jobs with career ladders or seniority pay. Instead, they are more likely to work in day labor or other casual jobs.

Because young black men with little education are imprisoned in such large numbers, the economic effects of incarceration on individual ex-convicts can add up to large economic disadvantages for minority communities. Neighborhoods with many people going to prison develop bad reputations that smear even the law abiding. In *When Work Disappears,* William Julius Wilson reports on interviews with Chicago employers which show how the stigma of criminality can attach to entire minority communities. Considering job candidates from the West Side, one employer observed, "Our black management people [would] say 'No, stay away from that area. That's a bad area ...' And then it came out, too, that sooner or later we did terminate everybody from that area for stealing ... [or] drinking." National statistics also show how imprisonment widens the inequality between groups. Estimates for 1998 show that the reduced earnings of ex-convicts contribute about 10 percent to the wage gap between black and white men. About 10 percent of the pay gap between all male college graduates and all high school drop-outs is due to the reduced wages that inmates earn after they are released.

The Price of Safety

The inequalities produced by the penal system are new. The state and federal governments have never imprisoned so many people, and this increase is the result not of more crime but of new policies toward crime. This expansion of imprisonment represents a more massive intrusion of government into the lives of the poor than any employment or welfare program. Young black men's sustained contact with official authority now sets them apart from mainstream America in a novel way.

The inegalitarian effects of criminal justice policy may be justified by gains in public safety. We have in this article treated the penal population primarily as disadvantaged and not as dangerous people, but a large proportion of prisoners are violent offenders. Many commit crimes again and again. Criminals may be poor men, but they also perpetrate crime in poor neighborhoods. From this viewpoint, the pro-liferation of prisons represents a massive investment in the public safety of disadvantaged urban areas.

But can enduring public safety be achieved by policies that deepen social inequality? A great deal of research indicates that effective crime con-trol depends on reducing economic divisions, not increasing them. There is a strong link between criminal behavior and economic disadvantage. To the extent that prison undermines economic op-portunities, the penal boom may be doing little to discourage crime in communities where most men have prison records. If high incarceration rates add to the stigma of residence in high-crime neighbor-hoods, the economic penalties of imprisonment may affect ex-convicts and law-abiding citizens alike. The criminal justice system is now a newly significant part of a uniquely American system of social inequality. Under these conditions, the puni-tive trend in criminal justice policy may be even tougher on the poor than it is on crime.

Questions for Critical Thinking

1. The authors explain how government policy on crime has resulted in an increase in poor men of color in prison. How does their explanation counter common media portrayals that poor men of color are more likely to be criminals?

2. The authors illustrate how the growth of the criminal justice system has contributed to greater inequality in the United States. Whose interests are served by such an expansion?

3. As the authors state, "effective crime control depends on reducing economic divisions," not expanding the prison system. What ideas do you have for reducing economic inequality in a way that may lead to a reduction in crime?

The Treacherous Triangle

Justice, Immigration Enforcement, and Child Welfare

SETH FREED WESSLER

The following essay, by investigative reporter Seth Freed Wessler, describes the intersections of the criminal justice system, immigration enforcement, and the family court systems as "a treacherous triangle" for a child that leads to the destruction of families. Through his discussion he illustrates how the everyday decisions taking place in criminal and immigration courts have real impacts on the relationships between parents and children.

Roberta's story starts when she was pulled over by local police in Phoenix, Arizona, while driving three of her five children home from a family party where she admits she had one too many beers. Local police administered a Breathalyzer and put her under arrest for drunken driving. Roberta was shuttled to the county jail and her three children were immediately placed in temporary foster care. She expected to bond out and quickly return to her children. And, if Roberta were a citizen, that's probably exactly what would have happened. But Roberta is not a citizen. She's an undocumented immigrant. So, despite the fact that she's a single mother of five who lived in the United States without any previous run-ins with law enforcement, Roberta was flagged for deportation by federal immigration authorities and moved to an immigration detention center in the desert an hour and a half south of her home. She lost contact with her children, all five of whom were placed in

foster care, and after seven months inside the detention center, Roberta was deported to Mexico without her children.

Roberta's story is not unique. Federal data obtained by the Applied Research Center (ARC) through a Freedom of Information Act (FOIA) request, and first published in *Shattered Families; The Perilous Intersection of Immigration Enforcement and the Child Welfare System,* shows that in the six month period between January and June 2011, the federal government deported over 46,000 parents of U.S. children.[1] In December 2012, ARC obtained additional federal data through another FOIA request that reveals that the federal government deported nearly 205,000 parents of U.S. citizen children during the time period between July 1, 2010, and September 30, 2012.[2] The number accounts for 23 percent of all deportations in that period.[3]

One of the most troubling effects of this mass deportation of parents and separation of families is that thousands of children languish in foster care for long periods and are sometimes put up for adoption, at least in part because of the deportation of their mother or father. Based on surveys with child welfare caseworkers, attorneys who represent parents and children in juvenile courts, and analyses of data from 22 states, the *Shattered Families* report conservatively estimated that as of late 2011, there were at least 5,100 foster children around the country who faced barriers to reunifying with their families because their mothers or fathers had been detained or deported by the federal government. These families are often separated for long periods of time, and sometimes children are permanently separated from their parents.

Although U.S. Immigration and Customs Enforcement (ICE) issued a memo in 2011 instructing its agents to use discretion to focus immigration enforcement efforts on people with "serious" criminal convictions while avoiding the deportation of people charged with low level crimes, or whose sole violation is that they lack proper immigration documentation, the most up-to-date data reveal that this discretion has scarcely been applied and many of those deported as a result of involvement with the criminal justice system have been convicted of minor violations.[4] Meanwhile, the ICE memo on prosecutorial discretion enumerated a set of factors to weigh while making deportation decisions. One of these factors is whether a potential deportee is a parent to a U.S. citizen child.[5] The recent data on parental deportations suggest that the memo has not significantly changed ICE practice. Indeed for Roberta, a DUI charge, the first blemish she's ever had on her record, made her subject to rapid movement into deportation. The consequences for her and her children are Spartan: they may never see each other again.

Expanded Role of Local Law Enforcement in Federal Immigration Enforcement

In recent years, there has been an expanding conflation of immigration and criminal laws and the systems that enforce them and, as a result, a growing proportion of deportees now come to the attention of federal immigration authorities through county and state criminal justice systems. The federal government's flagship deportation program, Secure Communities, is broadening jail-based immigration enforcement, creating a treacherous triangle of the criminal justice, immigration, and child welfare systems. The federal government under the Obama Administration rapidly expanded collaboration with and use of local law enforcement departments to identify noncitizens for deportation. If the Bush Administration's immigration enforcement strategy can be defined by its focus on workplace immigration raids, Obama's enforcement approach is defined by its focus on local law enforcement and jails. The Obama Administration has extended its enforcement infrastructure deeply into local jails in a strategic shift putatively aimed at deporting "criminal aliens" (noncitizens convicted of criminal offenses) rather than on immigrants who have only violated noncriminal immigration laws.

Secure Communities was piloted in 2008 and rapidly expanded under the Obama Administration. The deportation program uses local jails to identify immigrants for deportation. Currently, any time someone is booked into a local jail in the United States, his or her fingerprint data are automatically run through an FBI database. In jails where Secure Communities has been implemented, the FBI forwards that same data to ICE, which then determines the person's immigration status. ICE can issue a detainer to put an immigration hold on any arrested individual who is not a citizen, including lawful permanent residents of the United States, asking the local jail to continue detaining the arrested person until ICE arrives to move him or her to an immigration detention center. Secure Communities now operates in nearly all jails in the country and is scheduled to be implemented in all remaining counties by 2013.[6] Localities have no choice whether to participate in the program; it is mandatory and, as a partnership between the FBI and ICE, functions automatically.

President Obama and the heads of his U.S. Department of Homeland Security (DHS) and ICE regularly claim that they have deported record numbers of "criminal aliens," largely as a result of this program. And, they claim that the program is color-blind, immune from the racial profiling that's plagued previous federal–local immigration partnerships. However, both claims are shaky. Well over one-quarter of deportees who come to the attention of ICE through Secure Communities have no criminal conviction at all and are deported simply for violating immigration laws, like entering the United States without authorization.[7] Another 30 percent involve minor charges, including violations like driving without a license, a common charge against undocumented immigrants who, because of laws in most states, cannot obtain drivers' licenses.[8] In fact, fewer than 30 percent of Secure Communities deportations since the program was implemented have been a result of what ICE calls "level 1" convictions, or felonies.[9] As for the claim of color-blindness, although ICE may be correct that database immigration checks are run without regard for identity, the program cannot control for the discretion local police exercise in who they arrest and book into jail. In a jurisdiction where police are interested in targeting people who they think are immigrants, Secure Communities provides a surefire mechanism for getting people deported. Rather than apprehending people who have been convicted of serious criminal offenses, Secure Communities is much more akin to a dragnet that feeds off of local police practices. The result is that any non-citizen who comes into contact with local police for whatever reason is at risk of deportation.

Increased Risk of Separation

DHS' widespread use of local jails to detain noncitizens puts families at particular risk of separation. In jurisdictions where local police aggressively participate in immigration enforcement through programs like Secure Communities, children are more likely to be separated from their parents and face barriers to reunification. ARC measured the impact of a similar local immigration enforcement program called 287(g)—the name refers to a section of the Immigration and Nationality Act. Through 287(g), ICE deputized local police and jails to act as federal immigration agents, giving them authority to arrest and detain noncitizens.

The impact of aggressive policing and local enforcement is clear when comparing counties that are otherwise similar except for 287(g) programs.[10] In counties surveyed by ARC where local police signed 287(g) agreements with ICE, children in foster care were about 29 percent more likely to have detained or deported parents than in other counties (an average of 4.9 percent of foster care kids in 287(g) counties compared to 3.8 percent in others). The difference was statistically significant when variation in the size of counties' noncitizen populations and their proximity to the border were taken into account.

An attorney for children in Tucson, Arizona, explained to the author the impact of jail-based immigration enforcement while describing a current foster care case in which a mother was picked up on charges that were entirely unrelated to the children. Considering the nature of the relatively minor allegations, had she been a citizen, the attorney had little doubt that she would have bonded out of jail in a day or two.

The attorney described a mother who was otherwise "fit" to parent, but was separated from her children for an extended period because of the federal government's use of local jails as staging grounds for deportation. The mother was not released after a day or two, but rather moved to an immigration detention center and deported.

"In this particular case, it was her inability to be with her kids because of detention and deportation that got them into care. The kids are a little older and if she had been a citizen, the children would have made do for a day and then she would have been out and back with them."

The period of separation that was caused by the mother's detention and deportation, the attorney explained, "means it's considered to be neglect now by our state's statutory regime. This case has been open two months and the kids are still in foster care."[11]

Barriers to Reunification

Once parents with children in foster care are moved to federal immigration detention centers, they are severed from the vital lines of communication that connect them with their children, the child welfare system, juvenile court, and the court-appointed attorney. According to the ARC study, ICE has categorically refused to transport parents to their juvenile court hearings. While parents are sometimes able to appear telephonically in these hearings, all of the dozens of detained parents interviewed for *Shattered Families* missed at least one hearing because they were detained.

Moreover, detained mothers and fathers are nearly always denied access to the services they need to comply with their child welfare reunification plans. In general, jails and prisons provide few parenting, drug and alcohol, and other programs for parents. The federal immigration authorities, and the counties and private prison contractors paid to run many immigration detention centers, are even less likely to provide these services. Indeed, none of the six detention centers visited during the *Shattered Families* investigation made services available to detainees. And, ARC heard reports of county jails that provide some access to services to "regular" inmates, but refused similar access to ICE detainees held in the same facility.

In the Baker County jail in Florida, which has a contract with the federal government to hold ICE detainees, a British immigrant mother of a young daughter who was in foster care received a letter from her child welfare caseworker listing tasks she was required to complete to reunify with her daughter.

> The letter read as follows: This letter is to advise you that as part of your outstanding dependency case plan tasks, you are court ordered to complete:
>
> 1. Parent Educational Training for Teens
> 2. Psychological Evaluation and follow all Court approved recommendations
> 3. Substance Abuse Evaluation and follow all Court approved recommendations
> 4. Family Counseling upon release
> 5. Stable Housing and Income. . . .[12]

The mother could complete none of these requirements from within detention. The document that the caseworker sent her went on to read, "One of the tasks in your case plan is to visit with your child," but the caseworker would not drive the daughter to see her mother in the detention center located four hours away. According to a 2011 report by Human Rights Watch, detainees are on average transferred to detention centers 370 miles from their initial arrest or apprehension by immigration authorities.[13]

Paths of Separation

Detained and deported parents' children enter foster care for a variety of reasons, and the child welfare and immigration enforcement systems can intersect in a number of ways. Some children enter into the child welfare system solely because their parents are detained. Other families already have child welfare system involvement, but immigration enforcement derails the family reunification process. Though every case bares a unique set of facts, there are a number of common routes leading to the separation of families at the intersection of parental deportation and the children welfare system. In each of these scenarios, detention and deportation result in extended family separation.

Straight Path

One route is that children enter foster care as a direct result of their parents' arrest or detention. In these cases, when parents are detained by ICE directly or are arrested by police and then shuffled to immigration authorities through Secure Communities or another program, parents are not able to care for their children and their children enter into foster care.

Even if parents in these cases are eventually released from immigration detention through the discretion of immigration authorities, the fact that their children are in the custody of the child welfare system can mean that the family will not be immediately reunified. In Phoenix, Arizona, an attorney told the author of a case in which a 2-year-old girl was placed in foster care when her mother was pulled over by police and arrested because she was undocumented and was driving without a license. The author spoke with the girl's foster care provider who said without equivocation, "The only reason they're not back together yet is the bureaucracy of the system. Before they can return her to her mother, they have to verify that the mom has a stable home, everyone else in the home passes background checks and that takes time." He added that if the mother had not been detained, the child welfare system would never have been involved in this family's life. "None of these were made into problems until she was detained."

Parallel Path

The second common route entails ostensibly "normal" allegations of child maltreatment that first bring a family to the attention of the child welfare department, but because the mother or father is detained, reunification is not immediately possible. In some cases, when police are involved in child welfare investigations, a case that might have resulted in prompt reunification for a citizen parent leads instead to detention and extended separation. Parents in detention are often denied the due process right to advocate for themselves in juvenile court, and the child welfare system poses obstacles to reunifying families.

In many cases, children enter into the child welfare system after a parent is deported following abuse or neglect allegations against a remaining parent or relative. In Alleghany County, North Carolina, for example, Felipe Montes, the father of three young U.S. citizens, was deported to Mexico in late 2010 because of repeated driving violations.[14] His kids remained with their mother, Marie Montes, a U.S. citizen. Marie struggled to take care of the children alone. Her husband had been the primary wage earner and caregiver in their family and she had long struggled with mental health and substance abuse issues. The local child welfare department quickly removed the three young children from their mother, deeming her neglectful. Rather than quickly reuniting the boys with their father, a man who had never been found to be neglectful, the boys were placed

in foster homes. The child welfare department refused to consider placing the children with their father in Mexico. Even after Marie and Felipe told the department that they wanted the children sent to live with their father, who now lived with an uncle and aunt in Tamaulipas, Mexico, the child welfare system continued to move toward terminating both Felipe and Marie's parental rights. After nearly two years of separation, in November 2012, Felipe regained custody of his three children on a "trial" basis and as of the writing of this article, he expects the child welfare case to be fully closed in early 2013.[15]

Interrupted Path

The third route involves families that were already involved with the child welfare system when parents are detained. Immigration enforcement can interrupt the reunification process for families that are already involved with the child welfare system when parents are taken to detention facilities. A mother, a green card holder from Portugal who we'll call Magda, interviewed by the author in a Florida detention center, was just weeks away from fully reunifying with her son. The boy had been removed from her custody previously because of child maltreatment allegations stemming from substance abuse, but the family was well on its way to reuniting. Magda and her son were spending the afternoon together on one of their unsupervised biweekly visits when her son soiled his pants. With little money to spare, Magda walked across the street to a dollar store and stole the set of clothes he needed. She wanted to avoid taking her son back to the foster home without changing his clothes first. She didn't make it out the door. The security guard called the police, who arrested the mother for petty theft. The officers drove her son back to his foster home and the mother was placed in deportation proceedings because of the theft charge. From detention, she could do little to maintain contact with her son, and their path to reunification was interrupted. Though it's likely an arrest of this kind during a visit would interrupt any reunification process, the difference for Magda was that detention denied her the chance to continue efforts to reunify.

Child Welfare Practice after Parental Deportation

The intersection of child welfare and immigration enforcement is treacherous from all directions. Though detention and deportation separate families on the front end, once parents are deported, child welfare departments often lack clear policies to facilitate the reunification of children with their parents in other countries.

Currently, few child welfare departments systematically contact consulates when child welfare departments take custody of U.S. citizen children of a noncitizen parent. This lack of communication is significant because when foreign consulates are involved in these cases, children are sometimes reunified with their deported parents. Consulates can serve as a bridge between parents and child welfare departments. They can help mothers and fathers access case plan services in other countries, facilitate home studies, conduct searches for parents who may have been deported leaving behind children in foster care, and process passports so that children are allowed to leave the United States. Based on interviews, the practice of involving consulates when a foreign national is involved in a case is increasing in some jurisdictions, but in too many instances, parental deportation leads directly to extended and sometimes permanent family separation.

Without explicit policies to facilitate reunification with detained or deported parents, reunification decisions may be driven by systemic bias against placing children with their parents in other countries. One common barrier to the reunification of children with parents who have been deported is bias in child welfare systems, which manifests as a belief that children are better off in the United States, even if it means they will be in foster homes or placed for adoption. This bias can supersede the child welfare system's mandate to reunify families whenever possible.

Many of the attorneys, social workers, children's advocates, and judges interviewed in the *Shattered Families* investigation raised questions about prejudice against reunifying U.S. citizen children with their deported noncitizen parents. According to the *Shattered Families* research, these biases were especially pronounced from many children's attorneys, advocates, and caseworkers. A parent and child attorney in Brownsville, Texas, said,

> With the climate in Mexico, nobody wants to send any of the kids to that—it's unsafe there now. Most of the attorneys don't want to send the kids back to Mexico and their arguments are, one, poor conditions in that county and, two, they only get public education up to a certain age before the parents have to pay for it. Most of our parents don't have education themselves; they are poor and they don't have the ability to pay for further education.

Because child welfare systems are tasked primarily with reunifying children with "fit" parents, the impact of this bias raises serious due process questions about how poverty, immigration status, and national origin may be used inappropriately to determine parental fitness.

These biases can compound anxieties among child welfare attorneys and courts about giving up jurisdiction over a dependency case, even if that case was near closure. A judge in Pima County took this position explicitly: "As a general matter, everyone is hesitant about placing a kid in another country because, from a practical standpoint, we are going to lose control of the case. Once I place the child [in another country], the judge basically ends up being asked to dismiss the dependency." Without clear agreements with foreign consulates to take part in the transition of children from the United States to reunify with their parents, there's nothing to soothe these anxieties, and children can remain in foster care that might otherwise be reunified with their parents.

Recommendations

If the number of deported parents remains anywhere near the 2011 level, families will continue to be separated and children will continue to become stuck in foster care. This year, the Obama Administration offered a reprieve from deportation and work permits to young immigrants who entered or were brought into the United States without authorization before they were age 16 and who do not have criminal convictions. The deferred action for childhood arrivals policy could protect hundreds of thousands of young people from deportation. Yet some have asked, "What about these young immigrants' parents?" In September during a forum aired on Univision, the president was asked directly if he would consider granting a similar deferral of removal to parents of U.S. citizen children. President Obama did not offer a clear response, but the question placed such a policy shift on the table.[16]

Suspend Secure Communities

Meanwhile, immigrant rights advocates around the country are advocating for a suspension of the Secure Communities program. As *Shattered Families* found, the use of local jails in identifying non-citizens puts families at risk of separation and increases the chances that children in foster care will have parents who are detained and deported. Advocates call for an end to Secure Communities on the grounds that it is not the selective, targeted enforcement program that the administration claims it to be and that it separates families. In California, the legislature passed a bill that would have instructed local jails to refuse to participate in the program. The bill, called the TRUST Act, was ultimately vetoed by California Governor Jerry Brown, but a number of counties, including Cook County, home to Chicago, and Washington, D.C., have passed ordinances similar to the TRUST Act. By interrupting the pipeline from local jails to deportation, families might be spared separation or allowed the time and space to reunite.

Minimize the Use of Detention before Deportation

If the federal government ultimately decides to deport parents, minimizing the use of detention before deportation could help reduce the prevalence of foster care cases. Were mothers and fathers released on their own recognizance while their immigration cases proceed, they could fully participate in decision-making about their children. As things stand, detention often makes this nearly impossible.

Train Child Welfare Departments and Attorneys

Short of changing immigration policy, child welfare departments around the country are the frontline in preventing the prolonged separation of children from their deported parents. These departments, however, often lack clear policies and guidelines to ensure that detained immigrant parents are provided with appropriate due process. Child welfare departments and juvenile courts can implement trainings for child welfare staff and attorneys who represent children and parents in juvenile dependency hearings to improve their understanding of the circumstances facing detained immigrant parents.

Legislative and Administrative Policy Reforms

Child welfare policies, protocols, and guidelines can be developed to specifically address detained and deported immigrant parents. The California legislature recently passed two pieces of legislation that would help reunify families separated by immigration enforcement and the child welfare system. California legislation, the Reuniting Immigrant Families Act (SB 1064) would authorize juvenile court judges to provide detained or deported parents additional time to reunify with their children and require state child welfare authorities to offer guidance to counties about how to establish agreements with foreign consulates.[17] The bill would also prohibit child welfare departments from considering immigration status when making foster care placement decisions. A similar federal bill, the Help Separated Families Act (H.R. 6128), was introduced, but not yet passed in Congress.

Most components of the California and federal legislation could be adopted via administrative reforms at the state or federal level. For example, a number of county and state child welfare departments around the country have had Memorandum of Understanding (MOU) with foreign consulates for a number of years, most often with the Mexican consulate. These MOUs could be adopted without legislative action. Similarly, at least one state, Illinois, has a clear policy that excludes immigration status from consideration in potential kinship placements.[18] In addition to child welfare departments, juvenile courts could also enter into MOUs with foreign consulates directly, such as the agreement developed by Los Angeles County Juvenile Court and the Mexican consulate.

A second California bill, the Call for Kids Act (AB 2015), would provide incarcerated immigrant parents with clear information in their native language about their right to make two phone calls at the time of arrest, clearly post this right in the jail/police location, and provide an additional two phone calls at the time of their transfer from local law enforcement to a federal detention facility.[19] Because immigrants in the criminal justice system are often moved quickly to immigration detention, the additional phone calls could help parents with childcare arrangements at the time of transfer so that they do not simply disappear into detention. This bill will also help incarcerated parents in general, by providing all parents in the criminal justice system with greater access to the world outside their cells.

Roberta, the mother whose case was described at the opening of this chapter, was deported late last year and has still not been reunified with her children. According to a local legal services provider who has intermittent contact with Roberta, two of the kids have now been placed in the care of relatives, while three remain in foster care with nonrelatives. With no likely route for her to return to the United States given the mandatory ten-year bar for illegal entry and lack of responsiveness from the child welfare department, she and her children will likely be separated for years. The policy and practice changes discussed here could help to keep other families from facing a similar fate.

Notes

1. Wessler, S. F. (2012). *Shattered families: The perilous intersection of immigration enforcement and the child welfare system.* Applied Research Center. Retrieved from http://www.arc.org/shatteredfamilies.

2. U.S. Immigration and Customs Enforcement. *Deportation of Parents of U. C. Citizen Children July 1, 2010-September 30, 2013.* Accessed by Colorlines.com on December 12, 2012. http://colorlines.com/archives/2012/12/deportations of parents of us-born citizens 122012.html.

3. *Ibid.*

4. Preston, J. (June 6, 2012). Deportations continue despite U.S. review of backlog, *New York Times,* Retrieved from http://www.nytimes.com/2012/06/07/us/politics/deportations-continue-despite-us-review-of-backlog.html?r=2&smid=tw-share.

5. Morton, J. (2012). ICE Memorandum. *Exercising prosecutorial discretion consistent with the civil immigration enforcement priorities of the agency for the apprehension, detention, and removal of aliens.* Retrieved from http://www.icc.gov/doclib/secure-communities/pdf/prosecutrial-discretion-memo.pdf.

6. U.S. Immigration and Customs Enforcement. *Secure Communities: Activated jurisdictions.* Retrieved from http://www.ice.gov/doclib/secure-communities/pdf/sc-activated.pdf.

7. U.S. Immigration and Customs Enforcement. *Secure Communities: Monthly statistics through April 30, 2012.* Retrieved from http://www.icc.gov/doclib/foia/sc-stats/nationwide_interop_stats-fy2012-to-date.pdf.

8. *Ibid.* 6.

9. *Ibid.* 6.

10. *Ibid.* 1.

11. Anonymous interview by author, Tucson, Arizona. July 7, 2011.

12. Documents provided to author.

13. Human Rights Watch. *A costly move: Far and frequent transfers impede hearings for immigrant detainees in the United States.* Retrieved from http://www.htw.org/reports/2011/06/14/costly-move-0.

14. Seth Freed Wessler. "Deported Dad Begs North Carolina to Give Him Back His Kids," Colorlines. com, February 14, 2012. http://colorlines.com/archives/2012/02/deported_dad_begs_north_carolina_not_put_kids_into_adoption.html.

15. Seth Freed Wessler, "A Deported Father Wins a Long, Painful Fight to Keep His Kids," Colorlines. com November 28, 2012. http://colorlines.com/archives/2012/11/pc_judge_reunites_deported_father_with_three_us_citizen_children.html.

16. Rivas, J. (September 21, 2012). *Univision anchor cites Colorlines.com deportation investigation.* Colorlines.com. Retrieved from http://colorlines.com/archives/2012/09/univision_anchor_cites_colorlinescom_deportation_investigation_to_obama.html.

17. SB 1064, 2011–2012 Leg., Reg. Sess. (CA 2012). Retrieved from http://legiscan.com/gaits/text/574600.

18. Illinois Department of Children and Family Services. *Licensing, payment and placement of children with undocumented relatives. III. Policy guide 2008.01.* Retrieved from http://www.f2f.ca.gov/res/pdf/PolicyGuideLicensing.pdf.

19. AB 2015, 2011–2012 Leg., Reg Sess. (CA 2012). http://loginfo.legislature.ca.gov/faces/billTextClient.xhtml;jsessionid=fb26709e73be6c01b8866926a8c2?bill_201120120AB2015.

Questions for Critical Thinking

1. Wessler asserts that, although instructed to focus on immigration enforcement on people with serious criminal convictions, agents of Immigration and Customs Enforcement often target those with minor convictions. Why do you think this is? How does this reality reinforce or counter your own assumptions about immigration enforcement?

2. What policy changes do you see as necessary in our policies around immigration enforcement? How might these changes impact inequality on the basis of immigration status in the United States?

3. Wessler offers several recommendations to help alleviate the inequality that results from current immigration enforcement policies. What do you think of these? What additional recommendations do you have to offer?

The Digital Reproduction of Inequality

ESZTER HARGITTAI

The following essay, by communication studies professor and sociologist Eszter Hargittai, explores the notion of digital inequality, represented by differential access to online resources and technology depending on one's class position. As the author illustrates, differential access results in exacerbating social inequalities.

By the beginning of the twenty-first century, information and communication technologies (ICT) had become a staple of many people's everyday lives. The level of instantaneous connectivity—to others and to an abundance of information—afforded by advances in ICT is unprecedented. With economies increasingly dependent on knowledge-intensive activities, the unequal distribution of knowledge and information access across the population may be linked increasingly to stratification. No sooner did the Internet start diffusing to the general population in the mid-1990s than did debates spring up about its implications for social inequality. From the perspective of social mobility, digital media could offer people, organizations, and societies the opportunity to improve their positions regardless of existing constraints. From the point of view of social reproduction, however, ICT could exacerbate existing inequalities by increasing the opportunities available to the already privileged while leading to the growing marginalization of the disadvantaged.

Most initial attention concerning ICT's implications for social stratification focused on what segments of the population have access to the Internet or are Internet users (e.g., Bimber 2000; Hoffman and Novak 1998). Access is usually defined as having a network-connected machine in one's home or workplace. Use more specifically refers to people's actual use of the medium beyond merely having access to it. The term "digital divide" became a popular expression to sum up concerns about the unequal diffusion of the medium. The concept is most often understood in binary terms: someone either has access to the medium or does not, someone either uses the Internet or does not.

However, as an increasing portion of the population has gone online, a dichotomous approach is no longer sufficient to address the different dimensions of inequality associated with digital media uses. The term *digital inequality* better captures the spectrum of differences associated with ICT uses (DiMaggio et al. 2004). A more refined approach considers different aspects of the divide, focusing on such details as quality of equipment, autonomy of use, the presence of social support networks, experience and user skills, in addition to differences in types of uses (Barzilai-Nahon 2006; Dewan and Riggins 2006; DiMaggio et al. 2004; Mossberger, Tolbert, and Stansbury 2003; Norris 2001; van Dijk 2005; Warschauer 2003).

Originally appeared as Hargittai, E. (2008). The Digital Reproduction of Inequality. In Social Stratification. Edited by David Grusky, Boulder, CO: Westview Press. 936–944. © 2008 Eszter Hargittai.

Variation in basic usage rates continues to exist, so considering the core digital divide of access versus no access remains an important undertaking. However, to understand in a nuanced manner the implications of ICT for social inequality, it is important to analyze differences among users as well. This chapter will do both, starting with a historical look at connectivity patterns by population segments. This discussion is then followed by an explanation of why it is important to distinguish among users of digital media. A conceptual framework lays out the processes through which users' social position influences their ICT uses and how this in turn may contribute to social inequality even among the connected. Although the primary focus here is on Internet use in the United States, the main arguments made can be extended to the use of other digital devices in other national contexts as well.

The Haves and Have Nots

In 1995, the National Telecommunications Information Administration of the U.S. Department of Commerce published a report entitled "Falling Through the Net: A Survey of the 'Have Nots' in Rural and Urban America" in which policy makers analyzed data from the Current Population Survey about computer and modem use among Americans. Findings suggested that different segments of the population were using digital technologies at varying rates. In subsequent years, these reports began to focus increasingly on Internet access as opposed to computer use only, documenting continued differences among various population groups (NTIA 1998, 1999, 2000). The reports' titles highlighted concerns about inequality as they all began with the phrase "Falling Through the Net."

Breaking with tradition, the fifth report of the NTIA published in 2002, based on data collected in 2001, was called "A Nation Online: How Americans Are Expanding Their Use of the Internet" (NTIA 2002). The title of this last report no longer focused on differences. Rather, it highlighted the fact that more and more Americans were going online. While significant differences remained among various population segments regarding their rates of connectivity, the report focused on the growing number of people accessing the Internet through high-speed connections. This change in focus may imply that Internet use had reached universal levels, but that was not the case.

Overall findings from the reports suggested that while the Internet may have been spreading to an increasing portion of the American population, certain segments were much more likely to be online than others. In particular, men, younger people, whites, non-Hispanics, urban residents, the more highly educated, and those with higher income were more connected than their counterparts. Gender differences leveled off after a few years with respect to basic access (Ono and Zavodny 2003) although not regarding amount of use and skill (Hargittai and Shafer 2006). In contrast, all other differences in access among different population segments remained throughout the years.

Looking at adoption figures over time, we find that while all segments increased their participation significantly, disparities continued to persist. Figures 1 and 2 illustrate this point for income and education, respectively. As Figure 1 shows, people in all income brackets increased their participation over time, but the slopes in the higher income brackets are somewhat steeper, leading to an increased gap among groups over time. The data points in Figure 2 tell a similar story. Although the gap between those who have a college degree and graduate education narrowed over the years, all other gaps widened over time. In particular, the least educated—those with less than a high school degree—increased their connectivity minimally over the eight-year period. Overall, these trend data suggest that while all population segments may have become increasingly connected, serious divides persist with the most disadvantaged trailing behind the more privileged in significant ways.

We have less data on the diffusion of cell phones, but the little evidence that has surfaced suggests similar patterns of unequal distribution among the

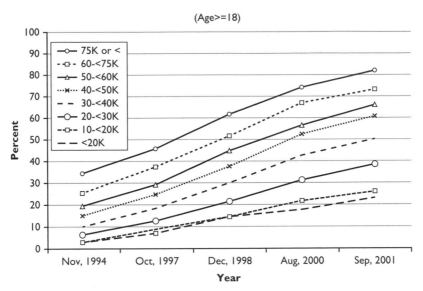

Figure 1 Internet Adoption by Level of Income in the United States, 1994–2001.

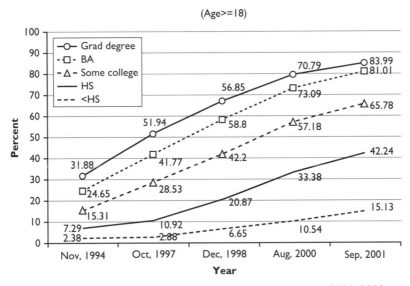

Figure 2 Internet Adoption by Level of Education in the United States, 1994–2001.

population. Looking at the earlier years of diffusion using data from 1994–1998, researchers found that mobile technology adoption was positively related to both income and education (Wareham, Levy, and Shi 2004). Based on data from 2006, Horrigan showed that people with lower levels of income were less likely to be users (Horrigan 2006). Analyses (by Hargittai for this chapter) of these same data collected by the Pew Internet and American Life Project also found that those with higher levels of education were more likely to own cell phones, and these findings are robust (also for income) when controlling for other factors. Moreover, those with higher income tend to own cell phones with more functionality (e.g., the ability to send and receive text messages, take photos and go online). While this literature is not as elaborate as the one on different rates of Internet connectivity, these findings clearly suggest that the digital divide expands beyond Internet use into the domain of mobile technology adoption as well.

Differences among the Connected

The uses of ICT can differ considerably with divergent outcomes for one's life chances. Therefore, it is imperative to examine variations in use among those who have crossed the digital divide fault line to the land of the connected. Baseline Internet use statistics do not distinguish among those who go online for no more than checking sports scores or TV schedules and those who use the medium for learning new skills, finding deals and job opportunities, participating in political discussions, interacting with government institutions, and informing themselves about health matters. Yet such differentiated uses can have significant implications for how ICT uses may relate to life outcomes. This section describes how various user characteristics and one's social surroundings influence digital media uses.

People's Internet uses do not happen in isolation of their societal position and the social institutions they inhabit. A refined approach to digital inequality recognizes that people's socioeconomic status influences the ways in which they have access to and use ICT. In addition to factors such as age, gender, race, ethnicity, disability status, education, and wealth, one's social surroundings are also relevant to one's ICT experiences. Figure 3 presents a graphical representation of this framework.

The basic premise is that the societal position that users inhabit influences aspects of their digital media uses, such as the technical equipment to which they have access and the level of autonomy they possess when using the medium. Autonomy of use is understood as the freedom to use digital

media when and where one wants to. Twenty-four-hour access at home can yield a much more autonomous user experience than having to drive half an hour to a public library where one competes with others for usage time and where filtering software limits the types of materials within reach. Similarly, a workplace that allows Web use without constraints results in a very different experience from a job environment where one's online actions are constantly monitored. Quality of equipment (available hardware, software, and connection speed) and autonomy of use can both be a function of one's socioeconomic status.

The use of and learning about digital media both happen in social contexts. In addition to autonomy of use, which itself is a certain social context, the availability of other users in one's social circles can have important implications for one's online experiences. The relevant mechanisms through which social networks matter can be grouped into two main categories: informal and more directed information exchange. The former refers to knowledge one amasses through everyday discussions with peers about digital media uses and includes suggestions passed along by others through email or at the water cooler. The latter highlights the importance of support networks when users encounter a specific problem during their experiences with ICT. When faced with a difficulty, it makes a difference

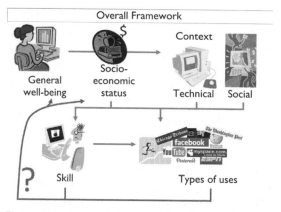

Figure 3 Framework for Studying the Implications of ICT Use for Social Inequality.

to have access to knowledgeable networks that help in finding a solution.

All of these factors then influence users' online abilities and what they are able to accomplish using digital media. While many online actions may seem trivial to the experienced user, most activities require some level of know-how. From recognizing what material is available online to being able to find it efficiently, from knowing how to contribute to online content production to knowing where to find relevant networks, from having the ability to evaluate content credibility to being vigilant about privacy and security concerns, informed uses of digital media rely on many important skills (Hargittai 2007b).

One's social position, the context of one's use, and one's online abilities then all have the potential to influence the types of uses to which one puts the medium. Some uses are more likely to yield beneficial outcomes than others. The next section will enumerate the ways in which ICT uses may improve, or in some cases impede, one's life chances.

How ICT Use Matters

The most pressing question for students of social inequality is whether the usage dimensions described above then loop back and translate into differences in users' socioeconomic position. What are the processes through which more informed and frequent uses of ICT may privilege some users over others? There are several ways in which differential ICT uses may influence access to the types of assets, resources, and valued goods that underlie stratification systems (Grusky 2008). The overarching idea is that certain types of ICT uses can result in increased human capital, financial capital, social capital, and cultural capital while other types of uses may outright disadvantage the uninformed.

With more and more jobs requiring the synthesis and analysis of varying types of information, employees with advanced Internet user skills can perform their jobs more effectively and efficiently. The Internet makes vast amounts of information

available *so long as* one knows how to locate desired material. While theoretically all public Web pages are equally available to all users, not everybody possesses the necessary skills to (1) recognize in all situations the types of content relevant to a task that can be found online; (2) find the information; (3) do so efficiently; and (4) carefully evaluate the results to avoid misinformation or, worse, fraudulent outcomes.

Even if people do not know how to perform certain tasks, advanced skills will allow them to find assistance online. Since skill encompasses the ability to find others who may have the desired information and efficiently contact them for guidance, even when lacking know-how most relevant to the task at hand, the skilled user can benefit through informed use of the medium. This all leads to more tasks getting done quicker and more efficiently with possibly higher-quality results than would be possible if relying on fewer resources. In addition to helping with the performance of on-the-job tasks, ICT also allow people to develop additional skills that may advantage them in the labor market. Free tutorials exist online for training in a myriad of domains from foreign languages to software applications, from design skills to networking to productivity enhancement tips.

Enterprising ways of using the Internet can save a person significant amounts of money. Several services exist that make comparison shopping very easy, allowing the user to find the best deals on an item without spending money on gas and time on driving from one store to the next. The use of auction sites expands options even further. Moreover, the especially knowledgeable can take advantage of other people's mistakes by searching for items with spelling mistakes thereby avoiding bidding wars given that misspelled items are seen by few (Hargittai 2006). In addition to savings through informed purchasing, people can also make money by selling products on the Web. While putting one's items on the market used to require significant upfront investment, ICT have lowered the barriers to entry for putting things up for sale accessible to a large buyer base, assuming one knows what services help with reaching the largest or most relevant purchasers.

The potential of ICT for expanding one's social networks is enormous, although efficient and relevant ways of doing so are not trivial and require some amount of know how. In some cases the Internet simply complements more traditional methods of networking while in others the medium is the main facilitator of a new relationship. The former refers to use of the tool to contact people who are already in one's extended network. The latter occurs thanks to various online interactions that can range from the exchange of information on a mailing list to the exchange of goods and services extending well beyond the Web. People find rides, coordinate meetings, and get emotional support from others online. But as with all other aspects of Internet use, skill matters. Finding the relevant communities and being sufficiently vigilant not to place oneself in harm's way are all important aspects of building social capital on the Web.

Familiarity with the latest trends can serve as status markers. Being able to discuss special topics in depth can help create bonds between people. Thanks to the Internet, certain subjects formerly much less accessible to the general public are more widely available. It is no longer necessary to go see a museum's special exhibition to have the facility to discuss what is on display since many galleries now put their pieces online. It is possible to develop a reasonably informed opinion about a restaurant halfway across the world simply by reading the many reviews available and constantly updated online. Knowing how to locate information about travel destinations—from driving directions to entertainment options—can yield more influence to the informed. Being able to draw on a myriad of topics while conversing with higher-ups can leave a good impression. While resources about diverse topics have long been available to the public, the ease and speed with which the Internet delivers information are unprecedented.

Informed users can be more engaged in the political process than those who rely exclusively on broadcast media for their political information seeking. Whether finding like-minded people or informing oneself in depth about the other side's perspective, the Internet allows for the exchange of political opinions much more than any other medium. Creating petitions and mobilizing others around a cause can be facilitated significantly with various online tools. Again, however, knowledge of what is available in this domain and how one can implement the services to benefit one's specific needs and interests is an essential part of any such undertaking.

The above are examples of how informed uses can have beneficial outcomes. There is another side to online actions, however. Uninformed uses may have outright problematic if not detrimental consequences. Do users stop to think about the context of, for example, an email message that requests confidential information from them? If everyone was aware of these issues, then phishing emails—messages that pretend to be from a reputable source to extract confidential information from users—would not lead to people giving up their passwords to Web sites that contain private information such as their bank accounts. Yet, we know that even among young adults—the generation that is growing up with these media— many lack the necessary knowledge to approach possibly malicious email with care (Hargittai 2008). While fraud has always existed, the scope of malicious activities and their consequences have skyrocketed.

Related to online social interactions discussed above, but sufficiently distinct to merit its own discussion, is one's reputation developed from one's online pursuits. Sending emails from the privacy of one's home or office leads many to behave less carefully than they would in a public social setting. Few interactions on the Web are truly anonymous yet many people do not realize this when sending critical messages or posting comments on Web sites. An unwelcome remark can have negative consequences if targeting the wrong person. Alternatively, critical comments by others can tarnish the reputation of the person under attack. In contrast, a well-thought-out online presence can result in significant benefits. Those who participate regularly in online discussions and maintain Web sites frequented by many can amass fame that can later translate into fortune as well.

Generally speaking, many of the skills needed to reap the benefits listed here—or sidestep negative implications—can be learned from one's immediate networks. Growing up in a household that has the latest gadgets and digital media resources will make a difference when a student then encounters these tools in the classroom. Having siblings who can navigate the technologies will help in the transfer of relevant know-how. Living in neighborhoods where many in one's proximity are also discovering the latest ICT options will allow for more opportunities to develop savvy in the domain of digital media than a situation in which one is isolated without access to relevant technologies and knowledgeable networks. Bourdieu's cultural capital (1973) applied to the twenty-first century must incorporate the differential exposure to, understanding, and use of ICT. Work looking at young adults' digital literacy has found a statistically significant positive relationship between Internet savvy and the parental education of respondents (Hargittai 2007b).

Overall, it is important to recognize that ICT do not nullify the effects of other variables on one's life chances. People's ICT uses happen in the context of their lives, influenced by their socioeconomic status and social surroundings. The question is whether ICT uses have an independent effect on life outcomes. Given the relative newness of the Internet and other digital media uses at a mass societal level, this field is in its infancy and lacks the longitudinal data necessary to answer many of the questions raised here. Nonetheless, preliminary findings seem to suggest that ICT reinforce inequalities more than alleviating differences. Although not without its critics (DiNardo and Pischke

1997), the general consensus seems to be that skill-biased technological change, and especially computerization, is an important source of the rise in earnings inequality in recent years (Krueger 1993). A more recent study found Internet use to have an independent effect on wage differences, suggesting tangible outcomes of being among the connected (DiMaggio and Bonikowski 2006).

Luxury Good or Essential Tool?

In 2001, then chair of the Federal Communication Commission Michael Powell likened the digital divide to a luxury car divide, stating: "I think there is a Mercedes divide, I would like to have one, but I can't afford one" (quoted in Clewley 2001).

Is Internet use simply a luxury item with people's connectivity—or lack thereof—merely a reflection of their preferences for the medium? As ICT become ever more central to our social infrastructure one can no longer participate meaningfully in our society without deep and ongoing usage of digital media. Once an entire society is built around these tools, they can no longer be considered simply as luxury goods. While the car and the telephone may have, at one time, been regarded as extravagant expenditures of the wealthy, once contemporary society was thoroughly built around these innovations they became necessities for operating in society and those who lacked them were socially excluded.

While it may be that some people opt out of ICT use based on an informed understanding of all that the Internet has to offer, much more likely is that people do not realize the many necessities and benefits of digital media. As an increasing number of activities between institutions and individuals move online—concerning both the public and the private sector—being a nonuser will have growing implications for people's access to various services. If government institutions assume a familiarity with and access to the medium, then lacking access to and understanding of such resources, some will be unable to interact with and navigate the system optimally.

Take, for example, the case of Medicare Part D in 2006. The government introduced a new system and required the elderly to make important choices about their health insurance. In response to concerns about the difficulty of navigating the system, the administration created a Web site and directed people to it for assistance with the program (Freese, Rivas, and Hargittai 2006). However, the resource was very complicated to navigate for many and the assumption that the elderly could access and understand the site was unfounded, as many were uninformed about or confused by the system. Similarly, more and more commercial services make material available on the Web and charge extra fees to those who interact with the company offline. When important government services are primarily accessible online and when there is an extra financial cost to handling matters with businesses offline, then having access to the Internet and knowing how to use it can no longer be considered an optional luxury item.

Conclusion

Disparities in people's Web-use abilities and uses have the potential to contribute to social inequalities rather than alleviate them. Those who know how to navigate the Web's vast landscape and how to use digital media to address their needs can reap significant benefits from it. In contrast, those who lack abilities in these domains may have a harder time dealing with certain logistics of everyday life, may miss out on opportunities, and may also obtain incorrect information from unreliable sources or come to rely on unsubstantiated rumors. Differentiated uses of digital media have the potential to lead to increasing inequalities benefiting those who are already in advantageous positions and denying access to better resources to the underprivileged. Merton's (1973) observation "Unto every one who hath shall be given" applies to this domain. Preliminary findings from this emerging field suggest that initial advantages translate into increasing returns over time for the digitally connected and digitally skilled.

References

Barzilai-Nahon, Karine. 2006. "Gaps and Bits: Conceptualizing Measurements for Digital Divide/s." *Information Society* 22: 269–278.

Bimber, B. 2000. "The Gender Gap on the Internet." *Social Science Quarterly* 81: 868–876.

Bourdieu, Pierre. 1973. "Cultural Reproduction and Social Reproduction." Pp. 71–112 in *Knowledge, Education, and Cultural Change*, edited by Richard Brown. London: Tavistock.

Clewley, Robin. 2001. "I Have a (Digital) Dream." In *Wired*, http://www.wired.com/politics/law/news/2001/04/43349.

Dewan, S., and F. Riggins. 2006. "The Digital Divide: Current and Future Research Directions." *Journal of the Association of Information Systems* 6: 298–337.

DiMaggio, Paul and Bart Bonikowski. 2006. "Make Money Surfing the Web? The Impact of Internet Use on the Earnings of U.S. Workers." *American Sociological Review*.

DiMaggio, Paul, Eszter Hargittai, Coral Celeste, and Steven Shafer. 2004. "Digital Inequality: From Unequal Access to Differentiated Use." Pp. 355–400 in *Social Inequality*, edited by Kathryn Neckerman. New York: Russell Sage Foundation.

DiNardo, John E., and Jorn-Steffen Pischke. 1997. "The Returns to Computer Use Revisited: Have Pencils Changed the Wage Structure Too?" *Quarterly Journal of Economics* 112: 291–303.

Freese, Jeremy, Salvador Rivas, and Eszter Hargittai. 2006. "Cognitive Ability and Internet Use Among Older Adults." *Poetics* 34: 236–249.

Grusky, David B. 2008. *Social Stratification: Class, Race, and Gender in Sociological Perspective*. Boulder, CO: Westview Press.

Hargittai, Eszter. 2006. "Hurdles to Information Seeking: Explaining Spelling and Typographical Mistakes in Users' Online Search Behavior." *Journal of the Association of Information Systems* 7. http://jais.aisnet.org/articles/default.asp?vol=7&art=1.

———. 2007b. "A Framework for Studying Differences in People's Digital Media Uses." In *Cyberworld Unlimited?*, edited by Nadia Kutscher and Hans-Uwe Otto. Wiesbaden: VS Verlag für Sozialwissenschaften/GWV Fachverlage GmbH. Pp. 121–137.

_____. 2008. "The Role of Expertise in Navigating Links of Influence." In *The Hyperlinked Society,* edited by Joseph Turow and Lokman Tsui. Ann Arbor: University of Michigan Press. Pp. 85–103 .

Hargittai, Eszter and Steven Shafer. 2006. "Differences in Actual and Perceived Online Skills: The Role of Gender." *Social Science Quarterly* 87(2): 432–448. June.

Hoffman, D. L., and T. P. Novak. 1998. "Bridging the Racial Divide on the Internet." Pp. 390–391 in *Science* 280(5362).

Horrigan, John. 2006. "Tech Users: What They Have, How It Matters." In KMB Video Journal Conference. St. Petersburg Beach, Florida.

Krueger, Alan. 1993. "How Computers Have Changed the Wage Structure: Evidence from Microdata, 1984–1989." *Quarterly Journal of Economics* 108: 33–60.

Merton, R. K. 1973. *The Sociology of Science: Theoretical and Empirical Investigations.* Chicago: University of Chicago Press.

Mossberger, Karen, Caroline J. Tolbert, and Mary Stansbury. 2003. *Virtual Inequality: Beyond the Digital Divide.* Washington, DC: Georgetown University Press.

National Telecommunications and Information Administration. 1998. "Falling Through the Net II: New Data on the Digital Divide." Washington, DC: NTIA.

_____. 1999. "Falling Through the Net: Defining the Digital Divide." Washington, DC: NTIA.

_____. 2000. "Falling Through the Net: Toward Digital Inclusion." Washington, DC: NTIA.

_____. 2002. "A Nation Online: How Americans Are Expanding Their Use of the Internet." Washington, DC: NTIA.

Norris, P. 2001. *Digital Divide: Civic Engagement, Information Poverty and the Internet in Democratic Societies,* New York: Cambridge University Press.

Ono, Hiroshi, and Madeline Zavodny. 2003. "Gender and the Internet." *Social Science Quarterly* 84: 111–121.

van Dijk, Jan A. G. M. 2005. *The Deepening Divide.* London: Sage Publications.

Wareham, Jonathan, Armando Levy, and Wei Shi. 2004. "Wireless Diffusion and Mobile Computing: Implications for the Digital Divide." *Telecommunications Policy* 28: 439–457.

Warschauer, M. 2003. *Technology and Social Inclusion.* Cambridge, MA: MIT Press.

Questions for Critical Thinking

1. Hargittai asserts that the use of information and communication technologies exacerbates social inequality, granting even greater benefits to those who already have access to a greater amount of resources. How does this occur?

2. Many have long argued that technologies like the internet will help to alleviate inequality because of the availability and accessibility of information to everyone. How does Hargittai's argument support or refute this assertion?

3. To alleviate inequality with regard to information and communication technologies, what policy changes do you think need to occur? Would it be possible to achieve these changes?

Winnebagos, Cherokees, Apaches, and Dakotas

The Persistence of Stereotyping of American Indians in American Advertising Brands

DEBRA MERSKIN

The following essay by journalism professor Debra Merskin examines how stereotypes of Native Americans are created and used in advertising to perpetuate stereotypes. The author asserts that these images build on long-standing assumptions about Native Americans by whites and reinforce an ideology that has resulted in many consumers failing to see this form of racism.

From early childhood on, we have all learned about "Indianness" from textbooks, movies, television programs, cartoons, songs, commercials, fanciful paintings, and product logos.[1] Since the turn of the century, American Indian images, music, and names have been incorporated into many American advertising campaigns and product images. Whereas patent medicines of the past featured "coppery, feather-topped visage of the Indian" (Larson, 1937, p. 338), butter boxes of the present show the doe-eyed, buckskin-clad Indian "princess." These stereotypes are pervasive, but not necessarily consistent—varying over time and place from the "artificially idealistic" (noble savage) to present-day images of "mystical environmentalists or uneducated, alcoholic bingo-players confined to reservations" (Mihesuah, 1996, p. 9). Yet today a trip down the grocery store aisle still reveals ice cream bars, beef jerky, corn meal,

baking powder, malt liquor, butter, honey, sour cream, and chewing tobacco packages emblazoned with images of American Indians. Companies that use these images of Indians do so to build an association with an idealized and romanticized notion of the past through the process of branding (Aaker & Biel, 1993). Because these representations are so commonplace (Land O' Lakes maiden, Jeep Cherokee, Washington Redskins logo), we often fail to notice them, yet they reinforce long-held stereotypical beliefs about Native Americans.

Trade characters such as Aunt Jemima (pancake mix), Uncle Rastus (Cream of Wheat), and Uncle Ben (rice) are visual reminders of the subservient occupational positions to which Blacks often have been relegated (Kern-Foxworth, 1994). Similarly, Crazy Horse Malt Liquor, Red Chief Sugar, and Sue Bee Honey similarly remind us of an oppressive past. How pictorial metaphors on product labels create and perpetuate stereotypes of American Indians is the focus of this study. McCracken's (1993) Meaning Transfer Model and Barthes's (1972) semiotic analysis of brand images serve as the framework for the analysis of four national brands. The following sections discuss how stereotypes are constructed and how they are articulated in, and perpetuated through, advertising.

Background

To understand how labels on products and brand names reinforce long-held stereotypical beliefs, we must consider beliefs already in place that facilitated this process. Goings (1994), in his study of African American stereotypes, points out that, "Racism was not a byproduct of the Civil War; it had clearly been around since the founding of the nation" (p. 7). Similarly, anti-Indian sentiments did not begin with the subjugation and dislocation efforts of the 1800s. Racial and ethnic images, part of American advertising for more than a century, were created in "less enlightened times" but have become a part of American popular culture and thought (Graham, 1993, p. 35) and persist today. The system of representation thereby becomes a "stable cultural convention that is taught and learned by members of a society" (Kates & Shaw-Garlock, 1999, p. 34).

Part of the explanation for the persistent use of these images can be found in the power and persuasiveness of popular culture representations. Goings's (1994) analysis of Black collectibles and memorabilia from the 1880s to the 1950s is a useful analogy for understanding the construction of Native American stereotypes in popular culture. He suggests that "collectible" items such as salt and pepper shakers, trade cards, and sheet music with images of happy Sambos, plump mammies, or wide-eyed pickaninnies served as nonverbal articulations of racism made manifest in everyday goods. By exaggerating the physical features of African American men and women, and making them laughable and useable in everyday items, these household objects reinforced beliefs about the place of Blacks in American society. Aunt Jemima, the roly-poly mammy; and Uncle Rastus, the happy slave chef (ironically both remain with us today) helped make Whites feel more comfortable with, and less guilty about, maintenance of distinctions on the basis of race well after Reconstruction. These items were meant for daily use, hence constantly and subtly reinforcing stereotypical beliefs.

Similarly, Berkhofer (1979) suggests that "the essence of the white image of the Indian has been the definition of American Indians in fact and in fancy as a separate and single other. Whether evaluated as noble or ignoble, whether seen as exotic or downgraded, the Indian as image was always alien to white" (p. xv). White images of Native Americans were similarly constructed through children's games, toys, tales, art, and theater of the 1800s. Whereas "Little Black Sambo" tales reinforced the construction of racist beliefs about Blacks, songs such as "Ten Little Indians" or "cowboy and Indian" games similarly framed Indian otherness in the White mind. Goings (1994) makes an important point about the source of the construction of objects that represent this way of thinking:

> It is important to note that Black memorabilia are figures from white American history. White Americans developed the stereotypes; white Americans produced the collectibles; and white American manufacturers and advertisers disseminated both the images and the objects to a white audience. (p. xix)

The maintenance of these kinds of beliefs satisfies the human need for psychological equilibrium and order, finding support and reinforcement in ideology. Defined as "typical properties of the 'social mind' of a group" (van Dijk, 1996, p. 56), ideologies provide a frame of reference for understanding the world. *Racist* ideologies serve several social functions operating to reproduce racism by legitimating social inequalities, thereby justifying racially or ethnically constructed differences. Racist ideology is used to (1) organize specific social attitudes into an evaluative framework for perceiving otherness, (2) provide the basis for "coordinated action and solidarity among whites," and (3) define racial and ethnic identity of the dominant group (van Dijk, 25–27). These beliefs and practices are thereby articulated in the production and distribution of racist discourse.

Theoretical Foundation

To every ad they see or hear, people bring a shared set of beliefs that serve as frames of reference for understanding the world around them. Beyond their obvious selling function, advertising images are about making meaning. Ads must "take into account not only the inherent qualities and attributes of the products they are trying to sell, but also the way in which they can make those properties mean something to us" (Williamson, 1978, p. 12).

Barthes (1972) describes these articulations as myth, that is, "a type of speech" or mode of signification that is conveyed by discourse that consists of many possible modes of representation including, but not limited to, writing, photography, publicity, and advertising. Myth is best described by the process of semiology (Barthes, 1972). Semiology "postulates a relation between two terms, a signifier and a signified" (Barthes, 1972, p. 112). The correlation of the terms *signifier, signified,* and *sign* is where associative meaning is made. What we see in an advertisement or product label, at first glance, are basic elements composed of linguistic signs (words) and iconic signs (visuals). Barthes (1972) uses a rose, for example, as a symbol of passion. Roses are not passion per se, but rather the roses (signifier) + concept of passion (signified) = roses (sign). He states that "the signifier is empty, the sign is full, it is a meaning" (Barthes, 1972, p. 113). Another example that involves race is the use of Aunt Jemima for maple syrup. We see the representation of a bandana-clad Black woman who suggests the mammy of the Deep South (signified). When placed on the bottle of syrup (sign), meaning is transferred to the otherwise ambiguous product—care giving, home cooking, and food sharing. The sign is formed at the intersection between a brand name and a meaning system that is articulated in a particular image. Quite simply, a sign, whether "object, word, or picture," has a "particular meaning to a person or group of people. It is neither the thing nor the meaning alone, but the two together" (Williamson, 1978, p. 17).

McCracken (1993, p. 125), who defines a brand as a "bundle or container of meaning," expanded on the Barthesian analysis and developed a framework for understanding the cultural relationship that brands have within society. His anthropological model (Figure 1) illustrates the meanings of brands. McCracken shows how brands assume meaning through advertising, combined with consumption behavior, and the nature of common knowledge that consumers bring to this system. The present study expands on this process by adding a reinforcement loop from consumer back to the culture where stereotypes are experienced and recirculated through the system.

A brand can have gendered meaning (maleness/femaleness), social standing (status), nationality (country meaning), and ethnicity/race (multicultural meaning). A brand can also stand for notions of tradition, trustworthiness, purity, family, nature, and so on. McCracken (1993) uses the Marlboro man as an example of these components with which a simple red and white box came to signify freedom, satisfaction, competence, maleness, and a quintessentially American, Western character. The product becomes part of the constellation of meanings that surrounds it and thereby "soaks up" meanings. When the rugged Marlboro man is situated on his horse, on the open plain, almost always alone, the meanings of the constellation become clear—freedom, love of the outdoors, release from the confines of industrialized society—he is a "real man," self-sufficient and individualistic. These meanings become part of a theme made up of prototypical content while simultaneously being "idealizations and not reality itself" (Schmitt & Simonson, 1997, p. 124).

Advertisements are created in such a way as to boost the commodity value of brand names by connecting them to images that resonate with the social and cultural values of a society. These images are loaded with established ideological assumptions that, when attached to a commodity, create the commodity sign. Tools of branding are thereby used to create a particular image in the mind of the consumer. According to van Dijk (1996), this pattern often serves to present an US versus THEM dichotomy, with US being White, "positive, tolerant, modern," and THEM being minorities who are "problematic, deviant and threatening"

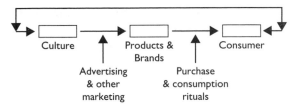

Figure 1 Meaning Model of Brand.
(*Source:* Revised from McCracken, 1993, p. 125.)

(pp. 26–27). Hence, attitudes, beliefs, and behavior that are racist serve to support a dominant ideology that focuses on difference and separatism.

These ideas and values are articulated through the construction, maintenance, and perpetuation of stereotypes. Stereotypes are overgeneralized beliefs that

get hold of the few simple, vivid, memorable, easily grasped, and widely recognized characteristics about a person, reduce everything about the person to those traits, exaggerate and simplify them, and fix them without change or development to eternity. (Hall, 1997, p. 258)

An example is the way the "Indian problem" of the 1800s has been shown in "cowboy and Indian" films. In his analysis of the representation of Indians in film, Strickland (1998, p. 10) asks, "What would we think the American Indian was like if we had only the celluloid Indian from which to reconstruct history?" (Strickland, 1998, p. 10). The cinematic representation includes the Indian as a

bloodthirsty and lawless savage; the Indian as enemy of progress; the Indian as tragic, but inevitable, victim; the Indian as a lazy, fat, shiftless drunk; the Indian as oil-rich illiterate; the Indian as educated half-breed unable to live in either a white or Indian world; the Indian as nymphomaniac; the Indian as noble hero; the Indian as stoic and unemotional; the Indian as the first conservationist. (Strickland, 1998, p. 10)

Champagne's (1994) analysis of Indians in films and theater suggests that the longevity of James Fenimore Cooper's *Last of the Mohicans,* evidenced

by its many film treatments, demonstrates that "Hollywood prefers to isolate its Indians safely within the romantic past, rather than take a close look at Native American issues in the contemporary world" (p. 719).

Natty Bumpo, in James Fenimore Cooper's *Deerslayer,* is a literary example of the male who goes from a state of "uncultured animality" to a state of "civilization and culture" (Green, 1993, p. 327). Larson (1937) describes how this stereotype was translated into a tool for marketing patent medicines:

No sooner had James Fenimore Cooper romanticized the Indian in the American imagination in his novels than patent-medicine manufacturers, quick to sense and take advantage of this new enthusiasm, used the red man as symbol and token for a great variety of ware. How the heart of the purchaser—filled, like as not, with the heroic exploits of Cooper's Indians—must have warmed as he gazed at the effigy, symbolic of "Nature's Own Remedy." (p. 338)

The female savage becomes an Indian princess who "renounces her own family, marries someone from the dominate culture and assimilates into it." (Green, 1993, p. 327), for example, Pocahontas. From this perspective, Indians are thought of as childlike and innocent, requiring the paternalistic care of Whites; that is, they are tamable. In her study of Indian imagery in *Dr. Quinn, Medicine Woman,* Bird (1996, p. 258) suggests that what viewers see is a White fantasy filled with White concerns around "guilt and retrospective outrage." Green's (1993) analysis of the use of male Indian images in ads posits that Natives continue to be portrayed according to stereotypical images: (1) noble savage (the stoic, innocent, child of nature), (2) civilizable savage (redeemable, teachable), and (3) bloodthirsty savage (fierce, predatory, cultureless, animalistic). Taken together, these studies suggest that historically constructed images and beliefs about American Indians are at the essence of stereotypical thinking that is easily translated into product images.

Method

To study the articulation of racist ideology in brand images, four currently available national products (Land O' Lakes butter, Sue Bee Honey, Big Chief [Monitor] Sugar, and Crazy Horse Malt Liquor) were analyzed according to Barthes's (1972) semiotic analysis. First, the material object was identified (signifier); second, the associative elements were identified (signified); and, third, these were brought together in what we as consumers recognize as the sign. Company websites, press releases, and product packages were used for visual and textual information. Several attempts to communicate directly with the companies yielded no response. Through this method of analysis we can see how these meanings are transferred to the different products on the basis of both race and gender.

Results

The following section presents a descriptive analysis of Land O' Lakes, Sue Bee Honey, Big Chief (Monitor) Sugar, and Crazy Horse Malt Liquor brand images.

Land O' Lakes

Although not the first national manufacturer to draw on the mystique of Indianness (that honor goes to Red Man Tobacco in 1904), Land O' Lakes is certainly one of the more prominent. In 1921, the Minnesota Cooperative Creameries Association opened for business in Arden Hills, Minnesota. This company served as the central shipping agent for a small group of small, farmer-owned dairy cooperatives (Morgan, 1986, p. 63). In 1924, the group wanted a different name and solicited ideas from farmers. Mrs. E. B. Foss and Mr. George L. Swift came up with the winning name—Land O' Lakes, "a tribute to Minnesota's thousands of sparkling lakes" (p. 63). The corporate website opens with a photograph of a quiet lake amid pine trees and blue sky. The copy under the photograph reads:

> Welcome to Land O' Lakes. A land unlike anywhere else on earth. A special place filled with

clear, spring-fed lakes. Rivers and streams that dance to their own rhythms through rich, fertile fields. It's the land we call home. And from it has flowed the bounty and goodness we bring to you, our neighbors and friends. (Land O' Lakes, 2000)

In addition, "The now famous Indian maiden was also created during the search for a brand name and trademark. Because the regions of Minnesota and Wisconsin were the legendary lands of Hiawatha and Minnehaha, the idea of an Indian maiden took form" (Land O' Lakes, 2000). A painting was sent to the company of an Indian maiden facing the viewer, holding a butter carton with a background filled with lakes, pines, flowers, and grazing cows.

At the Land O' Lakes corporate website, the director of communications includes a statement about the maiden image, where he agrees that the logo, the "Indian Maiden," has powerful connotations (Land O' Lakes). Hardly changed since its introduction in the 1920s, he says that Land O' Lakes has built on the "symbolism of the purity of the products" (Burnham, 1992). The company "thought the Indian maiden would be a good image. She represents Hiawatha and the Land of Gitchgoomee [sic] and the names of Midwest towns and streets that have their roots in the American Indian population" (Burnham, 1992).

The signifier is thereby the product, be it butter, sour cream, or other Land O' Lakes products. The Indian woman on the package is associated with youth, innocence, nature, and purity. The result is the generic "Indian maiden." Subsequently, the qualities stereotypically associated with this beaded, buckskinned, doe-eyed young woman are transferred to the company's products. Green's "noble savage" image is extended to include the female stereotype.

Sue Bee Honey

The Sioux Honey Association, based in Sioux City, Iowa, is a cooperative of honey producers, yielding 40 million pounds of honey annually (Sioux Honey Association, 2000). Corporate communications describe a change of the product name in 1964 from

Sioux Bee to Sue Bee, "to reflect the correct pronunciation of the name" (Sioux Honey Association, 2000). The brand name and image are reinforced on trucks (both real and toys), on the bottles and jars in which the honey is sold, and through collectibles such as coffee mugs and recipe books.

Sue Bee Honey also draws upon the child-of-nature imagery in an attempt to imbue qualities of purity into their products. If we were to view Sue Bee in her full form (as she is shown on many specialty items such as mugs, glasses, and jars) we would see that she is an Indian maiden on top, with braided hair and headband, and a bee below the waist. Changing the spelling of her name from "Sioux Bee" to "Sue Bee" could be interpreted in a variety of ways—possibly simply as a matter of pronunciation, as the company asserts, or as an effort to draw attention away from the savage imagery stereotypically attributed to members of this tribe and more toward the little girlishness of the image. In this case, the product is honey, traditionally associated with trees and forests and natural places. This association works well with the girl-child Indian stereotype. By placing the girl bee on the package of honey, consumers can associate the innocence, purity, and naturalness attributed to Native American females with the quality of the product.

In the tradition of Pocahontas, both the Land O' Lakes and the Sue Bee maidens symbolize innocence, purity, and virginity—children of nature. The maiden image signifies a female "Indianness." She is childlike, as she happily offers up perhaps honey or butter (or herself) that "is as pure and healthy as she is" (Dotz & Morton, 1996, p. 11). The maiden's image is used to represent attempts to get back to nature, and the association is that this can be accomplished through the healthy, wholesome products of Land O' Lakes. Both images are encoded with socially constructed meanings about female Indian sexuality, purity, and nature.

Monitor Sugar Company

Founded in 1901, the Monitor Sugar Company processes approximately 4% of U.S. beet production into sugar (granulated, powdered, brown, and icing; Monitor Sugar Company, 2000). For 60 years the company has been producing sugar from beets, relying on the image of an American Indian in full headdress to sell the sugar goods. The products are available on grocery store shelves and in bulk for institutions, delivered by trucks with the Big Chief logo emblazoned on the sides.

So, who is this Chief said to represent? Is he a bona fide tribal leader or a composite Indian designed to communicate naturalistic characteristics associated with Indians with the sugar? Green's (1993) savage typology suggests that this individual is a combination of the noble savage (natural) and the bloodthirsty savage (ferocious). He is proud, noble, and natural and yet he is wearing a ceremonial headdress that communicates strength and stoicism.

Crazy Horse Malt Liquor

A 40-ounce beverage that is sold in approximately 40 states (Metz & Thee, 1994), Crazy Horse Malt Liquor is brewed by the Heilman Brewing Company of Brooklyn, New York. Crazy Horse Malt Liquor employs the image of Tasunke Witko (Crazy Horse) on the label of its malt liquor. On the front of the bottle is an American Indian male wearing a headdress that appears to be an eagle feather bonnet, and there is a symbol representing a medicine wheel—both sacred images in Lakota and other Native cultures (Metz & Thee, 1994).

Image analysis shows that the sign is that of an actual Indian chief. Signified, however, are beliefs about Indians as warriors, westward expansion, how mighty the consumer might be by drinking this brand, and wildness of the American Western frontier.

This brand, perhaps more than any other, has come under public scrutiny because it is the image of a particular person. A revered forefather of the Oglala Sioux tribe of South Dakota, Crazy Horse died in 1877 (Blalock, 1992). The labels feature the prominent image of Chief Crazy Horse, who has long been the subject of stories, literature, and movies. Larger than life, he has played a role in American mythology.

Signifying Green's (1993) bloodthirsty savage image, Crazy Horse Malt Liquor makes use of American myths through image and association. Ironically, Crazy Horse objected to alcohol and warned his nation about the destructive effects of liquor (Specktor, 1995). As a sign, Crazy Horse represents a real symbol of early American life and westward expansionism. He was, according to the vice president of the Oglala Sioux Tribe, a "warrior, a spiritual leader, a traditional leader, a hero who has always been and is still revered by our people" (Hill, 1992; Metz & Thee, 1994, p. 50). This particular image brings together some interesting aspects of branding. Not only is the noble and bloodthirsty savage stereotype brought together in a proud, but ultimately defeated, Indian chief, but also this is an image of a real human being. The association of alcohol with that image, as well as targeting the Indian population, draws on assumptions of alcohol abuse.[2]

Discussion and Conclusions

Although there are dozens of possible examples of Native images on product labels, ranging from cigarette packages to sports utility vehicles, the examples discussed above illustrate the principles behind semiotics. The four presented here are significant examples of national brands employing stereotypical representations. When people are made aware of these products, they see how these images are consistently found in many products that employ Indian stereotypes either in product names or in their logos.

Many of these signs and symbols have been with us so long we no longer question them. Product images on packages, in advertisements, on television, and in films are nearly the only images non-Indians ever see of Native Americans. The covers of romance novels routinely feature Indian men sweeping beautiful non-Indian women off their feet as their bodices are torn away. These stereotypical representations of American Indians denies that they are human beings, and presents them as existing only in the past and as single, monolithic Indians (Merskin, 1998).

American Indians are certainly not the only racial or ethnic group to be discriminated against, overtly or covertly. Aunt Jemima and Rastus certainly have their origins in dehumanizing, one-dimensional images based on a tragic past. Yet, like Betty Crocker, these images have been updated. Aunt Jemima has lost weight and the bandana, and the Frito Bandito has disappeared (Burnham, 1992). But the Indian image persists in corporate marketing and product labeling.

These are highly visible and perhaps more openly discussed than images that appear on the products we see in grocery store aisles. An Absolut Vodka ad shows an Eskimo pulling a sled of vodka and a Grey Owl Wild Rice package features an Indian with braids, wearing a single feather, surrounded by a circle that represents (according to Grey Owl's distribution manager) the "oneness of nature" (Burnham, 1992). A partial list of others includes Apache helicopter, Jeep Cherokee, Apache rib doormats, Red Man Tobacco, Kleek-O the Eskimo (Cliquot Club ginger ale), Dodge Dakota, Pontiac, the Cleveland Indians, Mutual of Omaha, Calumet Baking Powder, Mohawk Carpet Mills, American Spirit cigarettes, Eskimo pies, Tomahawk mulcher, Winnebago Motor Homes, Indian Motorcycles, Tomahawk missiles, many high school sports teams, and the music behind the Hamm's beer commercials that begins "From the land of sky blue waters." And the list goes on.

Change is coming, but it is slow. For one thing, American Indians do not represent a significant target audience to advertisers. Representing less than 1% of the population, and the most economically destitute of all ethnic minority populations, American Indians are not particularly useful to marketers. Nearly 30% live below the official poverty line, in contrast with 13% of the general U.S. population (Cortese, 1999, p. 117). Without the population numbers or legal resources, it is nearly impossible for the voices of Natives to be heard, unlike other groups who have made some representational inroads. According to Westerman (1989), when minority groups speak, businesses are beginning to listen: "That's why Li'l Black Sambo and the Frito Bandito are dead. They were killed by the very ethnic groups they portrayed" (p. 28).

Not only does stereotyping communicate inaccurate beliefs about Natives to Whites, but also to Indians. Children, all children, are perhaps the most important recipients of this information for it is during childhood that difference is first learned. If, during the transition of adolescence, Native children internalize these representations that suggest that Indians are lazy, alcoholic by nature, and violent, this misinformation can have a life-long impact on perceptions of self and others. As Lippmann (1922/1961) wrote,

> The subtlest and most pervasive of all influences are those which create and maintain the repertory of stereotypes. We are told about the world before we see it. We imagine most things before we experience them. (p. 89)

By playing a game of substitution, by inserting other ethnic groups or races into the same situation, it becomes clear that there is a problem. Stereotypical images do not reside only in the past, because the social control mechanisms that helped to create them remain with us today.

Future research should continue to examine how the advertising and marketing practice of branding contributes to the persistent use of racist images on product labels. This study adds to the sparse literature on media representations of Native Americans in general and adds to Green's (1993) typology by including female counterparts to the male savage stereotypes. Future research could explore more images of Native Americans in ads and on products. Qualitative research with members of different tribes would add depth to this area of study.

Notes

1. Many people have preferences about terms used to describe America's indigenous peoples. "American Indian" is commonly used, as is "Native American, Native, and Indian." These terms are used interchangeably in recognition of individual preferences, without disregarding the weight each Heileman word carries.
2. Lawsuits are currently under way to limit Heilman Breweries' use of the name Crazy Horse Malt Liquor (Specktor, 1995). Several states have outlawed the sale of this beverage (Specktor, 1995). Also under review are important legal issues such as a tribe's sovereign power to exercise civil jurisdiction and the Witko family's right to protect the image of their ancestor.

References

Aaker, D., & A. L. Biel. (1993). *Advertising's role in building strong brands*. Mahwah, NJ: Lawrence Erlbaum.

Barthes, R. (1972). *Mythologies*. New York: The Noonday Press.

Berkhofer, R., Jr. (1979). *The white man's Indian: Images of the American Indian from Columbus to the present*. New York: Vintage Books.

Bird, S. E. (1996). Not my fantasy: The persistence of Indian imagery in *Dr. Quinn, Medicine Woman*. In S. E. Bird (Ed.), *Dressing in feathers: The construction of the Indian in American popular culture* (pp. 245–262). Boulder, CO: Westview Press.

Blalock, C. (1992). Crazy Horse controversy riles Congress: Controversies over Crazy Horse Malt Liquor and Black Death vodka. *Beverage Industry, 83*(9), 1–3.

Burnham, P. (1992, 27 May). Indians can't shake label as guides to good buys. *The Washington Times*, p. El.

Champagne, D. (1994). *Native America: Portrait of the peoples*. Detroit: Visible Ink.

Cortese, A. J. (1999). *Provocateur: Images of women and minorities in advertising*. New York: Rowman & Littlefield Publishers, Inc.

Dotz, W., & Morton, J. (1996). *What a character! 20th century American advertising icons*. San Francisco: Chronicle Books.

Goings, K. W. (1994). *Mammy and Uncle Mose: Black collectibles and American stereotyping*. Bloomington, IN: Indiana University Press.

Graham, R. (1993, 6 January). Symbol or stereotype: One consumer's tradition is another's racial slur. *The Boston Globe*, p. 35.

Green, M. K. (1993). Images of American Indians in advertising: Some moral issues. *Journal of Business Ethics, 12,* 323–330.

Hall, S. (1997). *Representation: Cultural representations and signifying practices.* London: Sage.

Hill, R. (1992). The non-vanishing American Indian: Are the modern images any closer to the truth? *Quill* (May), 35–37.

Kates, S. M., & Shaw-Garlock, G. (1999). The ever-entangling web: A study of ideologies and discourses in advertising to women. *Journal of Advertising 28*(2), 33–49.

Kern-Foxworth, M. (1994). *Aunt Jemima, Uncle Ben, and Rastus: Blacks in advertising yesterday, today, and tomorrow.* Westport, CT: Praeger.

Land O' Lakes. (2000). [On-line]. Available: http://www.landolakes.com.

Larson, C. (1937). Patent-medicine advertising and the early American press. *Journalism Quarterly, 14*(4), 333–339.

Lippmann, W. (1922/1961). *Public opinion.* New York: McMillan & Company.

McCracken, G. (1993). The value of the brand: An anthropological perspective. In D. Aaker & A. L. Biel (Eds.), *Brand equity in advertising: Advertising's role in building strong brands.* Mahwah, NJ: Lawrence Erlbaum.

Merskin, D. (1998). Sending up signals: A survey of American Indian media use and representation in the mass media. *The Howard Journal of Communications, 9,* 333–345.

Metz, S., & Thee, M. (1994). Brewers intoxicated with racist imagery. *Business and Society Review, 89,* 50–51.

Mihesuah, D. A. (1996). *American Indians: Stereotypes and realities.* Atlanta, GA: Clarity Press.

Monitor Sugar Company. (2000). [On-line]. Available: http://members.aol.com/asga/mon.htm.

Morgan, H. (1986). *Symbols of America.* New York: Penguin Books.

Schmitt, B., & Simonson, A. (1997). *Marketing aesthetics: The strategic management of brands, identity, and image.* New York: The Free Press.

Sioux Honey Association. (2000). [On-line]. Available: http://www.suebeehoney.com.

Specktor, M. (1995, January 6). Crazy Horse exploited to peddle liquor. *National Catholic Reporter, 31*(10), 3.

Strickland, R. (1998). The celluloid Indian. *Oregon Quarterly* (Summer), 9–10.

van Dijk, T. A. (1996). *Discourse, racism, and ideology.* La Laguna: RCEI Ediciones.

Westerman, M. (1989, March). Death of the Frito bandito: Marketing to ethnic groups. *American Demographics, 11,* 28–32.

Williamson, J. (1978). *Decoding advertisements: Ideology and meaning in advertising.* New York: Marion Boyars.

Questions for Critical Thinking

1. Merskin offers numerous examples of the continued misrepresentation of American Indians in advertising brands. Why do you think such distorted images continue?

2. Do you think that the stereotypes that Merskin discusses maintain the continued oppression of American Indians in the United States? Why or why not?

3. What will bring about more positive images of American Indians in advertising and other media? What obstacles prevent such positive portrayals?

The Prime-Time Plight of the Arab American after 9/11

Configuration of Race and Nation in TV Dramas

EVELYN ALSULTANY

The following essay by Evelyn Alsultany, an associate professor of American culture who studies the representations of Arab and Muslim Americans in U.S. mainstream media, examines the ways in which television dramas portray Arab Americans after 9/11. Alsultany discusses how television dramas contribute to the process of legitimizing racism directed at Arabs through plot lines that support the conflation of the categories of Arab and terrorist.

Two significant shifts occurred after September 11, 2001, in the representation of Arab and Muslim Americans in the U.S. media: an increase in representation and, in conjunction, an increase in sympathetic portrayals. Although there have been abundant stereotypical representations of Arabs in the U.S. media and most notably in Hollywood cinema, portrayals of Arab Americans have been scant.[1] Thus the first notable shift we witness is an increase in Arab *American* characters in U.S. mainstream television. As Jack G. Shaheen has tirelessly documented in *The TV Arab* (1984) and *Reel Bad Arabs: How Hollywood Vilifies a People* (2001), before 9/11 Arabs had predominantly been represented variously as villains, oppressed veiled women, exotic belly dancers, rich sheikhs with harems, and most remarkably as terrorists. While representations of Arabs and

Muslims as terrorists continue with increased dedication after 9/11, the second significant shift is that sympathetic portrayals that humanize Arab and Muslim Americans have entered the mainstream. Prime-time TV dramas—such as *The Guardian, The Education of Max Bickford,* and *7th Heaven*—have explicitly sought to counter representations of Arabs and Muslims as terrorists and fundamentalists, backward and uncivilized. Instead they present Arab and Muslim Americans as unfair targets of hate and discrimination. Through prime-time TV dramas, stories of Arab and Muslim Americans being misunderstood, detained, harassed, attacked, and murdered have entered U.S. living rooms, reaching millions of viewers.[2]

This shift toward representing Arab and Muslim Americans and portraying them sympathetically is particularly significant when considering how audiences have been positioned throughout the history of representations vis-à-vis Arabs and Muslims in the U.S. media.[3] Over the past four or five decades,[4] the majority of television and film representations of Arabs and Muslims have been as terrorists, seeking to elicit a celebration from the audience upon their murder (e.g., *True Lies, The Siege,* and *Executive Decision*). Within this historical framework, contemporary prime-time TV dramas evoking sympathy from viewers are

Evelyn Alsultany, "The Prime-Time Plight of the Arab American after 9/11: Configuration of Race and Nation in TV Dramas," from RACE AND ARAB AMERICANS BEFORE AND AFTER 9/11, edited by Amaney Jamal and Nadine Naber. © 2007 Syracuse University Press. Reprinted with permission.

a noteworthy development. Sympathy is a device used to gain audience identification and is usually associated with a "good" character as opposed to an "evil" one. In portraying Arab and Muslim Americans as victims of injustice, sympathy is sought from viewers, and an attempt is made to rework the hegemonic racial configuration that marks Arabs and Muslims as fanatical terrorists who threaten U.S. national security. Instead of presenting Arabs and Muslims as justifiable targets of hate, violence, and discrimination, some TV dramas represent Arab and Muslim Americans as unfair targets of misdirected fear and anger.

As the events of September 11 had the effect of confirming the stereotype of the Arab terrorist, some writers and producers of prime-time television programs created a new type of character and story line in an attempt to avert the dangerous potential of the stereotype. Characters that humanize Arab Americans were introduced along with story lines reflecting Arab and Muslim Americans in a post-9/11 predicament, caught between being associated with the terrorist attacks by virtue of ethnicity or religion and being American. Such TV episodes told the tale of the unjust backlash against Arab and Muslim Americans, seeking to garner audience sympathy as opposed to blame and hatred. Thus within some mainstream representations of Arabs and Muslims, there has been a shift from celebrating the murder of Arab terrorist characters to sympathizing with the plight of Arab Americans after 9/11.

This chapter examines a selection of TV dramas that represent the plight of Arab and Muslim Americans post-9/11. The central questions I pose are: How are Arab and Muslim Americans represented in TV dramas since 9/11? How are race, religion, citizenship, and nationalism configured in these representations? What kinds of explanations are offered about the current historical moment and alleged crisis in national security? What stories are being narrated to the U.S. public about Arab/Muslim Americans through the media? What is the relationship between media viewership and

citizenship? I argue that the TV dramas examined here, even when seeking to resist hegemonic racist configurations of the monolithic Arab Muslim terrorist, participate in reworking U.S. sovereignty through narrating ambivalence about racism in the case of Arab and Muslim Americans. I conclude by considering how media viewership is a form of virtual citizenship through which viewer-citizens are interpellated into national discourses through the virtual courtroom in TV dramas.

Ambivalent Racism, Momentary Multiculturalism, and Arab/Muslim Racialization

According to Giorgio Agamben, ambivalence is central to modern democratic sovereign power. By ambivalence, Agamben means regarding the same act as concurrently unjustifiable and necessary. Such a breach in logic comes to be reasoned through "exceptional" moments of crisis, which the state uses to call for a suspension of established codes and procedures to legitimize government abuses of power. Agamben claims that what characterizes modern democratic Western politics is that the exceptions have become the rule. The state of exception, he writes, becomes "the hidden foundation on which the entire political system rest[s]" (Agamben 1998, 9). Thus the United States is not necessarily in an exceptional state of crisis during this "war on terror," but rather operates through a perpetual "state of exception" to justify and enable exercising unilateral power, such as detaining, deporting, and denying due process to Arabs and Muslims, and waging wars in Afghanistan and Iraq.

By ambivalence in the case of Arab and Muslim Americans post-9/11, I am referring to an undecidedness about racism. Given that racism cannot be both good and bad and has been established as unjust over the past few decades since the civil rights movement, in order for this ambivalence to justify U.S. sovereign power, it would be necessary to reconfigure racism as bad in general but legitimate in the case of Arabs and Muslims after 9/11. News and talk shows often featured politicians and civil rights lawyers debating whether or not racial profiling is good or bad, right or wrong. Racism came to be articulated as wrong and indefensible and also reasoned as necessary for a short period of time (as if racialization and racism can be contained) because the United States is in an exceptional state of national security.

In order for this illogical ambivalence to acquire weight, race and racism had to be reconfigured after 9/11. This adjustment was accomplished through momentary diversity and simultaneous racialization and criminalization of Arabs and Islam. By momentary diversity, I am referring to a process by which the American citizen came to be ideologically redefined as diverse instead of white and united in the "war on terror," defined in opposition to Arabs and Islam, signified as terrorist and anti-American. Thus non-Arab, non-Muslim racialized groups became temporarily incorporated into the notion of American identity, while Arabs and Muslims were racialized as terrorist threats to the nation. By racialization, I am referring to the process of assigning derogatory meaning to particular bodies distinguished by ethnicity, nationality, biology, or geography, as well as legitimizing discourses, in this case the process by which the categories "Arab" and "terrorist" came to be conflated, consolidated, and interchangeable. Thus racism toward Arabs and Muslims is configured as legitimate and racism toward other groups illegitimate. Rachad Antonius (2002) refers to this process of justifying racism specifically towards Arabs and Muslims as producing "respectable racism." By defining racism toward Arabs and Muslims as legitimate or respectable, even necessary, not only are individual acts such as hate crimes or employment discrimination condoned, but government practices of detaining and deporting Arabs and Muslims without due process are enabled. By racializing Arabs and Islam, producing momentary diversity as the paradigm of U.S. citizenry, and articulating ambivalent racism, the Constitution and

principles of democracy come to be suspended based on the logic of the state of exception, and thus, according to Agamben (1998), furthers U.S. imperial power.

The TV dramas examined in this chapter on the surface appear to contest the dominant positioning of Arabs as terrorists, Islam as a violent extremist ideology, and Arabs and Islam as antithetical to U.S. citizenship and the U.S. nation. These TV programs are regarded as "liberal" or socially conscious as they take the stance that racism toward Arab and Muslim Americans post-9/11 is wrong, while other TV dramas do not (e.g., many TV dramas, such as *Threat Matrix, JAG, The Agency,* narrate that U.S. national security is at risk because of Arab Muslims). Nonetheless, despite somewhat sympathetic portrayals of Arab and Muslim Americans, they narrate the logic of ambivalence—that racism is wrong but essential—and thus participate in serving the U.S. government narratives.

I argue that, ultimately, discourses of the nation in crisis not only trump the Arab American plight, but also inadvertently support U.S. government initiatives in the "war on terror." I further claim that these prime-time stories seek to bring viewers into various national debates to participate in a form of virtual citizenship and serve as a racial project to redefine U.S. borders, U.S. citizens, and the position of Arabs and Muslims vis-à-vis the U.S. nation. This chapter specifically examines two episodes from the prime-time dramatic series *The Practice.*[5]

TV Dramas as Racial Projects

The programs examined are a sampling of the prime-time TV drama genre. Prime-time television, the 8–11 P.M. time slot, is the most sought-after time slot for television program producers because it lends itself to the largest viewing audience, targeting people at home after a standard nine-to-five workday. Nielsen ratings indicate that eighteen to thirty million viewers tune in to any given program during these prime-time hours on a major television network station (ABC, CBS, NBC, FOX). The majority of programs in this time slot are comedies (sitcoms), "reality" television programs, and dramas. Of these three prime-time genres, dramatic series are considered to be "quality television" because most address serious and realistic issues reflecting news stories.[6] They also tend to represent institutions of authority: a government agency, the police, or the legal system. *The Practice* is about the legal system. Broadcast on ABC from 1997 to 2004, it tells the story of lawyers and their cases and culminates with courtroom verdicts. It is part of a genre that includes *Law and Order, NYPD Blue,* and others that represent institutions of authority, and individuals seeking to pursue justice while confronting ethical and moral dilemmas. After 9/11, such prime-time dramas became forums to articulate and work through the events of 9/11.

TV dramas are critical sites for post-9/11 racial projects. Omi and Winant define a racial project as "simultaneously an interpretation, representation, or explanation of racial dynamics, and an effort to reorganize and redistribute resources along particular racial lines" (1994, 56). TV dramas interpret, represent, and explain the current racial dynamics in which Arabs, Arab Americans, Muslims, and Muslim Americans have come to be signified as terrorists, anti-American, and a threat to the United States and its citizens. TV dramas operate alongside a variety of other post-9/11 racial projects, such as the PATRIOT Act and government measures to detain, deport, and monitor Arabs, Arab Americans, Muslims, and Muslim Americans, that mark Arab bodies as dangerous and undeserving of citizenship rights. In other words, racialization is not only promoted on the state level, but operates through a complex web that includes media discourses, institutional measures, and individual citizenship acts (e.g., hate crimes).[7] TV dramas sometimes collaborate and at other times resist collaborating with government discourses. Either way, they explain these racial projects and the controversies surrounding them to the public and offer

viewers subject or citizenship positions in relation to such national debates.

As TV dramas narrate, explain, and debate government-initiated racial projects, they also operate as racial projects themselves. Through performing ideological work, rationalizing or contesting government measures that redistribute resources along racial lines (such as who gets a lawyer, who is eligible for citizenship, who gets a visa, a job, etc.), and articulating momentary diversity, they participate in defining and redefining racial dynamics (which bodies are threatening, deviant, suspect, criminal, terrorist, and un-American and therefore merit and justify denying rights). The connection between media and government is particularly palpable when examining these TV dramas that not only respond to and represent post-9/11 national debates, but also represent government agencies such as the police and court system. The story lines within the programs examined revolve around these institutions and therefore, I later argue, have a particular significance in positioning the audience as a virtual citizen. While other programs might encourage viewers to imagine themselves in relation to fashion or sexuality trends (MTV), or family (sitcoms), for example, these prime-time TV dramas encourage viewers to think about national issues and debates and their own relative position as citizens.

Debating Arab American Civil Rights in the Virtual Courtroom

The Practice takes viewers into the courtroom and after 9/11 into debates about the rights of Arab and Muslim Americans. On an episode entitled "Bad to Worse" (initially aired on December 1, 2002, and rebroadcast several times since), an airline seeks to bar Arabs from being passengers on their airplanes in the name of safety and security after 9/11. An Arab American man is suing the airline for discrimination, and the preliminary case goes to court. It is clear that the Arab American man, who is a university professor, is innocent and the unfair target of discrimination, but the case is heard to determine whether or not the racial profiling of Arabs and Muslims after 9/11 can be reasoned to be justifiable. Ms. Dole, a young white woman lawyer, is hired to defend the airline, whose slogan is "We Don't Fly Arabs," and it seeks to advertise and publicize itself as "the most security conscious airline in the new world." Ms. Dole is conflicted about defending the airline, aware of the racism and injustice inherent in the case, but takes it on to further her career. A debate ensues in the courtroom over whether racial profiling is justified and whether certain biases can be considered reasonable or whether there are legitimate forms of racism.

This particular episode and others correlate with actual events, as they represent specific occurrences. After 9/11, for example, there were instances of non-Arab passengers on airlines complaining about and refusing to fly with Arabs, Muslims, and South Asians who were mistaken for Arab, leading to their removal from flights. A Muslim man was escorted off his America West flight in New Jersey because other passengers were uncomfortable with his presence and therefore the pilot had *the right* to exclude him.[8] An Arab American Secret Service agent on his way from Washington, D.C., to President Bush's ranch in Texas was barred from an American Airlines flight because the pilot found him to be suspicious.[9] Dozens of Arab, Muslim, and South Asian Americans filed suits for being barred from flying, and many submitted complaints for the extra searches, extra security, and racial profiling. In Lincoln, Nebraska, a Muslim woman was asked to remove her *hijab* in public before boarding an American Airlines flight.[10] Meanwhile, news programs featured debates on whether or not it was just to profile Arab and Muslim Americans racially to ensure safety. Republican writer Ann Coulter, best known for her comment that the United States should invade Muslim countries, "kill their leaders and convert them to Christianity,"[11] furthered the national debate on racial profiling when she publicly expressed the opinion that airlines ought to

advertise the number of civil rights lawsuits filed against them by Arabs in order to boost business. When asked how Arabs should fly if discriminated against, she replied that they should use flying carpets.[12] Through the "Bad to Worse" episode of *The Practice,* the viewing audience participates in this debate as jurors in a virtual courtroom.

According to the debate within the virtual courtroom of *The Practice* about discrimination against Arab Americans, citizens have one of two options: political correctness or safety. The choice becomes clear, as there are grave consequences. If political correctness is chosen to avoid being racist, then safety is forfeited. As for electing safety over discrimination, not all racisms are alike in keeping with how the debate is framed: some are reasonable, others are not. Racism is reduced to political correctness and political correctness reduced to useless pleasant etiquette. Here is where we see the construction of the discourse of exceptionalism: racism is wrong except in certain cases and only during *exceptional* times of crisis. The CEO of Seaboard Airlines, the fictional airline represented in the episode, claims it would not be reasonable to discriminate against African Americans, but it would be and is reasonable to discriminate against Arabs, Arab Americans, Muslims, and Muslim Americans. As is often the case, "Arab," "Arab American," "Muslim," and "Muslim American" are conflated and used interchangeably as if they denote the same identity.[13] The attorney for the Arab American client, Mr. Furst, and the airline CEO debate the issue of political correctness versus safety in court:

MR. FURST: What if research showed that blacks were more likely to commit mayhem on a plane?

AIRLINE CEO: I would never exclude against blacks because I would consider that bias to be unreasonable. This prejudice isn't.

MR. FURST: There are 1.6 billion Muslims in the world. So you're discriminating against all of them because of the actions of 19? That's reasonable?

AIRLINE CEO: Start your own company and run it the way you'd like. I should get the same courtesy.

MR. FURST: We don't give people the right to be a bigot in this country.

AIRLINE CEO: How about the right to be safe?

The CEO's assumption is that Arabs and Muslims are a threat to flight security and in order to make passengers safe, airlines should have "the right" to bar Arabs from their flights. Moreover, as a CEO, he has "the right" to run his company as he desires. What "rights" will be protected? Do people have the "right" to be racist? The "right" to run their business as they wish? The "right" to be safe? Do Arab Americans have citizenship "rights"? According to the terms of this debate, safety trumps all other rights during times of crisis. Safety requires racism, and eliminating racism compromises safety. Ultimately, it is more important to be safe than it is not to discriminate; times are too urgent to be concerned with being politically correct. Furthermore, other racialized groups, in this case African Americans, are momentarily incorporated into the dominant conceptualization of American national identity during this "crisis" in order to consolidate the new racialized enemy. The inclusion of African Americans is necessary to the logic of exceptionalism. If we can simultaneously be racist against all racialized groups, then these are no longer exceptional times. It becomes necessary to consolidate groups that have been historically discriminated against into a coherent whole (U.S. citizens of all backgrounds united against the war on terror) in order for the logic of ambivalence within the argument to hold: that racism is both wrong and necessary against Arabs and Muslims at this time. Thus, momentary multiculturalism is used to racialize Arabs and Muslims and to create respectable or legitimate forms of racism. This debate surrounding the right to be racist and the right to be safe is elaborated in the closing arguments through defining the U.S. nation in crisis.

Mr. Furst and Ms. Dole each give heartfelt closing arguments invoking their children for additional emotional gravity. Mr. Furst says that his nine-year-old daughter recently told him that she was surprised to learn that African Americans used to be required by law to sit at the back of the bus, and he appeals to the court not to repeat a similar mistake with Arab Americans. Ms. Dole states that she cries for her son who is growing up in a world where planes are used as bombs, and therefore in order to create safety, it is unfortunately necessary to racially profile Arabs and Muslims.

The closing arguments center on defining the U.S. nation and its borders. Mr. Furst concedes that it is in fact reasonable to be suspicious of "Muslims" ("They blew up the World Trade Center for Gods sake!"), but encourages people to put those feelings aside and to consider larger and more important issues, namely "our civil rights," "our freedom," and how we define this country. In so doing, he sets up an "us"/"them" dichotomy: "they" blew up the World Trade Center, but "we" need to think about who "we" are as a people and whether or not "we" stand for equal rights; and although "they" violated "us," "we" cannot in turn violate "our" freedom. On the one hand, he defends his client's rights but at the same time he fails to acknowledge that his client is American, too, and also has the right to be safe. Importantly, Mr. Furst draws a parallel between barring Arabs from flying on airplanes and segregating African Americans from the white population to sit at the back of the bus. Through drawing this historical and comparative parallel, viewers are asked if perhaps presumed-reasonable racisms come to haunt "us" later. Do "we" agree that having blacks sit at the back of the bus is regrettable and shameful, and do "we" want to repeat this history by barring Arabs/Arab Americans from airplanes? He asks, haven't "we" learned the importance of judging people by their character and not by the color of their skin? Mr. Furst makes an important case against repeating a racist past and for defining the nation according to moral principles. His case, however, rests on acknowledging the public's right to be racist. Although he advocates not to act upon feelings of violation, Arab bodies are reinscribed as outside of American citizenship through appealing to "real" Americans not to be racist because greater moral principles are at stake.

In contrast, Ms. Dole argues that American citizens are entitled to security, and though racial profiling is "a terrible thing . . . it has become necessary." She states that although people want justice and revenge, what is most important is safety—and the desire for safety is not "paranoia" or unreasonable because the government tells us every day that we are still at risk. Not only is the courtroom, a site of national authority, represented, but government authority is also asserted when viewers are confronted with the discourse from the daily news about the crisis in national security. She continues that "we" are faced with an enemy and that enemy has clear features: they are Arab. Contributing to a broader historical mythology of the United States as a land of open borders, and neglecting a history of racist immigration restrictions, Dole says that America used to be a land with open borders, a place for any immigrant to fulfill the American dream, but that it is no longer possible so long as planes can be used as weapons. While Mr. Furst seeks to define the nation according to principles of freedom, civil rights, and equality, Ms. Dole instead shifts the discourse to defining the nation's borders: the borders should be closed and Arab Americans should be profiled in order to make U.S. citizens safe. Ms. Dole defines a nation in crisis and uses the very language from the Bill of Rights ("we the people") to argue for the suspension of its application in specific racialized configurations—vis-à-vis Arab and Muslim Americans.

The main question that is posed by this program is: Can we as a nation justify discriminating against Arabs, Arab Americans, Muslims, and Muslim Americans when we have been taught that discrimination is wrong? The answer, according to *The Practice,* comes in the form of the judge's verdict in which he states that he finds it "almost unimaginable" that whether or not it is

legally permissible to discriminate based on ethnicity is even being debated in court. He addresses Mr. Furst and Ms. Dole's closing arguments. To Mr. Furst, he says that he is being asked to waive legal and moral principles in the face of potentially boundless terrorism. To Ms. Dole, he says that he too loves being an American and became a judge to protect the freedoms provided by the Constitution. He concludes his verdict in the following way:

> The reality is that we make exceptions to our constitutional rights all the time. . . . none of them is absolute. The legal test for doing something so patently unconstitutional is basically: you better have a damn good reason. There has been one other long-standing reality in this country: If not safe, one can never be free. With great personal disgust, I am denying the plaintiff's motion for a TRO.

Although this episode seeks to demonstrate sympathy for Arab and Muslim Americans after 9/11 and repeatedly states that discrimination is unjust, representing what is considered to be a "liberal," "progressive," or "left" position, the ultimate message is that these times are unlike others and therefore normal rules do not apply. The judge recalls an article that he read in the *New York Times* written by Thomas L. Friedman in which he described the events of 9/11 as "beyond unimaginable." The writings of Friedman are used to justify an assault on Arab American civil liberties. Friedman, Foreign Affairs columnist for the *New York Times* and author of numerous books based on his many years of reporting in the Middle East, has gained mainstream status with his interpretations of 9/11 and other crises. He has won numerous Pulitzer Prizes for his reporting on the Sabra and Shatila massacre, the first Palestinian Intifada, and 9/11. He is considered a "liberal," however, he supported the U.S. invasion of Iraq in 2003 and his post-9/11 writings included encouraging the government to create a blacklist of those who critique the U.S. government for contributing to terrorism as opposed to counterterrorism. Friedman wrote in one of his *New York Times* columns that those who point to imperialism, Zionism, and colonialism as causes for terrorism are hatemongers who are in league with the terrorists (Friedman 2005). It is quite fitting that the mainstream, presumably liberal, writings of Friedman are used in the mainstream, presumably liberal story line of *The Practice* to articulate that the Constitution can be violated if there is a good reason. And, alas, there is a good reason, thus practicing discrimination against Arab and Muslim Americans is necessary and justifiable.

This is the formation of ambivalence Agamben identifies as necessary to the state of exception and sovereign rule. Ambivalence lies in defining racism as simultaneously wrong and necessary. Arab and Muslim Americans are unfairly victimized, but the real unfair victim in all of this is the U.S. nation and its citizens, who fear for their safety. By the show stating that what happened on 9/11 was unimaginable, the United States assumes a position of innocence, and the audience is not encouraged to imagine another perspective. The judge's words, "If not safe, one can never be free" evokes the president's rhetoric of freedom—"they hate us because we are free," and thus "we must discriminate in order to be free." Ultimately, despite representative sympathy, which comes in the form of deep regret and remorse surrounding the verdict, racism is legitimized: sacrifices to Arab and Muslim American civil rights must be made in the interim. This is not a verdict to celebrate: Dole is not proud; the judge is filled with disgust; and the Arab American man holds his wife as she cries. Within this apologetic moment, hatred toward Arabs is rendered "understandable," but the roots of terrorism are "beyond our imaginations."

This plight is indeed represented: it is established that Arab Americans are the unfair targets of discrimination after 9/11. Yet sympathy for the Arab American in the episode is compromised through discourses that hold more weight: namely, the right to be racist and national security threats. Discriminating against Arab Americans is reasonable at this time because, first, "they" committed

a terrorist act, and, second, the government tells us every day that we are still at risk of another terrorist attack. What comes to be represented is less the "plight" of the Arab Muslim after 9/11 and more the staging of the national debate on racial profiling and the national anxiety about flying with Arabs and Muslims. The Arab American man remains silent and unable to represent himself to the audience, sitting in the background not uttering one word, while his lawyer, a white man, speaks for him. Thus, the Arab American man remains a foreigner in the minds of American viewers. Furthermore, what America is "supposed to be" is debated in relation to Arab and Muslim Americans. Dole's closing remarks make a larger statement about how America has changed. She suggests that the United States should no longer be open to immigrants because "they" ruin America by making "us" unsafe. Through arguing for security, not only is racial profiling justified, but so are closed borders and new INS measures to detain and deport Arabs and Muslims.

Apparent here is the important function of racialization in creating the moment of exception so necessary to the abuse of government power. First, the nation in crisis needs to be established. Given the events of September 11, it is not difficult to make this point: we do not want terrorists, who are likely to be Arab and Muslim and who hate our freedom, to attack and kill again. Second, the necessity of exceptionalism needs to be established. In order to do that, a norm of democracy and freedom for all peoples regardless of race needs to be affirmed. Thus, it can be stated that it was wrong to discriminate against African Americans and gestures are made to bring disenfranchised racialized groups temporarily into the dominant designation of "American." Then, Arabs and Muslims need to undergo a process of racialization in which their potential threat to the nation becomes intertwined with their ethnic/racial background and religious beliefs. And lastly, it can be stated that racism is wrong but compulsory against this potentially threatening population at this particular exceptional time of crisis. Thus the logic is in place for the U.S. government to exercise power without constraint and use national crisis to justify acting outside of democratic legal conventions: implement the USA PATRIOT Act, invade Iraq, wage war in Afghanistan, hold prisoners in Guantanamo without legal recourse, and initiate mass deportations of Arabs and Muslims from the United States. This very logic comes to be articulated in TV dramas through portraying a sympathetic Arab American character, and while it seems that the audience might be encouraged to sympathize with the Arab American's post-9/11 plight, as opposed to celebrating the murder of Arab terrorists, viewers are presented with the very logic that supports U.S. imperial projects at home and abroad.

In War, Law Is Silent

Another episode of *The Practice,* entitled "Inter Anna Silent Leges"[14] (initially aired December 9, 2001), which translates from the Latin to "in war, law is silent," again represents the plight of Arab/Muslim Americans after 9/11. Similar to the episode examined above, it also appears to sympathize with Arab Americans while simultaneously narrating the U.S. nation in crisis, the logic of exceptionalism and ambivalence, the regretful need for security over liberty, and thus the logic to support government abuses of power. The story begins with the information that the U.S. government is unfairly detaining an Arab American man. As the plot develops, viewers learn that he has refused to speak to his wife and children and is apologetic to them for what he has done. What he has done remains a mystery to viewers, who are left to assume that he was involved with terrorism. It is ultimately revealed that the man is innocent and so intent on proving his loyalty to the United States that he has voluntarily given up his rights and agreed to be held prisoner in order to assist with the government's terrorism investigation.

Ms. Washington, an African American woman attorney, is hired by Dr. Ford, a white woman, to find and represent her husband, Bill Ford, the Arab

American man being detained by the government. She admits that her husband's "real name" is Bill Habib but they both use her maiden name, "Ford," signaling that white names are "safer" or more acceptable than Arab ones. Dr. Ford has been unable to get any information on her husband, and Ms. Washington quickly learns that the information is classified, requiring security clearance and that Mr. Habib is being detained without representation, which violates his rights as a U.S. citizen. Ms. Washington appears before a judge in court to argue against an FBI representative that she has a right to see her client. When she asks the FBI representative what Mr. Habib is being charged with, she is informed that he is not being charged with anything, but is being held as a material witness to something classified by the Foreign Intelligence Surveillance Act. The judge orders that Mr. Habib be permitted to see his lawyer and wife, stating that he will protect what is left of the Constitution. The FBI representative begins to challenge the judge's orders, but the judge warns him not to test his authority. The notion that courts have reduced power during times of war is set forth here, but the judge seeks to resist the complete suspension of the Constitution and uses his authority to allow Ms. Washington to see her client, Mr. Habib.

In addition to raising the issue of suspending the Constitution during war, this episode focuses on the government's practice of detention and their "voluntary interview program," both initiated after 9/11. It questions the possible injustice in detaining Arabs, Muslims, and South Asians and also the government's practice of not releasing information about the detainees. After 9/11, the Justice Department initiated a "voluntary interview program" through which they sought to interview thousands of Arab and Muslim immigrant men between the ages of eighteen and thirty-three, also referred to as those who "fit the criteria of people who might have information regarding terrorism."[15] The point of the "voluntary interview program" was to obtain assistance on the "war on terror." Many Arab and Muslim Americans feared that if they did not comply with being "voluntarily" interviewed, it would be perceived as unpatriotic and might jeopardize their citizenship and lead to detention or deportation. Also after 9/11, over a thousand Arabs, Muslims, and South Asians were rounded up and detained. The Justice Department refused to release information on the people detained—how many, their names, or what they were charged with.[16]

As Leti Volpp has written, "while the government refused to release the most basic information about these individuals—their names, where they were held, and the immigration or criminal charges filed against them—the public did know that the vast majority of those detained appeared to be Middle Eastern, Muslim, or South Asian. We knew, too, that the majority were identified to the government through suspicions and tips based solely on perceptions of their racial, religious, or ethnic identity" (2003, 148). Volpp's point is that the information released and concealed functioned to appease part of the population that could find comfort in the knowledge that the government was being proactive in fighting terrorism—knowledge and comfort based on the racialization of Arabs, Muslims, and South Asians. Detaining these particular racialized bodies comforted some and alarmed proponents of civil rights who demanded information and due process. In this episode of *The Practice,* the government's practice of detention and voluntary interviews of Arabs and Muslims is questioned. The judge acknowledges that the Constitution is put at risk by keeping Mr. Habib from speaking to his wife and children and demands that he be brought to the courtroom for his full citizenship rights.

Mr. Habib is first brought to the court conference room before being led into the courtroom. He is shackled, and his wife is instructed by a government official not to speak to him in case she is perceived to be giving him code. We learn that Mr. Habib has "voluntarily" turned himself in as an act of patriotism. Ms. Washington introduces herself to Mr. Habib as his lawyer and informs him

that he is about to have a hearing. Mr. Habib objects: he did not request a lawyer or a hearing (his wife had hired her). Mr. Habib worries about his family and their safety. His wife assures him that they are fine. Once in the courtroom for the hearing, Mr. Habib takes the stand:

Ms. WASHINGTON: Do you know why you're in custody?

Mr. HABIB: The government believes I may have information about someone. . . . I don't really know. He didn't do anything, but he may have known some people with ties to others who are wanted for questioning.

Ms. WASHINGTON: What information? What do they think you know?

FBI REPRESENTATIVE: Objection.

JUDGE: Sustained. You can't know that Ms. Washington.

Ms. WASHINGTON: You haven't talked to your family in weeks. Why did they keep you from speaking to your family?

Mr. HABIB: They didn't. I chose not to call my family.

Ms. WASHINGTON: Why?

Mr. HABIB: I was told anyone I spoke with would be subject to investigation. I do not want to bring my family into this. My wife and children were born here. They have no connection to any Arab, other than me.

Ms. WASHINGTON: Have you been interviewed?

Mr. HABIB: Many times.

Ms. WASHINGTON: Did you know you had the right to have an attorney present?

Mr. HABIB: I waived my rights.

Ms. WASHINGTON: You waived them? Voluntarily?

Mr. HABIB: I talked to them on my own. They didn't force me. Not in any way.

Ms. WASHINGTON: Did they make you afraid?

Mr. HABIB: Am I fearful, I guess I would say yes. But I have made all my decisions voluntarily.

Ms. Washington again questions Mr. Habib about his decision not to speak to his family, and he reiterates that he did not want to risk involving them in any way. The judge asks why Mr. Habib needs to be held in custody when he is clearly cooperating. The FBI representative says that Mr. Habib is helping through wiretaps and overseas contacts and that it is necessary to hold him as they are constantly learning new information.

> FBI REPRESENTATIVE: We can't risk losing him. Look. We're trying to get the information we need to stop the potential murder of thousands of Americans. That means depriving some Americans of their civil rights. I don't like it, but that's how it is.
>
> MS. WASHINGTON: You're imprisoning an innocent man.
>
> MR. HABIB: Ms. Washington, enough. If my country thinks I should be here, I will stay here.
>
> MS. WASHINGTON: Your country?
>
> MR. HABIB: Yes, I am an American. I am serving my country.

Ms. Washington, in disbelief, asks Mr. Habib if he has been tortured or mistreated. The judge asks him whether or not he objects to being held further. Mr. Habib clearly states that he has not been mistreated and that he is being held voluntarily. The judge concludes that Mr. Habib will remain in custody because "In war, law is silent."

Much like in the episode discussed above, viewers are presented with the plight of Arab/Muslim Americans after 9/11. In the prior episode, an Arab American man is barred from flying, and in this case, an Arab American man is detained by the government. Both men are innocent, but guilty by association. In this case, Bill Habib is helping the government because he might know someone who knows something about someone involved in terrorism. Mr. Habib accepts that he is guilty by association. He proclaims that he is American and that he wants to protect his family from interrogation because they are truly innocent, having no ties to any Arabs (all of whom are presumed terrorist suspects) except for him. Meanwhile, he is of Arab descent, has ties to the Arab world, and therefore accepts a degree of guilt and responsibility. A line

is drawn between innocent Americans, Arabs involved with terrorism, and helpful Arab Americans who can assist the U.S. government and prove their loyalty and patriotism. Although he is being unfairly detained with no rights or representation, it is justifiable to hold him and deprive his family of him and any information on him because it is a matter of national security. A similar message is repeated from the aforementioned episode: it is justifiable to suspend civil rights for the greater good and safety of the American citizenry because it is a time of crisis. Although unfair, it is both "voluntary" and necessary.

Accusations that the U.S. government is treating detainees unfairly are countered with Mr. Habib's insistence that he is not being held against his will. The fact that he has not contacted his family because he wants to protect them demonstrates that the U.S. government is being thorough in their questioning of all Arabs/Arab Americans and anyone associated with Arabs/Arab Americans in order to prevent another attack during this "war on terror." Nonetheless, "voluntarism" operates to excuse the government from abusing their power. If Mr. Habib and presumably other Arab, Muslim, and South Asian American detainees agree to being held, and voluntarily refuse legal representation, it excuses the government from wrongdoing and from abusing its power. If voluntary, then citizen-patriots are collaborating with the government in the "war on terror." Suspending civil rights comes to be rescripted: it is not a sovereign, totalitarian, or dictatorial endeavor, but a cooperative and well-intentioned one. Even if it is unfair to be in prison while assisting the government, not only is it an exceptional time of crisis and therefore necessary and justifiable now as opposed to during normal times, but it is voluntary: no one is being explicitly forced by the government.

Mr. Habib is very clear that he has made his own choices. Nonetheless, the question remains: what if he made different choices? What if he had chosen to have a lawyer, to call his family, to be released? He states that such choices come with consequences and thus he chose the options with fewer consequences. Within the terms of this discourse of crisis and exceptionalism, had Mr. Habib or the many men he represents refused, he would be a traitor-terrorist. As Judith Butler has written regarding September 11:

> Dissent is quelled, in part, through threatening the speaking subject with an uninhabitable identification. Because it would be heinous to identify as treasonous, as a collaborator, one fails to speak, or one speaks in throttled ways, in order to sidestep the terrorizing identification that threatens to take hold. This strategy of quelling dissent and limiting the reach of critical debate happens not only through a series of shaming tactics which have a certain psychological terrorization as their effect, but they work as well by producing what will and will not count as a viable speaking subject and a reasonable opinion within the public domain. (2004, xix)

If Mr. Habib had chosen a different path, not only would his family undergo investigation, but also he would inhabit the position of traitor. During times of war, the terms are binary and clear: good or evil, "with us or against us." This strategy of quelling dissent and limiting debate that Butler describes also operates through producing exceptionalism as an acceptable logic and thus justifies the suspension of Arab, Arab American, Muslim, and Muslim American civil rights. Thus the stories that the media tells and viewers receive are also restricted by the dominant discourse of national security. Critical debates, such as story lines that render terrorist acts as within our imaginations and comprehension, do not surface because such discourses are not permissible within the dominant available rhetorical spaces. For example, when the country music trio the Dixie Chicks voiced their disapproval of the U.S. war on Iraq during a concert in London, country music stations in the United States refused to play their albums, branding them as unpatriotic.[17] Similarly, when Linda Ronstadt, during a concert in Las Vegas, dedicated

a song to filmmaker Michael Moore in honor of his controversial film *Fahrenheit 9/11,* which criticizes the Bush administration's response to 9/11, hundreds of fans booed, left the theater immediately, and defaced posters of her.[18] If these speaking subjects become attacked, shamed, and terrorized in public spaces, what can pass through the mainstream media is also discursively restricted.

After 9/11, there were pressing debates over the treatment of Arab and Muslim Americans, and particularly over "voluntary interviews," detentions, deportations, and civil rights afforded to Arabs and Muslims—both American and not. The "Inter Arma Silent Leges" episode ends on the note that we are back to the times of interning people and unfairly suspecting people because of their racial/ethnic/religious identity. We have not learned from our mistakes and are engaged in repeating history—committing injustice and practicing racism. Ms. Dole, the defense attorney from the previous episode, interjects that the public is afraid and thus it is reasonable *though* unjust. Like the other episode of *The Practice,* this one, too, seeks to draw a parallel to injustices committed toward other racialized groups—in this case Japanese Americans during World War II. Japanese internment represents another exceptional time of crisis in which overt discrimination came to be seen as legitimate and necessary. A case is presented against the detention of Arabs and the violation of civil rights in light of a history of racism repeating itself. Regardless, the nation is constructed as being at risk and Arabs as threats to the nation, therefore such arguments for civil rights cannot be sustained when the nation is in crisis. Thus, like the aforementioned episode, this one also ends on a morose and apologetic note despite representing Arab Americans sympathetically through their post-9/11 plight: there is nothing to celebrate about this moment, but in crisis, injustice is justifiable and "in war, law is silent." Detention, discrimination, and racism are both wrong *and* essential. This ambivalence, justified through the politics of fear and rule of exception, enables the U.S. government to exercise sovereign power both within and outside its borders. This logic, articulated through TV dramas, is the same logic articulated by the U.S. government to the citizens about the current state of national crisis.

National Crisis and Virtual Citizenship

Representations of Arabs and Muslims have indeed shifted since 9/11. While representations of them as terrorists persist, some writers and producers of TV dramas have sought to make a difference through representing the plight of Arab and Muslim Americans post-9/11 to evoke sympathy from the viewing public. While such efforts should be commended, they need to be examined more closely to reveal whether they succeed in making prime-time mainstream interventions or further the official nationalist discourse that disavows racist views on the one hand while supporting racist policies and practices on the other, signifying newer and more complex forms of racism. Stuart Hall has claimed that even liberal writers and producers of media with the best of intentions who seek to subvert racial hierarchies inadvertently participate in inferential racism. Hall defines inferential racism as "apparently naturalized representations of events and situations relating to race, whether 'factual' or 'fictional,' which have racist premises and propositions inscribed in them as a set of unquestioned assumptions" (2000, 273). The writers and producers of the programs examined here are seeking to make an intervention and have good intentions, but they inadvertently support the government's discourse on the state of affairs and reinscribe the notion that the nation is in a state of crisis and that Arabs are a threat to the nation by naturalizing the government's discourse that we are in an exceptional state of crisis that merits U.S. sovereign measures.

Audience sympathy is evoked for the plight of the Arab American after 9/11, but the right to be racist and suspicious of Arab and Muslim Americans is affirmed, and government practices to profile racially, detain, deport, and terrorize Arabs and Muslims are accepted. Although Arab Americans are represented as victims and guilty only by their association to Arabs (non-Americans), the government's discourse about the continued Arab and Muslim threat to national security is narrated, and viewers are interpellated as citizens virtually participating in these national debates.[19] Viewers virtually sit in the courtroom, hear the various perspectives, and receive more information than offered in newspapers or the news media. Viewers' fears and biases are privileged over the Arab and Muslim American plight, and consoled and affirmed as reasonable during unreasonable times.

Mass media is an essential means through which meaning is produced and exchanged between citizens of a nation. As Stuart Hall, Toby Miller, David Morley, and other theorists of the media have demonstrated, representations perform ideological work, that is, they do not simply reflect reality but actively produce meaning that affects and shapes racial categories and national identity, TV dramas after 9/11 came to function as national narratives, as stories broadcast nationwide (and often even beyond the borders of the United States) with versions of what happened, why it happened, who is responsible, how it is being dealt with by the government, and how best to deal with it as citizens. News stories became the subjects of TV dramas and participated in a field of meaning about the place of Arabs and Muslims in the United States, and one site for the articulation of explanations, bringing the U.S. public into current debates about Arabs, Muslims, racial profiling, discrimination, and national security. TV dramas interpret, represent, and explain racial dynamics post-9/11 and in doing so, redefine U.S. borders, U.S. citizenship, and forms of patriotism. They offer a way to think about the current crisis and support the actions of the government.

Although how viewers will relate to and interpret these TV dramas is variable, the media is a powerful tool used to interpellate viewer-citizens into supporting the rule of exception—that is, into internalizing that the U.S. is a democratic government and that the suspension of due process, civil rights, and democratic principles is justifiable because of the exceptional state of crisis. The TV dramas examined here participate in the narrative that we are in a state of exception. They convey a message that U.S. residents are at risk and must give up some things now for the greater good later. The United States is figured as a good democratic country trying to spread peace in the world and therefore that the ends will justify the means. Perhaps it would be more accurate to state, as Agamben does, "means without ends."

The national discourse on Arab and Muslim threats to national security and the need to profile racially in order to attain safety can be considered a "technology" in the production of truth. Toby Miller defines a "technology" as a "popularly held logic" and truth as "an accepted fact" (1998, 4). True statements, according to Miller, are "contingent on the space, time, and language in which they are made and heard" (5). In other words, truth is produced through the ideological work performed by the media, such as prime-time television programs or government policies, and becomes part of our "common sense." Miller continues: "When these technologies congeal to forge loyalty to the sovereign state through custom or art, they do so through the cultural citizen" (4). The cultural citizen is interpellated into these logics and becomes a subject for their enactment. Truth is produced and attained not only at the juncture in which media representations and government hegemonic projects congeal and cooperate, but also more importantly through the interpellation of the viewer into citizenship. I argue that for some viewer-citizens, such interpellation takes place in the virtual courtroom. The stakes of the nation are defined in court—even virtual court: debates are enacted; racial projects are reasoned; ideological work to produce common sense is performed. As Miller has stated, "The audience participates in

the most uniformly global (but national), collective (yet private), and individually time consuming practice of meaning making in the history of the world . . . the concept and occasion of being an audience provide a textual link between society and person. . . . So viewing television involves solitary interpretation as well as collective behavior" (24). In other words, it involves imagining the self as part of a greater collective, in this case citizen of the United States. Not only is race formed and reformed at different historical moments to define borders, citizens, and enemies, but the public is also "formed and reformed on a routine basis through technologies of truth—popular logics for establishing fact" (5).

According to Hartley, we are all "citizens of media"; in other words, "participation in public-decision making is primarily conducted through media" (1999, 157). He writes, "It seems to me that what has in fact been occurring over the fifty-odd years that television has become established as the world's number-one entertainment resource and leisure-time pursuit is that a new form of citizenship has overlain the older, existing forms" (158). This new form of citizenship is one in which viewers-citizens are part of democratainment, "The means by which popular participation in public issues is conducted in the mediasphere" (209). In other words, "Audiences are understood as 'citizens of media' in the sense that it is through the symbolic, virtualized and mediated context of watching television, listening to radio and reading print media that publics participate in the democratic process on a day to day basis" (206–7).

Above all, what is defined through these TV dramas representing the plight of the Arab Muslim American is a nation in danger. The emphasis on the enduring threat Arabs and Muslims pose to U.S. national security operates to support national racial projects. As McAlister has written, "the continuing sense of threat provides support for the power of the state, but it also provides the groundwork for securing 'the nation' as a cultural and social entity. The 'imagined community' of the nation finds continuing rearticulation in the rhetoric of danger" (2001, 6). The rhetoric of the nation in danger, through the news media and TV dramas, has become accepted as truth and common sense. Discourses on safety and risk are a form of governmentality. In this case, "crisis" is used to justify racist views and practices; to racialize Arabs, Arab Americans, Muslims, and Muslim Americans as threats to the nation; and hence to use them as the contemporary racialized enemy through which the nation defines its identity and legitimizes its abuse of power.

Notes

1. Jamie Farr on *M.A.S.H.* (1972–83) and Hans Conreid on *The Danny Thomas Show* (1953–71) are the only consistent Arab American characters in the history of U.S. television. A few films have also featured Arab American characters that are not the embodiment of evil, such as Tony Shalhoub's character in *The Siege* and David Suchet in *A Perfect Murder*. Otherwise, Arab American actors have played stereotypical Arab roles or portray persons of other ethnicities (Italians, whites, etc.). See Shaheen (2002, 191–212).

2. For example, an estimated 25.2 million people in the United States tuned into *The West Wing's* post-9/11 special episode, according to Nielsen ratings.

3. Granted, how various audiences read and interpret media is not passive, but complex and varied. As José Esteban Muñoz (1999), Ien Ang (1991, 1995), Purnima Mankekar (1999), and others have demonstrated, audiences have agency; audiences accept, reject, resist, critique, identify, disidentify, and interpret the media with which they come into contact. Hence an insistence has arisen within cultural studies to examine not only the site of the production of an image, but also various sites for its reception. A thorough examination of reception is beyond the scope of this chapter, which seeks to examine dramatic televisual narratives produced for public consumption.

4. The inauguration of the state of Israel in 1948 and particularly the Arab–Israeli War of 1967 are turning points in representations of Arabs in the U.S. media. Before 1967, reflective of a Eurocentric colonial ideology (see Shohat and Stam 1994), Arab men were largely represented as rich and exotic, living in the desert outside of civilization with harems of women. Some were good and some evil. The good Arabs often required help from white men to defeat the evil Arabs. After 1967, Arab men came to be predominantly represented as terrorists, and Arab women became absent from representations (see Shohat 2006, 17–69; Naber 2000).

5. This study is part of a larger project that examines representations of Arab and Muslim Americans in the mainstream U.S. media after 9/11, including TV dramas, news reporting, and nonprofit advertising.

6. While reality television programs have gained a large prime-time audience, they do not carry the same reputation for quality as dramas that seek to reflect and engage with real-life issues facing individuals and the nation. Similarly, while some sitcoms do take on issues such as racism (most notably *The George Lopez Show* and *Whoopie*), most focus on interpersonal relationships.

7. See Volpp (2003).

8. See the Council on American–Islamic Relations' 2002 Civil Rights Report at http://www.cair-net.org/civilrights2002/.

9. "Inquiry into Secret Service Agent Barred from Flight." CNN.com. http://www.cnn.com/2001/US/12/28/rec.agent.airline.

10. Council on American–Islamic Relations' 2002 Civil Rights Report. http://www.cair-net.org/civilrights2002/.

11. See http://www.anncoulter.com (Sept. 13, 2001).

12. "An Appalling Magic," The Guardian Unlimited, May 17, 2003. http://www.guardian.co.uk/usa/story/0,12271,957670,00.html.

13. Omi and Winant have referred to this type of conflation as the consolidation of oppositional consciousness and attribute the erasure of difference and diversity within communities to being a common phenomenon of racism (1994, 66). To clarify, "Arab" refers to persons from a collective of countries in North Africa and West Asia.

There are approximately 300 million Arabs in the Middle East. "Arab American" refers to persons who are citizens or permanent residents of the United States and who trace their ancestry to North Africa or West Asia. There are approximately 3 million Arab Americans in the United States. "Muslim" refers to persons who practice the religion of Islam. It is estimated that there are 1.2 billion Muslims worldwide. "Muslim American" refers to persons who practice the religion of Islam and who are citizens or permanent residents of the United States; estimates are at 7 million.

14. "Inter Arma Silent Leges" is not in the Constitution, but it has become common wartime ideology for the courts to become deferential. The phrase came from Cicero's writings in B.C. Rome and has appeared time and again in U.S. legal documents during times of war. For example in the *Korematsu v. United States* case (323 U.S. 214, 219–20, 1994): "We uphold the exclusion order [of Japanese Americans from the West Coast] . . . hardships are part of war, and war is an aggregation of hardship."

15. "Ashcroft Announces 'Voluntary Interviews' with 3,000 U.S. Visitors." IslamOnline.net. http://www.islamonline.net/english/news/2002-03/21/article04.shtml.

16. "Hundreds of Arabs Still Detained." Mar. 13, 2002. CBS News. http://www.cbsnews.com/stories/2002/03/13/terror/main503649.shtml.

17. "Dixie Chicks Pulled from Air after Bashing Bush." Mar. 14, 2002. http://www.cnn.com/2003/SHOWBIZ/Music/03/14/dixie.chicks.reut/.

18. http://www.abc.net.au/news/newsitems/200407/sll58278.htm.

19. I borrow the term "interpellation" from Althusser (2001).

References

Agamben, Giorgio. 1998. *Homo Sacer: Sovereign Power and Bare Life.* Stanford, Calif.: Stanford Univ. Press.

Ang, Ien. 1991. *Desperately Seeking the Audience.* New York: Routledge.

———. 1995. *Living Room Wars: Rethinking Media Audiences for a Postmodern World.* New York: Routledge.

Althusser, L. 2001. *Lenin and Philosophy and Other Essays.* New York, Monthly Review Press.

Antonious, Rachad. 2002. "Un Racisme 'respectable.'" In *Les relations ethniques en question: Ce qui a change despuis de 11 septembre 2001,* edited by Jean Renaud, Linda Pietrantonio, and Guy Bourgeault, 253–71. Montreal: Univ. of Montreal Press.

Butler, Judith. 2004. *Precarious Life: The Powers of Mourning and Violence.* New York: Verso.

Friedman, Thomas L. 2005. "Giving the Hatemongers No Place to Hide," *New York Times,* July 22. http://www.nytimes.com/2005/07/22/opinion/22friedman.html?ex=1279684800&en=17fb5beb1 9b09d86&ei=5090&partner=rssuserland&emc=rss%3CBR%3E.

Hall, Stuart. 2000. "Racist Ideologies and the Media." In *Media Studies: A Reader,* edited by Paul Marris and Sue Thornham, 271–82. New York: New York Univ. Press.

Hartley, John. 1999. *The Uses of Television.* New York: Routledge.

Mankekar, Purnima. 1999. *Screening Culture, Viewing Politics: An Ethnography of Television, Womanhood, and Nation in Postcolonial India.* Durham, N.C.: Duke Univ. Press.

McAlister, M. (2001) *Epic Encounters: Culture, Media, & U.S Interests in the Middle East, 1945–2000.* California: University of California Press.

Miller, Toby. 1998. *Technologies of Truth: Cultural Citizenship and the Popular Media.* Minneapolis: Univ. of Minnesota Press.

Muñoz, José Esteban. 1999. *Disidentifications: Queers of Color and the Performance of Politics.* Minneapolis: Univ. of Minnesota Press.

Naber, Nadine. 2000. "Ambiguous Insiders: An Investigation of Arab American Invisibility." *Ethnic and Racial Studies* 23, no. 1 (Jan): 37–61.

Omi, Michael and Howard Winant. 1994. *Racial Formation in the United States: From the 1960s to the 1990s.* New York: Routledge.

Shaheen, Jack. 1984. *The TV Arab.* Madison: Univ. of Wisconsin Press, Popular Press.

———. 2001. *Reel Bad Arabs: How Hollywood Vilifies a People.* New York: Olive Branch Press.

———. 2002. "Hollywood's Muslim Arabs." In *A Community of Many Worlds: Arab Americans in New York City,* edited by Kathleen Benson and Philip M. Kayal, 191–212. New York: Museum of the City of New York/Syracuse University Press.

Shohat, Ella. 2006. "Gender and the Culture of Empire: Toward a Feminist Ethnography of the Cinema." In *Taboo Memories, Diasporic Voices,* 17–69. Durham, N.C.: Duke Univ. Press.

Shohat, Ella, and Robert Stam. 1994. *Unthinking Eurocentrism: Multiculturalism and the Media.* New York: Routledge.

Volpp, Leti. 2003. "The Citizen and the Terrorist." In *September 11 in History: A Watershed Moment?* Edited by Mary. L. Dudziak, 147–62. Durham, N.C.: Duke Univ. Press.

Questions For Critical Thinking

1. Alsultany discusses the ways in which television dramas portrayed Arab Americans after 9/11. How does her discussion help you to understand the portrayal of Arab Americans in new and different ways?

2. Many of the ideas discussed by the author can be applied to the ways in which the media represent a variety of marginalized groups in the United States. How does this reading help you to understand the ways in which the media influence your perceptions of others?

3. Understanding the role of the media in influencing our perceptions of ourselves and others helps us to become more media literate. How is this useful in understanding how to address problems of social inequality?

How the Right Made Racism Sound Fair— and Changed Immigration Politics

GABRIEL THOMPSON

The following essay, by journalist Gabriel Thompson, explores the power of language in constructing representations of immigrants in news media. As the author illustrates, these representations help to justify the continued inequality experienced by people of color, often regardless of their immigration status. Further, this essay demonstrates the powerful nature of language in influencing public perceptions and public policy.

In June of 2009, Sen. Charles Schumer took the stage in front of a capacity crowd at the Georgetown Law Center. The event was billed as "Immigration: A New Era," and Schumer, who chairs the Subcommittee on Immigration, Refugees and Border Security, was on campus to unveil his seven principles for a reform bill.

The first principle set the tone for his speech. "Illegal immigration is wrong, plain and simple," he said, before moving on to a linguistic primer for attendees. "People who enter the United States without our permission are illegal aliens. When we use phrases like 'undocumented workers,' we convey a message to the American people that their government is not serious about combating illegal immigration."

In total, Schumer used the term "illegal" 30 times and "alien" 9 times. It was a far cry from just three years earlier, when Schumer instead talked repeatedly about "undocumented" immigrants when speaking to a group of Irish Americans. But as the senator explained in 2009, he's choosing his words more purposefully these days.

And he is not alone. In the decade since the September 11 attacks, there has been a steady increase in language that frames unauthorized immigrants as a criminal problem. References to "illegals," "illegal immigrants" and their rhetorical variants now dominate the speech of both major political parties, as well as news media coverage of immigration.

In fact, Colorlines.com reviewed the archives of the nation's largest-circulation newspapers to compare how often their articles describe people as "illegal" or "alien" versus describing them as "undocumented" or "unauthorized." We found a striking and growing imbalance, particularly at key moments in the immigration reform debate. In 2006 and 2007, for example, years in which Congress engaged a pitched battle over immigration reform, the New York Times published 1,483 articles in which *people* were labeled as "illegal" or "alien"; just 171 articles used the adjectives "undocumented" or "unauthorized."

That imbalance isn't coincidental. In the wake of 9/11, as immigration politics have grown more heated and media organizations have worked to codify language they deem neutral, pollsters in both parties have pushed their leaders toward a punitive framework for discussing immigration.

Conservatives have done this unabashedly to rally their base; Democrats have shifted rhetoric with the hopes that it will make their reform proposals more palatable to centrists. But to date, the result has only been to move the political center ever rightward—and to turn the conversation about immigrants violently ugly.

Calling someone "illegal" or an "alien" has a whole host of negative connotations, framing that person as a criminal outsider, even a potential enemy of the state. But it does more, by also setting the parameters of an appropriate response. To label unauthorized immigrants as criminals who made an immoral choice suggests that they should be further punished—that their lives be made harder, not easier. Not surprisingly, then, as rhetoric has grown harsher on both sides (or "tougher," in the words of pollsters), legislation has followed suit. Border walls have been constructed, unmanned drones dispatched. Deportation numbers have continued a steady, record-breaking climb, while states pass ever-harsher laws.

These policy developments reflect—and find reflection in—a segment of the broader culture that is struggling with uneasy feelings about race and the ongoing transformation of the nation. When immigrants are targeted and murdered because of their status, and politicians joke about shooting them as livestock, we've moved to something beyond a simple policy debate. And at its swirling center is "the illegal"—a faceless and shadowy character who, it can be hard to remember, is actually a person.

The Language of Lawmaking

The art of choosing words has become big business in politics, for good reason. How a problem or solution is framed can be key to its chances of success.

Take, for example, Bush's plan in 2005 to privatize Social Security. Republicans trumpeted the idea, with Bush repeatedly referring to the creation of private accounts for individuals. Democrats campaigned vigorously to label the proposal as too risky and support for the idea plummeted; *privatizing* Social Security, it turned out, made Americans

uneasy. The Republicans then switched words. They talked about *personal* rather than private accounts and called media outlets to complain when they didn't adopt the new language. But by then it was too late and the proposal died.

That a single word can reframe an entire debate points to the power of language in evoking broad, often unexamined feelings. A *public* library or park may sound like a welcoming place to pass an afternoon; a *government* (or even worse, *government-run*) library or park, on the other hand, can bring to mind images of dull texts and rusty equipment.

"Words have entire narratives that go with them," says Geoffrey Nunberg, a linguist at University of California, Berkeley. "Government has acquired negative connotations, so public is what we call government when we don't want to say 'government.'"

When President Obama unveiled his health care proposal, he was careful to call the creation of a government-managed plan the "public option." As Republican strategist and pollster Frank Luntz told Fox News, "If you call it a 'public option,' the American people are split," but "if you call it the 'government option,' the public is overwhelmingly against it."

While language is always important, it has a special prominence when the discussion turns to immigration—and race. As Nunberg noted about the charged vocabulary around the topic: "The words refuse to be confined to their legal and economic senses; they swell with emotional meanings that reflect the fears and passions of the time."

Wetback. Alien. Illegal immigrant. These are powerful words, each of which has, at different times in our recent history, been the most popular term used to describe unauthorized immigrants. And while some anti-immigrant activists claim that words like "alien" or "illegal immigrant" are neutral, each conjures up a whole host of associations. Nunberg noted that in 1920 a group of college students was asked to define the word alien, and what they came up with—"a person who is hostile to this country," "an enemy from a foreign land"— hardly qualified as meeting its legal definition.

The same dynamic occurs today with illegal, especially when used to define a person rather than an action, such as working in the U.S. without authorization. "When two things bear the same name, there is a sense that they belong to the same category," Nunberg told me. "So when you say 'illegal,' it makes you think of people that break into your garage and steal your things."

"These are not small questions," agreed Frank Sharry, the executive director of America's Voice, a prominent immigrant advocacy group that has been a key player in Washington, D.C.'s word games. "The language, and who wins the framing of the language, likely will win the debate."

Prop 187: Before and After

The widespread belief that there is an "illegal immigrant" problem is a relatively recent phenomenon, according to Joseph Nevins, author of "Operation Gatekeeper: The Rise of the Illegal Alien and the making of the US–Mexico Boundary." As Nevins notes, the national platform of the Republican Party didn't mention a concern over "illegal immigration" until 1986. The Democrats—characteristically late and in a reactive mode—followed suit in 1996, adopting a similar stance as their counterparts.

That's one of the key patterns to understand in immigration debates over the past 15 years: Republicans take a stand; Democrats respond by agreeing with the critique but offering a slightly less harsh solution; Republicans get most of what they want.

It wasn't always that way. Back in the 1970s, the Carter administration, under INS Commissioner Leonel Castillo, sent out a directive forbidding the use of "illegal alien" and replaced it with "undocumented workers" or "undocumented alien." But as Nevins writes, "that linguistic sensitivity quickly disappeared."

The most significant turning point came in 1994 with the debate over California's Proposition 187, which barred undocumented immigrants from public schools and non-emergency health care. Today, Prop 187 is best remembered for propelling Republican Gov. Pete Wilson into the national

spotlight, but what's often overlooked is the Democratic response to the immigrant-bashing ballot measure—and the party's striking departure from Carter's framing of the debate.

First Democrats ignored Prop 187, then came out against it without much conviction. "I simply do not believe it will work," California's Democratic Sen. Dianne Feinstein explained. President Bill Clinton, fearing that he could lose the crucial state of California in 1996, responded to Prop 187 by dramatically beefing up border security and promising to crack down on "illegal aliens," while Feinstein proposed a toll for legal crossers and made repeated visits to the border to highlight her determination in sealing it.

A look at the Los Angeles Times' archives during the years of this debate shows an eruption in the use of "illegal" and "alien" to describe immigrants themselves. In 1994, the year Californians voted on Prop 187, the Times published 1,411 articles that labeled people "illegal" or "alien," either as an adjective or, in some cases, as a noun—as in "illegals." The same year, the Times published just 218 articles that used "undocumented" or "unauthorized" to describe people living in the country without papers.

When the Prop 187 dust settled, the immigration reform landscape had been dramatically altered. The law did not stand up to court challenge and was ultimately thrown out without being implemented. But the framework it ushered in proved lasting.

"The fact is, they agreed on all of the fundamentals with the Republicans," Nevins says of the Democratic response. "If you accept the framing that your opponents put forth, then you've lost the debate. And this helped lay the groundwork for the situation in which we find ourselves today."

Within two years, Clinton had signed two sweeping bills into law that would do "much of what Prop 187 called for," according to Andrew Wrote, author of "The Republican Party and Immigration Politics: From Proposition 187 to George W. Bush." The Illegal Immigration Reform and Immigrant Responsibility Act was enforcement-only legislation that, among other things, vastly expanded the grounds for deporting immigrants with legal status. The second bill, the Welfare Reform Act, stripped all non-citizens of many federal benefits. The pragmatist could argue that Clinton got in front of the issue by adopting harsh language and signing the bills; the pragmatist would also have to acknowledge, however, that Clinton got in front of the issue by signing strikingly anti-immigrant legislation.

Fifteen years later, President Obama, like Clinton, is still trying to appeal to the center by proving that he is serious about securing the border. In 2010, he sent 1,200 members of the National Guard to the border and signed a bill allocating $600 million to border enforcement, adding another 1,500 agents along with additional surveillance drones. At the same time, he has deported a record number of immigrants—many of whom have either no criminal record or low-level offenses, such as a traffic violation. And many of the enforcement tools Obama is currently flexing—from partnerships between ICE and local police to the flawed E-Verify program—actually have their roots in Clinton's 1996 bill.

"Changes on enforcement is the medicine that folks on our side have to accept," says Jeffrey Parcher, the communications director for the Center for Community Change, which helped coordinate an ultimately unsuccessful grassroots reform campaign in 2010. "The current narrative is that amnesty is some kind of gift, and in exchange for the gift we have to have enforcement. That is not a frame that we agree with, or that we endorse. But in the universe in which enough legislators sit in that box to prevent anything from passing, it's what we have to work with."

If true, it's a deliberately constructed universe. "Amnesty" became a bad word and "illegal" a good one because strategists on both sides of the partisan aisle assigned them those meanings.

"Words That Work"

For supporters of immigration reform, there was some reason for optimism during President George W. Bush's second term. Despite the House's passage of HR 4437 in 2005—a harsh bill introduced by Wisconsin Republican James Sensenbrenner that would have turned all unauthorized immigrants into felons—there was momentum among key Republicans for a comprehensive solution.

In 2006, the Senate passed a reform measure that offered a path to citizenship for most undocumented immigrants, provided that they enrolled in English classes and paid fines, as well as back taxes. The citizenship provisions, which did not include unauthorized immigrants who had been in the country for less than two years, were coupled with significant enforcement measures, including the doubling of border patrol agents within five years and more than 800 miles of border fencing and vehicle barriers. Among the bill's supporters were 23 Republicans.

Vocal members in the House, though, were quick to criticize the bill's citizenship provisions, limited as they were. "Amnesty is wrong because it rewards someone for illegal behavior," said Sensenbrenner. "And I reject the spin that the senators have been putting on their proposal. It is amnesty." The House stuck to its talking point, killing the measure and seeing Bush sign instead a bill adding 700 miles of border fencing.

"The right was defining the debate; the amnesty charge just killed us," Sharry concludes. "Their top line beat our top line. We said fix a broken immigration system and they said amnesty rewards lawbreakers. They had a visceral argument and we had something wonkish. We came to a gunfight with a knife."

A 2005 memo by GOP strategist Luntz perfectly captures the talking points relied upon by anti-reform Republicans to kill any reform measures. Luntz is known as a word genius for popularizing terms like "death tax" for estate tax and turning oil drilling into the friendlier-sounding "energy exploration." In his immigration memo, he instructed Republicans to "always refer to people crossing the border illegally as 'illegal immigrants'—NOT as 'illegals.'"

This was a nod to the long-term danger Republicans faced in demonizing undocumented immigrants: losing the Latino vote. As Luntz wrote,

"Republicans have made significant inroads into the Hispanic community over the past decade, and it would be a shame if poorly chosen words and overheated rhetoric were to undermine the credibility the party has built within the community." (Remember, this was 2005—pre–Tea Party.)

Such niceties aside, Luntz's memo was otherwise unrestrained in its attack on undocumented immigrants. In segments he labeled "Words That Work," he counseled Republicans to emphasize the following points:

> Let's talk about the facts behind illegal immigrants. They do commit crimes. They are more likely to drive uninsured. More likely to clog up hospital waiting rooms. More likely to be involved in anti-social behavior because they have learned that breaking the law brings more benefit to them than abiding by it.

Here was the Prop 187 argument rehashed, with an added pathology—that undocumented immigrants were prone to even broader criminal behavior. And now, one could also throw in the fear of terrorism. Another talking-point section advised Republicans to use the following phrases: "Right now, hundreds of illegal immigrants are crossing the border almost every day. Some of them are part of drug cartels. Some are career criminals. Some may even be terrorists."

The 25-page document is full of the same "overheated rhetoric" Luntz cautioned against and, importantly, became a playbook for Republicans' immigration politics moving forward, "If it sounds like amnesty, it will fail," promised Luntz—and he was right. He was also right to be concerned about just how far his party would go with his vitriolic ideas about brown-skinned immigrants.

But notably, Luntz's message is also the lesson many pro-reform politicians and advocates took from the 2006–2007 debate. Sharry joined forces with John Podesta at the Center for American Progress and enlisted a crew of top Democratic pollsters to work on messaging. Their first report, "Winning the Immigration Debate," was based on polling by Guy Molyneux of Peter Hart Associates and shared with politicians in 2008.

The report argued that Democrats should adopt a tougher tone when discussing reform. Instead of "offering a path to citizenship," which sounded to some like a giveaway, Democrats should use more coercive terms: immigrants would be *required* to pay taxes, learn English and pass criminal background checks. As the report states: "This message places the focus where voters want it, on what's best for the United States, not what we can/should do for illegal immigrants."

"Rather than educate [the public], you can convince them to do the right thing if you call it a requirement," Cecilia Munoz of the National Council of La Raza, told the Huffington Post. Her statement amounted to a strategic retreat: Democrats ought to focus less on challenging anti-immigrant claims (educating) and instead use messages that implicitly reinforce those claims (co-opting).

Sharry and Podesta also enlisted Stanley Greenberg to hone the message. Greenberg, a former Clinton pollster and influential Democratic strategist, was initially skeptical: in 2006 and 2007, his polling had shown that when Democrats discussed immigration reform they were vulnerable to attack. But the new framework, when presented to center and center-right voters, seemed to diffuse the amnesty charge.

Another person involved in the framing was Drew Westen, a psychology professor at Emory University and director of Westen Strategies, a messaging consulting firm, who was brought in by Media Matters for America. One of his conclusions echoed Schumer: Democrats should drop the words "undocumented worker" from their lexicon and instead use "illegal immigrant." Westen, who didn't respond to requests for an interview, told Politico that his advice to progressives is, "If the language appears fine to you, it is probably best not to use it. You are an activist, and by definition, you are out of the mainstream."

After the polls and focus groups, the messaging was in place. Democrats should lead with border security and enforcement, frame the legalization process as a requirement, and call people "illegal immigrants" instead of "undocumented." It was to be tough but not "overly punitive"—and it was notable in that it made no reference to any positive attributes undocumented immigrants might bring to the country.

Not everyone was pleased with the new framework. "This is oppressive language—punitive and restrictive," says Oscar Chacon, executive director of the National Alliance of Latin American & Caribbean Communities. According to Chacon, the 2008 report was "nothing but an effort by D.C. groups to justify their views with a public opinion survey" and it highlighted the Democrats' tendency to "accept more and more of the premises of the anti-immigrant lobby."

"We should be trying to change the way people think about the situation," contends Chacon, "instead of finding a way to make anti-immigrant sentiments tolerable."

Even among people involved in the Beltway Democrats' polling project there was dissension. "It's one thing to say that enforcement has to be a part of the solution, and another to say we have to call people illegal," says David Mermin of Lake Research Partners, who has been polling on immigration for a decade and worked with Sharry on honing the message. "We think there's a more nuanced way of saying it."

Journalism's Objective Bias

Whatever nuance is possible, it's increasingly missing from the public conversation on immigration.

A major turning point in news media's own language came in the wake of the September 11 attacks, as editors for the first time looked closely at how their publications described immigrants. Until then, the Associated Press Stylebook—a language bible for newsrooms—didn't have any entries related to unauthorized immigrants. But in 2003, reflecting government concerns about border security following 9/11, the AP determined it needed to come with up a specific term.

According to AP Deputy Standards Editor David Minthorn, the organization underwent extensive discussions, which included "reporters specializing in immigration and ethnic issues who are versed in the positions of all groups," as well as an overview of government and legal terminology. The AP settled on "illegal immigrant" as the "neutral" and preferred term, while noting that "illegal alien" and the shortened term of "illegal" should be avoided. Interestingly, that's precisely the message Luntz suggested in 2005.

The AP's decision locked in an industry standard for so-called neutral language on unauthorized immigration—and it focused on the person, not just the act. The Los Angeles Times' style book, for instance, calls for "illegal immigrant" as "the preferred, neutral, unbiased term that will work in almost all uses," as assistant managing editor Henry Fuhrmann recently explained to the paper's ombudsman. As a consequence, that "unbiased" language dominates news coverage of big immigration battles. In 2010, as Congress debated the DREAM Act and immigration became a leading issue in midterm elections, four of the five largest-circulation newspapers published a combined 1,549 articles that referred to people as "illegal" or "alien" in the headline or at least once in the text of the story; they published just 363 articles that referred to "undocumented" or "unauthorized" immigrants. (The four papers, in order of 2011 circulation numbers, include USA Today, the New York Times, the Los Angeles Times and the Washington Post; we did not search the archives of the Wall Street Journal, which is the largest paper, because it does not make the full text of its archives available on the database we used.)

In recent years, there has been push back on the criminalizing framework from journalists of color. In 2006 the National Association of Hispanic Journalists launched a campaign pressuring media agencies to stop using the term "illegal" to describe unauthorized immigrants. It was a time of raucous protest, with millions of immigrants across the country marching against Sensenbrenner's draconian House bill. (Notably, the bill's title—the Border Protection, Anti-Terrorism, and Illegal Immigration Control Act—perfectly captured the conflation of undocumented immigrants with terrorists that became common after 9/11.)

"Politicians and others were taking the rhetoric of the anti-immigrant groups, and using 'illegal' as a noun," says Ivan Roman, NAHJ's executive director. "We don't like the term illegal alien and we prefer not to use illegal immigrant—we prefer undocumented immigrant. And we think the news media needs to think critically about the terminology they use."

A more recent campaign, Drop the I-word, is being coordinated by Colorlines.com's publisher, the Applied Research Center. The campaign, which asks news organizations to not use the term "illegal" when discussing unauthorized migrants, finds inspiration from Holocaust survivor Elie Wiesel's phrase "no person is illegal," which he coined during the 1980s Central American sanctuary movement. (The British were the first to use "illegal" as a noun to refer to people, when describing Jews in the 1930s who entered Palestine without official permission.)

"Getting rid of the i-word is about our society asserting the idea that migrants are human beings deserving of respect and basic human rights," says Mònica Novoa, coordinator of the campaign. She says she has been disappointed with the number of otherwise sensitive journalists who continue to use the word, which she argues "points to how normalized the language has become."

And as the language has normalized, the broader public dialogue has grown increasingly harsh—and dangerous.

Part of the shift can be seen in the way formerly moderate Republicans have begun navigating political waters using the Tea Party as their compass. In 2007, Republican Sen. Lindsey Graham was adamant in his support of reform, arguing that, "We're not going to scapegoat people. We're going to tell the bigots to shut up." By last year, however, he'd moved to discussing an overhaul of the 14th

Amendment to end birthright citizenship for U.S.-born children of undocumented immigrants. Sen. John McCain has undergone a similar transformation: once a key proponent of reform, earlier this year he blamed wildfires in Arizona on undocumented immigrants, an absurd claim quickly refuted by the U.S. Forest Service. Longtime hardliners like Rep. Steve King of Iowa, who has called immigration a "slow moving Holocaust" and compared immigrants to livestock, are now finding more friends in Congress.

The new batch of Tea Party members openly use threatening images of brown-skinned immigrants to rally their base—in just the way Luntz warned against as he crafted the language politicians now hurl at immigrants. Sharron Angle, in an infamous commercial from her 2010 campaign against Nevada Sen. Harry Reid, featured Latinos ("illegals") sneaking along a border fence "putting our safety at risk" and labeled Reid as "the best friend an illegal alien ever had."

Angle lost, due in large measure to the Latino vote. But her campaign waged an unexpectedly meaningful threat to the long-term senator and Democratic leader. More and more people seem to believe that, with "illegals putting our safety at risk," drastic words (and actions) are needed.

In March, Kansas State Rep. Virgil Peck, during a debate about the use of gunmen in helicopters to kill wild hogs, suggested that such a tactic could also be a solution "to our illegal immigration problem." His statement was followed by Rep. Mo Brooks of Alabama, who made repeated calls for doing "anything short of shooting" undocumented immigrants.

In November 2008, that's just what a group of Long Island, N.Y., teenagers did when they stabbed Marcelo Lucero to death. Lucero, an undocumented immigrant from Ecuador, was the target of what the teens called "beaner hopping"—in which they roamed the streets searching for Latinos to attack. In the wake of the murder it was discovered that other immigrants had been beaten but not come forward due to fears about their immigration status. Another streak of violence targeting Latinos occurred in New York City's Staten Island in 2010, which included 10 attacks within a six-month period.

As the situation in Long Island attests, taking an accurate stock of hate crimes is a difficult task, as many undocumented immigrants are hesitant to report crimes to authorities. Existing statistics do point to an increase in attacks on Latinos during much of the last decade: from 2003–2007 the FBI reported hate crimes against Latinos increased by 40 percent, and last month California released data showing anti-Latino crimes jumped by nearly 50 percent from the previous year.

For Novoa, these types of statistics highlight the urgency behind the call to stop using "illegal" to describe unauthorized immigrants. "We need to change the current debate. It's hate-filled, racially charged, and inhumane—and it's driving up violence."

And all of this points to perhaps the greatest weakness in the Democratic response to Luntz's message. When one side is framing immigrants as criminals and potential terrorists, with some "joking" about slaughtering them like hogs, the other side likely needs to do more than co-opt poll-tested talking points. There's more at stake than votes. The Democratic strategy also holds a contradiction at its core: The more focus that is placed on the illegality of immigrants and the problems they cause, the less it makes sense to offer a path to legalization.

"All of that [polling] work is based on an assumption that this is a policy argument," Sharry acknowledges. "This is looking more like a front in a culture war, in which a rabid, well organized part of the Republican Party wants to expel millions of brown people from this country."

Questions for Critical Thinking

1. Thompson discusses the ways in which language is used to frame discussions and influence public policy around immigration. How does his discussion help you to better understand your own perceptions of immigrants and immigration?

2. How does your membership in a particular race category influence your understanding of or level of agreement with the author's discussion?

3. Considering the author's discussion, do you think it is possible to reduce or eliminate immigration stereotypes in our language?

Self, Identity, and the Naming Question

Reflections on the Language of Disability

IRVING KENNETH ZOLA

The following essay is by Irving Kenneth Zola, an author and activist in the areas of disability rights and medical sociology. Zola explores the importance of language in the naming of people with disabilities. Throughout his discussion, he draws on the similarities and differences with other oppressed groups in the United States.

> *"When I use the word, it means just what I choose it to mean—neither more nor less"*
>
> —Humpty Dumpty

I. The Power of Naming

Language . . . has as much to do with the philosophical and political conditioning of a society as geography or climate . . . people do not realize the extent to which their attitudes have been conditioned to ennoble or condemn, augment or detract, glorify or demean. Negative language inflicts the subconscious of most . . . people from the time they first learn to speak. Prejudice is not merely imparted or superimposed. It is metabolized in the bloodstream of society. What is needed is not so much a change in language as an awareness of the power of words to condition attitudes. [1]

A step in this awareness is the recognition of how deep is the power of naming in Western culture. According to the Old Testament, God's first act after saying "Let there be light" was to call the light "Day" and the darkness "Night." Moreover, God's first act after the creation of Adam was to bring in every beast of the field so that Adam could give them names; and "whatsoever Adam called every living creature, that was the name thereof" (Genesis 2:20). Thus what one is called tends "to stick" and any unnaming process is not without its difficulties and consequences [2]. While a name has always connoted some aspect of one's status (e.g., job, location, gender, social class, ethnicity, kinship), the mid-twentieth century seems to be a time when the issue of naming has assumed a certain primacy [3,4]. In the post–World War II era Erik Erikson [5] and Alan Wheelis [6] noted that "Who am I" or the issue of identity had become a major psychological concern of the U.S. population. The writings of C. Wright Mills [7] as well as the Women's Movement [8], however, called attention to the danger of individualizing any issue as only a "personal problem."

The power of naming was thus recognized not only as a personal issue but a political one as well. While social scientists focused more on the general "labeling" process [9–13] and the measurement of attitudes toward people with various chronic diseases and disabilities [14,15], a number of "liberation" or "rights" movements focused on the practical implications. They claimed that language was one of the mechanisms by which dominant groups kept others "in place" [16,17]. Thus, as minority groups sought to gain more control over their lives, the issue of naming—what they are called—was one of the first battlegrounds. The resolution of this was not always clear-cut. For some, the original stigmas became the banner: Negroes and coloreds become Blacks. For others, only a completely new designation would suffice—a "Ms" has caught on as a form of address but "womyn," "wimmin" have not been so successful in severing the vocabulary connection to "men."

People with disabilities are in the midst of a similar struggle. The struggle is confounded by some special circumstances which mitigate against the easy development of either a disability pride or culture [18,19]. While most minority group members grow up in a recognized subculture and thus develop certain norms and expectations, people with chronic diseases and disabilities are not similarly prepared. The nature of their experience has been toward isolation. The vast majority of people who are born with or acquire such conditions do so within families who neither have these conditions nor associate with others who do. They are socialized into the world of the "normal" with all its values, prejudices, and vocabulary. As one generally attempts to rise out of one's status, there is always an attempt to put this status in some perspective. The statements that one is more than just a Black or a woman, etc., are commonplace. On the other hand, where chronic illness and disability are concerned, this negation is almost total and is tantamount to denial. Proof of successful integration is embodied in such statements as "I *never* think of myself as handicapped" or the supreme compliment, "I *never* think of you as handicapped."

What then of the institutions where too many spend too much of their time—the long-term hospitals, sanitoria, convalescent and nursing homes? These are aptly labeled "total institutions" [20], but "total" refers to their control over our lives, not to the potential fullness they offer. The subcultures formed within such places are largely defensive and designed to make life viable within the institution.

Often this viability is achieved at such a cost that it cannot be transferred to the non-institutional world.

For most of their history, organizations of people with disabilities were not much more successful in their efforts to produce a viable subculture. Their memberships have been small in comparison to the potential disabled population, and they have been regarded more as social groups rather than serious places to gain technical knowledge or emotional support. And though there are some self-help groups which are becoming increasingly visible, militant and independent of medical influence, the movement is still in its infancy [21]. Long ago, Talcott Parsons articulated the basic dilemma facing such groups:

> The sick role is . . . a mechanism which . . . channels deviance so that the two most dangerous potentialities, namely group formation and successful establishment of the claim of legitimacy, are avoided. The sick are tied up, not with other deviants to form a "subculture" of the sick but each with a group of nonsick, his personal circle, and, above all, physicians. The sick thus become a statistical status and are deprived of the possibility of forming a solidary collectivity. Furthermore, to be sick is by definition to be in an undesirable state, so that it simply does not "make sense" to assert a claim that the way to deal with the frustrating aspects of the social system is for everyone to get sick. [22, p. 477]

A mundane but dramatic way of characterizing this phenomenon can be seen in the rallying cries of current liberation movements. As the "melting pot" theory of America was finally buried, people could once again say, even though they were three generations removed from the immigrants, that they were proud to be Greek, Italian, Hungarian, or Polish. With the rise of black power, a derogatory label became a rallying cry, "Black is beautiful." And when women saw their strength in numbers, they shouted "Sisterhood is powerful." But what about those with a chronic illness or disability? Could they yell, "Long live cancer," "Up with multiple sclerosis," "I'm glad I had polio!"? "Don't you wish you were blind!" Thus, the traditional reversing of the stigma will not so easily provide a basis for a common positive identity.

2. Some Negative Functions of Labeling

The struggle over labels often follows a pattern. It is far easier to agree on terms that should *not* be used than the designations that should replace them [23–25]. As with the racial, ethnic [26] and gender groups [27,28] before them, many had begun to note the negative qualities of certain "disability references" [29,30]. Others created quite useful glossaries [31].

Since, as Phillips [32] notes, the names one calls oneself reflect differing political strategies, we must go beyond a list of "do's" and "don'ts" to an analysis of the functions of such labeling [33–36]. As long ago as 1651, Thomas Hobbes—in setting his own social agenda—saw the importance of such clarifications, "seeing then that truth consists in the right ordering of names in our affirmations, a man that seeks precise truth has need to remember what every name he uses stands for; and to place it accordingly; or else he will find himself entangled in words as a bird in lime twigs; the more he struggles the more belimed" [37, p. 26].

There are at least two separate implications of such naming which have practical and political consequences. The first is connotational and associational. As Kenneth Burke [38, p. 4] wrote, "Call a man a villain and you have the choice of either attacking or avenging. Call him mistaken and you invite yourself to attempt to set him right." I would add, "Call a person sick or crazy and all their behavior becomes dismissable." Because someone has been labeled ill, all their activity and beliefs—past, present, and future—become related to and explainable in terms of their illness [20,39]. Once this occurs, society can deny the validity of anything which they might say, do, or stand for. Being seen as the object of medical treatment evokes the image of many ascribed traits, such as

weakness, helplessness, dependency, regressiveness, abnormality of appearance and depreciation of every mode of physical and mental functioning [17,40,41]. In the case of a person with a chronic illness and/or a permanent disability, these traits, once perceived to be temporary accompaniments of an illness, become indelible characteristics. "The individual is trapped in a state of suspended animation socially, is perpetually a patient, is chronically viewed as helpless and dependent, in need of cure but incurable" [17, p. 420].

A second function of labeling is its potential for spread, pervasiveness, generalization. An example of such inappropriate generalizing was provided in a study by Conant and Budoff [42]. They found that a group of sighted children and adults interpreted the labels "blind" and "legally blind" as meaning that the person was totally without vision—something which is true for only a small segment of people with that designation. What was problematic became a given. Another example of this process occurs when disability and person are equated. While it is commonplace to hear of doctors referring to people as "the appendicitis in Room 306" or "the amputee down the hall," such labeling is more common in popular culture than one might believe. My own analysis of the crime-mystery genre [43] noted that after an introductory description of characters with a disability, they are often referred to by their disability—e.g., "the dwarf," "the blind man," "the one armed," the "one-legged." This is usually done by some third person observer or where the person with the disability is the speaker. The disability is emphasized—e.g., "said the blind man." No other physical or social descriptor appears with such frequency.

Perhaps not unexpectedly, such stand-in appellations are most commonly applied to villains. They were commonplace during the heyday of the pulp magazines, where the disability was incorporated into their names—"One-Eyed Joe," "Scarface Kelly"—a tradition enshrined in the Dick Tracy comic strips. It is a tradition that continues, though with more subtlety. Today we may no longer have

"Clubfoot the Avenger," a mad German master-criminal who crossed swords for 25 years with the British Secret Service [44–51], but we do have "The Deaf Man," the recurring thorn in the side of Ed McBain's long-running (over 30 years) 87th Precinct novels [52–54]. All such instances can reinforce an association between disability, evil, and abnormality [55].

> A very old joke illustrates the pervasiveness of such labeling:

> A man is changing a flat tyre (sic) outside a mental hospital when the bolts from his wheel roll down a nearby sewer. Distraught, he is confronted by a patient watching him who suggests, "Why don't you take one bolt off each of the other wheels, and place it on the spare?" Surprised when it works, the driver says, "How come you of all people would think of that?" Replies the patient, "I may be crazy, but I'm not stupid."

This anecdote demonstrates the flaw in thinking that a person who is mad is therefore stupid or incapable of being insightful. As the social psychological literature has long noted, this is how stigma comes about—from a process of generalizing from a single experience, people are treated categorically rather than individually and are devalued in the process [56–58]. As Longmore so eloquently concludes, a "spoiling process" [59] results whereby "they obscure all other characteristics behind that one and swallow up the social identity of the individual within that restrictive category" [17, p. 419]. Peters puts it most concretely: "The label that's used to describe us is often far more important in shaping our view of ourselves—and the way others view us—than whether we sign, use a cane, sit in a wheelchair, or use a communication board" [23, p. 25].

While many have offered vocabulary suggestions to combat the above problems of connotation and pervasiveness, few have analytically delineated what is at stake in such name changes [17,60,61]. The most provocative and historically rooted analysis is an unpublished paper by Phillips [32] who delineates four distinct strategies which underlie the renaming. While she carefully notes that further investigation may change or expand her categorization, the very idea of her schema and the historical data describing the genesis of each "recoding" remain timely.

"Cripple" and "handicapped," as nouns or adjectives, she sees as primarily "names of acquiescence and accommodation," reflecting an acceptance of society's oppressive institutions. Terms such as "physically challenged" by so personalizing the disability run the risk of fostering a "blaming the victim" stance [62]. Such terms, as well as "physically different," "physically inconvenienced," not only may be so euphemistic that they confound the public as to who is being discussed but also contribute strongly to the denial of existing realities [33]. Two other strategies represent a more activist philosophy. "Handicapper" and "differently-abled" are "names of reaction and reflection" whose purpose is to emphasize "the can-do" aspects of having a disability. To the group of Michigan advocates who coined the term [63], a "Handicapper" determines the degree to which one's own physical or mental characteristics direct life's activities. Anger, says Phillips, is basic to "names of renegotiation and inversion" where the context sets the meaning. Perhaps the best examples occur when disability activists, in the privacy of their own circles, "talk dirty," referring to themselves as "blinks," "gimps," or telling "crip" jokes and expounding on the intricacies of "crip" time. More controversy arises, however, when people publicly proclaim such terms as a matter of pride. Recently, for example, many have written about the positive aspects of "being deaf" [64,65] or, even more dramatically, of being a "cripple" [66]. Kriegel [60,61] says that "cripple" describes "an essential reality," a way of keeping what needs to be dealt with socially and politically in full view. Nancy Mairs [67], a prize-winning poet who has multiple sclerosis, clearly agrees; and in the opening remarks of her essay, "On Being a Cripple," states it most vividly:

> The other day I was thinking of writing an essay on being a cripple. I was thinking hard in one of the

stalls of the women's room in my office building, as I was shoving my shirt into my jeans and tugging up my zipper. Preoccupied, I flushed, picked up my book bag, took my cane down from the hook, and unlatched the door. So many movements unbalanced me, and as I pulled the door open, I fell over backwards, landing fully clothed on the toilet seat with legs splayed in front of me: the old beetle-on-its-back routine. Saturday afternoon, the building deserted, I was free to laugh aloud as I wriggled back to my feet, my voice bouncing off the yellowish tiles from all directions. Had anyone been there with me, I'd have been still and faint and hot with chagrin.

I decided that it was high time to write the essay. First, the matter of semantics. I am a cripple. I choose this word to name me. I choose from among several possibilities, the most common of which are handicapped and disabled. I made the choice a number of years ago, without thinking, unaware of my motives for doing so. Even now, I'm not sure what those motives are, but I recognize that they are complex and not entirely flattering. People—crippled or not—wince at the word cripple, as they do not at handicapped or disabled. Perhaps I want them to wince. I want them to see me as a tough customer, one to whom the fates/gods/viruses have not been kind, but who can face the brutal truth of her existence squarely. As a cripple, I swagger. [67, p. 9]

When Phillips' very titles may imply an evaluation of the particular strategies, it is clear from her own caveats that while many may try to impose their terminology as "the correct language," "None feel really right" [23, p. 25].

3. Recontextualizing Names

The ultimate question, of course, is whether any of these renaming procedures, singly and alone, can deal with the connotational and generalization issues discussed previously. I would argue that the context of usage may be every bit as important (as Phillips implies) as the specific terminology. Thus

one of the reasons for all the negative associations to many terms is a result of such contexts. Here social scientists, researchers and clinicians are particularly at fault in the medicalizing of disability [55,68,69]. In their writings and in the transmission of these writings by the popular press and media, people with varying diseases and disabilities are inevitably referred to as "patients," a term which describes a role, a relationship and a location (i.e., an institution or hospital) from which many connotations, as previously noted, flow. For the 43 million people now designated as having a physical, mental or biological disability, only a tiny proportion are continually resident in and under medical supervision and are thus truly patients. Similarly, the terms "suffering from," "afflicted with" are projections and evaluations of an outside world. No person with a disability is automatically "suffering" or "afflicted" except in specific situations where they do indeed "hurt," are "in pain," or "feel victimized."

I am not arguing, however, for the complete elimination of medical or physical terminology. As DeFelice cautions, "The disabled movement has purchased political visibility at the price of physical invisibility. The crippled and lame had bodies, but the handicapped, or so the social workers say, are just a little late at the starting gate. I don't like that: it's banal. When we speak in metaphorical terms, we deny physical reality. The farther we get from our bodies, the more removed we are from the body politic . . ." [70].

One meaning I derive from his caution is that we must seek a change in the connotations and the pervasiveness of our names without denying the essential reality of our conditions. Thus biology may not determine our destiny, but, as with women, our physical, mental and biological differences are certainly part of that destiny [71, 72].

A way of contextualizing our relationship to our bodies and our disabilities may not be in changing terms but in changing grammars. Our continual use of nouns and adjectives can only perpetuate the equation of the individual equaling the disability.

No matter what noun we use, it substitutes one categorical definition for another. An adjective colors and thus connotes the essential quality of the noun it modifies. Such adjectives as "misshapen," "deformed," "defective," "invalid"—far from connoting a specific quality of the individual—tend to taint the whole person.

The same is true with less charged terms. Thus "a disabled car" is one which has totally broken down. Could "a disabled person" be perceived as anything less? Prepositions, on the other hand, imply both "a relationship to" and "a separation from." At this historical juncture the awkwardness in phrasing that often results may be all to the good, for it makes both user and hearer stop and think about what is meant, as in the phrases "people *of* color" and "persons *with* disabilities."

Distance and relationship are also at the heart of some very common verb usages. The first is between the active and passive tense. Note the two dictionary meanings:

Active   asserting that the person or thing represented by the grammatical subjects performs the action represented by the verb. [73, p. 12]

Passive   asserting that the grammatical subject to a verb is subjected to or affected by the action represented by that verb. [73, p. 838]

Thus in describing an individual's relationship to an assistive device such as a wheelchair, the difference between "being confined to a wheelchair" and "using" one is a difference not only of terminology but of control. Medical language has long perpetuated this "disabled passivity" by its emphasis on what medicine continually *does* to its "patients" rather than *with* them [74,75].

Similarly the issues of "connotation" and "pervasiveness" may be perpetuated by the differential use of the verbs "be" and "have." The French language makes careful distinctions between when to use "etre" (be) and when to use "avoir" (have). English daily usage is blurry, but another look at Webster's does show the possibilities:

be   to equal in meaning; to have same connotation as; to have identity with; to constitute the same class as. [73, p. 96]

have   to hold in possession; to hold in one's use; to consist of; to stand in relationship to; to be marked or characterized by; to experience; SYN—to keep, control, retain, or experience. [73, p. 526]

Like the issue of nouns versus prepositions, verbs can also code people in terms of categories (e.g., X is a redhead) instead of specific attributes (e.g., X has red hair), allowing people to feel that the stigmatized persons are fundamentally different and establishing greater psychological and social distance [76]. Thus, as between the active and passive tense, so it is between "I am. . . ." Both specify a difference in distance and control in relation to whatever it is one "is" or "has." And since renaming relates to alternative images of distance and control, grammar, which tends to be normative, concise, shared and long-lasting, may serve us better than sheer name change. Though I personally may have a generic preference (e.g., for "disability" over "handicap"), I am not arguing for any "politically correct" usage but rather examining the political advantages and disadvantages of each [36].

For example, there may be stages in the coping with a particular condition or in the perceived efficacy of a particular "therapy" (e.g., the 12 steps in Alcoholics Anonymous) when "ownership" and thus the use of "I am" is deemed essential. Those old enough to remember President Kennedy's words at the Berlin Wall, "*Ich bin ein Berliner*" (I am a Berliner), will recall the power of its message of kinship. Similarly, when we politically strategize as a minority group [77] and seek a kinship across disease and disability groups [78], the political coming-out may require a personal ownership best conveyed in terms of "I am. . . ."

On the other hand, there are times when the political goals involve groups for whom disease and disability is not a permanent or central issue. On my university campus, for a myriad of reasons, people with mobility impairments are virtually non-existent. Yet we are gradually retrofitting old buildings and guaranteeing accessibility in new ones. The alliance here is among women who are or may become pregnant, parents with small children, people with injuries or time-limited diseases, and others who perceive themselves at risk, such as aging staff or faculty. They rarely see themselves as disabled but often admit to having a temporary disability or sharing a part of "the disabled experience" (e.g., "Now I know what it's like to try to climb all those stairs"). Thus where coalition politics is needed, the concept of "having" versus "being" may be a more effective way of acknowledging multiple identities and kinship, as in our use of hyphenated personal and social lineages— e.g., Afro-American.

4. A Final Caveat

One of the sad findings in Phillips' study [32] is how divisive this struggle over names has become. People thus begin to chastise "non true-believers" and emphasize to others "politically correct" usage. In so doing, we may not only damage the unity so necessary to the cause of disability rights but also fail to see the forest for the trees. Our struggle is necessary because we live in a society which devalues, discriminates against and disparages people with disabilities [77,79]. It is not our task to prove that we are worthy of the full resources and integration of our society. The fault is not in us, not in our diseases and disabilities [41,62,80,81] but in mythical denials, social arrangement, political priorities and prejudices [82].

Here too, a renaming can be of service not of us but of our oppressors [83]. As Hughes and Hughes [84] note, when we turn the tables and create epithets for our oppressors, this may be a sign of a beginning cohesiveness. Thus the growing popularity of terms like TABs and MABs (temporarily or momentarily able-bodied) to describe the general population breaks down the separateness of "us" and "them" and emphasizes the continuity and inevitability of "the disability experience." Thus, too,

those who have created the terms "handicappism" [85] and "healthism" [68,86,87] equate these with all the structural "-isms" in a society which operates to continue segregation and discrimination. To return finally to the issue of naming, the words of Philip Dunne reflect well the choices and consequences of language:

> If we hope to survive in this terrifying age, we must choose our words as we choose our actions. We should think how what we say might sound to other ears as well as to our own. Above all, we should strive for clarity . . . if clarity [is] the essence of style, it is also the heart and soul of truth, and it is for want of truth that human freedom could perish [88, p. 14].

Notes

1. *Saturday Review,* Editorial, April 8, 1967.
2. LeGuin, U. K. She unnames them. *New Yorker,* January 21, p. 27, 1985.
3. Friedrich, O. What's in a name? *Time,* p. 16, August 18, 1986.
4. Vickery, H. Finding the right name for brand X. *Insight,* pp. 54–55, January 27, 1986.
5. Erikson, H. *Childhood and Society.* New York: Norton, 1950.
6. Wheelis, A. *The Quest for Identity.* New York: Norton, 1958.
7. Mills, C. W. *The Sociological Imagination.* Oxford: Oxford University Press, 1959.
8. Boston Women's Health Book Collective. *Women and Our Bodies* (In later revised versions, *Our Bodies Ourselves*). Boston: New England Free Press, 1970.
9. Becker, H. *Outsiders.* Glencoe, IL: The Free Press, 1963.
10. Becker, H. (Ed.) *The Other Side—Perspectives on Deviance.* Glencoe, IL: The Free Press, 1964.
11. Erikson, K. Notes on the sociology of deviance. *Social Problems* 9, 307–314, 1962.
12. Erikson, K. *Wayward Puritans: A Study in the Sociology of Deviance.* New York: Wiley, 1966.
13. Schur, E. *Crimes Without Victims.* Englewood Cliffs, N.J.: Prentice-Hall, 1965.
14. Siller, J. The measurement of attitudes toward physically disabled persons. In *Physical Appearance,*

Stigma, and Social Behavior: The Ontario Symposium (Edited by Herman, P. D.; Zanna M. P.; and Higgins E. T.), Vol. 3, pp. 245–288. Lawrence Hillsdale, NJ: Erlbaum Associates, 1986.

15. Yuker, H., Block, J. Z., and Young, J. H. *The Measurement of Attitudes Toward Disabled Persons.* Albertson, NY: Human Resources Center, 1966.

16. Gumperz, J. J. (Ed.) *Language and Social Identity.* Cambridge: Cambridge University Press, 1982.

17. Longmore, P. K. A note on language and the social identity of disabled people. *America Behavior Scientific* 28, (3), 419–423, 1985.

18. Johnson, M. Emotion and pride: the search for a disability culture. *Disability Rag,* January/February, pp. 1, 4–10, 1987.

19. Zola, I. K. Whose voice is this anyway? A commentary on recent collections about the experience of disability. *Medical Human Revision* 2 (1), 6–15, 1988.

20. Goffman, E. *Asylums.* New York: Anchor, 1961.

21. Crew, N., and Zola, I. K. et al. *Independent Living for Physically Disabled People.* San Francisco: Jossey–Bass, 1983.

22. Parsons, T. *The Social System.* Glencoe: The Free Press, 1951.

23. Peters, A. Developing a language. *Disability Rag,* March/April, 1986, p. 25.

24. Peters, A. The problem with "Gimp." *Disability Rag,* July/August, 1986, p. 22.

25. Peters, A. Do we have to be named? *Disability Rag,* November/December, 1986, pp. 31, 35.

26. Moore, R. B. *Racism in the English Language—A Lesson Plan and Study Essay.* The Council of Interracial Books for Children, New York, 1976.

27. Shear, M. Equal writes. *Womens Revision Book* 1 (11), 12–13, 1984.

28. Shear, M. Solving the great pronoun debate. *Ms.* pp. 106, 108–109, 1985.

29. Biklen, D., and Bogdan, R. Disabled—yes; handicapped—no: The language of disability, p. 5, insert in "Media Portrayals of Disabled People: A Study in Stereotypes." *Interracial Books Children Bull* 8 (3, 6, 7), 4–9, 1977.

30. Corcoran, P. J. Pejorative terms and attitudinal barriers—editorial. *Architectural Physics Medical Rehabilitation* 58, 500, 1977.

31. Shear, M. No more supercrip. *New Directions for Women,* p. 10, November–December 1986.

32. Phillips, M. J. What we call ourselves: Self-referential naming among the disabled. *Seventh Annual Ethnography in Research Forum.* University of Pennsylvania. Philadelphia. 4–6, April 1986.

33. Chaffee, N. L. Disabled . . . handicapped . . . and in the image of God?—Our language reflects societal attitudes and influences theological perception. Unpublished paper, 1987.

34. Gill, C. J. The disability name game. *New World for Persons with Disabilities* 13 (8), 2, 1987.

35. Gillet, P. The power of words—can they make you feel better or worse? *Accent on Living,* pp. 38–39, 1987.

36. Lindsey, K. The pitfalls of politically correct language. *Sojourner,* p. 16, 1985.

37. Hobbes, T. *Leviathan.* New York: Dutton, 1950.

38. Burke, K. *Attitudes Toward History,* revised ed. Hermes, Oakland, CA, 1959.

39. Ling, B. G., Cullen, F. T., Frank, J. and Wozniak, J. F. The social rejection of former mental patients: Understanding why labels matter. *American Journal Sociology* 1987, 92 (6), 1,461–1,500, 1987.

40. Goodwin, D. Language: Perpetualizing the myths. *Impact, Inc.* (Newsletter of Center for Independent Living, Alton, IL.). Vol. 1, No. 2, pp. 1–2, 1986.

41. Zola, I. K. *Missing Pieces: A Chronicle of Living with a Disability.* Philadelphia: Temple University Press, 1982.

42. Conant, S. and Budoff, M. The development of sighted people's understanding of blindness. *Journal Visual Impairment Blindness* 76, 86–96, 1982.

43. Zola, I. K. Any distinguishing features: Portrayal of disability in the crime-mystery genre. *Policy Studying Journal* 15 (3), 485–513, 1987.

44. Williams, V. *The Man with the Clubfoot.* London: Jenkins, 1918.

45. Williams, V. *The Secret Hand.* London: Jenkins, 1918.

46. Williams, V. *Return of Clubfoot.* London: Jenkins, 1918.

47. Williams, V. *Clubfoot the Avenger.* London: Jenkins, 1924.

48. Williams, V. *The Crouching Beast.* London: Hodder & Stoughton, 1928.

49. Williams, V. *The Gold Comfit Box.* London: Hodder & Stoughton, 1932.

50. Williams, V. *The Spider's Touch.* London: Hodder & Stoughton, 1936.

51. Williams, V. *Courier to Marrakesh*. London: Hodder & Stoughton, 1944.

52. McBain, E. *Fuzz*. New York: Doubleday, 1968.

53. McBain, E. *Let's Hear It for the Deaf Man*. New York: Random House, 1973.

54. McBain, E. *Eight Black Horses*. New York: Avon, 1985.

55. Conrad, P., and Schneider, J. W. *Deviance and Medicalization: From Badness to Sickness*. C. V. St. Louis: Mosby, 1980.

56. Ainlay, S. C., Becker, G., and Coleman, L. M. (Eds). *The Dilemma of Difference: A Multidisciplinary View of Stigma*. New York: Plenum, 1986.

57. Jones, E. E., Farina, A., Hastorf, A. H., Markus, H., Miller, D., and Scott R. *Social Stigma: The Psychology of Marked Relationships*. New York: W. H. Freeman, 1984.

58. Katz, I. *Stigma: A Social Psychological Analysis*. Hillsdale, NJ: Lawrence Erlbaum Associates, 1981.

59. Goffman, E. *Stigma: Notes on the Management of Spoiled Identity*. Prentice-Hall, NJ: Englewood Cliffs, 1963.

60. Kriegel, L. Uncle Tom and Tiny Tim: Reflection on the cripple as Negro. *American Scholar* 38, 412–430, 1969.

61. Kriegel L. Coming through manhood, disease and the authentic self. In: *Rudely Stamp'd: Imaginal Disability and Prejudice* (edited by Bicklen, D. and Bailey, L.), pp. 49–63. Washington, D.C.: University Press of America, 1981.

62. Ryan, W. *Blaming the Victim*. New York: Pantheon, 1970.

63. Gentile, E., and Taylor, J. K. Images, words and identity. Handicapper Programs. Michigan State University, East Lansing, MI, 1976.

64. *Disability Rag*. Cochlear implants: The final putdown. March/April, pp. 1, 4–8, 1987.

65. Innerst, C. A. Will to preserve deaf culture. *Insight*. November 24, pp. 50–51, 1986.

66. Milam, L. *The Crippled Liberation Front Marching Band Blues*. San Diego: MHO and MHO Works, 1984.

67. Mairs, N. On being a cripple. In *Plaintest: Essays*, pp. 9–20. Tucson, AZ: University of Arizona Press, 1986.

68. Zola, I. K. Medicine as an institution of social control. *Social Revenue* 20, 487–504, 1972.

69. Illich, I. *Medical Nemesis: The Expropriation of Health*. London: Calder & Boyars, 1975.

70. DeFelice, R. J. A crippled child grows up. *Newsweek,* November 3, p. 13, 1986.

71. Fine, M., and Asch, A. Disabled women: Sexism without the pedestal. *Journal Social Society Welfare* 8(2), 233–248, 1981.

72. Fine, M., and Asch, A. (Eds). *Women with Disabilities—Essays in Psychology, Culture, and Politics*. Philadelphia: Temple University Press, 1988.

73. *Webster's New Collegiate Dictionary*. Springfield, MA: Merriam, 1973.

74. Edelman, M. The political language of the helping professions. In *Political Language,* pp. 59–68. New York: Academic, 1977.

75. Szasz, T. S., and Hollender, M. H. A contribution to the philosophy of medicine: The basic models of the doctor-patient relationship. *AMA Arch. Internal Media* 97, 585–592, 1956.

76. Crocker, J., and Lutsky, N. Stigma and the dynamics of social cognition. In *The Dilemma of Difference: A Multidisciplinary View of Stigma* (Edited by Ainlay, S. C.), pp. 95–121. New York: Plenum, 1986.

77. Hahn, H. Disability policy and the problem of discrimination. *American Behaviour Scientist* 28, 293–318, 1985.

78. Harris, L. et al. Disabled *Americans' Self Perceptions: Bringing Disabled Americans into the Mainstream*. Study No. 854009. New York: International Center for the Disabled, 1986.

79. Scotch, R. K. *From Goodwill to Civil Rights: Transforming Federal Disability Policy*. Philadelphia: Temple University Press, 1984.

80. Crawford, R. You are dangerous to your health: the ideology of politics of victim blaming. *International Journal of Health Services* 7, 663–680, 1977.

81. Crawford, R. Individual responsibility and health politics. In *Health Care in America: Essays in Social History* (Edited by Reverby, S. and Rosner, D.), pp. 247–268. Philadelphia: Temple University Press, 1979.

82. Gleidman, J., and Roth, W. *The Unexpected Minority: Handicapped Children in America*. New York: Harcourt, Brace, Jovanovich, 1980.

83. Saxton, M. A. Peer counseling training program for disabled women. *Journal of Social Society Welfare* 8, 334–346, 1981.

84. Hughes, E., and Hughes, H. M. "What's in a name." In *Where People Meet—Racial and Ethnic*

Frontiers, pp. 130–144. Glencoe, IL: The Free Press, 1952.

85. Bogdan, R., and Biklen, D. "Handicappism." *Social Policy,* pp. 14–19, March/April, 1977.

86. Crawford, R. Healthism and the medicalization of everyday life. *International Journal of Health Services,* 10, 365–388, 1980.

87. Zola, I. K. Healthism and disabling medicalization. In *Disabling Professions* (Edited by Illich, I., Zola, I. K., McKnight, J., Caplan, J., and Shaiken, H.), pp. 41–69. London, Marion Boyars, 1977.

88. Dunne, P. Faith, hope, and clarity. *Harvard Magazine* 88 (4), 10–14, 1986.

Questions for Critical Thinking

1. Zola argues that those who occupy marginalized groups are not often given the opportunity to name themselves. How do you think this helps to maintain the oppression of marginalized groups?

2. Have you experienced names being imposed on you by others with greater social power? How does this impact your sense of self?

3. What resistance have you seen to efforts of members of marginalized groups (e.g., women, people of color, or people with disabilities) to name themselves? What are some ways that we can reduce such resistance?

The Florida State Seminoles
The Champions of Racist Mascots

DAVE ZIRIN

In this essay, sports editor David Zirin takes on the controversial topic of offensive mascots. Focusing primarily on the example of the Florida State Seminoles, he debunks the myth that this misrepresentation of Native Americans in sports imagery is endorsed by the Seminole Nation. Through his examination, he illustrates that this continued practice turns our attention away from dismantling the institutionalized racism that Native Americans continue to face.

It's easy to oppose the name of the Washington Redskins and call for owner Dan Snyder to change his beloved bigoted brand. After all, it's a dictionary-defined slur bestowed on the NFL franchise by their arch-segregationist, minstrel-loving founder. When you have Native American organizations, leading sportswriters, Republicans as well as Democrats in Congress and even the president say the time has come to change the name, it is not exactly difficult to get on board.

But what about the Florida State Seminoles, whose football team on Monday night won the Vizio/Dow Chemical/Blackwater/Vivid Video BCS National Championship Game? The NCAA, since 2005, has had formal restrictions against naming teams after Native American tribes, and yet there were the Seminole faithful: thousands of overwhelmingly Caucasian fans with feathers in their hair, doing the Tomahawk chop and whooping war chants on national television. Their passions were stirred into a frenzy by a white person, face smeared with war paint, dressed as the legendary chief Osceola riding out on a horse. As Stewart Mandel of *Sports Illustrated* gushed, "Chief Osceola plants the flaming spear in the Rose Bowl. Awesome." (Osceola was adopted after the school quietly retired their previous Native American mascot "Sammy Seminole.")

I have been to dozens of Redskins game and have never seen anything close to this kind of mass interactive minstrelsy. Yet there are no protests against this spectacle, no angry editorials and no politicians jumping on the issue. Why is that? Because as any Florida State fanatic will shout at you, the university has "a formal agreement with Seminole Nation" and that makes everything all right. Fans treat this much-touted agreement like they have a "racism amnesty card" in their back pocket. The approval of the Seminole Nation, they will tell you makes it all A-okay. Actually it doesn't. It doesn't first and foremost because the existence of this "agreement with the Seminole Nation" is a myth.

The agreement is with the Florida Seminole Tribal Council and not the Seminole Nation. The majority of Seminoles don't even live in Florida. They live in Oklahoma, one of the fruits of the Seminole Wars, the Indian Removal Act and The Trail of Tears. These Oklahoma Seminoles—who, remember, are the majority—oppose the name. On October 26, 2013, the Seminole Nation of

Oklahoma's governing body passed a resolution that read in part, "The Seminole Nation condemns the use of all American Indian sports team mascots in the public school system, by college and university level and by professional teams."

As for the Florida Seminole Tribal Council, it is the owner of a series of luxury casino hotels throughout the state where the Seminole "brand" is prominently on display. The Tribal Council also bought the Hard Rock Cafe for $965 million in cash in 2006, which thanks to the Seminoles' "first-nation status" now also offers gambling in its Florida locales. Hard Rock corporate called this "the perfect marriage of two kindred spirits." Seminole Nation Hard Rock Hotel and Casino T-shirts are available for purchase.

For the wealthy and powerful Florida Seminole tribal leaders, the cultural elevation of the football program is a part of their extremely lucrative gaming operation. Defending the school's use of the name is about defending its brand. That is why the chairman of the Florida Seminole Tribe of Florida, James Billie, said, "Anybody come here into Florida trying to tell us to change the name, they better go someplace else, because we're not changing the name."

Some might say that this is fine with them. After all, given the incalculable wealth stolen from Native American tribes over the centuries, what is wrong with them getting some of it back? That would be fine, except for the stubborn fact that gambling wealth flows into very few hands. The majority of Native Americans languish in dire poverty, with reservation poverty listed at 50 percent in the last census.

Another argument for the Florida State Seminoles' keeping their name is that it actually educates people and keeps the history from being eradicated. This is self-serving codswallop, like saying a Muhammad Ali mousepad teaches people about his resistance to the war in Vietnam. Branding and cultural appropriation is not history. It's anti-history. Take school mascot Chief Osceola as an example. If people in the stands and at home

actually knew who Osceola was, the ritual of his riding a horse and throwing a spear before games would be an outrage, and not just because the Seminoles, who lived and fought in swampy everglades, tended not to ride horses. Chief Osceola was a great resistance fighter and leader of the Second Seminole War in Florida.

As written in the terrific book *101 Changemakers: Rebels and Radicals who Changed US History*, "Osceola became an international symbol of the Seminole Nation's refusal to surrender. He was a renowned public speaker and a fierce fighter who was also an opponent of the US slave system. One of his two wives was a woman of African descent and it was not uncommon for escaped slaves to become a part of Seminole Nation. Osceola's army frustrated the entire US Government, five separate Army generals, at a cost to the US Treasury of more than 20 million dollars. . . . On October 21, 1837, Osceola met with US government officials to discuss a peace treaty. When he arrived, he was captured and imprisoned. Osceola's respect was so widespread that this maneuver was widely condemned and viewed as a dishonorable way to bring down the great warrior."

Osceola was nothing less than the American Mandela, but a Nelson Mandela who did not survive Robben Island. Imagine before a South African soccer game, a white person in black face, dressed like Mandela, running out to midfield to psyche up the crowd. Not even Rick Reilly would say that this was somehow educating people about African resistance to apartheid. No one is getting educated about Osceola or the Seminole Wars. Instead their heroic resistance has been translated for football purposes to being "tough." This "respect" for their toughness not only reduces a rich and varied Seminole culture to a savage culture of war, it is also an unspoken way to praise our own ability to engineer their conquest.

The last argument, which is perhaps the most common, is, "Changing the name of the Redskins or the Seminoles . . . where does the politically correct madness end? Do we stop using 'Giants' because it offends tall people? Or 'Cowboys' because it offends cowboys?" This kind of witticism is actually profoundly insulting because there was this thing called "history" that happened, and in this "history" giants were not subject to mass displacement and genocide. Once 100 percent of this country, Native Americans are now 0.9 percent, and we play sports on their graves. Their rituals and dress are our own commercialized entertainment. We turn our eyes to the field and away from the way institutionalized racism continues to define the lives of the overwhelming majority to Native Americans who do not own a stake in the Hard Rock Cafe. That gets us to the final problem with Seminole nation and all Native American mascoting. It makes us more ignorant about our own collective history. I'm not sure we can afford it.

Questions for Critical Thinking

1. How did reading this article help you to see the issue of sports symbols and mascots in new and different ways?
2. Do you think the use of American Indian/Native American mascots is problematic? Why or why not? How do you think your own status in society impacts your opinion?
3. What will bring about more positive images of American Indians in sports, advertising, and other media? What obstacles prevent such positive portrayals?

Climate of Fear

SOUTHERN POVERTY LAW CENTER

The following essay comes from the Southern Poverty Law Center, an organization that is dedicated to fighting inequality and seeking justice for oppressed groups and individuals. The focus of this piece is on the experiences of Latino immigrants following a violent incident that highlighted a growing national problem—violent hatred directed at all suspected undocumented immigrants, Latinos in particular. This essay demonstrates that the actions of people in social institutions, such as the criminal justice system and the government, often contribute to the creation of a climate of hate directed at immigrants.

Suffolk County, N.Y.—The night of Nov. 8, 2008, seven teenage males gathered in a park in Medford, N.Y., to drink beer and plot another round of a brutal pastime they called beaner-hopping. It consisted of randomly targeting Latino immigrants for harassment and physical attacks.

Five days earlier, three of them had gone on the hunt and beaten a Latino man unconscious, they later told police. "I don't go out and do this very often, maybe once a week," one of them said.

Two of the youths in the park had started their day just after dawn by firing a BB gun at Latino immigrant Marlon Garcia, who was standing in his driveway. Garcia was hit several times.

After leaving the park, the pack of seven drove around Medford. Unable to locate a victim, they set off for Patchogue, a nearby seaside village. Both communities are in Suffolk County, which occupies the eastern, less urban half of Long Island. In Patchogue, they caught sight of Hector Sierra walking downtown. They ran up to Sierra and began to punch him, but Sierra was able to flee.

Then, just before midnight, according to prosecutors, they spotted Ecuadorian immigrant Marcelo Lucero walking with a friend, Angel Loja. Lucero, 37, had come to the United States in 1992. He worked at a dry cleaning store and regularly wired money home to his ailing mother.

The seven teenagers jumped out of their vehicles and began taunting the two men with racial slurs. Loja fled, but the attackers surrounded Lucero and began punching him in the face. Trying to defend himself, Lucero removed his belt and swung it, striking one of the teens in the head. Enraged by that blow, 17-year-old Jeffrey Conroy, a star high school football and lacrosse player, allegedly pulled a knife, charged forward and stabbed Lucero in the chest, killing him.

All seven attackers were arrested a short time later. Conroy was charged with second-degree murder and manslaughter as a hate crime. The other six were charged with multiple counts of gang assault and hate crimes.

The local and national media gave the murder of Lucero extensive coverage. This was in part because it occurred less than four months after the highly publicized slaying of a Mexican immigrant in Shenandoah, Pa. Luis Ramírez, 25, was beaten to death by drunken high school football players in a case that sparked a national discussion and heightened awareness of the rising tide of anti-immigrant violence.[1]

In few places is that trend more viciously evident than in Suffolk County, where anti-immigrant sentiment has long run deep, and where a fast-growing Latino immigrant population has been victimized by a continuing epidemic of anti-immigrant hate crimes since the late 1990s.

In recent months, Southern Poverty Law Center (SPLC) researchers interviewed more than 70 Latino immigrants living in Suffolk County, along with more than 30 local religious leaders, human rights activists, community organizers and small business owners. Their accounts are remarkably consistent and demonstrate that although Lucero's murder represented the apex of anti-immigrant violence in Suffolk County to date, it was hardly an isolated incident.

Latino immigrants in Suffolk County live in fear. Low-level harassment is common. They are regularly taunted, spit upon and pelted with apples, full soda cans, beer bottles and other projectiles. Their houses and apartments are egged, spray-painted with racial epithets and riddled with bullets in drive-by shootings. Violence is a constant threat. Numerous immigrants reported being shot with BB or pellet guns, or hit in the eyes with pepper spray. Others said they'd been run off the road by cars while riding bicycles, or chased into the woods by drivers while traveling on foot. The SPLC recorded abundant first-hand accounts of immigrants being punched and kicked by random attackers, beaten with baseball bats or robbed at knifepoint.

Political leaders in the county have done little to discourage the hatred, and some have actively fanned the flames. County Executive Steve Levy, Suffolk's top elected official, has made hostile policies targeting undocumented immigrants a central theme of his administration since he was first elected in 2003. Others have done worse, with

public statements that all but endorsed violence. At a public hearing on immigration in August 2001, County Legislator Michael D'Andre of Smithtown said that if his own town should ever experience an influx of Latino day laborers like that of nearby communities, "We'll be up in arms; we'll be out with baseball bats." In March 2007, County Legislator Elie Mystal of Amityville said of Latino immigrants waiting for work on street corners, "If I'm living in a neighborhood and people are gathering like that, I would load my gun and start shooting, period. Nobody will say it, but I'm going to say it."

Most immigrants said they do not dare travel alone at night. Few let their children play outside unattended.

"We live with the fear that if we leave our houses, something will happen," said Luis, a Mexican who migrated to Suffolk County three years ago. "It's like we're psychologically traumatized from what happens here."

Like all but two immigrants contacted by the SPLC, Luis spoke for this report on the condition that, to avoid retaliation, he would be identified only by his first name and country of origin.

At best, the immigrants said, the police seem indifferent to their plight. At worst, the police contribute to it, in the form of racial profiling, selective enforcement and outright bullying. A detailed account provided by Agosto, a Guatemalan immigrant, was typical. Agosto said that in early 2008, he was waiting for work at *la placita* (little plaza), a day labor pick-up point in Brentwood, when a police car pulled up. The two officers inside told him he wasn't allowed to stand there and demanded to see his identification. When he replied that he didn't have his I.D. with him, the officers told him to get in the back of the squad car. "I thought they were giving me a ride home," he said. But when they arrived at his residence, the police officers got out of the car and told Agosto to find his I.D. When he unlocked the front door, he said, the officers barged in without asking permission to enter. The police ransacked his living quarters, rifling through drawers and knocking items off shelves.

"I was very nervous," Agosto said. "They kept pushing me and telling me to hurry up. I got even more nervous so it took me awhile to find my I.D. When you are undocumented, you get scared." When Agosto finally located his *cédula de identidad,* a Guatemalan government-issued I.D. card, the police looked it over then left. "I felt bad, like they were treating me like I was less than they were," he said. "It felt racist."

No immigrants reported serious physical abuse at the hands of Suffolk County law enforcement authorities. But time after time, they gave similar accounts of being pulled over for minor traffic violations and then interrogated, or being questioned harshly at nighttime checkpoints after watching Anglo drivers being waved through. A few said they'd been arrested for driving under the influence or for refusing to take a Breathalyzer test even though in fact they'd submitted to the test and registered well below the legal limit.

Evidence suggesting unequal enforcement of the motor vehicle code in Suffolk County is easily observed in the local courts that handle minor offenses. Latinos account for roughly 14% of Suffolk County's population, but on a typical day in a Suffolk County justice court, they make up nearly half the defendants appearing for motor vehicle violations. A review of the police blotters printed in Suffolk County daily newspapers yields similarly suggestive demographic evidence: almost every day, around 50% of the drivers listed as having been fined for a motor vehicle violation have Latino surnames.

The most common violation that Latino immigrants are tagged with is violation 509, for unlicensed driving. It carries a $185 fine on top of a $150 vehicle impound charge and $25 a day for vehicle storage. Failure to appear in court or to pay a fine leads to arrest warrants.

Law enforcement officers in Suffolk County tend not to exhibit the same enthusiasm for investigating hate crimes against Latinos as they do writing them tickets, according to immigrants and other county residents interviewed for this report.

Immigrants in Suffolk County don't trust the police. They say there's no point in reporting bias-motivated harassment, threats or assaults, even severe beatings, because from what they can tell, the police take the report and then do nothing. They say that when the police arrive on the scene of a hate crime, they often accept the version of events given by the assailant or assailants, even to the point of arresting the true victim in response to false claims that the immigrant started a fight. And they say that officers discourage hate crime victims from making formal complaints by questioning them about their immigration status.

In the days following the murder of Marcelo Lucero, the Congregational Church of Patchogue invited immigrants to the church to speak about hate crimes. In all, more than 30 Latino immigrants in Suffolk County came forward with detailed accounts of their own victimization. In response, the Suffolk County Legislature formed a task force to investigate the sources of racial tension in the county. To date, the task force has held one of at least four planned hearings.

Prosecutors, meanwhile, have announced new indictments that accuse the defendants in the Lucero murder of assaulting or menacing a total of eight other Latino immigrants.

On June 24, 2008, according to prosecutors, the teenagers set upon Robert Zumba, kicking him and pinning his arms while Conroy, the alleged knife-wielder in the Lucero slaying, sliced Zumba with a blade. Members of the group repeatedly victimized another man, José Hernández, in December 2007, prosecutors said. During one attack, Conroy allegedly held a pipe in one hand and smacked it against his opposite palm, threatening, "We're going to kill you."

Immigrants who have been the victims of hate-crime violence in Suffolk County report that in most cases the attackers are white males in their teens or 20s. A few reported being attacked by African-American males, or being lured by a white female to a nearby "party" where assailants lay in wait. Almost always, the reported attackers were young.

All seven youths accused of participating in the attack on Lucero reside in Patchogue or Medford—predominantly middle-class towns whose strip malls and pizzerias appear in sharp contrast to the lavish wealth on display elsewhere in the county. Suffolk County has one of the steepest wealth gradients in the country. Six of its ZIP codes are among the 100 wealthiest in the United States. The village of Sagaponack, one of a group of seaside communities collectively known as the Hamptons, is the most expensive ZIP code in the nation, with a median home sale price in 2005 of $2.8 million. It's home to investment bankers and real estate tycoons.

The parents of the alleged Lucero attackers include a teacher, a butcher, a store clerk, a deli owner and a former K-Mart operations manager. Latino immigrants may find work in Suffolk County's rich seaside communities, but they live in the more affordable inland towns, alongside middle- and working-class American families who are more likely to view the brown-skinned newcomers as competitors for jobs than hired help.

Immigrant advocates say that the violence committed by high school students and their slightly older peers is fueled by the immigrant-bashing rhetoric they absorb in the hallways and classrooms at school, in the news media, or in conversations at home.

Demographic change in Suffolk County has been rapid over the previous two decades. Some towns have gone from being practically all white to having a 15% Latino population, made up mostly of immigrants from Central America and Mexico, according to the latest census statistics. In Patchogue and Medford, the Latino population is 24%.

Although this influx has slowed since the U.S. economy faltered last year, the nativist backlash continues. It began in earnest in the late 1990s, when about 1,500 Mexican workers showed up over the course of a few years in the small, majority-white, middle-class hamlet of Farmingville. The hamlet's central location made it ideal for contractors looking to hire day laborers for jobs throughout

the county. That in turn made it attractive to immigrants drawn to the area by then-abundant employment opportunities in the landscaping, restaurant, and construction industries.

In 1998, a militant nativist group called Sachem Quality of Life formed in Farmingville and began disseminating propaganda that accused undocumented Latino immigrants of being inherently prone to rape, armed robbery and other violent crimes. Although Sachem Quality of Life is now defunct, the group, along with the Federation for American Immigration Reform and a smaller nativist group called American Patrol, heavily influenced the tone for public discourse on immigration in the area.

Nativist ideology now permeates many levels of society and government in Suffolk County. County Executive Levy in June 2006 mocked activists demonstrating against hate crime violence and the mass eviction of Latino immigrants based on the selective enforcement of zoning laws. "I will not back down to this one percent lunatic fringe," he said. "They evidently do not like me much because I am one of the few officials who are not intimidated by their politically correct histrionics."

That same year, a school board member in the Hamptons distributed an online petition to parents, teachers, and a school principal calling for undocumented immigrants to be prevented from receiving any "free services" in the U.S.

"Look, we need you to continue sending this around . . . [G]et as many viable names on here so that someone hears our voices," the E-mail read. "It seems the only voices they hear are the illegal immigrants who say 'foul play,' or the agencies backing them. We need to stop this and stop it in the bud!"

Also in 2006, the same official distributed an E-mail containing a "hilarious" mock description of a doll called Brentwood Barbie. "This Spanish-speaking only Barbie comes with a 1984 Toyota with expired temporary plates & 4 baby Barbies in the backseat (no car seats)," it read. "The optional Ken doll comes with a paint bucket lunch pail & is missing 3 fingers on his left hand. Green cards are not available for Brentwood Barbie or Ken."

In a February 2007 public hearing on proposed legislation, County Legislator Jack Eddington of Brookhaven singled out two immigration advocates who were speaking from the podium in Spanish and demanded to know if they were in the country legally. Eddington also warned undocumented immigrants, "You better beware" and "Suffolk County residents will not be victimized anymore."

Later in 2007, Levy was reelected with 96% of the vote.

Over the years, immigrant advocates have built an energetic movement in Suffolk County. Earlier this year, on the six-month anniversary of Lucero's murder, the Long Island Immigrant Alliance and The Workplace Project organized a vigil at the site of the killing. The event featured speakers from an array of groups, including the Fundación Lucero de América (Lucero Foundation America), along with Marcelo Lucero's brother, Joselo.

A few months before the vigil, some residents of eastern Long Island formed Neighbors in Support of Immigrants, in part to counter what they perceived as a takeover of local town council and community meetings by anti-immigrant zealots. In Patchogue, residents formed the Unity Coalition with the help of the New York Division of Human Rights to work to ease tensions in that community. A more established grassroots organization, Farmingdale Citizens for Viable Solutions, runs La Casa Comunal, a community center that serves Latino day laborers. The group also documents hate crimes.

Immigrant advocates cheered the news earlier this year that the Department of Justice had begun a criminal investigation into hate crimes against Latinos in Suffolk County. The federal agency also launched a probe into the way the Suffolk County Police Department, the main law enforcement agency in the county, has handled such crimes.

Nevertheless, the Latino immigrants interviewed for this report expressed little optimism that attitudes will change. If anything, they said, their situation is growing more perilous by the day. The weak economy means that more residents are out of work and looking for someone to blame. And many of the jobs for immigrants have dried up, forcing day laborers to spend more time traveling to and from their residence or waiting for work on street corners, making them all the more vulnerable.

Although most of the Latino immigrants who are victimized in Suffolk County are undocumented, their attackers have no way of knowing their immigration status. "They don't know if I'm legal or not so it must be because we're [Latino]," said Orlando, a Guatemalan immigrant who came to Suffolk County in 2005. "The racist people aren't going to change just because we get papers."

Notes

1. On May 26, 2010, Jeffrey Conroy, age 19, was sentenced to 25 years in prison for the first-degree manslaughter as a hate crime of Marcelo Lucero.

Questions for Critical Thinking

1. As this article demonstrates, the actions of people in social institutions such as the criminal justice system and the government often contribute to the creation of a climate of hate directed at immigrants. What do you see as the responsibilities of these officials in creating a safe and fair environment for all persons living in our communities?

2. As illustrated in the report, economic difficulties faced by middle- and working-class individuals often result in misplacing blame on immigrants. Where do you think such blame should be more appropriately placed?

3. The United States is a country made up largely of immigrants and the descendants of immigrants, and yet recent immigrants face increasing resistance in their efforts to be included in society. What do you see as solutions to this resistance?

Ruling Out Rape

LISA WADE, BRIAN SWEENEY, AMELIA SERAPHIA DERR, MICHAEL A. MESSNER, AND CAROL BURKE

The essay that follows explores the area of sexual assault as it relates to college campuses. Five experts in the field discuss how institutions deal with sexual assault and whether policies really protect victims.

Sexual assault is epidemic in the United States. Recent media reports, public outrage, and activism have been focused on the institutional settings in which these assaults occur. Colleges and universities, as well as the military and athletic programs, have come under increasing scrutiny as settings that not only fail to deter, but possibly foster rape.

Vanderbilt, Notre Dame, Maryville, Steubenville, Florida State, and the University of Missouri, to name a few, are among the recent highly-profiled institutions in which student athletes allegedly committed rapes that were ignored or downplayed by school administrators. The victims in these cases were treated with hostility by the schools, police, and even their peers who considered the reports of rape to be exaggerated responses to a party culture where "everyone is just trying to have fun" and where "stuff happens." Some of these victims have committed or attempted suicide.

Social consciousness around putting the victims of rape on trial may be evolving, but are the environments that foster these assaults really changing? President Obama recently promised women who have been sexually assaulted in college: "I've got your back." Should we be guardedly optimistic that this message from the top signals change, or do policy trends indicate attempts to protect institutions at the continued expense of victims? In this *Viewpoints*, five experts weigh in on the question of situational factors and institutional accountability around rape.

Lisa Wade reviews what we know about who commits rape on college campuses and the conditions that support this behavioral profile. She asserts that campus officials need to understand the interplay of cultural, psychological and situational causes for rape in order to make viable policy decisions. Brian Sweeney highlights the connection between alcohol consumption and sexual assault. He argues that campus policies that address binge drinking are doomed to fail unless they take into account that, for many young people, drinking and casual sex are rewarding. Amelia Seraphia Derr focuses on federal policies for reporting campus rape. She notes that colleges and universities are beginning to take these regulations more seriously, but raises concerns that they may trend in the direction of a "culture of compliance," where the fear of litigation that drives policy making could be counterproductive for prevention and support programs.

Michael A. Messner turns the lens on rape culture among male college athletes and asks what can be done. He's not convinced that current reform programs that target individual men and men's sports teams will mitigate sexual violence. He suggests we need a deeper understanding of the link between sexual domination, and the ways we celebrate male athletes and their violent domination in sports. Writing about a different, though familiar context, Carol Burke examines recent rape scandals in the military. She chronicles the mounting evidence for a high-level official blind eye on sexual assault and the resulting outrage among congresswomen who are calling for accountability. Is change in the offing? Read on and see what these experts have to say.

Understanding and Ending the Campus Sexual Assault Epidemic
Lisa Wade

College attendance is a risk factor for sexual assault. According to the U.S. Department of Justice, one in five women who attend college will be the victim of a completed or attempted sexual assault, compared to one in six women in the general population. Up to 90 percent of these women will know their attacker. Only about half will identify their experience as assault and fewer than 5 percent will report their experience to campus authorities or the police. Four percent of college men also report being sexually assaulted, overwhelmingly by other men.

Scholars have been working to gain a better understanding of the prevalence of rape on campuses, why it's infrequently reported to authorities, and what we can do about it. In a 2006 article, Elizabeth Armstrong and her collaborators point to cultural, psychological, and situational causes. In the effort to prevent sexual crimes, colleges and universities need to understand these interrelated causes and how they contribute to rates of sexual assault.

What are the psychological factors? A small number of men may be more predisposed to assault their peers than others. In a 2002 study by David Lisak and Paul Miller, 6 percent of male college students admitted to behavior that matched the legal definitions of sexual assault or rape. Of those men, two-thirds were serial rapists, with an average of six assaults each. Serial rapists plan their assaults, carefully choose their victim, use alcohol as a rape drug, and employ force, but only as a backup. Lisak and Miller find that these men are more likely than other men to engage in other forms of violence as well.

What about context? Some men may be inclined to harm others, but whether they do so is related to their opportunities. The right context can offer these men an opening to do so. Peggy Sanday first recognized the role that context plays in facilitating sexual assault. Studying fraternity parties, she found that some are generative of risk and others are less so. Parties that feature loud music, few places to sit, dancing, drinking, and compulsory flirting are, she explains, "rape prone." In these more dangerous places, rape culture camouflages the predatory behavior of serial rapists—like plying women with alcohol or pulling them into secluded areas—making it look normal and more difficult to interpret as criminal.

And then there's culture. Rape culture narratives—those that suggest that rape is simply a matter of miscommunication, that "date rape" isn't "real rape," that women frequently lie about being sexually assaulted for vengeance or out of shame—make it difficult for bystanders to justify intervening and for some victims to understand that their experience was a crime. Rape culture also gives rapists plausible excuses for their actions, making it difficult to hold them accountable, especially if members of the campus administration buy into these myths as well.

Armstrong and her colleagues show that all three of these causal factors interact together and with campus policy. Strict penalties for drinking alcohol in residence halls, for example, especially when strongly enforced, can push party-oriented students off campus to less safe places. Rape-friendly contexts offer a target-rich haven for the small percentage of individual men who are motivated to use force and coercion to attain sex. Rape culture contributes to concealing the predatory nature of their behavior to victims, their peers and, all too often, their advocates.

Currently, we're in the midst of a transformation in how colleges and universities handle sexual assault. While our understanding is far from complete, we know more than ever about the interaction of situational, cultural, and psychological causes. If institutions of higher education want to, they have the tools to reduce rates of sexual assault. And, even if they do not make this a priority, they face increasing pressure to do so. A strong national movement now aims to hold institutions accountable for ignoring, hiding, and mishandling sex crimes. Thanks largely to Know Your IX, 30 colleges submitted complaints to the U.S. Office for Civil Rights in 2013, nearly double the number from the year before. We should expect even higher numbers in 2014. Praising these activists, President Barack Obama announced that he was making the end of men's sexual violence against women a priority. The combination of "insider" and "outsider" politics, and a sympathetic media, is a promising recipe for change.

Drinking and Sexual Assault [Kids Just Wanna Have Fun]

Brian Sweeney

Getting wasted is fun, as is hooking up. In today's campus hookup culture, alcohol and sex often go together, and both can be rewarding experiences for young adults. Party culture glamorizes heavy drinking, making it seem less dangerous and, too often, causing students to dismiss the negative effects—whether getting puked on at a football game or being sexually assaulted—as "just stuff that happens." But sexual assault is a predictable result of party subcultures characterized by extreme drinking and sexual double standards. A majority of college rape victims are drunk when attacked, and

rapists use alcohol as a weapon to incapacitate their victims. Men—and other women, for that matter—may see overly drunk women as fair game, giving up their right to feminine protection because they have failed to be respectable and ladylike. Given the connection between intoxication and sexual assault, many ask, "Why not just tell women not to get so drunk?" But a mindset that places responsibility on women ignores the widespread attitudes and practices that encourage men's sexual predation and victimization of women in the first place.

To be clear, drinking, by itself, does not lead to sexual assault. Drinking heavily makes women more vulnerable, but it is overwhelmingly men who take advantage and rape. It is also men who stand by and watch their male friends ply women with drinks, block women from leaving rooms, and sometimes gang-rape women too drunk to walk home. Equipping women with "watch your drink, stay with your friends" strategies ignores both the fun of partying with abandon and the larger structures of domination that lead men to feel entitled to (drunk) women's bodies. Moreover, while rape-supportive beliefs are widespread, their influence over men's behavior is dependent on rape-supportive social and organizational arrangements—campus party culture and alcohol policy included.

Drinking subcultures have a long history on American college campuses, but since 1984 and the passage of the National Minimum Drinking Age Act, all 50 states have opted for billions in federal highway aid in exchange for passing Age-21 laws. As a result, many college campuses send mixed messages and endorse confused policies. Students are regularly fined and written up for drinking infractions but also educated about drinking responsibly. Students flock to so-called party schools and then spend most of their college years trying not to get caught—secretly "pre-gaming" with hard-alcohol in dorm rooms, hiding out in fraternity basements during party inspections, and nervously sweating as the bouncer checks for fake IDs. Alcohol becomes a coveted commodity, with many students seeking access to it and fortunate others wielding control of it.

Problems related to drinking exist, in part, because we have constructed a firewall between students and the adults who run universities—a divide that surely undermines our mission of creating safe and rich learning environments. We are allowing young people, unsupervised, to initiate each other into adulthood, often through rituals built around drinking. The campus pub is long gone at most schools, a relic of a bygone in loco parentis era when many professors lived among students and mentored them academically and socially. We could perhaps learn valuable lessons from a time when drinking was less illicit and student social life more open and watched over. Bringing drinking "aboveground" would disrupt some of the party scenes that sociological research has shown to be productive of sexual danger for women, would remove some of the constraints college administrators face in crafting effective alcohol education and policy, and would embolden sexual assault victims to come forward, reducing their fears of being punished for drinking violations.

Many schools are trying to get students to drink more responsibly. Since 2008, over 125 college and university presidents and chancellors have signed on to the Amethyst Initiative, which calls for "informed and dispassionate public debate" on Age-21 drinking laws. The supporters of the initiative, while not explicitly endorsing a lowering of the drinking age, believe Age-21 laws drive drinking underground, leading to dangerous binge drinking and reckless behavior among students. Five years after its inception, it is unclear if anything will come of the Amethyst Initiative. Federal and state government officials seem stubbornly unwilling to open discussion on Age-21 laws. And yet, because the initiative focuses on moderate and responsible drinking among students rather than abstinence, its ideas should have traction in correcting party cultures that, as they are currently organized, produce both fun and sexual danger. What is fairly certain is that sexual assault policies that ignore

the collective, rewarding nature of drunken, erotically charged revelry will likely fail among many young adults.

A Culture of Compliance vs. Prevention
Amelia Seraphia Derr

The under-reporting of campus sexual assaults has become a social problem. Students around the country are waging protests and demanding accountability from university administrators who have been accused of making light of alarming rates of sexual violence on college campuses. In 2011 the U.S. Department of Education Office of Civil Rights, in reaction to a Department of Justice report on the serious under-reporting of campus sexual assaults, and with the encouragement of Vice President Joe Biden, issued a Dear Colleagues Letter (DCL) on the topic of sexual violence. Specifically, the DCL emphasized and reiterated the legally mandated expectations for systems of reporting and adjudicating cases of sexual violence, for training staff, and for developing prevention and support programs.

Legislated reporting of sexual assault is the fruit of efforts dating back to the 1972 issuance of Title IX of the Education Amendments, which included sexual violence along with a variety of other forms of gender discrimination. In 1986 the Clery Act clarified and expanded the reporting requirements that were part of Title IX by establishing clear expectations for support services for students who are victims of sexual violence, and for the types of sexual violence-related reports that colleges and universities must file annually.

This legislative action intensified in 2011 when Bob Casey (D-PA) learned of Title IX violation complaints against Swarthmore College, alleging under-reporting cases of sexual misconduct, and took action. He introduced the Campus Sexual Violence Elimination Act (The SaVE Act), which became law with the passage of the Violence Against Women Reauthorization Act in August

2013. This act closes a serious gap in the existing law by requiring clearer and more publicized policies, education on student's rights, "bystander education" for the purpose of prevention, expanded reporting requirements, mandated prevention programs, and procedural rights for the accuser and accused.

This federal-level attention has created a sense of urgency in higher education, prompting university administrators to revisit policies on sexual assault to ensure compliance. But does it actually help change an organizational environment that is highly conducive to assault?

Institutionalizing accountability is essential; policies are a sustainable tool for addressing sexual violence on campuses. Evidence of the effectiveness of such policies can be seen in the fact that since the 2011 DCL there has been a steep increase in the number of Title IX and Clery Act complaints filed. According to the U.S. Department of Education, 62 Title IX complaints dealing with issues of sexual violence and harassment were filed between Oct. 1, 2012 and Sept. 30, 2013 alone.

However, a heightened regulatory environment may create a culture of compliance where the fear of litigation—rather than expert knowledge on prevention—drives policy-making. Institutional priorities and resources are directed differently depending on whether a university focuses on compliance-based reporting policies or prevention and support programs (which also include reporting policies, but within a framework of victim advocacy rather than institutional protection). For example, the DCL states that "if a school knows or reasonably should know about a potential sexual assault it is required to take immediate action." Ambiguity about what this means may prompt universities to adopt a mandated reporting policy for adult-aged students similar to those in place for minors or other vulnerable populations in order to avoid litigation.

Duke University (along with University of Montana, Swarthmore, and several others) has instituted such a policy, naming almost all of its 34,000 employees as mandated reporters. When staff or faculty members realize that students are about to share a concern with them, they must inform the student that the information they share will be reported to the designated administrator, with or without the student's permission. Duke University states that reports have increased since this policy was adopted. However, some victim's advocates oppose the practice. They counter that campus policies that mandate reporting irrespective of the victim's desire perpetuate a campus environment of silence and isolation and limit victims' options for confiding in trusted sources. A student Resident Assistant (RA) at Swarthmore, where RAs are considered mandated reporters, was recently fired from her position because she refused to break confidentiality by identifying a victim. Critics warn that these policies could ultimately lead to decreased reporting from victims who feel there is no safe space for them to turn in confidence. This is especially likely to be the case at a campus with few or insufficient survivor support services.

The real issue is how to move beyond a culture of compliance to a culture of prevention. In response to the requirements of the Campus SaVE Act, university policies should foreground survivor self-determination, provide strong perpetrator-prevention programs, offer robust victim support services, and promote increased dialogue about sexual violence with all members of the university community. These efforts will take us beyond the high visibility that reporting requirements have had, and into the areas of support and education required for true change.

Can Locker Room Rape Culture Be Prevented?
Michael A. Messner

Recipe for sexual assault: Assemble a group of young men. Promise them glory for violently dominating other groups of young men. Bond the group with aggressive joking about the sexual domination of women. Add public adulation that permeates the group with the scent of entitlement. Provide mentors who thrived as young men in this same system. Allow to simmer.

What have we cooked up? Horrendous sexual assaults on unconscious girls by high school football players in Steubenville and Maryville as well as an ongoing parade of sexual assault accusations against college football players, most recently at Florida State, Vanderbilt, and the United States Naval Academy. Do we over-emphasize cases of football player sexual misconduct because of their high profile? Perhaps. But research by sociologist Todd Crosset since the 1990s has shown that men who play intercollegiate sports are more likely than non-athletes to commit sexual assault—especially those in high-status sports that valorize violence.

Of course most football or ice hockey athletes don't rape women. Recently, some male athletes have even formed organizations to stop violence against women. "Male Athletes Against Violence" has done peer education at the University of Maine for years. And since 1993, Northeastern University's Mentors in Violence Prevention program has created a template for a national proliferation of sports-based programs that deploy a "bystander" approach to violence prevention. These programs attempt to disrupt the ways that high status male groups—like sports teams and fraternities—layer protective silence around members who perpetrate violence against women. A bystander approach teaches men to intervene to stop sexual assaults before they happen—for instance, stepping in when seeing one's teammates dragging an inebriated woman to a back room. A good man, the bystander approach teaches, steps forward not only to keep a woman safe, but also to keep the team safe from public trouble.

The years of silence surrounding Penn State University football coach Jerry Sandusky's serial sexual assaults of children is one example of the absolute failure by high-profile university coaches and administrators to model the responsible bystander behavior they say their young athletes should engage in. This case showed that, rather than resulting simply from the actions of one bad man, sexual assault is embedded in the routine values and culture of silence in organizations.

A number of years ago, I assisted psychologist Mark Stevens—a pioneer in working with athletes to prevent sexual violence—in an intervention with a college football program after members of the team were accused of sexually assaulting a woman at an off-campus party. Before the first of two workshops, I asked Stevens if he really thought that a few hours of talk could change the culture of sexual dominance that so commonly cements football team members' loyalties while simultaneously putting women and vulnerable men at risk. Stevens answered no. "But," he added, "if we can empower one or two guys who, down the road, might intervene in a situation to stop a sexual assault, then our work will have made the world safer for at least one woman."

I still worry that such interventions do less to prevent acts of violence than they do to contain the public relations nightmare that sexual assaults create for athletics departments. Confirming that fear, a man I recently interviewed told me that he had been hired by a big-time college sports program to institute a violence prevention program, only to find it "incredibly disappointing" when he learned his employers had hired him mostly to work with male athletes of color to keep them eligible to play sports. "I thought that they were genuinely ready to do something, you know, make some changes . . . I got kind of duped. I had this particular background [in violence prevention] so that was really enticing for them, and they had no intention of actually letting me do any of that work."

While some schools have adopted sexual assault prevention programs for some of their men's sports teams, we just don't know how well they work. We need good research that points to how, or under what conditions prevention programs within institutions like football (or the military) can actually succeed in mitigating gender-based violence. To have such an impact, I believe these interventions

will need to confront how sexism is routinely intertwined with male entitlement and celebratory
violence. To be truly successful, I suspect, such
a program would render the game itself to be no
longer football as we know it.

Failure to Serve and Protect

Carol Burke

Military scandals in the past two years have
brought new attention to old problems: sexual
harassment, sexual assault, and the potential for
bias in the handling of these crimes. The general
who commanded the 82nd Airborne was charged
with forcible sodomy, indecent acts, and violating
orders, and was issued a reprimand and ordered to
pay a $20,000 fine. The commanders in charge of
Lackland Air Force Base apparently didn't realize
that, over a two-year period, 62 recruits were assaulted by 33 drill instructors. Even those tasked
with preventing sexual assault were charged with
the crimes they had pledged to thwart. A lieutenant colonel who headed the Sexual Harassment
and Assault Response Prevention program at Fort
Campbell, Kentucky, was arrested and charged
with stalking an ex-wife and sending her threatening emails in violation of a restraining order. A
lieutenant colonel in charge of the Air Force Sexual
Assault Prevention and Response Program was
charged with the sexual battery of a stranger in a
parking lot. His alleged victim, according to witnesses, took justice into her own hands and after
pushing away the drunken officer, ran after him
and punched him in the face. At trial, the officer
was acquitted.

Ultimately, the scandal that ignited the outrage
of several congresswomen was Lieutenant General
Craig Franklin's decision to overturn Lieutenant
Colonel James Wilkerson's court-martial conviction for sexual assault. To Franklin, it seemed in-
congruous that a man "who adored his wife and
his 9-year-old son," a man who as a pilot had
flown in the same unit as him, and a man who
had been selected "for promotion to full colonel,

a wing inspector general, a career officer" could
be a sexual predator. So Franklin exercised the
power granted him and other commanders under
the Uniform Code of Military Justice (UCMJ) to
reverse any verdict without explanation. Although
this might have looked at the time like the decision
of an out-of-touch commander from his lonely and
lofty post, identifying more with the plight of the
accused than of the victim, emails related to the
case revealed that generals of even higher rank
than Franklin's supported his decision.

According to the Defense Department's own
survey, 26,000 anonymous respondents claimed
that they had been sexually assaulted in 2012, yet
only 3,374 complaints were officially reported in
that year. The incendiary mix of the skyrocketing
rates of assault and the apparent indifference of
some commanders to the plight of victims captured
the attention of many women in Congress, and
they demanded reform. These congresswomen,
joined by some of their male colleagues, took aim
at the heart of military culture, the sacrosanct military justice system, which can only be as impartial
as the commander who oversees it. Senator Kristin
Gillibrand (D-NY) proposed a two-part judicial
system akin to those of many of our NATO Allies,
a system that would take the most serious crimes
like murder and sexual assault out of the chain of
command and ensure that decisions to investigate,
prosecute, and convict could not be arbitrarily
reversed by a commander. In a statement issued
December 20, 2013, Gillibrand said, "Nowhere in
America do we allow a boss to decide if an employee was sexually assaulted or not, except in the
United States military."

Senator Claire McCaskill (D-MO) fashioned a
more moderate compromise that left the investigation and adjudication of crimes of sexual assault
in the hands of commanders but that lifted the
five-year statute of limitations on courts-martial
for sex-related crimes, criminalized retaliation by
commanders (but not by peers), provided counsel
for victims, and did away with the "good soldier
defense." The compromise carried the day, much to

the chagrin of victims who regard the UCMJ as a system that often denies them justice.

For several years now the Department of Defense has required mandatory training intended to prevent sexual assault and sexual harassment, crafted public service announcements for broadcast on military TV stations, established hotlines for victims, and posted pleas in bathrooms on bases here and abroad for bystanders to step in when they see abuse taking place. Unfortunately, these costly efforts have failed to build trust in a military judicial system. Victims see these public campaigns as the military's efforts to protect the institution and not them. As long as the investigation and adjudication of sexual assault cases remain within such a command-centric judicial system, the partiality of a single individual can easily trump justice.

Questions for Critical Thinking

1. Gendered expectations of sexuality often contribute to an environment that fosters sexual assault. How might gender equality among college women and men in their sexual behavior reduce the incidence of rape?

2. Do you think some college party environments perpetuate a rape culture? If so, how? If not, why don't you think so?

3. Issues of rape and sexual assault are of particular concern on college campuses. Why do you think this is? What steps can all members of campus communities take to reduce or eliminate this concern?

Cyberbullying, School Bullying, and Psychological Distress

A Regional Census of High School Students

SHARI KESSEL SCHNEIDER, LYDIA O'DONNELL, ANN STUEVE,
AND ROBERT W. S. COULTER

Drawing on data from a regional census of high school students, the following essay documents the prevalence of cyberbullying, school bullying victimization, and negative consequences for the targets of that bullying. The authors' findings demonstrate that those students perceived to be gay, lesbian, bisexual, and/or transgendered were more likely to be targets of this form of violence and that such bullying had negative consequences for the school performance and mental health of these students. The conclusions of the authors confirm the need to establish structural changes to prevent this trend from continuing.

Recent national attention to several cases of suicide among youth victims of cyberbullying[1,2] has raised concerns about its prevalence and psychological impact. Most states now have legislation in place that requires schools to address electronic harassment in their antibullying policies,[3] yet schools lack information about cyberbullying correlates and consequences and how they may differ from those of school bullying. To inform schools' efforts, research is needed that examines the overlap between cyberbullying and school bullying and identifies which youths are targeted with either or both types of bullying. It is also necessary to understand whether the psychological correlates of cyberbullying are similar to those of school bullying and whether students targeted with both forms of bullying are at increased risk of psychological harm.

With reports indicating that 93% of teens are active users of the Internet and 75% own a cell phone, up from 45% in 2004,[4] there is great potential for cyberbullying among youths. Yet the extent of cyberbullying victimization and its prevalence relative to school bullying is unclear. Studies have found that anywhere from 9% to 40% of students are victims of cyberbullying,[5–7] and most suggest that online victimization is less prevalent than are school bullying and other forms of offline victimization.[8,9] Strikingly few reports provide information on youths' involvements in bullying both online and on school property.

Cyberbullying has several unique characteristics that distinguish it from school bullying. Electronic communications allow cyberbullying perpetrators to maintain anonymity and give them the capacity to post messages to a wide audience.[10] In addition, perpetrators may feel reduced responsibility and accountability when online compared with face-to-face situations.[11,12] These features suggest that youths who may not be vulnerable to school bullying could, in fact, be targeted online through covert methods. The limited number of studies that address the overlap between school and cyberbullying victimization has wide variation in findings, indicating that anywhere from about one third to more than three quarters of youths bullied online are also bullied at school.[11,13,14]

The distinct features of cyberbullying have led to questions about the sociodemographic characteristics of cyberbullying victims compared with those of school bullying victims. Although numerous studies of school bullying have found that boys are more likely to be victims,[15,16] the extent of gender differences in cyberbullying is unclear.[5] Some studies have found that girls are more likely to be victims of cyberbullying,[9,10] yet other studies have found no gender differences.[8,17,18] Age is another characteristic in which cyberbullying patterns may differ from traditional bullying. Although there is a decreasing prevalence of traditional bullying from middle to high school,[16] some studies suggest that cyberbullying victimization increases during the middle school years,[8,10] and others have found no consistent relationship between cyberbullying and age.[11,19] Sexual orientation has been consistently linked with traditional bullying.[20-22] Despite recent media attention to cases of suicide among sexual minority youths who have been cyberbullied,[23] accounts of the relationship between cyberbullying and sexual orientation are primarily anecdotal, with little documentation of the extent to which nonheterosexual youths are victimized. The wide range of definitions and time frames used to assess cyberbullying complicates the comparison of the prevalence and correlates of cyberbullying across studies, and rapid advances in communications technology render it difficult to establish a comprehensive and static definition. Furthermore, there is wide variation in the age and other demographic characteristics of the samples, with many studies employing small, nonrepresentative samples.

In addition to comparing the sociodemographics of cyberbullying victims with those of school

bullying victims, it is important to understand whether cyberbullying is linked with negative school experiences, as is the case with school bullying. School bullying is widely known to be associated with many negative indicators, including lower academic achievement, lower school satisfaction, and lower levels of attachment and commitment to school, known as school bonding.[24,25] Because most cyberbullying occurs outside school,[19,26] it is uncertain whether a similar relationship exists for cyberbullying. A few studies have linked cyberbullying to negative school experiences, such as lower academic performance[27] and negative perceptions of school climate.[8] Although these studies suggest that cyberbullying may be a contributing factor, more research is needed to determine the extent to which school attachment and performance are related to cyberbullying experiences.

The known link between school bullying and psychological harm, including depression and suicidality,[28-31] has also raised concerns about how cyberbullying is related to various forms of psychological distress. An emerging body of research has begun to identify psychological correlates of cyberbullying that are similar to the consequences of traditional bullying, including increased anxiety and emotional distress.[6,11,32] There are also reports that online victimization may be linked with more serious distress, including major depression,[33,34] self-harm, and suicide.[31,35,36] Although studies consistently identify a relationship between cyberbullying and psychological distress, it is not known whether reports of psychological distress are similar among cyberbullying and school bullying victims or what levels of distress are experienced by those who report being victimized both online and at school.

In this study, we used data collected from more than 20 000 students from the second wave of the MetroWest Adolescent Health Survey to examine patterns and correlates of bullying victimization. We first examined the prevalence of cyberbullying and school bullying and the degree of overlap between the 2 forms of victimization. Next, looking at youths who experienced cyberbullying only, school bullying only, or both types of bullying, we identified sociodemographic and individual-level school characteristics associated with each type of victimization. Finally, we analyzed the relationship between type of bullying victimization and multiple indicators of psychological distress, ranging from depressive symptoms to suicide attempts.

Methods

The MetroWest Adolescent Health Survey is a biennial census survey of high school students in the western suburbs and small cities of the Boston metropolitan area that has the goal of monitoring trends to inform local and regional school and community policies and practices. The region is home to 26 high schools serving predominantly middle- and upper-middle class families. The survey employs a census rather than sampling procedure so that each district can monitor student behaviors and identify health issues that may vary by grade, gender, and other sociodemographic characteristics.

In fall 2008, 22 of 26 high schools in the region participated in the survey; these schools serve 86% of all public high school students in the region. Pencil and paper, anonymous surveys were conducted with all 9th- through 12th-grade students present on the day of administration. Parents and guardians were notified in advance and given the opportunity to view the survey and opt out their child(ren); students also provided assent. Youths (n=20 406) completed the surveys, for a participation rate of 88.1% (range, 75.2%–93.7%). Reflecting differences in school size, the number of students participating at each site ranged from 303 to 1815.

Measures

To facilitate comparison with state and national data, most items in the Metro-West Adolescent Health Survey were drawn from the Centers for Disease Control and Prevention's Youth Risk Behavior Survey[37] and the Massachusetts Youth Risk Behavior Survey.[38]

Bullying.

Students were asked about cyberbullying victimization and school bullying victimization in the past 12 months. Cyberbullying was measured with the following question: "How many times has someone used the Internet, a phone, or other electronic communications to bully, tease, or threaten you?" School bullying was measured by the following question: "During the past 12 months, how many times have you been bullied on school property?" with bullying defined as "being repeatedly teased, threatened, hit, kicked, or excluded by another student or group of students." Responses from these 2 questions were categorically grouped into 4 categories of bullying victimization: cyberbullying victim only, school bullying victim only, both cyber and school bullying victim, and neither.

Psychological distress.

Depressive symptoms, suicidal ideation (seriously considering suicide), and suicide attempts (any attempt and an attempt requiring medical treatment) were measured using items about behavior in the past 12 months.[37] Self-injury was assessed by the item "How many times did you hurt or injure yourself on purpose? (For example, by cutting, burning, or bruising yourself on purpose)."[38] Responses were dichotomized into yes or no categories.

Sociodemographics.

Sociodemographic characteristics included gender, grade (9–12), race/ethnicity (Asian, African American or Black, Hispanic or Latino, Caucasian or White, or mixed or other), and sexual orientation (responses grouped as "heterosexually identified" vs "nonheterosexually identified," the latter of which encompassed gay or lesbian, bisexual, other, and not sure).

Individual-level school characteristics.

School performance was measured through self-reported grades coded as "mostly As," "mostly Bs," "mostly Cs," and a combined category encompassing "mostly Ds," "mostly Fs," and un-graded or other. School attachment was measured using a 5-item scale from the National Longitudinal Study of Adolescent Health[39]; scale scores were divided into tertiles (low, medium, high).

School size.

Schools were grouped into 3 categories on the basis of the size of student enrollment: <750 students, 750–1250 students, and >1250 students.

Results

Table 1 presents the sociodemographic characteristics of participants. Three quarters (75.2%) of the youths were non-Hispanic White, consistent with regional demographics. About 6% of youths reported that they were gay or lesbian, bisexual, other, or not sure (nonheterosexually identified youths).

Prevalence and Overlap of Cyberbullying and School Bullying Victimization

Overall, 15.8% of students reported cyberbullying, and 25.9% reported school bullying in the past 12 months. The overlap between cyberbullying and school bullying was substantial: 59.7% of cyberbullying victims were also school bullying victims, and 36.3% of school bullying victims were also cyberbullying victims. When categorized into 4 groups on the basis of reports of cyber and school bullying victimization, one third of all students were bullying victims: 6.4% were victims of cyberbullying only, 16.5% of students were victims of school bullying only, and 9.4% were victims of both school and cyberbullying.

Correlates of Bullying Victimization

Regarding overall cyberbullying and school bullying victimization, reports of cyberbullying were higher among girls than among boys (18.3% vs 13.2%), whereas reports of school bullying were similar for both genders (25.1% for girls, 26.6% for boys). Although cyberbullying decreased slightly from 9th grade to 12th grade (from 17.2% to 13.4%), school bullying decreased by nearly half (from 32.5% to 17.8%). Nonheterosexually identified

Table 1 Sociodemographics and School-Related Characteristics of Study Sample: MetroWest Adolescent Health Survey, Massachusetts, 2008

Characteristics	No. (%)
Sociodemographics	
Gender	
Girl	10 218 (50.4)
Boy	10 050 (49.6)
Grade	
9th	5446 (26.8)
10th	5312 (26.2)
11th	5075 (25.0)
12th	4458 (22.0)
Race/ethnicity	
Asian	786 (3.9)
African American	564 (2.8)
Hispanic	1186 (5.8)
White	15 265 (75.2)
Mixed/other	2497 (12.3)
Sexual orientation	
Heterosexually identified	18 795 (93.7)
Nonheterosexually identified	1261 (6.3)
School-related characteristics	
Self-reported school performance	
Mostly As	6072 (31.0)
Mostly Bs	9947 (50.8)
Mostly Cs	2477 (12.6)
Mostly Ds or Fs	1090 (5.6)
Self-reported school attachment	
Highest tertile	7066 (35.1)
Medium tertile	5953 (29.6)
Lowest tertile	7095 (35.3)
School enrollment	
<750 students	2402 (11.8)
750–1250 students	8576 (42.0)
>1250 students	9428 (46.2)

youths were far more likely than were heterosexually identified youths to report cyberbullying (33.1% vs 14.5%) and school bullying (42.3% vs 24.8%). There were no differences in overall reporting of cyberbullying or school bullying by race/ethnicity.

Table 2 displays the sociodemographic and individual-level school correlates of bullying victimization when categorized into the following 4 groups: cyberbullying victim only, school bullying victim only, both, and neither. Whereas there was little difference by gender, race/ethnicity, and grade, nonheterosexually identified youths were more likely to be victims of cyberbullying only, compared with those who self-identify as heterosexual (10.5% vs 6.0%). Youths who reported lower school performance and lower school attachment were also more likely to be victimized with cyberbullying only; for example, students who received mostly Ds and Fs were twice as likely to be cyber-only victims compared with students who received mostly As (11.3% vs 5.2%).

In contrast to reports of the cyber-only group, victimization on school property decreases substantially from 21.4% in 9th grade to 10.6% in 12th grade. There was little difference by gender or race/ethnicity. Consistent with the cyber-only group, nonheterosexually identified youths were at higher risk of school-only victimization (19.5% vs 16.3%); school-only victimization was also associated with lower school attachment.

Although there was little difference by gender for the other victimization groups, girls were more likely than were boys to be victims of both types of bullying (11.1% vs 7.6%). Like the cyber-only and school-only groups, sexual orientation was associated with reports of both cyber and school victimization; 22.7% of nonheterosexually identified youths were victims of both types of bullying compared with 8.5% of heterosexually identified youths. In addition, the associations between dual forms of victimization and school variables were stronger: students who received mostly Ds and Fs were more than twice as likely as were students who received mostly As to be victims of both forms of bullying (16.1% vs 7.4%), and students in the lowest school attachment tertile were nearly 3 times as likely to report both forms of victimization than were students in the highest tertile (14.9% vs 5.6%). Thus, youths who were in lower grades and nonheterosexually identified youths were more likely to be

victims of one or both types of bullying, as were students who reported lower grades and lower levels of school attachment.

Bullying Victimization and Psychological Distress

Table 3 presents bivariate associations between types of bullying victimization (cyber-only, school-only, both, or neither) and 5 indicators of psychological distress. Bullying victimization was consistently and robustly associated with an increased likelihood of psychological distress across all measures from depressive symptoms and suicidal ideation to reports of self-injury and suicide attempts. Furthermore, the relationship between victimization and distress was strongest among students who were victims of both cyber and school victimization, followed by victims of cyberbullying only and then victims of school bullying only. For example, reports of depressive symptoms were highest among victims of both cyber and school bullying (47.0%), followed by cyber-only victims (33.9%), and school-only victims (26.6%) compared with 13.6% of nonvictims. Similarly, attempted suicide was highest among victims of both cyber and school bullying (15.2%); however, it was also elevated among cyber-only victims (9.4%) and school-only victims (4.2%) compared with students reporting neither form of victimization (2.0%).

Table 4 displays logistic regressions modeling the relationship between type of bullying victimization and psychological distress, adjusting for the sociodemographic and individual-level school variables identified earlier as significant correlates of victimization. Consistent with the bivariate associations, there were strong relationships between bullying victimization and psychological distress across all indicators of distress. Overall, the risks of experiencing psychological distress were greatest for victims of both cyber and school bullying. For example, compared with nonvictims, victims of both cyber and school bullying were more than 4 times as likely to report depressive symptoms (adjusted odds ratio (AOR) = 4.38; 99% CI = 3.76, 5.10), suicidal ideation (AOR = 4.51; 99% CI = 3.78, 5.39),

Table 2 Sociodemographic and Individual-Level School-Related Correlates of Bullying Victimization: MetroWest Adolescent Health Survey, Massachusetts, 2008

Characteristics	Cyberbullying victim only, No. (%)	School bullying victim only, No. (%)	Cyber and school bullying victim, No. (%)	Neither, No. (%)
Sociodemographics correlates				
Gender*				
Girl	723 (7.2)	1564 (15.5)	1118 (11.1)	6697 (66.3)
Boy	546 (5.6)	1718 (17.5)	751 (7.6)	6812 (69.3)
Grade*				
9th	327 (6.1)	1146 (21.4)	596 (11.1)	3293 (61.4)
10th	329 (6.3)	961 (18.4)	554 (10.6)	3376 (64.7)
11th	335 (6.7)	724 (14.5)	411 (8.2)	3529 (70.6)
12th	275 (6.3)	463 (10.6)	310 (7.1)	3324 (76.0)
Race/ethnicity*				
White	858 (5.7)	2474 (16.4)	1400 (9.3)	10332 (68.6)
Non-White/mixed	413 (8.4)	822 (16.8)	481 (9.8)	3179 (64.9)
Sexual orientation*				
Heterosexually identified	1125 (6.0)	3046 (16.3)	1583 (8.5)	12888 (69.1)
Nonheterosexually identified	131 (10.5)	243 (19.5)	282 (22.7)	589 (47.3)
Individual-level school-related correlates				
School performance*				
Mostly As	312 (5.2)	1002 (16.6)	448 (7.4)	4266 (70.8)
Mostly Bs	598 (6.1)	1642 (16.7)	896 (9.1)	6679 (68.0)
Mostly Cs	191 (8.0)	399 (16.6)	293 (12.2)	1516 (63.2)
Mostly Ds and Fs	117 (11.3)	145 (14.0)	167 (16.1)	606 (58.6)
School attachment*				
Highest tertile	364 (5.2)	891 (12.7)	393 (5.6)	5385 (76.6)
Medium tertile	348 (5.9)	965 (16.3)	435 (7.3)	4174 (70.5)
Lowest tertile	552 (7.9)	1442 (20.6)	1048 (14.9)	3974 (56.6)
Total	1275 (6.4)	3311 (16.5)	1889 (9.4)	13582 (67.7)

Note. All measures are for the past 12 months.

*$P<.001$ for association between bullying victimization and sociodemographic or student-level school correlate.

and self-injury (AOR = 4.79; 99% CI = 4.06, 5.65), and more than 5 times as likely to report a suicide attempt (AOR = 5.04; 99% CI = 3.88, 6.55) and a suicide attempt requiring medical treatment (AOR = 5.42; 99% CI = 3.56, 8.26). Victims of cyberbullying only were also at a heightened, but somewhat lower risk of psychological distress (AORs from 2.59 to 3.44). The risk was still notable, but even lower, among victims of school bullying only (AORs from 1.51 to 2.20) compared with nonvictims.

Table 3 Psychological Correlates of Bullying Victimization: MetroWest Adolescent Health Survey, Massachusetts, 2008

Bullying victimization	Depressive symptoms,* No. (%)	Suicidal ideation,* No. (%)	Self-injury,* No. (%)	Suicide attempt,* No. (%)	Suicide attempt with medical treatment,* No. (%)
Cyber victim only	429 (33.9)	228 (18.1)	305 (24.0)	119 (9.4)	42 (3.3)
School victim only	878 (26.6)	464 (14.1)	511 (15.5)	138 (4.2)	45 (1.4)
Both cyber and school victim	884 (47.0)	561 (30.0)	712 (37.8)	286 (15.2)	123 (6.6)
Neither	1839 (13.6)	836 (6.2)	1102 (8.1)	275 (2.0)	86 (0.6)
Total	4030 (20.2)	2089 (10.5)	2630 (13.2)	818 (4.1)	296 (1.5)

Note. All measures are for the past 12 months.

*$P<.001$ for association between victimization and indicator of psychological distress.

Discussion

We examined data from a large, school-based census of more than 20 000 youths to document the co-occurrence of cyberbullying and school bullying and their association with psychological distress. We have provided evidence of a substantial overlap between cyberbullying and school bullying victimization and called attention to particularly vulnerable populations, including nonheterosexually identified youths. We also found an association between both types of bullying and indicators of school success. Finally, we have highlighted the relationship between victimization and psychological distress, documenting a substantially elevated risk of distress among victims of both cyber and school bullying. These findings show a clear need for prevention efforts that address both forms of victimization.

Although almost all states now mandate schools to address cyberbullying in their anti-bullying policies,[3] there is great flexibility in how much emphasis schools place on efforts to prevent cyberbullying, which occurs mostly outside school.[19,26] We found substantial overlap between cyberbullying and school bullying: nearly two thirds of all cyberbullying victims reported they were also bullied at school, and conversely, more than one third of school bullying victims also reported

cyberbullying. This indicates the importance of prevention approaches that address both modes of victimization.

Another important reason for schools to address cyberbullying is the link between victimization and school attachment and self-reported school performance. This is true even for the 6% of students who were victimized only through cyberbullying. Although this cross-sectional survey cannot make attributions of causality, cyberbullying may be a contributing factor to negative school experiences, suggesting the need for schools to incorporate cyberbullying into their antibullying programs and policies. Efforts to increase student engagement in school, connectedness to peers and teachers, and academic success may also promote a climate in which school and cyberbullying are less likely to occur.

Our findings identified several groups that were particularly susceptible to victimization. It is not surprising to learn that cyberbullying victimization and dual victimization were more prevalent among nonheterosexually identified youths, who are known to suffer from higher rates of victimization in school settings.[20–22] Nearly one quarter (23%) were victims of both cyber and school bullying, compared with only 9% of heterosexually identified youths. These disproportionate reports

Table 4 Associations of Bullying Victimization and Psychological Distress among High School Students: MetroWest Adolescent Health Survey, 2008

Characteristics	Depressive symptoms, No. or OR (95% CI)	Suicidal ideation, No. or OR (95% Cf)	Self-injury, No. or OR (95% CI)	Suicide attempt, No. or OR (95% CI)	Suicide attempt with medical treatment, No. or OR (95% CI)
Unadjusted					
Students	19 990	19 953	19 975	19 988	19 877
Bullying victimization					
Cyber victim only	3.26 (2.76, 3.85)	3.35 (2.71, 4.13)	3.56 (2.95, 4.29)	5.00 (3.73, 6.71)	5.36 (3.28, 8.75)
School victim only	2.31 (2.04, 2.60)	2.49 (2.13, 2.92)	2.07 (1.78, 2.40)	2.11 (1.60, 2.77)	2.16 (1.34, 3.48)
Both cyber and school victim	5.64 (4.93, 6.46)	6.52 (5.56, 7.64)	6.86 (5.92, 7.94)	8.64 (6.88, 10.86)	10.93 (7.57, 15.80)
Neither (Ref)	1.00	1.00	1.00	1.00	1.00
Adjusted					
Students	18 815	18 784	18 796	18 812	18 735
Bullying victimization					
Cyber victim only	2.61 (2.17, 3.13)	2.59 (2.06, 3.25)	2.83 (2.30, 3.48)	3.44 (2.48, 4.76)	3.39 (1.99, 5.77)
School victim only	2.19 (1.92, 2.50)	2.20 (1.86, 2.62)	1.84 (1.57, 2.17)	1.63 (1.20, 2.20)	1.51 (0.89, 2.55)
Both cyber and school victim	4.38 (3.76, 5.10)	4.51 (3.78, 5.39)	4.79 (4.06, 5.65)	5.04 (3.88, 6.55)	5.42 (3.56, 8.26)
Neither (Ref)	1.00	1.00	1.00	1.00	1.00
Gender					
Girl	2.19 (1.97, 2.44)	1.59 (1.39, 1.82)	2.34 (2.05, 2.66)	1.29 (1.04, 1.59)	1.11 (0.79, 1.57)
Boy (Ref)	1.00	1.00	1.00	1.00	1.00
Grade					
9th	0.70 (0.60, 0.81)	0.76 (0.63, 0.93)	0.96 (0.80, 1.15)	1.04 (0.77, 1.42)	0.81 (0.50, 1.30)
10th	0.82 (0.71, 0.95)	0.92 (0.76, 1.11)	1.18 (0.98, 1.41)	1.06 (0.78, 1.44)	0.82 (0.51, 1.33)
11th	1.02 (0.88, 1.18)	0.93 (0.77, 1.13)	1.13 (0.94, 1.35)	1.05 (0.77, 1.44)	0.79 (0.48, 1.30)
12th (Ref)	1.00	1.00	1.00	1.00	1.00
Race/ethnicity					
White (Ref)	1.00	1.00	1.00	1.00	1.00
Non-White/mixed	1.25 (1.12, 1.41)	1.15 (0.99, 1.33)	1.02 (0.89, 1.18)	1.55 (1.25, 1.94)	1.38 (0.97, 1.98)
Sexual orientation					
Heterosexually identified (Ref)	1.00	1.00	1.00	1.00	1.00
Nonheterosexually identified	2.36 (1.97, 2.83)	3.43 (2.83, 4.16)	4.12 (3.42, 4.96)	5.17 (4.05, 6.60)	5.34 (3.69, 7.74)
School performance					
Mostly As (Ref)	1.00	1.00	1.00	1.00	1.00
Mostly Bs	1.44 (1.27, 1.63)	1.28 (1.09, 1.52)	1.27 (1.10, 1.48)	1.64 (1.22, 2.21)	1.21 (0.75, 1.96)
Mostly Cs	2.17 (1.83, 2.58)	1.70 (1.37, 2.12)	1.82 (1.49, 2.23)	2.79 (1.98, 3.94)	2.05 (1.19, 3.55)
Mostly Ds and Fs	2.71 (2.17, 3.38)	2.41 (1.85, 3.14)	2.28 (1.77, 2.94)	3.90 (2.67, 5.71)	3.31 (1.87, 5.87)

School attachment

Highest tertile (Ref)	1.00	1.00	1.00	1.00	1.00
Medium tertile	1.23 (1.07, 1.43)	1.26 (1.03, 1.53)	1.18 (0.99, 1.40)	1.09 (0.78, 1.52)	0.98 (0.55, 1.75)
Lowest tertile	2.69 (2.36, 3.07)	2.50 (2.10, 2.98)	2.12 (1.81, 2.47)	2.09 (1.58, 2.77)	2.11 (1.33, 3.37)

Note. CI—confidence interval; OR—odds ratio. All measures are for the past 12 months.

of bullying involvement, combined with the high prevalence of psychological distress among non-heterosexually identified youths,[40] show a clear need for antibullying programs and policies to address and protect students who identify as gay, lesbian, or bisexual or who may be questioning their sexual orientation. We also noted gender differences in victimization patterns. Girls were more likely than were boys to report cyberbullying, especially in combination with school bullying. Several other studies support the higher prevalence of cyberbullying victimization among girls.[9,10]

There is a robust relationship between cyberbullying victimization and all forms of psychological distress along the continuum from depression to suicide attempts. Importantly, whereas all 3 victim groups examined in this study reported elevated psychological distress, victims of cyberbullying alone reported more distress than did victims of school bullying alone. Moreover, the risk of psychological distress was most marked for victims of both cyber and school bullying, who were more than 4 times as likely to experience depressive symptoms and more than 5 times as likely to attempt suicide as were nonvictims. Our study not only provides further evidence of the link between cyberbullying and psychological distress[30,34,36] but also points to an even greater need to identify and support victims of both cyber and school bullying.

This study has several limitations. First, cyberbullying and school victimization were assessed using self-reported single items. There is no current consensus among researchers on how to measure cyberbullying, and the changing nature of communications technology makes it difficult to establish a fixed definition. In addition, some youths reporting both cyberbullying and school bullying may have answered positively to both questions because they were victims of cyberbullying that occurred on school property. The psychological distress indicators were also assessed using single self-report items; although these items are widely used, they are not diagnostic. The cross-sectional nature of the analysis means that we cannot attribute causality or temporality to the relation between bullying and distress. Furthermore, this study does not consider students' roles as perpetrators. These involvements may also be associated with increased psychological distress and negative school factors.[41,42] We also did not explore contextual influences on these behaviors and the complex roles that bystanders—students and parents and adults in the school community—play in escalating, condoning, tolerating, or preventing cyberbullying and school bullying. These are important areas for further research.

Despite these limitations, our study has several unique strengths. Many studies of cyberbullying are conducted online and, therefore, may have a bias toward the experiences of students who use the Internet more frequently. In fact, time spent online and computer proficiency have been related to cyberbullying behavior.[17] This school-based study included a more diverse group of students in terms of exposure to and use of electronic media. In addition, the sample size was large, permitting examination of behaviors within relatively small subgroups, such as nonheterosexually identified youths, and of infrequent forms of psychological distress, such as suicide attempts. At the same time, however, the results are regional, and generalizability to other populations, including youths in urban and rural schools, may be limited.

In summary, our study provides a better understanding of cyberbullying and its relationship to school bullying, which is critical to informing school-based prevention efforts and engaging parents and other community members in combating this significant public health issue. Our findings underscore the need for prevention efforts that address all forms of bullying victimization and their potential for harmful consequences both inside and outside school.

References

1. Deutsch L. Prosecutors: cyber law applies to suicide case. *Associated Press.* August 13, 2008. Available at: http://www.usatoday.com/news/nation/2008-08-12-327594069_x.htm. Accessed September 8, 2011.

2. Kennedy H. Phoebe Prince, South Hadley High School's "new girl" driven to suicide by teenage cyber bullies. *New York Daily News.* March 29, 2010.

3. Hinduja S., Patchin JW. *State Cyberbullying Laws: A Brief Review of State Cyberbullying Laws and Policies.* Cyberbullying Research Center. Available at: http://cyberbullying.us/Bullying_and_Cyberbullying_Laws.pdf. Accessed February 9, 2011.

4. Lenhart A, Purcell K, Smith A, Zickuhr K. *Social Media and Mobile Internet Use Among Teens and Adults.* Pew Research Center Publications; 2010. Available at: http://pewinternetorg/~/media//Files/Reports/2010/PIP_Social_Media_and_Young_Adults_Report_Final_with_toplines.pdf. Accessed February 9, 2011.

5. Tokunaga RS. Following you home from school: a critical review and synthesis of research on cyberbullying victimization. *Comput Human Behav.* 2010;26(3): 277–287.

6. Ybarra ML, Mitchell KJ, Wolak J, Finkelhor D. Examining characteristics and associated distress related to Internet harassment: findings from the second Youth Internet Safety Survey. *Pediatrics.* 2006;118(4): et169–et177.

7. David-Ferdon C, Hertz MF. *Electronic Media and Youth Violence: A CDC Issue Brief for Researchers.* Atlanta, GA: Centers for Disease Control and Prevention; 2009.

8. Williams KR, Guerra NG. Prevalence and predictors of Internet bullying. *J Adolesc Health.* 2007;41(6 suppl 1): S14–S21.

9. Wang J, Iannotti RJ, Nansel TR. School bullying among adolescents in the United States: physical, verbal, relational, and cyber. *J Adolesc Health.* 2009;45(4):368–375.

10. Kowalski RM, Limber SP. Electronic bullying among middle school students. *J Adolesc Health.* 2007;41(6 suppl 1):S22–S30.

11. Juvonen J, Gross EF. Extending the school grounds?—Bullying experiences in cyberspace. *J Sch Health.* 2008;78(9): 496–505.

12. Mishna F, Saini M, Solomon S. Ongoing and online: children and youth's perceptions of cyber bullying. *Child Youth Serv Rev.* 2009;31(12):1222–1228.

13. Twyman K, Saylor C, Taylor LA, Comeaux C. Comparing children and adolescents engaged in cyberbullying to matched peers. *Cyberpsychol Behav Soc Netw.* 2010; 13(2):195–199.

14. Ybarra ML, Diener-West M, Leaf PJ. Examining the overlap in Internet harassment and school bullying: implications for school intervention. *J Adolesc Health.* 2007;41(6 suppl 1):S42–S50.

15. Carlyle KE, Steinman KJ. Demographic differences in the prevalence, co-occurrence, and correlates of adolescent bullying at school. *J Sch Health.* 2007;77(9):623–629.

16. Nansel TR, Overpeck M, Pilla RS, Ruan WJ, Simons-Morton B, Scheidt P. Bullying behaviors among US youth: prevalence and association with psychosocial adjustment. *JAMA.* 2001;285(16):2094–2100.

17. Hinduja S, Patchin JW. Cyberbullying: an exploratory analysis of factors related to offending and victimization. *Deviant Behav.* 2008;29(2):129–156.

18. Ybarra ML, Mitchell KJ. Youth engaging in online harassment: associations with caregiver–child relationships, Internet use, and personal characteristics. *J Adolesc.* 2004;27(3):319–336.

19. Smith PK, Mahdavi J, Carvalho M, Fisher S, Russell S, Tippett N, Cyberbullying: its nature

and impact in secondary school pupils. *J Child Psychol Psychiatry.* 2008;49(4): 376–385.

20. Birkett M, Espelage DL, Koenig B. LGB and questioning students in schools: the moderating effects of homophobic bullying and school climate on negative outcomes. *J Youth Adolesc.* 2009;38(7):989–1000.

21. Espelage DL, Aragon SR., Birkett M, Koenig BW. Homophobic teasing, psychological outcomes, and sexual orientation among high school students: what influence do parents and schools have? *School Psych Rev.* 2008;37(2):202–216.

22. Berlan ED, Corliss HIL, Field AE, Goodman E, Austin SB. Sexual orientation and bullying among adolescents in the Growing Up Today study. *J Adolesc Health.* 2010; 46(4);366–371.

23. Schwartz J. Bullying, suicide, punishment *New York Times.* October 2, 2010.

24. Dake JA, Price JK, Telljohann SK. The nature and extent of bullying at school. *J Sch Health.* 2003;73(5):173–180.

25. Spriggs AL, Iannotti RJ, Nansel TR, Haynie DL. Adolescent bullying involvement and perceived family, peer and school relations: commonalities and differences across race/ethnicity. *J Adolesc Health.* 2007;41(3):283–293.

26. Agatston PW, Kowalski R, Limber S. Students' perspectives on cyber bullying. *J Adolesc Health.* 2007;41(6 suppl 1):S59–S60.

27. Beran T, Qing L. The relationship between cyberbullying and school bullying. *J Student Wellbeing.* 2007;1(2):15–33.

28. Brunstein Klomek A, Marrocco F, Kleinman M, Schonfeld IS, Gould MS. Bullying, depression, and suicidality in adolescents. *J Am Acad Child Adolesc Psychiatry.* 2007;46(1):40–49.

29. Klomek AB, Marrocco F, Kleinman M, Schonfeld IS, Gould MS. Peer victimization, depression, and suicidality in adolescents. *Suicide Life Threat Behav.* 2008;38(2):166–180.

30. Kim YS, Leventhal B., Bullying and suicide. A review. *Int J Adolesc Med Health.* 2008;20(2): 133–154.

31. Brunstein Klomek A, Sourander A, Gould M. The association of suicide and bullying in childhood to young adulthood: a review of cross-sectional

and longitudinal research findings. *Can J Psychiatry.* 2010;55(5):282–288.

32. Tynes B, Giang M. P01–298 online victimization, depression and anxiety among adolescents in the US. *Eur Psychiatry.* 2009;24(suppl 1):S686.

33. Ybarra ML, Mitchell KJ. Online aggressor/targets, aggressors, and targets: a comparison of associated youth characteristics. *J Child Psychol Psychiatry.* 2004;45(7): 1308–1316.

34. Mitchell KJ, Ybarra M, Finkelhor D. The relative importance of online victimization in understanding depression, delinquency, and substance use. *Child Maltreat.* 2007;12(4):314–324.

35. Hay C, Meldrum R. Bullying victimization and adolescent self-harm: testing hypotheses from general strain theory. *J Youth Adolesc.* 2010;39(5): 446–459.

36. Hinduja S, Patchin JW. Bullying, cyberbullying, and suicide. *Arch Suicide Res.* 2010;14(3):206–221.

37. Centers for Disease Control and Prevention. *2007 Youth Risk Behavior Survey.* Available at: http://www.cdc.gov/Healthy Youth/yrbs/questionnaire_rationale.htm. Accessed April 12, 2010.

38. Massachusetts Department of Elementary and Secondary Education and Massachusetts Department of Public Health. *Health and Risk Behaviors of Massachusetts Youth, 2007: The Report,* 2008. Available at: http://www.doe.mass.edu/cnp/hprograms/yrbs/2007YRBS.pdf. Accessed April 20, 2010.

39. Harris KM, Halpern CT, Whitsel E, et al. *The National Longitudinal Study of Adolescent Health: Research Design.* Available at: http://www.cpc.unc.edu/projects/addhealth/design. Accessed April 26, 2010.

40. Mustanski BS, Garofalo R, Emerson EM. Mental health disorders, psychological distress, and suicidality in a diverse sample of lesbian, gay, bisexual, and transgender youth. *Am J Public Health.* 2010;100(12):2426–2432.

41. Kaltiala-Heino R, Rimpelä M, Rantanen P, Rimpelä A. Bullying at school—an indicator of adolescents at risk for mental disorders. *J Adolesc.* 2000;23(6):661–674.

42. Juvoven J, Graham S, Schuster MA. Bullying among young adolescents: the strong, the weak, and the troubled. *Pediatrics.* 2003;112(6 pt 1):1231–1237.

Questions for Critical Thinking

1. The authors of this essay illustrate how school bullying and cyberbullying are becoming more prevalent in society. What factors do you think contribute to their growth?

2. How is violence or the threat of violence used to maintain the status quo? For example, have you seen homophobia used to reinforce rigid gender roles?

3. What are some ways in which we can work toward eliminating school bullying and cyberbullying?

Experiencing Difference and Inequality in Everyday Life

Introduction

In Part I we examined the ways in which categories of difference are constructed and then transformed into systems of inequality. We continued this discussion in Part II with an exploration of how systems of inequality are maintained as oppression and privilege through the role of social institutions, language, and violence. In this section we will gain a more thorough understanding of the construction and maintenance of these systems by examining the experiences of difference and inequality in everyday life.

The Importance of Hearing Personal Accounts

The readings in this section help to put a face on what we have discussed thus far. Although theoretical explanations and statistical information can help us to understand the prevalence of inequality in our society, as well as the ways in which systems of oppression and privilege interconnect, the picture that they offer is far from complete. Through the examination of lived experiences we gain a more complete awareness of how categories of difference are constructed and how systems of oppression and privilege are manifested in everyday life.

Stephanie Wildman and Adrienne Davis's discussion on the existence of systems of privilege in "Making Systems of Privilege Visible" (Reading 35)—particularly around whiteness—shows us the effect of **privilege** on one's **life chances.** By reading Jon Ronson's encounters with negative stereotypes in "You May Know Me from Such Roles as Terrorist #4" (Reading 36), we gain a greater understanding of how attitudes about oppressed groups become internalized. Furthermore, the stories of living life as a member of a marginalized group and its accompanying stereotypes allow us to more fully comprehend how such **internalized oppression** results in the desire to **pass**—to deny one's membership in an oppressed group and to attempt to portray oneself as a member of a less stigmatized group. Each of the readings in this section demonstrates the daily grind of oppression and the perks of privilege and deepens our understanding of these issues.

Additional readings in this section demonstrate the impact of the structural factors that construct and maintain inequality, discussed in Parts I and II, on the everyday experiences of individuals. For example, Ellis Cose articulates the effect of discrimination and stereotypes on African Americans in his article "A Dozen Demons" (Reading 37). Further, Tram Nguyen, in "Separated by Deportation" (Reading 39), tells of the experiences of Abdullah Osman and other Somali refugees, representing the impact of equating Muslims with terrorists in the post-9/11 United States, disrupting the lives and livelihoods of people seeking refuge from their war-torn home countries. These and other readings in this section bring into graphic detail the everyday consequences of systems of inequality.

It is important to point out that, although each of us experiences oppression and privilege each day, to examine the various factors of our own experiences while simultaneously living them is like a fish trying to examine the water in which it swims. To fully understand experiences of oppression and privilege we must stand at a distance from these experiences. The accounts in this section provide us with the opportunity to stand outside and to look in on the experiences of others. By reading the stories in this section we will gain a greater understanding of the impact of oppression and privilege, not only on the lives of others but also on our own lives.

Personal Accounts and "Deconstructing" Stereotypes

At the foundation of our prejudice regarding those whom we see as different from ourselves are **stereotypes**—rigid, oversimplified, and often exaggerated beliefs that are applied both to a category of people and to each individual in the category. We learn these stereotypes through the process of socialization. They are fostered by the policies and practices of social institutions, as well as by our tendency to interact with people like ourselves, and we often have difficulty deconstructing or exposing the falsehoods in these stereotypes. Generally, it is not until we have frequent contact with those about whom we possess stereotypes that we are able to debunk them—and sometimes not even then. Through the sharing of personal experiences, the readings in this section provide a great deal of information that will serve to counter our stereotypes. As you read, be aware of the stereotypes that you possess and note your reactions when you encounter new information that challenges them.

The Lived Experience of the Matrix of Domination

To this point we have engaged in a primarily theoretical discussion of the matrix of domination. In examining the ways in which categories of difference are constructed and transformed into systems of inequality, we have noted some of the commonalities in the ways in which these categories are constructed. Further, our examination of the role of social institutions, language, and violence in maintaining systems of oppression and privilege has helped us to understand the similar foundations on which such systems rest. The readings in this section reveal the interrelationships of systems of oppression and privilege by providing us with an opportunity to witness the matrix of domination as lived experience. As you read the selections in this section, look closely to see how different systems of oppression and privilege interrelate in the stories the authors share. In addition, notice how some experience both oppression and privilege and how many experience more than one form of oppression simultaneously.

Keep This in Mind

Although reading personal accounts can serve to further our understanding of systems of oppression and privilege, it is important not to overgeneralize. The anecdotal evidence of a personal story does not in and of itself prove anything. Indeed, it is often anecdotal evidence that gets in the way of our fully seeing and accepting that systems of oppression and privilege exist. In addition, when we read the personal experiences of a member of a marginalized group, there is often the danger of expecting the writer to speak for the experiences of all members of that group. To avoid these pitfalls, it is important to keep in mind the readings of the previous two sections. By understanding the experiences of the different groups examined in previous sections, we will better understand the experiences of the individuals discussed here. In addition, the readings here confirm the theoretical and statistical discussions elsewhere in this text.

A Final Note

As stated in Part I, a fundamental component to understanding the impact of systems of inequality is to employ our **empathy** skills—the ability to understand the experiences of others, although you have not shared those experiences. The readings in this section are provided to aid you in honing your empathy skills. As you read these accounts, be mindful of how they increase your understanding of experiences with which you are not familiar. As you become more informed about the experiences of others, you will further your understanding of the construction, maintenance, and impact of systems of oppression and privilege.

Making Systems of Privilege Visible

STEPHANIE M. WILDMAN WITH ADRIENNE D. DAVIS

The following essay, written by law professors Stephanie Wildman and Adrienne Davis, discusses the existence of systems of privilege, often rendered invisible in our language. Through their discussion, they reveal these privileges, illustrating their effect on one's life chances.

The notion of privilege, although part of the consciousness of popular culture, has not been recognized in legal language and doctrine. This failure to acknowledge privilege, to make it visible in legal doctrine, creates a serious gap in legal reasoning, rendering us unable to address issues of systemic unfairness.

The invisibility of privilege strengthens the power it creates and maintains. The invisible cannot be combated, and as a result privilege is allowed to perpetuate, regenerate, and re-create itself. Privilege is systemic, not an occasional occurrence. Privilege is invisible only until looked for, but silence in the face of privilege sustains its invisibility.

Silence is the lack of sound and voice. Silence may result from a desire for quiet; it may signify intense mental concentration; it may also arise from oppression or fear. Whatever the reason, when there is silence, no criticism is expressed. What we do not say, what we do not talk about, allows the status quo to continue. To describe these unspoken systems means we need to use language. But even when we try to talk about privilege, the language

we use inhibits our ability to perceive the systems of privilege that constitute the status quo.

How Language Veils the Existence of Systems of Privilege

Language contributes to the invisibility and regeneration of privilege. To begin the conversation about subordination, we sort ideas into categories such as race and gender. These words are part of a system of categorization that we use without thinking and that seems linguistically neutral. Race and gender are, after all, just words.

Yet when we learn that someone has had a child, our first question is usually "Is it a girl or a boy?" Why do we ask that, instead of something like "Are the mother and child healthy?" We ask, "Is it a girl or a boy?" according to philosopher Marilyn Frye, because we do not know how to relate to this new being without knowing its gender.[1] Imagine how long you could have a discussion with or about someone without knowing her or his gender. We place people into these categories because our world is gendered.

Similarly, our world is also raced, and it is hard for us to avoid taking mental notes as to race. We use our language to categorize by race, particularly, if we are white, when that race is other than white. Marge Shultz has written of calling on a Latino student in her class.[2] She called him Mr. Martínez, but his name was Rodríguez. The class tensed up at her error; earlier that same day another professor had called him Mr. Hernández, the name of the defendant in the criminal law case under discussion. Professor Shultz talked with her class, at its next session, about her error and how our thought processes lead us to categorize in order to think. She acknowledged how this process leads to stereotyping that causes pain to individuals. We all live in this raced and gendered world, inside these powerful categories, that make it hard to see each other as whole people.

But the problem does not stop with the general terms "race" and "gender." Each of these categories contains the images, like an entrance to a tunnel with many passages and arrows pointing down each possible path, of subcategories. Race is often defined as Black and white; sometimes it is defined as white and "of color." There are other races, and sometimes the categories are each listed, for example, as African American, Hispanic American, Asian American, Native American, and White American, if whiteness is mentioned at all. All these words, describing racial subcategories, seem neutral on their face, like equivalent titles. But however the subcategories are listed, however neutrally the words are expressed, these words mask a system of power, and that system privileges whiteness.

Gender, too, is a seemingly neutral category that leads us to imagine subcategories of male and female. A recent scientific article suggested that five genders might be a more accurate characterization of human anatomy, but there is a heavy systemic stake in our image of two genders.[3] The apparently neutral categories male and female mask the privileging of males that is part of the gender power system. Try to think of equivalent gendered titles, like king and queen, prince and princess, and you will quickly see that male and female are not equal titles in our cultural imagination.

Poet and social critic Adrienne Rich has written convincingly about the compulsory heterosexuality that is part of this gender power system.[4] Almost everywhere we look, heterosexuality is portrayed as the norm. In Olympic ice-skating and dancing, for example, a couple is defined as a man partnered with a woman.[5] Heterosexuality is privileged over any other relationship. The words we use, such as "marriage," "husband," and "wife," are not neutral, but convey this privileging of heterosexuality. What is amazing, says Rich, is that there are any lesbians or gay men at all.[6]

Our culture suppresses conversation about class privilege as well as race and gender privileges. Although we must have money or access to money to obtain human necessities such as food, clothing, and shelter, those fundamental needs are recognized only as an individual responsibility. The notion of privilege based on economic wealth is viewed as a radical, dangerous idea, or an idiosyncratic throwback to the past, conjuring up countries with monarchies, nobility, serfs, and peasants. Yet even the archaic vocabulary makes clear that no one wants to be categorized as a have-not. The economic power system is not invisible—everyone knows that money brings privilege. But the myth persists that all have access to that power through individual resourcefulness. This myth of potential economic equality supports the invisibility of the other power systems that prevent fulfillment of that ideal.

Other words we use to describe subordination also mask the operation of privilege. Increasingly, people use terms like "racism" and "sexism" to describe disparate treatment and the perpetuation of power. Yet this vocabulary of "isms" as a descriptive shorthand for undesirable, disadvantaging treatment creates several serious problems.

First, calling someone a racist individualizes the behavior and veils the fact that racism can occur only where it is culturally, socially, and legally supported. It lays the blame on the individual rather than the systemic forces that have shaped that individual and his or her society. White people know they do not want to be labeled racist; they become concerned with how to avoid that label, rather than worrying about systemic racism and how to change it.

Second, the isms language focuses on the larger category, such as race, gender, sexual preference. Isms language suggests that within these larger categories two seemingly neutral halves exist, equal parts in a mirror. Thus Black and white, male and female, heterosexual and gay/lesbian appear, through the linguistic juxtaposition, as equivalent subparts. In fact, although the category does not take note of it, Blacks and whites, men and women, heterosexuals and gays/lesbians are not equivalently situated in society. Thus the way we think and talk about the categories and subcategories that underlie the isms allows us to consider them parallel parts, and obscures the pattern of domination and subordination within each classification.

Similarly, the phrase "isms" itself gives the illusion that all patterns of domination and subordination are the same and interchangeable. The language suggests that someone subordinated under one form of oppression would be similarly situated to another person subordinated under another form. Thus, a person subordinated under one form may feel no need to view himself/herself as a possible oppressor, or beneficiary of oppression, within a different form. For example, white women, having an ism that defines their condition—sexism—may not look at the way they are privileged by racism. They have defined themselves as one of the oppressed.

Finally, the focus on individual behavior, the seemingly neutral subparts of categories, and the apparent interchangeability underlying the vocabulary of isms all obscure the existence of systems of privilege and power. It is difficult to see and talk about how oppression operates when the vocabulary itself makes these systems of privilege invisible. "White supremacy" is associated with a lunatic fringe, not with the everyday life of well-meaning white citizens. "Racism" is defined by whites in terms of specific, discriminatory racist actions by others. The vocabulary allows us to talk about discrimination and oppression, but it hides the mechanism that makes that oppression possible and efficient. It also hides the existence of specific, identifiable beneficiaries of oppression, who are not always the actual perpetrators of discrimination. The use of isms language, or any focus on discrimination, masks the privileging that is created by these systems of power.

Thus the very vocabulary we use to talk about discrimination obfuscates these power systems and the privilege that is their natural companion. To remedy discrimination effectively we must make the power systems and the privileges they create visible and part of the discourse. To move toward a unified theory of the dynamics of subordination, we have to find a way to talk about privilege. When we discuss race, sex, and sexual orientation, each needs to be described as a power system that creates privileges in some people as well as disadvantages in others. Most of the literature has focused on disadvantage or discrimination, ignoring the element of privilege. To really talk about these issues, privilege must be made visible.

What Is Privilege?

What then is privilege? We all recognize its most blatant forms. "Men only admitted to this club." "We will not allow African Americans into that school." Blatant exercises of privilege certainly exist, but they are not what most people think of as our way of life. They are only the tip of the iceberg, however.

When we try to look at privilege we see several elements. First, the characteristics of the privileged group define the societal norm, often benefiting those in the privileged group. Second, privileged group members can rely on their privilege and avoid objecting to oppression. Both the conflation of privilege with the societal norm and the implicit option to ignore oppression mean that privilege is rarely seen by the holder of the privilege.

A. The Normalization of Privilege

The characteristics and attributes of those who are privileged group members are described as societal norms—as the way things are and as what is normal in society.[7] This normalization of privilege means that members of society are judged, and succeed or fail, measured against the characteristics that are held by those privileged. The privileged characteristic is the norm; those who stand outside are the aberrant or "alternative."

For example, a thirteen-year-old-girl who aspires to be a major-league ballplayer can have only a low expectation of achieving that goal, no matter how superior a batter and fielder she is. Maleness is the foremost "qualification" of major-league baseball players. Similarly, those who legally are permitted to marry are heterosexual. A gay or lesbian couple, prepared to make a life commitment, cannot cross the threshold of qualification to be married.

I had an example of being outside the norm recently when I was called to jury service. Jurors are expected to serve until 5 P.M. During that year, my family's life was set up so that I picked up my children after school at 2:40 and made sure that they got to various activities. If courtroom life were designed to privilege my needs, then there would have been an afternoon recess to honor children. But in this culture children's lives and the lives of their caretakers are the alternative or other, and we must conform to the norm.

Even as these child care needs were outside the norm, I was privileged economically to be able to meet my children's needs. What many would have described as mothering, not privilege—my ability to pick them up and be present in their after-school lives—was a benefit of my association with privilege.

Members of the privileged group gain many benefits by their affiliation with the dominant side of the power system. This affiliation with power is not identified as such; often it may be transformed into and presented as individual merit. Legacy admissions at elite colleges and professional schools are perceived to be merit-based, when this process of identification with power and transmutation into qualifications occurs. Achievements by members of the privileged group are viewed as the result of individual effort, rather than privilege. . . .

B. Choosing Whether to Struggle against Oppression

Members of privileged groups can opt out of struggles against oppression if they choose. Often this privilege may be exercised by silence. At the same time that I was the outsider in jury service, I was also a privileged insider. During *voir dire,* each prospective juror was asked to introduce herself or himself. The plaintiff's and defendant's attorneys then asked additional questions. I watched the

defense attorney, during voir dire, ask each Asian-looking male prospective juror if he spoke English. No one else was asked. The judge did nothing. The Asian American man sitting next to me smiled and flinched as he was asked the questions. I wondered how many times in his life he had been made to answer such a question. I considered beginning my own questioning by saying, "I'm Stephanie Wildman, I'm a professor of law, and yes, I speak English." I wanted to focus attention on the subordinating conduct of the attorney, but I did not. I exercised my white privilege by my silence. I exercised my privilege to opt out of engagement, even though this choice may not always be consciously made by someone with privilege.

Depending on the number of privileges someone has, she or he may experience the power of choosing the types of struggles in which to engage. Even this choice may be masked as an identification with oppression, thereby making the privilege that enables the choice invisible.

. . . Privilege is not visible to its holder; it is merely there, a part of the world, a way of life, simply the way things are. Others have a *lack,* an absence, a deficiency.

Systems of Privilege

Although different privileges bestow certain common characteristics (membership in the norm, the ability to choose whether to object to the power system, and the invisibility of its benefit), the form of a privilege may vary according to the power relationship that produces it. White privilege derives from the race power system of white supremacy. Male privilege[8] and heterosexual privilege result from the gender hierarchy.[9] Class privilege derives from an economic, wealth-based hierarchy.

Visualizing Privilege

For me the struggle to visualize privilege has most often taken the form of the struggle to see my white privilege. Even as I write about this struggle, I fear that my own racism will make things worse, causing me to do more harm than good. Some readers may be shocked to see a white person contritely acknowledge that she is racist. I do not say this with pride. I simply believe that no matter how hard I work at not being racist, I still am. Because part of racism is systemic, I benefit from the privilege that I am struggling to see.

Whites do not look at the world through a filter of racial awareness, even though whites are, of course, members of a race. The power to ignore race, when white is the race, is a privilege, a societal advantage. The term "racism/white supremacy" emphasizes the link between discriminatory racism and the privilege held by whites to ignore their own race.

As bell hooks explains, liberal whites do not see themselves as prejudiced or interested in domination through coercion, yet "they cannot recognize the ways their actions support and affirm the very structure of racist domination and oppression that they profess to wish to see eradicated."[10] The perpetuation of white supremacy is racist.

All whites are racist in this use of the term, because we benefit from systemic white privilege. Generally whites think of racism as voluntary, intentional conduct, done by horrible others. Whites spend a lot of time trying to convince ourselves and each other that we are not racist. A big step would be for whites to admit that we are racist and then to consider what to do about it.[11]

Notes

1. See Marilyn Frye, The Politics of Reality: Essays in Feminist Theory 19–34 (1983) (discussing sex marking, sex announcing, and the necessity to determine gender).
2. Angela Harris and Marge Shultz, "A(nother) Critique of Pure Reason": Toward Civic Virtue in Legal Education, 45 Stan. L. Rev. 1773, 1796 (1993).
3. Anne Fausto-Sterling, The Five Sexes: Why Male and Female Are Not Enough, Sciences, Mar./Apr. 1993. (Thanks to Gregg Bryan for calling my attention to this article.) See also Frye, supra note 1, at 25.

4. Adrienne Rich, Compulsory Heterosexuality and Lesbian Existence, in Blood, Bread, and Poetry, Selected Prose 1979–1985 (1986).
5. See Stephanie M. Wildman and Becky Wildman-Tobriner, Sex Roles Iced Popular Team? S.F. Chron., Feb. 25, 1994, at A23.
6. Rich, supra note 4, at 57 ("Heterosexuality has been both forcibly and subliminally imposed on women").
7. Richard Delgado and Jean Stefancic, Pornography and Harm to Women: "No Empirical Evidence?" 53 Ohio St. L. J. 1037 (1992) (describing this "way things are." Because the norm or reality is perceived as including these benefits, the privileges are not visible.)
8. Catharine A. MacKinnon, Toward a Feminist Theory of the State 224 (1989).
9. Sylvia Law, Homosexuality and the Social Meaning of Gender, 1988 Wis. L. Rev. 187, 197 (1988); Marc Fajer, Can Two Real Men Eat Quiche Together? Storytelling, Gender-Role Stereotypes, and Legal Protection for Lesbians and Gay Men, 46 U. Miami L. Rev. 511, 617 (1992). Both articles describe heterosexism as a form of gender oppression.
10. bell hooks, Overcoming White Supremacy: A Comment, in Talking Back: Thinking Feminist, Thinking Black 113 (1989).
11. See also Jerome McCristal Culp Jr., Water Buffalo and Diversity: Naming Names and Reclaiming the Racial Discourse, 26 Conn. L. Rev. 209 (1993) (urging people to name racism as racism).

Questions for Critical Thinking

1. Wildman and Davis discuss the ways in which language hides systems of privilege in the United States. What are some of the ways in which you are privileged by your class, race, gender, education, etc.? What makes it difficult to recognize this privilege?
2. How is the invisibility of white privilege a privilege in and of itself?
3. How might recognizing the various ways that we are privileged help to reduce or eliminate inequality?

You May Know Me from Such Roles as Terrorist #4

JON RONSON

The following essay offers a reflection on the negative stereotypes experienced by Muslim American actors in the United States. Through the author's discussion, we gain an understanding of how the media plays a significant role in the perpetuation of false images of Muslim Americans.

The right-wing action hero gave Maz Jobrani hope. This was 2001. Maz had been trying to make it as an actor in Hollywood for three years, but things were going badly for him. He was earning peanuts as an assistant at an advertising agency. But then his agent telephoned: Did Maz want to play a terrorist in a Chuck Norris movie? So Maz read the screenplay for The President's Man: A Line in the Sand, and he found within it a moment of promising subtlety.

"Chuck Norris plays a professor of Middle Eastern studies," Maz tells me. We're sitting in a coffee shop in Westwood, Los Angeles. Maz is a goateed man in his early forties who was born in Tehran but moved with his family to the San Francisco Bay Area when he was 6. "There's a scene where he's talking to his students about Afghanistan. One of the students raises his hand and says something like, 'Uh, professor, they're all fanatics, so why don't we just kill them all?' And the Chuck Norris character goes, 'Now, now. They're not all bad.' And I thought, 'Wow! A nuance!'"

The nuance gave Maz hope. Did this mean they'd allow him to make his character nuanced? Maz was aware that fixating on this one line might have been self-deluding, like a drowning man clutching driftwood in a hurricane. But he agreed to take the part.

Then, at the wardrobe fitting, they handed him his turban.

"I said, 'Whoa, whoa! No! Afghans in America don't wear turbans. Plus, this guy's a terrorist. He's not going to draw attention to himself. You tell the producers I want to bring authenticity to this character.' The wardrobe supervisor replied, 'All right, all right, I'll talk to them.'"

The message came back from Chuck Norris's people that the turban was mandatory.

And then came Maz's death. It was the one thing he'd been excited about, because the script alluded to a short fight immediately preceding it. Hand-to-hand combat with Chuck Norris!

"But on the day of the scene," Maz says, "Chuck Norris told his son, who was the director, 'Oh, I'll just take a gun and I'll shoot him.' Oh, great! I don't even get a fight!"

"So how exactly did you get shot?" I ask Maz.

"Okay, so I'm about to set off a bomb at a refinery," he replies. "Chuck Norris runs in. I run away, because I'm scared. He gets behind the computer and starts dismantling the bomb, because he's a genius. I come running back in carrying an Uzi. And I try to shoot him. But he takes out his gun and shoots me." Maz shrugs. "I start to yell, 'Allah—' Bang! I'm down. I don't even get 'Allahu Akbar!' out. It was horrible, man."

Maz shakes his head at the memory. It was humiliating. Actually, it was worse than humiliating—it was a harbinger. Maz understood, as he lay dead in that refinery, that Hollywood didn't want him to be an actor. Hollywood wanted him to be a caricature. "I started acting in junior high," he says. "I was in Guys and Dolls. I was Stanley Kowalski. In my head, before coming to Hollywood, I thought, 'I can play anything.'" But instead he'd become the latest iteration in Hollywood's long history of racist casting, reducing his religion and culture to a bunch of villainous, cartoonish psychopaths. He knew he had to get out.

I glance at my phone. It's 1 p.m. We're running late to meet three of Maz's friends at a nearby Lebanese restaurant. We jump into Maz's car.

Maz refuses to take terrorist parts nowadays. He's primarily a stand-up comedian instead, a very funny and successful one. In fact, he's just published a memoir, I'm Not a Terrorist, But I've Played One on TV. But Maz's friends at the restaurant haven't been so lucky. They still make their livings as actors, which means they still play terrorists all the time.

Maz and I hurry into the restaurant, apologizing for being late. We order a mezze plate for five. These men have been killed while committing acts of terrorism on Homeland and 24, in The Kingdom and Three Kings and True Lies, and in too many other films and shows to list. We've barely sat down when Waleed Zuaiter, a Palestinian-American actor in his early forties, recounts for me his death scene on Law & Order: Criminal Intent. This was about a year after September 11. "I play a guy from a sleeper cell," Waleed says. "I'm checking my e-mails. I hear the cops come in, and the first thing I go for is my box cutter. There's literally a box cutter in the scene."

"Was this in an office?" I ask Waleed.

"It was in my home!" he replies. "I just happened to have a box cutter lying around." Waleed shakes his head, bemused. "The cops burst in, and next thing you know I've got the box cutter to some guy's neck. And then one of the cops shoots me."

"I die in Iron Man," says Sayed Badreya, an Egyptian man with a salt-and-pepper beard. "I die in Executive Decision. I get shot at by—what's his name?—Kurt Russell. I get shot by everyone. George Clooney kills me in Three Kings. Arnold blows me up in True Lies . . ."

As Sayed and Waleed and the others describe their various demises, it strikes me that the key to making a living in Hollywood if you're Muslim is to be good at dying. If you're a Middle Eastern actor and you can die with charisma, there is no shortage of work for you.

Here's another irony in the lives of these men: While they profoundly wish they didn't have to play terrorists, much of our lunch is taken up with them swapping tips on clever ways to stand out at terrorist auditions.

"If I'm going in for the role of a nice father, I'll talk to everybody," Sayed tells the table. "But if you're going for a terrorist role, don't fucking smile at all those white people sitting there. Treat them like shit. The minute you say hello, you break character."

"But it's smart at the end of the audition to break it," adds Hrach Titizian, who at 36 is the youngest actor here. "'Oh, thanks, guys.' So they know it's okay to have you on set for a couple of weeks."

Then Waleed says something you don't often hear actors say, because most actors regard their competition with dread: "Whenever it's that kind of role and we see each other at the auditions, it's so comforting. We're not in this alone. We're in this together."

We're in this together. By this Waleed is referring to a uniquely demeaning set of circumstances. I'm sure practically all actors, Muslim or otherwise, feel degraded. Most have no power over their careers—what roles they can play, how their performances are edited. But Muslim actors are powerless in unusually hideous ways. The last time one became a big star in America was back in 1962—Omar Sharif in Lawrence of Arabia. These days they get offered terrorist roles and little else. And we—the paying public—barely even notice, much less worry about it. Where's the outrage? There is none, except from the actors themselves.

These roles are ethically nightmarish for them, and the stress can wreak havoc on their lives. Waleed's father, for instance, threatened never to talk to him again if he ever played a terrorist. I thought that was bad enough. But then I meet another actor who had it much worse.

Ahmed Ahmed was raised a strict Muslim in Riverside, California, by his Egyptian-immigrant parents—a mother who learned English from watching soap operas, and a gas-station-attendant father who ended up buying an automotive shop. The day Ahmed told them he was quitting college to try his luck in Hollywood, his father asked if he was gay and didn't speak to him for seven years.

When I meet Ahmed at the French Roast Café in downtown New York City, he echoes Waleed's thoughts about the camaraderie among these actors. "It's always the same guys at every audition. Waleed, Sayed Badreya . . . You're all sitting in a row in the waiting room. Oftentimes the casting o∞ce is right next to you. The door's shut, but you can hear what's going on."

"What do you hear?" I ask him.

"Oh, you know," he says. "'ALLAHU AKBAR!' And then . . ." Ahmed switches to the voice of a bubbly casting director. "'Thank you! That was great!' And the guy walks out, sweating. And you walk in and they're, 'Hey! Thanks for coming in! Whenever you're ready!' And you're thinking, 'How do I do it differently from the guy before me? Do I go louder?'"

When he auditioned for Executive Decision, he went louder. Executive Decision is, I realize as I talk to people from this world, considered the ground zero (as it were) of ludicrous portrayals of Islamic terrorists. This was 1996, and Ahmed was in his mid-twenties. "My agent had called me. 'There's this film. It's a $55 million action suspense thriller starring Kurt Russell, Halle Berry, and Steven Seagal. They want to bring you in to read for one of the parts.' I said, 'What's the part?' She said, 'Terrorist Number Four.' I said, 'I don't want to do it.' She said, 'It's three weeks of work. It pays $30,000.'"

And so Ahmed read for the part. "My lines were 'Sit down and obey or I will kill you in the name of Allah.' And the director goes, 'Brilliant! Do it again. But this time, can you give me more of that Middle Eastern, you know . . .' I go, 'Anger?' He goes, 'Yes! Yes! Angry!'"

Feeling a flash of actual anger, Ahmed decided to ridicule the process by going stupidly over-the-top.

"And the next day," he says, "my agent calls me up: 'You booked it.'"

By the time Executive Decision came out later that year, Ahmed says, his life had "become dark. Boozing on the Sunset Strip. After-hours parties. I'd wake up at 2 p.m. and do it all over again. It's the same people in the clubs every night. Everyone's trying to fill a void."

"Were you doing all that boozing because you felt guilty for playing terrorists?" I ask him.

"There was an element of that," he replies. "There was an element of not working between those parts. And then I had an epiphany. I called my agent: 'Hey! Don't send me out on these terrorist parts anymore. I'll be open for anything else, but not the terrorist stuff.'" Ahmed pauses. "After that, she never called."

"How often did she call before then?" I ask him.

"Oh, three or four times a week."

And so Ahmed made a decision: "Get the fuck out of Hollywood." He went to Mecca. And what he saw there were "four and a half million people dressed in white—rich, poor, walking side by side, asking for blessings from God."

For ten solid years after his trip to Mecca, Ahmed quit acting and became a stand-up comedian. He still performs regularly, but he says he'll take a terrorist role from time to time if a good one comes along. After all, he notes, nobody accuses Robert De Niro of betraying other Italian-Americans when he plays a mobster.

The evening after our lunch in Westwood, I visit Sayed Badreya, the older Egyptian actor, at his Santa Monica apartment. When I arrive, he's online, looking at photographs of Arabian horses.

"I'm involved in breeding them," he says, "because I don't know if I can keep playing these same parts." He says his daughter was once asked at school what her father did for a living and she replied, "He hijacks airplanes."

Sayed takes his work seriously and has always gone to great lengths to research his roles. In 1991, he started attending a mosque in Culver City, one that was known to attract some militant worshippers, so he could study Islamic radicalism up close. A few years later, some of the mosque's worshippers went to a movie and recognized Sayed. Back at the mosque after Friday prayers, they surrounded him. "They were yelling, right in my face: 'You're helping the Zionist Jews of Hollywood in their agenda to make Islam look bad. For money, you're giving up your heritage.'"

"How were you responding?" I ask.

"I felt guilty," he says. "I knew they were sort of right. But I yelled back at them, 'We have to take their money to make our own movie and tell our own story!' We were yelling so hard we were showering each other with spit."

"What was the movie of yours they saw?" I ask him.

"Executive fucking Decision," he says.

Sayed says he does all he can to intersperse his terrorist roles with more helpful portrayals of Muslims. He wrote and starred in a well-regarded film, AmericanEast, charting the struggles of Muslims in America post-9/11. But he has to play terrorists to pay the bills, so he at least tries to be a realistic one. He does side work as a technical consultant, advising directors on the accuracy of their films. He worked in this capacity on Executive Decision. "We had a really beautiful moment in an Arabic wedding scene," Sayed says. "And the producer, Joel Silver, saw it and said, 'No, no. This is nice. I want a fucking bad Arab. We don't want a good Arab.'"

Almost all of the wedding scene was cut from the film, Sayed says. But here's a scene that wasn't cut: One of the terrorists takes a quick break from killing people to read the Koran. "If I'm playing a guy chosen to hijack a plane, that means I'm one of the top soldiers. I'm going on a mission. I'm not going to Mecca. He might recite something in his head if he's religious, but he's not going to open the Bible. But producers get really sensitive if you say, 'No, that's not accurate.'"

In an e-mailed statement, Joel Silver denied the "bad Arab" incident, adding, "Any editorial decisions, made twenty years ago, were strictly creative, and not to perpetuate any stereotypes." I didn't hear back from any of the other producers or directors I approached. Not Peter Berg (The Kingdom, another film that has a bad reputation with Muslim actors for its portrayal of the Islamic world), nor Stephen McEveety (Mel Gibson's collaborator on The Passion of the Christ and the producer of The Stoning of Soraya M., in which an Iranian husband has his wife stoned to death), nor Joel Surnow, the co-creator of 24. Maz told me that his most offensive acting offer ever was for a Joel Surnow production—Fox's short-lived comedy The 1/2 Hour News Hour. Maz says he was asked to audition for a sketch about a Middle Eastern architect pitching to rebuild the twin towers. The joke was that his design included a bull's-eye right on the building. Howard Gordon, the man behind Homeland and 24, is the only producer I persuade to talk to me. He calls me from his car.

"I came to this issue when I was accused of having Islamophobia in 24," he says. "We had a family, essentially, of terrorists on the show. The Muslim Public Affairs Council provided an education for me on the power of images."

"What did they say?"

"They asked me to imagine what it might be like to be a Muslim, to have people fear my faith," he replies. "I felt very sympathetic. I didn't want to be a midwife to xenophobia."

Since then, he says, he has done his best. And people have noticed. When I was having lunch with Maz and the other actors at the Lebanese restaurant in Westwood, Howard was one of the only mainstream producers they praised. (Three Kings' David O. Russell was another.)

"Anyone with a conscience has to take this seriously," Howard tells me. "I'd often hidden behind the defense that 24 was a counterterrorism show. We rationalized to ourselves that our primary task was to tell a compelling story." But the truth, he knew, was darker than that: "We all have our personal biases and fears—I suspect we're wired to feel threatened by the 'other.' And I include myself in that category."

In the lobby of a chichi old hotel in Midtown Manhattan, Anthony Azizi warns me that this interview might get heated. And indeed it does. If you want to know the impact that a lifetime of doing these movies can have on a man, spend some time with Anthony Azizi.

Anthony is a veteran of various CSIs and NCISs and 24. His death scene in 24, he says, made it onto a Yahoo list of best deaths ever. (His throat gets slit with a credit card.) He's a big, handsome, intense man who is not, by the way, a Muslim. He's a member of the Iranian spiritualist faith the Bahá'í.

"Hollywood has the power to snap its fingers and make whoever it wants a star," he begins. "It specifically and purposefully doesn't want to see an Arab or a Middle Eastern star. There's too much prejudice and racism—and the people running it, I don't need to go into the specifics of their backgrounds. . . ."

I think I know what he's getting at. But all sorts of producers—not just Jews—are behind insensitive movie portrayals of Muslims. There's Chuck Norris. There's John Musker, director of 1992's Aladdin, in which all the "good Arabs" have American accents and all the "bad Arabs" have pseudo-Middle Eastern accents. Stephen McEveety (The Stoning of Soraya M.) is Catholic.

Anthony carries on, turning his anger toward Jon Stewart's Rosewater, in which the Mexican actor Gael García Bernal plays the Iranian-Canadian reporter Maziar Bahari. "Man, if I saw Jon Stewart, you'd have to hold me back. How dare you hire a Mexican-American to play an Iranian-American, with all these amazing Iranian-American artists. I can't stand it. I'm sick of it. I speak Spanish fluently. . . ."

He effortlessly slides into perfect Spanish for a few seconds, then returns to being Anthony. "Why am I not being hired for Mexican or Latino roles?" he says. "You play my roles, but I can't play yours, and I speak Spanish just as well? Go fuck yourself." Anthony picks up my recorder. "Go fuck yourself, Jon Stewart!" he yells. "Have me on your show if you have the balls! You don't have the balls!"

He's really shouting now. The hotel receptionists keep glancing nervously over at us, wondering whether to intervene. "Hollywood people are pussies!" he rants. "They're racist! They don't want to say, 'I just built a Middle Eastern star!' Here's how I see it—and this is probably the most controversial thing I'll ever say: The only Middle Eastern star was Omar Sharif. The minute he had a relationship with a Jewish-American woman named Barbra Streisand was the death knell for any other Arab-American actor's career. Hear it again! The minute he had a sexual relationship with a Jewish . . ."

"I don't underst—" I start to say.

"How dare you make that an incident where no Arab-American actor can ever get a career again!"

Finally I get my question out, or at least some of it: "But what's the connection between Omar Sharif purportedly having an affair with Barbra Streisand and—"

"I think there's a certain type of producer that doesn't want to see that happen," he says. "They don't want their gem—Barbra Streisand was the gem of the Jewish community—sleeping with the Arab heathen! It caused huge riots in Egypt, too. I'd say the same thing to the Egyptian community. . . ."

Sure, Anthony's Barbra Streisand outburst is crazy. If there is a racist conspiracy in Hollywood to rob Middle Eastern actors of roles, it's not a great idea to rail against it with a racist-conspiracy theory of one's own. But think about what Anthony has been subjected to in his career. He and the other men in this story are going through something that future generations will regard as outrageous. They're the bloodthirsty Red Indians surrounding the settlers' wagons in Stagecoach. They're the black savages in The Birth of a Nation (who were played by white actors in blackface). They are the people Hollywood will be apologizing to tomorrow.

"Don't question my talent," Anthony says. "I should be a star by now. But I'm not. So you explain why."

Perhaps the closest this community has to a star is Navid Negahban. He played, most famously, Abu Nazir in Homeland and also the Iraqi in American Sniper who helps the U.S. military locate "the butcher." He was Ali, the stoner in The Stoning of Soraya M.

"Everyone I've met seems really talented," I tell Anthony. "So why do you think Navid, of all of you. . . .?"

"He's hot right now, playing bad guys," Anthony replies. "He loves to play those roles. I love Navid. He's my brother. But there's no longevity in those roles. You always get whacked. Everybody who's still alive in Homeland is white! Where is Abu Nazir? He got whacked, 'cause he's brown."

Getting to meet Navid isn't easy. One minute he's filming in upstate New York, the next he's doing motion capture as a video-game character in Los Angeles before flying off to shoot a movie in Morocco. But I manage to catch him for an hour at a coffee shop near Columbus Circle in New York City. He's already there, chatting with another on-screen terrorist, Herzl Tobey (The Shield, 24, Homeland). They've been working on a movie together upstate, so Navid has brought him along to meet me. Navid is very dashing, with an old-fashioned matinee-idol air to him.

"I'm sure you've had a few of the others say, 'I won't do terrorists anymore,'" he says as I sit down.

"Yes," I say.

"I've told them that's the biggest mistake," says Navid. "If we don't play those roles, the character becomes a caricature. [The producers] might get some actor from a different background who looks Middle Eastern." Herzl nods, adding, "The writer is sitting here in America, writing about a world he's completely unfamiliar with. So of course he won't be able to write it with the full depth and sensuality that comes with that world. It's up to us to bring that depth."

I tell Navid that I've noticed that the more prominent the Middle Eastern actor, the more awesome the death. Back when Maz was just starting out, he barely got "Allah" out before Chuck Norris shot him. But Navid is at the top of the pecking order, the closest thing we have to Omar Sharif. I ask him to remind me how Abu Nazir died on Homeland.

"Oh, he was graceful," Navid replies. "It was so . . ." He smacks his lips. "He's sitting very gracefully on the floor. On his knees. He's ready. The soldiers run in. Everybody's yelling. But he's calm. He's just looking at all of them very, very calmly. And then he reaches into his pocket and they shoot him. And there's a Koran in his pocket." Navid smiles wistfully. "That was beautiful," he says. "I die well."

Questions for Critical Thinking

1. How does the author's discussion of negative stereotypes experienced by Muslim American actors in the United States help you to understand the impact of these stereotypes?

2. What are the sources of your own perceptions of Muslims? How has this impacted your reactions to media and other coverage of incidents involving terrorism?

3. How does US foreign policy and other practices shape perceptions of Arabs, Arab Americans, and those that follow Islam? How have these things impacted the overall reaction in the United States to violent events and whether to label them terrorism?

A Dozen Demons

ELLIS COSE

In the essay that follows, journalist Ellis Cose identifies twelve ways in which stereotyping and subtle racism hinder progress and undermine the self-confidence of African Americans in corporate America. His experiences illustrate the importance of recognizing the intersection of race and class.

In the workplace, the continuing relevance of race takes on a special force, partly because so much of life, at least for middle-class Americans, is defined by work, and partly because even people who accept that they will not be treated fairly in the world often hold out hope that their work will be treated fairly—that even a society that keeps neighborhoods racially separate and often makes after-hours social relations awkward will properly reward hard labor and competence. What most African Americans discover, however, is that the racial demons that have plagued them all their lives do not recognize business hours—that the stress of coping extends to a nonwork world that is chronically unwilling (or simply unable) to acknowledge the status their professions ought to confer.

The coping effort, in some cases, is relatively minor. It means accepting the fact, for instance, that it is folly to compete for a taxi on a street corner with whites. It means realizing that prudence dictates dressing up whenever you are likely to encounter strangers (including clerks, cops, and doormen) who can make your life miserable by

mistaking you for a tramp, a slut, or a crook. And it means tolerating the unctuous boor whose only topic of party conversation is blacks he happens to know. But the price of this continual coping is not insignificant. In addition to creating an unhealthy level of stress, it puts many in such a wary state of mind that insults are seen where none were intended, often complicating communications even with sensitive, well-meaning whites who unwittingly stumble into the racial minefield.

What is it exactly that blacks spend so much time coping with? For lack of a better phrase, let's call them the dozen demons. This is not to say that they affect blacks only; as will become clear, members of other racial minority groups are often plagued by them as well. Nor is it to say that there are only twelve, or that all black Americans encounter every one. Still, if you're looking for a safe bet, you could not find one more certain than this: that any random gathering of black American professionals, asked what irks or troubles them, will eventually end up describing, in one guise or another, the following items.

1. *Inability to fit in.* During the mid 1980s, I had lunch in the Harvard Club in Manhattan with a newsroom recruiter from the *New York Times*. The lunch was primarily social, but my companion was also seeking help in identifying black, Hispanic, and Asian-American journalists he could lure to

the *Times*. Though he had encountered plenty of people with good professional credentials, he was concerned about an attribute that was torturously difficult to gauge: the ability to fit into the often bewildering culture of the *Times*. He was desperate to hire good minority candidates, he said, yet hiring someone who could produce decent copy was not enough. He wanted people with class, people who could be "*Times* people."

As we talked, it became clear that he was focusing on such things as speech, manners, dress, and educational pedigree. He had in mind, apparently, a certain button-down sort, an intellectual, nonthreatening, quiet-spoken type—something of a cross between William F. Buckley and Bill Cosby. Someone who might be expected to have his own membership at the Harvard or Yale Club. Not surprisingly, he was not having much success. That most whites at the *Times* fit no such stereotype seemed not to have occurred to him. I suggested, rather gingerly, that perhaps he needed to expand his definition of a "*Times* person," that perhaps some of those he was eliminating for seemingly superficial reasons might have all the qualities the *Times* required.

Even as I made the argument, I knew that it was unpersuasive. Not because he disagreed—he did not offer much of a rebuttal—but because he and many similarly placed executives almost instinctively screened minority candidates according to criteria they did not apply to whites. The practice has nothing to do with malice. It stems more, I suspect, from an unexamined assumption that whites, purely because they are white, are likely to fit in, while blacks and other minority group members are not. Hence, he found it necessary to search for specific assurances that those he brought into the fold had qualities that would enable them, despite their color, to blend into the great white mass.

2. *Exclusion from the club*. Even the ability to fit in, however, does not necessarily guarantee acceptance. Many blacks who have made huge efforts to get the right education, master the right accent, and dress in the proper clothes still find that certain

doors never seem to open, that there are private clubs—in both a real and a symbolic sense—they cannot join. . . .

In 1990, in testimony before the U.S. Senate Judiciary Committee, Darwin Davis, senior vice president of the Equitable Life Assurance Society, told of the frustrations he and some of his black friends had experienced in trying to join a country club. "I have openly approached fellow executives about memberships. Several times, they have said, 'My club has openings; it should be no problem. I'll get back to you.' Generally, one of two things happens. They are too embarrassed to talk to me or they come right out and tell me they were shocked when they made inquiries about bringing in a black. Some have even said they were told to get out of the club if they didn't like the situation as it is."

Davis, a white-haired, elegant, and genial raconteur who loves to play golf, told the Senate panel that his interest was not merely in the game but in the financial costs of exclusion. He was routinely reduced to entertaining golf-playing clients at a public course with poor facilities. "The best I can offer my client is a hamburger and a beer in a plastic cup. My competitor takes this client . . . where they have a great lunch and drinks, and use of the locker room and showers. Then, they get their shoes shined. I am out of the ball game with this client." Whenever he found out that a customer played golf, he became "anxious because I know I am on thin ice." It was "disheartening and demeaning," he added, "to know that it doesn't matter how hard I work, how proficient an executive I become, or how successful I become. I will be denied this one benefit that success is supposed to confer on those who have achieved."

Two years after his testimony, Davis told me his obsession with private clubs sprang in part from concerns about his children. Several years before, he had visited a club as a guest and happened to chance upon a white executive he knew. As they were talking, he noticed the man wave at someone on the practice range. It turned out that he had brought his son down to take a lesson from the club pro. Davis was suddenly struck by a depressing thought. "Damn!" he said to himself. "This is being perpetuated all over again.... I have a son the same age as his. And when my son grows up he's going to go through the same crap I'm going through if I don't do something about this. His son is learning how to ... socialize, get lessons, and do business at a country club." His own son, Davis concluded, would "never ever be able to have the same advantages or even an equal footing."

3. *Low expectations.* Shortly after I arrived to take over the editorial pages of the New York *Daily News,* I was visited by a black employee who had worked at the paper for some time. More was on his mind than a simple desire to make my acquaintance. He had also come to talk about how his career was blocked, how the deck was stacked against him—how, in fact, it was stacked against any black person who worked there. His frustration and anger I easily understood. But what struck me as well was that his expectations left him absolutely no room to grow. He believed so strongly that the white men at the *Daily News* were out to stymie black achievement that he had no option but failure, whatever the reality of the situation.

Even those who refuse to internalize the expectation of failure are often left with nagging doubts, with a feeling, as journalist Joe Boyce puts it, "that no matter what you do in life, there are very few venues in which you can really be sure that you've exhausted your potential. Your achievement is defined by your color and its limitations. And even if in reality you've met your fullest potential, there's an aggravating, lingering doubt ... because you're never sure. And that makes you angry."

During the late 1970s, I met a Harvard student, Mark Whitaker, who was interning for a summer in *Newsweek*'s Washington bureau. Whitaker made it clear that he intended to go far. He had it in mind to become editor of *Newsweek*. I didn't know whether to be amused by his arrogance, awed by his ambition, or amazed by his naivete. I asked Whitaker—the product of a mixed (black/white) union—whether he had considered that his race might hold him back. He answered that maybe it would, but that he was not going to permit his color to smother his aspirations. He would not hold himself back. If he was to be stopped, it would be by someone else.

More than a decade later, when Whitaker had become a *Newsweek* assistant managing editor, I reminded him of our earlier conversation. He laughed his precocious comments off, attributing them to the ignorance and arrogance of youth. We both knew better, of course—just as we knew that many young blacks, for a variety of reasons, never even reach the point of believing that success was within their grasp.

Conrad Harper, former head of the Association of the Bar of the City of New York and a partner in Simpson Thacher & Barlett, said that throughout the years he had seen plenty of young associates "bitterly scarred by not being taken first as lawyers ... but always first as African Americans." He had also seen affirmative action turned into a stigma and used as a club to beat capable people down. If someone's competency is consistently doubted, "the person begins to question his own abilities." The result, he added, is not only a terrible waste of talent, but in some cases psychological damage.

4. *Shattered hopes.* After two years toiling at an eminent law firm, the young associate walked away in disgust and became a public defender. For more than a year after leaving, he was "so filled with rage, I couldn't even talk about it much." A soft-spoken Mexican American, he bristles with emotion as he recalls those years.

He believes that he and other minority group hires simply never got a shot at the big assignments, which invariably went to white males. This sense of disappointment, he makes plain, was felt by all the nonwhites in his class. He remembers one in particular, a black woman who graduated with honors from Yale. All her peers thought she was headed for the stars. Yet when she was rated periodically, she was never included in the first tier but at the top of the second.

If he had been alone in his frustration, he says, one could reject his complaint as no more than a case of sour grapes. "But the fact that all of us were having the same kinds of feelings" means something more systemic was at work. He acknowledges that many whites had similar feelings, that in the intensely competitive environment of a top law firm, no one is guaranteed an easy time. But the sense of abandonment, he contends, was exacerbated for nonwhites. By his count, every minority group member who entered the firm with him ended up leaving, having concluded that nonwhites—barring the spectacularly odd exception—were not destined to make it in that world.

5. *Faint praise.* For a year and a half during the early 1980s, I was a resident fellow at the National Research Council–National Academy of Sciences, an august Washington institution that evaluates scientific research. One afternoon, I mentioned to a white colleague who was also a close friend that it was a shame the NRC had so few blacks on staff. She replied, "Yes, it's too bad there aren't more blacks like you."

I was stunned enough by her comment to ask her what she meant. She answered, in effect, that there were so few really intelligent blacks around who could meet the standards of the NRC. I, of course, was a wonderful exception. Her words, I'm sure, were meant as a compliment, but they angered me, for I took her meaning to be that blacks (present company excluded) simply didn't have the intellect to hang out with the likes of her.

My colleague's attitude seemed to disallow the possibility of a better explanation for the scarcity of blacks than the supposedly low intellectual quality of the race. Perhaps there were so few blacks at the NRC—because they simply were not sought out, or because they were encouraged to believe, from childhood on, that they could never master the expertise that would land them in such a place. The ease with which she dismissed such possibilities in favor of a testimonial to my uniqueness disappointed and depressed me.

Blacks who have been singled out as exceptions often experience anger at the whites who commend them. One young woman, a Harvard-trained lawyer with a long list of "firsts" behind her name, had another reason for cringing whenever she was held up as a glistening departure from the norm for her race. "I don't like what it does to my relationships with other blacks," she said.

6. *Presumption of failure.* A year or so prior to my Harvard Club chat with the *Times* recruiter, I was visited at my office (then in Berkeley, California) by a *Times* assistant managing editor. I took him to lunch, and after a few drinks we fell into a discussion of people at the *Times,* among them a talented black editor whose career seemed to have stalled. Was he in line, I asked, for a high-level editorship that would soon be vacant? My companion agreed that the editor would probably do very well in the job, but then he pointed out that a black person had never held such a post at the *New York Times.* The *Times* would have to think hard, he indicated, before changing that, for they could not afford to have a black journalist fail in such a visible position. I didn't know whether the man even wanted the job (he later told me he might have preferred something else); I know that he didn't get it, that (at least in the eyes of one *Times* assistant managing editor in 1985) his prior work and credentials could not offset the questions raised by his color. Failure at the highest levels of the *Times* was a privilege apparently reserved for whites.

The *Times'* executive's reasoning reminded me of an encounter with a newspaper editor in Atlanta who had contacted me several years earlier. He had an editorial writer's position to fill and was interested in giving me a crack at it. I was intrigued enough to go to Atlanta and spend an evening with the man. We discovered we shared many interests and friends and hit it off famously. Still, I wondered: Why in the world was he recruiting me? Interesting though Atlanta might be, and as well as he and I got along, there had never been much chance that I would leap at the job. In no way did it represent a career advancement, and the editor's budget would barely permit him to pay the salary I was already making. As the evening wore on, I put the question to him bluntly. Why did he not offer the job to someone in his newsroom for whom it would be a real step up? His answer I found more than a little unsettling. One black person, he said, had already come on staff and not performed very well. He could not afford another black failure, so he had gone after someone overqualified in an attempt to buy himself insurance.

I'm sure he was not surprised that I turned the job down. . . . I don't doubt . . . that similar preconceptions still exist, that before many executives even ask whether a minority person can do a job, they ask whether they are prepared to take a flyer on a probable failure.

7. *Coping fatigue.* When Armetta Parker headed for Midland, Michigan, to take a job as a public relations professional at the Dow Chemical Company, she assumed that she was on her way to big-time corporate success. A bright, energetic black woman then in her early thirties, Parker had left a good position at a public utility in Detroit to get on the Fortune 100 fast track.

"Dow was everything I expected and more, and everything I expected and less," she says. The town of nearly forty thousand had only a few hundred black families, and virtually no single black people her own age. Though she expected a certain amount of social isolation, "I didn't expect to get the opportunity to take a really hard look at me, at what was important to me and what wasn't." She had to face that fact that success, in that kind of corporate environment, meant a great deal of work and no social life, and that it also required a great deal of faith in people who found it difficult to recognize competence in blacks. . . .

Nonetheless, Parker did extremely well, at least initially. Her first year at the company, she made it into "The Book"—the roster of those who had been identified as people on the fast track. But eventually she realized that "I was never going to be vice president of public affairs for Dow Chemical." She believed that her color, her gender, and her lack

of a technical degree all were working against her. Moreover, "even if they gave it to me, I didn't want it. The price was too high." Part of that price would have been accepting the fact that her race was not seen as an asset but as something she had to overcome. And her positive traits were probably attributed to white genes, she surmised, even though she is no more "white" than most American blacks. Even her way of talking drew attention. Upon meeting her, one colleague remarked with evident pleasure and astonishment, "You don't speak ghettoese." She had an overwhelming sense that what he meant was "You're almost like us, but not enough like us to be acceptable." . . . She realized that "good corporate jobs can be corporate handcuffs. You have to decide how high of a price you're willing to pay."

8. *Pigeonholing.* Near the end of his brashly brilliant tenure as executive editor of the *Washington Post,* Ben Bradlee observed how much both Washington and the *Post* had changed. Once upon a time, he told me, one would not have thought of appointing a black city editor. Now one could not think of not seriously considering—and even favoring—a black person for the assignment.

Bradlee, I realized, was making several points. One was about himself and his fellow editors, about how they had matured to the extent that they valued all managerial talent—even in blacks. He was also acknowledging that blacks had become so central to Washington's political, economic, and social life that a black city editor had definite advantages, strictly as a function of race. His third point, I'm sure, was wholly unintended but clearly implied: that it was still possible, even for the most enlightened management, to classify jobs by color. And logic dictates that if certain managerial tasks are best handled by blacks, others are best left to whites.

What this logic has meant in terms of the larger corporate world is that black executives have landed, out of all proportion to their numbers, in community relations and public affairs, or in slots where their only relevant expertise concerns blacks and other minorities. The selfsame racial assumptions that make minorities seem perfect for certain initially desirable jobs can ultimately be responsible for trapping them there as others move on.

9. *Identity troubles.* The man was on the verge of retiring from his position as personnel vice president for one of America's largest companies. He had acquired the requisite symbols of success: a huge office, a generous compensation package, a summer home away from home. But he had paid a price. He had decided along the way, he said matter-of-factly, that he could no longer afford to be black.

I was so surprised by the man's statement that I sat silent for several seconds before asking him to explain. Clearly he had done nothing to alter his dark brown complexion. What he had altered, he told me, was the way he allowed himself to be perceived. Early in his career, he had been moderately outspoken about what he saw as racism within and outside his former corporation. He had learned, however, that his modest attempts at advocacy got him typecast as an undesirable. So when he changed jobs, he decided to disassociate himself from any hint of a racial agenda. The strategy had clearly furthered his career, even though other blacks in the company labeled him an Uncle Tom. He was aware of his reputation, and pained by what the others thought, but he had seen no other way to thrive. He noted as well, with evident pride, that he had not abandoned his race, that he had quietly made it his business to cultivate a few young blacks in the corporation and bring their careers along; and could point to some who were doing very well and would have been doing considerably worse without his intervention. His achievements brought him enough pleasure to balance out the distress of not being "black."

Putting aside for the moment what it means to be "black," the fear of being forced to shed one's identity in order to prosper is not at all uncommon. Georgetown University law professor Anita Allen tells of a worried student who asked whether her diction would have to be as precise as Allen's

if she was to be successful as a lawyer. She feared, it seemed, not merely having to change her accent, but being required to discard an important part of herself.

10. *Self-censorship and silence. . . .* [M]any blacks find their voices stilled when sensitive racial issues are raised. A big-city police officer once shared with me his frustration at waiting nineteen years to make detective. In those days before affirmative action, he had watched, one year after another, as less qualified whites were promoted over him. And each year he had swallowed his disappointment, twisted his face into a smile, and congratulated his white friends as he hid his rage—so determined was he to avoid being categorized as a race-obsessed troublemaker. And he had endured other affronts in silence, including a vicious beating by a group of white cops while carrying out a plainclothes assignment. As an undercover officer working within a militant black organization, he had been given a code word to whisper to a fellow officer if the need arose. When he was being brutalized, he had screamed out the word and discovered it to be worthless. His injuries had required surgery and more than thirty stitches. When he was asked by his superior to identify those who had beat him, he feigned ignorance; it seems a fellow officer had preceded his commander and bluntly passed along the message that it was safer to keep quiet.

Even though he made detective years ago, and even though, on the side, he managed to become a successful businessman and an exemplary member of the upwardly striving middle class, he says the anger still simmers within him. He worries that some day it will come pouring out, that some luckless white person will tick him off and he will explode, with tragic results. Knowing him, I don't believe he will ever reach that point. But I accept his fear that he could blow up as a measure of the intensity of his feelings, and of the terrible cost of having to hold them in.

11. *Mendacity.* Even more damaging than self-imposed silence are the lies that seem an integral part of America's approach to race. Many of the

lies are simple self-deception, as when corporate executives claim their companies are utterly color-blind. Some stem from unwillingness to acknowledge racial bias, as when people who have no intention of voting for a candidate of another race tell pollsters that they will. And many are lies of business, social, or political convenience, as was the case with Massachusetts Senator Edward Brooke in the early 1970s.

At the time, Brooke was the highest-ranking black politician in America. His name was routinely trotted out as a vice presidential possibility, though everyone involved knew the exercise was a farce. According to received wisdom, America was not ready to accept a black on the ticket, but Brooke's name seemed to appear on virtually everyone's list. During one such period of vice-presidential hype, I interviewed Brooke for a newspaper profile. After asking the standard questions, I could no longer contain my curiosity. Wasn't he tired, I asked, of the charade of having his name bandied about when no one intended to select him? He nodded wearily and said yes, he was.

To me, his response spoke volumes, probably much more than he'd intended. But I took it as his agreement that lies of political convenience are not merely a nuisance for those interested in the truth but a source of profound disgust and cynicism for those on whose behalf the lies are supposedly told.

12. *Guilt by association.* In the mid 1980s, I was unceremoniously tossed out of Cafe Royale, a restaurant that catered to yuppies in San Francisco, on the orders of a maitre d' who apparently mistook me for someone who had caused trouble on a previous occasion. I sued the restaurant and eventually collected a few thousand dollars from its insurance company. But I will never forget the fury I experienced at being haughtily dismissed by an exalted waiter who would not suffer the inconvenience of having to distinguish one black person from another.

My first real understanding of how poisonous such an attitude could be came to me at the age of twelve or thirteen, when I went to Marshall Field's department store in downtown Chicago in search of a Mother's Day gift. While wandering from one section of the store to another, I gradually became aware that someone was shadowing me. That someone, I ascertained, was a plain-clothes security guard. Apparently I fit his profile of a shoplifter. For several minutes, I roamed through the store, trying to ignore him, but he was determined not to be ignored. Little by little, he made his surveillance more obvious, until we were practically walking in lock step. His tactics unsettled me so much that I could no longer concentrate on shopping. Finally, I whirled to face him.

He said nothing, merely glared as my outrage mounted. *How dare he treat me like a criminal,* I thought, *simply because I'm black.* I screamed something at him; I don't remember what. Whatever it was, it had no effect; he continued to stare at me with a look somewhere between amusement and disdain. I stalked out of the store, conceding him the victory, burning with anger and humiliation. . . .

[Many commentators argue] that America's cities have become so dangerous, largely as a result of young black thugs, that racial discrimination is justified—and is even a necessary tool of survival when directed at young black men. . . .

This rationalization strikes me, to put it mildly, as dangerous. For it inevitably takes one beyond the street, and beyond those black males who are certifiably dangerous. It quickly takes one into society at large, where blacks in no way connected with street crime find themselves victims of street-crime stereotypes. Members of the law-abiding black middle class also have sons, as do those countless African Americans without substantial financial resources who have tried to pound into their children, from birth, that virtue has its rewards, that there is value in following a moral path and shunning the temptations of the street. . . .

Countless members of the black middle class are in fact volunteering every spare moment in an attempt to do whatever they can (working in homeless shelters, volunteering in literacy programs, serving as formal mentors) to better the lives of those in the so-called underclass. At the same time, however, many who belong to America's black privileged class are struggling with problems of their own that are largely unseen or dismissed.

Questions for Critical Thinking

1. Cose outlines many of the "demons" that African Americans experience as a result of racism. How are these demons common to all people of color?

Are there different demons some groups may face that others do not?

2. Did the author discuss any demons that surprised you or that you were not aware of? How do you think your own status in society influences your reaction?

3. How does the author's discussion demonstrate that racism comes in a variety of forms that are, in most cases, less blatant than in the past? How does such covert racism make it difficult to bring about racial equality?

The Story of My Body

JUDITH ORTIZ COFER

In the following essay, author Judith Ortiz Cofer recounts her experiences as a Puerto Rican child coming to the United States and the impact that constructions of race and beauty had on her perceptions of self. At one moment literally learning to become invisible, Cofer demonstrates the impact of societal constructions of difference and inequality on the individual.

> *Migration is the story of my body.*
> —*Victor Hernández Cruz*

Skin

I was born a white girl in Puerto Rico but became a brown girl when I came to live in the United States. My Puerto Rican relatives call me tall; at the American school, some of my rougher classmates called me Skinny Bones, and the Shrimp because I was the smallest member of my classes all through grammar school until high school, when the midget Gladys was given the honorary post of front row center for class pictures and scorekeeper, bench warmer, in P.E. I reached my full stature of five feet in sixth grade.

I started out life as a pretty baby and learned to be a pretty girl from a pretty mother. Then at ten years of age I suffered one of the worst cases of chicken pox I have ever heard of. My entire body, including the inside of my ears and in between my toes, was covered with pustules which in a fit of panic at my appearance I scratched off my face, leaving permanent scars. A cruel school nurse told me I would always have them—tiny cuts that looked as if a mad cat had plunged its claws deep into my skin. I grew my hair long and hid behind it for the first years of my adolescence. This was when I learned to be invisible.

Color

In the animal world it indicates danger: the most colorful creatures are often the most poisonous. Color is also a way to attract and seduce a mate. In the human world color triggers many more complex and often deadly reactions. As a Puerto Rican girl born of "white" parents, I spent the first years of my life hearing people refer to me as *blanca*, white. My mother insisted that I protect myself from the intense island sun because I was more prone to sunburn than some of my darker, *trigueño*[1] playmates. People were always commenting within my hearing about how my black hair contrasted so nicely with my "pale" skin. I did not think of the color of my skin consciously except when I heard the adults talking about complexion. It seems to me that the subject is much more common in the conversation of mixed-race peoples than in mainstream United States society, where it is a touchy and sometimes even embarrassing topic to discuss, except in a political context. In Puerto Rico I heard many conversations about skin color. A pregnant woman could say, "I hope my baby doesn't turn out *prieto*" (slang for "dark" or "black") "like my husband's grand-mother, although she was a good-looking *negra*[2] in her time." I am a combination of both, being olive-skinned—lighter than my mother yet darker than my fair-skinned father. In America, I am a person of color, obviously a Latina. On the Island I have been called everything from a *paloma blanca,*[3] after the song (by a black suitor), to *la gringa.*[4]

My first experience of color prejudice occurred in a supermarket in Paterson, New Jersey. It was Christmastime, and I was eight or nine years old. There was a display of toys in the store where I went two or three times a day to buy things for my mother, who never made lists but sent for milk, cigarettes, a can of this or that, as she remembered from hour to hour. I enjoyed being trusted with money and walking half a city block to the new, modern grocery store. It was owned by three good-looking Italian brothers. I liked the younger one with the crew-cut blond hair. The two older ones watched me and the other Puerto Rican kids as if they thought we were going to steal something. The oldest one would sometimes even try to hurry me with my purchases, although part of my pleasure in these expeditions came from looking at everything in the well-stocked aisles. I was also teaching myself to read English by sounding out the labels in packages: L&M cigarettes, Borden's homogenized milk, Red Devil potted ham, Nestle's chocolate mix, Quaker oats, Bustelo coffee, Wonder bread, Colgate toothpaste, Ivory soap, and Goya (makers of products used in Puerto Rican dishes) everything—these are some of the brand names that taught me nouns. Several times this man had come up to me, wearing his blood-stained butcher's apron, and towering over me had asked in a harsh voice whether there was something he could help me find. On the way out I would glance at the younger brother who ran one of the registers and he would often smile and wink at me.

It was the mean brother who first referred to me as "colored." It was a few days before Christmas, and my parents had already told my brother and me that since we were in Los Estados[5] now, we would get our presents on December 25 instead of Los Reyes, Three Kings Day, when gifts are exchanged in Puerto Rico. We were to give them a wish list that they would take to Santa Claus, who apparently lived in the Macy's store downtown—at least that's where we had caught a glimpse of him when we went shopping. Since my parents were timid about entering the fancy store, we did not approach the huge man in the red suit. I was not interested in sitting on a stranger's lap anyway. But I did covet Susie, the talking schoolteacher doll that was displayed in the center aisle of the Italian brothers' supermarket. She talked when you pulled a string on her back. Susie had a limited repertoire of three sentences: I think she could say: "Hello, I'm Susie Schoolteacher," "Two plus two is four," and one other thing I cannot remember. The day the older brother chased me away, I was reaching to touch Susie's blond curls. I had been told many times, as most children have, not to touch anything in the store that I was not buying. But I had been looking at Susie for weeks. In my mind, she was my doll. After all, I had put her on my Christmas wish list. The moment is frozen in my mind as if there were a photograph of it on file. It was not a turning point, a disaster, or an earth-shaking revelation. It was simply the first time I considered—if naively—the meaning of skin color in human relations.

I reached to touch Susie's hair. It seems to me that I had to get on tip-toe, since the toys were stacked on a table and she sat like a princess on top of the fancy box she came in. Then I heard the booming "Hey, kid, what do you think you're doing!" spoken very loudly from the meat counter. I felt caught, although I knew I was not doing anything criminal. I remember not looking at the man, but standing there, feeling humiliated because I knew everyone in the store must have heard him yell at me. I felt him approach, and when I knew he was behind me, I turned around to face the bloody butcher's apron. His large chest was at my eye level. He blocked my way. I started to run out of the place, but even as I reached the door I heard him shout after me: "Don't come in here unless you gonna buy something.

You PR kids put your dirty hands on stuff. You always look dirty. But maybe dirty brown is your natural color." I heard him laugh and someone else too in the back. Outside in the sunlight I looked at my hands. My nails needed a little cleaning as they always did, since I liked to paint with watercolors, but I took a bath every night. I thought the man was dirtier than I was in his stained apron. He was also always sweaty—it showed in big yellow circles under his shirt-sleeves. I sat on the front steps of the apartment building where we lived and looked closely at my hands, which showed the only skin I could see, since it was bitter cold and I was wearing my quilted play coat, dungarees, and a knitted navy cap of my father's. I was not light pink like my friend Charlene and her sister Kathy, who had blue eyes and light brown hair. My skin is the color of the coffee my grandmother made, which was half milk, *leche con café* rather than *café con leche*.[6] My mother is the opposite mix. She has a lot of café in her color. I could not understand how my skin looked like dirt to the supermarket man.

I went in and washed my hands thoroughly with soap and hot water, and borrowing my mother's nail file, I cleaned the crusted watercolors from underneath my nails. I was pleased with the results. My skin was the same color as before, but I knew I was clean. Clean enough to run my fingers through Susie's fine gold hair when she came home to me.

Size

My mother is barely four feet eleven inches in height, which is average for women in her family. When I grew to five feet by age twelve, she was amazed and began to use the word tall to describe me, as in "Since you are tall, this dress will look good on you." As with the color of my skin, I didn't consciously think about my height or size until other people made an issue of it. It is around the preadolescent years that in America the games children play for fun become fierce competitions where everyone is out to "prove" they are better than others. It was in the playground and sports fields that my size-related problems began. No matter how familiar

the story is, every child who is the last chosen for a team knows the torment of waiting to be called up. At the Paterson, New Jersey, public schools that I attended, the volleyball or softball game was the metaphor for the battlefield of life to the inner city kids—the black kids versus the Puerto Rican kids, the whites versus the blacks versus the Puerto Rican kids; and I was 4F,[7] skinny, short, bespectacled, and apparently impervious to the blood thirst that drove many of my classmates to play ball as if their lives depended on it. Perhaps they did. I would rather be reading a book than sweating, grunting, and running the risk of pain and injury. I simply did not see the point in competitive sports. My main form of exercise then was walking to the library, many city blocks away from my barrio.

Still, I wanted to be wanted. I wanted to be chosen for the team. Physical education was compulsory, a class where you were actually given a grade. On my mainly all A report card, the C for compassion I always received from the P.E. teachers shamed me the same as a bad grade in a real class. Invariably, my father would say: "How can you make a low grade for *playing games?*" He did not understand. Even if I had managed to make a hit (it never happened) or get the ball over that ridiculously high net, I already had a reputation as a "shrimp," a hopeless nonathlete. It was an area where the girls who didn't like me for one reason or another—mainly because I did better than they on academic subjects—could lord it over me; the playing field was the place where even the smallest girl could make me feel powerless and inferior. I instinctively understood the politics even then; how the not choosing me until the teacher forced one of the team captains to call my name was a coup of sorts—there, you little show-off, tomorrow you can beat us in spelling and geography, but this afternoon you are the loser. Or perhaps those were only my own bitter thoughts as I sat or stood in the sidelines while the big girls were grabbed like fish and I, the little brown tadpole, was ignored until Teacher looked over in my general direction and shouted, "Call Ortiz," or, worse, "Somebody's *got* to take her."

No wonder I read Wonder Woman comics and had Legion of Super Heroes daydreams. Although I wanted to think of myself as "intellectual," my body was demanding that I notice it. I saw the little swelling around my once-flat nipples, the fine hairs growing in secret places; but my knees were still bigger than my thighs, and I always wore long- or half-sleeve blouses to hide my bony upper arms. I wanted flesh on my bones—a thick layer of it. I saw a new product advertised on TV. Wate-On. They showed skinny men and women before and after taking the stuff, and it was a transformation like the   ninety-seven-pound-weakling-turned-into-Charles-Atlas ads that I saw on the back covers of my comic books. The Wate-On was very expensive. I tried to explain my need for it in Spanish to my mother, but it didn't translate very well, even to my ears—and she said with a tone of finality, eat more of my good food and you'll get fat—anybody can get fat. Right. Except me. I was going to have to join a circus someday as Skinny Bones, the woman without flesh.

Wonder Woman was stacked. She had a cleavage framed by the spread wings of a golden eagle and a muscular body that has become fashionable with women only recently. But since I wanted a body that would serve me in P.E., hers was my ideal. The breasts were an indulgence I allowed myself. Perhaps the daydreams of bigger girls were more glamorous, since our ambitions are filtered through our needs, but I wanted first a powerful body. I daydreamed of leaping up above the gray landscape of the city to where the sky was clear and blue, and in anger and self-pity, I fantasized about scooping my enemies up by their hair from the playing fields and dumping them on a barren asteroid. I would put the P.E. teachers each on their own rock in space too, where they would be the loneliest people in the universe, since I knew they had no "inner resources," no imagination, and in outer space, there would be no air for them to fill their deflated volleyballs with. In my mind all P.E. teachers have blended into one large spiky-haired woman with a whistle on a string around her neck and a volleyball under one arm. My Wonder Woman fantasies of revenge were a source of comfort to me in my early career as a shrimp.

I was saved from more years of P.E. torment by the fact that in my sophomore year of high school I transferred to a school where the midget, Gladys, was the focal point of interest for the people who must rank according to size. Because her height was considered a handicap, there was an unspoken rule about mentioning size around Gladys, but of course, there was no need to say anything. Gladys knew her place: front row center in class photographs. I gladly moved to the left or to the right of her, as far as I could without leaving the picture completely.

Looks

Many photographs were taken of me as a baby by my mother to send to my father, who was stationed overseas during the first two years of my life. With the Army in Panama when I was born, he later traveled often on tours of duty with the Navy. I was a healthy, pretty baby. Recently, I read that people are drawn to big-eyed round-faced creatures, like puppies, kittens, and certain other mammals and marsupials, koalas, for example, and, of course, infants. I was all eyes, since my head and body, even as I grew older, remained thin and small-boned. As a young child I got a lot of attention from my relatives and many other people we met in our barrio. My mother's beauty may have had something to do with how much attention we got from strangers in stores and on the street. I can imagine it. In the pictures I have seen of us together, she is a stunning young woman by Latino standards: long, curly black hair, and round curves in a compact frame. From her I learned how to move, smile, and talk like an attractive woman. I remember going into a bodega[8] for our groceries and being given candy by the proprietor as a reward for being *bonita*, pretty.

I can see in the photographs, and I also remember, that I was dressed in the pretty clothes, the stiff, frilly dresses, with layers of crinolines underneath, the glossy patent leather shoes, and, on special occasions, the skull-hugging little hats and the white gloves that were popular in the late fifties and early sixties. My mother was proud of my looks, although I was a bit too thin. She could dress me up like a doll and take me by the hand to visit relatives, or go to the Spanish mass at the Catholic church and show me off. How was I to know that she and the others who called me "pretty" were representatives of an aesthetic that would not apply when I went out into the mainstream world of school?

In my Paterson, New Jersey, public schools there were still quite a few white children, although the demographics of the city were changing rapidly. The original waves of Italian and Irish immigrants, silk-mill workers, and laborers in the cloth industries had been "assimilated." Their children were now the middle-class parents of my peers. Many of them moved their children to the Catholic schools that proliferated enough to have leagues of basketball teams. The names I recall hearing still ring in my ears: Don Bosco High versus St. Mary's High, St. Joseph's versus St. John's. Later I too would be transferred to the safer environment of a Catholic school. But I started school at Public School Number 11. I came there from Puerto Rico, thinking myself a pretty girl, and found that the hierarchy for popularity was as follows: pretty white girl, pretty Jewish girl, pretty Puerto Rican girl, pretty black girl. Drop the last two categories; teachers were too busy to have more than one favorite per class, and it was simply understood that if there was a big part in the school play, or any competition where the main qualification was "presentability" (such as escorting a school visitor to or from the principal's office), the classroom's public address speaker would be requesting the pretty and/or nice-looking white boy or girl. By the time I was in sixth grade, I was sometimes called by the principal to represent my class because I dressed neatly (I knew this from a progress report sent to my mother, which I translated for her) and because all the "presentable" white girls had moved to the Catholic schools (I later surmised this part). But I

was still not one of the popular girls with the boys. I remember one incident where I stepped out into the playground in my baggy gym shorts and one Puerto Rican boy said to the other: "What do you think?" The other one answered: "Her face is OK, but look at the toothpick legs." The next best thing to a compliment I got was when my favorite male teacher, while handing out the class pictures, commented that with my long neck and delicate features I resembled the movie star Audrey Hepburn. But the Puerto Rican boys had learned to respond to a fuller figure: long necks and a perfect little nose were not what they looked for in a girl. That is when I decided I was a "brain." I did not settle into the role easily. I was nearly devastated by what the chicken pox episode had done to my self-image. But I looked into the mirror less often after I was told that I would always have scars on my face, and I hid behind my long black hair and my books.

After the problems at the public school got to the point where even nonconfrontational little me got beaten up several times, my parents enrolled me at St. Joseph's High School. I was then a minority of one among the Italian and Irish kids. But I found several good friends there—other girls who took their studies seriously. We did our homework together and talked about the Jackies. The Jackies were two popular girls, one blonde and the other red-haired, who had women's bodies. Their curves showed even in the blue jumper uniforms with straps that we all wore. The blonde Jackie would often let one of the straps fall off her shoulder, and although she, like all of us, wore a white blouse underneath, all the boys stared at her arm. My friends and I talked about this and practiced letting our straps fall off our shoulders. But it wasn't the same without breasts or hips.

My final two and a half years of high school were spent in Augusta, Georgia, where my parents moved our family in search of a more peaceful environment. Then we became part of a little community of our Army-connected relatives and friends. School was yet another matter. I was enrolled in a huge school of nearly two thousand students that had just that year been forced to integrate. There were two black girls and there was me. I did extremely well academically. As to my social life, it was, for the most part, uneventful— yet it is in my memory blighted by one incident. In my junior year, I became wildly infatuated with a pretty white boy. I'll call him Ted. Oh, he was pretty: yellow hair that fell over his forehead, a smile to die for—and he was a great dancer. I watched him at Teen Town, the youth center at the base where all the military brats gathered on Saturday nights. My father had retired from the Navy, and we had all our base privileges—one other reason we moved to Augusta. Ted looked like an angel to me. I worked on him for a year before he asked me out. This meant maneuvering to be within the periphery of his vision at every possible occasion. I took the long way to my classes in school just to pass by his locker, I went to football games, which I detested, and I danced (I too was a good dancer) in front of him at Teen Town— this took some fancy footwork, since it involved subtly moving my partner toward the right spot on the dance floor. When Ted finally approached me, "A Million to One" was playing on the jukebox, and when he took me in his arms, the odds suddenly turned in my favor. He asked me to go to a school dance the following Saturday. I said yes, breathlessly. I said yes, but there were obstacles to surmount at home. My father did not allow me to date casually. I was allowed to go to major events like a prom or a concert with a boy who had been properly screened. There was such a boy in my life, a neighbor who wanted to be a Baptist missionary and was practicing his anthropological skills on my family. If I was desperate to go somewhere and needed a date, I'd resort to Gary. This is the type of religious nut that Gary was: when the school bus did not show up one day, he put his hands over his face and prayed to Christ to get us a way to get to school. Within minutes a mother in a station wagon, on her way to town, stopped to ask why we weren't in school. Gary informed her that the Lord had sent her just in time to find us a way to get

there in time for roll call. He assumed that I was impressed. Gary was even good-looking in a bland sort of way, but he kissed me with his lips tightly pressed together. I think Gary probably ended up marrying a native woman from wherever he may have gone to preach the Gospel according to Paul. She probably believes that all white men pray to God for transportation and kiss with their mouths closed. But it was Ted's mouth, his whole beautiful self, that concerned me in those days. I knew my father would say no to our date, but planned to run away from home if necessary. I told my mother how important this date was. I cajoled and pleaded with her from Sunday to Wednesday. She listened to my arguments and must have heard the note of desperation in my voice. She said very gently to me: "You better be ready for disappointment." I did not ask what she meant. I did not want her fears for me to taint my happiness. I asked her to tell my father about my date. Thursday at breakfast my father looked at me across the table with his eyebrows together. My mother looked at him with her mouth set in a straight line. I looked down at my bowl of cereal. Nobody said anything. Friday I tried on every dress in my closet. Ted would be picking me up at six on Saturday: dinner and then the sock hop at school. Friday night I was in my room doing my nails or something else in preparation for Saturday (I know I groomed myself nonstop all week) when the telephone rang. I ran to get it. It was Ted. His voice sounded funny when he said my name, so funny that I felt compelled to ask: "Is something wrong?" Ted blurted it all out without a preamble. His father had asked who he was going out with. Ted had told him my name. "Ortiz? That's Spanish, isn't it?" the father had asked. Ted had told him yes, then shown him my picture in the yearbook. Ted's father had shaken his head. No. Ted would not be taking me out. Ted's father had known Puerto Ricans in the Army. He had lived in New York City while studying architecture and had seen how the spics lived. Like rats. Ted repeated his father's words to me as if I should understand *his* predicament when I heard why he was breaking our date. I don't remember what I said before hanging up. I do recall the darkness of my room that sleepless night and the heaviness of my blanket in which I wrapped myself like a shroud. And I remember my parents' respect for my pain and their gentleness toward me that weekend. My mother did not say "I warned you," and I was grateful for her understanding silence.

In college, I suddenly became an "exotic" woman to the men who had survived the popularity wars in high school, who were not practicing to be worldly: they had to act liberal in their politics, in their lifestyles, and in the women they went out with. I dated heavily for a while, then married young. I had discovered that I needed stability more than social life. I had brains for sure and some talent in writing. These facts were a constant in my life. My skin color, my size, and my appearance were variables—things that were judged according to my current self-image, the aesthetic values of the time, the places I was in, and the people I met. My studies, later my writing, the respect of people who saw me as an individual person they cared about, these were the criteria for my sense of self-worth that I would concentrate on in my adult life.

Notes

1. *trigueño:* Brown-skinned.
2. *negra:* Black.
3. *paloma blanca:* White dove.
4. *la gringa:* A white, non-Latina woman.
5. *Los Estados:* "The States"—that is, the United States.
6. *leche con café . . . café con leche:* Milk with coffee (light brown) . . . coffee with milk (dark brown).
7. 4F: Draft-board classification meaning "unfit for military service"; hence, not physically fit.
8. *bodega:* Market.

Questions for Critical Thinking

1. Cofer's discussion illustrates that the way we see our bodies is influenced by dominant societal values and beliefs. How do you see your own perceptions of your body influenced by societal beliefs and values? How do these perceptions change in different situations?
2. Cofer experiences particular difficulties with regard to her body and dominant attitudes about gender. Do you think males experience similar problems? Why or why not?
3. Are the experiences Cofer relates simply examples of childhood difficulties everyone experiences or are they examples of larger issues? What makes you think this?

Separated by Deportation

TRAM NGUYEN

In an excerpt from his book We Are All Suspects Now, *author Tram Nguyen tells of the experiences of Abdullah Osman and other Somali refugees, representing the impact of equating Muslims with terrorists in the post-9/11 United States, disrupting the lives and livelihoods of people seeking refuge from their war-torn home countries. His descriptions bring into graphic detail the everyday consequences of systems of inequality.*

It was February 2003 in Minneapolis, and Abdullah Osman zipped his jacket as he crossed Cedar Street. His wife Sukra's brown eyes lit up as he entered their apartment, and his three-year-old daughter, Maria, in a pink sweatsuit with her braids bouncing, wrapped her limbs around his leg. Sukra asked if it was warm outside. He replied with a firm no, returning her smile with his eyes. "The sun must be lying then," she said, disappointment on her face.

Sukra, a petite woman in a patterned headscarf, grew up at the equator and was still adjusting to the Minnesota cold. After nearly a decade of separation, she and Abdullah were reunited less than five years ago in Minneapolis.

Unlike the stark exterior of their housing project, the inside of the Osmans' one-bedroom apartment burst with color and felt like an oasis. A Persian rug covered the linoleum living room floor. Throughout the tidy room lay Maria's toys—a purple and pink bike with training wheels, a large stuffed bear, other things that roll and squeak. Next to a computer desk stood an entertainment center, where a television was turned on to morning cartoons. A poster of the Kenyan city of Mombasa—a city that once provided its own refuge for Sukra and her family—hung above the doorway. The apartment's most distinguishing feature was an intricately patterned sectional foam sofa that circled the perimeter of the living room. "We have to have space for a lot of relatives," explained Sukra, her long headscarf draped over her upper body.

In 1999, Sukra, twenty-four, was able to join Abdullah in Minneapolis. She spoke and wrote Somali and Kiswahili, and became fluent in English after six months in the United States. She worked as an education specialist at a public elementary school, where she prepared lesson plans, translated materials for Somali students, and served as a liaison to Somali parents. Soft-spoken with a gentle smile, Sukra had earned respect within the school. "The Somali kids will listen to me even more than their teachers," she said proudly, "especially when it comes to discipline."

Abdullah worked in construction in 1996, until a wrist injury forced him to seek less-physical work. For several years he was a bus driver for Minneapolis Public Schools, and supplemented his income by driving a taxi during evenings, weekends, and school holidays. "When people first came, they mostly worked at the meat factory," he recalled. "Now there are more jobs. And the state helps people here if they are in need. We love Minnesota."

The Cedar-Riverside neighborhood where they lived is the heart of the largest Somali community in the United States. It's a neighborhood where cafés and organic food stores, several independent theaters, and music venues that cater to the local college crowd sit alongside money-transfer agencies, halal grocers, and a Somali mall with fabrics, furniture, and other East African products. On a Sunday morning, the streets and cafés were filled with men drinking spicy tea and conversing in Somali. Many read the local Somali newspaper, which contained news of current events in Somalia and local job postings. Tall, handsome, and sharply dressed in a sweater, dark blue jeans, and black leather shoes, Abdullah, thirty-three, walked between the snowdrifts and ice patches that covered the sidewalks. He greeted almost every passerby with a warm smile, typically accompanied by a hug or a handshake.

Toward the end of 1991 the State Department began resettling refugees from Somalia's civil war, and chose Minneapolis–St. Paul as one of several resettlement destinations. Community organizations and social service agencies now estimate the city's Somali population at 35,000, more than 70 percent of whom entered the country through the U.S. refugee resettlement program.[1] Most others have been granted, or are seeking, asylum. With its robust local economy and liberal political culture, Minneapolis was a place where Somali refugees felt accepted and found opportunity. "If you want an education, you can get it," Abdullah marveled. His optimism was natural and infectious. "You can get money, food. You can raise your children, and you can find people to help them if you're having trouble. My child, Maria, is lucky. A lot of people don't have what I have. My brothers' children in Somalia aren't so lucky."

For Somalis, Minneapolis had been a safe haven, where they could reestablish family connections, and an economic base from which to support relatives abroad. But after September 11, the haven was becoming a more complicated place.

Abdullah walked casually into the Merkato café and restaurant on Sixth and Cedar. Brown tracks of snow covered the linoleum floor of the sparsely furnished café. Simple stackable chairs with black vinyl seats surrounded bare tables. Unframed posters of East African landscapes and handwritten Somali signs adorned the walls. One man, his jacket unzipped, scarf askew, and open mouth spewing bits of breakfast onto the floor, greeted Abdullah. They left the café and walked together down the street, where Abdullah bought him a cup of tea. "He's crazy," Abdullah said simply of the man's mental illness. Like a large family, people in the Somali community take care of each other. "You will never see a homeless Somali," Abdullah explained. "Someone will take them in. If I know them, they can sleep in my living room." Further down the street, Abdullah encountered a shorter, stocky man with a slight beard and of similar age. It was Omar, a friend he last saw in a refugee camp in Kenya.

For the past several years, encounters like this were as consistent as the cold winters. When Abdullah arrived in Minneapolis in 1996, there were 200 to 300 Somalis in the city. Now, more than twice that number live in the Osmans' building alone, and the community has spread throughout the suburbs and around the state.

"I moved into that building right away, and I've lived in the same apartment ever since," Abdullah said, signaling across the street to the Cedar-Riverside Plaza. Five concrete towers rise nearly forty stories above the Mississippi River and the campus of the University of Minnesota. From a distance they resemble the drab, institutional public housing projects built in inner cities during the 1950s and 1960s. Although the plaza's sixteen hundred units are occupied mostly by Somalis, local cab drivers refer to the complex as the United Nations towers because of the diversity of nationalities it contains. For thousands of new immigrants from all over the world, the plaza has represented the beginning of their pursuit of an American dream.

Abdullah's long-sleeved shirt hid most of the scars that covered his body, which he received during a decade of war, violence, and flight across borders and oceans. Until 1990 Abdullah lived in Mogadishu, a large industrialized Red Sea city that was Somalia's capital and a business and cultural hub for East Africa. His family was from the majority clan. "It was a lot like race and minorities in the U.S." according to Abdullah. While he and his brother, sister, and father enjoyed a middle-class lifestyle, other minority clans were more likely to be poor. Sukra was from a minority clan, and despite her feelings for Abdullah, a relationship between them was forbidden in their communities. As a teenager Abdullah helped Sukra's mother care for their family, which allowed him to spend time with her pretty daughter.

* * *

The Osmans' twenty-seventh-story apartment window overlooked the Hubert Humphrey Institute, a brick building housing the University of Minnesota's school of public affairs departments. Abdullah and Sukra were close enough to see into the office window of Ali Galaydh, a professor of international development. In his tweed jacket, checkered shirt, and brightly colored tie, Galaydh seemed to blend in to the academy. Yet just two decades ago, Galaydh was Somalia's minister of industry and the youngest member of former dictator Mohammed Siad Barre's cabinet. Now he lived with his wife and three daughters in a Minneapolis suburb. He still felt the weight of a peaceful resolution to Somalia's crisis on his shoulders.

"Most people want to go back," said Galaydh, "especially the older people. My mom is from a nomadic clan, and before they would go to a new location, they would always send a scout. My mom was sitting on a rocking chair and looking out the window at the cold, and she said to me, who scouted this place? She has papers, but she wants to go back to our village in Somalia." While Galaydh had not abandoned hope, he was sober in his assessment

of Somalia's prospects for the near future. "Some people pray for world peace," he said, "I pray to Almighty Allah that the weather in Minnesota would be more clement."

His sad eyes belied the academic detachment in his voice as he traced Somalia's route to civil war. "Because of the superpower rivalry, the U.S.S.R. wanted a foothold in the Horn of Africa. Somalia was a strategic location—the U.S. already had a presence in Ethiopia, and it was on the Red Sea. It was seen as the gateway to Africa."

The Soviet Union invested heavily in the armed forces of Somalia, and the military soon became the dominant force in the country. In 1969 the president was assassinated. The new leader, Siad Barre, dissolved the national assembly, banned political parties, and established a Supreme Revolutionary Council with the power to rule by decree.

"With Barre, Somalia fell into one-man rule," explained Galaydh. "There was disenchantment with a government that killed religious leaders, with the loss of democratic culture, and with corruption." Throughout the 1980s, discontent with Somalia's government intensified. Several armed movements formed, mostly operating from Ethiopia through hit-and-run tactics. The United States, meanwhile, continued to support Barre's regime, pouring hundreds of millions into arms in return for the use of military bases from which it could intervene in the Middle East.[2]

"I then realized what was going on," Galaydh continued. "Siad Barre would find the resistance fighters, and he would not only punish them but also their families. He would kill their next of kin and destroy their property." Galaydh and several other ministers defected in 1982. When resistance fighters captured urban areas in the north in 1988 and 1989, Siad Barre responded with extreme force—including aerial bombings of civilian neighborhoods. "That's when people really started to leave. They fled to the Gulf States, Ethiopia, Djibouti, the U.K., the U.S., and Canada. That was before the total collapse."

In January of 1991 a civil uprising forced Barre to flee the capital. Anarchy ensued. In Mogadishu, armed militias vying for power launched artillery with little regard for civilian casualties.

While Galaydh was safe in the United States, Abdullah and Sukra were still in Mogadishu. "There were tanks rolling through the streets," Abdullah remembered. "We were just trying to survive. All of us were shot—my brother, sister, and my father." Abdullah pointed to a scar on his leg where a bullet passed through as they were fleeing. "There were no doctors; no hospitals. You could get bandages, but you had to treat the wounds yourselves. You would just wrap yourself up and try to continue. We ran so we wouldn't get killed."

Abdullah's family escaped to a boat on the Red Sea and an uncertain future as refugees. "There were two to three hundred people packed onto a boat intended for a hundred and fifty. We only drank water for five days," said Abdullah.

After a seven-day journey at sea, their boat was the first to arrive at the undeveloped site of a United Nations refugee camp. It was a barren and remote location in the Kenyan desert, far from any population center. "We spent two weeks sleeping under a tree in hard rain before the UN officials arrived," Abdullah said. "When the UN came they counted us, then gave us tents and water tanks and two blankets a person." UN rations included corn, wheat, flour, and cooking oil. Occasionally they received kidney beans and a little sugar. While there were no cities nearby, neighboring farmers raised goats. "You would trade a pound of flour for a cup of goat's milk, and that's how you fed your children," Abdullah said.

Sukra's family remained in Somalia. "I can remember my dad saying, 'they just want to overthrow the government, then things will get better.' But all of your belongings could be stolen at any time. If you have girls, they get raped." Each new ruler was worse than the last, and soon Sukra's family had to flee Mogadishu. "They were bombing everything," she said. "We had to step over dead people, and sometimes we had to step on them, to

get out." She raised her foot and pointed her toe down, as if she could still feel the flesh under her shoes. "There were empty houses everywhere, with only dead bodies inside."

Different armed factions occupied the roads that led out of the city. The factions were largely based on clanship, and often showed little mercy for people from other clans. "All of the clans have different dialects, and you had to try to guess which clan the men were from and try to speak in their dialect," Sukra remembered. "Maybe someone recognizes you, or maybe they don't believe you. If so, you're probably going to be dead." Still not yet a teenager, Sukra watched her brother and her sister die as they tried to escape Mogadishu.

Sukra and her family traveled overland to Chisimayu, another coastal city hundreds of miles south. The war followed them. In 1992, after three months imprisoned in their homes by militia forces, they escaped to the Red Sea and boarded a boat for the Kenyan city of Mombasa. "They packed eighty people on a forty-person boat. We had no food, no personal belongings," Sukra said. "The boat would stop every day, and then charge us another thousand Somali rupees to continue on." They arrived at a UN camp on the border between Kenya and Somalia. That camp became home for the next seven years.

By 2002, there were more than 300,000 Somali refugees living in UN camps in twelve countries around the world.[3] Refugee camps in Kenya are by far the most extensive, hosting over 140,000 Somali refugees. Many camps issued each person three kilograms of maize every fifteen days, only eight hundred calories per day per person. Maize has to be cooked, which requires firewood. People had to leave the camps to get firewood, and they were often raped or robbed. Wheat and oil, which they were supposed to receive, were scarce. There were well-stocked markets in most camps, so fortunate people relied on money sent from abroad.

Most refugee camps in Kenya were connected by the *taar*, or telegram. But Abdullah and Sukra had to rely on mail or an occasional phone call, for which Kenyan Telecom would charge a significant fee. In the early 1990s, soon after arriving in Kenya, Abdullah's older brother had been granted refugee status and passage to the United States. In 1996 he was able to sponsor Abdullah, his younger brother, his older sister, and their father to come to Minnesota through the refugee resettlement program. When Abdullah arrived, he found a temporary construction job and moved into his apartment in the Cedar-Riverside Plaza.

Abdullah soon found permanent work cleaning rental cars for Avis at the Minneapolis airport, and began sending money not only to his family, but to Sukra and her mother as well. "Abdullah told me, 'I want you to learn English because you will need it when you come to America,'" Sukra recounted. "So I took English classes in the camp from some North Americans, for a small fee."

In 1999, Sukra was able to get support from family members abroad to finance her passage to the United States. She was nineteen, and it was the first time she had ever been out of sight of her family. She had no documents. "I was too afraid to even look up during the trip. I didn't want to be found out," Sukra said. "But you know you're going there to help your family, so you hold onto that." Sukra arrived in San Diego, California, where she applied for asylum. After five months Sukra's asylum petition was accepted, and she moved to Minnesota to meet Abdullah. They were married six months later.

"This is home to us. This is where we came, this is where our community is," Sukra said. She and Abdullah continued to send money back to Kenya to other relatives in refugee camps, including Abdullah's mother. In January of 2001, Sukra gave birth to Maria.

"I was happy. I had my family, a job, money to pay rent, to buy clothes. We have families in Kenya and Somalia that need food, so we need to work," said Abdullah. "I felt like a man, like I had life, opportunity."

* * *

On Friday, June 16, 2001, Abdullah woke up at 10:00 AM to start his taxi shift. He found his first fare on Cedar Street, where he would drive a Somali man to a car repair shop three miles away. The man asked Abdullah to wait outside while he checked to see if the repairs were complete. While he waited, two men came to his window.

"One of them asked me to lend them twenty dollars," Abdullah recounted. "He said they would give me their address and I could come and pick up the money later. I told them my shift had just started so I didn't have any money." Abdullah had never met either of the men, but when they started knocking on his window, he decided it was time to leave.

"I thought they were just crazy," Abdullah said. "I didn't think they would attack me."

When Abdullah tried to get out of the car to get his passenger, one man slammed his door shut on him, then opened it and pulled him to the ground. The man hit him repeatedly. "He was much bigger and stronger than me. He had me pinned on my back and was punching me in the head," Abdullah said. "He hit me in the face, in my eyes and in my mouth." The man took the fifty dollars that were in Abdullah's shirt pocket to pay for the daily taxi rental. Then the assailant's keychain, attached to a razorblade, fell out of his pocket.

"We both saw it and reached for it, and I got it first. He was holding my wrist, but I shook it free and slashed at his arm," Abdullah said. When the razor cut the man's shoulder, he released Abdullah and ran down the street.

Three other men, who had been watching the attack, began to approach Abdullah. Frightened and in shock, Abdullah hurried to his cab and drove away. He realized that he should go back to the scene and contact the police. By the time he returned to the repair shop, the police were already there. "I was bleeding from my eyes, and from my arm," Abdullah remembered, displaying a six-inch scar between his elbow and wrist from when the man threw him to the ground. "But the people [at the scene] said I was the one who tried to kill somebody. The police threw me against the car and handcuffed me. They never asked me my side of the story."

Abdullah was held in jail for three days. He was not charged with a crime and was released. But two months later, while Abdullah was at work, the sheriff showed up at the Osmans' apartment door with a warrant for his arrest.

"I asked to see the warrant because I didn't believe it," recalled Sukra. "They said they didn't send notification because they thought he would flee. I said, from what? He didn't do anything wrong, so why would he flee? And where would he go? They searched the house, and even picked up the sofas to see if he was hiding."

After a call from the sheriff, Abdullah turned himself in that day. He remained in jail for eleven days until his family and friends were able to raise the $10,000 bail. His court date was set for April 2002. Abdullah hired a criminal-defense attorney based in downtown Minneapolis, who quickly learned that Abdullah's assailant had been found guilty of seven prior felonies, mostly for assault. "My attorney told me to sleep easy," Abdullah recalled. "I had never had any problems with the law. He told me that because I was working at the time, and it was self-defense, and that I was a family man, that the case would be easily dismissed." Abdullah went back to work, and life returned to normal for a brief month. Then came September 11.

* * *

On October 1, 2001, which was the start of the 2002 fiscal year, President Bush refused to sign the annual Presidential Determination that allows an allotted number of refugees to enter the United States. The virtual moratorium lasted until November 21, when Bush issued an order allowing 70,000 people to be resettled in the coming year, 10,000 less than the number set in 2001. Of this number, only 27,000 refugees were actually admitted.[4] Five thousand Somali refugees had been admitted from October 2000 to October 2001. In the following year, less than 200 Somali refugees entered the United States.[5] Asylum applications continue to face difficulty.

While identifying countries that might harbor terrorists, Secretary of State Colin Powell told the Senate Foreign Relations Committee at a 2002 hearing, "A country that immediately comes to mind is Somalia because it is quite a lawless place without much of a government. Terrorism might find fertile ground there and we do not want that to happen."[6] This focus on Somalia paralleled the restrictions on refugee acceptance and asylum. According to Craig Hope, director of the Episcopal Church's refugee resettlement office, "No one is going to say it's because of September 11, but that's the reason. They're being screened and watched carefully."

Soon after, Attorney General John Ashcroft's Justice Department launched a series of aggressive campaigns against immigrants. In Minnesota, the Somali community began to hear of arrests. Omar Jamal, a vocal Somali activist and director of the Somali Justice Advocacy Center in St. Paul, was accused of concealing his previous Canadian residency when he applied for asylum in 1997. Convicted in federal court a few years later, Jamal faced deportation. Another crucial blow to the community was the arrest of Mohamed Abshir Musse, a seventy-six-year-old former Somali general. His visa expired in September 2002 despite his application for renewal, and when he reported to the immigration office to comply with the new special registration program, officials ordered his deportation. Called by one former U.S. ambassador "the greatest living Somali," he has been credited for saving the lives of innumerable American soldiers during violent conflicts in the 1990s. Several members of Congress and former ambassadors sponsored a bill on his behalf. Despite the clout of his supporters, he may still be deported.[7]

"We will see a lot more asylum revocation cases, and we may lose," said Michele Garnett McKenzie, director of the Refugee and Immigration Program at the Minnesota Advocates for Human Rights. A young attorney and Minnesota native, McKenzie played a central role in connecting Minnesota immigrants with pro bono legal defense. "It might be because there's more money in the pipeline for enforcement. The local ICE [Immigration and Customs Enforcement, formerly INS] might be getting more federal support. They view it as a war-on-terrorism issue rather than an immigration issue. So there's more investigation into asylum cases."

In the case of Milagros Jimenez, asylum problems were combined with a new immigration enforcement policy, the Absconder Apprehension Initiative, resulting in what many local immigrants saw as a highly political arrest in 2002. Jimenez came to Minneapolis from Peru with her son in 1996, seeking asylum from the armed conflict with guerillas that had embroiled her son's father. She overcame the loneliness and fear of new-immigrant life to become involved with ISAIAH, a progressive faith-based organization in Minnesota. Eventually, she became the organization's first Latina organizer, despite the language barrier and her trepidations. "Sometimes we want to live like hiding, in the shadows. When we came to this country, we lost our self-confidence. You need to build your confidence again," she explained. "I knew it was risky, but I felt like I need to do it."

The risk became real as Jimenez began organizing statewide for banks and other institutions to accept the *matricular consular,* the Mexican ID, in lieu of a driver's license for undocumented immigrants. Three days before a rally where they were expecting up to two thousand people to participate, Jimenez left a late-night meeting to see an unmarked car and two men waiting for her. They had her name from an existing list of "absconders" with outstanding deportation orders, and handcuffed her and put her in the back seat without explaining anything. Jimenez was driven hours outside of the Twin Cities to a jail where she was detained for four weeks. After her release on bond, she joined hundreds of immigrants around the country ordered to wear ankle bracelets while they waited for their deportation hearings. Minneapolis was part of an eight-city pilot program started in the summer of 2004 as a house-arrest alternative to detention.[8] While it was accepted as "better than jail" by some immigrants and advocates, the electronic monitoring was hardly the solution that many were hoping for. As Jimenez went about her work in a hospital clinic, the heavy metal shackle on her leg was "terrible, so humiliating" and made her feel like a criminal.

"They're only trying to save a buck," said Jorge Saavedra, of Minneapolis' Centro Legal. "The number one issue for immigrants that end up in the enforcement system is a virtual lack of due process, especially since Sept. 11."[9]

* * *

Like other immigrants, Abdullah and Sukra Osman felt the chilling effect of September 11 on their adopted city.

"I was very afraid. As a person who has been through war, you know there is going to be isolation, and people targeted," said Sukra. "And it happened here. A community leader was killed, a girl got beaten up, someone was thrown off a bridge. We couldn't go out at night. I was afraid to go on the freeway to my job, because I thought someone would see me and harass me.

"And it's not like Somalia, where you can blend in and escape. Here you are so different from everyone else, so you can't hide. You stand out."

In a front-page article on October 14, 2001, the *Minneapolis Star Tribune* speculated that local Somalis had contributed to a charity linked to Osama bin Laden.[10] A day later, Ali Warsame Ali, a sixty-six-year-old retired Somali businessman, was punched in the head while waiting for a bus and died of his injuries.[11] Many community residents linked the newspaper article to a rise in hate crimes and to Ali's death. A demonstration organized by the Confederation of Somali Community drew more than five hundred Somalis to protest. "People had their headscarves pulled, their car windows smashed. My brother had a symbol of Allah in his window and it was smashed," recalled Mohamud

Noor, chairman of the Confederation's board. "Ali died because of a hate crime after September 11. There are issues of prejudice that have arisen since September 11, because of the generalization of Muslims." Somalis were even afraid to send money to relatives overseas. "People were worried," explained Noor. "If I send money, will I be targeted? Will I be linked to al-Qa'ida? Will I be targeted as a terrorist? People were afraid that the questioning process would be extended to them—that they might lose their refugee status and the benefits that come with it."

The fear that money transfers to relatives would result in government suspicion and retaliation was not unfounded. On September 23, 2001, just twelve days after the strike on the World Trade Center, President Bush announced "a strike on the financial foundation of the global terror network." This initiative targeted Islamic charities, banks, and financial institutions, including local hawalas, or money-transfer agencies. Over 40 percent of Somalia's GDP is from remittances from relatives living abroad, mostly in Europe and North America.[12] "I would say ninety-five percent of Somalis send money home, more than that," said Ahmed Omar, an owner of Barwaaqo Financial Services. It is one of dozens of hawalas that serve Minneapolis's Somali community. "People will send one hundred dollars a month to a family of five in Somalia, maybe two or three hundred to camps in Kenya because the expenses are higher. That will be enough to keep people fed, and put kids in school.

"We're still scared that they are going to come in, shut us down, or arrest us for something," Omar continued. Business slowed at Barwaaqo. Other hawalas, in Minneapolis–St. Paul, Seattle, and cities across the nation, were shut down completely. Al Barakaat, the largest hawala operating in Somalia, was one of them. "Millions of dollars were lost when they froze all of Al Barakaat's accounts around the world," Omar said. "Hawalas are like a bank for Somalis. They trust and know them, and will put all of their money in their accounts. I don't think people are getting their money back." Wire transfer agencies such as Western Union do not operate in Somalia. Hawalas are not only the trusted choice, they are often the only lifeline between those who made it out of war-torn Somalia to their relatives who remain behind. "A lot of people have suffered [from these closures]," Omar said.

September 11 affected the three most important things for Somalis in the United States—feeling safe in a place they can call home, being able to reunite with family members, and supporting relatives who live in poverty abroad. For Abdullah and many others, their life and liberty are also at stake.

* * *

Just seven months after September 11, Abdullah was scheduled for trial. Suddenly his case, which had seemed like a sure victory, had turned on its head. "My lawyer told me that I would never win the case. My name is Abdullah. I am Muslim, and I used a box cutter," he said, bitterness and incredulity in his voice. "My lawyer said that no jury would ever acquit me."

In March of 2002, shortly before his April court appearance, his attorney offered him a settlement option. If he pled guilty, he could serve eight months in a work release program. "He told me I could work and be with my family during the day, or I could go to a trial that we'll definitely lose and face five years in prison," Abdullah recalled. "He said, 'You're a Somali Muslim, and you can't win because of September 11.'"

Abdullah and Sukra considered hiring another attorney. All were reluctant to take his case and would only do so for a high price. "Another lawyer wanted fourteen thousand dollars, and he said we would probably lose," Sukra said. "We were thinking, what choice do we have?"

Abdullah pled guilty. He was taken to a work release facility under the assumption that he would be able to go to work the next morning. When he arose at 4:00 AM, the officers told him they hadn't completed his paperwork, and that he wouldn't be able to work that day.

Then at 9:00 AM, two officers entered his cell. "One pushed his knee into my back while I was sleeping, grabbed my arms and pulled them back and cuffed me," said Abdullah. "He told me to collect my things, but they were up on a shelf and I had my hands cuffed behind my back. He threw my stuff on the floor and I had to squat down to pick it up."

The officers asked Abdullah if he was a citizen. When he explained that he was a refugee, they told him that he was no longer "eligible to be in society." Under a 1996 immigration law, noncitizens convicted of crimes that fell under the category of "aggravated felonies" are subject to consequences that include detention and deportation. Abdullah spent the next eight months in twenty-three-hour lockdown in the county jail, where he was allowed outside for less than three hours a week. During that time, he had no access to a doctor. His only solace was in weekend visits, through glass windows, from his wife and daughter.

"County jails are designed to house inmates for three weeks or a month before trials, not for extended stays," said Michele Garnett McKenzie of the Minnesota Advocates for Human Rights. "There are no programs for inmates, no education options, and few services."

After several weeks, Abdullah's health began to deteriorate. He had a neck injury from a recent car accident, but despite his pleas he was not allowed to see a doctor or receive any therapy. He began to lose weight. Sukra, with help from family and friends, hired an immigration lawyer to try to get him transferred to an immigration facility.

"We wanted to do anything to get him out of that jail," she recalled.

On November 20, 2002, immigration officials moved Abdullah from the county jail through various facilities until they placed him in the Sherburne county jail in Elk River, Minnesota. "I spent three days moving around with no food, water, blanket, nothing. Not even in refugee camps did I go that long without food," Abdullah said. "Everywhere we went they said, lunch is over, or dinner

is over. Or, they would say, you won't eat pork, so there's no food." During his three months in Elk River, Sukra and Maria could only see him through a television screen. He was again denied medical treatment. "They said there was no budget, and blamed it on the immigration department. They would take other inmates out of prison to get care, but not immigrants."

During the period of his detention at Elk River, Abdullah was driven forty miles southwest to the state's immigration court in Bloomington, where a judge would decide whether he would be deported to Somalia. Minnesota had two full-time immigration judges, Joseph R. Dierkes and Kristin W. Olmanson, both of whom were located across from the INS building in Bloomington. Which judge a detainee sees is a matter of chance. "I had scars from war. We are in an interclan marriage, which isn't approved of. We brought a witness from the United Nations to testify about how dangerous Somalia is," Abdullah recounted. "One judge never sends people to Somalia. The other judge automatically sentences people to deportation. When she [Olmanson] was chosen as our judge, our lawyer and other people we knew said we had a one percent chance of winning. To her, the danger didn't matter."

Abdullah and Sukra found another attorney to help them appeal his deportation order to the Board of Immigration. For the next several months, Abdullah was shipped all over the nation. They took him first to Rush State Prison in Minnesota. "It was one of the best places I had been," he said. "I got some education, some treatment for my neck, and was able to get a sore tooth removed." On July 9, 2002, prison guards told Abdullah to pack his belongings. They moved him back to Elk River for one night, and the next day, at 3:00 AM, they told him to pack up again. They flew him to Jefferson City, Oklahoma, on a U.S. Marshals Service air transport. By 8:00 PM he was once again in a county jail. "They didn't even give me a toothbrush. There were flies everywhere. There were seventy-five or eighty people in one room. It was worse than any refugee camp. I saw people vomit blood," Abdullah remembered. "Even in Somalia if we get arrested, family can come visit, and bring food. Here all they served was beans and rice, every day."

The conditions became worse. "I was right next to the air-conditioning vent and I was cold, so I asked to be moved to an empty bunk nearby so I could sleep. Because of that they put me in solitary for a week," Abdullah said. "I threatened to call my lawyer and they put me back in a bunk. They wouldn't give me a doctor or let me see a nurse or anything. I understand that people get arrested, but at least they should get food and medical treatment. But that's not true in the U.S. People died in the Oklahoma jail. When I would ask for care they would say they had to contact Washington, D.C. I never saw a doctor."

Abdullah's travels between prisons were not over. After three months in Oklahoma, he was moved to a detention facility in Texas for nearly two months. "Every two days, they would give me a bologna sandwich. I never ate pork before that, but I had no choice. I had to survive," he said. "I saw a lot of things in county jail and immigration that I've never seen in other countries. There is nothing for immigrants."

Moving immigration detainees to different facilities around the country is "a tried-and-true tactic of deportation officials to deny people access to friends, family, counsel," said McKenzie. "It's an old-fashioned immigration enforcement tool, to make it harder for them to pursue their case." In Minnesota, advocates had been pushing for better conditions in detention. "We were making progress with the bar association to get a monitoring project into facilities for immigrant detainees," said McKenzie. "But since September 11 we've had no access [to the facilities]. People haven't felt able to pursue it."

* * *

Abdullah's final appeals to the Board of Immigration were denied. On November 20, 2003, he received a letter saying he would be sent home

under supervision until his final removal. He had been in county jails or state prisons for a year and eight months. When he arrived at home, Sukra was shocked at how thin he was.

"I was thrilled when he was released, I was so excited," remembered Sukra. "But he's still not free. We had written so many support letters. We had spent almost fifteen thousand dollars on lawyers. But none of it mattered."

Abdullah's deportation depended on the outcome of legal battles that were about to be fought all the way to the Supreme Court. In a case involving the deportation of Somali nationals living in Seattle, the Ninth Circuit Court of Appeals ruled in January 2003 that deportation requires acceptance by the government of the deportee's home country. Somalia is the only nation in the world that the U.S. Department of State categorizes as having no functioning government. Without official government acceptance, the court ruled that deportations would violate international law.

This ruling, however, came with a loophole. Cases already going through the courts in other jurisdictions were not affected by the Seattle ruling. Minneapolis is in the Eighth Circuit Court of Appeals, which ruled in February 2003 for the deportation of Somali immigrant Keyse Jama. Convicted of third-degree assault in 1999, Jama had been detained by immigration officials for nearly four years after serving his one-year sentence. His appeal to the U.S. Supreme Court was being watched around the nation for the precedent it would set on Somali deportations. In court papers, the Justice Department maintained that deportation to Somalia is "a vital tool to protect the security of this nation's borders."[13] Abdullah's fate and that of more than three thousand other Somalis with deportation orders hinged on the outcome of Jama's case.

* * *

While the Osmans struggled through imprisonment and legal battles, Ali Galaydh, the professor and government minister, was mired in conflicts on a different scale. In 2000, the president of Somalia's neighbor state, Djibouti, hosted thousands of Somalis, including elders, community leaders, and the heads of warring factions, for a five-month peace and reconciliation conference. By its end they had agreed to establish a national charter (an interim constitution), and elect a national assembly. Another former minister under Barre's regime became president, and Galaydh became the first prime minister of Somalia's Transitional National Government in October 2000. It was the closest Somalia had come to a recognized central authority in more than a decade.

After fleeing Somalia, Galaydh taught at Harvard's Center for International Affairs until 1989, and at Syracuse's Maxwell School of Public Policy from 1989 until 1996. He had also started a transnational telecommunications company in Dubai to help develop industry in Somalia. Despite this experience, "there was nothing I ever learned or taught that could prepare me for what we were trying to do (with the transitional government)," Galaydh admitted. The president soon began to veer away from democratic principles, instead adopting strong-arm tactics reminiscent of Barre's government. Galaydh, who disagreed with the president's methods, was ousted while he was in the United States negotiating for antiterrorism funds in the wake of September 11.

At the end of its three-year mandate, the Transitional National Government that Galaydh and millions of Somalis had hoped would lead the nation to peace and economic recovery was in disarray. There was no central authority once again. "Unlike civil wars in other countries, there are no identifiable groups fighting," Galaydh explained. "The media talks about the warlords, most of whom are in Mogadishu. At best, they control a certain neighborhood in the city. They don't even have the force to dominate other neighborhoods, let alone stabilize the whole country. These are messy little wars with no winners."

It wasn't until 2004 when another transitional government was put together, this time brought about after talks that began in 2002 and were sponsored by the neighboring countries of Ethiopia, Ghana, and Kenya. By summer of 2004, the Somali leadership, based out of Kenya, had put together a parliament and elected a president.

"Unfortunately, the president they elected is a warlord, one of the more brutal ones. Now the issue is how to go back to Somalia," said Galaydh. "Their work will be cut out for them, because there is nothing on the ground in terms of a civil service, in terms of even a security detail for the president and his key people."

If the transitional government was afraid for its safety in Somalia, advocates in the United States believed that deportees would face a much worse situation, especially those without strong clan and family connections. In May 2002, the body of a Somali man deported from the United States was discovered near a Mogadishu factory.[14] The man had been kidnapped the previous evening. "If you come from the U.S. with blue jeans and nice sneakers you can get killed, or they will kidnap you and force relatives in the U.S. to cough up ten thousand dollars or more," Galaydh explained. "The absence of government institutions and the lawlessness are a threat to life."

On January 12, 2005, the Supreme Court ruled in a 5–4 decision in favor of Keyse Jama's deportation, ending the hopes of thousands that U.S. and international law could protect them from being sent back.

★ ★ ★

Since 1997, immigration authorities have deported 196 Somali nationals.[15] Of those people, 49 were deported for criminal charges, such as Abdullah's, and 147 were deported on visa violations or other issues related to immigration, like those of Omar Jamal or Mohammed Abshir Musse. Toward the end of 2004, there were 3,568 Somalis with deportation orders. About 4,000 more Somalis had deportation cases still tied up in the courts, bringing the estimated number of people affected by the Supreme Court ruling up to 8,000.[16]

In Minneapolis, chaos and alarm followed news of the ruling. A few weeks after the announcement, Somali lawyer Hassan Mohamud was preparing to pull together a hasty meeting to try to answer some of the community's urgent questions. Who are the people affected? Will they be deported, how will they be deported, and where will they go? An imam as well as a lawyer, Mohamud sat in his downtown Legal Aid office wondering what he could tell them.

"We contacted immigration, they are not answering and we don't know what to do," Mohamud said. "Logistically we don't have enough information—about where to ship and how to ship. They were saying, okay we can ship them by determining everyone's clan and then ship them where their clan has a majority. But there's no clan power—it's not a matter of who do you belong to, it's a matter of safety and there's no safe place in Somalia."

Abdullah and Sukra were waiting like everyone else to find out what would happen next. They had been living in limbo for more than three years. Abdullah's legal options had already run dry back in the winter of 2003. After submitting thirty-five job applications in a month, Abdullah finally found an employer who would look past his criminal record. Still, because of his conviction, he was paid much less than his coworkers. He now drove two hours each way for an eight-dollars-an-hour job without benefits. "It's all I can get, so I have to hold onto it," he said. Once a month, he checked in at the local immigration office. "They can come anytime and take me away," Abdullah said in a quiet, desperate tone. "They don't have to say anything."

Abdullah said goodbye to his family as he stepped out of his apartment. "My daughter is so beautiful," he said. Moments later Maria poked her head out of their doorway to play a game of peek-a-boo with her father as he walked away. He covered his face, pretending to hide, then raised his arms as if he were going to chase her into the apartment. She squealed with delight and ran inside, only to pop her head out later and say goodbye again. He smiled as he zipped up his jacket and entered the elevator. "She has lots of friends in the building," he said. "She knows all of their elevator buttons." Maria is a U.S. citizen, and if Abdullah is deported, she and Sukra cannot risk their lives to join him in Somalia. If he is deported, he will never be permitted to return. Having survived years apart, through war, poverty, injury, and death, they have always treasured their hours together. Now they must live with the knowledge that any one could be their last.

Notes

1. Author interview with Saeed Fahia, executive director of Confederation of Somali Community in Minnesota, Minneapolis, January 20, 2005.
2. Stephen Zunes, "The Long and Hidden History of the U.S. in Somalia," AlterNet, posted January 17, 2002, www.alternet.org/story/12253.
3. Office of the United Nations High Commissioner for Refugees, "Somalia," *Global Appeal 2002*, www.unhcr.ch/Pubs/fedrs/ga2002/ga2002toc.htm.
4. James Ziglar, commissioner of U.S. Immigration and Naturalization Service, testimony before the Senate Committee on the Judiciary, Subcommittee on Immigration, February 12, 2002.
5. Confederation of Somali Community in Minnesota, February 2005.
6. Toby Harnden, "Powell Orders Watch on 'Lawless Country,'" *Daily Telegraph*, January 10, 2002.
7. Eric Black, "U.S. Diplomats Fighting for Somali," *Minneapolis Star-Tribune*, March 6, 2003.
8. Heron Marquez Estrada, "Federal Government to Release Some Immigration Detainees in State," *Minneapolis Star-Tribune*, June 19, 2004.
9. Ibid.
10. Greg Gordon, Joy Powell, Kimberly Hayes Taylor, "Terror Group May Have Received Local Funds," *Minneapolis Star-Tribune*, October 14, 2001.
11. Human Rights Watch, *We Are Not the Enemy: Hate Crimes against Arabs, Muslims, and Those*

Perceived to Be Arab or Muslim after September 11, Report, November 2002.

12. Author interview with Ali Galaydh, Minneapolis, January 21, 2005.
13. Mary Beth Sheridan, "For Somalis a Home and a Haven," *Washington Post,* December 27, 2002.
14. Author interview with Hassan Mohamud of the Legal Aid Society of Minneapolis and U.S. Committee for Refugees and Immigrants, Minneapolis, January 22, 2005.
15. INS document, January 13, 2003.
16. Florangela Davila, "Ruling Could Lead to Deportations," *Seattle Times,* January 13, 2005.

Questions for Critical Thinking

1. Nguyen discusses the impact of targeting the Somali community after the events of September 11, 2001. How does this reading help you to understand the impact of discrimination not only on individual lives but also on families and communities?
2. How did this reading help you to understand the reasons immigrants have for coming to the United States and remaining despite their illegal status?
3. Considering Nguyen's discussion, do you think it is possible to change negative perceptions of immigrants to the United States?

"Gee, You Don't Seem Like an Indian from the Reservation"

BARBARA CAMERON

In the following essay, author Barbara Cameron recounts her experiences growing up Native American in South Dakota. Her encounters with racism and racial violence had long-lasting and penetrating impacts on her sense of self.

One of the very first words I learned in my Lakota language was *wasicu,* which designates white people. At that early age, my comprehension of wasicu was gained from observing and listening to my family discussing the wasicu. My grandmother always referred to white people as the "wasicu sica" with emphasis on *sica,* our word for terrible or bad. By the age of five I had seen one Indian man gunned down in the back by the police and was a silent witness to a gang of white teenage boys beating up an elderly Indian man. I'd hear stories of Indian ranch hands being "accidentally" shot by white ranchers. I quickly began to understand the wasicu menace my family spoke of.

My hatred for the wasicu was solidly implanted by the time I entered first grade. Unfortunately in first grade I became teacher's pet so my teacher had a fondness for hugging me, which always repulsed me. I couldn't stand the idea of a white person touching me. Eventually I realized that it wasn't the white skin that I hated, but it was their culture of deceit, greed, racism, and violence.

During my first memorable visit to a white town, I was appalled that they thought of themselves as superior to my people. Their manner of living appeared devoid of life and bordered on hostility even for one another. They were separated from each other by their perfectly, politely fenced square plots of green lawn. The only lawns on my reservation were the lawns of the BIA[1] officials or white Christians. The white people always seemed so loud, obnoxious, and vulgar. And the white parents were either screaming at their kids, threatening them with some form of punishment or hitting them. After spending a day around white people, I was always happy to go back to the reservation where people followed a relaxed yet respectful code of relating with each other. The easy teasing and joking that were inherent with the Lakota were a welcome relief after a day with the plastic faces.

I vividly remember two occasions during my childhood in which I was cognizant of being an Indian. The first time was at about three years of age when my family took me to my first pow-wow. I kept asking my grandmother, "Where are the Indians? Where are the Indians? Are they going to have bows and arrows?" I was very curious and strangely excited about the prospect of seeing real live Indians even though I myself was one. It's a memory that has remained with me through all these years because it's so full of the subtleties of my culture. There was a sweet wonderful aroma in the air from the dancers and from the traditional food booths. There were lots of grandmothers and grandfathers with young children running about. Pow-wows in the Plains usually last for three days, sometimes longer, with Indian people traveling from all parts of our country to dance, to share food and laughter, and to be with each other. I could sense the importance of our gathering times and it was the beginning of my awareness that my people are a great and different nation.

The second time in my childhood when I knew very clearly that I am Indian occurred when I was attending an all-white (except for me) elementary school. During Halloween my friends and I went trick or treating. At one of the last stops, the mother knew all of the children except for me. She asked me to remove my mask so she could see who I was. After I removed my mask, she realized I was an Indian and quite cruelly told me so, refusing to give me the treats my friends had received. It was a stingingly painful experience.

I told my mother about it the next evening after I tried to understand it. My mother was outraged and explained the realities of being an Indian in South Dakota. My mother paid a visit to the woman, which resulted in their expressing a barrage of equal hatred for one another. I remember sitting in our pick-up hearing the intensity of the anger and feeling very sad that my mother had to defend her child to someone who wasn't worthy of her presence.

I spent a part of my childhood feeling great sadness and helplessness about how it seemed that Indians were open game for the white people, to kill, maim, beat up, insult, rape, cheat, or whatever atrocity the white people wanted to play with. There was also a rage and frustration that has not died. When I look back on reservation life, it seems that I spent a great deal of time attending

the funerals of my relatives or friends of my family. During one year I went to funerals of four murder victims. Most of my non-Indian friends have not seen a dead body or have not been to a funeral. Death was so common on the reservation that I did not understand the implications of the high death rate until after I moved away and was surprised to learn that I've seen more dead bodies than my friends will probably ever see in their lifetime.

Because of experiencing racial violence, I sometimes panic when I'm the only non-white in a roomful of whites, even if they are my closest friends; I wonder if I'll leave the room alive. The seemingly copacetic gay world of San Francisco becomes a mere dream after the panic leaves. I think to myself that it's truly insane for me to feel the panic. I want to scream out my anger and disgust with myself for feeling distrustful of my white friends and I want to banish the society that has fostered those feelings of alienation. I wonder at the amount of assimilation which has affected me and how long my "Indianness" will allow me to remain in a city that is far removed from the lives of many Native Americans.

"Alienation" and "assimilation" are two common words used to describe contemporary Indian people. I've come to despise those two words because what leads to "alienation" and "assimilation" should not be so concisely defined. And I generally mistrust words that are used to define Native Americans and Brown People. I don't like being put under a magnifying glass and having cute liberal terms describe who I am. The "alienation" or "assimilation" that I manifest is often in how I speak. There isn't necessarily a third world language but there is an Indian way of talking that is an essential part of me. I like it, I love it, yet I deny it. I "save" it for when I'm around other Indians. It is a way of talking that involves "Indian humor" which I know for sure non-Indian people would not necessarily understand.

Articulate. Articulate. I've heard that word used many times to describe third world people. White people seem so surprised to find brown people who can speak fluent English and are even perhaps educated. We then become "articulate." I think I spend a lot of time being articulate with white people. Or as one person said to me a few years ago, "Gee, you don't seem like an Indian from the reservation."

I often read about the dilemmas of contemporary Indians caught between the white and Indian worlds. For most of us, it is an uneasy balance to maintain. Sometimes some of us are not so successful with it. Native Americans have a very high suicide rate.

> When I was about 20, I dreamt of myself at the age of 25–26, standing at a place on my reservation, looking to the North, watching a glorious, many-colored horse galloping toward me from the sky. My eyes were riveted and attracted to the beauty and overwhelming strength of the horse. The horse's eyes were staring directly into mine, hypnotizing me and holding my attention. Slowly from the East, an eagle was gliding toward the horse. My attention began to be drawn toward the calm of the eagle but I still did not want to lose sight of the horse. Finally the two met with the eagle sailing into the horse causing it to disintegrate. The eagle flew gently on.

I take this prophetic dream as an analogy of my balance between the white [horse] and Indian [eagle] worlds. Now that I am 26, I find that I've gone as far into my exploration of the white world as I want. It doesn't mean that I'm going to run off to live in a tipi. It simply means that I'm not interested in pursuing a society that uses analysis, research, and experimentation to concretize their vision of cruel destinies for those who are not bastards of the Pilgrims; a society with arrogance rising, moon in oppression, and sun in destruction.

Racism is not easy for me to write about because of my own racism toward other people of color, and because of a complex set of "racisms" within the Indian community. At times animosity exists between half-breed, full-blood, light-skinned Indians, dark-skinned Indians, and non-Indians who attempt to pass as Indians. The U.S. government

has practiced for many years its divisiveness in the Indian community by instilling and perpetuating these Indian versus Indian tactics. Native Americans are the foremost group of people who continuously fight against premeditated cultural genocide.

I've grown up with misconceptions about Blacks, Chicanos, and Asians. I'm still in the process of trying to eliminate my racist pictures of other people of color. I know most of *my* images of other races come from television, books, movies, newspapers, and magazines. Who can pinpoint exactly where racism comes from? There are certain political dogmas that are excellent in their "analysis" of racism and how it feeds the capitalist system. To intellectually understand that it is wrong or politically incorrect to be racist leaves me cold. A lot of poor or working class white and brown people are just as racist as the "capitalist pig." We are *all* continually pumped with gross and inaccurate images of everyone else and we *all* pump it out. I don't think there are easy answers or formulas. My personal attempts at eliminating my racism have to start at the base level of those mindsets that inhibit my relationships with people.

Racism among third world people is an area that needs to be discussed and dealt with honestly. We form alliances loosely based on the fact that we have a common oppressor, yet we do not have a commitment to talk about our own fears and misconceptions about each other. I've noticed that liberal, consciousness-raised white people tend to be incredibly polite to third world people at parties or other social situations. It's almost as if they make a point to SHAKE YOUR HAND or to introduce themselves and then run down all the latest right-on third world or Native American books they've just read. On the other hand it's been my experience that if there are several third world gay people at a party, we make a point of avoiding each other, and spend our time talking to the whites to show how sophisticated and intelligent we are. I've always wanted to introduce myself to other third world people but wondered how I would introduce myself or what would I say. There are so many things I would want to say, except sometimes I don't want to remember I'm Third World or Native American. I don't want to remember sometimes because it means recognizing that we're outlaws.

At the Third World Gay Conference in October 1979, the Asian and Native American people in attendance felt the issues affecting us were not adequately included in the workshops. Our representation and leadership had minimal input, which resulted in a skimpy educational process about our struggles. The conference glaringly pointed out to us the narrow definition held by some people that third world means black people only. It was a depressing experience to sit in the lobby of Harambee House with other Native Americans and Asians, feeling removed from other third world groups with whom there is supposed to be this automatic solidarity and empathy. The Indian group sat in my motel room discussing and exchanging our experiences within the third world context. We didn't spend much time in workshops conducted by other third world people because of feeling unwelcomed at the conference and demoralized by having an invisible presence. What's worse than being invisible among your own kind?

It is of particular importance to us as third world gay people to begin a serious interchange of sharing and educating ourselves about each other. We not only must struggle with the racism and homophobia of straight white America, but must often struggle with the homophobia that exists within our third world communities. Being third world doesn't always connote a political awareness or activism. I've met a number of third world and Native American lesbians who've said they're just into "being themselves," and that politics has no meaning in their lives. I agree that everyone is entitled to "be themselves" but in a society that denies respect and basic rights to people because of their ethnic background, I feel that individuals cannot idly sit by and allow themselves to be co-opted by the dominant society. I don't know what moves a person to be politically active or to attempt to raise

the quality of life in our world. I only know what motivates my political responsibility . . . the death of Anna Mae Aquash—Native American freedom fighter—"mysteriously" murdered by a bullet in the head; Raymond Yellow Thunder—forced to dance naked in front of a white VFW club in Nebraska—murdered; Rita Silk-Nauni—imprisoned for life for defending her child; my dear friend Mani Lucas-Papago—shot in the back of the head outside of a gay bar in Phoenix. The list could go on and on. My Native American History, recent and past, moves me to continue as a political activist.

And in the white gay community there is rampant racism which is never adequately addressed or acknowledged. My friend Chrystos from the Menominee Nation gave a poetry reading in May 1980, at a Bay Area feminist bookstore. Her reading consisted of poems and journal entries in which she wrote honestly from her heart about the many "isms" and contradictions in most of our lives. Chrystos' bluntly revealing observations on her experiences with the white-lesbian-feminist community are similar to mine and are probably echoed by other lesbians of color.

Her honesty was courageous and should be representative of the kind of forum our community needs to openly discuss mutual racism. A few days following Chrystos' reading, a friend who was in the same bookstore overheard a white lesbian denounce Chrystos' reading as anti-lesbian and racist.

A few years ago, a white lesbian telephoned me requesting an interview, explaining that she was taking Native American courses at a local university, and that she needed data for her paper on gay Native Americans. I agreed to the interview with the idea that I would be helping a "sister" and would also be able to educate her about Native American struggles. After we completed the interview, she began a diatribe on how sexist Native Americans are, followed by a questioning session in which I was to enlighten her mind about why Native Americans are so sexist. I attempted to rationally answer her inanely racist and insulting questions, although my inner response was to tell her to remove herself from my house. Later it became very clear how I had been manipulated as a sounding board for her ugly and distorted views about Native Americans. Her arrogance and disrespect were characteristic of the racist white people in South Dakota. If I tried to point it out, I'm sure she would have vehemently denied her racism.

During the Brigg's initiative scare, I was invited to speak at a rally to represent Native American solidarity against the initiative. The person who spoke prior to me expressed a pro-Bakke sentiment which the audience booed and hissed. His comments left the predominantly white audience angry and in disruption. A white lesbian stood up demanding that a third world person address the racist comments he had made. The MC, rather than taking responsibility for restoring order at the rally, realized that I was the next speaker and I was also T-H-I-R-D-W-O-R-L-D!! I refused to address the remarks of the previous speaker because of the attitudes of the MC and the white lesbian that only third world people are responsible for speaking out against racism. *It is inappropriate for progressive or liberal white people to expect warriors in brown armor to eradicate racism.* There must be co-responsibility from people of color and white people to equally work on this issue. It is not just MY responsibility to point out and educate about racist activities and beliefs.

Redman, redskin, savage, heathen, injun, american indian, first americans, indigenous peoples, natives, amerindian, native american, nigger, negro, black, wet back, greaser, mexican, spanish, latin, hispanic, chicano, chink, oriental, asian, disadvantaged, special interest group, minority, third world, fourth world, people of color, illegal aliens—oh, yes, about them, will the U.S. government recognize that the Founding Fathers (you know George Washington and all those guys) are this country's first illegal aliens.

We are named by others and we are named by ourselves.

Epilogue . . .

Following writing most of this, I went to visit my home in South Dakota. It was my first visit in eight years. I kept putting off my visit year after year because I could not tolerate the white people there and the ruralness and poverty of the reservation. And because in the eight years since I left home, I came out as a lesbian. My visit home was overwhelming. Floods and floods of locked memories broke. I rediscovered myself there in the hills, on the prairies, in the sky, on the road, in the quiet nights, among the stars, listening to the distant yelps of coyotes, walking on Lakota earth, seeing Bear Butte, looking at my grandparentws' cragged faces, standing under wakiyan, smelling the Paha Sapa [Black Hills], and being with my precious circle of relatives.

My sense of time changed, my manner of speaking changed, and a certain freedom with myself returned.

I was sad to leave but recognized that a significant part of myself has never left and never will. And that part is what gives me strength—the strength of my people's enduring history and continuing belief in the sovereignty of our lives.

Note

1. Bureau of Indian Affairs.

Questions for Critical Thinking

1. Cameron discusses the hatred that she felt toward white people at a very early age. How is this hatred different from the racism that whites direct at American Indians?
2. What are some ways of eliminating the hatred that Cameron felt?
3. How does equating the contempt members of marginalized groups possess for whites with the racism that whites direct at people of color keep us from finding solutions to racism?

The Transgender Crucible

SABRINA RUBIN ERDELY

The following essay details the experiences of CeCe McDonald, a transgender woman who endured homelessness and other hardships as a teen and was later charged with murder when defending herself from an attacker. Her experiences of survival despite the violence she has faced have helped to transform her into a hero for the rights of transgender people.

Dozen eggs, bacon, maybe some biscuits: CeCe McDonald had a modest shopping list in mind, just a few things for breakfast the next day. It was midnight, the ideal time for a supermarket run. Wearing a lavender My Little Pony T-shirt and denim cutoffs, CeCe grabbed her purse for the short walk to the 24-hour Cub Foods. She preferred shopping at night, when the darkened streets provided some relief from the stares, whispers and insults she encountered daily as a transgender woman. CeCe, 23, had grown accustomed to snickers and double takes—and was practiced in talking back to strangers who'd announce, "That's a man!" But such encounters were tiring; some days a lady just wanted to buy her groceries in peace.

And so it was that on a warm Saturday night in June 2011, CeCe and four friends, all African-Americans in their twenties, found themselves strolling the tree-lined streets of her quiet working-class Longfellow neighborhood in Minneapolis, toward a commercial strip. Leading the way was CeCe's roommate Latavia Taylor and two purse-carrying gay men—CeCe's makeshift family, whom she called "cousin" and "brothers"—with CeCe, a fashion student at a local community college, and her lanky boyfriend trailing behind. They were passing the Schooner Tavern when they heard the jeering.

"Faggots."

Gathered outside the dive bar were a handful of cigarette-smoking white people, looking like an aging biker gang in their T-shirts, jeans and bandannas, motorcycles parked nearby. Hurling the insults were 47-year-old Dean Schmitz, in a white button-down and thick silver chain, and his 40-year-old ex-girlfriend Molly Flaherty, clad in black, drink in hand. "Look at that boy dressed as a girl, tucking his dick in!" hooted Schmitz, clutching two beer bottles freshly fetched from his Blazer, as CeCe and her friends slowed to a stop. "You niggers need to go back to Africa!"

Chrishaun "CeCe" McDonald stepped in front of her friends, a familiar autopilot kicking in, shunting fury and fear to a distant place while her mouth went into motion. "Excuse me. We are people, and you need to respect us," CeCe began in her lisping delivery, one acrylic-nailed finger in the air, her curtain of orange microbraids swaying. With her caramel skin, angled jaw and square chin, friends called her "CeCe" for her resemblance to the singer Ciara; even her antagonist Flaherty would later describe CeCe as "really pretty." 'We're just trying to walk to the store," CeCe continued, raising her voice over the blare of Schmitz and Flaherty's free-associating invective: "bitches with dicks," "faggot-lovers," "niggers," "rapists." The commotion was drawing more patrons out of the bar—including a six-foot-eight, 310-pound biker in leather chaps—and CeCe's boyfriend, Larry Thomas, nervously called to Schmitz, "Enjoy your night, man—just leave us alone." CeCe and her friends turned to go. Then Flaherty glanced at Schmitz and laughed.

"I'll take all of you bitches on!" Flaherty hollered, and smashed CeCe in the side of her face with a glass tumbler.

Just like that, a mundane walk to the store turned into a street brawl, in a near-farcical clash of stereotypes. Pandemonium erupted as CeCe and Flaherty seized each other by the hair; the bikers swung fists and hurled beer bottles, hollering "beat that faggot ass!"; and CeCe's friends flailed purses and cracked their studded belts as whips. When the two sides separated, panting and disoriented, Flaherty was curled up amid the broken glass screaming, mistakenly, that she'd been knifed, and CeCe stood over her, her T-shirt drenched with her own blood. Touching her cheek, CeCe felt a shock of pain as her finger entered the open wound where Flaherty's glass had punctured her salivary gland. Purse still over her shoulder, CeCe fast-walked from the scene. She'd made it more than a half-block away when she heard her friends calling, 'Watch your back!'

CeCe whirled around to see Schmitz heading toward her: walking, then running, his face a twist of wild, unrestrained hatred. CeCe felt terror burst out from that remote place where she normally locked it away. She didn't know that Schmitz's veins were pounding with cocaine and meth. She didn't know of his lengthy rap sheet, including convictions for assault. Nor did she know that under Schmitz's shirt, inked across his solar plexus, was a four-inch swastika tattoo. All CeCe needed to see was the look on his face to know her worst fears were coming true: Her young life was about to end as a grim statistic, the victim of a hate crime.

"Come here, bitch!" Schmitz roared as he closed in. CeCe pedaled backward, blood dripping from her slashed face.

"Didn't y'all get enough?" CeCe asked, defiant and afraid, while her hand fished into her large handbag for anything to protect herself. Her fingers closed on a pair of black-handled fabric scissors she used for school. She held them up high as a warning, their five-inch blades glinting in the parking-lot floodlights. Schmitz stopped an arm's length away, raising clenched fists and shuffling his feet in a boxing stance. His eyes were terrible with rage.

"Bitch, you gonna stab me?" he shouted. They squared off for a tense moment: the furious white guy, amped up on meth, Nazi tattoo across his belly; the terrified black trans woman with a cartoon pony on her T-shirt; the scissors between them. CeCe saw Schmitz lunge toward her and braced herself for impact. Their bodies collided, then separated. He was still looking at her.

"Bitch—you stabbed me!"

"Yes, I did," CeCe announced, even as she wondered if that could possibly be true; in the adrenaline of the moment, she'd felt nothing. Scanning Schmitz over, she saw no sign of injury—though in fact he'd sustained a wound so grisly that CeCe would later recall to police that the button-down shirt Schmitz wore that night was not white but "mainly red. Like one of them Hawaiian shirts." CeCe waited until he turned to rejoin his crowd. Then she and Thomas ran arm in arm down the block toward the nearly empty Cub Foods parking lot, where they waited for police to arrive.

They didn't see the scene unfolding behind them: how Schmitz took a few faltering steps, uttered, "I'm bleeding," then lifted his shirt to unleash a geyser of blood. CeCe had stabbed him in the chest, burying the blade almost three and a half inches deep, slicing his heart. Blood sprayed the road as Schmitz staggered, collapsed and, amid his friends' screams, died. When CeCe and Thomas waved down a police car minutes later, she was promptly handcuffed and arrested.

Given the swift political advances of the transgender movement, paired with its new pop-culture visibility, you'd be forgiven for believing that to be gender-nonconforming today is to be accepted, celebrated, even trendy—what with trans models in ads for American Apparel and Barneys; Facebook's more than 50 gender options for users to choose from; and Eurovision song-contest winner Conchita Wurst, who accepted the trophy in an evening gown and a full beard. When this spring Secretary of Defense Chuck Hagel recommended a review of the military's ban on allowing trans people to serve openly—by one estimate, trans people are as much as twice as likely as the general U.S. population to serve in the armed forces—his announcement seemed to herald a new era of recognition. But the appearance of tolerance belies the most basic day-to-day reality: No community living in America today is as openly terrorized as transgender women, especially trans women of color. "Every day a trans person says, 'I may die today,'" says trans woman Miasha Forbes. "You ready yourself for war each day." Leaving the house on a typical day, a trans woman prepares herself to endure indignities unimaginable to most of us: to be pelted by rocks, called slurs or referred to not as "she" or even "he," but rather as "it."

"Just being trans out on the street is cause for our lives to be in danger," says trans actress Laverne Cox, who says she envisioned her Orange Is the New Black character, Sophia Burset, as a homage to CeCe McDonald. "So many times I've been walking on the street as a trans woman and been harassed, called a man—one time I was kicked," she adds. "Any of them could have escalated into someone doing me harm. I very easily could be CeCe."

Living with a gender identity different from one's birth anatomy (a phenomenon thought to affect as many as one in 10,000 people) means that trans women live with constant anxiety of being recognized as trans—"getting spooked" or "getting clocked"—because reactions can be harsh to the extreme. Though transgender people make up

perhaps 10 percent of the LGBT community, they account for a shocking proportion of its hate-crime statistics, with trans people nearly twice as likely to be threatened as their LGB peers. And trans people all too often meet with violent deaths: Of the 25 reported anti-LGBT homicides in 2012, according to the National Coalition of Anti-Violence Programs, transgender people accounted for more than half of the victims. All of those trans homicide victims were trans women of color.

Highlighting the danger, transgender murders tend to be gruesome, often involving torture and mutilation, as in the 2012 California murder of 37-year-old Brandy Martell, who was shot in the genitals; or the brutal hatchet slaying last July in Philadelphia of 31-year-old Diamond Williams, whose body was hacked to pieces and strewn in an overgrown lot. After Williams' alleged killer reportedly confessed that he'd killed Williams, a prostitute he'd solicited, when he'd realized she was trans—commonly known as the "trans panic defense"—online commenters were quick to agree "the cross-dresser had it coming": that Williams' transgender status was an act of duplicity whose logical punishment was death. "It's socially sanctioned to say that," says Cox. "If a guy is even attracted to her, then she has to die. What is that?" And when these cases go unresolved, as they often do—like last summer's vicious Harlem beating death of 21-year-old Islan Nettles, reportedly after a catcalling admirer turned vengeful—the lack of resolution seems a further reminder to trans women of their own disposability. It's telling that the closest thing the trans community has to a long-running Pride event is Transgender Day of Remembrance, a day of mourning for victims of violence.

"It takes a toll. This life is not an easy life," says trans woman Anya Stacy Neal. "Trust me, if this was a choice, I would have packed it up a long time ago."

As the sisterhood is picked off one by one, each gets a chilling vision of her own fate. "You rarely hear of a trans woman just living a long life and then dying of old age," says CeCe today, seated at a friend's Minneapolis dining-room table with her legs crossed ladylike at the knee. Wearing a striped cardigan that she opens to reveal, laughing, a T-shirt reading IT'S ALL ABOUT ME, CeCe's an animated run-on talker with a lip ring and a warm, open nature, whose cadences recall the church days of her youth, mouth opening wide to flash a tongue stud. "You never hear, 'She passed on her own, natural causes, old age,' no, no, no," she continues, ticking off on her fingers. "She's either raped and killed, she's jumped and killed, stalked and killed—or just killed." Which is why, amid all the death and sorrow, CeCe, whose jagged life experience embodies the archetypal trans woman's in so many ways, has become an LGBT folk hero for her story of survival—and for the price she paid for fighting back.

* * *

By age eight, CeCe McDonald was fascinated by the beauty rituals of the women in her family. Watching reverently from a doorway as her mother and aunts clucked over outfits, swiped on lipstick and examined themselves in the mirror—casually engaged in the intimate, luxuriant rites of femininity—she ached to join them someday. "Even seeing my grandma get ready for church, putting on her pearl earrings and her White Diamonds perfume, it was really powerful," remembers CeCe. "I felt like I was a guest in their presence, these superwomen who are fucking fabulous and have these great shoes and cute clothes. And I thought, 'Yeah! That's the person that I am.'"

From earliest childhood CeCe had felt at odds with her boy's body, boyish clothes and boy's name (a name that she still can't discuss without anguish). She'd always felt such an irrepressible girlishness. In grade school she walked with graceful wrists and swishing hips, to the consternation of her family. CeCe was the oldest of seven, raised on Chicago's gritty South Side by a single mother; a dozen family members crammed under one roof,

where no one could fail to notice young CeCe sashaying in her mother's heels. "You need to pray that out of you," her religious family instructed, and at night, CeCe tearfully pleaded with God to take away her sinful attraction to boys. Better yet, she prayed to awaken a girl, in the body He had surely meant for her.

She redoubled her prayers as other kids began to mock her femininity, and their taunts turned violent. CeCe was chased through the neighborhood, beaten up and, around seventh grade, attacked by five high schoolers yelling "kill that faggot," who kicked her in the mouth so savagely that her incisor tore through the skin above her lip. Such bullying is the norm for transgender kids, nearly nine out of 10 of whom are harassed by peers, and 44 percent of whom are physically assaulted. But no number of beatings could change CeCe. In school she'd dash into the girls' bathroom when the coast was clear, frightened of being seen in the boys' room sitting down to pee. She joined the cheer-leading squad—gleefully doing splits at basketball games—coming to class in her mom's blouse or platform shoes, though she'd change back into boy clothes before returning home, fearful of her family's wrath, and of losing the love of her mother, who was trying to persuade CeCe onto a more traditional path.

"It kind of scared me," says mom Christi McDonald of CeCe's femininity. "I know it's a cruel world, and if you're different it's hard for people to accept you." Christi bought CeCe baggy jeans and dropped hints about cute girls, just as when CeCe was smaller Christi had urged her to draw pictures of Superman instead of sketching dresses. "I kept questioning him, 'Why are you doing this?'" Christi says, adjusting her pronouns to add, "I just wanted a peaceful life for her."

CeCe had always tried staying in her mom's good graces by being a responsible, diligent child, constantly neatening the house, making the beds and whipping up recipes inspired by cooking shows, but nonetheless she felt her mother grow distant. CeCe was unable to find sanctuary with her family, and tensions grew in the crowded three-bedroom house. One day, an uncle found an undelivered love note she'd written to a boy and, CeCe says, knocked her to the kitchen floor and choked her. She ran away from home, never to return. She was 14.

She crashed with friends before taking up residence in a glorified drug den where other runaways congregated. CeCe tried to see the bright side of her family's rejection: She was finally free to be herself. The first time she tried on a bra and panties, she felt a shiver of recognition that she was headed in the right direction. Instead, she fell right through a trapdoor. She'd reached a crucial point in the too-typical trans woman's narrative, in which, cut loose at a young age from family, she falls directly into harm's way. Up to 40 percent of U.S. homeless youth are LGBT. Adrift without money, shelter, education or a support system, they're exposed to myriad dangers. According to one study, 58 percent of LGBT homeless youth are sexually assaulted (compared with 33 percent of their hetero peers). Drug and alcohol use is rampant. CeCe grew up fast. "Honey, I think there's not too much in this world that I haven't heard or seen or done," she tells me. "And a lot of that is sad."

She learned to sell crack and marijuana. Out in the streets, her appearance in girls' clothing was met with outbursts of violence, as when a man once threw an empty 40-ounce bottle at her head, knocking her unconscious; another time, a stranger pulled a knife. Even more traumatic, a handsome man lured CeCe into his home with an invitation to smoke weed—"I was like, 'Oh, my goodness, this is so cool.' Very naive, thinking everybody is good"—then pushed her face-forward onto his bed and anally raped her. The assault changed CeCe profoundly, crystallizing how expendable she was in the eyes of the world. Never had she felt so degraded, and so certain no one would care. Living in poverty and unpredictability so extreme that she sometimes found herself sleeping on park benches and eating grass to fill her belly, CeCe decided to offer herself in the one last arena where she felt she had worth.

At 15, CeCe was a child prostitute working the strip off Belmont Avenue in Boys-town, climbing into men's cars to earn up to $1,000 on a Saturday night. In choosing the sex trade, CeCe was heading down a well-worn path. Studies of urban trans-gender women have found that upward of 50 percent had engaged in sex work. It's a risky job, in which the threat of violence is only one hazard. Transgender women are considered the fastest-growing HIV-positive population in the country, with a meta-analysis showing that nearly 28 percent of trans women in America have the virus. Bearing the highest risk are trans women in sex work, who are four times more likely to be living with HIV than other female sex workers.

CeCe got through each sex act by thinking about the cash, which not only kept her and her friends stocked with food and weed and liquor, but granted her the illusion of power. No longer merely a homeless trans teen, she recast herself as a fierce independent woman getting her coin, a sexy Donna Summer lyric sprung to life. "There is some type of pride in that," says CeCe. "I felt like, 'No bitch can touch me, I gets all the men, with all the money, and who gonna do something about it?' And that made me feel like I was on top." She also reveled in the ego boost of having her femininity affirmed for the very first time, her paying clientele proof of her irresistibility. But despite the pep talks she gave herself, CeCe was sickened by the way she'd turned her own body into a commodity available to anyone. "They saw me as an object; they saw me as their fantasy. And for a long time that's how I viewed myself, as a fantasy." She set a price on her own life, permitting sex without condoms for a premium.

"I became this soulless drone," says CeCe. She entertained a dim hope she'd get AIDS and die. She was tired of internalizing hostility and worthlessness, mentally exhausted from constantly scanning for danger. Such daily burdens take a heavy toll: Though the suicide-attempt rate in the general population is estimated to be 4.6 percent, the National Transgender Discrimination Survey found that an extraordinary 41 percent of trans respondents had attempted suicide, with the rate soaring to 64 percent for sexual-assault victims. The first time CeCe attempted suicide, it was with pills washed down with a bottle of NyQuil. The second time, she crushed up a pile of pills and drank it down with juice. Asked how many times she tried to kill herself, CeCe has to think for a long moment; it's hard to sort out, since her late teens were basically an extended death wish. So much so that when one night a man on a street corner pointed a gun at her, shouting, "Faggot, I'll kill you," CeCe just looked at him and said, "Shoot me."

Surely it would have been far easier for CeCe if she'd given up, renounced her womanhood and opted to live life as a gay man. And yet even in her darkest despair, CeCe never considered retreat an option. If she was going to continue living, it was going to be as a lady. For her there was no decision-making; she felt she couldn't "choose" to be a man, because she'd never been male to begin with.

"I wasn't born a boy," she says heatedly. "I was born a baby." Like many trans women, CeCe disputes her basic narrative as that of a boy who grew up to be a woman. Rather, hers is a story of mistaken identity, of a person assigned the wrong gender at birth. She doesn't know why she was created with a boy's anatomy but with the mind and soul of a girl; all she could do was work with the mixed-up results. "If the Creator, whoever He-She-They are, wanted me to be a certain way, that's how They would've made me," CeCe declares at the bohemian Minneapolis coffee shop Cafe South-Side, which serves as a local LGBT hub. "But until then, until all this shit is figured out? I'm-a rock this. Till the wheels fall off," she says, one balletic hand in the air testifying, flashing electric-yellow fingernails. Across the table a friend, a lesbian poet in Buddy Holly glasses, laughs with appreciation, as does the proprietress behind the cash register. "Till the wheelsfalloff. Mmmph!" CeCe exclaims with a flourish. "Crop tops and all, trust and believe that!"

That unflagging enthusiasm for her feminine identity, fused with her magnetic talent for making friends, helped push CeCe forward through her teenage years, until in 2008 she found herself as a 20-year-old living in St. Paul. "Hiiii! Y'all taking job applications?" she'd sing as she strode into yet another retail store or restaurant. Reluctantly checking "male" on her application, CeCe would subtly scan people's faces for that telltale twinge of discomfort, a sure sign that no job would be forthcoming; trans people have reported twice the unemployment rate as the general population. She tried not to let her spirits sink when she didn't get a callback. CeCe was intent on finding a job, which was a cornerstone of her plan to turn her life around.

She'd taken a Greyhound bus to the Twin Cities two years earlier on a whim, hoping to escape her Chicago misery and start anew. Instead she'd been floundering, in and out of shelters, flirting with coke and meth addictions, jailed for shoplifting and other misdemeanors, and hospitalized for suicidal ideation. But she'd also started visiting a drop-in youth center, where she learned how to regain control of her life bit by bit. "CeCe caught my attention right away," says her case manager Abby Beasley. "Her energy, she's just so bubbly, laughing constantly, just a real loving person. I put more work into her than I did anybody else, trying to help her stabilize her life."

Education was a first step: CeCe earned her GED, then enrolled in Minneapolis Community and Technical College, focusing on fashion design. Estrogen came next. A doctor diagnosed CeCe with gender dysphoria—determining that there was an incongruity between her biological sex and her gender identity—after which she started wearing a hormone patch on her hip, the cost covered by state medical assistance. CeCe watched with amazement as over the following months she developed smooth skin, fuller hips and, most fulfilling of all, breasts. Finally seeing her outer self match her inner self "was definitely something like a relief," she remembers. In an important move for CeCe, she called her mother to re-establish ties after years of separation. "Are those real?" Christi exclaimed when she finally got her first glimpse of CeCe post-hormones, and CeCe laughed in reply.

A legal name change tied a ribbon on CeCe's transition, a bureaucratic process that yielded a government ID identifying her by her carefully chosen new name: Chrishaun Reed Mai'luv McDonald. It was a name she liked for its mystique and personality; Chrishaun was also her aunt's name, keeping her tethered just a little bit to her past.

Secure in her identity at last, CeCe felt something free up within herself. And with confidence also came a new ability to stand up to street harassment; for perhaps the first time, she felt herself truly worth defending. "It's not OK that you called me a tranny," she'd lecture a surprised heckler. 'You're gonna apologize, and then you're gonna go home and think about why you turned my pretty smile into an ugly mug." Satisfied, she'd coolly walk on, her self-respect growing with each small triumph.

"She looked like someone who knew where she was heading in life," says Larry Thomas, who caught sight of CeCe at a corner store and, knowing full well she was trans, gave her his phone number—thus beginning, in fits and starts, that thing that eludes so many trans women: an actual in-the-daylight relationship. Thomas was a straight man who usually kept his "flings" with trans women on the down-low. But CeCe began occupying much of his time, and she started to wonder if she wasn't doomed to live a lonely life after all.

Then came more good fortune, when in May 2011, after a decade of couch-surfing homelessness, CeCe moved into the very first apartment of her own. It was a two-bedroom oasis she shared with a roommate. Though still unemployed—CeCe paid her rent with general assistance and SSI—she was certain now that she was a college student with a permanent address, that remaining piece of the puzzle would be forthcoming.

"I was feeling really accomplished," remembers CeCe wistfully as she stands on the sidewalk looking up at the weather-beaten three-story brick apartment building on an early spring day. She tries

flashing her patented wide smile, but it evaporates. We're taking a tour through her old neighborhood, and in skinny jeans, cropped jacket and a colorful head scarf, CeCe points at the second-floor window where she once lived, so full of potential and promise—a period that lasted for a single, shining month.

"I was just so happy with myself," she says, taking a fretful pull off her Newport. "I was unstoppable." She stubs out her cigarette and heads resolutely toward the passenger seat of my car for the next, most difficult stop on this sightseeing trip.

We drive slowly down East 29th Street, tracing the path CeCe walked just after midnight on June 5th, 2011. CeCe hasn't been back here since that fateful night, and as a maroon brick building with neon Bud Light signs comes into view, she clamps a hand to her belly. "Oooh, Jesus. I just get that little feeling inside," she says. We pull up alongside Schooner Tavern. "So. This is the bar," CeCe says, then in a sudden panic buries her face in her hands and hyperventilates, whispering, "Oh, my God. Oh, Lord, Lord, Lord. Oh, my goodness, Jesus Christ." A half-block past the bar CeCe speaks again, her voice trembling. "And somewhere at this point," she says, "is where I stabbed him."

In a police interrogation room hours after the stabbing, CeCe had given a full confession. "I was only trying to defend myself," CeCe sobbed. Police interviews with nearly a dozen witnesses would paint a consistent picture of the events of that night: Dean Schmitz and Molly Flaherty started the confrontation, Flaherty had triggered the fight by breaking a glass on CeCe's face, and Schmitz had pursued CeCe when she'd tried to escape—all precisely the way CeCe recounted in her confession. But no witness had seen exactly how the stabbing had transpired. "I didn't jab him; I didn't force the scissors into him; he was coming after me," CeCe insisted to detectives. "He ran into the scissors." And yet in Hennepin County Jail, CeCe was shocked to learn she was charged with second-degree murder. She faced up to 40 years in prison.

Dressed in orange scrubs, CeCe would cry and stare at the white brick walls of her cell for hours on end, her thoughts a tangle. There was the horrific knowledge that someone had died by her hand. And there was the agony that the life she'd been trying so hard to build had been decimated in an instant. "There wasn't a moment when I wasn't in pain mentally and spiritually, and even beating myself up for defending myself," CeCe says. She had nothing but time to obsess because she was locked alone in her cell for 23 hours a day. The jail had determined that for her own safety, she be held in solitary confinement.

Trans women have a difficult time behind bars, where they show up in disproportionate numbers; one survey found 16 percent of trans women had been to jail, compared to 2.7 percent of the general population. Once in prison they pose a dilemma, because, as a study of seven California prisons revealed, 59 percent of transgender inmates reported being sexually abused, compared to 4.4 percent of the general inmate population. A common solution, then, is to put them in solitary. For CeCe, who'd previously spent short stints in men's jails, the brain-racking isolation was a form of confinement she'd never known before. "There's no room for sanity," she says of her subsequent mental collapse. When her former caseworker Abby Beasley visited, Beasley was shocked at the sight of CeCe on the other side of the glass, scared and shaken, her left cheek swollen to the size of a golf ball.

"Whatever you can do to help me, please," CeCe begged.

Beasley notified the Trans Youth Support Network, a Minneapolis organization, which secured CeCe a pro bono lawyer. The case immediately galvanized the local trans and queer community, who saw CeCe's attack as something that could easily have happened to any of them, and hailed her as a hero. "CeCe was attacked in a racist, transphobic incident that could have killed her," says Billy Navarro Jr. of the Minnesota Transgender Health Coalition, who helped found the Free CeCe

campaign. "And then how is she treated? She is prosecuted for having the audacity to survive."

Her support base grew after the Florida shooting death of Trayvon Martin, which stoked a national debate over race, self-defense and justice. CeCe's supporters argued that unlike George Zimmerman, who would be acquitted of all charges, CeCe had been faced with an actual threat, against which she had stood her ground. But they feared the justice system would view CeCe, as a black trans woman, unkindly. A petition advocating for CeCe's release gathered more than 18,000 signatures from across the country. As supporters in FREE CECE T-shirts held rallies outside the jail and packed the courthouse for each hearing, defense lawyer Hersch Izek set about building a case.

"CeCe was defending herself against a racist, a bigot, someone who had all sorts of issues against the LGBT community," says Izek, an aging hippie with long, sparse gray hair, a tie-dyed tie and a Bob Marley poster on his office wall. "And you couldn't understand what she did, and what this so-called victim did, without that context." The Hennepin County Attorney's Office, however, presented the scenario as simply the slaying of an unarmed man by a person with a weapon—who had a legal obligation to flee the scene. Minnesota forbids the use of deadly force in self-defense if you can avoid being harmed, for example, by running away. Prosecutors speculated that what had in fact occurred between CeCe and Schmitz was the very definition of intentional, unprovoked murder. "CeCe took shears and thrust them into his heart and killed him," says Hennepin County Attorney Michael Freeman. "We try to treat every case being blind to sex, sexual orientation, economic status. And it's not being insensitive to CeCe to say this was a bar fight. The bottom line is, did her actions result in the death of another? The answer is yes."

The months leading to trial saw the judge's rulings laying waste to CeCe's defense case. Evidence of Schmitz's swastika tattoo was deemed inadmissible, since CeCe never saw the tattoo—it had no bearing on her mindset at the time of the killing—and because, Judge Daniel Moreno wrote, "the tattoo does not establish that [Schmitz] intended to threaten, fight or kill anyone." Schmitz's prior assault convictions were deemed irrelevant, and the judge would allow only limited testimony about the toxicology report showing Schmitz was high on meth, feeding his aggression. The defense's bid to include expert testimony about the lives of transgender women also failed. "The idea was to show the violence transgender individuals face, to bolster the self-defense claim," says Izek. "We'd have to be educating the jury about what it meant to be transgender. That would be difficult. Most wouldn't even know what that meant."

Seated at the defense table with a headache on the morning of the trial, May 2nd, 2012, CeCe looked at the mostly white jury staring back at her. She knew those expressions all too well. She'd been intent on seeing her case through, but glancing at those tasked with deciding her fate, she gave up. "These people weren't going to let me win," she says. She accepted a deal and pleaded guilty to second-degree manslaughter. Her supporters in the courtroom cried as the judge led her through her admission of guilt. CeCe tried her best to choke back tears as she was led from the courtroom, overwhelmed by what was next for her: A 41-month sentence in a state men's prison.

In a tiny office that serves as the de facto Free CeCe headquarters, Navarro, a burly, bearded trans man in overalls, checks his computer for CeCe's fan mail. "Somebody wants to know if you got a tank top?" he asks.

"Oh, T-GIRLS ROCK?" CeCe asks, distracted by her phone.

"Yeah. Can you tweet a picture of you wearing it?" Navarro shoots her an adoring grin. This crammed room tucked next door to Cafe South-Side is known as the "Shot Clinic" for its main attraction: a brightly lit closet, inside of which a volunteer is currently administering a hormone injection to a trans man. This building serves as headquarters for three Minnesota transgender organizations. Together, the groups have knitted a

vibrant infrastructure for the local trans community: improving health care access, arranging support groups, promoting trans artists and hosting parties and concerts. Their grassroots efforts have created a trans refuge, and have earned the Twin Cities a reputation as two of the nation's most trans-friendly, alongside San Francisco, New York and Seattle, each of which boasts similar community-driven hubs tailored around its members' unique needs. The idea for this Shot Clinic, for example, was born of a rather specific need. "Billy's scared of needles," Navarro says of himself faux-bashfully. So he implemented a program that trains volunteers to administer hormones to the squeamish. Fifteen to 20 patients now come in each week; bags of oranges lay around the office for those wanting to perfect their needle-stick technique.

A patient emerges from the closet, face slack with relief, and reports of today's injection volunteer: "He seems to know what he's doing!" Everyone laughs, with CeCe's guffaw, as always, loudest of all. Here, CeCe has found sanctuary. Everyone who bustles through the tiny office pauses to beam at her or give her a squeeze, and she opens her arms to each. She's at home in this space, cherished and protected, but also a star; no matter where she's standing, everyone aligns in her direction.

"She's legendary," one friend says later, and CeCe lets out an open-mouthed cackle. "I like that! Legendary," she repeats.

CeCe was released from the Minnesota Correctional Facility in St. Cloud in January after 19 months, her sentence reduced for good behavior and for the 275 days she'd served prior to trial. While in prison she'd been intent on staying positive and grateful for having continued access to her hormones, and having her own cell with a TV, where she'd escape the hyper-masculinity of her fellow inmates for Sex and the City marathons on E!. She says she never encountered violence, kept mostly to herself and even made a couple of friends. Mostly, she tried to work on recovering, and on remaining sane. When she was notified that Molly Flaherty was being prosecuted for attacking her, CeCe declined to testify, viewing it as a pointless act of vengeance potentially bad for her own mental health. (Flaherty pleaded guilty to third-degree assault and was sentenced to six months in jail.) "It's easy, especially for a person who's been through so much, to be a cruel and coldhearted person. But I chose not to be," CeCe says.

Outside encouragement helped. During her incarceration, the Free CeCe campaign continued spreading via social media, with chapters as far-off as Paris and Glasgow sending her mail. Upon CeCe's release, prominent trans activist Janet Mock asked her Twitter followers to tweet about what CeCe meant to them, and the outpouring of responses sent the hashtag #BecauseOfCeCe trending. CeCe is a little awestruck by her celebrity status. She's been stunned to come across a photo online of her own face tattooed upon a stranger's arm. She's been asked to help lead Seattle's Pride parade. Her parole officer has let her travel to New York and San Francisco to parlay her fame into activism and to film a documentary, Free CeCe, coproduced by Laverne Cox.

And yet to see CeCe trudging down the street from the Shot Clinic to the place she's calling home, you'd never know she's having her moment. Despite a strong network of friends, and the continued affections of her boyfriend—both lifelines to her—she's struggling. She has residual PTSD and trust issues. She's unemployed, and with a felony on her record, she's less hopeful about the job applications she's been filling out. For now, CeCe is living on food stamps and the remaining funds raised by the Free CeCe campaign; for her housing, she's crashing with a kind supporter in a small spare bedroom.

"My story wouldn't have been important had I been killed. Because it's like nobody cares," CeCe says forcefully at her dining-room table, as day turns to evening. A shiny, sickle-shaped scar cuts across the jawbone of her left cheek, a permanent reminder of her tragic walk to the supermarket. "But fortunately for me, I'm a survivor. I'm not gonna beat myself up for being a woman, I'm not gonna beat myself up for being trans, I'm not gonna beat myself up for defending myself." She smacks her lips for punctuation. "'Cause I am a survivor," she repeats in a voice sharp with conviction, while watching carefully for my assent. CeCe's still trying to come to terms with the way that evening disrupted her life, and the ground she must regain. Underneath her aura of loving positivity, she's angry as she grapples to understand her significance to a community that needs her inspiration so badly, and what it means to be heralded as a survivor, when her day-to-day survival feels so frustratingly precarious. She still has to get to the grocery store, after all, and despite all CeCe has been through, she still waits until nightfall.

Questions for Critical Thinking

1. The experiences of CeCe McDonald illustrate the ways in which violence is used as a form of social control. What are some of the ways in which violence is used against people of color and those who identify as transgender to maintain stratification based on race, sex, and gender?

2. Beyond the direct violence exhibited in this essay, what are some of the barriers that people who identify as transgender continue to face in society? How do these barriers impact all of us, regardless of our gender identity?

3. How might the acceptance of people who identify as transgender help to reduce problems of inequality based on sex and gender in society?

Nickel-and-Dimed

On (Not) Getting by in America

BARBARA EHRENREICH

The following essay is an excerpt from the book Nickel and Dimed: On (Not) Getting by in America *by journalist Barbara Ehrenreich. In this ethnographic study on low-wage jobs in America, Ehrenreich's experiences illustrate the complexity of barriers faced by workers in such occupations in the United States.*

At the beginning of June 1998 I leave behind everything that normally soothes the ego and sustains the body—home, career, companion, reputation, ATM card—for a plunge into the low-wage workforce. There, I become another, occupationally much diminished "Barbara Ehrenreich"—depicted on job-application forms as a divorced homemaker whose sole work experience consists of housekeeping in a few private homes. I am terrified, at the beginning, of being unmasked for what I am: a middle-class journalist setting out to explore the world that welfare mothers are entering, at the rate of approximately 50,000 a month, as welfare reform kicks in. Happily, though, my fears turn out to be entirely unwarranted: during a month of poverty and toil, my name goes unnoticed and for the most part unuttered. In this parallel universe where my father never got out of the mines and I never got through college, I am "baby," "honey," "blondie," and, most commonly, "girl."

My first task is to find a place to live. I figure that if I can earn $7 an hour—which, from the want ads, seems doable—I can afford to spend $500 on rent, or maybe, with severe economies, $600. In the Key West area, where I live, this pretty much confines me to flophouses and trailer homes—like the one, a pleasing fifteen-minute drive from town, that has no air-conditioning, no screens, no fans, no television, and, by way of diversion, only the challenge of evading the landlord's Doberman pinscher. The big problem with this place, though, is the rent, which at $675 a month is well beyond my reach. All right, Key West is expensive. But so is New York City, or the Bay Area, or Jackson Hole, or Telluride, or Boston, or any other place where tourists and the wealthy compete for living space with the people who clean their toilets and fry their hash browns.[1] Still, it is a shock to realize that "trailer trash" has become, for me, a demographic category to aspire to.

So I decide to make the common trade-off between affordability and convenience, and go for a $500-a-month efficiency thirty miles up a two-lane highway from the employment opportunities of Key West, meaning forty-five minutes if there's no road construction and I don't get caught behind some sun-dazed Canadian tourists. I hate the drive, along a roadside studded with white crosses commemorating the more effective head-on collisions, but it's a sweet little place—a cabin, more or less, set in the swampy back yard of the converted mobile home where my landlord, an affable TV repairman, lives with his bartender girlfriend. Anthropologically speaking, a bustling trailer park would be preferable, but here I have a gleaming white floor and a firm mattress, and the few resident bugs are easily vanquished.

Besides, I am not doing this for the anthropology. My aim is nothing so mistily subjective as to "experience poverty" or find out how it "really feels" to be a long-term low-wage worker. I've had enough unchosen encounters with poverty and the world of low-wage work to know it's not a place you want to visit for touristic purposes; it just smells too much like fear. And with all my real-life assets—bank account, IRA, health insurance, multiroom home—waiting indulgently in the background, I am, of course, thoroughly insulated from the terrors that afflict the genuinely poor.

No, this is a purely objective, scientific sort of mission. The humanitarian rationale for welfare reform—as opposed to the more punitive and stingy impulses that may actually have motivated it—is that work will lift poor women out of poverty while simultaneously inflating their self-esteem and hence their future value in the labor market. Thus, whatever the hassles involved in finding child care, transportation, etc., the transition from welfare to work will end happily, in greater prosperity for all. Now there are many problems with this comforting prediction, such as the fact that the economy will inevitably undergo a downturn, eliminating many jobs. Even without a downturn, the influx of a million former welfare recipients into the low-wage labor market could depress wages by as much as 11.9 percent, according to the Economic Policy Institute (EPI) in Washington, D.C.

But is it really possible to make a living on the kinds of jobs currently available to unskilled people? Mathematically, the answer is no, as can be shown by taking $6 to $7 an hour, perhaps subtracting a dollar or two an hour for child care, multiplying by 160 hours a month, and comparing the result to the prevailing rents. According to the National Coalition for the Homeless, for example, in 1998 it took, on average nationwide, an hourly

wage of $8.89 to afford a one-bedroom apartment, and the Preamble Center for Public Policy estimates that the odds against a typical welfare recipient's landing a job at such a "living wage" are about 97 to 1. If these numbers are right, low-wage work is not a solution to poverty and possibly not even to homelessness.

It may seem excessive to put this proposition to an experimental test. As certain family members keep unhelpfully reminding me, the viability of low-wage work could be tested, after a fashion, without ever leaving my study. I could just pay myself $7 an hour for eight hours a day, charge myself for room and board, and total up the numbers after a month. Why leave the people and work that I love? But I am an experimental scientist by training. In that business, you don't just sit at a desk and theorize; you plunge into the everyday chaos of nature, where surprises lurk in the most mundane measurements. Maybe, when I got into it, I would discover some hidden economies in the world of the low-wage worker. After all, if 30 percent of the workforce toils for less than $8 an hour, according to the EPI, they may have found some tricks as yet unknown to me. Maybe—who knows?—I would even be able to detect in myself the bracing psychological effects of getting out of the house, as promised by the welfare wonks at places like the Heritage Foundation. Or, on the other hand, maybe there would be unexpected costs—physical, mental, or financial—to throw off all my calculations. Ideally, I should do this with two small children in tow, that being the welfare average, but mine are grown and no one is willing to lend me theirs for a month-long vacation in penury. So this is not the perfect experiment, just a test of the best possible case: an unencumbered woman, smart and even strong, attempting to live more or less off the land.

On the morning of my first full day of job searching, I take a red pen to the want ads, which are auspiciously numerous. Everyone in Key West's booming "hospitality industry" seems to be looking for someone like me—trainable, flexible, and with suitably humble expectations as to pay. . . .

Most of the big hotels run ads almost continually, just to build a supply of applicants to replace the current workers as they drift away or are fired, so finding a job is just a matter of being at the right place at the right time and flexible enough to take whatever is being offered that day. This finally happens to me at one of the big discount hotel chains, where I go, as usual, for housekeeping and am sent, instead, to try out as a waitress at the attached "family restaurant," a dismal spot with a counter and about thirty tables that looks out on a parking garage and features such tempting fare as "Polish [sic] sausage and BBQ sauce" on 95-degree days. Phillip, the dapper young West Indian who introduces himself as the manager, interviews me with about as much enthusiasm as if he were a clerk processing me for Medicare, the principal questions being what shifts can I work and when can I start. I mutter something about being woefully out of practice as a waitress, but he's already on to the uniform: I'm to show up tomorrow wearing black slacks and black shoes; he'll provide the rust-colored polo shirt with HEARTHSIDE embroidered on it, though I might want to wear my own shirt to get to work, ha ha. At the word "tomorrow," something between fear and indignation rises in my chest. I want to say, "Thank you for your time, sir, but this is just an experiment, you know, not my actual life."

So begins my career at the Hearthside, I shall call it, one small profit center within a global discount hotel chain, where for two weeks I work from 2:00 till 10:00 P.M. for $2.43 an hour plus tips.[2] In some futile bid for gentility, the management has barred employees from using the front door, so my first day I enter through the kitchen, where a red-faced man with shoulder-length blond hair is throwing frozen steaks against the wall and yelling, "Fuck this shit!" "That's just Jack," explains Gail, the wiry middle-aged waitress who is assigned to train me. "He's on the rag again"—a condition occasioned, in this instance, by the fact that the cook on the morning shift had forgotten to thaw out the steaks. For the next eight hours, I run after the agile

Gail, absorbing bits of instruction along with fragments of personal tragedy. All food must be trayed, and the reason she's so tired today is that she woke up in a cold sweat thinking of her boyfriend, who killed himself recently in an upstate prison. No refills on lemonade. And the reason he was in prison is that a few DUIs caught up with him, that's all, could have happened to anyone. Carry the creamers to the table in a monkey bowl, never in your hand. And after he was gone she spent several months living in her truck, peeing in a plastic pee bottle and reading by candlelight at night, but you can't live in a truck in the summer, since you need to have the windows down, which means anything can get in, from mosquitoes on up.

At least Gail puts to rest any fears I had of appearing overqualified. From the first day on, I find that of all the things I have left behind, such as home and identity, what I miss the most is competence. Not that I have ever felt utterly competent in the writing business, in which one day's success augurs nothing at all for the next. But in my writing life, I at least have some notion of procedure: do the research, make the outline, rough out a draft, etc. As a server, though I am beset by requests like bees: more iced tea here, ketchup over there, a to-go box for table fourteen, and where are the high chairs, anyway? Of the twenty-seven tables, up to six are usually mine at any time, though on slow afternoons or if Gail is off, I sometimes have the whole place to myself. There is the touch-screen computer-ordering system to master, which is, I suppose, meant to minimize server–cook contact, but in practice requires constant verbal fine-tuning: "That's gravy on the mashed, okay? None on the meatloaf," and so forth—while the cook scowls as if I were inventing these refinements just to torment him. Plus, something I had forgotten in the years since I was eighteen: about a third of a server's job is "side work" that's invisible to customers—sweeping, scrubbing, slicing, refilling, and restocking. If it isn't all done, every little bit of it, you're going to face the 6:00 P.M. dinner rush defenseless and probably go down in flames. I screw up dozens of times at the beginning, sustained in my shame entirely by Gail's support—"It's okay, baby, everyone does that sometime"—because, to my total surprise and despite the scientific detachment I am doing my best to maintain, I care. . . .

On my first Friday at the Hearthside there is a "mandatory meeting for all restaurant employees," which I attend, eager for insight into our overall marketing strategy and the niche (your basic Ohio cuisine with a tropical twist?) we aim to inhabit. But there is no "we" at this meeting. Phillip, our top manager except for an occasional "consultant" sent out by corporate headquarters, opens it with a sneer: "The break room—it's disgusting. Butts in the ashtrays, newspapers lying around, crumbs." This windowless little room, which also houses the time clock for the entire hotel, is where we stash our bags and civilian clothes and take our half-hour meal breaks. But a break room is not a right, he tells us. It can be taken away. We should also know that the lockers in the break room and whatever is in them can be searched at any time. Then comes gossip; there has been gossip; gossip (which seems to mean employees talking among themselves) must stop. Off-duty employees are henceforth barred from eating at the restaurant, because "other servers gather around them and gossip." When Phillip has exhausted his agenda of rebukes, Joan complains about the condition of the ladies' room and I throw in my two bits about the vacuum cleaner. But I don't see any backup coming from my fellow servers, each of whom has subsided into her own personal funk; Gail, my role model, stares sorrowfully at a point six inches from her nose. The meeting ends when Andy, one of the cooks, gets up, muttering about breaking up his day off for this almighty bullshit.

Just four days later we are suddenly summoned into the kitchen at 3:30 P.M., even though there are live tables on the floor. We all—about ten of us—stand around Phillip, who announces grimly that there has been a report of some "drug activity" on the night shift and that, as a result, we are now to be a "drug-free" workplace, meaning that all new hires will be tested, as will possibly current

employees on a random basis. I am glad that this part of the kitchen is so dark, because I find myself blushing as hard as if I had been caught toking up in the ladies' room myself: I haven't been treated this way—lined up in the corridor, threatened with locker searches, peppered with carelessly aimed accusations—since junior high school. Back on the floor, Joan cracks, "Next they'll be telling us we can't have sex on the job." When I ask Stu what happened to inspire the crackdown, he just mutters about "management decisions" and takes the opportunity to upbraid Gail and me for being too generous with the rolls. From now on there's to be only one per customer, and it goes out with the dinner, not with the salad. He's also been riding the cooks, prompting Andy to come out of the kitchen and observe—with the serenity of a man whose customary implement is a butcher knife—that "Stu has a death wish today."

The other problem, in addition to the less-than-nurturing management style, is that this job shows no sign of being financially viable. You might imagine, from a comfortable distance, that people who live, year in and year out, on $6 to $10 an hour have discovered some survival stratagems unknown to the middle class. But no. It's not hard to get my co-workers to talk about their living situations, because housing, in almost every case, is the principal source of disruption in their lives, the first thing they fill you in on when they arrive for their shifts. After a week, I have compiled the following survey:

- Gail is sharing a room in a well-known downtown flophouse for which she and a roommate pay about $250 a week. Her roommate, a male friend, has begun hitting on her, driving her nuts, but the rent would be impossible alone.
- Claude, the Haitian cook, is desperate to get out of the two-room apartment he shares with his girlfriend and two other, unrelated, people. As far as I can determine, the other Haitian men (most of whom only speak Creole) live in similarly crowded situations.

- Annette, a twenty-year-old server who is six months pregnant and has been abandoned by her boyfriend, lives with her mother, a postal clerk.
- Marianne and her boyfriend are paying $170 a week for a one-person trailer.
- Jack, who is, at $10 an hour, the wealthiest of us, lives in the trailer he owns, paying only the $400-a-month lot fee.
- The other white cook, Andy, lives on his dry-docked boat, which, as far as I can tell from his loving descriptions, can't be more than twenty feet long. He offers to take me out on it, once it's repaired, but the offer comes with inquiries as to my marital status, so I do not follow up on it.
- Tina and her husband are paying $60 a night for a double room in a Days Inn. This is because they have no car and the Days Inn is within walking distance of the Hearthside. When Marianne, one of the breakfast servers, is tossed out of her trailer for subletting (which is against the trailer-park rules), she leaves her boyfriend and moves in with Tina and her husband.
- Joan, who had fooled me with her numerous and tasteful outfits (hostesses wear their own clothes), lives in a van she parks behind a shopping center at night and showers in Tina's motel room. The clothes are from thrift shops.[3]

It strikes me, in my middle-class solipsism, that there is gross improvidence in some of these arrangements. When Gail and I are wrapping silverware in napkins—the only task for which we are permitted to sit—she tells me she is thinking of escaping from her roommate by moving into the Days Inn herself. I am astounded: How can she even think of paying between $40 and $60 a day? But if I was afraid of sounding like a social worker, I come out just sounding like a fool. She squints at me in disbelief, "And where am I supposed to get a month's rent and a month's deposit for an apartment?" I'd been feeling pretty smug about my $500 efficiency, but of course it was made possible only by the $1,300 I had allotted myself for start-up costs when I began my low-wage life: $1,000 for the first month's rent and deposit, $100 for initial groceries and cash in my pocket, $200 stuffed away for emergencies. In poverty, as in certain propositions in physics, starting conditions are everything.

There are no secret economies that nourish the poor; on the contrary, there are a host of special costs. If you can't put up the two months' rent you need to secure an apartment, you end up paying through the nose for a room by the week. If you have only a room, with a hot plate at best, you can't save by cooking up huge lentil stews that can be frozen for the week ahead. You eat fast food, or the hot dogs and styrofoam cups of soup that can be microwaved in a convenience store. If you have no money for health insurance—and the Hearthside's niggardly plan kicks in only after three months—you go without routine care or prescription drugs and end up paying the price. Gail, for example, was fine until she ran out of money for estrogen pills. She is supposed to be on the company plan by now, but they claim to have lost her application form and need to begin the paperwork all over again. So she spends $9 per migraine pill to control the headaches she wouldn't have, she insists, if her estrogen supplements were covered. Similarly, Marianne's boyfriend lost his job as a roofer because he missed so much time after getting a cut on his foot for which he couldn't afford the prescribed antibiotic.

My own situation, when I sit down to assess it after two weeks of work, would not be much better if this were my actual life. The seductive thing about waitressing is that you don't have to wait for payday to feel a few bills in your pocket, and my tips usually cover meals and gas, plus something left over to stuff into the kitchen drawer I use as a bank. But as the tourist business slows in the summer heat, I sometimes leave work with only $20 in tips (the gross is higher, but servers share about 15 percent of their tips with the busboys and bartenders). With wages included, this amounts to about the minimum wage of $5.15 an hour. Although the sum in the drawer is piling up, at the present rate of accumulation it will be more than a hundred dollars short of my rent when the end of the month comes around. Nor can I see any expenses to cut. True, I haven't gone the lentil-stew route yet, but that's because I don't have a large cooking pot, pot holders, or a ladle to stir with (which cost about $30 at Kmart, less at thrift stores), not to mention onions, carrots, and the indispensable bay leaf. I do make my lunch almost every day—usually some slow-burning, high-protein combo like frozen chicken patties with melted cheese on top and canned pinto beans on the side. Dinner is at the Hearthside, which offers its employees a choice of BLT, fish sandwich, or hamburger for only $2. The burger lasts longest, especially if it's heaped with gut-puckering jalapenos, but by midnight my stomach is growling again.

So unless I want to start using my car as a residence, I have to find a second, or alternative, job. I call all the hotels where I filled out housekeeping applications weeks ago—the Hyatt, Holiday Inn, Econo Lodge, Hojo's, Best Western, plus a half dozen or so locally run guesthouses. Nothing. Then I start making the rounds again, wasting whole mornings waiting for some assistant manager to show up, even dipping into places so creepy that the front-desk clerk greets you from behind bulletproof glass and sells pints of liquor over the counter. But either someone has exposed my real-life housekeeping habits—which are, shall we say, mellow—or I am at the wrong end of some infallible ethnic equation: most, but by no means all, of the working housekeepers I see on my job searches are African Americans, Spanish-speaking, or immigrants from the Central European post-Communist world, whereas servers are almost invariably white and monolingually English-speaking. When I finally get a positive response, I have been identified once again as server material. Jerry's, which is part of a well-known national family restaurant chain and physically attached here to another budget hotel chain, is ready to use me at once. The prospect is

both exciting and terrifying, because, with about the same number of tables and counter seats, Jerry's attracts three or four times the volume of customers as the gloomy old Hearthside. . . .

I start out with the beautiful, heroic idea of handling the two jobs at once, and for two days I almost do it: the breakfast/lunch shift at Jerry's, which goes till 2:00, arriving at the Hearthside at 2:10, and attempting to hold out until 10:00. In the ten minutes between jobs, I pick up a spicy chicken sandwich at the Wendy's drive-through window, gobble it down in the car, and change from khaki slacks to black, from Hawaiian to rust polo. There is a problem, though. When during the 3:00 to 4:00 P.M. dead time I finally sit down to wrap silver, my flesh seems to bond to the seat. I try to refuel with a purloined cup of soup, as I've seen Gail and Joan do dozens of times, but a manager catches me and hisses "No eating!" though there's not a customer around to be offended by the sight of food making contact with a server's lips. So I tell Gail I'm going to quit, and she hugs me and says she might just follow me to Jerry's herself.

But the chances of this are minuscule. She has left the flophouse and her annoying roommate and is back to living in her beat-up old truck. But guess what? she reports to me excitedly later that evening: Phillip has given her permission to park overnight in the hotel parking lot, as long as she keeps out of sight, and the parking lot should be totally safe, since it's patrolled by a hotel security guard! With the Hearthside offering benefits like that, how could anyone think of leaving? . . .

Management at Jerry's is generally calmer and more "professional" than at the Hearthside, with two exceptions. One is Joy, a plump, blowsy woman in her early thirties, who once kindly devoted several minutes to instructing me in the correct one-handed method of carrying trays but whose moods change disconcertingly from shift to shift and even within one. Then there's B.J., a.k.a. B.J.-the-bitch, whose contribution is to stand by the kitchen counter and yell, "Nita, your order's up, move it!" or, "Barbara, didn't you see you've got another table out there? Come on, girl!" Among other things, she is hated for having replaced the whipped-cream squirt cans with big plastic whipped-cream-filled baggies that have to be squeezed with both hands— because, reportedly, she saw or thought she saw employees trying to inhale the propellant gas from the squirt cans, in the hope that it might be nitrous oxide. On my third night, she pulls me aside abruptly and brings her face so close that it looks as if she's planning to butt me with her forehead. But instead of saying, "You're fired," she says, "You're doing fine." The only trouble is I'm spending time chatting with customers: "That's how they're getting you." Furthermore I am letting them "run me," which means harassment by sequential demands: you bring the ketchup and they decide they want extra Thousand Island; you bring that and they announce they now need a side of fries; and so on into distraction. Finally she tells me not to take her wrong. She tries to say things in a nice way, but you get into a mode, you know, because everything has to move so fast. . . .[4]

I make the decision to move closer to Key West. First, because of the drive. Second and third, also because of the drive: gas is eating up $4 to $5 a day, and although Jerry's is as high-volume as you can get, the tips average only 10 percent, and not just for a newbie like me. Between the base pay of $2.15 an hour and the obligation to share tips with the busboys and dishwashers, we're averaging only about $7.50 an hour. Then there is the $30 I had to spend on the regulation tan slacks worn by Jerry's servers—a setback it could take weeks to absorb. (I had combed the town's two downscale department stores hoping for something cheaper but decided in the end that these marked-down Dockers, originally $49, were more likely to survive a daily washing.) Of my fellow servers, everyone who lacks a working husband or boyfriend seems to have a second job: Nita does something at a computer eight hours a day; another welds. Without the forty-five-minute commute, I can picture myself working two jobs and having the time to shower between them.

So I take the $500 deposit I have coming from my landlord, the $400 I have earned toward the next month's rent; plus the $200 reserved for emergencies, and use the $1,100 to pay the rent and deposit on trailer number 46 in the Overseas Trailer Park, a mile from the cluster of budget hotels that constitute Key West's version of an industrial park. Number 46 is about eight feet in width and shaped like a barbell inside, with a narrow region— because of the sink and the stove—separating the bedroom from what might optimistically be called the "living" area, with its two-person table and half-sized couch. The bathroom is so small my knees rub against the shower stall when I sit on the toilet, and you can't just leap out of the bed; you have to climb down to the foot of it in order to find a patch of floor space to stand on. Outside, I am within a few yards of a liquor store, a bar that advertises "free beer tomorrow," a convenience store, and a Burger King—but no supermarket or, alas, laundromat. By reputation, the Overseas park is a nest of crime and crack, and I am hoping at least for some vibrant, multicultural street life. But desolation rules night and day, except for a thin stream of pedestrian traffic heading for their jobs at the Sheraton or 7-Eleven. There are not exactly people here but what amounts to canned labor, being preserved from the heat between shifts.

In line with my reduced living conditions, a new form of ugliness arises at Jerry's. First we are confronted—via an announcement on the computers through which we input orders—with the new rule that the hotel bar is henceforth off-limits to restaurant employees. The culprit, I learn through the grapevine, is the ultra-efficient gal who trained me—another trailer-home dweller and a mother of three. Something had set her off one morning, so she slipped out for a nip and returned to the floor impaired. This mostly hurts Ellen, whose habit it is to free her hair from its rubber band and drop by the bar for a couple of Zins before heading home at the end of the shift, but all of us feel the chill. Then the next day, when I go for straws, for the first time I find the dry-storage room locked. Ted, the portly assistant manager who opens it for me, explains that he caught one of the dishwashers attempting to steal something, and, unfortunately, the miscreant will be with us until a replacement can be found—hence the locked door. I neglect to ask what he had been trying to steal, but Ted tells me who he is—the kid with the buzz cut and the earring. You know, he's back there right now.

I wish I could say I rushed back and confronted George to get his side of the story. I wish I could say I stood up to Ted and insisted that George be given a translator and allowed to defend himself, or announced that I'd find a lawyer who'd handle the case pro bono. The mystery to me is that there's not much worth stealing in the dry-storage room, at least not in any fenceable quantity: "Is Gyorgi here, and am having 200—maybe 250—ketchup packets. What do you say?" My guess is that he had taken—if he had taken anything at all—some Saltines or a can of cherry-pie mix, and that the motive for taking it was hunger.

So why didn't I intervene? Certainly not because I was held back by the kind of moral paralysis that can pass as journalistic objectivity. On the contrary, something new—something loathsome and servile—had infected me, along with the kitchen odors that I could still sniff on my bra when I finally undressed at night. In real life I am moderately brave, but plenty of brave people shed their courage in concentration camps, and maybe something similar goes on in the infinitely more congenial milieu of the low-wage American workplace. Maybe, in a month or two more at Jerry's, I might have regained my crusading spirit. Then again, in a month or two I might have turned into a different person altogether—say, the kind of person who would have turned George in.

But this is not something I am slated to find out. When my month-long plunge into poverty is almost over, I finally land my dream job—housekeeping. I do this by walking into the personnel office of the only place I figure I might have some credibility, the hotel attached to Jerry's, and confiding urgently that I have to have a second job

if I am to pay my rent and, no, it couldn't be front-desk clerk. "All right," the personnel lady fairly spits, "so it's housekeeping," and she marches me back to meet Maria, the housekeeping manager, a tiny, frenetic Hispanic woman who greets me as "babe" and hands me a pamphlet emphasizing the need for a positive attitude. The hours are nine in the morning till whenever, the pay is $6.10 an hour, and there's one week of vacation a year. I don't have to ask about health insurance once I meet Carlotta, the middle-aged African-American woman who will be training me. Carla, as she tells me to call her, is missing all of her top front teeth.

On that first day of housekeeping and last day of my entire project—although I don't yet know it's the last—Carla is in a foul mood. We have been given nineteen rooms to clean, most of them "checkouts," as opposed to "stay-overs," that require the whole enchilada of bed-stripping, vacuuming, and bathroom-scrubbing. When one of the rooms that had been listed as a stay-over turns out to be a checkout, Carla calls Maria to complain, but of course to no avail. "So make up the motherfucker," Carla orders me, and I do the beds while she sloshes around the bathroom. For four hours without a break I strip and remake beds, taking about four and a half minutes per queen-sized bed, which I could get down to three if there were any reason to. We try to avoid vacuuming by picking up the larger specks by hand, but often there is nothing to do but drag the monstrous vacuum cleaner—it weighs about thirty pounds—off our cart and try to wrestle it around the floor. Sometimes Carla hands me the squirt bottle of "BAM" (an acronym for something that begins, ominously, with "butyric"; the rest has been worn off the label) and lets me do the bathrooms. No service ethic challenges me here to new heights of performance. I just concentrate on removing the pubic hairs from the bathtubs, or at least the dark ones that I can see. . . .

When I request permission to leave at about 3:30, another housekeeper warns me that no one has so far succeeded in combining housekeeping at the hotel with serving at Jerry's: "Some kid did it once for five days, and you're no kid." With that helpful information in mind, I rush back to number 46, down four Advils (the name brand this time), shower, stooping to fit into the stall, and attempt to compose myself for the oncoming shift. So much for what Marx termed the "reproduction of labor power," meaning the things a worker has to do just so she'll be ready to work again. The only unforeseen obstacle to the smooth transition from job to job is that my tan Jerry's slacks, which had looked reasonably clean by 40-watt bulb last night when I handwashed my Hawaiian shirt, prove by daylight to be mottled with ketchup and ranch-dressing stains. I spend most of my hour-long break between jobs attempting to remove the edible portions with a sponge and then drying the slacks over the hood of my car in the sun.

I can do this two-job thing, is my theory, if I can drink enough caffeine and avoid getting distracted by George's ever more obvious suffering.[5] The first few days after being caught he seemed not to understand the trouble he was in, and our chirpy little conversations had continued. But the last couple of shifts he's been listless and unshaven, and tonight he looks like the ghost we all know him to be, with dark half-moons hanging from his eyes. At one point, when I am briefly immobilized by the task of filling little paper cups with sour cream for baked potatoes, he comes over and looks as if he'd like to explore the limits of our shared vocabulary, but I am called to the floor for a table. I resolve to give him all my tips that night and to hell with the experiment in low-wage money management. At eight, Ellen and I grab a snack together standing at the mephitic end of the kitchen counter, but I can only manage two or three mozzarella sticks and lunch had been a mere handful of McNuggets. I am not tired at all, I assure myself, though it may be that there is simply no more "I" left to do the tiredness monitoring. What I would see, if I were more alert to the situation, is that the forces of destruction are already massing against me. There is only one cook on duty, a young man named

Jesus ("Hay-Sue," that is) and he is new to the job. And there is Joy, who shows up to take over in the middle of the shift, wearing high heels and a long, clingy white dress and fuming as if she'd just been stood up in some cocktail bar.

Then it comes, the perfect storm. Four of my tables fill up at once. Four tables is nothing for me now, but only so long as they are obligingly staggered. As I bev table 27, tables 25, 28, and 24 are watching enviously. As I bev 25, 24 glowers because their bevs haven't even been ordered. Twenty-eight is four yuppyish types, meaning everything on the side and agonizing instructions as to the chicken Caesars. Twenty-five is a middle-aged black couple, who complain, with some justice, that the iced tea isn't fresh and the tabletop is sticky. But table 24 is the meteorological event of the century: ten British tourists who seem to have made the decision to absorb the American experience entirely by mouth. Here everyone has at least two drinks—iced tea and milk shake, Michelob and water (with lemon slice, please)—and a huge promiscuous orgy of breakfast specials, mozz sticks, chicken strips, quesadillas, burgers with cheese and without, sides of hash browns with cheddar, with onions, with gravy, seasoned fries, plain fries, banana splits. Poor Jesus! Poor me! Because when I arrive with their first tray of food—after three prior trips just to refill bevs—Princess Di refuses to eat her chicken strips with her pancake-and-sausage special, since, as she now reveals, the strips were meant to be an appetizer. Maybe the others would have accepted their meals, but Di, who is deep into her third Michelob, insists that everything else go back while they work on their "starters." Meanwhile, the yuppies are waving me down for more decaf and the black couple looks ready to summon the NAACP.

Much of what happened next is lost in the fog of war. Jesus starts going under. The little printer on the counter in front of him is spewing out orders faster than he can rip them off, much less produce the meals. Even the invincible Ellen is ashen from stress. I bring table 24 their reheated main courses, which they immediately reject as either too cold or fossilized by the microwave. When I return to the kitchen with their trays (three trays in three trips), Joy confronts me with arms akimbo: "What is this?" She means the food—the plates of rejected pancakes, hash browns in assorted flavors, toasts, burgers, sausages, eggs. "Uh, scrambled with cheddar," I try, "and that's . . ." "NO," she screams in my face. "Is it a traditional, a super-scramble, an eye-opener?" I pretend to study my check for a clue, but entropy has been up to its tricks, not only on the plates but in my head, and I have to admit that the original order is beyond reconstruction. "You don't know an eye-opener from a traditional?" she demands in outrage. All I know, in fact, is that my legs have lost interest in the current venture and have announced their intention to fold. I am saved by a yuppie (mercifully not one of mine) who chooses this moment to charge into the kitchen to bellow that his food is twenty-five minutes late. Joy screams at him to get the hell out of her kitchen, please, and then turns on Jesus in a fury, hurling an empty tray across the room for emphasis.

I leave. I don't walk out; I just leave. I don't finish my side work or pick up my credit-card tips, if any, at the cash register or, of course, ask Joy's permission to go. And the surprising thing is that you can walk out without permission, that the door opens, that the thick tropical night air parts to let me pass, that my car is still parked where I left it. There is no vindication in this exit, no fuck-you surge of relief, just an overwhelming, dank sense of failure pressing down on me and the entire parking lot. I had gone into this venture in the spirit of science, to test a mathematical proposition, but somewhere along the line, in the tunnel vision imposed by long shifts and relentless concentration, it became a test of myself, and clearly I have failed. Not only had I flamed out as a housekeeper/server, I had even forgotten to give George my tips, and, for reasons perhaps best known to hardworking, generous people like Gail and Ellen, this hurts. I don't cry, but I am in a position to realize, for the first time in many years, that the tear ducts are still there, and still capable of doing their job.

When I moved out of the trailer park, I gave the key to number 46 to Gail and arranged for my deposit to be transferred to her. She told me that Joan is still living in her van and that Stu had been fired from the Hearthside. I never found out what happened to George.

In one month, I had earned approximately $1,040 and spent $517 on food, gas, toiletries, laundry, phone, and utilities. If I had remained in my $500 efficiency, I would have been able to pay the rent and have $22 left over (which is $78 less than the cash I had in my pocket at the start of the month). During this time I bought no clothing except for the required slacks and no prescription drugs or medical care (I did finally buy some vitamin B to compensate for the lack of vegetables in my diet). Perhaps I could have saved a little on food if I had gotten to a supermarket more often, instead of convenience stores, but it should be noted that I lost almost four pounds in four weeks, on a diet weighted heavily toward burgers and fries.

How former welfare recipients and single mothers will (and do) survive in the low-wage workforce, I cannot imagine. Maybe they will figure out how to condense their lives—including child-raising, laundry, romance, and meals—into the couple of hours between full-time jobs. Maybe they will take up residence in their vehicles, if they have one. All I know is that I couldn't hold two jobs and I couldn't make enough money to live on with one. And I had advantages unthinkable to many of the long-term poor—health, stamina, a working car, and no children to care for and support. Certainly nothing in my experience contradicts the conclusion of Kathryn Edin and Laura Lein, in their recent book *Making Ends Meet: How Single Mothers Survive Welfare and Low-Wage Work,* that low-wage work actually involves more hardship and deprivation than life at the mercy of the welfare state. In the coming months and years, economic conditions for the working poor are bound to worsen, even without the almost inevitable recession. As mentioned earlier, the influx of former welfare recipients into the low-skilled workforce will have a depressing effect on both wages and the number of jobs available. A general economic downturn will only enhance these effects, and the working poor will of course be facing it without the slight, but nonetheless often saving, protection of welfare as a backup.

The thinking behind welfare reform was that even the humblest jobs are morally uplifting and psychologically buoying. In reality they are likely to be fraught with insult and stress. But I did discover one redeeming feature of the most abject low-wage work—the camaraderie of people who are, in almost all cases, far too smart and funny and caring for the work they do and the wages they're paid. The hope, of course, is that someday these people will come to know what they're worth, and take appropriate action.

Notes

1. According to the Department of Housing and Urban Development, the "fair-market rent" for an efficiency is $551 here in Monroe County, Florida. A comparable rent in the five boroughs of New York City is $704; in San Francisco, $713; and in the heart of Silicon Valley, $808. The fair-market rent for an area is defined as the amount that would be needed to pay rent plus utilities for "privately owned, decent, safe, and sanitary rental housing of a modest (non-luxury) nature with suitable amenities."

2. According to the Fair Labor Standards Act, employers are not required to pay "tipped employees," such as restaurant servers, more than $2.13 an hour in direct wages. However, if the sum of tips plus $2.13 an hour falls below the minimum wage, or $5.15 an hour, the employer is required to make up the difference. This fact was not mentioned by managers or otherwise publicized at either of the restaurants where I worked.

3. I could find no statistics on the number of employed people living in cars or vans, but according to the National Coalition for the Homeless's 1997 report "Myths and Facts about Homelessness,"

nearly one in five homeless people (in twenty-nine cities across the nation) is employed in a full- or part-time job.

4. In *Workers in a Lean World: Unions in the International Economy* (Verso, 1997), Kim Moody cites studies finding an increase in stress-related workplace injuries and illness between the mid 1980s and the early 1990s. He argues that rising stress levels reflect a new system of "management by stress," in which workers in a variety of industries are being squeezed to extract maximum productivity, to the detriment of their health.

5. In 1996, the number of persons holding two or more jobs averaged 7.8 million, or 6.2 percent of the workforce. It was about the same rate for men and for women (6.1 versus 6.2), though the kinds of jobs differ by gender. About two thirds of multiple jobholders work one job full-time and the other part-time. Only a heroic minority—4 percent of men and 2 percent of women—work two full-time jobs simultaneously. (From John F. Stinson Jr., "New Data on Multiple Jobholding Available from the CPS," in the *Monthly Labor Review,* March 1997.)

Questions for Critical Thinking

1. In this reading, the author illustrates some of the factors that perpetuate social stratification on the basis of class in the United States. How did the author's experiences broaden your understanding of these factors? What information did you already know?

2. Reflecting on what you read, how do you think factors of race influence the author's experiences? In other words, would her experiences have been similar if she were a woman of color?

3. Economic policymakers in the United States rarely have had experience in trying to live on low-wage employment. Do you think their actions as policymakers would be influenced if they had the opportunity to have the experiences Ehrenreich did in this experiment?

Not Poor Enough

SUSAN SHEEHAN

The following essay details the experiences of an elderly woman named Cassie Stromer. Living on less than $10,000 annually, Stromer is above what the US government has established as the threshold for poverty. As a result, she does not qualify for full Medicaid benefits. Her experiences provide a clear illustration of how constructions of poverty do not adequately reflect the everyday realities of the poor.

Cassie Stromer, a petite seventy-six-year-old woman with bottle-blond hair and off-blue eyes, lives in Mount Vernon House, a pleasant four-story red brick apartment complex in Alexandria, Virginia. She has good memories of a colorful past—three husbands, numerous boyfriends, five children, lots of jobs—but her current life is not so good. She was reared in rural Tennessee, and first came to Virginia to work when she was fifteen. She never finished high school. For a short period after separating from the father of her children, she went on welfare, but she found it demeaning. For a while, she worked two full-time jobs, from which she got home at midnight. Cassie doesn't brood over a past marked by poverty. She liked her jobs—at drugstores, at doughnut shops, waiting on tables in restaurants, serving as a hostess at hotels, working in the advertising department of a local newspaper, babysitting.

Cassie is fortunate to live at Mount Vernon House, which opened in 1983; it is one of the few privately owned and operated buildings in northern Virginia subsidized by the Department of Housing and Urban Development. To apply for an apartment there, a single person must be at least sixty-two or disabled and have an annual income no higher than $30,450. Cassie was sixty-eight when she moved there, in 1996. This year, her income will be $9,654—$686 from Social Security every month and a monthly pension of $118.51 from the newspaper, for which she worked for twenty years.

Last year, Cassie's rent was seventy-two dollars a month. "That's on the low end of what our hundred and forty-one residents pay," the property manager for Mount Vernon House, La-Rita Timberlake, says. "As a general rule, residents pay about thirty per cent of their income minus medical bills for rent. HUD makes up the difference."

Cassie Stromer's income puts her in the lowest third of women over sixty-five living alone in America. The official poverty level is $9,310 a year. As it happens, Cassie would be better off if her income were considerably below that amount, rather than some three hundred dollars above it, because her income is regarded as too high for her to receive full Medicaid benefits.

Cassie suffers from neuropathy, a dysfunction of the peripheral nerves, which typically causes numbness or weakness. The neuropathy began in Cassie's big toe ten or twelve years ago; it has spread to her legs, arms, and hands. "I can't do much with my hands," she says. "I can't peel potatoes. When water hits my fingers, they hurt. I can walk, but standing hurts. The tops of my feet feel like people are pouring hot water on them and the bottoms feel like I'm stepping on coals."

In 2003, this is where Cassie's monthly income of $790.51 went after she paid her rent: about $66 for electricity; $50 for her telephone; and $45 for her cable TV. (Television is Cassie's primary form of recreation: she watches several daytime soaps, listens to the news, sometimes looks at the country-music channel, and in the evening watches one or two favorite shows, like "NYPD Blue" or "Law & Order.") Her prescription-drug bills averaged $328 a month. These expenses left Cassie with $230, which was supplemented with ten dollars a month in food stamps, the amount given to individuals who have a net income between $434 and $1,236 a month. Ten dollars has been the monthly minimum payment since 1978; advocates for the poor have been trying, without success, to raise it to twenty-five dollars.

In Alexandria, the Rising Hope United Methodist Mission Church and the United Community Ministries provide bags of groceries for residents who sign up. Still, Cassie estimates that she spends more than a hundred dollars a week on food and other products not covered by food stamps—paper towels, Kleenex, toilet tissue, laundry and cleaning products, toothpaste, shampoo, deodorant, vitamins, and other personal-care items.

"I've gotten away from eating bacon and eggs in the morning," Cassie says. "But I have to start the day with breakfast-type food, like cold cereal. I try to eat a nutritious dinner." She likes to drink juice and milk—and one cup a day of Dunkin' Donuts coffee—and to eat fresh fruit and vegetables, salads, and meat or chicken several evenings a week. A recent dinner consisted of a baked potato with sour cream, a can of asparagus, and some fresh tomatoes (the vegetables were donated by Rising Hope and the United Community Ministries). When her prescription bills and her medical co-payments are on the low side in a given month, she has ten dollars a week to spend on quarters for the washer and dryer, and bus fare. A friend drives her to church most Sundays, and she puts a dollar in the collection plate when she can.

Cassie was born in Harlan, Kentucky, on February 20, 1928, and moved with her parents to the small town of Sneedville, Tennessee, in the early nineteen-thirties. She was the sixth of seven children born to Henry Monroe Depew, a Baptist minister and a farmer, and Mahalie Seals Depew. A sister died as an infant about two years before Cassie's birth, and her younger brother died when she was five.

The family was poor, and one winter, Cassie recalls, "there wasn't enough to eat, so my grandmother stepped in and helped, because she always did a lot of canning." Cassie didn't feel poor, however. Few people in Sneedville were much better off than the Depews, and she didn't resent those who were.

As a child, Cassie had her share of chores—setting out tobacco, chopping chicken heads off with an axe, planting corn—but most of her early memories are warm ones. "I didn't start school until I was eight," she says. That wasn't unusual in the nineteen-thirties. June Seal, a childhood friend, recalls her as an attractive, slender girl with brown hair. Cassie likes to talk about the year she was "the most popular girl in the school." She was a good student.

In 1943, when Cassie was fifteen, she spent the summer in northern Virginia, where an older sister, who was married to a bus driver, was living. For the next several summers, Cassie worked at drugstores in or near Alexandria, staying either with her sister or at a Y or sharing an apartment with a friend. She returned to high school each fall, but stopped going six weeks before graduation. "I'd had enough of geometry and chemistry by then," she says. "I'd learned that poetry was easy to remember, and words that didn't rhyme—I think they call it prose—was hard. I had my high-school ring, and it never mattered that I didn't graduate. When anyone asked me how many years of school I'd done, I said twelve. No one ever asked to see my diploma."

While still in high school, Cassie married a sailor from North Carolina, but after he got out of the Navy she refused to move there with him, and the marriage was annulled. A few years later, she married again. Cassie's second husband, Bob, was a baker. Their first daughter was born in 1951, when Cassie was twenty-three, and their second in 1955. Cassie made babysitting arrangements for her daughters and kept working at a drugstore. Ten days after the birth of her first son, in 1956, she moved with her family from an apartment to a small house that the couple had bought for $13,750 in the Virginia Hills section of Alexandria, and she stopped working. A third daughter was born in 1958, a second son in 1961. "There were no birth-control pills back then," she says. "I guess if pills had been available I'd have had only two children. But once they were born I was glad to have all five."

Cassie enjoyed being home with the children. "I remember watching the first episode of 'General Hospital,' in 1963, while I was ironing clothes for the five kids," she says. For some months, Cassie babysat for another woman's four children in her house. At another point, when Cassie couldn't pay the pediatrician, she took a job at a dough-nut shop, working the evening shift until 1 A.M. The marriage deteriorated as Bob began drinking heavily, and she left him, she says, after he hit her during a quarrel. "I took my five kids and my three cents to the house of friends across the street, and they let us stay overnight," she says. Social work-ers found a house for her to rent in Falls Church, Virginia, but although Cassie occasionally worked part time as a waitress while the older girls took care of their younger siblings, she couldn't make ends meet and had to go on welfare. Bob paid only forty dollars a week in child support. The house in Virginia Hills had appreciated in value, but she learned that her husband had borrowed money against it and hadn't paid the water bills. "There were so many liens against the house I wound up

with less than a thousand dollars after it was sold," she says. "I put it in savings accounts in the kids' names and gradually spent it on clothes for them." She lived for a while in a rented house in a run-down neighborhood, and then moved to a series of apartments. She eventually got off welfare, and worked at a variety of jobs. "I'm pretty sure I mar-ried Bernie Stromer while I was a keypunch opera-tor," she says. Stromer was the manager of a small hotel in Alexandria. "I'm certain I was attracted to him mostly because he didn't drink. I can't stand alcohol or cigarettes."

Cassie then got a job in the advertising depart-ment of the Alexandria *Gazette*. When she was at the newspaper, she was often away from her desk. Stromer would call and then accuse her—falsely, she says—of carrying on a romance with an advertising salesman there. "The one thing worse than a drink-ing man is a jealous man," she says. "I got a divorce after six years. I sold my three engagement rings and wedding bands to a gold dealer." After the divorce, Cassie worked at the *Gazette* from 7 A.M. to 4 P.M. and at a Peoples Drug from 4:30 P.M. until 11 P.M.

There are eight photograph albums on the top shelf of one of the two closets in Cassie's bedroom at Mount Vernon House. Taped to the pages are photographs of Cassie, starting at the age of seven, and of her children and grandchildren. "My oldest daughter was awarded a full scholarship to Bar-nard and later graduated from law school," she says. "She never wanted to practice law, so she prepares cases for a law firm in Washington, D.C. My second daughter is divorced. She lives with her older sister and works as a legal secretary. My older son works as a security guard in Tennessee, and he's studying ac-counting. He has two daughters. One is away at col-lege, the other lives with him and is in high school. My third daughter is happily married. She and her husband have lived in Virginia, California, Missis-sippi, and Delaware. They've settled in Florida with their two children. They both work. My younger son is single. He's a land surveyor in Virginia." Here and there in the pages of the albums are photographs of Cassie taken at the weddings of her children.

Cassie's children help her out when they can. One of her daughters buys her shoes and also sends her padded socks, which are much more expensive than regular socks but are more comfortable for those suffering from neuropathy. She also sends Cassie checks from time to time, and gave her a forty-dollar Wal-Mart gift certificate last Christmas. One of her sons sent her a check for forty dollars for Christmas. Another daughter is especially helpful, Cassie says, in situations where "there is an emergency or I let her know I really want to do something and I ask her ahead of time"—buying her a hundred and thirty-seven dollars' worth of groceries, for instance, one month when Cassie was out of money. A third daughter telephones often, visits weekly, shops for her, and writes out her checks and mails them, saving Cassie from having to buy stamps. And each week, if there is enough in Cassie's bank account, she withdraws twenty-five dollars for her mother to use as spending money. "The kids got their own lives," Cassie says. "Mortgages or rent, house repairs, car payments, school bills, and vet bills. There's an old saying: 'It takes one mother to take care of five children, but oftentimes five children can't take care of a mother.'"

In one album is the business card of Cassie Stromer, Advertising Manager of the *Gazette*, "America's Oldest Daily Newspaper, Established in 1784," which was still a daily when Cassie went to work there, in 1970. The *Gazette* later merged with the Alexandria *Port Packet*, and became a weekly. "The company published seven other small papers, and I laid out the ads for the *Walter Reed Stripe*, the *Bolling Beam*, the *Pentagram News*, and the others," she says. In another album is a clipping from the *Gazette* with a photograph of Cassie and a number of her colleagues, taken on the occasion of their production of "14 prize-winning advertisements in the 1988 Newspaper Advertising Contest sponsored by the Virginia Press Association."

Two years later, when Cassie was sixty-two, she returned to work from a vacation and received unwelcome news. "My boss handed me a long list of additional jobs he wanted me to do," she says. "I was already doing the work of two people, so I told him he could take his list and shove it. I quit and gave him an hour and a half's notice."

Cassie worked for a time at an apartment-building switchboard, and then, finally, retired. To supplement her retirement income, she took a job babysitting for the six-week-old twins of a prosperous couple. "Some nights, I also took care of another couple's two children from 6 P.M. until midnight," she says. "They paid me more than I'd ever been paid in my life—sometimes even a hundred dollars a night." Frightened by a number of burglaries in her apartment building, she moved to Mount Vernon House in 1996. She was dating a retired Army enlisted man, and they enjoyed travelling together.

"We often flew, but one time he rented a Lincoln Town Car," she says. "He treated me better than any man I've ever known. He paid for everything. We took trips to Las Vegas, we went to Florida to visit my daughter, to Virginia Beach to visit his daughter, and to Kentucky to visit his son." Eventually, the man decided to move to another part of Virginia. Cassie didn't want to leave Alexandria, and the relationship ended. Afterward, Cassie became depressed, and sought help from a local mental-health center. She continues to see a therapist every two weeks. "I find it easier to talk to psychologists and psychiatrists than to most of my friends," she says. "They listen better." With the therapist's help, Cassie has received prescriptions at nominal cost for Paxil, an anti-depressant, and Trazadone, another anti-depressant. Virginia law requires that everyone taking medication under the aegis of a mental-health agency be seen every three months by a psychiatrist. "I look forward to his visits," Cassie says. "He's handsome."

In 1991, Catherine Cole, a spirited woman now in her early fifties, was hired to be the director of resident services at Mount Vernon House. "Most people who live there are in situations similar to Cassie's," she says. "They weren't born with advantages. They didn't become doctors or lawyers or business executives. They were hair-dressers, food-service workers, private-school teachers, auto mechanics, and housekeepers. Some owned homes but couldn't afford to keep them up. Some moved here from trailer parks. The majority have spent most of their adult lives in Fairfax County. A fair number knew at least one other person before they moved here."

There are residents who are less healthy than Cassie. Some women walk around carrying oxygen tanks, a few men and women use wheelchairs. The *Mount Vernon Post*, a monthly newsletter for the residents, recently published a "Lobby Do's and Don'ts" that included "DO NOT BLOW YOUR HORN on motorized scooters in the lobby."

Part of the service director's job is providing entertainment for the residents, and this includes organizing parties to celebrate holidays. At the most recent Halloween party, Cole told Halloween jokes she had found on the Internet, passed out slices of pumpkin pie to the thirty people gathered for the occasion, and handed out prizes for the best costumes. Cassie was wearing a peach-colored top, jacket, and slacks—the closest color she had to orange. She was not among the fifteen residents who showed up, the following week, for a presentation by the Cunningham Funeral Home of Alexandria on the subject of funeral planning.

Regular activities are listed on the calendar published in the *Mount Vernon Post*. At 9:30 A.M. on Tuesdays, the Mount Vernon House van takes residents to a Wal-Mart or a shopping center. On Fridays, Fastran, a Fairfax County shuttle service for the elderly and the handicapped, takes them to a grocery store. Cassie, who doesn't feel well most mornings, prefers to go grocery shopping on weekend afternoons with one of her daughters. She does use Fastran for medical appointments.

A Bible-study group meets at Mount Vernon House on Tuesdays at 4 P.M., and bingo is played at 7 P.M. Movies are often shown on Wednesday evenings. For a while, a swing band rehearsed on Monday evenings in the lobby. The service director arranges occasional trips to dinner theatres in the Washington area and to the American Music

Theatre, in Lancaster, Pennsylvania. "The Lancaster trip costs forty-six dollars, but you can pay in installments," Cassie says. "Two of my daughters will pay for me to go on outings, but the bus ride to Lancaster is long and it shakes you to pieces."

Each year, the Mount Vernon House Tenants' Association raises money for a Christmas dinner by holding a bazaar. The most recent dinner included ham, turkey, stuffing, succotash, green beans, sweet potatoes, mashed potatoes, gravy, cranberry sauce, rolls, apple crisp, and pumpkin pie with whipped cream. Cassie observed that most of the Asian residents sat at one long table and most of the Latinos at another, and that the two or three people who hang out together every day in the lobby sat together and didn't talk to anyone else. "This place is more clannish than junior high school," she said. Still, when a friend came over to her apartment to address Christmas cards to people from Sneedville, the *Gazette*, and other chapters of her life (Cassie's ability to write is limited by her neuropathy and by macular degeneration), she studied the Mount Vernon House directory and chose cards for forty-nine residents, and signed "Love, Cassie" on each card. Cassie keeps the cards that she receives each Christmas until she has dispatched her cards the following December. She was sad when she came across the card that her friend Lucille had sent her. Seven or eight residents of Mount Vernon House, among them Lucille, died the previous year. "I miss Lucille," Cassie says. She also misses another friend, named Warren, who left her his collection of Beanie Babies. Cassie can't afford to send her grandchildren birthday and Christmas presents, but she has been sending Beanie Babies to her youngest granddaughter, who wrote her a thankyou note.

Ellen Cook, a large cheerful woman with only two upper front teeth, is among a handful of original residents, as is Cassie's friend Rachel Tucker, a lively, hundred-and-one-year-old African-American woman, who goes out nearly every day to visit one of her sons, who is blind. "Rachel can still thread a needle without using glasses," Cassie says admiringly. Rachel is the only resident with a key to Cassie's apartment. When Cassie prepares a dinner of baked chicken, egg noodles, and canned kale, she delivers a plate to Rachel. When Rachel fixes ribs, cabbage, or tapioca pudding, she takes some to Cassie.

Mount Vernon House is not an assisted-living facility. Its residents must be able to fend for themselves. Housekeeping help is provided by a county program called Share Care, and, once every week or so, someone comes to change Cassie's bed, scrub her bathroom and kitchen, and vacuum the worn indoor–outdoor carpeting that covers the concrete floor in the bedroom, living room, and hall.

"It's enlightened fiscal policy to enable residents to stay at Mount Vernon House," Cathy Cole says. "Assisted-living facilities are far more expensive, and they're rarely subsidized."

The medical needs of most of this country's old or disabled citizens fall under the jurisdiction of two Great Society programs created in 1965, Medicare and Medicaid. Medicare, a federal system of health insurance available to old people generally, does not provide full medical coverage. Medicaid is jointly administered by the federal government and the states, and covers medical costs for individuals and families with low incomes or with disabilities. Within broad national guidelines, each of the fifty states determines the income at which its residents become eligible for Medicaid. In Virginia, an old person with insignificant assets is eligible for comprehensive Medicaid benefits only if her personal income is no higher than eighty per cent of the poverty level, or $7,448. For those whose income, like Cassie's, is no higher than a hundred and twenty per cent of the poverty level, Medicaid does pay some of the Medicare premiums, but not the first hundred dollars in doctor bills that Cassie incurs each year, and she has to pay twenty per cent of the "usual and customary" fees that doctors charge for their services or, if she is admitted to a hospital, the $876 deductible for a hospital stay of up to sixty days.

Last November, after much debate, Congress significantly modified the Medicare program, authorizing it, for the first time in its history, to bear some of the costs of prescription drugs. The bill doesn't go into effect until 2006, but people whose income is less than $12,576 are now eligible to apply for an annual transitional benefit amounting to a six-hundred-dollar credit on various prescription cards. The new prescription-card system is cumbersome, however, and many of those who are eligible for the cards, including Cassie, find the application process too complicated to follow. Even with the cards, Cassie would be left with the prospect of having to pay thousands of dollars in additional prescription bills this year and next year.

On one visit to the pharmacy, Cassie had five prescriptions filled. Three were to alleviate the pain of neuropathy—Ultram, Keppra, and lidocaine patches (which she applies to the tops of her feet for twelve-hour periods). The fourth, Patanol drops, soothes her eyes, easing the unpleasantness of macular degeneration. The fifth, potassium pills, relieves cramps in her legs. The pharmacy bill that day came to $562.45. Last year, Cassie's entire pharmacy bill was $3,940.50.

"Up until I retired, my health was pretty good," Cassie says. "I was busy working and raising five children and putting one foot in front of the other, and I think it's lucky I couldn't see further down the road, to where I am today—on the borderline of Medicare and Medicaid, which ain't a nice place to be."

"I'd estimate that about one-third of Mount Vernon House's residents are eligible for Medicaid and another few have private health insurance," Cathy Cole says. "The majority, however, fall between the cracks. Their income is a couple of hundred dollars a month too high for them to qualify for Medicaid, and with Medicare alone they cannot afford to pay for all of their medical costs."

Cassie's only hope of qualifying for comprehensive Medicaid—and then only for a period of up to six months at a time—is to be placed on a "spend-down." Mount Vernon House gives residents like Cassie a plastic envelope and tells them to put all their medical bills in it—their co-pays, their prescription bills, and their receipts for all out-of-pocket medical expenses, including transportation to medical appointments. The spend-down is calculated by taking Cassie's monthly income—$790.51 in 2003—and first subtracting a twenty-dollar "disregard." $770.51 is multiplied by six, which amounts to $4,623.06. That figure is then compared with the "medically needy" figure for a single person in northern Virginia, which is $2,071 for a six-month period. The difference, $2,552.06, is Cassie's spend-down. If, in a six-month period, she has $2,552.06 in medical expenses, she will qualify for Medicaid for the remainder of that six-month period. In the eight years that Cassie has been at Mount Vernon House, she has met the Medicaid spend-down once. "It was wonderful to have a Medicaid card," Cassie says. "Prescriptions cost me only a dollar or two apiece. But, by the time I'd met the spend-down amount, the six months of Medicaid coverage was almost up, and before I knew it I was without Medicaid again." A friend remembers coming to visit Cassie at Mount Vernon House. "She was in pain, but she cut one of the pills she took for neuropathy in half, because it was expensive," the friend says.

"People like Cassie believe that their problem lies in having too much income," Steven L. Myers, the executive director of the Virginia Poverty Law Center, says. "In my opinion, the problem is, rather, that Virginia's Medicaid eligibility—eighty per cent of poverty—is too low. We struggled to get the General Assembly to raise it from seventy-four per cent to eighty per cent. That six-per-cent increase was helpful to thousands of people. I know of one woman who spent down and qualified for Medicaid a few years ago. She was on that spend-down long enough to get a free pair of prescription eyeglasses. Now Virginia Medicaid no longer covers eye-glasses. Spend-downs work for some people with catastrophic illnesses. They don't work for people with chronic health problems. I'm convinced that most upper-income people in the country don't know that our safety-net programs aren't as generous as they believe them to be. They assume that the aged, the blind, and the disabled

receive Medicaid at a hundred per cent of poverty. Virginia is a very bad place in which to be elderly and poor."

Cassie Stromer is a fastidious person. After she makes coffee, she doesn't simply rinse out the drip machine's glass carafe; she fills it with fresh water, puts a filter in the plastic cone, and boils the water. Every couple of months, she pours vinegar into the carafe, boils the vinegar, and then repeats the process with water to get rid of the vinegar's pungent odor. She changes her towels and bed linens frequently. The laundry room at Mount Vernon House is less than ideal, she says. "Just four washers and dryers, and sometimes one is broken."

Before Cassie puts fifty cents in a washer, she sprays Lysol in it, and before inserting coins in the dryer she empties the lint tray. She usually doesn't leave the laundry room until her clothes are dry. "People waiting for a machine will change the delicate cycle to high heat so your clothes will be done faster, and that'll ruin them," she says. "Other times, they'll take out your things when they're still wet and they'll use what's left of your money to dry their own clothes."

That happened one day last year, when Cassie left her quilt in a dryer unattended and returned to her apartment. She was already upset because earlier in the day someone had reported her for using two machines at a time and she had been reprimanded. "If I use one machine at a time, I'll be in the laundry room for seven hours," she says. "That's my whole day. And that's the only rule I ever break. Everyone should be allowed to break one goddam rule. I've never reported anyone for using two machines." When Cassie discovered the damp quilt on top of the dryer, she carried it back to her apartment, hung it over the shower rod in her bathroom, and turned on the heat lamp. She owned only one quilt and wanted it on her bed by evening. She started to walk toward her La-Z-Boy recliner in the living room and collided with a small table in the hall that held her microwave. She fell, bumping her head. She lost consciousness briefly, came to, picked herself up, and made it to the recliner. A friend stopped by, saw the bump, and dialled 911. An ambulance took her to a nearby hospital, where she spent six days, returning to Mount Vernon House the day before Thanksgiving. She had been "peeked at and poked at" by numerous doctors—all of whom subsequently sent bills—and had had many X-rays and CAT scans. She had not broken any bones, but she had broken her lower denture. The denture had been made some fifteen or twenty years earlier, when she was still at the *Gazette* and had dental insurance. There is virtually no dentistry that the poor can afford in Virginia; even Medicaid offers dental benefits only to children.

When Cassie received an unexpected rent rebate check from Fairfax County for a hundred dollars later that month, she cashed the check and stashed the hundred dollars in her bedroom, thinking that she might be able to save up for new dentures. Her mouth felt uncomfortable without the lower plate, and she couldn't easily chew meat or raw broccoli, celery, and carrots, which are among her favorite foods.

In January, Cassie's ophthalmologist prescribed TobraDex drops to relieve some irritation in her left eye. When a neighborhood pharmacy delivered the prescription, the bill was $63.23. Cassie had only seventeen dollars. "Shit, shit, shit," she said as she walked to the bedroom and took out fifty dollars of the squirrelled-away hundred dollars. She gave the delivery boy sixty-five dollars—the sum she owed and a tip.

As Cassie's birthday approached, in February, she had only twenty dollars left in her bedroom cache: she had dipped into the denture fund to buy groceries. She telephoned the dentist who had made her original dentures and learned that new ones would cost twenty-seven hundred dollars, but he encouraged her to bring in the broken lower denture. "If the break is clean, I can glue it together and that would last for a while," he said. Cassie had him do the glue repair.

In May, Cassie got some good news. Because of a formula involving her medical expenses, her rent was being reduced from $72 a month to $42. In September, however, she received a notice from the state, telling her that her $58 Medicare premium would no longer be covered, meaning that she would have to pay it herself.

Earlier this month, Cassie's lower denture broke again. "This time it shattered," she says. "It's harder to eat now. I can't really chew anything." She has to cut her food up into small pieces. She says there's nothing she can do about it. "I don't have any more money today than I did last February, and I won't have any more tomorrow."

Questions for Critical Thinking

1. The experiences of Cassie Stromer illustrate that current definitions of what is considered poor are inadequate. Despite this, official definitions of poverty remain relatively unchanged. Why do you think this is?

2. What are some of your own assumptions about the poor? How does Stromer's experience affirm or challenge these assumptions? How is your reaction impacted by your own class position?

3. What are some ways that the definitions of poverty can be changed to provide aid to those who need it?

Learning to Fight

GEOFFREY CANADA

The following excerpt is from the memoir Fist Stick Knife Gun, *by educator Geoffrey Canada. His personal recount of childhood experiences in his neighborhood offers an illustration of the role of violence in constructing masculinity.*

On Union Avenue, failure to fight would mean that you would be set upon over and over again. Sometimes for years. Later I would see what the older boys did to Butchie.

Butchie was a "manchild," very big for his age. At thirteen he was the size of a fully grown man. Butchie was a gentle giant. He loved to play with the younger boys and was not particularly athletic. Butchie had one flaw: he would not fight. Everyone picked on him. The older teenagers (fifteen and sixteen) were really hard on him. He was forever being punched in the midsection and chest by the older boys for no reason. (It was against the rules to punch in the face unless it was a "fair fight.")

I don't know what set the older boys off, or why they picked that Saturday morning, but it was decided that Butchie had to be taught a lesson. The older boys felt that Butchie was giving the block a bad reputation. Everyone had to be taught that we didn't tolerate cowards. Suddenly two of them grabbed Butchie. Knowing that something was wrong, that this was not the rough and tumble play we sometimes engaged in, Butchie broke away. Six of the older boys took off after him. Butchie zigzagged between the parked cars, trying desperately to make it to his building and the safety of his apartment. One of the boys cut him off and, kicking and yelling, Butchie was snagged.

By the time the other five boys caught up, Butchie was screaming for his mother. We knew that his mother often drank heavily on the weekends and were not surprised when her window did not open and no one came to his aid. One of the rules of the block was that you were not allowed to cry for your mother. Whatever happened you had to "take it like a man." A vicious punch to the stomach and a snarled command, "Shut the fuck up," and Butchie became quiet and stopped struggling. The boys marched him up the block, away from his apartment. Butchie, head bowed, hands held behind his back, looked like a captured prisoner.

There are about twelve of us younger boys out that morning playing football in the street. When the action started we stopped playing and prepared to escape to our individual apartment buildings. We didn't know if the older boys were after us, too—they were sometimes unpredictable—and we nervously kept one eye on them and one on a clear avenue of escape. As they marched Butchie down the block it became apparent that we were meant to learn from what was going to happen to Butchie, that they were really doing this for us.

The older boys took Butchie and "stretched" him. This was accomplished by four boys grabbing

Butchie, one on each arm, one on each leg. Then they placed him on the trunk of a car (in the early 1960s the cars were all large) and pulled with all their might until Butchie was stretched out over the back of the car. When Butchie was completely, helplessly exposed, two of the boys began to punch him in his stomach and chest. The beating was savage. Butchie's cries for help seemed only to infuriate them more. I couldn't believe that a human body could take that amount of punishment. When they finished with him, Butchie just collapsed in the fetal position and cried. The older boys walked away talking, as if nothing had happened.

To those of us who watched, the lesson was brutal and unmistakable. No matter who you fought, he could never beat you *that* bad. So it was better to fight even if you couldn't win than to end up being "stretched" for being a coward. We all fought, some with more skill and determination than others, but we all fought.

The day my brother John went out to play on the block and had to fight Paul Henry there was plenty of wild swinging and a couple of blows landed, but they did no real damage. When no one got the better of the other after six or seven minutes, the fight was broken up. John and Paul Henry were made to shake hands and became best of friends in no time.

John was free. He could go outside without fear. I was still trapped. I needed help figuring out what would happen when I went outside. John was not much help to me about how the block worked. He was proud that he could go out and play while we were still stuck in the house. I mentioned something about going downstairs and having Ma come down to watch over me and John laughed at me, called me a baby. He had changed, he had accepted the rules—no getting mothers to fight your battles. His only instructions to me were to fight back, don't let the boys your age hit you without hitting back. Within a week I decided I just couldn't take it, and I went downstairs.

The moment I went outside I began to learn about the structure of the block and its codes of conduct. Each excursion taught me more. The first thing I learned was that John, even though he was just a year older than me, was in a different category than I was. John's peers had some status on the block; my peers were considered too young to have any.

At the top of the pecking order were the young adults in their late teens (seventeen, eighteen, and nineteen). They owned the block; they were the strongest and the toughest. Many of them belonged to a gang called the Disciples. Quite a few had been arrested as part of a police crackdown on gangs in the late fifties and early sixties. Several came out of jail during my first few years on Union Avenue. They often spent large amounts of time in other areas of the Bronx, so they were really absentee rulers.

At this time there were some girls involved in gang activities as well; many of the larger male gangs had female counterparts whose members fought and intimidated other girls. On Union Avenue there was a group of older girls who demanded respect, and received it, from even the toughest boys on the block. Some of these girls were skilled fighters, and boys would say "she can fight like a boy" to indicate that a girl had mastered the more sophisticated techniques of fistfighting. Girls on Union Avenue sometimes found themselves facing the same kind of violence as did boys, but this happened less often. All in all there was less pressure on girls to fight for status, although some did; for girls to fight there usually had to be a major triggering incident.

But status was a major issue for boys on the block. The next category in the pecking order was the one we all referred to as the "older boys," fifteen and sixteen years old. They belonged to a group we sometimes called the Young Disciples, and they were the real rulers of Union Avenue. This was the group that set the rules of conduct on the block and enforced law and order. They were the ones who had stretched Butchie.

Next were boys nine, ten, and eleven, just learning the rules. While they were allowed to go into the street and play, most of them were not allowed off the block without their mother's permission. My brother John belonged to this group.

The lowest group was those children who could not leave the sidewalk, children too young to have any status at all. I belonged to this group and I hated it. The sidewalk, while it provided plenty of opportunity to play with other children, seemed to me to be the sidelines. The real action happened in the street.

There were few expectations placed on us in terms of fighting, but we were not exempt. There was very little natural animosity among us. We played punchball, tag, and "red light, green light, one-two-three." It was the older boys who caused the problems. Invariably, when the older boys were sitting on the stoop and one of them had a brother, or cousin amongst us, it would be he who began the prelude to violence.

I'd been outside for more than a week and thought that I had escaped having to fight anyone because all the boys were my friends. But sure enough, Billy started in on me.

"David, can you beat Geoff?"

David looked at me, then back at Billy. "I don't know."

"What! You can't beat Geoff? I thought you was tough. You scared? I know you ain't scared. You betta not be scared."

I didn't like where this conversation was heading. David was my friend and I didn't know Billy; he was just an older boy who lived in my building. David looked at me again and this time his face changed; he looked threatening; he seemed angry.

"I ain't scared of him."

I was lost. Just ten minutes before David and I were playing, having a good time. Now he looked like I was his worst enemy. I became scared, scared of David, scared of Billy, scared of Union Avenue. I looked for help to the other boys sitting casually on the stoop. Their faces scared me more. Most of them barely noticed what was going on, the rest were looking half interested. I was most disheartened by the reaction of my brother John. Almost in a state of panic, I looked to him for help. He looked me

directly in the eye, shook his head no, then barely perceptibly pointed his chin toward David as if to say, Quit stalling; you know what you have to do. Then he looked away as if this didn't concern him at all.

The other sidewalk boys were the only ones totally caught up in the drama. They knew that their day would also come, and they were trying to learn what they could about me in case they had to fight me tomorrow, or next week, or whenever.

During the time I was sizing up my situation I made a serious error. I showed on my face what was going on in my head. My fear and my confusion were obvious to anyone paying attention. This, I would later learn, was a rookie mistake and could have deadly consequences on the streets.

Billy saw my panic and called to alert the others. "Look at Geoff; he's scared. He's scared of you, David. Go kick his ass."

It was not lost on me that the questioning part of this drama was over. Billy had given David a direct command. I thought I was saved, however, because Billy had cursed. My rationale was that no big boy could use curses at a little boy. My brother would surely step in now and say, "C'mon, Billy, you can't curse at my little brother. After all, he's only seven." Then he would take me upstairs and tell Ma.

When I looked at John again I saw only that his eyes urged me to act, implored me to act. There would be no rescue coming from him. What was worse, the other older boys had become interested when Billy yelled, "Kick his ass," and were now looking toward David and me. In their eyes this was just a little sport, not a real fight, but a momentary distraction that could prove to be slightly more interesting than talking about the Yankees, or the Giants, or their girlfriends. They smiled at my terror. Their smiles seemed to say, "I remember when I was like that. You'll see, it's not so bad."

Thinking on your feet is critical in the ghetto. There was so much to learn and so much of it was so important. It was my brother's reaction that clued me in. I knew John. He was a vicious tease at times, but he loved me. He would never allow me to be harmed and not help or at least go for help. He was telling me I had to go through this alone. I knew I could run upstairs, but what about tomorrow? Was I willing to become a prisoner in my apartment again? And what about how everyone was smiling at me? How was I ever going to play in the street with them if they thought I was such a baby? So I made the decision not to run but to fight.

I decided to maximize the benefits the situation afforded. I said, not quite with the conviction that I'd hoped for, "I'm not afraid of David. He can't beat me. C'mon, David, you wanna fight?"

There was only one problem—I didn't know how to fight. I hadn't seen Dan taking back John's coat, or John's fight with Paul Henry. But a funny thing happened after I challenged David. When I looked back at him, he didn't look quite so confident. He didn't look like he wanted to fight anymore. This gave me courage.

Billy taunted David, "You gonna let him talk to you like that? Go on, kick his ass."

Then Paul Henry chimed in, "Don't be scared, little Geoff. Go git him."

I was surprised. I didn't expect anyone to support me, especially not Paul Henry. But as I would learn later, most of these fights were viewed as sport by the bystanders. You rooted for the favorite or the underdog. Almost everyone had someone to root for them when they fought.

David put up his balled-up fists and said, "Come on." I didn't know how to fight, but I knew how to pretend fight. So I "put up my dukes" and stood like a boxer. We circled one another.

"Come on."

"No, *you* come on."

Luckily for me, David didn't know how to fight either. The older boys called out encouragement to us, but we didn't really know how to throw a punch. At one point we came close enough to one another for me to grab David, and we began to wrestle. I was good at this, having spent many an hour wrestling with my three brothers.

Wrestling wasn't allowed in a "real" fight, but they let us go at it a few moments before they broke

us up. The older boys pronounced the fight a tie and made us shake hands and "be friends." They rubbed our heads and said, "You're all right," and then gave us some pointers on how to really fight. We both basked in the glory of their attention. The other sidewalk boys looked at us with envy. We had passed the first test. We were on our way to becoming respected members of Union Avenue.

David and I became good friends. Since we'd had a tie we didn't have to worry about any other older boys making us fight again. The rule was that if you fought an opponent, and could prove it by having witnesses, you didn't have to fight that person again at the command of the older boys. This was important, because everyone, and I mean everyone, had to prove he could beat other boys his age. Union Avenue, like most other inner-city neighborhoods, had a clear pecking order within the groups as well as between them when it came to violence. The order changed some as boys won or lost fights, but by and large the same boys remained at the top. New boys who came on the block had to be placed in the pecking order. If they had no credentials, no one to vouch for their ability, they had to fight different people on the block until it could be ascertained exactly where they fit in. If you refused to fight, you moved to the bottom of the order. If you fought and lost, your status still remained unclear until you'd won a fight. Then you'd be placed somewhere between the person you lost to and the person you beat.

The pecking order was important because it was used to resolve disputes that arose over games, or girls, or money, and also to maintain order and discipline on the block. Although we were not a gang, there were clear rules of conduct, and if you broke those rules there were clear consequences. The ranking system also prevented violence because it gave a way for boys to back down; if everybody knew you couldn't beat someone and you backed down, it was no big deal most of the time.

My "fight" with David placed me on top of the pecking order for boys on the sidewalk. I managed to get through the rest of the summer without having to fight anyone else. I had learned so much about how Union Avenue functioned that I figured I would soon know all I needed about how to survive on the block.

Questions for Critical Thinking

1. Canada describes the way in which he and other boys in his neighborhood were taught to be violent. How do his experiences demonstrate how violence as a masculine characteristic is a social construct?

2. What functions are served by socializing boys to fight?

3. What would men's relationships (to other men as well as to women) look like if they were not socialized to learn how to fight? Would the prevalence of social inequality be impacted in any way? If so, how? If not, why not?

Resistance and Social Change

Introduction

Throughout this text we have explored how elements of the social structure construct categories of difference with regard to race, class, gender, and sexuality and transform them into systems of oppression and privilege. In Part I we examined why such categories are constructed as well as the social factors involved in the process of transforming them into systems of inequality. In Part II we explored the significance of social institutions in maintaining these systems of inequality as systems of oppression and privilege. The readings in Part III provided us with personal representations illustrating how such systems impact daily lives. The readings in each of the preceding sections have prepared us for the task of this one—to understand the ways in which we can work toward the transformation of systems of oppression and privilege into a system of equal access to opportunity.

Beginning the work of transforming systems of oppression and privilege is often difficult. When we first become aware of systems of inequality, many of us are overwhelmed and do not have a clear idea of where to begin to bring about positive social change. Furthermore, as we discuss later in this section, many of us are motivated to work for social change because of the pain that we or someone close to us experienced as a result of systems of oppression. Because of our proximity to the injustice, we may not feel physically or emotionally capable of challenging the system.

Starting to transform systems of oppression and privilege is also hindered by the role of social institutions in maintaining these systems. As discussed in Part II, social institutions work to maintain systems of inequality based on ideologies that endorse and justify the interests of the dominant group. As a result, they are not likely to be open to challenges. Actions to bring about positive social change are therefore met with resistance on the parts of these institutions and discredited, if not omitted from history altogether. For example, in April 1989 in Beijing, China, a massive demonstration of Chinese students for democratic reform began on Tiananmen Square. Joined by workers, intellectuals, and civil servants until over one million people filled the square, the protestors demanded that the leadership of the country resign. The government responded on June 3 and 4 with troops and tanks, killing thousands to quell a "counter-revolutionary rebellion." Government reaction to these protests has been followed by silence. There is no public discussion of the incident in China, except for occasional government accounts defending the actions of the military. Editors of newspapers in China delete even vague references to the protests. Groups and individuals protesting injustice in the United States have been met with similar acts of resistance (e.g., the World Trade Organization protests in Seattle[1]; the use of the USA PATRIOT Act to limit actions of antiwar protestors[2]; or the introduction of legislation in Minnesota that would increase penalties and charge demonstrators the cost of policing protests in response to Black Lives Matter protests blocking busy interstates in the Twin Cities.) and attempts to render their political activism invisible (e.g., the lack of media coverage of peace rallies and antiwar protests since September 11[3]). Faced with the possibility of opposition and, moreover, lacking an awareness of previous efforts to transform systems of oppression and privilege, those who would begin work toward positive social change face major difficulty.

Finally, beginning the work of transforming systems of oppression and privilege into systems of equal access to opportunity is often difficult because we underestimate our ability to impact these systems. In essence, we doubt that we will be able to bring about change. However, as Margaret Mead said, "Never doubt that a small group of thoughtful, committed citizens can change the world; indeed, it's the only thing that ever has." Efforts to create social equality are often begun by everyday individuals.

The readings in this section examine the various ways individuals and groups have worked to create positive social change. Those who bring about social change come from all walks of life. As you read these selections, consider the systems of oppression and privilege that you would like to see change—and the ways in which you would like to go about working for this change. Create your own image of what a system of equal access to opportunity would look like.

Before beginning this process, it is important to remember that difference is not always negative. On the contrary, the preservation of a distinct identity is often central to working toward positive social change. Differences are not problematic; rather, as stated in Part I of this text, it is when the meanings and values applied to these *differences* transform them into systems of *inequality* that such constructs become problematic. As we work to find solutions to inequality, it is important that we seek not to eliminate difference but rather to transform the ways in which difference has been established into a system where each individual is seen as valuable.

What Is Social Change?

To transform systems of oppression and privilege into systems of equality, it is important that we understand the concept of social change. **Social change**—fundamental alterations in the patterns of culture, structure, and social behavior over time—is always occurring. It can result from a variety of actions and can be inspired from a number of motivations. From individual actions to collective behavior, efforts and movements to transform systems of oppression and privilege work toward **positive social change**—changing patterns of the social structure and social behavior in an effort to reduce oppression and increase inclusion for all members of society.

Such efforts often involve conflicts in **ideology.** As we discussed in Part II, the maintenance of systems of oppression depends on the presence of ideologies that provide the basis of inequality. The clash in ideology that results from challenging beliefs, values, and attitudes that see members of certain groups as inferior or superior is generally seen as disruptive to the social order and may result in strong reactions on the part of those interested in maintaining the power of the dominant group. For example, on November 14, 1960, Ruby Bridges became the first black child in the history of the US South to enter an all-white school. Although only in first grade and six years old, she was an agent for social change—and also represented a clash in ideology with the racially segregated South. As a result, she needed to be escorted by US marshals on the first day of school and spent her first year in that school in a class of one because all the parents pulled their children out of school to protest the integration. Although such clashes in ideology may act as deterrents for those wanting to transform systems of oppression, the reality that dominant ideologies do not always win out in the end can also serve as encouragement.

What are the Goals of Social Change?

When seeking positive social change, we must have a clear idea of the goals we are working toward. Just as there are divergent approaches to positive social change, there are also many goals. The general goal in seeking to transform systems of oppression is to develop systems in which all have access to important resources and none is advantaged at the expense of others, but specific goals of positive social change are defined by those who seek them. As you read this section, consider the injustices that have come to matter to you and imagine how you would like to see these injustices transformed.

For some, discussions of social change are centered around a goal of creating a society based on a system of **social justice**—a system in which each member of society has the opportunity and power to fully participate in the social system. As mentioned in Part I, in the United States we have a system based on a **civil rights** framework. Such a framework is based on the concept of majority rule, where the will of the majority becomes the will for all, with some people inevitably losing. A *social justice* framework stands in contrast to such a system and provides the opportunity for each member of society to benefit. It relies on three principles.

The first principle is that *people have options*. These options relate to having access to resources and can include opportunity for work, adequate health care, access to housing, freedom from harassment or discrimination, and so on. In some ways, the United States can be seen as meeting this principle, in that with our vast resources it appears that we all have the *option* of access to these resources. For example, with regard to opportunity for work and career choice, many of us who grew up in the United States were presented with the notion that anyone has the option to be president. You do not need to be of any particular race, class, gender, or sexuality to have this option.

The second principle of a social justice framework is that *people are aware of their options*. In such a framework we must be made aware of our opportunities to access important resources such as attending college, applying for jobs, purchasing property, and receiving adequate health care. Considering again the opportunity to become president, many of us who grew up in the United States heard that this was a possibility and thus we were aware of this option. Indeed, we often heard such messages along with Horatio Alger stories and notions of achieving the "American Dream." Many of these messages were rooted in the assumption that the United States is a **meritocracy**—a system in which people's success is a result of their talents, abilities, and efforts. However, the notion of a meritocracy ignores the advantages that are given to some and denied to others. In a socially just system, people are aware of their options and their opportunities and are not hindered by unfair disadvantages.

The third and final principle of a socially just system is that *people have the power to act on their options.* This is where the system of civil rights—and thus the system of the United States—departs from that of a social justice framework. As noted above, the assumption of a meritocracy sits at the core of the American Dream. A system of oppression and privilege that derives from the social construction of difference results in an unequal distribution of power. Because of this unequal distribution, it is not our individual talents, abilities, and efforts that lead to our ability to succeed, but our access to power. Power, typically viewed as an ability to control people or things, can be defined in many ways. In the case of running for president, one's power directly relates to the amount of money one is able to raise to run a successful campaign. For example, according to the *United States Federal Elections Commission* in 2016, the two major presidential candidates for president (Clinton and Trump) spent in excess of $585 million and $350 million, respectively. From our discussion in Part II of the distribution of income and wealth in the United States, it is obvious that there are few people, particularly African Americans and other people of color, who possess or have access to the financial resources and other forms of power to be able to act on their option to become president. Considering this, it is clear that a civil rights system departs from one based on social justice.

A social justice framework is one of many possibilities in framing our efforts to transform systems of oppression and privilege. Another possible framework relies on **empowerment**—a process of defining ourselves rather than being defined by others. In a system based on empowerment, those who have experienced oppression are given the opportunity to create their own power in improving their own circumstances. Whatever specific goal each of us sets our sights on, we must establish our own strategies for working toward that goal. Many of the readings in this section offer insights that may be useful in establishing these strategies. These strategies include efforts to resist corporate power, as illustrated through Anmol Chaddha's discussion of opposing Walmart in the article "Good for the 'Hood?" (Reading 46); the importance of integrating issues of racial and class inequality, as in Eric Holt-Giménez and Yi Wang's exploration of the role of food justice to address issues of hunger and food insecurity in "Reform or Transformation? The Pivotal Role of Food Justice in the U.S. Food Movement" (Reading 48); and the role of a human rights framework in the Black Lives Matter movement, rooted in the history of the black freedom struggle as explained by Fredrick C. Harris in "The Next Civil Rights Movement?" (Reading 50). These examples are intended to broaden our understanding of how to build effective movements to bring about positive social change.

What Motivates Work for Social Change?

Much work has been done in a variety of contexts to bring about positive social change to transform systems of oppression and privilege. The factors that precipitate such work come from a variety of sources. Work for positive social change can be motivated by personal experiences; at other times, it is motivated by dissatisfaction with social systems on the part of large groups of people. To understand how to create positive social change, it is important to understand what has motivated others to become involved in such efforts.

Motivation for working toward positive social change can come from factors related to the social system. For example, according to Neil Smelser (1962), when important aspects of a social system appear to be out of joint, such as when standards of living are not what people expect them to be, people may experience **structural strain.** As an illustration, consider the notion that the United States is thought to be an affluent society. Whether our economy is in a state of recession or boom, poverty rates continue to be high. Further, as illustrated in Part I, such poverty rates are arbitrarily determined and do not necessarily reflect the experience of poverty accurately. According to Smelser, as the strain from this situation accumulates over time, individuals become motivated to use courses of action not defined by existing institutional arrangements. As people begin to see the strain as a problem in need of a solution, they develop shared ideas about how they should respond to it.

At other times, motivation for working toward positive social change requires precipitating factors, such as the recent mobilization on many campuses and in numerous cities to work for peace in response to the war in Iraq and Afghanistan. Other precipitating factors can be hearing stories of social injustice experienced on the part of individuals. For example, the Matthew Shepard and James Byrd, Jr. Hate Crimes Prevention Act passed in 2009. Much of the motivation for working on such legislation arose from the brutal killings of James Byrd,[4] Matthew Shepard,[5] Billy Jack Gaither,[6] Juana Vega,[7] and Scotty Joe Weaver.[8] Indeed, increasing incidents of antigay hate crimes were reported after the narrow passage in 2008 of Proposition 8 in California, an antigay piece of legislation that provides that only marriage between a man and a woman is valid or recognized in California. Overall, the FBI reported an increase in hate crimes in the United States in 2015, with attacks against Muslims increasing the most sharply. Acts of brutality such as these, motivated by hatred for someone seen as different or other, have motivated individuals, organizations, and government officials to work to enact legislation to reduce the likelihood that hate crimes will continue to occur.

Whether the motivation for working toward positive social change comes from witnessing inconsistencies between structural values, hearing stories of violence committed by those who hate, our own personal experiences with inequality, or some other source, taking on the challenge of working to improve our social environment does not occur unless we can imagine a reality that differs from what already exists. Returning to Part I, one of the fundamental aspects of critical thinking is the ability to imagine alternative ways of thinking. For example, if children experienced an inclusive representation of history, how might that positively impact their perceptions of their own race as well as those of others? What lasting impact might that have on constructions of race and the interactions of those who identify as belonging to different race categories? Critical thinking is a fundamental tool for those desiring to create positive social change. Imagining alternatives to the current social order can provide us not only with the motivation to work for positive social change but also with a goal and some strategies for achieving that goal.

Who Creates Positive Social Change?

When we think of positive social change, we often think of large **social movements**—sustained, organized collective effort. In addition, we tend to think of those who work toward such change as being charismatic leaders with large groups of followers. Thus, if asked who were great makers of social justice, we may mention names such as Martin Luther King, Malcolm X, Emma Goldman, Gandhi, Cesar Chavez, and Jane Addams. Moreover, many of us may imagine activists as fitting a radical image that we do not see ourselves fitting into. In any event, we rarely identify ourselves when describing agents of change.

Although it is true that a great deal of the positive social change that has occurred in our society has involved the organization of movements and the participation of great leaders, the earlier example of Ruby Bridges illustrates that such social transformation has also involved the actions of a wide array of individuals coming from all walks of life. Thus, there is no model activist. An activist can be anyone with the motivation and ideas of how to transform a situation of inequality.

For example, in 1996 Kelli Peterson, a Salt Lake City East High School student, created a group that provided safe space for support and dialogue for lesbian, gay, and bisexual students and their allies at her school. Many studies and reports have indicated the need for such a group. For example, a study conducted by the Gay, Lesbian, and Straight Education Network found that

> 84 percent of LGBT students reported that they have been verbally harassed; 82.9 percent stated that teachers or administrators rarely, if ever, intervened when they witnessed homophobic comments; 55 percent of transgender

students reported being physically harassed because of their gender identity; 41 percent of lesbian, gay and bisexual students said that they had been physically harassed because of their sexual orientation; and 64.3 percent of LGBT students reported that, because of their sexual orientation, they felt unsafe at school.

When Kelli attempted to establish a gay/straight alliance, the school board voted to ban all noncurricular clubs rather than allow the alliance to be formed. Through her commitment and motivation, however, she worked to organize students, faculty, and community members to overturn the decision. The gay/straight alliance now meets regularly at Salt Lake City East High School, offering a safer environment for lesbian, gay, bisexual, and transgender students and their allies.

Just as each of us participates in constructing categories of difference and systems of oppression and privilege, we can also participate in transforming them into systems of equality. Once we locate our source of motivation and establish a new vision of what is possible, we are well on our way toward creating this change.

Where Does Positive Social Change Occur?

Just as a vast array of social activists and endless contributing factors transform categories of difference, there are also a large number of contexts within which we can enact positive social change. Further, as categories of difference are constructed and transformed into systems of inequality in a variety of contexts—institutional, interpersonal, and internal—so, too, can we work to transform systems of oppression in all contexts.

The first site of working toward positive social change is often the internal context—within ourselves. We are able to begin this work once we are able to transform how we view ourselves and our memberships within a system of oppression. To be effective agents for social change, we often must transform the negative perceptions we have of ourselves before we are able to effectively work at transforming systems of oppression in other contexts. This often involves a transformation of identity through the restoration of dignity and overcoming a previously stigmatized status.

Transforming systems of oppression within ourselves requires that we examine not only our own internalized oppression but also how we have internalized oppressive attitudes about others. One of the reasons systems of oppression persist is that individuals in those systems, regardless of their location in them, internalize the ideas of the dominant group. As Patricia Hill Collins notes in "Toward a New Vision" (Reading 45), we often fail to see how our own ideas and behaviors perpetuate someone else's subjugation. She quotes Audre Lorde as saying,

> The true focus of revolutionary change is never merely the oppressive situations which we seek to escape but that piece of the oppressor which is planted deep within each of us. (1984, 123)

As this quote illustrates, if we desire to engender positive social change, we must first examine not only the ideas we have internalized that oppress ourselves but also those notions that perpetuate the oppression of others.

Transformations of systems of oppression and privilege can also occur in interpersonal contexts. Indeed, it is at this level that a great deal of positive social change begins. Here we can often use the dynamics of our interpersonal relationships as a source of leverage in seeking to transform inequality. Love between family members, commitment between spouses/partners, philosophical or religious alliances between members of communities, political coalitions between members of an organization, and so on can all provide a foundation that makes challenges regarding oppressive or discriminatory behavior more likely to be heard and seen as valid.

We can also seek to transform systems of oppression and privilege within institutional contexts. This can involve seeking to transform the institution from within, with members of the institution using their power to create change in individuals and policies. For example, a teacher can use her or his position within the institution to change students through using a curriculum that is inclusive and focuses on transformation rather than perpetuation of systems of oppression. Additionally, a social scientist can use knowledge and skills as a researcher and status as a member of an academic institution to demonstrate the importance of transforming difference within other institutions. Further, institutions can establish policies and procedures that set precedents for the more inclusive treatment of marginalized groups. For example, when President Harry S. Truman officially desegregated the military in 1948, he helped to establish a precedent for future inclusion of blacks and African Americans in the United States.

Transforming systems of oppression and privilege within institutional contexts also involves individuals outside the institution who use a variety of means to pressure it to change. The use of methods such as protests, boycotts (withdrawal of support, usually through money), and informing the public of the institution's discriminatory policies and practices have been effective in bringing about change within these contexts.

It is important to note here, however, that institutions in the United States are generally organized around systems of oppression and privilege, as the readings in this text have made clear. As a result, we are often limited in the amount of change that can occur within these structures. For example, a woman who works in a large corporation that is dominated by males may risk loss of advancement, if not job security, if she challenges the institution's sexist hiring and operating practices. In addition, we should not expect that positive change will result merely because members of marginalized groups are present in powerful positions within these organizations. The success of marginalized *individuals* within an organization should not be assumed to reflect a positive change in institutional policies toward that *group*. We often assume that gender inequality will cease to exist in the workplace as more women obtain positions of prestige and authority. As illustrated in Part II, however, social policies that ignore the patriarchal structure on which they are built and assume that institutional changes will occur on the individual level will inevitably fail. These failures, in turn, will be blamed on the subordinated individual rather than on the social structure itself.

Regardless of the context within which we focus our efforts to generate positive social change, such change is possible from a variety of starting points. As you read this section, take note of the strategies and tools used and think critically about the possibilities that they reveal for you to transform systems of oppression and privilege in your own social world.

Strategies: The Importance of Coalition

As the previous discussion indicates, there are a variety of ways in which we can work to transform systems of oppression and privilege. However, it is difficult, and perhaps dangerous, to try to discern which is the *best* strategy. Indeed, such debates over strategies for generating positive social change have often stood in the way of creating any change at all and have generally only served to perpetuate inequality. However, it is important to note here that, regardless of the strategies we choose to use in the formation of positive social change, it is important to build coalitions and work across categories of difference.

Throughout this text, the connections between forms of oppression have been made clear. Systems of oppression share similarities in how they are established and maintained as well as in their effect. Thus, if we seek to transform such systems, we need to examine their foundations and the underlying aspects of the social structure that serve to perpetuate them. Such a *system-based rather* than *issue*-based focus not only enables us to build coalitions but also *requires* us to do so.

As Collins notes in "Toward a New Vision" (Reading 45), we often get caught up in asserting that there is one type of oppression that is most important, and all others, as a result, become less important. As mentioned earlier, such a debate is not only endless but also likely to defeat all efforts to transform systems of oppression and privilege. Rather than focusing on ranking oppressions, Collins argues, we need to focus on how systems of stratification interconnect. As we discussed in Parts I and II, Collins sees these systems as operating within a matrix of domination. Significant problems occur when we miss these parallels and interconnections. Understanding the interconnections among various forms of oppression will help us to forge stronger alliances and coalitions. In addition, it is important that we understand the ideological foundations shared by various forms of stratification. We cannot hope to eradicate one form of inequality if others remain intact. While these alliances and coalitions may be difficult to develop and maintain, they are necessary if we are to eradicate all forms of domination.

Further Barriers to Creating Positive Social Change

While coalition building presents an effective strategy for transforming categories of difference, it also can present a variety of barriers, institutional as well as personal, to bringing about positive social change. In addition to these barriers, we may face other obstacles in both interpersonal and institutional contexts.

Social control mechanisms, which reward conformity and punish or discourage nonconformity, are effective means of regulating the behavior of societal members. These mechanisms also create barriers to transforming systems of oppression by thwarting efforts to bring about positive social change. Anne Wilson Schaef (1981) offers an example of one such mechanism. Focusing on the social control of women, she uses the term *stoppers* to refer to anything that keeps women where the dominant group wants them to be. People seeking to create positive social change often face such stoppers, regardless of the form of oppression that they may be seeking to transform. For example, heterosexual men who challenge other men on their sexism may experience challenges to their masculinity or have their heterosexuality called into question by other men. Women who speak out against sexism risk being called lesbians or facing physical violence. People of color who speak out about racism in their workplace face accusations of being too angry or having an agenda. People who speak out against the war risk being called un-American or having their civil liberties curtailed.[9]

Stoppers also exist within institutional contexts and can have a more severe impact than those that occur on an individual level. As mentioned at the beginning of this essay, efforts to transform systems of oppression and privilege are often met with resistance on the part of institutions. For example, the social institution of the state may enact policies seeking to repress the efforts of those working to transform systems of oppression and privilege. The experiences of political prisoners, including Angela Davis[10] and Leonard Peltier,[11] offer clear examples of the ways in which institutions may work to prevent the transformation of systems of oppression.

Again, to effectively transform systems of oppression and privilege, it is important to be aware of individual as well as institutional barriers. Having this awareness will enable us to create effective strategies for moving beyond them.

Conclusion

Despite the barriers we face when seeking to transform systems of oppression and privilege, opportunities for bringing about such change continually present themselves. As mentioned earlier, there is no single cause for inequality, and thus there is no single solution. Thinking critically about categories of difference and structures of inequality can present us with endless options for generating positive social change. By challenging our assumptions and being aware of our own standpoint, we can become more aware of how our own ideas perpetuate someone else's subjugation. By imagining alternative ways of constructing our social world, we are able to establish goals for our social action. Finally, by employing a reflexive analysis, we are able to challenge dominant ideas and question rigid belief systems. Such questions and challenges will provide a good foundation for creating a structure where each individual is seen as valuable. As you read the selections in the final chapters of this text, take note of how your process of critical thinking helps you to become aware of your own goals for transforming systems of oppression and privilege.

Notes

1. For a discussion of the World Trade Organization protests, see Alexander Cockburn and Jeffrey St. Clair, *Five Days That Shook the World: Seattle and Beyond* (New York: Verso, 2000).
2. For more information on the USA PATRIOT Act, go to http://www.aclu.org/keep-america-safe-free.
3. *The Nation*, December 31, 2001, 8.
4. James Byrd, forty-nine, was beaten unconscious and then dragged by a chain to his death from the back of a pickup truck after accepting a ride from three white men in Jasper, Texas, in June 1998. One of the men, John William King, was found guilty and given the death penalty for his role in the killing. Another man, Lawrence Brewer, was also found guilty and sentenced to death. The third suspect, Shawn Berry, was sentenced to life in prison. Byrd's body was dismembered in the assault and many of his body parts were found about a mile from his torso. When he was found, his body was so badly disfigured that Byrd had to be identified by fingerprints.
5. Matthew Shepard, a University of Wyoming student, was lured from a bar and attacked by two men, allegedly because they presumed he was gay. He

was struck eighteen times in the head with a pistol and left to die on a fence outside Laramie in October 1998. He was found unconscious eighteen hours after he was kidnapped and died five days later. One of his attackers, Russell Henderson, was sentenced to two consecutive life sentences after pleading guilty. The other man accused in the murder, Aaron McKinney, was sentenced to life without parole.

6. The body of Billy Jack Gaither, a thirty-nine-year-old textile worker, was found in rural Sylacauga, Alabama, some forty miles southeast of Birmingham, on February 20, 1999. Two men, Steven Eric Mullins and Charles Monroe Butler Jr., confessed to the killing in early March after waiving their right to counsel. After bludgeoning Gaither with an axe handle, the men burned the victim's remains. They then drove his car to a deserted location and burned it as well.

7. Juana Vega was murdered in November 2001 by Pablo Parrilla, the brother of her partner. Upset about his sister's relationship with a woman, he shot Vega five times and then repeatedly hit her with the gun and kicked her motionless body. Parrilla confessed to the killing, and following a seven-day trial, a jury found him guilty. He was sentenced to life imprisonment with extended supervision eligibility after forty-five years. Parrilla has appealed this decision.

8. The severely burned and decomposed body of Scotty Joe Weaver was found in July 2004 by a man driving an all-terrain vehicle in Minnette, Alabama. Christopher Gaines, twenty; Nichole Kelsay, eighteen; and Robert Porter, eighteen, were arrested on July 24 and charged with capital murder, according to the Associated Press. Police say they robbed Weaver of $65.00 to $85.00 and then beat, cut, and strangled him before setting him on fire. The district attorney argues that Weaver's identity as a gay man played a key role in the killing.

9. Armed government agents detained Nancy Oden, Green Party USA coordinating committee member, on November 1, 2001, at Bangor International Airport in Bangor, Maine, as she attempted to board an American Airlines flight to Chicago. Her name had been flagged by airport computers because of the Green Party's opposition to the war in Afghanistan.

10. A retired professor of history at the University of California–Santa Cruz, Davis was placed on the FBI's Ten Most Wanted list in 1970, after she was accused of planning the kidnapping of three imprisoned African American activists in San Quentin and supplying the gun that killed four people during the incident. She was incarcerated on charges of murder, kidnapping, and conspiracy, and her case was taken up by supporters across the country. In 1972, after eighteen months in jail, she was tried and acquitted of all crimes.

11. On June 26, 1975, two FBI agents and one Native American were killed in a shootout on the Pine Ridge Indian Reservation. This firefight led to what many see as the false incarceration of American Indian Movement member Leonard Peltier. Now fifty-four years old, Peltier is serving his twenty-fourth year of

incarceration in Leavenworth Penitentiary in Kansas. He stands accused of the murders of the two FBI agents. To date, no credible evidence has been presented to suggest that he is guilty. All others who have been brought to trial regarding this incident were acquitted on the basis of self-defense.

References

Lorde, Audre. 1984. *Sister Outsider.* Trumansberg, NY: Crossing Press.

Schaef, Anne Wilson. 1981. *Women's Reality: An Emerging Female System in the White Male Society.* Minneapolis, MN: Winston Press.

Smelser, Neil J. 1962. *Theory of Collective Behavior.* New York: Free Press.

Toward a New Vision

Race, Class, and Gender as Categories of Analysis and Connection

PATRICIA HILL COLLINS

The following essay, written by sociologist Patricia Hill Collins, considers a challenge faced by those working for positive social change: while we are often aware of our own situations and where we lack privilege, we often fail to see how our own ideas and behaviors perpetuate someone else's inequality. Collins calls on us to consider reconceptualizing categories of race, class, and gender and to overcome the barriers of our own experiences of inequality to build the coalitions necessary to bring about social justice.

> *The true focus of revolutionary change is never merely the oppressive situations which we seek to escape, but that piece of the oppressor which is planted deep within each of us.*
> —Audre Lorde, *Sister Outsider, 123*

Audre Lorde's statement raises a troublesome issue for scholars and activists working for social change. While many of us have little difficulty assessing our own victimization within some major system of oppression, whether it be by race, social class, religion, sexual orientation, ethnicity, age or gender, we typically fail to see how our thoughts and actions uphold someone else's subordination. Thus, white feminists routinely point with confidence to their oppression as women but resist seeing how much their white skin privileges them. African-Americans who possess eloquent analyses of racism often persist in viewing poor white women as symbols of white power. The radical left fares little better. "If only people of color and women could see their true class interests," they argue, "class solidarity would eliminate racism and sexism." In essence, each group identifies the type of oppression with which it feels most comfortable as being fundamental and classifies all other types as being of lesser importance.

Oppression is full of such contradictions. Errors in political judgment that we make concerning how we teach our courses, what we tell our children, and which organizations are worthy of our time, talents and financial support flow smoothly from errors in theoretical analysis about the nature of oppression and activism. Once we realize that there are few pure victims or oppressors, and that each one of us derives varying amounts of penalty and privilege from the multiple systems of oppression that frame our lives, then we will be in a position to see the need for new ways of thought and action.

To get at that "piece of the oppressor which is planted deep within each of us," we need at least two things. First, we need new visions of what oppression is, new categories of analysis that are inclusive of race, class, and gender as distinctive yet interlocking structures of oppression. Adhering to a stance of comparing and ranking oppressions—the proverbial, "I'm more oppressed than you"—locks us all into a dangerous dance of competing

Patricia Hill Collins. "Toward a New Vision: Race, Class, and Gender as Categories of Analysis and Connection." Race, Sex & Class, Vol. 1, No. 1, Fall 1993. Reprinted with permission of the author.

for attention, resources, and theoretical supremacy. Instead, I suggest that we examine our different experiences within the more fundamental relationship of damnation and subordination. To focus on the particular arrangements that race or class or gender takes in our time and place without seeing these structures as sometimes parallel and sometimes interlocking dimensions of the more fundamental relationship of domination and subordination may temporarily ease our consciences. But while such thinking may lead to short-term social reforms, it is simply inadequate for the task of bringing about long-term social transformation.

While race, class and gender as categories of analysis are essential in helping us understand the structural bases of domination and subordination, new ways of thinking that are not accompanied by new ways of acting offer incomplete prospects for change. To get at that "piece of the oppressor which is planted deep within each of us," we also need to change our daily behavior. Currently, we are all enmeshed in a complex web of problematic relationships that grant our mirror images full human subjectivity while stereotyping and objectifying those most different than ourselves. We often assume that the people we work with, teach, send our children to school with, and sit next to . . . will act and feel in prescribed ways because they belong to given race, social class or gender categories. These judgments by category must be replaced with fully human relationships that transcend the legitimate differences created by race, class and gender as categories of analysis. We require new categories of connection, new visions of what our relationships with one another can be. . . .

[This discussion] addresses this need for new patterns of thought and action. I focus on two basic questions. First, how can we reconceptualize race, class and gender as categories of analysis? Second, how can we transcend the barriers created by our experiences with race, class and gender oppression in order to build the types of coalitions essential for social exchange? To address these questions I contend that we must acquire both new theories of

how race, class and gender have shaped the experiences not just of women of color, but of all groups. Moreover, we must see the connections between the categories of analysis and the personal issues in our everyday lives, particularly our scholarship, our teaching and our relationships with our colleagues and students. As Audre Lorde points out, change starts with self, and relationships that we have with those around us must always be the primary site for social change.

How Can We Reconceptualize Race, Class and Gender as Categories of *Analysis*?

To me, we must shift our discourse away from additive analyses of oppression (Spelman, 1982; Collins, 1989). Such approaches are typically based on two key premises. First, they depend on either/or, dichotomous thinking. Persons, things and ideas are conceptualized in terms of their opposites. For example, Black/White, man/woman, thought/feeling, and fact/opinion are defined in oppositional terms. Thought and feeling are not seen as two different and interconnected ways of approaching truth that can coexist in scholarship and teaching. Instead, feeling is defined as antithetical to reason, as its opposite. In spite of the fact that we all have "both/and" identities (I am both a college professor and a mother—I don't stop being a mother when I drop my child off at school, or forget everything I learned while scrubbing the toilet), we persist in trying to classify each other in either/or categories. I live each day as an African-American woman—a race/gender specific experience. And I am not alone. Everyone has a race/gender/class specific identity. Either/or, dichotomous thinking is especially troublesome when applied to theories of oppression because every individual must be classified as being either oppressed or not oppressed. The both/and position of simultaneously being oppressed and oppressor becomes conceptually impossible.

A second premise of additive analyses of oppression is that these dichotomous differences must be ranked. One side of the dichotomy is typically labeled dominant and the other subordinate. Thus, Whites rule Blacks, men are deemed superior to women, and reason is seen as being preferable to emotion. Applying this premise to discussions of oppression leads to the assumption that oppression can be quantified, and that some groups are oppressed more than others. I am frequently asked, "Which has been most oppressive to you, your status as a Black person or your status as a woman?" What I am really being asked to do is divide myself into little boxes and rank my various statuses. If I experience oppression as a both/and phenomenon, why should I analyze it any differently?

Additive analyses of oppression rest squarely on the twin pillars of either/or thinking and the necessity to quantify and rank all relationships in order to know where one stands. Such approaches typically see African-American women as being more oppressed than everyone else because the majority of Black women experience the negative effects of race, class and gender oppression simultaneously. In essence, if you add together separate oppressions, you are left with a grand oppression greater than the sum of its parts.

I am not denying that specific groups experience oppression more harshly than others—lynching is certainly objectively worse than being held up as a sex object. But we must be careful not to confuse this issue of the saliency of one type of oppression in people's lives with a theoretical stance positing the interlocking nature of oppression. Race, class and gender may all structure a situation but may not be equally visible and/or important in people's self-definitions. In certain contexts, such as the antebellum American South and contemporary South America, racial oppression is more visibly salient, while in other contexts, such as Haiti, El Salvador and Nicaragua, social class oppression may be more apparent. For middle-class White women, gender may assume experiential primacy unavailable to poor Hispanic women struggling with the ongoing issues of low-paid jobs and the frustrations of the welfare bureaucracy. This recognition that one category may have salience over

another for a given time and place does not minimize the theoretical importance of assuming that race, class and gender as categories of analysis structure all relationships.

In order to move toward new visions of what oppression is, I think that we need to ask new questions. How are relationships of domination and subordination structured and maintained in the American political economy? How do race, class and gender function as parallel and interlocking systems that shape this basic relationship of domination and subordination? Questions such as these promise to move us away from futile theoretical struggles concerned with ranking oppressions and towards analyses that assume race, class and gender are all present in any given setting, even if one appears more visible and salient than the others. Our task becomes redefined as one of reconceptualizing oppression by uncovering the connections among race, class and gender as categories of analysis.

I. The Institutional Dimension of Oppression

Sandra Harding's contention that gender oppression is structured along three main dimensions—the institutional, the symbolic and the individual—offers a useful model for a more comprehensive analysis encompassing race, class and gender oppression (Harding 1986). Systemic relationships of domination and subordination structured through social institutions such as schools, businesses, hospitals, the workplace and government agencies represent the institutional dimension of oppression. Racism, sexism and elitism all have concrete institutional locations. Even though the workings of the institutional dimension of oppression are often obscured with ideologies claiming equality of opportunity, in actuality, race, class and gender place Asian-American women, Native American men, White men, African-American women and other groups in distinct institutional niches with varying degrees of penalty and privilege.

Even though I realize that many . . . would not share this assumption, let us assume that the institutions of American society discriminate, whether by design or by accident. While many of us are familiar with how race, gender and class operate separately to structure inequality, I want to focus on how these three systems interlock in structuring the institutional dimension of oppression. To get at the interlocking nature of race, class and gender, I want you to think about the antebellum plantation as a guiding metaphor for a variety of American social institutions. Even though slavery is typically analyzed as a racist institution, and occasionally as a class institution, I suggest that slavery was a race, class, gender specific institution. Removing any one piece from our analysis diminishes our understanding of the true nature of relations of domination and subordination under slavery.

Slavery was a profoundly patriarchal institution. It rested on the dual tenets of White male authority and White male property, a joining of the political and the economic within the institution of the family. Heterosexism was assumed and all Whites were expected to marry. Control over affluent White women's sexuality remained key to slavery's survival because property was to be passed on to the legitimate heirs of the slave owner. Ensuring affluent White women's virginity and chastity was deeply intertwined with maintenance of property relations.

Under slavery, we see varying levels of institutional protection given to affluent White women, working class and poor White women and enslaved African women. Poor White women enjoyed few of the protections held out to their upper class sisters. Moreover, the devalued status of Black women was key in keeping all White women in their assigned places. Controlling Black women's fertility was also key to the continuation of slavery, for children born to slave mothers themselves were slaves.

African-American women shared the devalued status of chattel with their husbands, fathers and sons. Racism stripped Blacks as a group of legal rights, education and control over their own persons. African-Americans could be whipped, branded, sold, or killed, not because they were poor, or because they were women, but because they were Black. Racism ensured that Blacks would continue to serve Whites and suffer economic exploitation at the hands of all Whites.

So we have a very interesting chain of command on the plantation—the affluent White master as the reigning patriarch, his White wife helpmate to serve him, help him manage his property and bring up his heirs, his faithful servants whose production and reproduction were tied to the requirements of the capitalist political economy and largely propertyless, working class White men and women watching from afar. In essence, the foundations for the contemporary roles of elite White women, poor Black women, working class White men and a series of other groups can be seen in stark relief in this fundamental American social institution. While Blacks experienced the most harsh treatment under slavery, and thus made slavery clearly visible as a racist institution, race, class and gender interlocked in structuring slavery's systemic organization of domination and subordination.

Even today, the plantation remains a compelling metaphor for institutional oppression. Certainly the actual conditions of oppression are not as severe now as they were then. To argue, as some do, that things have not changed all that much denigrates the achievements of those who struggled for social change before us. But the basic relationships among Black men, Black women, elite White women, elite White men, working class White men and working class White women as groups remain essentially intact.

A brief analysis of key American social institutions most controlled by elite White men should convince us of the interlocking nature of race, class and gender in structuring the institutional dimension of oppression. For example, if you are from an American college or university, is your campus a modern plantation? Who controls your university's political economy? Are elite White men overrepresented among the upper administrators and trustees controlling your university's finances and policies? Are elite White men being joined by growing numbers of elite White women helpmates? What kinds of people are in your classrooms grooming the next generation who will occupy these and other decision-making positions? Who are the support staff that produce the mass mailings, order the supplies, fix the leaky pipes? Do African-Americans, Hispanics or other people of color form the majority of the invisible workers who feed you, wash your dishes, and clean up your offices and libraries after everyone else has gone home?

If your college is anything like mine, you know the answers to these questions. You may be affiliated with an institution that has Hispanic women as vice-presidents for finance, or substantial numbers of Black men among the faculty. If so, you are fortunate. Much more typical are colleges where a modified version of the plantation as a metaphor for the institutional dimension of oppression survives.

2. The Symbolic Dimension of Oppression

Widespread, societally sanctioned ideologies used to justify relations of domination and subordination comprise the symbolic dimension of oppression. Central to this process is the use of stereotypical or controlling images of diverse race, class and gender groups. In order to assess the power of this dimension of oppression, I want you to make a list, either on paper or in your head, of "masculine" and "feminine" characteristics. If your list is anything like that compiled by most people, it reflects some variation of the following:

Masculine	*Feminine*
aggressive	passive
leader	follower
rational	emotional
strong	weak
intellectual	physical

Not only does this list reflect either/or dichotomous thinking and the need to rank both sides of the dichotomy, but ask yourself exactly which men and women you had in mind when compiling these characteristics. This list applies almost exclusively to middle class White men and women. The allegedly "masculine" qualities that you probably listed are only acceptable when exhibited by elite White men, or when used by Black and Hispanic men against each other or against women of color. Aggressive Black and Hispanic men are seen as dangerous, not powerful, and are often penalized when they exhibit any of the allegedly "masculine" characteristics. Working class and poor White men fare slightly better and are also denied the allegedly "masculine" symbols of leadership, intellectual competence, and human rationality. Women of color and working class and poor White women are also not represented on this list, for they have never had the luxury of being "ladies." What appear to be universal categories representing all men and women instead are unmasked as being applicable to only a small group.

It is important to see how the symbolic images applied to different race, class and gender groups interact in maintaining systems of domination and subordination. If I were to ask you to repeat the same assignment, only this time, by making separate lists for Black men, Black women, Hispanic women and Hispanic men, I suspect that your gender symbolism would be quite different. In comparing all of the lists, you might begin to see the interdependence of symbols applied to all groups. For example, the elevated images of White womanhood need devalued images of Black womanhood in order to maintain credibility.

While the above exercise reveals the interlocking nature of race, class and gender in structuring the symbolic dimension of oppression, part of its importance lies in demonstrating how race, class and gender pervade a wide range of what appears to be universal language. Attending to diversity in our scholarship, in our teaching, and in our daily lives provides a new angle of vision on interpretations of reality thought to be natural, normal and "true." Moreover, viewing images of masculinity and femininity as universal gender symbolism, rather than as symbolic images that are race, class and gender specific, renders the experiences of people of color and of nonprivileged White women and men invisible. One way to dehumanize an individual or group is to deny the reality of their experiences. So when we refuse to deal with race or class because they do not appear to be directly relevant to gender, we are actually becoming part of someone else's problem.

Assuming that everyone is affected differently by the same interlocking set of symbolic images allows us to move forward toward new analyses. Women of color and White women have different relations to White male authority and this difference explains the distinct gender symbolism applied to both groups. Black women encounter controlling images such as the mammy, the matriarch, the mule and the whore, that encourage others to reject us as fully human people. Ironically, the negative nature of these images simultaneously encourages us to reject them. In contrast, White women are offered seductive images, those that promise to reward them for supporting the status quo. And yet seductive images can be equally controlling. Consider, for example, the views of Nancy White, a 73-year-old Black woman, concerning images of rejection and seduction:

> My mother used to say that the black woman is the white man's mule and the white woman is his dog. Now, she said that to say this: we do the heavy work and get beat whether we do it well or not. But the white woman is closer to the master and he pats them on the head and lets them sleep in the house, but he ain't gon' treat neither one like he was dealing with a person. (Gwaltney 1980, 148)

Both sets of images stimulate particular political stances. By broadening the analysis beyond the confines of race, we can see the varying levels of rejection and seduction available to each of us due to our race, class and gender identity. Each of us lives with an allotted portion of institutional privilege and penalty, and with varying levels of rejection and seduction inherent in the symbolic images applied to us. This is the context in which we make our choices. Taken together, the institutional and symbolic dimensions of oppression create a structural backdrop against which all of us live our lives.

3. The Individual Dimension of Oppression

Whether we benefit or not, we all live within institutions that reproduce race, class and gender oppression. Even if we never have any contact with members of other race, class and gender groups, we all encounter images of these groups and are exposed to the symbolic meanings attached to those images. On this dimension of oppression, our individual biographies vary tremendously. As a result of our institutional and symbolic statuses, all of our choices become political acts.

Each of us must come to terms with the multiple ways in which race, class and gender as categories of analysis frame our individual biographies. I have lived my entire life as an African-American woman from a working class family and this basic fact has had a profound impact on my personal biography. Imagine how different your life might be if you had been born Black, or White, or poor, or of a different race/class/gender group than the one with which you are most familiar. The institutional treatment you would have received and the symbolic meanings attached to your very existence might differ dramatically from that you now consider to be natural, normal and part of everyday life. You might be the same, but your personal biography might have been quite different.

I believe that each of us carries around the cumulative effect of our lives within multiple structures of oppression. If you want to see how much you have been affected by this whole thing, I ask you one simple question—who are your close friends? Who are the people with whom you can share your hopes, dreams, vulnerabilities, fears and victories? Do they look like you? If they are all the same, circumstance may be the cause. For the first seven years of my life I saw only low income Black people. My friends from those years reflected the composition of my community. But now that I am an adult, can the defense of circumstance explain the patterns of people that I trust as my friends and colleagues? When given other alternatives, if my friends and colleagues reflect the homogeneity of one race, class and gender group, then these categories of analysis have indeed become barriers to connection.

I am not suggesting that people are doomed to follow the paths laid out for them by race, class and gender as categories of analysis. While these three structures certainly frame my opportunity structure, I as an individual always have the choice of accepting things as they are, or trying to change them. As Nikki Giovanni points out, "we've got to live in the real world. If we don't like the world we're living in, change it. And if we can't change it, we change ourselves. We can do something" (Tate 1983, 68). While a piece of the oppressor may be planted deep within each of us, we each have the choice of accepting that piece or challenging it as part of the "true focus of revolutionary change."

How Can We Transcend the Barriers Created by Our Experiences with Race, Class and Gender Oppression in order to Build the Types of Coalitions Essential for Social Change?

Reconceptualizing oppression and seeing the barriers created by race, class and gender as interlocking categories of analysis is a vital first step. But we must transcend these barriers by moving toward race, class and gender as categories of connection, by building relationships and coalitions that will bring about social change. What are some of the issues involved in doing this?

1. Differences in Power and Privilege

First, we must recognize that our differing experiences with oppression create problems in the relationships among us. Each of us lives within a system that vests us with varying levels of power and privilege. These differences in power, whether structured along axes of race, class, gender, age or sexual orientation, frame our relationships. African-American writer June Jordan describes her discomfort on a Caribbean vacation with Olive, the Black woman who cleaned her room:

> . . . even though both "Olive" and "I" live inside a conflict neither one of us created, and even though both of us therefore hurt inside that conflict, I may be one of the monsters she needs to eliminate from her universe and, in a sense, she may be one of the monsters in mine. (1985, 47)

Differences in power constrain our ability to connect with one another even when we think we are engaged in dialogue across differences. Let me give you an example. One year, the students in my course "Sociology of the Black Community" got into a heated discussion about the reasons for the upsurge of racial incidents on college campuses. Black students complained vehemently about the apathy and resistance they felt most White students expressed about examining their own racism. Mark, a White male student, found their comments particularly unsettling. After claiming that all the Black people he had ever known had expressed no such beliefs to him, he questioned how representative the viewpoints of his fellow students actually were. When pushed further, Mark revealed that he had participated in conversations over the years with the Black domestic worker employed by his family. Since she had never expressed such strong feelings about White racism, Mark was genuinely shocked by class discussions. Ask yourselves whether that domestic worker was in a position to speak freely. Would it have been wise for her to do so in a situation where the power between the two parties was so unequal?

In extreme cases, members of privileged groups can erase the very presence of the less privileged. When I first moved to Cincinnati, my family and I went on a picnic at a local park. Picnicking next to us was a family of White Appalachians. When I went to push my daughter on the swings, several of the children came over. They had missing, yellowed and broken teeth, they wore old clothing and their poverty was evident. I was shocked. Growing up in a large eastern city, I had never seen such awful poverty among Whites. The segregated neighborhoods in which I grew up made White poverty all but invisible. More importantly, the privileges attached to my newly acquired social class position allowed me to ignore and minimize the poverty among Whites that I did encounter. My reactions to those children made me realize how confining phrases such as "well, at least they're not Black," had become for me. In learning to grant human subjectivity to the Black victims of poverty, I had simultaneously learned to demean White victims of poverty. By applying categories of race to the objective conditions confronting me, I was quantifying and ranking oppressions and missing the very real suffering which, in fact, is the real issue.

One common pattern of relationships across differences in power is one that I label "voyeurism." From the perspective of the privileged, the lives of people of color, of the poor, and of women are interesting for their entertainment value. The privileged become voyeurs, passive onlookers who do not relate to the less powerful, but who are interested in seeing how the "different" live. Over the years, I have heard numerous African-American students complain about professors who never call on them except when a so-called Black issue is being discussed. The students' interest in discussing race or qualifications for doing so appear unimportant to the professor's efforts to use Black students' experiences as stories to make the material come alive for the White student audience. Asking Black students to perform on cue and provide a Black experience for their White classmates can be seen as voyeurism at its worst.

Members of subordinate groups do not willingly participate in such exchanges but often do so because members of dominant groups control the institutional and symbolic apparatuses of oppression. Racial/ethnic groups, women, and the poor have never had the luxury of being voyeurs of the lives of the privileged. Our ability to survive in hostile settings has hinged on our ability to learn intricate details about the behavior and world view of the powerful and adjust our behavior accordingly. I need only point to the difference in perception of those men and women in abusive relationships. Where men can view their girlfriends and wives as sex objects, helpmates and a collection of stereotypes—categories of voyeurism—women must be attuned to every nuance of their partners' behavior. Are women "naturally" better in relating to people with more power than themselves, or have circumstances mandated that men and women develop different skills? . . .

Coming from a tradition where most relationships across difference are squarely rooted in relations of domination and subordination, we have much less experience relating to people as different but equal. The classroom is potentially one powerful and safe space where dialogues among individuals of unequal power relationships can occur. The relationship between Mark, the student in my class, and the domestic worker is typical of a whole series of relationships that people have when they relate across differences in power and privilege. The relationship among Mark and his classmates represents the power of the classroom to minimize those differences so that people of different levels of power can use race, class and gender as categories of analysis in order to generate meaningful dialogues. In this case, the classroom equalized racial difference so that Black students who normally felt silenced spoke out. White students like Mark, generally unaware of how they had been privileged by their whiteness, lost that privilege in the classroom and thus became open to genuine dialogue . . . .

2. Coalitions around Common Causes

A second issue in building relationships and coalitions essential for social change concerns knowing the real reasons for coalition. Just what brings people together? One powerful catalyst fostering group solidarity is the presence of a common enemy. African-American, Hispanic, Asian-American, and women's studies all share the common intellectual heritage of challenging what passes for certified knowledge in the academy. But politically expedient relationships and coalitions like these are fragile because, as June Jordan points out:

> It occurs to me that much organizational grief could be avoided if people understood that partnership in misery does not necessarily provide for partnership for change. When we get the monsters off our backs all of us may want to run in very different directions. (1985, 47)

Sharing a common cause assists individuals and groups in maintaining relationships that transcend their differences. Building effective coalitions involves struggling to hear one another and developing empathy for each other's points of view. The coalitions that I have been involved in that lasted and that worked have been those where commitment to a specific issue mandated collaboration as the best strategy for addressing the issue at hand.

Several years ago, master degree in hand, I chose to teach in an inner-city parochial school in danger of closing. The money was awful, the conditions were poor, but the need was great. In my job, I had to work with a range of individuals who, on the surface, had very little in common. We had White nuns, Black middle class graduate students, Blacks from the "community," some of whom had been incarcerated and/or were affiliated with a range of federal anti-poverty programs. Parents formed another part of this community, Harvard faculty another, and a few well-meaning White liberals from Colorado were sprinkled in for good measure.

As you might imagine, tension was high. Initially, our differences seemed insurmountable. But as time passed, we found a common bond that we each brought to the school. In spite of profound differences in our personal biographies, differences that in other settings would have hampered our ability to relate to one another, we found that we were all deeply committed to the education of Black children. By learning to value each other's commitment and by recognizing that we each had different skills that were essential to actualizing that commitment, we built an effective coalition around a common cause. Our school was successful, and the children we taught benefited from the diversity we offered them.

. . . None of us alone has a comprehensive vision of how race, class and gender operate as categories of analysis or how they might be used as categories of connection. Our personal biographies offer us partial views. Few of us can manage to study race, class and gender simultaneously. Instead, we each know more about some dimensions of this larger story and less about others. . . . Just as the members of the school had special skills to offer to the task of building the school, we have areas of specialization and expertise, whether scholarly, theoretical, pedagogical or within areas of race, class or gender. We do not all have to do the same thing in the same way. Instead, we must support each other's efforts, realizing that they are all part of the larger enterprise of bringing about social change.

3. Building Empathy

A third issue involved in building the types of relationships and coalitions essential for social change concerns the issue of individual accountability. Race, class and gender oppression form the structural backdrop against which we frame our relationship—these are the forces that encourage us to substitute voyeurism . . . for fully human relationships. But while we may not have created this situation, we are each responsible for making individual, personal choices concerning which elements of race, class and gender oppression we will accept and which we will work to change.

One essential component of this accountability involves developing empathy for the experiences of individuals and groups different than ourselves. Empathy begins with taking an interest in the facts of other people's lives, both as individuals and as groups. If you care about me, you should want to know not only the details of my personal biography but a sense of how race, class and gender as categories of analysis created the institutional and symbolic backdrop for my personal biography. How can you hope to assess my character without knowing the details of the circumstances I face?

Moreover, by taking a theoretical stance that we have all been affected by race, class and gender as categories of analysis that have structured our treatment, we open up possibilities for using those same constructs as categories of connection in building empathy. For example, I have a good White woman friend with whom I share common interests and beliefs. But we know that our racial differences have provided us with different experiences. So we talk about them. We do not assume that because I am Black, race has only affected me and not her or that because I am a Black woman, race neutralizes the effect of gender in my life while accenting it in hers. We take those same categories of analysis that have created cleavages in our lives, in this case, categories of race and gender, and use them as categories of connection in building empathy for each other's experiences.

Finding common causes and building empathy is difficult, no matter which side of privilege we inhabit. Building empathy from the dominant side of privilege is difficult, simply because individuals from privileged backgrounds are not encouraged to do so. For example, in order for those of you who are White to develop empathy for the experiences of people of color, you must grapple with how your white skin has privileged you. This is difficult to do, because it not only entails the intellectual process of seeing how whiteness is elevated in institutions and symbols, but it also involves the often painful process of seeing how your whiteness has shaped your personal biography. Intellectual stances against the institutional and symbolic dimensions of racism are generally easier to maintain than sustained self-reflection about how racism has shaped all of our individual biographies. Were and are your fathers, uncles, and grandfathers really more capable than mine, or can their accomplishments be explained in part by the racism members of my family experienced? Did your mothers stand silently by and watch all this happen? More importantly, how have they passed on the benefits of their whiteness to you?

These are difficult questions, and I have tremendous respect for my colleagues and students who are trying to answer them. Since there is no compelling reason to examine the source and meaning of one's own privilege, I know that those who do so have freely chosen this stance. They are making conscious efforts to root out the piece of the oppressor planted within them. To me, they are entitled to the support of people of color in their efforts. Men who declare themselves feminists, members of the middle class who ally themselves with anti-poverty struggles, heterosexuals who support gays and lesbians, are all trying to grow, and their efforts place them far ahead of the majority who never think of engaging in such important struggles.

Building empathy from the subordinate side of privilege is also difficult, but for different reasons. Members of subordinate groups are understandably reluctant to abandon a basic mistrust of members of powerful groups because this basic mistrust has traditionally been central to their survival. As a Black woman, it would be foolish for me to assume that White women, or Black men, or White men or any other group with a history of exploiting African-American women have my best interests at heart. These groups enjoy varying amounts of privilege over me and therefore I must carefully watch them and be prepared for a relation of domination and subordination.

Like the privileged, members of subordinate groups must also work toward replacing judgments by category with new ways of thinking and acting. Refusing to do so stifles prospects for effective coalition and social change. Let me use another example from my own experiences. When I was an undergraduate, I had little time or patience for the theorizing of the privileged. My initial years at a private, elite institution were difficult, not because the coursework was challenging (it was, but that wasn't what distracted me) or because I had to work while my classmates lived on family allowances (I was used to work). The adjustment was difficult because I was surrounded by so many people who took their privilege for granted. Most of them felt entitled to their wealth. That astounded me.

I remember one incident of watching a White woman down the hall in my dormitory try to pick out which sweater to wear. The sweaters were piled up on her bed in all the colors of the rainbow, sweater after sweater. She asked my advice in a way that let me know that choosing a sweater was one of the most important decisions she had to make on a daily basis. Standing knee-deep in her sweaters, I realized how different our lives were. She did not have to worry about maintaining a solid academic average so that she could receive financial aid. Because she was in the majority, she was not treated as a representative of her race. She did not have to consider how her classroom comments or basic existence on campus contributed to the treatment her group would receive. Her allowance protected her from having to work, so she was free to spend her time studying, partying, or in her case, worrying about which sweater to wear. The degree of inequality in our lives and her unquestioned sense of entitlement concerning that inequality offended me. For a while, I categorized all affluent White women as being superficial, arrogant, overly concerned with material possessions, and part of my problem. But had I continued to classify people in this way, I would have missed out on making some very good friends whose discomfort with their inherited or acquired social class privileges pushed them to examine their position.

Since I opened with the words of Audre Lorde, it seems appropriate to close with another of her ideas. . . .

> Each of us is called upon to take a stand. So in these days ahead, as we examine ourselves and each other, our works, our fears, our differences, our sisterhood and survivals, I urge you to tackle what is most difficult for us all, self-scrutiny of our complacencies, the idea that since each of us believes she is on the side of right, she need not examine her position. (1985)

I urge you to examine your position.

References

Gwaltney, John Langston. 1980. *Drylongso: A Self-Portrait of Black America*. New York: Vintage.

Harding, Sandra. 1986. *The Science Question in Feminism*. Ithaca, New York: Cornell University Press.

Jordan, June. 1985. *On Call: Political Essays*. Boston: South End Press.

Lorde, Audre. 1984. *Sister Outsider*. Trumansberg, New York: The Crossing Press.

_____. 1985. "Sisterhood and Survival." Keynote address, conference on the Black Woman Writer and the Diaspora, Michigan State University.

Spelman, Elizabeth. 1982. "Theories of Race and Gender: The Erasure of Black Women." *Quest* 5: 36–62.

Tate, Claudia. ed. 1983. *Black Women Writers at Work*. New York: Continuum.

Questions for Critical Thinking

1. Collins argues that we often fail to see how our own ideas and behaviors perpetuate someone else's oppression. What are some ideas or behaviors that you possess that perpetuate the inequality of others?

2. What makes it difficult to recognize the ways that we participate in transforming difference into inequality?

3. How can recognizing the ways we participate in perpetuating inequality move us toward a more equal society?

Good for the 'Hood?

ANMOL CHADDHA

The following essay, written by sociologist Anmol Chaddha, provides an example of recent efforts to bring about social change by resisting the negative impact of Walmart on poor, urban neighborhoods. Through their resistance, these communities are able to build coalitions to express their needs and redefine the terms of economic development.

At the corner of Grand and Kilpatrick Avenues in Chicago, the Reverend Joseph Kyles addressed a rally last May. "Tomorrow morning," he said, "we need you to pray for the City Council to vote for Wal-Mart in this community." That Rev. Kyles would be preaching the virtues of a corporate retail behemoth was no fluke. It was part of a strategy by Wal-Mart executives to cultivate support among black city council members and church leaders for building two stores in Chicago—each about the size of ten football fields. It is also part of a broader strategy to bring Wal-Mart to the 'hood— touting not just lower prices but also racial equity.

Having built its base in rural areas in the 1960s and extending to suburban markets in the last two decades, Wal-Mart began approaching poor, urban neighborhoods most noticeably in 2003, when it tried to open a store in Inglewood, a poor city near Los Angeles. From there, the company moved to Chicago and New York City. Initial plans to open a store in Queens, New York, were dropped earlier but Wal-Mart executives say they are determined to find another site in New York. With over $280 billion in annual sales and 3,500 stores across the United States, the company is now selling itself as a solution to urban racial inequality.

The pitch goes like this: Wal-Mart is good for poor people of color because they get jobs and also get to buy cheap goods. What executives don't mention is that the jobs come with notoriously low wages and that the company has cracked down on union organizing. But Wal-Mart executives know that poor people of color are in no position to be picky about who brings what jobs to the community. As the largest private employer in the United States, with over 1.2 million workers, Wal-Mart is also the leading employer of African American and Latino workers.

Using race as a selling point for economic development projects in distressed urban areas is not just the handiwork of Wal-Mart. In 2001, developers promoted the Staples Center sports complex in Los Angeles as a boon for a hurting local economy, insisting that it would create jobs for people of color who lived nearby. A 450-foot-tall Marriott hotel is going up on 125th Street in Harlem, and Ikea is planning to open its biggest U.S. furniture store in Brooklyn. All make the same argument: they are helping poor people of color.

Amidst this urban gold rush for developers, communities of color are forced to choose between the very real need for jobs and having a voice in economic development.

Lessons from Inglewood

Willie Cole, a middle-aged black mother, knows firsthand the economic hardships that face the poor neighborhoods of Los Angeles. She was unemployed for two years until she landed a cashier job at a Wal-Mart that opened in Crenshaw in 2003. Although her position typically pays less than $20,000 annually, she stuck with it and was promoted into a management-training program a year later.

Cole represents Wal-Mart's best public relations argument for opening stores in poor urban areas. In fact, the company featured her in a television commercial promoting its contributions to these communities. "When Wal-Mart came in," she says in the ad, dressed in her store uniform and standing near Crenshaw High School, "they let us know that they cared." The spot has been broadcast nationally, and it received heavy airplay in Inglewood leading up to a special election there in April 2004. Wal-Mart had collected signatures for a local ballot initiative that would have exempted the company from the standard environmental reviews and public hearings required to open a store.

In Inglewood, where 47 percent of the residents are black and 46 percent are Latino, Wal-Mart claimed it would create several hundred much-needed jobs. That was attractive to a small city with an official unemployment rate that was approaching double digits. What the massive retail chain failed to mention was that its entrance has been blocked in over 200 so-called "site fights" in states such as Virginia, Vermont and Oregon. Critics, led forcefully by labor unions, denounce the company for paying low wages, providing inadequate health care benefits, displacing local businesses and contributing to undesirable sprawl. The average Wal-Mart salary is at the federal poverty level for a family of four. A study at the University of California, Berkeley, estimates that California pays $86 million in public benefits to Wal-Mart employees whose low incomes qualify them for food stamps, health care and subsidized housing—programs that are funded by taxpayers. Recent studies have identified Wal-Mart as the leading employer of workers receiving public health benefits in Alabama, Connecticut, Georgia, Tennessee, Washington and West Virginia.

When the company gathered the necessary signatures to force a special election in Inglewood, the Los Angeles Alliance for a New Economy (LAANE) formed the Coalition for a Better Inglewood with labor, religious and community allies. "We began organizing grocery workers and local small business owners to present the case against Wal-Mart to community leaders," says Tracy Gray-Barkan, senior research analyst at LAANE. The community-based organization already had some experience with local economic development issues. In 2001, it helped broker a deal with the Staples Center, getting the developers to sign a Community Benefits Agreement that required them to hire local residents, provide living-wage jobs and construct parks. Organizers in Inglewood walked into a tough fight with Wal-Mart. Just a month before the April 2004 election, polling showed residents supporting Wal-Mart's plan by a two-to-one margin, and one of its most prominent supporters was the town's black mayor, Roosevelt Dorn. Over the following weeks, the Coalition for a Better Inglewood reached out to community residents with information on the quality of Wal-Mart jobs and its effect on local business. In this heavily black and Latino city, the groups brought attention to allegations of racial discrimination in hiring by Wal-Mart, as well as a gender discrimination lawsuit that had been filed against the company, covering 1.6 million female Wal-Mart employees.

Although black Congresswoman Maxine Waters and the Reverend Jesse Jackson both lashed out against Wal-Mart's labor practices, many traditional civil rights groups stayed away. John Mack, president of the Los Angeles chapter of the Urban League, which received $65,000 over two years from Wal-Mart, told the *Los Angeles Times,* "I'd rather have a person on somebody's payroll—even if it isn't at the highest wage—than on the unemployment roll." Wal-Mart, by its own account, has made donations to the NAACP, National Council of La Raza, the Congressional Black Caucus, the Organization of Chinese Americans and the League of United Latin American Citizens.

Despite over $10 million spent on the initiative by Wal-Mart, including a newspaper advertisement that publicized its financial support of black and Latino organizations, Inglewood voters rejected the initiative 61 percent to 39 percent. The store would have been the first Wal-Mart Supercenter in a major urban area.

Ultimately, it may have been Wal-Mart's own brashness that helped organizers. The debate in Inglewood was not simply over whether Wal-Mart jobs are good or bad. The company was asking to skip the standard review procedures that normally require the city to consider the impacts of a development project. By bringing attention to Wal-Mart's attempt to circumvent the development process, organizers also framed the fight around the principles of how decisions in Inglewood are made about economic development. "The issue was about community control and community voice," says Gray-Barkan of LAANE.

The Inglewood initiative provided a spark for the Los Angeles City Council to consider an ordinance proposed by a coalition of labor groups, clergy and community organizations. In August 2004, the Council passed the ordinance, which requires a study of the economic impacts of any proposed superstore and allows the community to weigh the potential benefits and costs of the project. Whereas the Inglewood fight was a reaction to a plan initiated by Wal-Mart, "the Los Angeles City Council ordinance is a proactive process for residents to have a say in what gets developed in their communities," says Gray-Barkan.

A Harder Challenge in Chicago

Last May, just two weeks after the special election in Inglewood, the Chicago City Council met to discuss proposed zoning changes that would allow the construction of a Wal-Mart Supercenter on the South Side and another on the West Side.

It was a heated debate since Wal-Mart employed many of the same tactics it had used in Inglewood. "It brought the same seductive claims of jobs and low prices to black communities," explains Dorian Warren, an expert on race and organized labor who is currently a post-doctoral fellow with University of Chicago's School of Public Policy.

Just as it had done in Southern California, the company appealed to black church leaders and City Council members, "Any job is better than no job," the Reverend Ronald Wilks said at the time.

While the City Council debated, a coalition formed, led by Jobs With Justice, a national workers' rights organization. It included unions and progressive black church leaders who decided that it might not be politically feasible to ban Wal-Mart from Chicago, given how much residents needed jobs. Instead, the groups began pushing for a Community Benefits Agreement that would require Wal-Mart to pay higher wages and hire local residents.

To promote its position, Wal-Mart organized a town-hall meeting with religious leaders in the Austin neighborhood, the potential site of the South Side store, and flew out a black executive from its Arkansas headquarters. The ministers presented a demand that surprised the company: hire ex-offenders, a growing population on the West and South Sides that are excluded from employment opportunities. While Wal-Mart promoted its jobs as valuable opportunities for local residents, it made no promises to hire ex-offenders. Instead, Wes Gillespie, the black executive, presented himself to the church leaders as an example of the opportunities provided by Wal-Mart. And Alton Murphy, a black Wal-Mart district manager, quoted from the Bible when asked about the quality of Wal-Mart jobs. "Whatever you do," he recited from Colossans 3:23, "work at it with all your heart, as working for the Lord, not for men."

Despite the company's efforts to build support, not all of the ministers were sold on the plan. The 8,500-member Trinity United Church of Christ on the South Side became a center of opposition to Wal-Mart, and its leaders directly linked the store's attractive low prices to its low-paying jobs. "Whenever price means more to you than principle," wrote Trinity's pastor, the Reverend Jeremiah Wright, in the church newsletter, "you have defined yourself as a prostitute." Wright charged that Wal-Mart's backers among the City Council and the black religious community were "pimping" black residents and their economic hardships.

While Wal-Mart was reaching out to the black community, the United Food and Commercial Workers Local 881 could not easily build a coalition across race lines. According to Chicago labor expert Warren, "a few unions—particularly in the building trades—had historically excluded black men from well-paying union jobs by keeping them out of apprenticeship programs." In the minds of many black leaders, the rapid deindustrialization of the inner city combined with the racism of some building trades unions was largely responsible for the severe joblessness on the South and West Sides.

So when the union spoke of fighting Wal-Mart, it only stirred more resentment. "Some of these same unions never say a thing about the lack of African Americans in the trades," Alderman Isaac Carothers of the West Side complained at a City Council meeting.

Organizers opposing Wal-Mart also faced a more difficult challenge than in Inglewood. Where the company had asked to circumvent the standard review process in Inglewood, in Chicago the debate was over whether Wal-Mart was a good or bad option for residents. More importantly, perhaps, the two Chicago neighborhoods where Wal-Mart proposed its stores and whose residents are more than 90 percent African-American, face an employment crisis even worse than Inglewood. And organizers in Chicago did not have the benefit of taking the issue directly to local residents, since it was not an initiative to be decided by the voters. It was a City Council vote, and that made the fight over Wal-Mart vulnerable to council members who historically do not vote against an economic development proposal in another member's district if that alderman is in favor of the project (the

practice is so prevalent that it's known as "aldermanic perogative").

As it did during the Inglewood fight, Wal-Mart made contributions to the local NAACP and gave a $5,000 contribution to City Council member Emma Mitts, who loudly voiced support for the construction of a Wal-Mart in her West Side district. In what was apparently an attempt to demonstrate its support of the community, the company donated 50 calculators to Austin High School in the district.

The morning after Rev. Kyles asked residents to pray for the approval of the two Wal-Mart stores, the City Council gave a split decision. It rejected the South Side location and approved the proposed store on the West Side. The approval of one store and the rejection of the other had much to do with the politics among members of the City Council, but it also reflected the tensions between the real need to create any jobs and the demand that these actually be good jobs. In what had been described as the most controversial City Council issue in two decades, all but two black aldermen supported the West Side Wal-Mart.

After the vote, a coalition of labor, religious and community groups began pushing for a local ordinance that would attach certain standards to the jobs at large stores like Wal-Mart. It would require so-called "big-box stores" to pay a $10 living wage, provide health benefits and remain neutral in efforts by its workers to form a union. The ordinance, which is still being debated by the City Council, is "a way to regulate the terms on which these stores will come in to the community," explains Chirag Mehta, a researcher at the Center for Urban Economic Development at the University of Illinois at Chicago. In response, the Reverend James Demus, director of the Chicago Southside's NAACP that received a donation from Wal-Mart, testified against the ordinance in early hearings.

Unfinished Business

While Martin Luther King's 1963 "I Have a Dream" speech is the most familiar refrain of the civil rights movement, the full title of the rally was the "March on Washington for Jobs and Freedom." That is, King viewed the struggle for civil rights as linked to economic justice. In many ways, the enduring racial economic inequality since then is the unfinished business of the civil rights movement.

"It has been one of the weak links of racial justice organizing over the last three decades," says Warren, the University of Chicago expert on race and labor. "We have been unable to answer what our fundamental demands are around economic justice," he adds, "and how they relate to racial justice."

Since the rhetoric of race is being used strategically by developers, economic development is now the only area of urban policy that emphasizes issues of race—however hollow that talk may be. There is no similar discussion from local politicians when discussing education or health disparities.

All the economic development plans underway in New York, for example, require buy-in from poor communities of color. Developers are even going to absurd lengths to use race as a selling point. One proposal for the redevelopment of the Victoria Theater—a few doors down from the legendary Apollo Theater—includes a "Harlem-themed restaurant" with a menu that includes such items as a "Zora Neale Hurston salad . . . Miles Davis omelette and a Denzel burger."

For now, Wal-Mart has lost in New York City. Following the battles in Inglewood and Chicago, Wal-Mart's urban strategy continued east to Queens, New York. The proposed site there would have given Wal-Mart a store in nine of the ten largest U.S. urban markets. (The only city being left out is Detroit, which has been dealing with its own economic devastation.) But early reports of Wal-Mart's plans to open in Queens provoked an immediate outcry from labor groups that made a difference in a city where labor still yields power. By the end of February, the developer had dropped the Wal-Mart store from its proposal.

Recognizing that the promise of low-wage jobs is often being promoted to win the support of communities of color, New York City Councilman Charles Barron explains, "We need to distinguish between economic development and economic exploitation." In Barron's district, which includes some of the poorest sections of Brooklyn, a cinema complex recently opened with the promise of jobs for community residents. "All we got was a bunch of popcorn-selling jobs," says Barron.

Pitching proposals to poor communities who are desperate for jobs, private developers are able to exploit the failure of public policy to create jobs in these communities. "There are plenty of other ways to create jobs," says Councilman Barron, who argues for increased investment in public infrastructure such as hospitals and schools to revitalize poor areas like his Brooklyn district. "Private developers," he continues, "manipulate the race question for their financial gain."

In response to Wal-Mart and other development projects, groups in urban communities around the country are using a variety of tools to broker deals that also address other vital areas of economic development, such as housing. Some organizations are pushing for "inclusionary zoning," a regulation that requires developers to set aside residential units in a new development as affordable housing. Other community groups, including ones in New York, want to attach standards to jobs at Wal-Mart if it does open a store somewhere else in the city. Besides its low wages, the lack of adequate health care provided to workers places an unfair burden on the public health care system, many critics charge. A coalition of labor, community groups and responsible employers has sponsored a bill in the city council called the Health Care Security Act, which would require businesses in certain industries to either provide health coverage to their workers or pay fees that the city would use to provide public care to the workers. If passed, the bill would cover any Wal-Mart Superstores that would open in the city.

Organizers view Community Benefits Agreements and related tools as a critical first step in laying the groundwork for a long-term goal of redefining the terms of economic development.

"As long as private developers set the agenda and groups respond by asking for Community Benefits Agreements or inclusionary zoning," says Dorian Warren, the expert on race and labor from the University of Chicago, "we may just be trying to get a piece of the pie. We need to ask, 'What does a different pie look like?'"

Questions for Critical Thinking

1. Chaddha reviews the ways in which various groups organized against having Walmart in their community. Why were they opposed to Walmart? How did the policies and practices of Walmart contribute to inequality?

2. How did this reading expand your ideas of what is involved in working for positive social change?

3. What lessons can movements for social justice learn from the people involved in this movement?

Seeing More Than Black & White
Latinos, Racism, and the Cultural Divides

ELIZABETH MARTINEZ

In the essay that follows, sociologist Elizabeth Martinez offers some explanations for the difficulty the United States has with viewing issues of race beyond a black–white dichotomy and calls for inclusion when discussing racial issues. Especially keeping in mind our increasing diversity as a nation and the ever-growing complexity of race, she asserts that our effectiveness in working toward racial justice will only come when we move beyond black and white.

A certain relish seems irresistible to this Latina as the mass media have been compelled to sit up, look south of the border, and take notice. Probably the Chiapas uprising and Mexico's recent political turmoil have won us no more than a brief day in the sun. Or even less: liberal Ted Koppel still hadn't noticed the historic assassination of presidential candidate Colosio three days afterward. But it's been sweet, anyway.

When Kissinger said years ago "nothing important ever happens in the south," he articulated a contemptuous indifference toward Latin America, its people, and their culture which has long dominated U.S. institutions and attitudes. Mexico may be great for a vacation, and some people like burritos, but the usual image of Latin America combines incompetence with absurdity in loud colors. My parents, both Spanish teachers, endured decades of being told kids were better off learning French.

U.S. political culture is not only Anglo-dominated but also embraces an exceptionally stubborn national self-centeredness, with no global vision other than relations of domination. The U.S. refuses to see itself as one nation sitting on a continent with 20 others all speaking languages other than English and having the right not to be dominated.

Such arrogant indifference extends to Latinos within the U.S. The mass media complain, "people can't relate to Hispanics"—or Asians, they say. Such arrogant indifference has played an important role in invisibilizing La Raza (except where we become a serious nuisance or a handy scapegoat). It is one reason the U.S. harbors an exclusively white-on-Black concept of racism. It is one barrier to new thinking about racism which is crucial today. There are others.

Good-bye White Majority

In a society as thoroughly and violently racialized as the United States, white–Black relations have defined racism for centuries. Today the composition and culture of the U.S. are changing rapidly. We need to consider seriously whether we can afford to maintain an exclusively white/Black model of racism when the population will be 32 percent Latin/Asian/Pacific American and Native American—in short, neither Black nor white—by the year 2050. We are challenged to recognize that multi-colored racism is mushrooming, and then strategize how to resist it. We are challenged to move beyond a dualism comprised of two white supremacist inventions: Blackness and Whiteness.

At stake in those challenges is building a united anti-racist force strong enough to resist contemporary racist strategies of divide-and-conquer. Strong enough in the long run, to help defeat racism itself. Doesn't an exclusively Black/white model of racism discourage the perception of common interests among people of color and thus impede a solidarity that can challenge white supremacy? Doesn't it encourage the isolation of African Americans from potential allies? Doesn't it advise all people of color to spend too much energy understanding our lives in relation to Whiteness, and thus freeze us in a defensive, often self-destructive mode?

No "Oppression Olympics"

For a Latina to talk about recognizing the multi-colored varieties of racism is not, and should not be, yet another round in the Oppression Olympics. We don't need more competition among different social groupings for that "Most Oppressed" gold. We don't need more comparisons of suffering between women and Blacks, the disabled and the gay, Latino teenagers and white seniors, or whatever. We don't need more surveys like the recent much publicized Harris Poll showing that different peoples of color are prejudiced toward each other—a poll patently designed to demonstrate that us coloreds are no better than white folk. (The survey never asked people about positive attitudes.)

Rather, we need greater knowledge, understanding, and openness to learning about each other's histories and present needs as a basis for working together. Nothing could seem more urgent in an era when increasing impoverishment encourages a self-imposed separatism among people of color as a desperate attempt at community survival. Nothing could seem more important as we search for new social change strategies in a time of ideological confusion.

My call to rethink concepts of racism in the U.S. today is being sounded elsewhere. Among academics, liberal foundation administrators, and activist-intellectuals, you can hear talk of the need for a new "racial paradigm" or model. But new thinking seems to proceed in fits and starts, as if dogged by a fear of stepping on toes, of feeling threatened, or of losing one's base. With a few notable exceptions, even our progressive scholars of color do not make the leap from perfunctorily saluting a vague multiculturalism to serious analysis. We seem to have made little progress, if any, since Bob Blauner's 1972 book *Racial Oppression in America*. Recognizing the limits of the white–Black axis, Blauner critiqued White America's ignorance of and indifference to the Chicano/a experience with racism.

Real opposition to new paradigms also exists. There are academics scrambling for one flavor of ethnic studies funds versus another. There are politicians who cultivate distrust of others to keep their own communities loyal. When we hear, for example, of Black/Latino friction, dismay should be quickly followed by investigation. In cities like Los Angeles and New York, it may turn out that political figures scrapping for patronage and payola have played a narrow nationalist game, whipping up economic anxiety and generating resentment that sets communities against each other.

So the goal here, in speaking about moving beyond a bipolar concept of racism is to build stronger unity against white supremacy. The goal is to see our similarities of experience and needs. If that goal sounds naive, think about the hundreds of organizations formed by grassroots women of different colors coming together in recent years. Their growth is one of today's most energetic motions and it spans all ages. Think about the multicultural environmental justice movement. Think about the coalitions to save schools. Small rainbows of our own making are there, to brighten a long road through hellish times.

It is in such practice, through daily struggle together, that we are most likely to find the road to greater solidarity against a common enemy. But we also need a will to find it and ideas about where, including some new theory.

The West Goes East

Until very recently, Latino invisibility—like that of Native Americans and Asian/Pacific Americans—has been close to absolute in U.S. seats of power, major institutions, and the non-Latino public mind. Having lived on both the East and West Coasts for long periods, I feel qualified to pronounce: an especially myopic view of Latinos prevails in the East. This, despite such data as a 24.4 percent Latino population of New York City alone in 1991, or the fact that in 1990 more Puerto Ricans were killed by New York police under suspicious circumstances than any other ethnic group. Latino populations are growing rapidly in many eastern cities and the rural South, yet remain invisible or stigmatized—usually both.

Eastern blinders persist. I've even heard that the need for a new racial paradigm is dismissed in New York as a California hangup. A black Puerto Rican friend in New York, when we talked about experiences of racism common to Black and brown, said "People here don't see Border Patrol brutality against Mexicans as a form of police repression," despite the fact that the Border Patrol is the largest and most uncontrolled police force in the U.S. It would seem that an old ignorance has combined with new immigrant bashing to sustain divisions today.

While the East (and most of the Midwest) usually remains myopic, the West Coast has barely begun to move away from its own denial. Less than two years ago in San Francisco, a city almost half Latino or Asian/Pacific American, a leading daily newspaper could publish a major series on contemporary racial issues and follow the exclusively Black–white paradigm. Although millions of TV viewers saw massive Latino participation in the April 1992 Los Angeles uprising, which included 18 out of 50 deaths and the majority of arrests, the mass media and most people labeled that event "a Black riot."

If the West Coast has more recognition of those who are neither Black nor white, it is mostly out of

fear about the proximate demise of its white majority. A second, closely related reason is the relentless campaign by California Gov. Pete Wilson to scapegoat immigrants for economic problems and pass racist, unconstitutional laws attacking their health, education, and children's future. Wilson has almost single-handedly made the word "immigrant" mean Mexican or other Latino (and sometimes Asian). Who thinks of all the people coming from the former Soviet Union and other countries? The absolute racism of this has too often been successfully masked by reactionary anti-immigrant groups like FAIR blaming immigrants for the staggering African-American unemployment rate.

Wilson's immigrant bashing is likely to provide a model for other parts of the country. The five states with the highest immigration rates—California, Florida, New York, Illinois and Texas—all have a governor up for re-election in 1994. Wilson's tactics won't appear in every campaign but some of the five states will surely see intensified awareness and stigmatization of Latinos as well as Asian/Pacific Islanders. *Editor's Note:* While the specific references are dated, the larger reality is still true: immigration remains a controversial issue in local and regional elections.

As this suggests, what has been a regional issue mostly limited to western states is becoming a national issue. If you thought Latinos were just "Messicans" down at the border, wake up—they are all over North Carolina, Pennsylvania and 8th Avenue Manhattan now. A qualitative change is taking place. With the broader geographic spread of Latinos and Asian/Pacific Islanders has come a nationalization of racist practices and attitudes that were once regional. The west goes east, we could say.

Like the monster Hydra, racism is growing some ugly new heads. We will have to look at them closely.

The Roots of Racism and Latinos

A bipolar model of racism—racism as white on Black—has never really been accurate. Looking for the roots of racism in the U.S. we can begin with the genocide against American Indians which made possible the U.S. land base, crucial to white settlement and early capitalist growth. Soon came the massive enslavement of African people which facilitated that growth. As slave labor became economically critical, "blackness" became ideologically critical; it provided the very source of "whiteness" and the heart of racism. Franz Fanon would write, "colour is the most outward manifestation of race."

If Native Americans had been a crucial labor force during those same centuries, living and working in the white man's sphere, our racist ideology might have evolved differently. "The tawny," as Ben Franklin dubbed them, might have defined the opposite of what he called "the lovely white." But with Indians decimated and survivors moved to distant concentration camps, they became unlikely candidates for this function. Similarly, Mexicans were concentrated in the distant West; elsewhere Anglo fear of them or need to control was rare. They also did not provide the foundation for a definition of whiteness.

Some anti-racist left activists have put forth the idea that only African Americans experience racism as such and that the suffering of other people of color results from national minority rather than racial oppression. From this viewpoint, the exclusively white/Black model for racism is correct. Latinos, then, experience exploitation and repression for reasons of culture and nationality— not for their "race." (It should go without saying that while racism is an all-too-real social fact, race has no scientific basis.)

Does the distinction hold? This and other theoretical questions call for more analysis and more expertise than one article can offer. In the meantime, let's try on the idea that Latinos do suffer for their nationality and culture, especially language. They became part of the U.S. through the 1846–48 war on Mexico and thus a foreign population to be colonized. But as they were reduced to cheap or semi-slave labor, they quickly came to suffer for their "race"—meaning, as non-whites. In the Southwest of a super-racialized nation

the broad parallelism of race and class embrace Mexicans ferociously.

The bridge here might be a definition of racism as "the reduction of the cultural to the biological," in the words of French scholar Christian Delacampagne now working in Egypt. Or: "racism exists wherever it is claimed that a given social status is explained by a given natural characteristic." We know that line: Mexicans are just naturally lazy and have too many children, so they're poor and exploited.

The discrimination, oppression and hatred experienced by Native Americans, Mexicans, Asian/Pacific Islanders, and Arab Americans are forms of racism. Speaking only of Latinos, we have seen in California and the Southwest, especially along the border, almost 150 years of relentless repression which today includes Central Americans among its targets. That history reveals hundreds of lynchings between 1847 and 1935, the use of counterinsurgency armed forces beginning with the Texas Rangers, random torture and murder by Anglo ranchers, forced labor, rape by border lawmen, and the prevailing Anglo belief that a Mexican life doesn't equal a dog's in value.

But wait. If color is so key to racial definition, as Fanon and others say, perhaps people of Mexican background experience racism less than national minority oppression because they are not dark enough as a group. For White America, shades of skin color are crucial to defining worth. The influence of those shades has also been internalized by communities of color. Many Latinos can and often want to pass for whites; therefore, White America may see them as less threatening than darker sisters and brothers.

Here we confront more of the complexity around us today, with questions like: What about the usually poor, very dark Mexican or Central American of strong Indian or African heritage? (Yes, folks, 200,000–300,000 Africans were brought to Mexico as slaves, which is far, far more than the Spaniards who came.) And what about the effects of accented speech or foreign name, characteristics that may instantly subvert "passing"?

What about those cases where a Mexican-American is never accepted, no matter how light-skinned, well-dressed or well-spoken? A Chicano lawyer friend coming home from a professional conference in suit, tie and briefcase found himself on a bus near San Diego that was suddenly stopped by the Border Patrol. An agent came on board and made a beeline through the all-white rows of passengers direct to my friend. "Your papers." The agent didn't believe Jose was coming from a U.S. conference and took him off the bus to await proof. Jose was lucky; too many Chicanos and Mexicans end up killed.

In a land where the national identity is white, having the "wrong" nationality becomes grounds for racist abuse. Who would draw a sharp line between today's national minority oppression in the form of immigrant-bashing, and racism?

None of this aims to equate the African American and Latino experiences; that isn't necessary even if it were accurate. Many reasons exist for the persistence of the white/Black paradigm of racism; they include numbers, history, and the psychology of whiteness. In particular they include centuries of slave revolts, a Civil War, and an ongoing resistance to racism that cracked this society wide open while the world watched. Nor has the misery imposed on Black people lessened in recent years. New thinking about racism can and should keep this experience at the center.

A Deadly Dualism

The exclusively white/Black concept of race and racism in the U.S. rests on a western, Protestant form of dualism woven into both race and gender relations from earliest times. In the dualist universe there is only black and white. A disdain, indeed fear, of mixture haunts the Yankee soul; there is no room for any kind of multi-faceted identity, any hybridism.

As a people, La Raza combines three sets of roots—indigenous, European, and African—all in widely varying degrees. In short we represent a profoundly un-American concept: *mestizaje* (pronounced mess-tee-zah-hey), the mixing of peoples and emergence of new peoples. A highly racialized society like this one cannot deal with or allow room for *mestizaje*. It has never learned to do much more than hiss "miscegenation!" Or, like that Alabama high school principal who recently denied the right of a mixed-blood pupil to attend the prom, to say: "your parents made a mistake." Apparently we, all the millions of La Raza, are just that—a mistake.

Mexicans in the U.S. also defy the either–or, dualistic mind in that, on the one hand, we are a colonized people displaced from the ancestral homeland with roots in the present-day U.S. that go back centuries. Those ancestors didn't cross the border; the border crossed them. At the same time many of us have come to the U.S. more recently as "immigrants" seeking work. The complexity of Raza baffles and frustrates most Anglos; they want to put one neat label on us. It baffles many Latinos too, who often end up categorizing themselves racially as "Other" for lack of anything better. For that matter, the term "Latino" which I use here is a monumental simplification; it refers to 20-plus nationalities and a wide range of classes.

But we need to grapple with the complexity, for there is more to come. If anything, this nation will see more *mestizaje* in the future, embracing innumerable ethnic combinations. What will be its effects? Only one thing seems certain: "white" shall cease to be the national identity.

A glimpse at the next century tells us how much we need to look beyond the white/Black model of race relations and racism. White/Black are real poles, central to the history of U.S. racism. We can neither ignore them nor stop there. But our effectiveness in fighting racism depends on seeing the changes taking place, trying to perceive the contours of the future. From the time of the Greeks to the present, racism around the world has had certain commonalties but no permanently fixed character. It is evolving again today, and we'd best labor to read the new faces of this Hydra-headed monster. Remember, for every head that Hydra lost it grew two more.

Sometimes the problem seems so clear. Last year I showed slides of Chicano history to an Oakland high school class with 47 African Americans and three Latino students. The images included lynchings and police beatings of Mexicans and other Latinos, and many years of resistance. At the end one Black student asked, "Seems like we have had a lot of experiences in common—so why can't Blacks and Mexicans get along better?" No answers, but there was the first step: asking the question.

Questions for Critical Thinking

1. Martinez offers some explanations for the difficulty the United States has with viewing issues of race beyond a black–white dichotomy. What do you think of her explanations?

2. Has the reality that whites will no longer be a majority in the United States impacted race relations positively or negatively?

3. How might expanding issues of race beyond the black–white dichotomy help us to move toward a system of equal access to opportunity with regard to race?

Reform or Transformation?

The Pivotal Role of Food Justice in the U.S. Food Movement

ERIC HOLT-GIMÉNEZ AND YI WANG

A sixth of the world's population is now hungry, just as a sixth of the US population is "food insecure." These severe levels of hunger and insecurity share root causes, located in the political economy of a global, corporate food system. As the authors illustrate, food justice is centrally positioned to influence the direction of a change in this system. What will be of particular importance is how addressing issues of racial and class inequality is integrated into this change.

The global food crisis has pushed the U.S. food movement to a political juncture. A sixth of the world's population is now hungry—just as a sixth of the U.S. population is "food insecure." These severe levels of hunger and insecurity share root causes, located in the political economy of a global, corporate food regime. Because of its political location between reformist calls for food security and radical calls for food sovereignty, food justice is pivotally placed to influence the direction of food-systems change. This placement subjects the concept of food justice to multiple claims, definitions, and practices that tend either to affirm a structural focus on resource redistribution, or to dilute its political meaning by focusing on food access. How issues of race and class

are resolved will influence the political direction of the food justice movement's organizational alliances: toward reform or toward transformation. How the food justice movement "pivots" may determine the degree to which it is able to bring about substantive changes to the U.S. food system.

Background: The Global Food Crisis, Hunger and Food Security

The global food price crisis of 2008 ushered in record levels of hunger for the world's poor at a time of record global harvests as well as record profits for the world's major agrifoods corporations (Lean 2008). The combination of increasing hunger in the midst of wealth and abundance unleashed a flurry of worldwide "food riots" (including in the United States) not seen for many decades. In June 2008, the World Bank reported that global food prices had risen 83 percent in three years and the Food and Agriculture Organization of the United Nations (FAO) cited a 45 percent increase in their world food price index in just nine months (Wiggins and Levy 2008). Despite a brief drop in the food price index, retail food prices remained high through 2010 and into 2011 when the index spiked again to record levels (FAO 2011). According to the United Nations World

"Reform or Transformation? The Pivotal Role of Food Justice in the U.S. Food Movement," Eric Holt-Giménez and Yi Wang, published in Race/Ethnicity: Multidisciplinary Global Contexts (published by Indiana University Press); Kirwan Institute for the Study of Race and Ethnicity at The Ohio State University.

Food Program, more than 90 percent of the world's hungry—most of whom are peasant farmers—are simply too poor to buy enough food (WFP 2011). Some of the planet's hungry people live in the Global North, though hunger is measured as "food insecurity" and social safety nets are more readily available. Levels of food insecurity in the United States mirror global patterns; more than 50 million people are now food insecure and one in nine Americans are on food stamps (Nord et al. 2010).

Food insecurity in the United States is characterized by a nationwide epidemic of diet-related diseases that result in an estimated $240 billion a year in health costs (Schlosser 2001) that fall disproportionately on low-income communities of color (Baker et al. 2006). In these neighborhoods, food access is often limited to the cheap, high-fat, high-salt, high-calorie, processed food available at gas stations, liquor stores, corner stores, and fast food outlets (Herrera, Khanna, and Davis 2009; Mamen 2007; Morton and Blanchard 2007; Parker 2005). When available, fruits, vegetables, and low-fat dairy products are often of inferior quality and are more expensive at these establishments than in supermarkets and grocery stores (Perry and Harries 2007). Lack of access to affordable, fresh, and healthy food, when combined with preexisting health disparities in regions with high socioeconomic inequality, has led to a dramatic increase in obesity, heart disease, cancer, diabetes, immunity disorders, and hypertension (Alkon and Norgaard 2009).

Dealing with what food-systems analyst Raj Patel (2007) describes as crises of the "stuffed and starved" has produced a wide array of initiatives that, while linked through their focus on food, are largely divided between those who want to preserve the political economy of the existing global food system and those who seek to change it. The former tend to be from government and industry; the latter make up the global "food movement." The food movement itself, however, is diverse and subject to social divides.

The Rise and Divides of Food Movements

Even before the onset of the current food price crisis, the decades-long increase in hunger, food insecurity, diet-related diseases—fueled by low-nutrient, highly processed food—gave rise to social movements for community food security and food justice (Winne 2008), food sovereignty (Wittman, Desmarais, and Wiebe 2010), food democracy (Lang 2005), new agrarianism (Jackson, Berry, and Coleman 1984), food safety (Nestle 2002), anti-hunger (Berg 2008), and Slow Food that is "good, clean and fair" (Petrini 2005). This past decade has seen a boom in documentaries that both attack the industrial agrifoods complex and champion local, organic, sustainable food systems. These titles include Super Size Me (Spurlock 2004), The Future of Food (Garcia 2004), The World According to Monsanto (Robin 2008), Food Inc. (Kenner 2009), and King Corn (Woolf 2007).

These efforts have loosely come to be identified as the "food movement." Journalism professor Michael Pollan, one of the mainstream media's prominent food celebrities, asserts that "[t]he food movement coalesces around the recognition that today's food and farming economy is 'unsustainable'—that it can't go on in its current form much longer without courting a breakdown of some kind, whether environmental, economic, or both. . . ." For Pollan, the food movement is "splintered" in its origins, "[unified] as yet by little more than the recognition that industrial food production is in need of reform because its social/environmental/public health/animal welfare/gastronomic costs are too high" (Pollan 2010).

This recognition leads to calls for quality, environmental sustainability, and safety of food (e.g., fresh, organic, local) as well as for the reaffirmation of environmental values and community relationships associated with halcyon days of a reconstructed agrarian past. These make up what Alkon and Agyeman (2011a) refer to as the dominant food-movement narrative. Grounded in the social base of predominantly white, middle-class consumers, this narrative has become an important reference in the mainstream media. However, it also tends to render the food histories and realities of low-income people and people of color invisible.

An emblematic example of this narrative at work is the ubiquitous food-movement adage to fix the food system by "voting with your fork" (Pollan 2006). This strategy not only takes the access and purchasing power of the predominantly white, middle-class consumer for granted, but also it assumes that our food system can be reformed through informed consumer choice, and ignores the ways working-class and people of color have historically brought about social change (Guthman 2008). But, as one Slow Food leader counsels, "If dinner is a democratic election . . . in many electoral districts . . . there are no polling stations [and] there is only one candidate, the incumbent: fast food" (Viertel 2011). The notion that the food system can be transformed through individual acts of consumption—rather than through lobbying, organizing, boycotts, mobilization, or direct action—fits nicely within the prevailing neoliberal economic rhetoric: that unregulated capitalist markets yield the most efficient allocation of resources (Harvey 2005). The prominence of the privileged in the food-movement narrative, along with its "whiteness" (Slocum 2007), reflects the uneasy dualism between the trend of "quality food" for higher-income consumers and "other food" consumed by the masses (Goodman and Goodman 2008 6).

On the ground, the food movement's dominant narrative is, arguably, skin deep. Its widespread growth through farmers' markets, Community Supported Agriculture (CSAs), and high-end organic/"locavore" restaurants and retail chains has also been paralleled by less-celebrated expansions of the community food security movement (CFS), the food justice movement (FJ), and the

food-sovereignty movement (FS) over the last ten years. While not rejecting the need for "good," "real," sustainable, or organic food, the agendas of these movements are focused on the lack of good food access, social and distributional inequities, institutional racism and classism, and the need to address labor, gender, and human rights in the food system (Holt-Giménez, Patel, and Shattuck 2009; Gottlieb and Joshi 2010 Alkon and Agyeman 2011a,b).

These developments suggest that below the surface of its amorphous "splintering," the food movement is segmented in ways that reflect social hierarchies of race and class in the food system. As we will explore further in this article, this segmentation has important implications for movement-based strategies for food-systems change.

Community Food Security, Food Justice, and Food Sovereignty: Adding Voices, Being Heard, or Forging a New Narrative?

The CFS is a broad-based movement that grew to national prominence with the formation of the Community Food Security Coalition (CFSC), a nonprofit group founded in 1994. With more than 250 affiliated organizations, the CFSC is representative of the diversity within the U.S. food movement. The CFSC refers to Hamm and Bellows's (2003) definition of community food security as "a condition in which all community residents obtain a safe, culturally acceptable, nutritionally adequate diet through a sustainable food system that maximizes community self-reliance and social justice" (CFSC 2004; 2010). The Coalition supports food-system alternatives by advocating for new business models, cooperative ownership of retail outlets, direct marketing, urban agriculture, community gardens and urban greening projects, community nutrition education, and community-driven agricultural research (Pothukuchi and Kaufman 1999). By focusing on community, the CFSC takes the notion of food security beyond long-standing governmental programs that typically focus on individual and household food access (Mooney and Hunt 2009).

The CFS framework also calls for increased funding to safety-net welfare programs such as the federal Supplemental Nutrition Assistance Program (food stamps); school lunch and breakfast programs; the Special Supplemental Nutrition Program for Women, Infants, and Children; the Child and Adult Care Food Program; and food banks (Anderson and Cook 1999; McCullum et al. 2004).

CFS frames food-system inequities in terms of food production and acquisition rather than structural inequality, resulting in an emphasis on enhancing food skills and alternative means of food access for low-income households, coupled with a Washington D.C.–focused lobbying effort for increased forms of food aid and support for community food systems (Tarasuk 2001; McCullum et al. 2004). Politically, CFS seeks strategic partnerships with government, industry, and major anti-hunger organizations to enhance food security programs, food access, and to promote anti-poverty measures (NAHO 2009). By working actively for government reforms and industry partnerships to improve the "other food" consumed by low-income people, CFS movement strives to mainstream food security into the existing food system.

CFS's efforts to incorporate food-security issues into the dominant food-movement narrative is not without its contradictions. While the movement has gained political currency with the Obama administration's initiative for Healthy Food Financing and First Lady Michelle Obama's "Let's Move" campaign against childhood obesity, many food activists feel the administration's staunch support for agribusiness and food retail monopolies (reaching new heights with the Let's Move/Walmart partnership) goes against CFS's core principles of self-reliance and social justice:

Imagine if the national answer to the food crisis took the form of a huge, publicly financed flood of corporations like WalMart and Tesco opening up stores in inner city neighborhoods using the exact same economic model they're using now. We could expect low wages, the destruction of small businesses and local economies, and all of the awful labor and supply chain practices we're familiar with.... [We need] good, living-wage jobs that pay meaningful earnings and teach meaningful skill sets.... [Instead] poor urban communities will see their economies tied to the wealth and resource extraction from rural communities with the usual negative consequences for local economies and the environment. (Ahmadi 2011)

The Food Justice movement (FJ) overlaps broadly with CFS, but tends to be more progressive than reformist in that it addresses specifically the ways in which people of color in low-income communities are disproportionately and negatively impacted by the industrial food system. In their recent book on the movement, Gottlieb and Joshi (2010, 229) describe FJ as a social movement with "multiple layers ... [of] producers, processors, workers, eaters, or communities," for whom race, ethnicity, class, and gender issues are at the forefront of an agenda that includes a mix of "producing food, local preference, environment, economic development, healthy food for all, preparing, cooking & eating, and public health & nutrition."

The food-justice movement emerged from several corners, including movements for environmental justice (Bullard 1994), working-class communities of color dealing with diet-related diseases (Herrera, Khanna, and Davis 2009), critiques of racism in the food system (Self 2003; Allen 2008) as well as critiques of racism in the food movement itself (Slocum 2007; Guthman 2008). Food justice formulates its food-security discourse in the "context of institutional racism, racial formation, and racialized geographies" (Alkon and Norgaard 2009). The Detroit Black Community Food Security Network, for example, articulates an explicit analysis of structural racism in the food system and a policy platform that includes eliminating "barriers to African-American participation and ownership in all aspects of the food system," as well as a "redistribution of wealth through cooperative community ownership" (Detroit Black Community Food Security Network 2010). According to FJ advocate Brahm Ahmadi of the People's Community Market in Oakland, California:

> Food justice asserts that no one should live without enough food because of economic constraints or social inequalities. . . . The food justice movement is a different approach to a community's needs that seeks to truly advance self-reliance and social justice by placing communities in leadership of their own solutions and providing them with the tools to address the disparities within our food systems and within society at large. (Ahmadi 2010)

In a debate on COMFOOD, a popular food security/food justice list-serve, Hank Herrera, another longtime FJ advocate from Dig Deep Farms in Oakland, California, offers up the following principles:

> Food justice must address structural inequity, structural violence and structural racism. Food justice work must result in ownership of the means of production and exchange of food by the people who consume the food. Food justice work is the incredibly difficult work of building new local healthy food systems, not opposing the global food industry. Food justice emerges from the economic justice work of Dr. King and represents the next wave of the civil rights movement. Food justice cannot reproduce systems of power, privilege and capital that create and maintain food apartheid. (Herrera 2011)

As Herrera's principles suggest, many food-justice activists engaged in the hard, grassroots work of building new food systems simply do not have the time, resources, or inkling to actively oppose the global food industry. Nonetheless, many see a role for food justice in addressing systemic change by engaging in political and policy processes as well as activism and movement mobilization (Steel 2010; Wekerle 2004).

In its more radical forms, FJ asserts economic democracy for underserved communities of color, including the transfer of ownership, property, and leadership to those most negatively affected by the industrial food System.[1] FJ's radical roots reflect the community work of the Black Panther Party nearly half a century ago. According to Black Panther co-founder Bobby Seale:

> One of the party's important lasting legacies is grassroots programmatic organizing such as the Free Breakfast for Children Program which evolved to a point where forty-nine Black Panther chapters and branches in association with many other organizations across the United States were feeding 250,000 kids five days a week each morning before school. We had no government money or War on Poverty money to start the programs—we did it ourselves with donations. (Shames 2006, 12–13)

Accomplished long before community organizing developed its dependence on funding from philanthropic foundations, the Black Panther's free breakfast program predated the nation's school breakfast legislation of 1973. Food was part of a much larger program for black liberation and community autonomy as expressed in the October 1966 Black Panther Party Platform and Program. The first point in the program demanded freedom and the power for the black community to determine its own destiny. The last point, invoking the Declaration of Independence and calling for a black plebiscite, was introduced with the statement

> "We want land, *bread*, housing, education, clothing, justice and peace. . . ."
> (Shames, 13–14, emphasis added)

The platform was radical not only because it addressed the egregious manifestations of racism, such as underemployment, economic exploitation, police brutality, and a skewed criminal justice system (and suggested black communities might secede from the United States), but because the Black Panthers sought to dismantle the capitalist structures of racism.

The call among many of today's FJ activists for local control over food and dismantling racism in the food system echoes some of the liberation politics of the Black Panthers. Less common today are the structural critiques of capitalism and racism that were integral to the Black Panther's political work.

The food-justice movement confronts both the effects of structural racism on the ground and the failure of the dominant social change paradigms to take structural racism into account. Its discourse invokes the notion of a grassroots-driven transition to a more equitable and sustainable food system. Thus, just as the Environmental Justice Paradigm established at the People of Color Environmental Leadership Summit in 1991 sought to emphasize the issues of race, class, and leadership in the face of the mainstream "New Environmental Paradigm" dominated by middle-class white activists (Taylor 2000; Bullard 2010), FJ struggles to make its voice heard above the mainstream food-movement narrative.

Food sovereignty is another radical trend for food-system transformation based on the notion of entitlement and redistribution of food-producing resources. The discourse is framed by a more radical interpretation of food justice that sees access to food, land, and water as a human right, works for the democratization of the food system in favor of the poor and underserved, and specifically advocates dismantling the present global food system (Patel 2009; Wittman, Desmarais, and Wiebe 2010).

While the food-sovereignty movement has its origins in the peasant struggles for land and livelihoods in the Global South, the call has been increasingly taken up by family farms and the more radical food justice organizations in the United States and Europe. The draft mission statement of

the recently formed U.S. Food Sovereignty Alliance states as follows:

> The US Food Sovereignty Alliance works to end poverty, rebuild local food economies, and assert democratic control over the food system. We believe all people have the right to healthy, culturally appropriate food, produced in an ecologically sound manner. As a US-based food justice, anti-hunger, labor, environmental, and faith-based alliance, we uphold the right to food as a basic human right and work to connect our local and national struggles to the international movement for food sovereignty. (U.S. Food Sovereignty Alliance 2010)

The food-sovereignty movement seeks to dismantle global markets and the monopoly power of corporations at local, national, and international scales, and advocates redistributing and protecting productive assets such as seeds, water, land, and processing and distribution facilities. The rights of labor and immigrants figure prominently in this trend, as advocated by the national Food Chain Workers Alliance and the Community to Community Alliance of Washington state. Direct action is practiced by organizations like the Coalition of Immokalee Workers and Students for Fair Food. Reminiscent of the United Farm Worker (UFW) mobilizations of the 1960s, these groups seek to achieve labor justice and an end to modern-day slavery in the tomato fields through student–farmworker coalitions and national boycotts.

Poverty, hunger, and community demands for healthy food access continually pull low-income communities of color toward food aid and food-access solutions coming from mainstream food security and anti-hunger groups, as well as toward the cheap industrial food solutions offered by low-end food retail chains such as Walmart, Food 4 Less, and Dollar Stores (Holt-Giménez, Wang, and Shattuck 2011). While anti-hunger and food-security advocates often prefer affordable access to bad food over no food at all, this puts them at odds with food-justice and food-sovereignty groups who distrust these large agrifood corporations

(Gottlieb and Joshi 2010, 215). Indeed, because they produce poor health outcomes and drain precious local food dollars from underserved communities, the pervasiveness of programs that channel surplus industrial food to low-income people of color could itself be considered an insidious form of racism. They also tend to divert attention from the structural causes of food insecurity and diet-related disease, and can bind local food-security efforts to the very industrial food system that is making their community members sick.

Caught between the urgency of access and the imperative of equity, the food-justice movement shifts, overlaps, and bridges with the efforts of the CFS and food-sovereignty movements, attempting to address racism and classism on one hand while trying to fix a broken food system on the other. This produces a "both/and" food justice narrative in which ". . . the lack of fresh food access [is seen as] both an equity disparity and a system failure" (Gottlieb and Joshi 2010, 299).

One difficulty with this narrative—fairly generalized within the food-justice movement—is that it separates the system from the disparity. The food system may be dysfunctional in that it does not serve the better interests of the environment, peasants, family farmers, or low-income people of color, but it is certainly not broken. During the food crisis of 2008, and again in 2010, quarterly profits for the world's agri-food monopolies (seed and input suppliers, grain traders, retailers) grew by some 80 percent, so the system clearly works well for those who run it (Holt-Giménez, Patel, and Shattuck 2009). "Equity disparity" and "system failure" do not sufficiently describe the profound, ongoing systemic exploitation that girds the global food system.

But understanding that racial and class disparities are a structurally integrated part of the present food system does not, in and of itself, resolve the strategic problem of how to proceed—practically and politically. In the following sections, we construct a "regime/movement" framework for understanding food systems and food movements,

taking into account the historical tendencies of capitalist food systems and the strategic importance of alliance building to overcome the system/disparity dilemma.

The Corporate Food Regime[2]

Our food systems are part of a corporate food regime that is performing exactly as a late-capitalist system would be expected: it efficiently creates and concentrates wealth through market expansion, compound economic growth, technological innovation, and, increasingly, financial speculation (Magdoff and Tokar 2010; Harvey 2010). In addition to noting the cornucopian abundance frequently associated with the corporate food regime, it is important to recall that it was built over two centuries of violent, global-scale dispossession, and accumulation, a good part of which took place in North America. The regime continues to rely extensively on the direct and indirect appropriation and exploitation of land, labor, and capital, both at home and abroad.

A food regime is a "rule-governed structure of production and consumption of food on a world scale" (McMichael 2009). The first global food regime spanned the period from the late 1800s through the Great Depression and linked food imports from southern and American colonies to European industrial expansion. The second food regime began after World War II and reversed the flow of food from the northern to the southern hemisphere to fuel Cold War industrialization in the Third World.

Today's corporate food regime, ushered in by the neoliberal policies of Ronald Reagan and Margaret Thatcher in the 1980s, is characterized by the monopoly market power of agrifood corporations, globalized grain-fed meat production, giant retail, and growing links between food and fuel. This regime is controlled by a far-flung agrifood industrial complex made up of huge oligopolies including Monsanto, Archer Daniels Midland, Cargill, Conagra, and Walmart. Together, these corporations dominate the government agencies and multilateral organizations that make and enforce the regime's rules, regulations, and projects for trade, labor, property, and technology, including the World Bank and International Monetary Fund (IMF), the UN World Food Program, USAID, the USDA, and big philanthropy.

Liberalization and Reform

Like the capitalist economic system of which they are a part, global food regimes historically alternate between periods of economic liberalization characterized by unregulated markets, privatization, and massive concentrations of wealth, followed by devastating economic and financial busts—the costs of which are socialized and paid for by citizens, consumers, workers, and taxpayers. This eventually leads to social unrest, which, when sufficiently widespread, threatens profits and governability. Governments then usher in reformist periods in which markets, supply, and consumption are re-regulated to stem the crisis and restore stability to the regime. In cases where governments are incapable of reform—as witnessed in 2011 in Egypt and other countries in northern Africa—rebellion and revolution can become likely avenues of social change.

Infinitely unregulated markets would eventually destroy both society and the natural resources that the regime depends on for its reproduction. Therefore, while the "mission" of reform is to mitigate the social and environmental externalities of the corporate food regime, its "job" is identical to that of the liberal trend: preserving the corporate food regime. Though liberalization and reform may appear politically distinct, they are actually two phases of the same system. While both tendencies exist simultaneously, they are rarely ever in equilibrium, with either liberalization or reform hegemonic at any period of time. Reformists dominated the global food regime from the New Deal in the 1930s until our current era of neo-liberal "globalization" in the 1980s. The current neo-liberal phase has been characterized by deregulation, privatization, and the growth and consolidation of

global corporate monopoly power in food systems around the globe.

With the recurrent global food crises, desperate calls for reform have sprung up worldwide. However, less than 5 percent of the US$ 22 billion in promised aid to end the crisis has actually been committed, and most government and multilateral solutions (e.g., Feed the Future, Global Agriculture and Food Security Program, Global Harvest) simply call for more of the same policies that brought about the crisis to begin with: extending liberal (free) markets, privatizing common resources (including forests and the atmosphere), proprietary technological "fixes" including genetically modified seeds, and protecting monopoly concentration. Collateral damage to community food systems is mitigated by weak safety nets—including food aid from the World Food Program and U.S. food banks or food stamps. Unless there is strong pressure from civil society, reformists will not likely affect (much less reverse) the present neo-liberal direction of the corporate food regime.

From Coping to Regime Change: The Pivotal Role of Food Justice

The current food and health crises reflect a socially inequitable and economically volatile corporate food regime. Unless there are profound changes to this regime, it will repeat its cycles of liberalization and reform, plunging neighborhood food systems, rural communities, and the environment into ever graver crises. While moderate food system reforms—such as increasing food stamps or relocating grocery stores—are certainly needed to help vulnerable communities cope with crises, because they address the proximate rather than the root causes of hunger and food insecurity (Holt-Giménez, Patel, and Shattuck 2009), they will not alter the fundamental balance of power within the food system and in some cases may even reinforce existing, inequitable power relations. Fixing the dysfunctional food system—in any sustainable sense—requires regime change.

If the history of U.S. capitalism and social change is a reliable guide, we can be assured that substantive changes to the corporate food regime will not come simply from within the regime itself, but from a combination of intense social pressure and political will. Today's food-system "reforms" and the rush of anti-hunger alliances between agrifood monopolies, government, and big philanthropy (Global Harvest, AGRA, AGree, etc.) are attempts to mitigate the negative effects of food price volatility, not end global hunger or substantively challenge neo-liberal control over the food system. Food-system change will come from powerful and sustained social pressure that forces reformists to roll back neo-liberalism in the food system. Much of this pressure could come from the food movement—if it overcomes its divides.

As we indicated earlier in this article, the food-sovereignty movement and some food-justice organizations have a radical critique of the corporate food regime. These groups call for structural, redistributive reforms of basic entitlements, for example, for property, labor, capital, and markets. Other food-justice groups (and some CFS organizations) advance a progressive agenda on the basis of sustainable family farming and rights of access to healthy food. These radical and progressive trends overlap significantly in their approaches, demographics, and types of organization (e.g., CFS, FJ, and FS). While the progressive trend focuses on local ownership of production and on improving the service and delivery aspects of the food system, the radical trend directs more of its energy at structural changes to capitalist food systems. When taken together, both trends seek to change the rules and practices of food systems, locally, nationally, and internationally. In this regard they are two sides of the same food movement. Their strategic alliance could go a long way toward overcoming the food movement's system/disparity dilemma.

Food-movement organizations are fluid and have different and changing positions on food-system issues such as GMOs, domestic hunger programs, food aid, supply management, land reform, and trade. Depending on their ideology, political awareness, support base, and funding, food-movement organizations will adopt a range of stances and will consciously (or unconsciously) form alliances with groups and institutions across regime and movement trends. While some organizations are solidly neo-liberal, reformist, progressive, or radical, others are much harder to categorize because they adopt politically divergent positions on different issues (for example, a reformist position on labor, but a radical position on GMOs). Some organizations say one thing, yet do another. Rather than ascribing fixity to organizations, an appreciation of their heterogeneous and fluid political nature, coupled with an analysis of their positions on specific issues, can help identify opportunities for alliance building for food-system change.

As the world's fuel, financial, and climate crises exacerbate the food crisis, the systemic differences between the food regime and food movements will likely deepen. However, unlike the symbiotic relationship between neo-liberal and reformist trends in the food regime, in which the latter helps to stabilize the food regime following a crisis caused by the former, there is nothing intrinsically stable about the relationship between the progressive and radical trends that will keep them from splitting under pressure. The fragmentation and segmentation of the U.S. food movement already cedes political ground to the corporate food regime, whose reformist trends are busy co-opting food security and its related terms, among them "community," "organic," "local," and "fair."

Overcoming the present (and future) divisions within the food movement will require strong alliances and the clarity to distinguish superficial change from structural change. This in turn depends not only on clear vision and practice of the desired changes, but also means making strategic and tactical sense of the matrix of actors, institutions, and projects at work within local–global food politics. The dominant food-movement narrative is not only color-blind, but it also does not distinguish between the neo-liberal/reformist trends in the food regime (of which it is unconsciously a part) and the progressive and radical trends of the food movement itself. The challenge for building a powerful food movement is to reach beyond the dominant (and depoliticizing) food-movement narrative to build strategic political alliances and construct a new narrative. But who should reach; to whom; and on what basis?

Addressing this challenge, Gottlieb and Joshi (2011, 232–33) identify FJ as a key political trend within the U.S. food movement and claim it is facing a "pivotal moment" that requires an "overarching theory of food system change." They call on FJ to organize existing food groups into a larger social movement, to develop a theory of change, an agenda that is both incremental and structural, and to link to other social movements, worldwide.

We agree with this assessment, and suggest that in addition to its pivotal moment, because it is located between, and in many ways also spans, radical and progressive trends within the food movement, the food-justice movement occupies a "pivotal position." The way FJ organizations organize, theorize, set agendas, and build alliances will have a direct influence on the balance of forces that will serve to stabilize, reform, or transform the corporate food regime. If FJ organizations build reformist alliances, the corporate food regime will be strengthened. If they build radical alliances, the food movement will be strengthened. The former scenario will not lead to regime change, while the latter at least opens the possibility of a strong food movement capable of pushing substantive reforms.

On what basis could these alliances be built? The structural exploitation of resources, markets, and communities—at home and abroad—is foundational to the corporate food regime. Racial disadvantages are structured into the corporate food regime, reproducing a hierarchical social structure into our food systems (Winant 2001). The flood of cheap, unhealthy, and fast food into the void left by the exodus of food retail outlets from low-income communities of color is part of the racialized dispossession affecting immigrants and people of color in both rural and urban areas (Minkoff-Zern et al. 2011). For example, the recent drive by monopoly food retailers to gobble up real estate in underserved urban communities follows on this trend (Holt-Giménez, Wang, and Shattuck 2011). These racialized enclosures are no less structural issues than the wholesale dispossession of peasants occurring as a result of the massive global land grabs exploding across the Global South (Grain 2008). Land itself is one basis for local–global alliance building.

Engaging with the structural aspects of food justice requires addressing race and class in relation to dispossession and control over land, labor, and capital in the food system. For reforms to actually reverse the trends of dispossession and concentration—and lead to transformation—they must be redistributive (Borras 2007). This means that FJ needs to build alliances to address ownership and redistribution over the means of production and reproduction, including credit, land, processing, markets, and retail as well as labor and immigrant rights—all areas of dispossession within the food-value chain of the corporate food regime. The most likely partners for these structural alliances are in local and international food-sovereignty movements and other organizations working within the radical trend of the food movement.

Granted, no amount of fresh produce will solve the underlying socioeconomic problems of chronic unemployment, labor exploitation, crumbling public education, land and real estate speculation, and violence visited upon underserved communities of color. But within a historicized framework of structural racism, the centrality of food to a community's collective cultural identities provides links between racial identity and activism (Pulido 2000). Food-justice activism is an important social change driver that, if allied with other, radical social movements, could seriously challenge the corporate food regime's structural inequities.

Solving the food crisis requires dismantling racism and classism in the food system and transforming the food regime. This challenges the food-justice movement to forge alliances that advance equitable and sustainable practices on the ground while mobilizing politically for broad, redistributive reforms. This pivotal praxis may yet produce a new, powerful food movement narrative: the narrative of liberation.

Notes

We would like to thank Annie Shattuck for her work on earlier versions of this paper, as well as the three anonymous reviewers for their helpful comments. All the usual disclaimers apply.

1. These demands have a solid material basis. In West Oakland, California, one of the city's lowest-income neighborhoods, an estimated $65 million per year is spent on food, $48 million of which "floats" out of the community (People's Community Market 2009). This amount represents some 1,000 potential jobs paying $45,000 a year. Figures are similarly high for other low-income urban communities in which grocery stores have abandoned the inner city for the suburbs (Mamen 2007). This is one reason many FJ activists prefer the term "food apartheid" over "food deserts," as the former provides a more accurate description of the political–economic depth of structural racism in the U.S. food system (Ahmadi 2010; Cook 2010; Workman 2010).

2. For a more extensive, global analysis of the corporate food regime and its relation to the global food movement, see Holt-Giménez and Shattuck (2011).

Works Cited

Ahmadi, Brahm. 2011. Racism and food justice: The case of Oakland. In *Food Movements Unite!*, ed. Eric Holt-Giménez, 149–62. Oakland, CA: Food First Books.

———. 2010. Structural Racism in the U.S. Food System. Oakland, CA: Food First Books.

Alkon, Alison Hope, and Julian Agyeman. 2011a. Introduction: The food movement as polyculture. In *Cultivating Food Justice: Race, Class, and Sustainability*, 1–20. Food, Health and Environment; series ed. Robert Gottlieb. Cambridge, MA: MIT Press.

———, eds. 2011b. *Cultivating food justice: Race, class, and sustainability*. Cambridge, MA: MIT Press.

Alkon, Alison Hope, and Kari Marie Norgaard. 2009. Breaking the food chains: An investigation of food justice activism. *Sociological Inquiry* 79: 289–305.

Allen, Patricia. 2008. Mining for justice in the food system: Perceptions, practices, and possibilities. *Agriculture and Human Values* 25: 157–61.

Anderson, Molly, and John T. Cook. 1999. Community food security: Practice in need of theory? *Agriculture and Human Values* 16: 141–50.

Baker, Elizabeth A., Mario Schootman, Ellen Barnidge, and Cheryl Kelly. 2006. The role of race and poverty in access to foods that enable individuals to adhere to dietary guidelines. *Preventing Chronic Disease* 3: 1–11.

Berg, Joel. 2008. *All you can eat: How hungry is America?* New York: Seven Stories Press.

Borras, Saturnino M. Jr. 2007. *Pro-poor land reform: A critique*. Ottawa: University of Ottawa Press.

Bullard, Robert D. 1994. *Unequal protection: Environmental justice and communities of color*. San Francisco: Sierra Club Books.

———. 2010. Environmental justice in the 21st Century. http://www.ejrc.cau.edu/ejinthe21century.htm (accessed June 30, 2011).

CFSC Community Food Security Coalition. 2004. About CFSC. http://www.foodsecurity.org/aboutcfsc.html (accessed June 30, 2011).

———. 2010. What is community food security? http://www.foodsecurity.org/views_cfs_faq.html (accessed June 30, 2011).

Cook, Christopher. 2010. Covering food deserts. University of Southern California Annenberg School for Communication. http://www.reportingonhealth.org/resources/lessons/covering-food-deserts (accessed June 30, 2011).

Detroit Black Community Food Security Network. 2010. A City of Detroit policy on food security: "Creating a food-secure Detroit." http://detroitblackfoodsecurity.org/policy.html (accessed June 30, 2011).

FAO. 2011. FAO Food Price Index. Food and Agriculture Organization of the United Nations,

March 7. http://www.fao.org/worldfoodsituation/wfs-home/foodpricesindex/en/ (accessed June 30, 2011).

Garcia, Deborah Koons. 2004. The future of food. Documentary. Lily Films.

Goodman, David, and Michael K. Goodman. 2008. "Alternative food networks," in Rob Kitchin and Nigel Thrift, *Encyclopedia of Human Geography.* Oxford: Elsevier.

Gottlieb, Robert, and Anupama Joshi. 2010. *Food justice.* Cambridge, MA: MIT Press.

Grain. 2008. Seized: The 2008 landgrab for food and financial security. Grain Briefing. http://www.grain.org/briefings/?id=212 (accessed June 30, 2011).

Guthman, Julie. 2008. "If only they knew": Color blindness and universalism in California alternative food institutions. *The Professional Geographer* 60: 387–97.

Hamm, Michael W., and Anne C. Bellows. 2003. Community food security and nutrition educators. *Journal of Nutrition Education and Behavior* 35: 37–43.

Harvey, David. 2005. *A brief history of neoliberalism.* Oxford: Oxford University Press.

———. 2010. *The enigma of capital: And the crises of capitalism.* Oxford: Oxford University Press.

Herrera, Henry. Unpublished correspondence. Oakland, California, April 24, 2011.

Herrera, Henry, Navina Khanna, and Leon Davis. 2009. Food systems and public health: The community perspective. *Journal of Hunger & Environmental Nutrition* 4: 430–45.

Holt-Giménez, Eric, and Annie Shattuck. 2011. "Food Crises, Food Regimes and Food Movements: Rumblings of Reform or Tides of Transformation?" *Journal of Peasant Studies* 38(1): 109–144.

Holt-Giménez, Eric, Raj Patel, and Annie Shattuck. 2009. *Food rebellions! Crisis and the hunger for justice.* Oakland: Food First Books.

Holt-Giménez, Eric, Yi Wang, and Annie Shattuck. 2011. "The urban and northern face of global land grabs." Paper presented at the presented at the International Conference on Global Land Grabbing, Brighton, UK, April 6–8.

Jackson, Wes, Wendell Berry, and Bruce Coleman, eds. 1984. *Meeting the expectations of the land:*

Essays in sustainable agriculture and stewardship. San Francisco: North Point Press.

Kenner, Robert. 2009. Food, Inc. Documentary. Magnolia Pictures, Participant Media.

Lang, Tim. 2005. Food control or food democracy? Reengaging nutrition with society and the environment. *Public Health Nutrition* 8(6A): 730–37.

Lean, Geoffrey. 2008. Multinationals make billions in profit out of growing global food crisis. *The Independent,* May 4.

Magdoff, Fred, and Brian Tokar. 2010. *Agriculture and food in crisis: Conflict, resistance, and renewal.* New York: Monthly Review Press.

Mamen, Katy. 2007. Facing Goliath: Challenging the impacts of supermarket consolidation on our local economies, communities, and food security. Oakland, CA: The Oakland Institute.

McCullum, Christine, David Pelletier, Donald Barr, Jennifer Wilkins, and Jean-Pierre Habicht. 2004. Mechanisms of power within a community-based food security planning process. *Health Education & Behavior* 31: 206–222.

McMichael, Philip. 2009. A food regime genealogy. *Journal of Peasant Studies* 36: 139–69.

Minkoff-Zern, Laura-Anne, Nancy Peluso, Jennifer Sowerwine, and Christy Getz. 2011. Race and regulation: Asian immigrants in California agriculture. In *Cultivating Food Justice: Race, Class, and Sustainability,* ed. Alison Alkon and Julian Agyeman, 65–86. Cambridge, MA: MIT Press.

Mooney, Patrick H., and Scott A. Hunt. 2009. Food security: The elaboration of contested claims to a consensus frame. *Rural Sociology* 74: 469–97.

Morton, Lois Wright, and Troy C. Blanchard. 2007 *Starved for access: Life in rural America's food deserts.* Columbia, MO: University of Missouri Press.

NAHO. 2009. Roadmap to end childhood hunger in America by 2015. National Anti-Hunger Organizations. http://www.foodsecurity.org/policy/NAHO-Roadmap_to_End_Hunger.pdf (accessed June 30, 2011).

Nestle, Marion. 2002. Food politics: How the food industry influences nutrition and health. In *California Studies in Food and Culture.* Berkeley: University of California Press.

Nord, Mark, Alisha Coleman-Jensen, Margaret Andrews, and Steven Carlson. 2010. Household food security in the United States, 2009. Economic Research Report. U.S. Department of Agriculture, November 10. http://www.ers.usda.gov/publications/err108/ (accessed June 30, 2011).

Parker, Lynn. 2005. Obesity, food insecurity and the federal child nutrition programs: Understanding the linkages. Food Research and Action Center.

Patel, Raj. 2007. *Stuffed and starved: Markets, power and the hidden battle for the world food system.* London: Portobello Books.

———. 2009. Food Sovereignty. *Journal of Peasant Studies* 36: 663–706.

People's Community Market. 2009. Market Gap Study. Unpublished.

Perry, Duane, and Caroline Harries. 2007. The need for more supermarkets in Chicago. Philadelphia: The Food Trust.

Petrini, Carlo. 2005. *Slow food nation: Why our food should be good, clean, and fair.* Bra, Italy: Slow Food Editore.

Pollan, Michael. 2006. Voting with your fork. http://pollan.blogs.nytimes.com/2006/05/07/voting-with-your-fork/ (accessed June 30, 2011).

———. 2010. The food movement, rising. *New York Review of Books,* June 10. http://www.nybooks.com/articles/archives/2010/jun/10/food-movement-rising/ (accessed June 30, 2011).

Pothukuchi, Kameshwari, and Jerome Kaufman. 1999. Placing the food system on the urban agenda: The role of municipal institutions in food systems planning. *Agriculture and Human Values* 16: 213–24.

Pulido, Laura. 2000. Rethinking environmental racism: White privilege and urban development in Southern California. *Annals of the Association of American Geographers* 90: 12–40.

Robin, Marie-Monique. 2008. The world according to Monsanto. Documentary. National Film Board of Canada, ARTE France, Image & Compagnie, WDR, and Les Productions Thalie.

Schlosser, Eric. 2001. *Fast food nation: The dark side of the all-American meal.* New York: Harper Perennial.

Self, Robert O. 2003. *American Babylon: Race and the struggle for postwar Oakland.* Princeton, NJ: Princeton University Press.

Shames, Stephen. 2006. *The Black Panthers.* New York: Aperture Foundations Books.

Slocum, Rachel. 2007. Whiteness, space and alternative food practice. *Geoforum* 38: 520–33.

Spurlock, Morgan. 2004. *Super size me.* Documentary. Samuel Goldwyn Films; Roadside Attractions.

Steel, Anim. 2010. Youth and food justice: Lessons from the Civil Rights movement. Food First/Institute for Food and Development Policy.

Tarasuk, Valerie. 2001. A critical examination of community-based responses to household food insecurity in Canada. *Health Education & Behavior* 28: 487–99.

Taylor, Dorceta E. 2000. The rise of the environmental justice paradigm: Injustice framing and the social construction of environmental discourses. *American Behavioral Scientist* 43: 508–580.

U.S. Food Sovereignty Alliance. 2010. Food sovereignty PMA resolution. http://www.usfoodsovereigntyalliance.org/foodsovereigntypma/food-sovereignty-pma-resolution (June 30, 2011).

Viertel, Josh. 2011. Beyond voting with your fork: Moving past enlightened eating, to movement building. In *Food Movements Unite!,* ed. Eric Holt-Giménez, 137–48. Oakland, CA: Food First Books.

Wekerle, Gera R. 2004. Food justice movements: Policy, planning, and networks. *Journal of Planning Education and Research* 23: 378–86.

WFP. 2011. Hunger FAQs. World Food Program. http://www.wfp.org/hunger/faqs (accessed June 30, 2011).

Wiggins, Steve, and Stephanie Levy. 2008. Rising food prices: A global crisis. Briefing Paper #37. Overseas Development Institute. London. http://www.odi.org.uk/resources/download/1009.pdf (accessed June 30, 2011).

Winant, Howard. 2001. *The world is a ghetto: Race and democracy since World War II.* New York: Basic Books.

Winne, Mark. 2008. *Closing the food gap.* Boston: Beacon Press.

Wittman, Hannah, Annette Aurelie Desmarais, and Nettie Wiebe. 2010. *Food sovereignty: Reconnecting food, nature and community.* Oakland, CA: Food First Books.

Woolf, Aaron. 2007. King Corn. Mosaic Films.

Workman, Mandy Lynn. 2010. Food deserts & growing hunger in the US: The USDA's response, Oakland Food Policy Council, http://www.oaklandfood.org/blog/entry/587521/-food-deserts-growing-hunger-in-the-us-the-usda%E2%80%99s-response%C2%A0ID-177 (accessed June 30, 2011).

Questions for Critical Thinking

1. In this article, the authors discuss the important topic of food justice. In what ways is this issue new to you? Can you think of examples of barriers to food access in your own communities?
2. The authors discuss the root causes of severe levels of hunger in our communities. How does their discussion inform your understanding of how to go about making structural change to achieve food justice?
3. What new insights does this reading give you with regard to personally being involved in making social change around issues of food justice?

Voices of a New Movimiento

ROBERTO LOVATO

The final essay in this text, written by Robert Lovato, discusses why it is important to organize for change. Highlighting the ways in which this new movimiento *goes beyond single-minded organizing tactics, the author provides examples of how activists merge traditional labor and civil rights strategies and tactics with more global, networked—and personalized—ones.*

Under cover of an oak tree on a tobacco farm deep in the heart of rural North Carolina, Leticia Zavala challenges the taller, older male migrant farm workers with talk of a boycott and *legalización*.

"We will not get anything without fighting for it," declares the intense 5-foot-1 organizer with the Farm Labor Organizing Committee (FLOC). Pen and notebook in hand, Zavala hacks swiftly through the fear and doubt that envelop many migrants. She speaks from a place, an experience, that most organizers in this country don't know: Her earliest childhood and adolescent memories are of migrating each year with her family between Mexico and Florida. "We have five buses and each of you has to decide for yourselves if you want to go to Washington with us," she says. After some deliberation most of the workers, many of whom have just finished the seven-day trek from Nayarit, Mexico, opt to get on another bus and join the May 1 *marcha* and boycott. They trust her, as do the more than 500 other migrant workers from across

the state who heed the call from one of the new leaders of the *movimiento* that is upon us.

Asked why she thinks FLOC was so successful in mobilizing farm workers (the union made history after a stunning 2004 victory that secured representation and a contract for more than 10,000 H-2A "guest" workers who labor on strawberry, tobacco, yam, cucumber and other farms), Zavala talks about "the importance of networks" and the need to respond to the globalization of labor through the creation of a "migrating union." She and other FLOC organizers have followed migrant workers to Mexico, where the organization has an office—and then have followed them back over several months. She also points to the vision, strategies and tactics shared by her mentor, FLOC founder Baldemar Velásquez, who passed on to her the advice that Martin Luther King Jr. gave him during the Poor People's Campaign in 1967: "When you impact the rich man's ability to make money, anything is negotiable."

But when you ask her what is most important in the twenty-first-century matrix of successful organizing, the bespectacled, bright-eyed Zavala will bring you back to basics: "One of the biggest successes of the union is that it takes away loneliness."

The 26-year-old Zavala's vision, experience and learning are a telling reflection of how the leaders of the *movimiento* merge traditional labor and civil rights strategies and tactics with more global,

---

networked—and personalized—organizing to meet the challenges of the quintessentially global issue of immigration. While it's important to situate the immigrant struggle within the context of the ongoing freedom struggles of African-Americans, women (like Zavala, an extraordinary number of *movimiento* leaders are *mujeres*) and others who have fought for social justice in the United States, labeling and framing it as a "new civil rights movement" risks erasing its roots in Latin American struggles and history.

The mainstream narrative of the movement emphasizes that single-minded immigrants want legalization—and how "angry Hispanics" and their Spanish-language radio DJ leaders mobilized in reaction to HR 4437 (better known as the Sensenbrenner immigration bill, which would criminalize the undocumented). But Zavala and other *movimiento* leaders across the country say that while it's true that the Sensenbrenner bill provided a spark, explaining this powerful movement of national and even global significance as a reaction to DJ-led calls to "*marchar!*" leaves many things—and people—out of the picture.

This time, there is no Martin Luther King or César Chávez centering and centralizing the movement. Instead, grassroots leaders like Zavala mix, scratch and dub different media (think MySpace.com and text messaging, radio and TV, butcher paper and bullhorns) while navigating the cultural, political and historical currents that yoke and inspire the diverse elements making up this young, decentralized, digital-age *movimiento*.

At the older end of the age and experience spectrum (the average Latino is 26) is 44-year-old Juan José Gutiérrez. He started organizing in the late 1970s, distributing mimeographed copies of the radical newspaper *Sin Fronteras* to immigrant workers in the face of hostility from the anti-Communist right. The director of Latino Movement USA and a key figure in the recent (and, to some, controversial) May 1 boycott, Gutiérrez has logged thousands of miles and met hundreds of leaders in his efforts to build one of many vibrant movement networks.

"Since January, I've been to about thirty-five different cities and seen old and new leadership coming together to create something that has never been seen before," says Gutiérrez, who migrated to Los Angeles from Tuxpan, Jalisco, Mexico, when he was 11. "The [Spanish-language] DJs played a role, an important role, but they let us put our message in their medium. You can trace this movement all the way back to 1968."

Unlike the *movimiento* leaders who cut their teeth organizing in left-leaning Latin America, Gutiérrez traces his political roots to post–civil rights East LA; he and many of the most important Mexican and Chicano immigrant rights leaders in LA—including union leader Maria Elena Durazo, longtime activist Javier Rodriguez and LA Mayor Antonio Villaraigosa—came out of the Centro de Acción Social Autónomo (Center for Autonomous Social Action), or CASA, a seminal Chicano political organization founded by legendary leaders Bert Corona and Soledad "Chole" Alatorre in 1968. One of the central tasks of CASA, which from its inception had a strong working-class and trade union orientation, was organizing undocumented workers. Gutiérrez and others who have covered the country spiderlike for years see a direct line from the organizing around the amnesty law of 1986, which legalized 3 million undocumented workers, to immigrant rights organizing in California (home to one of every three immigrants in the United States), the fight against Proposition 187 of 1994 (which tried to deny health and education benefits to the children of the undocumented) and the historic shift of the AFL–CIO in 2000, when it decided to undertake immigrant organizing.

Having hopped back and forth among many of the more than 200 cities and towns that staged actions in April and May, Gutiérrez sees different kinds of leaders emerging from the grassroots: "There are, of course, the undocumented, who are also leading things in local communities; there are legal immigrants getting involved, because they have friends and family who are affected by the anti-immigrant policies; and there are immigrants from different countries who bring their own political, sometimes radical, experiences from places like Guatemala and El Salvador."

One of the "radical" legacies that New York immigrant rights leader Miguel Ramírez has carried with him since fleeing El Salvador is an intensely collective outlook on personal and political identity. Ramírez, who heads the Queens-based Centro Hispano Cuzcatlán, recalls how one of his US-born colleagues told him to "correct" the résumé he used to apply for his first organizing job in New York. "He [the friend] told me I had to take out the 'we,'" says 53-year-old Ramírez, whose bushy mustache often lifts to reveal a disarming smile. "I didn't know it was wrong to write, 'We organized a forum, we organized a workshop, we organized a network.'"

The experience and approach of Ramírez, who left his homeland in 1979 after many of his fellow students at the University of El Salvador were persecuted and killed, show that the US *movimiento* is as much the northernmost expression of a resurgent Latin American left as it is a new, more globalized, human rights–centered continuation of the Chicano, civil rights and other previous struggles that facilitated immigrant rights work here.

Ramírez, who estimates that since migrating he's helped organize more than 100 marches—all of them "very disciplined and without incidents"—is informed by the experience of organizing students, campesinos and others in revolutionary El Salvador, where one of every three Salvadorans adopted radicalized politics during the war. Lacking the wealth and pro-US government politics of Cuban-Americans and other, more conservative immigrant groups, Ramírez and many Salvadoran immigrants (most of whom were denied legal status and benefits granted to Cubans, Vietnamese and others) created organizations that then formed vast multi-issue, mass-based networks challenging the foreign and domestic policies of the most powerful country on earth.

This robust legacy energizes Ramírez and Centro Hispano Cuzcatlán, which organizes around worker rights, housing and immigration, as they play definitive roles in the construction of local networks like the Immigrant Communities in Action coalition. Through the coalition, Centro joined Indian, Pakistani, Korean, Filipino, Bangladeshi, Indonesian and other groups that have organized some of the country's most diverse marches.

Reflecting the historic and ongoing tensions between more election- and legislative-focused immigrant rights advocates in Washington and local and regional players, Ramírez, like the younger Zavala, calmly insists the *movimiento* must look beyond the upcoming elections and even the pending immigration bill. "In the end, it's an issue of power, one that can only be addressed by constant organizing."

US-born Latinos also feel Ramírez's urgency about organizing around immigration. Their ranks include teens and twentysomethings relatively new to politics, along with veterans like Wisconsin's Christine Neumann-Ortiz, who was influenced by several Latin American movements as well as the struggle against California's Proposition 187.

"To see those thousands of people marching against Prop 187 was an inspiration," says Ortiz, who heads Voces de la Frontera, an immigrant worker center in the belly of the anti-immigrant beast, James Sensenbrenner's Milwaukee. "I was very impressed that there was that kind of response [to Prop 187]. We used that as a lesson," says Ortiz, who was one of the main organizers of marches of 30,000 and 70,000 people, some of the largest marches ever in a state with a storied progressive past.

Ortiz was not caught off guard by the *movimiento*. "I'm happy to be alive to see this shift," she states from one of Voces's three offices in Wisconsin, "but I'm not at all surprised. We've been building up networks of people over many years."

She and other activists point to years of service and advocacy on behalf of immigrants, which built up good will and trust in the community, as being defining factors in the ability to rally people into political action.

Founded in Austin, Texas, with a mission to build solidarity between US and Mexican maquiladora workers following the signing of the NAFTA accords in nearby San Antonio in 1994, Voces de la Frontera embodies a local–global sensibility. Ortiz started the Milwaukee Voces in November 2001 in response to the growing needs of Milwaukee's fast-growing Latino immigrant population. Like the settlement houses and mutual aid societies and other organizations that supported German and other white European immigrant workers of previous, more progressive eras in Wisconsin and elsewhere, Voces provides a critical support structure for the mostly Mexican and Central American workers in the agricultural, hotel and restaurant, construction and manufacturing industries in HR 4437 country.

Sensenbrenner "wants to leave a legacy. So did McCarthy. Immigrants in Wisconsin know his hypocrisy better than anyone," says Ortiz, whose German and Mexican immigrant heritage portends the not-so-distant future of once wholly white Wisconsin. "He is encroaching on his own base. Dairy farmers in his own district are revolting because he's attacking their economic base. This can't last in the long term," she says, as if eyeing developments in post-Prop 187 California, where short-term anti-immigrant backlash led to a longer-term movement that gave Los Angeles its first Latino (and progressive) mayor—and gave the *movimiento* a vision of its potential.

Like organizers in Los Angeles, Chicago and other cities, Ortiz and Voces have built strong and deep relationships with the local Spanish-language media. But they're also keenly aware of who's leading the charge. "We had lists of more than 4,000 workers before the radio stations or Sensenbrenner came into the picture," Ortiz explains.

As they continue to organize and lobby around the immigration debate in Congress, around the inevitable backlash at the local and state levels and around a more proactive agenda, Ortiz and many of the other leaders of the immigrant rights movement are keeping their eyes on a larger prize, beyond the issue of immigration. "We're going to change this country," she says, adding, "We've gained public sympathy for immigrants. We've gained recognition and power, and we are an inspiration to the larger movement for change." She is especially motivated when she describes the effect of the *movimiento* on the generations to come. Like the "Hmong students who went to a Sensenbrenner town hall meeting in South Alice [a Milwaukee suburb] and chanted 'Si se puede, Si se puede' at him." Asked if the backlash will damage the *movimiento*, Ortiz responds, "In the long run this will make us stronger and build our movement."

Questions for Critical Thinking

1. Lovato discusses the reasons that it is important to organize for change beyond electoral politics. Why does he think this is so important?

2. As is often said, the United States is made up predominantly of immigrants and their descendants. In what ways are recent immigrants treated in similar ways to those of the past? In what ways are they treated differently? What do you think needs to occur to provide more access to equal opportunity for recent waves of immigrants?

3. After reading this text, what do you see as important issues of social inequality? What are you willing to do to address these issues?

The Next Civil Rights Movement?

FREDRICK C. HARRIS

In the essay that follows, author Fredrick Harris, professor of political science and director of the Center on African-American Politics and Society at Columbia University, discusses how the Black Lives Matter movement's appeal to human rights has deep roots in the history of the black freedom struggle. As he illustrates, black America's struggle for human rights is once again gaining strength and will, hopefully, result in long-lasting positive social change.

Kareem Jackson, a St. Louis hip-hop artist who goes by the name Tef Poe, was interviewed this February by a BBC talk show host about why the Black Lives Matter movement was necessary. A leader in the organization Hands Up United, which was founded in the wake of Michael Brown's murder, Poe explained: "One of the negligent areas of the civil rights movement is that we did not move the moral compass of racism to the right direction."

Though the 1960s movement addressed the civil and political rights that were denied to black people—access and use of public accommodations, the right to vote, and ensuring fair employment and housing opportunities—it did not directly confront the racialized degradation black people endured, and many continue to endure, at the hands of the police. What the Black Lives Matter protests have done, however, is not only put police reform on the policy agenda but demanded that American society reconsider how it values black lives.

Tef Poe had not been directly involved in politics until Brown's death. He was a struggling hip-hop artist who occasionally wrote a column for the *Riverfront Times*, an independent newspaper in St. Louis. One day, while checking his Instagram account, Poe noticed a post that shook him. It was a photograph of Brown's stepfather holding up a hand-written sign that read simply, "My unarmed child has been murdered by the Ferguson police." As he watched the wave of anger, disgust, and disbelief mount on his social media feed within hours of the shooting, Tef Poe knew he had to go to Ferguson. This is how he—along with legions of people across the country—was transformed into an activist, not just concerned with civil and political rights but with black humanity.

The protests that have erupted since the deaths of Brown and other casualties of police brutality have been extraordinary. Seemingly out of nowhere, a multiracial, multigenerational movement asserting black humanity in response to racist police killings and vigilante violence has ripped across the country. The police brutality and killings are not, to be sure, new; the emerging movement against them, however, is. The upsurge in anti-racist organizing is a break from what we normally consider black activism in the United States. Each periodic wave of activism for the last half century—whether centered on electoral politics or protests—has traced its lineage to the "golden age" of the 1960s. But while there is a great deal of nostalgia in these comparisons, core activists of the Black Lives Matter movement have been quick to remind us that this current wave of protest "is not your grandmamma's civil rights movement."

In a purely tactical sense, that assessment is correct. The movement's use of technology to mobilize hundreds of thousands of people through social media is light years away from the labor that was once required to mobilize black people and their allies during the 1960s or even a few years ago. Jo Ann Robinson of the all-black Women's Political Council in Montgomery, for instance, spent hours using a hand-driven mimeograph machine to crank out over 52,000 leaflets that announced a mass protest after Rosa Parks's arrest in 1955.

Today, social media—particularly Twitter—can reach individuals throughout the nation and across the world in milliseconds, drastically slashing the time it takes to organize protests. As a recent *New York Times Magazine* spread noted, through Twitter, core Black Lives Matter activists like Johnetta Elzie and DeRay Mckesson, who are based in St. Louis, now have the ability to frame events and direct the actions of hundreds of thousands of people across the nation at their fingertips. Not only is social media a tool for mobilization, but the intense reporting on police brutality via social media also influences print and television coverage, which means that attention to such incidents has multiplied. Twitter and Facebook have, in this way, become documentary tools for Black Lives Matter activists, a way for them to become citizen journalists capturing the protests and police responses in almost real time. Indeed, for this reason, the spontaneity and the intensity of Black Lives Matter is more akin to other recent movements—Occupy Wall Street and the explosive protests in Egypt and Brazil—than 1960s activism.

Similarly, images of police violence are helping put pressure on municipal police departments to address these issues. Unlike the images of brutality that sparked outrage in the past—photographs of lynch victims hanging from trees during the age

of Jim Crow or newspaper images of brutalized black bodies lying in a coroner's office—we are now able to witness and document police violence as it happens. Videos from handheld phones and surveillance cameras have shown Marlene Pinnock being beaten by a California highway patrol officer, the ambush police shooting of John Crawford at a Walmart in Ohio, the chokehold death of Eric Garner in Staten Island, the drive-by police shooting of twelve-year-old Tamir Rice in Cleveland, and the crippling condition of Freddie Gray as he was arrested in Baltimore, before he eventually died.

But it is not only technological and tactical differences that separate Black Lives Matter activists from their civil rights predecessors. When activists remind us that the Black Lives Matter movement is different from the civil rights movement, they are making a conscious decision to avoid mistakes from the past. They are rejecting the charismatic leadership model that has dominated black politics for the past half century, and for good reason.

This older model is associated with Martin Luther King and the clergy-based, male-centered hierarchal structure of the organization he led, the Southern Christian Leadership Conference. In the ensuing years, this charismatic model has been replicated, most notably through organizations like Jesse Jackson's Rainbow PUSH Coalition and Al Sharpton's National Action Network, but also by hundreds of other locally based activist organizations across the country. But Black Lives Matter activists today recognize that granting decision-making power to an individual or a handful of individuals poses a risk to the durability of a movement. Charismatic leaders can be co-opted by powerful interests, place their own self-interest above that of the collective, be targeted by government repression, or even be assassinated, as were Martin Luther King and Malcolm X. The dependence of movements on charismatic leaders can therefore weaken them, even lead to their collapse.

Instead, core activists of the Black Lives Matter movement have insisted on a group-centered model of leadership, rooted in ideas of participatory democracy. The movement has modeled itself after the Student Nonviolent Coordinating Committee (SNCC), the 1960s organization that helped black Americans gain legal access to public spaces and the right to vote. Black Lives Matter organizers also operate on the principle that no one person or group of individuals should speak for or make decisions on behalf of the movement. They believe, as the legendary civil rights activist Ella Baker believed, that "strong people don't need strong leaders."

In some ways, the new tools of technology—particularly social media and especially Twitter—have facilitated the emergence of just such a bottom-up insurgency led by ordinary people, and have displaced the top-down approach of old guard civil rights organizations. But this model has also been adopted by design. For many young black Americans, leaders like Jesse Jackson and Al Sharpton, as well as heads of civil rights organizations such as the NAACP and the National Urban League, are no longer seen as the gatekeepers of the movement's ideals or the leaders who must broker the interests of black communities with the state or society. Additionally, with the exception of Al Sharpton's National Action Network, which has represented families of victims but has been less effective accomplishing police and prison reform, policing and mass incarceration have not been aggressively pursued by these more traditional organizations. And none, certainly, have adopted the disruptive protest tactics—the street marches, die-ins, bridge and tunnel blockades, and the intense publicity campaigns—that have helped Black Lives Matter force these issues onto the national political agenda.

Unlike the civil rights movement, the focus of Black Lives Matter—on policing in black and brown communities, on dismantling mass incarceration—is also being articulated less as a demand for specific civil or political rights, and more as a broader claim for "black humanity." This insistence on black humanity has repeatedly been used by Black Lives Matter activists as a catalyst for political action. "If you can see a dead black boy lie in the street for four and a half hours and that doesn't make you angry, then you lack humanity," said Ashley Yates, a Ferguson activist and co-founder of Millennial Activists United, at a rally last October. Evoking humanity is used to express communal anger against police brutality, but also to mobilize those who aren't acting. Yates explained further:

> And at the very core of this is humanity—Black Lives Matter. We matter. We matter. Black lives matter because they are lives. Because we are human. Because we eat. Because we breathe. Because he [Michael Brown] had a dream, because he made rap songs, they may have had cuss words in them. Yeah. He was human. And when we neglect to see that we end up where we are today.

Activists like Yates have also used the claim of humanity to challenge the politics of respectability, a black middle-class ideology that has its origins in the turn-of-the-twentieth century response to black people's loss of civil and political rights following Reconstruction's collapse. The politics of respectability is invested in changing the personal behavior and culture of poor and working-class black people, rather than squarely addressing the structural barriers that keep them locked into a perpetual state of marginality.

This appeal to humanity too has deep—though hidden—roots in the history of the black freedom struggle. The eighteenth-century anti-slavery campaign roused the consciousness of nations by pleading to those who kept them and profited from their bondage, "Am I Not a Man and a Brother?" The agitation of the anti-lynching campaigns of the first half of the twentieth century highlighted the inhumanness of mob violence against black people. Striking garbage workers fighting for a living wage in Memphis in 1968 carried with them placards proclaiming, "I am a Man." But with the successful passage of major civil rights legislation—specifically the 1964 Civil Rights Act, 1965 Voting Rights Act, and the 1968 Fair Housing Act—and the expansion of these laws in subsequent decades, the language of civil rights came to dominate both the ideas and the strategies of leaders and organizations concerned with racial inequality.

With Black Lives Matter, we now have a revival of these historical roots. Its recognition that all black lives deserve humanity, regardless of their gender, class, or sexual orientation, has breathed new life into the legacy of the black freedom struggle. Today's new—and much larger—movement is also articulating the national struggle for racial justice as a broader one for human rights.

In 1951, the "We Charge Genocide" campaign—which included William Patterson, Paul Robeson, W. E. B. Du Bois, Claudia Jones, and family members of victims of racial violence such as Josephine Grayson and Rosalie McGee—petitioned the United Nations to examine human rights abuses against black Americans. The petitioners sought to frame their claims—that African Americans were being persecuted, denied the right to vote, and "pauperized" because of their race—as a question of both black humanity and as a human rights issue: "[A]bove all we protest this genocide as human beings whose very humanity is denied and mocked."

The horrific evidence compiled for the petition, culled from stories in black newspapers and accounts collected by civil rights and labor organizations from 1945 to 1951, is eerily similar to the accounts we hear today. We may be more familiar with the evidence that petitioners document in the Jim Crow South, but the incidents recorded outside it are especially revealing. In many pockets of the urban North, the policing of black migrants was merely a parallel to the Jim Crow violence that terrorized them in the South.

For instance, in February 1946 in Freeport, Long Island, a policeman shot and killed two unarmed black men, wounded a third, and arrested a fourth for "disorderly conduct." The men had objected to being denied service in a café. The Freeport police, in a move that resembles the police's response to protesters in Ferguson, "threw a cordon around the bus terminal and stationed men with tommy guns and tear gas there, saying that they wanted to 'prevent a possible uprising of local Negroes.'"

Three months later in Baltimore, police shot and killed Wilbur Bundley. "Nine witnesses stated that he was shot in the back while running," the petition reports. In July, Lucy Gordy James, a member of a prominent family of "Negro business people in Detroit," was "beaten severely" by three police officers. "She sued the officers for $10,000 damages, charging illegal arrest, assault, and maltreatment." And in 1951 in Philadelphia, "forty police officers killed an unarmed 21-year-old Negro youth, Joseph Austin Conway, allegedly being sought for questioning in a robbery. He died in a hail of bullets while seeking to draw fire away from his family and neighbors." This catalogue of disaster—to quote James Baldwin—is documented in over 200 pages.

In the 1950s, Malcolm X and Martin Luther King also used the language of human rights to internationalize the issue of racial inequality in the United States. During his travels abroad, Malcolm X enlisted the assistance of heads of states in Africa and the Middle East to condemn the United States for their treatment of black Americans. He discovered that by framing the mistreatment of black Americans as an international human rights issue instead of a national civil rights one, "those grievances can then be brought into the United Nations and be discussed by people all over the world." For him, as long as the discussion was centered on civil rights, "your only allies can be the people in the next community, many of whom are responsible for your grievance." Malcolm X wanted "to come up with a program that would make our grievances international and make the world see that our problem was no longer a Negro problem or an American problem but a human problem."

In framing racial discrimination in human rights terms, the Black Lives Matter movement is today picking up the baton of civil rights activists before them. The parents of Trayvon Martin and Jordan Davis have raised the issue of discriminatory policing with members of the UN Committee on the Elimination of All Forms of Racial Discrimination in Geneva. The parents of Mike Brown along with representatives of organizations in Ferguson and

Chicago traveled to Geneva to share information about their cases with the UN Committee Against Torture in November 2014. Brown's parents submitted a statement to the Committee that read in part, "The killing of Mike Brown and the abandonment of his body in the middle of a neighborhood street is but an example of the utter lack of regard for, and indeed dehumanization of, black lives by law enforcement personnel." Following its examination of the United States, the Committee Against Torture recommended that it undertake independent and prompt investigations into allegations of police brutality and expressed concerns about racial profiling and the "growing militarization of policing activities." After it reviewed the human rights record of the United States, a review procedure of the UN Human Rights Council recommended strengthening legislation to combat racial discrimination and addressing excessive use of force by the police.

When Anthony Scott saw the video of his brother Walter Scott being shot as he fled a North Charleston police officer, he remarked, "I thought that my brother was gunned down like an animal." It is a curious thing for black people in the twenty-first century to once again have to claim their humanity.

We live in a society where people are more likely to be convicted of animal cruelty than police officers are likely to be charged for the murder of unarmed black, brown, and poor people. But with the Black Lives Matter movement, black America's struggle for human rights is once again gaining strength. Hopefully this time, we can win the more than century-long campaign that has demanded of our nation simply to see us as human.

Questions for Critical Thinking

1. In this essay, Fredrick Harris discusses how the Black Lives Matter movement's appeal to human rights has deep roots in the history of the black freedom struggle. How did his argument help you to understand this movement in new and different ways?

2. Harris points to the importance of recognizing that this movement is less about a demand for specific civil or political rights and more about a broader claim for "black humanity." Why is this an important distinction?

3. What are the conditions necessary for building effective coalitions to bring about positive social change for all with regard to the Black Lives Matter movement?